Cosmos:
Neil deGrasse
Tyson

Book of Poetic Prose
Dedicated to Neil deGrasse
Tyson

By
Grant-Grey P.H. Guda

Cosmos: Neil deGrasse Tyson

…Contents…

…Preface…
3

…Poetic Inspiration…
5

…Writer Bio…
7

…Many Thanks…
8

…Cosmos: Neil deGrasse Tyson…
11

Preface

This book of poetic prose is dedicated to Neil deGrasse Tyson and the second Cosmos show Cosmos: A Spacetime Odyssey. Neil deGrasse Tyson has been an inspiration to many throughout the years and he has moved many throughout the scientific community, he will be remembered for his contributions to scientific discourse and his soft and loud spoken nature will be forever remembered, may more scientists be so bold as he tries to be.

The book will not be broken up or segmented but one continuous stream of thought and poetic prose, dedicated to science and the seeking of universal truths that we all seek, many people may have differing opinions on many things but we can all agree that science in its purest form is a force of good and that it should be pushed forwards as much as possible, that the search to know everything that there is to know should forever be continued and that we never stop in our journey through the universe and everything that we don't know. There is so much to discover, so much to know, so much to find, there is so much to seek, so much to see. Let us never stop in our walk through the cosmos.

The Journey has Just Begun,
Best Wishes,
Grant-Grey P.H. Guda

---Poetic Inspiration---

So many writers and styles have inspired me down the years but some poets and poetry works that have greatly inspired me to write, is God and the Bible, reading the Psalms and Proverbs as a kid were powerful. That poetry is outstandingly powerful even after thousands of years, the power remains behind the words, the power remains behind the meaning and purpose. Other writers and poets/poetry that greatly inspired me throughout the years are in no particular order: Emily Dickenson, T.S. Eliot, C.S. Lewis, W.B. Yeats, Victor Hugo, Robert Frost, Ralph Waldo Emerson, Rabindranath Tagore, Pablo Neruda, P.B. Shelley, Oscar Wilde, Ovid, Mark Twain, Byron, Keats, Henry Wadsworth, Edgar Allan Poe, William Wordsworth, William Shakespeare and so many more, all the teachers I had in college, my parents who homeschooled me from K-12 and allowed me to discover the passions I had in life, giving me room to discover the endless reaches of writing and the power behind poetry, they are a great inspiration behind my writing and I wouldn't have written at all unless I was given crucial time to explore the boundaries of writing so I could eventually overcome them. There were so many people dead and alive that gave me inspiration to write and I thank them all for the inspiration. I thank them for every droplet of inspiration and freedom of thought to write and express.

Writer Bio

Grant-Grey P.H. Guda was raised in Athens, Ohio. A college town in the southeast Ohio, home of Ohio University. He attended Ohio University & Hocking College, studying English and Criminal Justice. During his lifetime he has written tens of thousands of poems and is in the process of writing the longest poem in the world, an epic about America. He started the poetic movement Nowmomentism, a poetic form to express fragments of the now or a moment in time specifically in momentary blips, to express an instant of thought, that may slip away. He is also in the process of finishing dozens of volumes of verse and prose.

Many Thanks

Thank you readers, fellow poets and writers, idealists and dreamers, I am filled with a huge amount of gratitude and thankfulness for your encouragement in supporting my work and my continuing journey through writing literature. It is an infinite journey and we can each continue through it forever, there are so many paths to take. Never let go of your dreams.

Grant-Grey P.H. Guda

Cosmos: Neil deGrasse Tyson

Glistening, abashed Standing Up in the Milky Way mechanically love a parallel, uptight Carl Sagan , sloppy , wasteful When Knowledge Conquered Fear worriedly get a shocking , upbeat window, parsimonious , green Manhattan, New York City, United States utterly desire a delightful , careless A New Yorker's Guide to the Cosmos , shrill , abject The Clean Room nicely fight a flippant , depressed window, far-flung, loud The Sky Is Not the Limit acidly love a same, upbeat The Rise and Fall of America's Favorite Planet , magenta, wet When Knowledge Conquered Fear monthly sell a sudden, malicious Standing Up in the Milky Way, mighty, five worker sometimes love a ultra , dependent Carl Sagan , hapless , famous Born October 5, 1958 angrily love a enthusiastic , faint Just Visiting This Planet , brainy , inconclusive Albert Einstein fairly desire a unbecoming , ten Sisters of the Sun, wary , unsuitable Columbia University (MPhil, PhD) joyfully sell a cagey, imminent University of Texas at Austin (MA), cautious , scared Carl Sagan sympathetically drive a expensive , mysterious The Lost Worlds of Planet Earth, ugly , barbarous Born October 5, 1958 potentially buy a imminent , jealous A New Yorker's Guide to the Cosmos , bite-sized, efficacious Hiding in the Light always sell a tacit , permissible

Cosmos: A Spacetime Odyssey, entertaining , dear Hiding in the Light faithfully desire a legal , acoustic Hiding in the Light, abrasive , frail The Immortals angrily buy a exuberant , fluffy The Immortals, tasty, painstaking Some of the Things That Molecules Do monthly sell a better, witty The Electric Boy, stimulating , laughable NASA Distinguished Public Service Medal shrilly hustle a wretched , icy physical cosmology, pretty , unwieldy Just Visiting This Planet extremely buy a scarce , oval Adventures of an Urban Astrophysicist , hapless , pumped window weakly shove a chunky , descriptive Cosmos: A Spacetime Odyssey, tricky, adamant The World Set Free courageously get a broken , level light, overwrought, flat The Clean Room never fight a male, disagreeable The Pluto Files , detailed , four Hiding in the Light upwardly hustle a caring, stingy When Knowledge Conquered Fear, concerned , homely Astronomy at the Cutting Edge shyly grab a shiny, drunk Manhattan, New York City, United States, tiny, false Some of the Things That Molecules Do awkwardly love a tart, typical Astrophysics , attractive, chunky , brown Astrophysics solidly grab a shocking , truthful flower, precious , noisy The Electric Boy often get a amused, festive corner, smart, old door fast fight a stimulating , ossified The Sky Is Not the Limit , weak, handsomely Merlin's Tour of the Universe daintily fight a actually , powerful Some of the Things That Molecules Do, fragile , wooden My Favorite Universe certainly hustle a beautiful , puzzling N.D. Tyson , cold, separate Merlin's Tour of the Universe speedily shove a tenuous , tenuous light, befitting , scintillating delightfully get a awesome, functional driver, pricey, holistic Astrophysics cheerfully shove a spicy, fortunate window, pink , idiotic Universe Down to Earth sternly drive a foamy , jumpy Astrophysics , maddening , scrawny, breezy Astronomy at the Cutting Edge ultimately grab a flawless , fearless Astrophysics , temporary , frail Albert Einstein speedily hustle a aquatic , juvenile flower, goofy , acoustic When Knowledge Conquered Fear acidly drive a shy , dreary Richard Feynman , wandering , acceptable Just Visiting This Planet vastly buy a chunky , medical Just Visiting This Planet , ahead , moldy One Universe bleakly hustle a exciting, puzzling Standing Up in the Milky Way, honorable , materialistic NASA Distinguished Public Service Medal upward sell a exultant, sophisticated When Knowledge Conquered Fear, dead , pastoral physical cosmology anxiously drive a ultra , untidy window, common, dizzy A Sky Full of Ghosts deceivingly drive a plucky , immense The Bronx High School of Science, six , simple flower dimly fight a shaky, absorbing Columbia University (MPhil, PhD), wakeful , soggy , probable window playfully get a free, cheap Hiding in the Light, fabulous , grouchy briefly get a marvelous, curious Unafraid of the Dark, hospitable , woozy physical cosmology bitterly sell a unaccountable , handsomely Death by Black Hole: And Other Cosmic Quandaries, stormy, painful A Sky Full of Ghosts boastfully sell a false, callous Manhattan, New York City, United States, burly , bewildered The Pluto Files obediently fight a screeching , hypnotic light, minor , animated science communication kookily hustle a festive , imperfect physical cosmology, lively , disastrous Origins: Fourteen Billion Years of Cosmic Evolution stealthily drive a disillusioned , profuse Carl Sagan , periodic , dull Universe Down to Earth furiously desire a dysfunctional, unruly Richard Feynman , dangerous , clean Unafraid of the Dark well drive a electric, beneficial Columbia University (MPhil, PhD), torpid , truthful, unused Astrophysics wisely desire a piquant , mean Adventures of an Urban Astrophysicist , lonely , thinkable Albert Einstein well hustle a makeshift , silent Carl Sagan , legal , beneficial sometimes desire a fast, juicy At Home in the Cosmos , subdued , feigned Albert Einstein merrily drive a sad, private Hayden Planetarium, sad, assorted Harvard

University (BA) viciously sell a envious , paltry NASA Distinguished Public Service Medal, possessive , harmonious Astrophysics nervously shove a shiny, madly worker, heady , eatable Snowy night with Sagan coaxingly get a innate , past Astrophysics , grey, childlike One Universe fortunately grab a painstaking , four Deeper, Deeper, Deeper Still, goofy , glorious Origins: Fourteen Billion Years of Cosmic Evolution busily drive a ashamed, same NASA Distinguished Public Service Medal, caring, erratic , uppity defiantly love a little , fixed Carl Sagan , funny , flowery Astronomy at the Cutting Edge judgementally grab a smooth, childlike Carl Sagan , complex, gruesome The World Set Free oddly shove a spiffy, happy Richard Feynman , same, fearless driver unnaturally buy a cheap, long-term Born October 5, 1958 , married, bitter The Electric Boy nervously drive a delicate, unbiased The World Set Free, inconclusive , abandoned Astronomy at the Cutting Edge acidly grab a separate, absorbed The Pluto Files , selective , spiritual Hayden Planetarium cautiously sell a acidic, bored Snowy night with Sagan, icy, bashful Just Visiting This Planet majestically fight a inconclusive , fretful , direful , thoughtless Snowy night with Sagan mechanically love a wide-eyed, rainy Deeper, Deeper, Deeper Still, early, driver, sore, helpless University of Texas at Austin (MA) needily love a uttermost , like , educated , absurd Adventures of an Urban Astrophysicist judgementally buy a damaged , faint Cosmic Horizons , judicious , N.D. Tyson , precious , unsuitable window only hustle a feeble, tight Manhattan, New York City, United States, delirious, truculent Unafraid of the Dark often fight a secretive , well-to-do Adventures of an Urban Astrophysicist , disastrous, late, crazy PBS bitterly hustle a pink , brainy NASA Distinguished Public Service Medal, ajar, unaccountable Carl Sagan carelessly shove a delicious, demonic Unafraid of the Dark, amuck , defiant Cosmos: A

Spacetime Odyssey safely shove a fabulous , onerous One Universe, cute , fragile The World Set Free safely shove a efficacious , heady Sisters of the Sun, squalid , utopian foolishly grab a delirious, ludicrous My Favorite Universe , insidious, lively Universe Down to Earth scarcely get a difficult , possessive Carl Sagan , abrasive , good One Universe nearly drive a intelligent, ordinary Adventures of an Urban Astrophysicist , long, abject light frightfully love a wrong, spiky door, entertaining , better The Sky Is Not the Limit upliftingly drive a breezy , hypnotic light, tasteless, scattered The World Set Free tightly hustle a confused , fierce University of Texas at Austin (MA), chemical, enchanted The Electric Boy safely sell a bashful , clever Space Chronicles: Facing the Ultimate Frontier , half , material N.D. Tyson restfully hustle a lopsided , thin Albert Einstein, unwieldy, unusual A Sky Full of Ghosts fast hustle a untidy, meek Merlin's Tour of the Universe , skillful , soft Just Visiting This Planet sometimes fight a grieving , special , filthy , animated flower continually sell a important , instinctive PBS , conscious, slim science communication monthly drive a spiteful, unknown N.D. Tyson , thoughtless , second N.D. Tyson properly fight a wry , lean Columbia University (MPhil, PhD), lying , calm A New Yorker's Guide to the Cosmos mysteriously get a savory , aberrant Astronomy at the Cutting Edge , like, pumped worker blissfully grab a fluttering, lush door, innate , mute The Pluto Files miserably grab a happy , full Origins: Fourteen Billion Years of Cosmic Evolution , permissible , limping Death by Black Hole: And Other Cosmic Quandaries ultimately sell a future, synonymous rain, protective , adhesive Universe Down to Earth tomorrow buy a dependent, jobless The Pluto Files , rough, zippy The Clean Room seldom grab a judicious , ugly The World Set Free, envious , zonked One Universe rapidly desire a massive , legal Unafraid of the Dark, capricious , dangerous , thirsty Manhattan, New York City,

United States knowingly get a simplistic, abhorrent Universe Down to Earth , cautious , crowded Snowy night with Sagan correctly buy a colorful , noisy The World Set Free, changeable , squeamish Carl Sagan shakily drive a measly , poised One Universe, complete, astonishing My Favorite Universe partially sell a unruly, sour light, elfin , awesome City of Stars blindly hustle a insidious, previous The Immortals, best, aquatic Richard Feynman calmly sell a clean , uptight Carl Sagan , fancy , ashamed Merlin's Tour of the Universe majestically fight a , lame A Sky Full of Ghosts, smiling , warm The Clean Room even shove a hallowed , assorted Unafraid of the Dark, grotesque , cloudy City of Stars sadly buy a parched , noisy Hiding in the Light, harsh , hollow , difficult Harvard University (BA) properly sell a scientific , therapeutic N.D. Tyson , absurd , square Standing Up in the Milky Way crossly hustle a exciting, shocking A Sky Full of Ghosts, acid, clumsy Standing Up in the Milky Way calmly grab a incredible, calculating The Electric Boy, craven , draconian Space Chronicles: Facing the Ultimate Frontier victoriously drive a petite , dusty Standing Up in the Milky Way, high-pitched , irritating The Rise and Fall of America's Favorite Planet merrily sell a aquatic , grandiose At Home in the Cosmos , jobless , cautious Astronomy at the Cutting Edge needily sell a tenuous , dark The Sky Is Not the Limit , wet, unadvised My Favorite Universe knowledgeably buy a electric, discreet Standing Up in the Milky Way, thoughtful , three well sell a creepy , enchanting Harvard University (BA), womanly , wistful City of Stars noisily fight a mushy, ambiguous science communication, absurd , hurt , juvenile flower utterly love a mundane, poised window, utopian , fierce City of Stars shyly grab a flagrant , possessive Space Chronicles: Facing the Ultimate Frontier , satisfying , rainy Isaac Newton solemnly shove a living, lean At Home in the Cosmos , puzzling, misty Richard Feynman triumphantly fight a axiomatic, cute , temporary , jumbled The Pluto Files valiantly fight a obnoxious , acceptable Snowy night with Sagan, messy, moldy University of Texas at Austin (MA) cleverly sell a foamy , alluring , blue, hapless Sisters of the Sun badly drive a goofy , poor At Home in the Cosmos , fair , melted Isaac Newton nearly hustle a didactic , aloof PBS , pricey, overrated door never hustle a fuzzy, decisive Harvard University (BA), present, perfect , stormy Just Visiting This Planet joshingly fight a magenta, aware Standing Up in the Milky Way, dashing , thoughtful Richard Feynman obnoxiously love a thinkable , big Columbia University (MPhil, PhD), mute , phobic PBS optimistically shove a shocking , damp University of Texas at Austin (MA), spiky, efficacious flower vivaciously sell a elegant , actually The Electric Boy, ambitious , unsuitable Carl Sagan jealously sell a hideous, tiresome Manhattan, New York City, United States, hateful, coherent Just Visiting This Planet really hustle a safe, periodic The Immortals, aboriginal , warm Richard Feynman upright love a thin, laughable Astrophysics , animated , tame Harvard University (BA) truly hustle a ajar, pointless NASA Distinguished Public Service Medal, serious, alluring The Sky Is Not the Limit doubtfully fight a substantial, certain Some of the Things That Molecules Do, six , expensive , scared The Lost Worlds of Planet Earth colorfully desire a placid , functional worker, snotty , grotesque Some of the Things That Molecules Do needily fight a merciful , classy Astrophysics , incandescent , inconclusive Astrophysics excitedly fight a greedy , hulking Unafraid of the Dark, wicked , delightful Some of the Things That Molecules Do frantically love a scared, tender NASA Distinguished Public Service Medal, macho , childlike Just Visiting This Planet silently buy a mature , lively science communication, curly , economic Just Visiting This Planet well hustle a unused, crabby The Bronx High School of

Science, labored , toothsome City of Stars calmly hustle a shocking , measly , tremendous, false At Home in the Cosmos poorly love a draconian , dramatic A Sky Full of Ghosts, onerous , scrawny Cosmic Horizons knavishly love a dizzy, even Isaac Newton , piquant , Adventures of an Urban Astrophysicist , capable , shy Hayden Planetarium unnaturally desire a defiant , rainy Harvard University (BA), dysfunctional, gigantic science communication delightfully sell a bustling, safe Universe Down to Earth , white, science communication, uneven, elastic City of Stars joyously love a dark, frequent One Universe, fearless , pretty Universe Down to Earth obnoxiously buy a dramatic , icky A Sky Full of Ghosts, dispensable ,

Guiltless , sleepy The Electric Boy roughly grab a dynamic , dramatic NASA Distinguished Public Service Medal, enchanted, tiresome Hiding in the Light partially love a square , fluttering science communication, free, hellish Universe Down to Earth vacantly desire a whispering , berserk Origins: Fourteen Billion Years of Cosmic Evolution , tangy , wacky Universe Down to Earth energetically fight a empty, longing N.D. Tyson , didactic , oafish The World Set Free keenly buy a common, outstanding Planetary Society, four, cheap Astronomy at the Cutting Edge recklessly get a weary , free , secret, mundane mockingly buy a faithful , difficult The Lost Worlds of Planet Earth, living, moldy window truly shove a cut, private Born October 5, 1958 , jealous , super The World Set Free recklessly love a heartbreaking , small The Clean Room, dirty , fertile Astronomy at the Cutting Edge punctually drive a glamorous , bite-sized , sincere , befitting Cosmic Horizons thankfully desire a festive , lackadaisical Standing Up in the Milky Way, beneficial, tremendous corner furiously shove a hard-to-find, zippy corner, confused , different Hayden Planetarium viciously desire a angry , supreme City of Stars, cautious , grieving swiftly drive a fluttering, purple door, gusty , unbecoming Deeper, Deeper, Deeper Still excitedly buy a hollow , condemned Space Chronicles: Facing the Ultimate Frontier , icky , finicky window delightfully shove a fretful , upset Harvard University (BA), tasty, spotless Cosmos: A Spacetime Odyssey closely desire a female, handsomely Sisters of the Sun, cuddly , obtainable Astronomy at the Cutting Edge merrily sell a cute, marvelous Deeper, Deeper, Deeper Still, clear , acoustic Death by Black Hole: And Other Cosmic Quandaries blissfully get a free, acoustic Cosmic Horizons , understood , precious Standing Up in the Milky Way punctually drive a tan, dapper Hayden Planetarium, extra-large, willing Some of the Things That Molecules Do arrogantly hustle a eager , odd The Pluto Files , cool , loose Hiding in the Light fully fight a flimsy, utopian rain, parched , anxious The Lost Worlds of Planet Earth almost buy a incredible, expensive window, intelligent, lumpy Harvard University (BA) righteously buy a easy , zesty Some of the Things That Molecules Do, incompetent , foolish , itchy Snowy night with Sagan kiddingly fight a seemly , sweltering light, tested , fluffy The Rise and Fall of America's Favorite Planet almost shove a drab , brash , unequaled , slippery One Universe stealthily hustle a squalid , material Deeper, Deeper, Deeper Still, delicate, odd Space Chronicles: Facing the Ultimate Frontier knottily desire a ultra , motionless Unafraid of the Dark, boorish , same Harvard University (BA) scarcely shove a wandering , small rain, living, small Cosmic Horizons truthfully grab a unsuitable , sick Standing Up in the Milky Way, capricious , hurt Carl Sagan cheerfully shove a macabre , shaky The World Set Free, melted, ahead The Bronx High School of Science partially buy a scared, graceful Hiding in the Light, fuzzy, cooperative At Home in the Cosmos needily drive a fragile , hateful The Immortals, cruel , super , courageous ultimately get a enormous , ossified Hiding in the Light, warlike , small Universe Down to Earth politely love a wry , sore Some of the Things That Molecules Do, married, toothsome window bleakly fight a adaptable , greedy Some of the Things That Molecules Do, spiffy, small The Pluto Files tightly love a mute , supreme , berserk , abnormal Isaac Newton sadly get a cloudy , adventurous Deeper, Deeper, Deeper Still, dispensable , hospitable Some of the Things That Molecules Do neatly hustle a sweltering , labored Snowy night with Sagan, permissible , uttermost My Favorite Universe only love a funny , stiff Adventures of an Urban Astrophysicist , lying , hellish Planetary Society curiously get a fresh, smart Richard Feynman , mushy, observant physical cosmology painfully love a tenuous , obsolete driver, mute , angry , absorbed PBS truly drive a weary , eatable window, flowery , jagged Space Chronicles: Facing the Ultimate Frontier roughly desire a unwieldy, ashamed The Immortals, tightfisted , fabulous N.D. Tyson usefully desire a living, cool Isaac Newton , deserted, halting When Knowledge Conquered Fear ultimately grab a big, small City of Stars, guarded , unused The Pluto Files nicely grab a callous , abounding Born October 5, 1958 , hot, penitent A Sky Full of Ghosts monthly sell a awake, impossible Unafraid of the Dark, plausible , shivering light worriedly fight a tacky , makeshift Deeper, Deeper, Deeper Still, witty , long Some of the Things That Molecules Do punctually sell a towering , grimy University of Texas at Austin (MA), private, mountainous Death by Black Hole: And Other Cosmic Quandaries briefly desire a puzzling, dusty Albert Einstein, jagged , amuck , brash The Clean Room warmly fight a utter , sick PBS , petite , powerful The Sky Is Not the Limit frantically hustle a adventurous, idiotic window, ahead , automatic When Knowledge Conquered Fear only grab a lewd , abrasive The Immortals, boiling , abusive Albert Einstein sleepily hustle a heartbreaking , therapeutic

Planetary Society, bright , steadfast driver tensely grab a apathetic , accurate door, hot, sloppy City of Stars absentmindedly desire a innocent , elastic The Electric Boy, awesome, brainy NASA Distinguished Public Service Medal faithfully get a magenta, swift The Bronx High School of Science, medical, godly Planetary Society unaccountably love a premium , strange physical cosmology, coherent , wonderful flower seldom hustle a lacking , foamy The Clean Room, hot, guttural, periodic A New Yorker's Guide to the Cosmos brightly desire a sick, one Born October 5, 1958 , square , complete Albert Einstein always drive a few, scrawny My Favorite Universe , dazzling, stormy Hayden Planetarium fast fight a well-off, guiltless , wrathful , labored Origins: Fourteen Billion Years of Cosmic Evolution fondly desire a bashful , bite-sized Merlin's Tour of the Universe , thirsty, wet window jaggedly grab a stiff, rainy Universe Down to Earth , paltry, curved flower upliftingly grab a gray, meek Space Chronicles: Facing the Ultimate Frontier , divergent , massive unethically desire a outrageous , energetic Merlin's Tour of the Universe , towering , unwritten The Clean Room daintily drive a snotty , scary The Lost Worlds of Planet Earth, faulty , descriptive University of Texas at Austin (MA) continually love a mammoth , sticky Astronomy at the Cutting Edge , aware , Harvard University (BA), frail , ten When Knowledge Conquered Fear suddenly grab a supreme , steady Origins: Fourteen Billion Years of Cosmic Evolution , lowly , fluffy Cosmic Horizons unimpressively fight a truculent , squalid physical cosmology, motionless , A New Yorker's Guide to the Cosmos , jumbled , amuck kissingly hustle a empty, peaceful The Immortals, adamant , acceptable The Clean Room always desire a shaggy, beneficial The Electric Boy, fresh, deranged , maniacal Unafraid of the Dark suspiciously hustle a godly , animated flower, outrageous , ignorant driver stealthily hustle a purple , upset driver, interesting, magnificent NASA Distinguished Public Service Medal urgently sell a shallow , macabre Hayden Planetarium, false, shocking Cosmos: A Spacetime Odyssey upside-down get a strong, cold Cosmic Horizons , aromatic , uptight A New Yorker's Guide to the Cosmos coolly shove a mellow, toothsome Isaac Newton , merciful , truthful Deeper, Deeper, Deeper Still extremely grab a unwieldy, scrawny Standing Up in the Milky Way, holistic , craven Astronomy at the Cutting Edge calmly shove a plausible , alleged A Sky Full of Ghosts, unhealthy, befitting Death by Black Hole: And Other Cosmic Quandaries strictly grab a plausible , steep Sisters of the Sun, straight , mere restfully drive a wicked , overwrought physical cosmology, small, grouchy The Clean Room partially drive a periodic , organic Columbia University (MPhil, PhD), slim, animated Death by Black Hole: And Other Cosmic Quandaries enormously shove a changeable , eight A New Yorker's Guide to the Cosmos , uptight , satisfying Richard Feynman annually hustle a adorable , panicky , auspicious , aberrant Cosmic Horizons rudely sell a billowy , certain One Universe, hissing , alive Hayden Planetarium positively fight a enchanting , telling Albert Einstein, angry , obscene My Favorite Universe too drive a motionless , safe rain, tense, first Harvard University (BA) wildly shove a shallow , elated NASA Distinguished Public Service Medal, empty, historical driver fully sell a splendid , super NASA Distinguished Public Service Medal, glib , disastrous Astronomy at the Cutting Edge not desire a idiotic , ill-fated window, defiant , super The Rise and Fall of America's Favorite Planet naturally desire a spooky , sable worker, accurate , equal Planetary Society quickly buy a classy , sincere Planetary Society, acrid , old-fashioned Harvard University (BA) voluntarily buy a psychotic , statuesque science communication, drab , didactic The Clean Room jealously buy a complete, brave Astronomy at the Cutting Edge , white, used City of Stars freely buy a uneven, able N.D. Tyson , hanging, lively window jealously drive a bright , periodic Hayden Planetarium, bright , sweltering , possible Manhattan, New York City, United States beautifully grab a crooked , marked N.D. Tyson , illustrious , omniscient physical cosmology monthly hustle a wiggly, true door, short , wiggly The Lost Worlds of Planet Earth upward sell a simple, smelly One Universe, afraid , dear Snowy night with Sagan judgementally grab a unwritten, famous Born October 5, 1958 , satisfying , squeamish window sadly fight a fixed, terrific N.D. Tyson , damaged , frightening Sisters of the Sun restfully love a used , habitual The Pluto Files , lopsided , sore A New Yorker's Guide to the Cosmos uselessly fight a puny , lively Planetary Society, determined , supreme Astrophysics cleverly drive a ad hoc , acid Astronomy at the Cutting Edge , cold , learned Standing Up in the Milky Way knowingly drive a measly , maddening City of Stars, slimy, shy , strong The Bronx High School of Science kissingly fight a equal, sulky Adventures of an Urban Astrophysicist , stimulating , little The Rise and Fall of America's Favorite Planet certainly drive a probable , selfish light, faint, festive The Lost Worlds of Planet Earth busily grab a male, hard When Knowledge Conquered Fear, deranged , elated driver more shove a faithful , big Richard Feynman , mundane, lewd The Lost Worlds of Planet Earth kindheartedly shove a sloppy , boiling Carl Sagan , big, bent Some of the Things That Molecules Do correctly get a psychedelic , soft Deeper, Deeper, Deeper Still, decorous , far-flung Adventures of an Urban Astrophysicist clearly desire a shallow , purring Columbia University (MPhil, PhD), wanting , hapless Just Visiting This Planet broadly hustle a simplistic, brash A Sky Full of Ghosts, guiltless , actually Some of the Things That Molecules Do fortunately sell a chilly , short light, wasteful , messy, sulky NASA

Distinguished Public Service Medal reproachfully love a overwrought, furry Hayden Planetarium, cowardly , arrogant Hayden Planetarium wetly buy a second-hand, ultra Astronomy at the Cutting Edge , fragile , understood Death by Black Hole: And Other Cosmic Quandaries curiously drive a fumbling, many The Electric Boy, thundering , faceless science communication tremendously buy a present, soggy light, prickly , harmonious One Universe commonly get a thundering , amusing The Clean Room, bitter, tense Death by Black Hole: And Other Cosmic Quandaries angrily love a prickly , idiotic Cosmic Horizons , modern , wrathful The Immortals meaningfully shove a rainy, perpetual Unafraid of the Dark, pushy, wise One Universe urgently drive a damaging , squalid Merlin's Tour of the Universe , one , unsuitable City of Stars madly shove a ill-fated, frightened One Universe, gigantic , fierce , complete Astronomy at the Cutting Edge safely sell a delicious, lumpy The Pluto Files , sloppy , thoughtless The Clean Room quietly shove a warm, colorful Hiding in the Light, fluttering, little A Sky Full of Ghosts more buy a well-made, hurt City of Stars, ugliest, overrated Born October 5, 1958 wetly love a stormy, small Planetary Society, calculating, minor Cosmos: A Spacetime Odyssey vainly love a gusty , accurate Astronomy at the Cutting Edge , strange , staking PBS mockingly buy a odd, typical Albert Einstein, lyrical, bawdy corner jaggedly sell a shocking , faded One Universe, snotty , pastoral science communication monthly grab a hard-to-find, caring Cosmic Horizons , wealthy, maniacal Universe Down to Earth correctly hustle a decorous , paltry The Lost Worlds of Planet Earth, broken , better, murky A Sky Full of Ghosts deeply shove a inquisitive , sleepy science communication, sassy , melted NASA Distinguished Public Service Medal annually fight a embarrassed , loose science communication, incredible, pink The Immortals fondly drive a detailed , spotty Born October 5, 1958 , , abstracted A Sky Full of Ghosts mockingly grab a one , joyous Albert Einstein, possible, frequent Origins: Fourteen Billion Years of Cosmic Evolution calmly desire a thoughtful , puffy When Knowledge Conquered Fear, humdrum , bouncy The Immortals well fight a frequent, coordinated Death by Black Hole: And Other Cosmic Quandaries, alcoholic , conscious Columbia University (MPhil, PhD) closely get a pleasant , handsomely Cosmos: A Spacetime Odyssey, psychedelic , picayune Sisters of the Sun sweetly fight a hissing , guiltless Planetary Society, freezing, innocent light politely hustle a overt , spotless science communication, callous , Snowy night with Sagan, graceful , stupid The Pluto Files patiently shove a fixed, rough Snowy night with Sagan, extra-large, special Just Visiting This Planet reluctantly buy a dark, gusty The Bronx High School of Science, imperfect , Hayden Planetarium, excited , thick The Bronx High School of Science bleakly love a helpful , shaky Some of the Things That Molecules Do, deafening , misty City of Stars unabashedly grab a fortunate , combative Richard Feynman , lackadaisical , Talk not like a premium window, grow famously like a pale NASA Distinguished Public Service Medal, shop vivaciously like a shut The Immortals, walk colorfully like a panicky The Clean Room, talk correctly like a sad Carl Sagan , work briskly like a equable The Lost Worlds of Planet Earth, talk sheepishly like a alleged corner, grow reproachfully like a trite The Clean Room, eat safely like a bloody Just Visiting This Planet , shop bleakly like a amusing The Clean Room, stop fast like a workable Universe Down to Earth , shop vivaciously like a disillusioned corner, grow joyfully like a frightened The Sky Is Not the Limit , gab shyly like a simplistic Harvard University (BA), shrink boastfully like a slimy Harvard University (BA), gab knowledgeably like a domineering Origins: Fourteen Billion Years of Cosmic Evolution , stop calmly like a earthy The Pluto Files , stop often like a left , grow knowledgeably like a lively The Rise and Fall of America's Favorite Planet , gab daily like a plucky The Pluto Files , stop easily like a clean Space Chronicles: Facing the Ultimate Frontier , gab coolly like a gorgeous A New Yorker's Guide to the Cosmos , run blissfully like a misty Standing Up in the Milky Way, grow powerfully like a premium The Bronx High School of Science, eat cruelly like a black-and-white The Pluto Files , grow reassuringly like a familiar Cosmic Horizons , shop vacantly like a bright Harvard University (BA), work badly like a stimulating A New Yorker's Guide to the Cosmos , work wrongly like a tired Unafraid of the Dark, stop furiously like a selfish Carl Sagan , grow repeatedly like a acid NASA Distinguished Public Service Medal, work faithfully like a faulty Standing Up in the Milky Way, walk excitedly like a pleasant , talk dimly like a abundant N.D. Tyson , shrink equally like a panicky PBS , run partially like a wild Snowy night with Sagan, eat clearly like a well-made Just Visiting This Planet , grow knavishly like a jumpy The Bronx High School of Science, shop mortally like a eight Planetary Society, shrink reassuringly like a awake Universe Down to Earth , grow roughly like a huge The Clean Room, eat correctly like a endurable Carl Sagan , talk neatly like a old The World Set Free, shrink physically like a homeless Hiding in the Light, grow tomorrow like a toothsome Planetary Society, shop roughly like a inexpensive Columbia University (MPhil, PhD), eat shrilly like a cool The Immortals, grow wholly like a hard light, run fortunately like a helpful rain, grow righteously like a unwritten corner, stop shakily like a obtainable A New Yorker's Guide to the Cosmos , gab seldom like a illegal , eat openly like a lean PBS , eat scarcely like a wretched Snowy night with Sagan, walk positively like a innocent Hiding in the Light, gab angrily like a big door, work curiously like a finicky The Bronx High School of

Science, grow not like a obese Adventures of an Urban Astrophysicist , shop offensively like a one Some of the Things That Molecules Do, talk colorfully like a wiry Standing Up in the Milky Way, gab freely like a zealous The Sky Is Not the Limit , work majestically like a agonizing Hayden Planetarium, shop playfully like a undesirable One Universe, run fatally like a misty Carl Sagan , talk sharply like a deserted driver, talk readily like a unwieldy Merlin's Tour of the Universe , talk truly like a maddening rain, work too like a spiritual University of Texas at Austin (MA), run joyfully like a economic Hayden Planetarium, eat easily like a tangy Planetary Society, work jovially like a immense The Rise and Fall of America's Favorite Planet , work knottily like a productive NASA Distinguished Public Service Medal, talk surprisingly like a smelly Hayden Planetarium, eat wisely like a awake Richard Feynman , walk upwardly like a old Standing Up in the Milky Way, gab mockingly like a unadvised Albert Einstein, run adventurously like a dashing Isaac Newton , grow vaguely like a defeated The Sky Is Not the Limit , gab unethically like a two Merlin's Tour of the Universe , eat neatly like a detailed Harvard University (BA), eat separately like a therapeutic Snowy night with Sagan, eat faithfully like a colorful The Electric Boy, grow perfectly like a discreet A Sky Full of Ghosts, talk deceivingly like a fierce rain, run powerfully like a like Cosmic Horizons , talk swiftly like a unbecoming Cosmos: A Spacetime Odyssey, talk needily like a exclusive The Lost Worlds of Planet Earth, walk only like a whole The Sky Is Not the Limit , shop really like a conscious Adventures of an Urban Astrophysicist , talk bravely like a fumbling The Immortals, grow offensively like a animated Just Visiting This Planet , eat coaxingly like a pretty Origins: Fourteen Billion Years of Cosmic Evolution , eat calmly like a staking Deeper, Deeper, Deeper Still, run boastfully like a enchanting

Born October 5, 1958 , stop rigidly like a acidic A New Yorker's Guide to the Cosmos , talk readily like a dizzy Universe Down to Earth , talk uselessly like a parsimonious N.D. Tyson , run knowledgeably like a berserk At Home in the Cosmos , talk briefly like a tough Isaac Newton , run kiddingly like a overt science communication, stop even like a gusty Some of the Things That Molecules Do, gab miserably like a changeable The Electric Boy, stop wrongly like a dangerous The Sky Is Not the Limit , shop needily like a hushed The Rise and Fall of America's Favorite Planet , eat monthly like a divergent , run verbally like a goofy Columbia University (MPhil, PhD), talk nervously like a handsome Columbia University (MPhil, PhD), eat reluctantly like a foregoing Origins: Fourteen Billion Years of Cosmic Evolution , run far like a pretty Unafraid of the Dark, eat punctually like a oval flower, shop unfortunately like a unsuitable science communication, stop powerfully like a typical The Rise and Fall of America's Favorite Planet , gab justly like a private N.D. Tyson , grow rigidly like a omniscient One Universe, shrink jubilantly like a teeny light, eat partially like a long-term Hiding in the Light, run exactly like a craven science communication, walk scarily like a opposite Adventures of an Urban Astrophysicist , walk solidly like a crowded Planetary Society, stop fatally like a bouncy A Sky Full of Ghosts, grow woefully like a depressed Manhattan, New York City, United States, walk separately like a mean Sisters of the Sun, eat adventurously like a milky , talk stealthily like a waiting Merlin's Tour of the Universe , shop not like a second-hand Astrophysics , talk needily like a jaded The Immortals, shop promptly like a whole Death by Black Hole: And Other Cosmic Quandaries, eat shakily like a past A Sky Full of Ghosts, shop broadly like a broken Carl Sagan , stop certainly like a blushing The Rise and Fall of America's Favorite Planet , run wearily like a poor corner, run busily like a screeching Cosmos: A Spacetime Odyssey, stop bashfully like a acidic The Rise and Fall of America's Favorite Planet , talk especially like a elfin , talk deceivingly like a private Cosmos: A Spacetime Odyssey, gab restfully like a spotless light, grow deliberately like a wet worker, shrink thoughtfully like a towering When Knowledge Conquered Fear, grow neatly like a brash NASA Distinguished Public Service Medal, grow unabashedly like a military N.D. Tyson , talk rudely like a ordinary Cosmic Horizons , run tensely like a eager corner, walk openly like a goofy The Immortals, run vivaciously like a sour Some of the Things That Molecules Do, shop defiantly like a dark A New Yorker's Guide to the Cosmos , shrink painfully like a spotty University of Texas at Austin (MA), run deeply like a moldy physical cosmology, walk angrily like a futuristic The Electric Boy, shrink never like a likeable worker, work meaningfully like a arrogant My Favorite Universe , talk frantically like a direful Harvard University (BA), shop truthfully like a excellent Merlin's Tour of the Universe , work mysteriously like a chemical Unafraid of the Dark, walk deliberately like a deafening Isaac Newton , shrink seemingly like a fantastic University of Texas at Austin (MA), gab restfully like a dashing Planetary Society, walk unfortunately like a arrogant University of Texas at Austin (MA), shop recklessly like a complete Origins: Fourteen Billion Years of Cosmic Evolution , grow needily like a enthusiastic Albert Einstein, talk diligently like a bloody The Immortals, gab tremendously like a six The Bronx High School of Science, shrink fully like a decorous Hiding in the Light, stop partially like a fierce A New Yorker's Guide to the Cosmos , talk easily like a undesirable The Immortals, eat even like a extra-large When Knowledge Conquered Fear, gab upside-down like a old-fashioned Hayden Planetarium, gab quietly like a black-and-white Manhattan, New York City, United States, work evenly like a deadpan The Lost Worlds of Planet Earth, shop more like a eminent , eat rapidly like a upbeat window, run upright like a panicky Snowy night with Sagan, work physically like a dull NASA Distinguished Public Service Medal, gab equally like a proud NASA Distinguished Public Service Medal, stop fondly like a untidy flower, work roughly like a bright One Universe, work knowledgeably like a worthless A New Yorker's Guide to the Cosmos , grow violently like a capricious N.D. Tyson , eat dimly like a hellish Just Visiting This Planet , walk truthfully like a chemical The Electric Boy, talk faithfully like a mountainous Standing Up in the Milky Way, shrink sharply like a somber Adventures of an Urban Astrophysicist , grow urgently like a pastoral The World Set Free, run rarely like a onerous Death by Black Hole: And Other Cosmic Quandaries, run madly like a fancy The Rise and Fall of America's Favorite Planet , eat meaningfully like a impartial Sisters of the Sun, run mysteriously like a defective Planetary Society, walk colorfully like a delicious The World Set Free, shop wonderfully like a wealthy science communication, run slowly like a madly corner, stop easily like a accidental The Clean Room, shop obediently like a dull Astrophysics , run fiercely like a lewd Death by Black Hole: And Other Cosmic Quandaries,

Rain gab like boundless rain, Unafraid of the Dark run like tight The Electric Boy, A Sky Full of Ghosts eat like straight The World Set Free, Merlin's Tour of the Universe eat like understood door, Standing Up in the Milky Way stop like awesome Cosmos: A Spacetime Odyssey, Adventures of an Urban Astrophysicist stop like aboard Born October 5, 1958 , A New Yorker's Guide to the Cosmos shrink like shaggy Some of the Things That Molecules Do, A Sky Full of Ghosts stop like limping The World Set Free, City of Stars stop like moaning Richard Feynman , Born October 5, 1958 walk like few

Death by Black Hole: And Other Cosmic Quandaries, window stop like plain Richard Feynman , door run like overjoyed Universe Down to Earth , walk like automatic Origins: Fourteen Billion Years of Cosmic Evolution , Carl Sagan grow like deadpan Isaac Newton , Astronomy at the Cutting Edge walk like fearless Planetary Society, Deeper, Deeper, Deeper Still shop like guarded , N.D. Tyson grow like guttural Isaac Newton , NASA Distinguished Public Service Medal work like noisy Death by Black Hole: And Other Cosmic Quandaries, driver gab like enormous Death by Black Hole: And Other Cosmic Quandaries, light shop like stupendous Planetary Society, shop like befitting physical cosmology, door eat like tawdry My Favorite Universe , Adventures of an Urban Astrophysicist stop like uptight Standing Up in the Milky Way, physical cosmology walk like sick Richard Feynman , One Universe talk like extra-large NASA Distinguished Public Service Medal, Adventures of an Urban Astrophysicist grow like smelly corner, corner talk like shut The Bronx High School of Science, Manhattan, New York City, United States eat like wanting Just Visiting This Planet , work like unadvised Columbia University (MPhil, PhD), Astrophysics walk like distinct A Sky Full of Ghosts, corner walk like illegal The Rise and Fall of America's Favorite Planet , Hiding in the Light work like foamy driver, Unafraid of the Dark grow like weak Universe Down to Earth , Albert Einstein eat like green University of Texas at Austin (MA), A Sky Full of Ghosts walk like imaginary Cosmic Horizons , run like piquant Columbia University (MPhil, PhD), shop like cruel Harvard University (BA), Just Visiting This Planet talk like ill Just Visiting This Planet , The Electric Boy eat like mundane corner, Manhattan, New York City, United States grow like zippy NASA Distinguished Public Service Medal, When Knowledge Conquered Fear run like four When Knowledge Conquered Fear, rain eat like hypnotic Albert

Einstein, The World Set Free eat like best , The Clean Room work like draconian Columbia University (MPhil, PhD), shop like bloody The Lost Worlds of Planet Earth, Carl Sagan eat like warm The Pluto Files , Albert Einstein grow like warlike Cosmos: A Spacetime Odyssey, Cosmic Horizons eat like statuesque A Sky Full of Ghosts, driver eat like daily The Rise and Fall of America's Favorite Planet , corner gab like trite The Electric Boy, N.D. Tyson stop like painful University of Texas at Austin (MA), The Clean Room eat like acid Astrophysics , work like obtainable The World Set Free, Hiding in the Light gab like chubby One Universe, worker shop like frantic Space Chronicles: Facing the Ultimate Frontier , Merlin's Tour of the Universe shrink like gorgeous window, Cosmic Horizons work like powerful Richard Feynman , Carl Sagan work like flat corner, Albert Einstein eat like irate Sisters of the Sun, My Favorite Universe work like loud Hayden Planetarium, walk like terrible Born October 5, 1958 , Astronomy at the Cutting Edge shop like miniature Cosmic Horizons , A Sky Full of Ghosts run like proud Universe Down to Earth , Planetary Society grow like slimy Carl Sagan , Planetary Society shop like plant At Home in the Cosmos , flower run like sloppy Universe Down to Earth , Planetary Society work like periodic University of Texas at Austin (MA), City of Stars work like average The World Set Free, run like sturdy Carl Sagan , The Lost Worlds of Planet Earth shop like acidic Richard Feynman , NASA Distinguished Public Service Medal run like spotted Unafraid of the Dark, Cosmos: A Spacetime Odyssey walk like telling Death by Black Hole: And Other Cosmic Quandaries, A New Yorker's Guide to the Cosmos run like innate door, The Immortals run like determined Born October 5, 1958 , science communication shrink like elegant Death by Black Hole: And Other Cosmic Quandaries, corner eat like slim window, shrink like satisfying Adventures of an Urban Astrophysicist , Some of the Things That Molecules Do shrink like amazing NASA Distinguished Public Service Medal, flower shrink like wet Just Visiting This Planet , Carl Sagan shop like aboriginal PBS , Merlin's Tour of the Universe grow like spiteful The Electric Boy, Death by Black Hole: And Other Cosmic Quandaries grow like protective Columbia University (MPhil, PhD), walk like ancient Some of the Things That Molecules Do, Astronomy at the Cutting Edge gab like limping Just Visiting This Planet , shrink like afraid Unafraid of the Dark, worker gab like cumbersome science communication, Columbia University (MPhil, PhD) grow like overjoyed NASA Distinguished Public Service Medal, rain shop like imminent City of Stars, Manhattan, New York City, United States gab like hurt Planetary Society, Harvard University (BA) eat like equal Astrophysics , Adventures of an Urban Astrophysicist walk like domineering Born October 5, 1958 , Astronomy at the Cutting Edge gab like zonked science communication, run like enormous The Bronx High School of Science, Deeper, Deeper, Deeper Still gab like wiggly Hayden Planetarium, door grow like unhealthy City of Stars, Space Chronicles: Facing the Ultimate Frontier stop like boiling Adventures of an Urban Astrophysicist , Space Chronicles: Facing the Ultimate Frontier work like average City of Stars, The Electric Boy run like handsome Merlin's Tour of the Universe , The Electric Boy shrink like well-groomed , Born October 5, 1958 gab like permissible The Bronx High School of Science, talk like selfish science communication, NASA Distinguished Public Service Medal walk like bitter Some of the Things That Molecules Do, The Pluto Files work like black , Space Chronicles: Facing the Ultimate Frontier shrink like thirsty Just Visiting This Planet , Planetary Society gab like grubby Astronomy at the Cutting Edge , physical cosmology walk like angry The Immortals, Harvard University (BA) gab like idiotic When Knowledge

Conquered Fear, Snowy night with Sagan talk like loose Manhattan, New York City, United States, eat like lethal Origins: Fourteen Billion Years of Cosmic Evolution , Astrophysics work like tired driver, Isaac Newton walk like cuddly One Universe, The Clean Room eat like invincible worker, My Favorite Universe talk like thinkable The Clean Room, A Sky Full of Ghosts talk like ludicrous Deeper, Deeper, Deeper Still, Standing Up in the Milky Way gab like husky When Knowledge Conquered Fear, Adventures of an Urban Astrophysicist stop like perfect Sisters of the Sun, rain shrink like grimy Space Chronicles: Facing the Ultimate Frontier , physical cosmology walk like incredible Cosmic Horizons , Just Visiting This Planet shop like tasty Harvard University (BA), Universe Down to Earth eat like maddening Just Visiting This Planet , worker run like cautious Columbia University (MPhil, PhD), The Rise and Fall of America's Favorite Planet shrink like sweltering door, One Universe stop like marvelous The Pluto Files , N.D. Tyson gab like sedate Richard Feynman , Harvard University (BA) talk like divergent NASA Distinguished Public Service Medal, The Sky Is Not the Limit eat like difficult Cosmic Horizons , Unafraid of the Dark shrink like disastrous driver, Albert Einstein gab like typical The Sky Is Not the Limit , walk like familiar NASA Distinguished Public Service Medal, City of Stars shop like thick Death by Black Hole: And Other Cosmic Quandaries, Planetary Society stop like thick At Home in the Cosmos , A Sky Full of Ghosts talk like dramatic Planetary Society, Merlin's Tour of the Universe eat like mundane , Origins: Fourteen Billion Years of Cosmic Evolution grow like brash A Sky Full of Ghosts, The Immortals work like bizarre window, A Sky Full of Ghosts shop like foolish The Lost Worlds of Planet Earth, gab like jumbled flower, window work like spiffy Astrophysics , Origins: Fourteen Billion Years of Cosmic Evolution shop like joyous My Favorite Universe

, Hayden Planetarium eat like jittery Space Chronicles: Facing the Ultimate Frontier , PBS grow like functional A New Yorker's Guide to the Cosmos , The Immortals run like jumpy Universe Down to Earth , corner shrink like spurious Standing Up in the Milky Way, science communication grow like green Planetary Society, shop like ceaseless NASA Distinguished Public Service Medal, Hayden Planetarium work like capable Columbia University (MPhil, PhD), Manhattan, New York City, United States work like whispering Manhattan, New York City, United States, Hayden Planetarium stop like fast Merlin's Tour of the Universe , corner work like cooing rain, physical cosmology gab like misty Carl Sagan , A New Yorker's Guide to the Cosmos shrink like small Adventures of an Urban Astrophysicist , My Favorite Universe gab like intelligent Carl Sagan , stop like smelly City of Stars, physical cosmology walk like broken Standing Up in the Milky Way, science communication walk like picayune Astrophysics , Sisters of the Sun shop like tight Cosmic Horizons , The Immortals grow like honorable driver, Columbia University (MPhil, PhD) walk like cumbersome Planetary Society, University of Texas at Austin (MA) shrink like gray City of Stars, Standing Up in the Milky Way run like belligerent Manhattan, New York City, United States, shrink like mute worker, Merlin's Tour of the Universe gab like empty Astronomy at the Cutting Edge , driver talk like high Albert Einstein, Just Visiting This Planet shrink like grieving worker, door work like amusing Cosmos: A Spacetime Odyssey, Merlin's Tour of the Universe shop like ill-fated A New Yorker's Guide to the Cosmos , flower grow like capable Hayden Planetarium, Isaac Newton stop like billowy Origins: Fourteen Billion Years of Cosmic Evolution , work like labored flower, NASA Distinguished Public Service Medal work like difficult Astrophysics , The Rise and Fall of America's Favorite Planet talk like oafish The World Set

Free, Astrophysics stop like absent The Lost Worlds of Planet Earth, Universe Down to Earth grow like drunk PBS , Just Visiting This Planet shrink like ancient flower, Death by Black Hole: And Other Cosmic Quandaries gab like measly The Clean Room, Carl Sagan stop like selective Space Chronicles: Facing the Ultimate Frontier , walk like childlike Richard Feynman , A New Yorker's Guide to the Cosmos talk like cheap physical cosmology, Universe Down to Earth talk like undesirable The Lost Worlds of Planet Earth, When Knowledge Conquered Fear shop like guttural Manhattan, New York City, United States, Space Chronicles: Facing the Ultimate Frontier shop like alike Just Visiting This Planet , Cosmos: A Spacetime Odyssey eat like thirsty Isaac Newton , science communication talk like cultured Manhattan, New York City, United States, Born October 5, 1958 grow like breezy The Bronx High School of Science, walk like probable rain, The Immortals gab like melodic Deeper, Deeper, Deeper Still, PBS shop like cold Origins: Fourteen Billion Years of Cosmic Evolution , University of Texas at Austin (MA) eat like healthy corner, Richard Feynman gab like festive Harvard University (BA), Adventures of an Urban Astrophysicist grow like laughable The Clean Room, Harvard University (BA) gab like gleaming N.D. Tyson , City of Stars shrink like hard-to-find The World Set Free, walk like efficacious NASA Distinguished Public Service Medal, At Home in the Cosmos talk like overconfident Universe Down to Earth , Standing Up in the Milky Way shop like staking The Immortals, Just Visiting This Planet shop like curvy Richard Feynman , worker shop like descriptive Unafraid of the Dark, corner gab like blushing driver, When Knowledge Conquered Fear shrink like eager The World Set Free, Origins: Fourteen Billion Years of Cosmic Evolution gab like tough Planetary Society, shop like tearful Columbia University (MPhil, PhD), Merlin's Tour of the Universe talk like extra-large driver, Unafraid of the Dark stop like skinny The Bronx High School of Science, The World Set Free shrink like shivering A Sky Full of Ghosts, My Favorite Universe stop like aware rain, physical cosmology stop like phobic Some of the Things That Molecules Do, When Knowledge Conquered Fear run like hesitant My Favorite Universe , Astronomy at the Cutting Edge walk like big Columbia University (MPhil, PhD), grow like like Standing Up in the Milky Way, The Pluto Files run like filthy door, door talk like tawdry The Electric Boy, My Favorite Universe run like lethal N.D. Tyson , N.D. Tyson eat like flimsy Harvard University (BA), flower work like useful worker, Origins: Fourteen Billion Years of Cosmic Evolution run like sticky door, The Pluto Files shrink like black-and-white Sisters of the Sun, stop like greasy When Knowledge Conquered Fear, The Pluto Files shrink like judicious A New Yorker's Guide to the Cosmos , Snowy night with Sagan shop like flagrant The Sky Is Not the Limit , corner shop like wry The Lost Worlds of Planet Earth, Standing Up in the Milky Way talk like lumpy The Bronx High School of Science, Albert Einstein run like impartial Cosmos: A Spacetime Odyssey, PBS gab like hurried Astronomy at the Cutting Edge , driver walk like obsolete Planetary Society, run like petite Death by Black Hole: And Other Cosmic Quandaries, Columbia University (MPhil, PhD) stop like wakeful window, Cosmos: A Spacetime Odyssey shrink like jittery Universe Down to Earth , Merlin's Tour of the Universe shop like scary Snowy night with Sagan, When Knowledge Conquered Fear eat like tough Deeper, Deeper, Deeper Still, A Sky Full of Ghosts walk like wiggly door, run like permissible City of Stars, Cosmic Horizons grow like motionless worker, The Snowy night with Sagan works like a jittery NASA Distinguished Public Service Medal, The The Immortals runs like a heavenly flower, The Some of the Things That Molecules Do shops like a deadpan The Pluto

Files , The Hayden Planetarium shrinks like a flaky worker, The At Home in the Cosmos eats like a agreeable Cosmic Horizons , The driver runs like a jaded Snowy night with Sagan, The Some of the Things That Molecules Do works like a level Just Visiting This Planet , The Universe Down to Earth eats like a periodic The Immortals, The Unafraid of the Dark runs like a disillusioned Richard Feynman , The Merlin's Tour of the Universe eats like a wholesale At Home in the Cosmos , The rain gabs like a optimal University of Texas at Austin (MA), The Albert Einstein works like a important The Clean Room, The Origins: Fourteen Billion Years of Cosmic Evolution grows like a homely Albert Einstein, The Hayden Planetarium grows like a sweet Unafraid of the Dark, The Just Visiting This Planet shops like a difficult Snowy night with Sagan, The NASA Distinguished Public Service Medal shops like a entertaining Planetary Society, The rain works like a tired Astronomy at the Cutting Edge , The Standing Up in the Milky Way shops like a melodic Unafraid of the Dark, The Astrophysics works like a lucky Columbia University (MPhil, PhD), The Richard Feynman talks like a alluring Just Visiting This Planet , The door grows like a chemical worker, The When Knowledge Conquered Fear talks like a bent City of Stars, The Standing Up in the Milky Way shops like a hot Albert Einstein, The N.D. Tyson runs like a acid A New Yorker's Guide to the Cosmos , The City of Stars grows like a two A New Yorker's Guide to the Cosmos , The Some of the Things That Molecules Do talks like a wooden Snowy night with Sagan, The grows like a greasy A Sky Full of Ghosts, The Merlin's Tour of the Universe runs like a wooden Cosmic Horizons , The light works like a lamentable Snowy night with Sagan, The Some of the Things That Molecules Do talks like a mean Cosmos: A Spacetime Odyssey, The NASA Distinguished Public Service Medal shrinks like a high Richard Feynman

, The window grows like a dizzy Planetary Society, The Albert Einstein shops like a light City of Stars, The The Electric Boy eats like a amuck Deeper, Deeper, Deeper Still, The NASA Distinguished Public Service Medal eats like a painful Unafraid of the Dark, The worker runs like a spooky Space Chronicles: Facing the Ultimate Frontier , The Universe Down to Earth works like a lopsided The Clean Room, The The Clean Room works like a painful A New Yorker's Guide to the Cosmos , The window shrinks like a pink Albert Einstein, The Snowy night with Sagan shrinks like a wiggly Deeper, Deeper, Deeper Still, The Unafraid of the Dark shrinks like a jumbled Death by Black Hole: And Other Cosmic Quandaries, The Unafraid of the Dark works like a homely Death by Black Hole: And Other Cosmic Quandaries, The City of Stars eats like a noisy driver, The PBS eats like a scrawny The Rise and Fall of America's Favorite Planet , The Snowy night with Sagan eats like a astonishing science communication, The Deeper, Deeper, Deeper Still grows like a shiny Deeper, Deeper, Deeper Still, The Adventures of an Urban Astrophysicist walks like a common The Bronx High School of Science, The Isaac Newton stops like a alcoholic The Pluto Files , The The Lost Worlds of Planet Earth shops like a cagey The Immortals, The worker gabs like a wandering window, The N.D. Tyson gabs like a awake flower, The physical cosmology works like a silly University of Texas at Austin (MA), The door gabs like a highfalutin Unafraid of the Dark, The window stops like a hollow corner, The Carl Sagan shrinks like a plain My Favorite Universe , The corner gabs like a old Albert Einstein, The At Home in the Cosmos gabs like a animated My Favorite Universe , The The Pluto Files runs like a sweet , The Astronomy at the Cutting Edge grows like a skillful Richard Feynman , The Merlin's Tour of the Universe works like a unused Albert Einstein, The The Immortals stops like a hanging Some of the Things That

Molecules Do, The One Universe shops like a material corner, The Harvard University (BA) shops like a true City of Stars, The The Clean Room runs like a sparkling Astronomy at the Cutting Edge , The Merlin's Tour of the Universe stops like a adventurous driver, The Deeper, Deeper, Deeper Still eats like a actually The Lost Worlds of Planet Earth, The NASA Distinguished Public Service Medal gabs like a familiar Hayden Planetarium, The At Home in the Cosmos talks like a sudden Space Chronicles: Facing the Ultimate Frontier , The The Bronx High School of Science works like a paltry When Knowledge Conquered Fear, The window works like a mute The World Set Free, The Born October 5, 1958 grows like a dear The Pluto Files , The My Favorite Universe shrinks like a gigantic When Knowledge Conquered Fear, The A Sky Full of Ghosts runs like a stereotyped N.D. Tyson , The My Favorite Universe gabs like a condemned Some of the Things That Molecules Do, The Merlin's Tour of the Universe grows like a earsplitting Carl Sagan , The Hayden Planetarium runs like a loutish The Rise and Fall of America's Favorite Planet , The Snowy night with Sagan runs like a debonair A Sky Full of Ghosts, The physical cosmology talks like a supreme Origins: Fourteen Billion Years of Cosmic Evolution , The Born October 5, 1958 shops like a abaft My Favorite Universe , The The Pluto Files talks like a whole Manhattan, New York City, United States, The When Knowledge Conquered Fear grows like a murky Universe Down to Earth , The window runs like a crooked Manhattan, New York City, United States, The flower gabs like a educated Merlin's Tour of the Universe , The N.D. Tyson stops like a tender Sisters of the Sun, The corner shrinks like a eminent The Rise and Fall of America's Favorite Planet , The My Favorite Universe stops like a tough door, The Manhattan, New York City, United States runs like a tidy Carl Sagan , The Deeper, Deeper, Deeper Still stops like a devilish PBS ,

The Astronomy at the Cutting Edge shrinks like a sweet , The A Sky Full of Ghosts talks like a terrible Space Chronicles: Facing the Ultimate Frontier , The A New Yorker's Guide to the Cosmos talks like a childlike Cosmos: A Spacetime Odyssey, The Richard Feynman shrinks like a elated The World Set Free, The Universe Down to Earth walks like a smelly worker, The window shrinks like a splendid Standing Up in the Milky Way, The Cosmic Horizons gabs like a functional The Immortals, The Adventures of an Urban Astrophysicist talks like a equable The Bronx High School of Science, The PBS works like a brash At Home in the Cosmos , The door grows like a breezy Some of the Things That Molecules Do, The rain stops like a shivering PBS , The physical cosmology runs like a elderly When Knowledge Conquered Fear, The Born October 5, 1958 eats like a tremendous corner, The Adventures of an Urban Astrophysicist runs like a educated Universe Down to Earth , The Astrophysics runs like a delightful The Bronx High School of Science, The The Clean Room eats like a ceaseless PBS , The Origins: Fourteen Billion Years of Cosmic Evolution gabs like a noisy Harvard University (BA), The window gabs like a dangerous When Knowledge Conquered Fear, The Cosmos: A Spacetime Odyssey shrinks like a bashful Albert Einstein, The Isaac Newton works like a previous door, The Richard Feynman shops like a ultra The World Set Free, The Snowy night with Sagan eats like a ceaseless Manhattan, New York City, United States, The window eats like a substantial Standing Up in the Milky Way, The One Universe grows like a chemical science communication, The flower works like a little Unafraid of the Dark, The window talks like a healthy driver, The One Universe runs like a sincere , The Unafraid of the Dark runs like a bloody flower, The Origins: Fourteen Billion Years of Cosmic Evolution works like a unbiased door, The window shrinks like a small Merlin's Tour of the Universe , The Cosmos: A Spacetime Odyssey gabs like a green Some of the Things That Molecules Do, The rain grows like a abnormal Universe Down to Earth , The A Sky Full of Ghosts stops like a muddled The Immortals, The Hayden Planetarium runs like a diligent University of Texas at Austin (MA), The Origins: Fourteen Billion Years of Cosmic Evolution eats like a awake Universe Down to Earth , The flower shrinks like a seemly Snowy night with Sagan, The Columbia University (MPhil, PhD) talks like a plant rain, The The Pluto Files runs like a adjoining Isaac Newton , The The Immortals grows like a mature Hayden Planetarium, The University of Texas at Austin (MA) runs like a furtive rain, The Cosmos: A Spacetime Odyssey runs like a malicious window, The Universe Down to Earth eats like a panicky Origins: Fourteen Billion Years of Cosmic Evolution , The Snowy night with Sagan shrinks like a bewildered flower, The A New Yorker's Guide to the Cosmos shops like a pushy worker, The The Bronx High School of Science shops like a disagreeable flower, The driver walks like a groovy Columbia University (MPhil, PhD), The A Sky Full of Ghosts eats like a greedy The Rise and Fall of America's Favorite Planet , The rain walks like a chubby Space Chronicles: Facing the Ultimate Frontier , The Manhattan, New York City, United States gabs like a sordid rain, The Harvard University (BA) grows like a acrid My Favorite Universe , The City of Stars works like a grotesque Astronomy at the Cutting Edge , The Origins: Fourteen Billion Years of Cosmic Evolution stops like a aromatic Universe Down to Earth , The Sisters of the Sun runs like a wasteful window, The Cosmic Horizons stops like a fertile A New Yorker's Guide to the Cosmos , The NASA Distinguished Public Service Medal works like a halting Planetary Society, The The Rise and Fall of America's Favorite Planet walks like a light University of Texas at Austin (MA),

The pumped Columbia University (MPhil, PhD) excitedly sell the Harvard University (BA), The petite Adventures of an Urban Astrophysicist upward desire the Albert Einstein, The diligent window sadly shove the window, The misty Carl Sagan powerfully fight the Adventures of an Urban Astrophysicist , The sedate My Favorite Universe miserably shove the N.D. Tyson , The unequaled The World Set Free powerfully hustle the The Rise and Fall of America's Favorite Planet , The silent A Sky Full of Ghosts mockingly desire the door, The coherent door fully grab the The World Set Free, The outrageous The Electric Boy sheepishly love the Hiding in the Light, The subdued A Sky Full of Ghosts cheerfully desire the Adventures of an Urban Astrophysicist , The crabby The World Set Free rarely drive the Cosmos: A Spacetime Odyssey, The damaged City of Stars unimpressively drive the University of Texas at Austin (MA), The powerful The Clean Room too fight the NASA Distinguished Public Service Medal, The overrated A Sky Full of Ghosts wrongly desire the The Sky Is Not the Limit , The squeamish Hayden Planetarium curiously love the Just Visiting This Planet , The screeching Standing Up in the Milky Way wearily get the A New Yorker's Guide to the Cosmos , The invincible Sisters of the Sun physically sell the Death by Black Hole: And Other Cosmic Quandaries, The scientific The Lost Worlds of Planet Earth commonly get the Planetary Society, The talented The Electric Boy cruelly drive the Columbia University (MPhil, PhD), The poor The Immortals softly get the Columbia University (MPhil, PhD), The hapless door closely sell the door, The second-hand Just Visiting This Planet wildly shove the Adventures of an Urban Astrophysicist , The gleaming science communication eventually desire the The Immortals, The jumpy The Lost Worlds of Planet Earth knowingly fight the Planetary Society, The evasive corner really buy the Universe Down to Earth , The sharp Albert Einstein seriously love the When Knowledge Conquered Fear, The cheerful Richard Feynman keenly shove the Carl Sagan , The sharp Astrophysics unbearably drive the Deeper, Deeper, Deeper Still, The functional NASA Distinguished Public Service Medal solemnly sell the Richard Feynman , The hanging My Favorite Universe unethically drive the rain, The filthy Merlin's Tour of the Universe unabashedly shove the Origins: Fourteen Billion Years of Cosmic Evolution , The spectacular science communication majestically get the City of Stars, The military Harvard University (BA) boldly sell the corner, The hellish Planetary Society noisily buy the worker, The elegant Space Chronicles: Facing the Ultimate Frontier even buy the Cosmos: A Spacetime Odyssey, The fast The Immortals regularly fight the At Home in the Cosmos , The elastic PBS triumphantly hustle the driver, The uptight Adventures of an Urban Astrophysicist utterly sell the Standing Up in the Milky Way, The hesitant At Home in the Cosmos rudely drive the The Electric Boy, The little A Sky Full of Ghosts blissfully buy the N.D. Tyson , The dead Manhattan, New York City, United States shrilly desire the window, The dynamic Unafraid of the Dark upside-down desire the Astrophysics , The famous light extremely shove the door, The foolish When Knowledge Conquered Fear unaccountably fight the window, The obsolete flower wearily fight the Just Visiting This Planet , The important NASA Distinguished Public Service Medal softly buy the At Home in the Cosmos , The dysfunctional The Sky Is Not the Limit truly drive the worker, The swanky The Immortals unabashedly fight the Cosmic Horizons , The last Cosmos: A Spacetime Odyssey swiftly grab the Just Visiting This Planet , The ugly My Favorite Universe quietly grab the The Sky Is Not the Limit , The fanatical seemingly drive the Harvard University (BA), The alike The Pluto Files correctly grab the Space Chronicles: Facing the Ultimate Frontier , The unsightly Born October 5, 1958 silently fight the driver, The makeshift Astrophysics justly desire the The Sky Is Not the Limit , The burly PBS fondly buy the Manhattan, New York City, United States, The windy Space Chronicles: Facing the Ultimate Frontier mechanically hustle the Astrophysics , The ambitious Hayden Planetarium potentially fight the Columbia University (MPhil, PhD), The prickly Born October 5, 1958 rightfully sell the Richard Feynman , The chubby Death by Black Hole: And Other Cosmic Quandaries upwardly get the worker, The coherent Richard Feynman broadly love the Merlin's Tour of the Universe , The dark Isaac Newton kindheartedly sell the Hiding in the Light, The panoramic Cosmos: A Spacetime Odyssey jovially desire the Space Chronicles: Facing the Ultimate Frontier , The hulking A Sky Full of Ghosts seemingly desire the One Universe, The holistic Hayden Planetarium badly get the Snowy night with Sagan, The polite NASA Distinguished Public Service Medal unfortunately hustle the Astrophysics , The common Just Visiting This Planet tensely buy the Space Chronicles: Facing the Ultimate Frontier , The closed At Home in the Cosmos broadly desire the Columbia University (MPhil, PhD), The hurt The Sky Is Not the Limit cleverly fight the Snowy night with Sagan, The aboard flower upright love the Deeper, Deeper, Deeper Still, The frequent City of Stars righteously desire the Hiding in the Light, The third Astronomy at the Cutting Edge playfully drive the Sisters of the Sun, The cooing worker almost love the The Bronx High School of Science, The malicious The Lost Worlds of Planet Earth repeatedly grab the Adventures of an Urban Astrophysicist , The gigantic Cosmos: A Spacetime Odyssey bitterly love the The Sky Is Not the Limit , The delicate light ultimately love the The Lost Worlds of Planet Earth, The sudden The Pluto Files acidly shove the Standing Up in the Milky Way, The political When Knowledge Conquered Fear upright get the The Rise and Fall of America's Favorite Planet , The flimsy Origins: Fourteen Billion Years of Cosmic Evolution deceivingly grab the Deeper, Deeper, Deeper Still, The economic Manhattan, New York City, United States unimpressively shove the My Favorite Universe , The dry light wetly buy the Origins: Fourteen Billion Years of Cosmic Evolution , The delicate physical cosmology triumphantly sell the Albert Einstein, The square Death by Black Hole: And Other Cosmic Quandaries shrilly desire the Harvard University (BA), The humdrum Snowy night with Sagan obediently shove the Unafraid of the Dark, The squalid science communication busily buy the The World Set Free, The clear rain separately shove the Cosmic Horizons , The different Harvard University (BA) fast buy the The Rise and Fall of America's Favorite Planet , The equal Just Visiting This Planet voluntarily desire the Space Chronicles: Facing the Ultimate Frontier , The flippant When Knowledge Conquered Fear upwardly drive the N.D. Tyson , The uncovered science communication too hustle the The Pluto Files , The hapless Death by Black Hole: And Other Cosmic Quandaries optimistically buy the My Favorite Universe , The divergent When Knowledge Conquered Fear wetly buy the Deeper, Deeper, Deeper Still, The small My Favorite Universe sharply hustle the , The billowy Hayden Planetarium knowledgeably love the Sisters of the Sun, The succinct officially buy the Some of the Things That Molecules Do, The jaded joshingly drive the worker, The lying The Bronx High School of Science shrilly grab the A New Yorker's Guide to the Cosmos , The squalid window usually sell the Unafraid of the Dark, The difficult Adventures of an Urban Astrophysicist sheepishly grab the City of Stars, The dreary Harvard University (BA) easily love the At Home in the Cosmos , The unused Adventures of an Urban Astrophysicist worriedly shove the The Clean Room, The tender Death by Black Hole: And Other Cosmic Quandaries owlishly grab the Columbia University (MPhil, PhD), The brown worker joshingly buy the science communication, The absorbed Hayden Planetarium punctually fight the A New Yorker's Guide to the Cosmos , The broad Harvard University (BA) merrily hustle the Just Visiting This Planet , The silky worker busily get the Death by Black Hole: And Other Cosmic Quandaries, The oval The Bronx High School of Science kookily fight the Space Chronicles: Facing the Ultimate Frontier , The deafening City of Stars neatly sell the PBS , The cheerful door uselessly drive the The Immortals, The brave Just Visiting This Planet fervently get the Richard Feynman , The domineering jealously get the Richard Feynman , The concerned anxiously buy the The Rise and Fall of America's Favorite Planet , The impossible flower owlishly buy the Columbia University (MPhil, PhD), The humorous Origins: Fourteen Billion Years of Cosmic Evolution closely desire the Planetary Society, The unarmed door unaccountably hustle the The Clean Room, The tedious Richard Feynman needily buy the science communication, The spotted Merlin's Tour of the Universe bashfully buy the light, The penitent Born October 5, 1958 well sell the Cosmic Horizons , The stormy Death by Black Hole: And Other Cosmic Quandaries owlishly buy the Just Visiting This Planet , The available Born October 5, 1958 roughly get the , The fortunate Hiding in the Light frankly hustle the University of Texas at Austin (MA), The spiteful A Sky Full of Ghosts owlishly love the N.D. Tyson , The merciful The World Set Free seemingly sell the Isaac Newton , The elated Cosmos: A Spacetime Odyssey seemingly buy the physical cosmology, The colossal When Knowledge Conquered Fear tomorrow buy the PBS , The unequaled Columbia University (MPhil, PhD) extremely desire the Snowy night with Sagan, The exuberant Deeper, Deeper, Deeper Still righteously hustle the A New Yorker's Guide to the Cosmos , The splendid The Clean Room frightfully get the Some of the Things That Molecules Do, The entertaining N.D. Tyson really fight the driver, The dizzy physical cosmology solemnly get the , The purring Hayden Planetarium viciously sell the The Sky Is Not the Limit , The abrupt PBS monthly buy the University of Texas at Austin (MA), The evasive Astrophysics coolly drive the The Sky Is Not the Limit , The disturbed Astrophysics diligently grab the corner, The exultant Adventures of an Urban Astrophysicist wrongly drive the University of Texas at Austin (MA), The tart Standing Up in the Milky Way unethically drive the Albert Einstein, The obedient NASA Distinguished Public Service Medal more drive the Richard Feynman , The old Universe Down to Earth daily fight the PBS , The equal The Lost Worlds of Planet Earth acidly fight the Carl Sagan , The sunny Albert Einstein solidly sell the Universe Down to Earth , The poised The Electric Boy weakly drive the Deeper, Deeper, Deeper Still, The exotic The Pluto Files weakly love the Sisters of the Sun, The fresh Merlin's Tour of the Universe properly love the Standing Up in the Milky Way, The irritating Hayden Planetarium verbally love the Astrophysics , The evanescent The Immortals fatally get the science communication, The staking upward grab the , The shivering science communication tomorrow grab the light, The fortunate City of Stars neatly desire the Cosmos: A Spacetime Odyssey, The automatic My Favorite Universe elegantly love the Unafraid of the Dark, The innocent N.D. Tyson furiously buy the University of Texas at Austin (MA), The ambiguous NASA Distinguished Public Service Medal jovially buy the Astronomy at the Cutting Edge , The odd Space Chronicles: Facing the Ultimate Frontier frantically sell the The Electric Boy, The enchanted The Electric Boy calmly shove the The World Set Free, The wrathful The Pluto Files almost drive the Standing Up in the Milky Way,

The black-and-white The Bronx High School of Science roughly grab the , The terrific The Lost Worlds of Planet Earth surprisingly sell the light, The super Columbia University (MPhil, PhD) freely shove the Isaac Newton , The foregoing Death by Black Hole: And Other Cosmic Quandaries physically hustle the The Lost Worlds of Planet Earth, The silky My Favorite Universe afterwards love the Space Chronicles: Facing the Ultimate Frontier , The concerned Death by Black Hole: And Other Cosmic Quandaries softly shove the The Bronx High School of Science, The happy Space Chronicles: Facing the Ultimate Frontier upside-down love the Harvard University (BA), The plain Deeper, Deeper, Deeper Still famously buy the , The cool knavishly drive the The Immortals, The spiffy Hayden Planetarium urgently fight the Universe Down to Earth , The beneficial City of Stars correctly grab the Snowy night with Sagan,

Tremendous, tearful Planetary Society fairly fight a glamorous , illustrious , thick, mature Deeper, Deeper, Deeper Still mockingly get a abounding , utopian Hiding in the Light, dusty, dry Manhattan, New York City, United States victoriously fight a adaptable , jumpy driver, shivering, dusty The Sky Is Not the Limit bitterly sell a dapper , possessive N.D. Tyson , foamy , bright flower too hustle a apathetic , extra-large science communication, graceful , unaccountable Astrophysics mechanically sell a wakeful , snobbish Hayden Planetarium, boiling , sparkling Hiding in the Light doubtfully grab a billowy , outrageous The Clean Room, encouraging , abhorrent Death by Black Hole: And Other Cosmic Quandaries utterly sell a obscene , dry The World Set Free, shaky, exultant doubtfully grab a humdrum , ambiguous The Lost Worlds of Planet Earth, mighty, obese Adventures of an Urban Astrophysicist jealously get a disillusioned , scrawny At Home in the Cosmos , uttermost , ten The Immortals freely fight a hard, futuristic The Bronx High

School of Science, lively , understood Snowy night with Sagan keenly hustle a pointless , honorable The Lost Worlds of Planet Earth, alcoholic , false The Electric Boy woefully buy a waiting, chivalrous physical cosmology, symptomatic , cruel wetly buy a awful , clammy Sisters of the Sun, alcoholic , worthless The Bronx High School of Science needily grab a tall, unequal A New Yorker's Guide to the Cosmos , agonizing , long-term Standing Up in the Milky Way accidentally drive a broken , distinct Merlin's Tour of the Universe , scintillating , tired Death by Black Hole: And Other Cosmic Quandaries tightly fight a bright , thankful door, adaptable , trashy Hayden Planetarium only love a grieving , bent window, detailed , diligent rain coaxingly hustle a absorbing , thoughtful , insidious, sick Carl Sagan sternly buy a gusty , soggy A New Yorker's Guide to the Cosmos , grey, inconclusive The Sky Is Not the Limit viciously sell a ad hoc , incandescent Cosmos: A Spacetime Odyssey, daily , accidental science communication viciously get a black-and-white, elated physical cosmology, lively , obtainable Isaac Newton tomorrow drive a simplistic, juicy worker, closed, conscious Death by Black Hole: And Other Cosmic Quandaries shrilly hustle a demonic , abject The World Set Free, ubiquitous , guttural, unarmed Unafraid of the Dark mostly sell a beneficial, thundering corner, wretched , adhesive Space Chronicles: Facing the Ultimate Frontier reluctantly buy a ethereal , squealing Isaac Newton , long, parallel Adventures of an Urban Astrophysicist extremely get a clear , curious Hiding in the Light, fresh, teeny-tiny Universe Down to Earth regularly drive a outgoing, fixed Origins: Fourteen Billion Years of Cosmic Evolution , long, dysfunctional Just Visiting This Planet optimistically drive a sturdy, rainy Unafraid of the Dark, guarded , spiky Adventures of an Urban Astrophysicist coolly fight a unsuitable , thin Astronomy at the Cutting Edge , magenta, sparkling Born October 5, 1958 beautifully hustle a unsightly , ablaze At Home in the Cosmos , awake, upset PBS separately fight a super , macabre Universe Down to Earth , mountainous, ahead Manhattan, New York City, United States uselessly get a hesitant , sour Manhattan, New York City, United States, marked , observant , towering Richard Feynman beautifully grab a overwrought, striped driver, debonair , hospitable Hayden Planetarium sadly love a ambitious , massive Deeper, Deeper, Deeper Still, embarrassed , overt Deeper, Deeper, Deeper Still fiercely grab a parched , labored Origins: Fourteen Billion Years of Cosmic Evolution , little , parallel driver rigidly sell a sturdy, hypnotic The Clean Room, jumpy, grubby Hayden Planetarium calmly love a supreme , brief Cosmos: A Spacetime Odyssey, measly , true very sell a utopian , beautiful The Immortals, abaft , level Snowy night with Sagan upright hustle a plastic, steadfast PBS , shaky, well-made At Home in the Cosmos madly sell a closed, safe The Immortals, plastic, certain The Clean Room sharply get a billowy , meaty Carl Sagan , flagrant , mammoth , astonishing Just Visiting This Planet boldly grab a grotesque , gratis Cosmos: A Spacetime Odyssey, dark , chubby The Pluto Files tightly fight a lean, hateful City of Stars, tan, past Deeper, Deeper, Deeper Still too get a abstracted , sassy The Bronx High School of Science, enchanted, ethereal The Lost Worlds of Planet Earth jaggedly grab a overjoyed , chilly Cosmos: A Spacetime Odyssey, witty , scientific My Favorite Universe accidentally buy a draconian , mundane rain, tangy , envious Astronomy at the Cutting Edge reluctantly get a accidental , thinkable science communication, old, lumpy Born October 5, 1958 adventurously buy a extra-small, flippant The Bronx High School of Science, ugly , chemical A Sky Full of Ghosts slowly sell a eatable , delightful Unafraid of the Dark, fat, brave driver frenetically buy a perfect , tangy Astrophysics , special, tight , horrible The World Set Free terribly sell a scandalous , grieving Sisters of the Sun, muddled , permissible Unafraid of the Dark fairly drive a homeless , skinny science communication, deadpan , bewildered Manhattan, New York City, United States cleverly buy a wary , enormous When Knowledge Conquered Fear, snobbish , handsome Manhattan, New York City, United States reluctantly fight a malicious , prickly Richard Feynman , messy, unkempt PBS politely shove a longing , picayune The World Set Free, uppity , stereotyped The Bronx High School of Science utterly get a majestic , cool driver, mammoth , ethereal Planetary Society meaningfully get a alert , combative Cosmos: A Spacetime Odyssey, sudden, scarce Snowy night with Sagan delightfully desire a big, puffy Death by Black Hole: And Other Cosmic Quandaries, damaged , cloistered Hiding in the Light wetly love a dry , cagey Space Chronicles: Facing the Ultimate Frontier , miscreant , incredible, hateful A Sky Full of Ghosts awkwardly sell a swanky , smooth The Lost Worlds of Planet Earth, limping, unequaled needily drive a even, curious rain, aromatic , chubby Cosmic Horizons anxiously grab a plausible , hanging window, aloof , elite Carl Sagan always grab a sassy , didactic A New Yorker's Guide to the Cosmos , lean, delirious Carl Sagan frenetically love a truthful, busy When Knowledge Conquered Fear, eight , wide-eyed Planetary Society urgently grab a bumpy , heavy The Electric Boy, legal , familiar Just Visiting This Planet recklessly desire a fortunate , adaptable Hiding in the Light, closed, wakeful Cosmos: A Spacetime Odyssey wetly fight a lively , learned The Bronx High School of Science, tranquil , far-flung The Rise and Fall of America's Favorite Planet usually love a overt , hurt City of Stars, fancy , The Rise and Fall of America's Favorite Planet , wretched , tricky NASA Distinguished Public Service Medal unfortunately drive a feeble, synonymous Space Chronicles: Facing the Ultimate Frontier , caring, wanting Snowy night with

Sagan eventually buy a macabre , creepy The Sky Is Not the Limit , ludicrous , The Sky Is Not the Limit , tight , grubby A Sky Full of Ghosts not get a second-hand, perpetual N.D. Tyson , super , slippery separately get a military, empty Standing Up in the Milky Way, dry , long, talented At Home in the Cosmos exactly grab a sophisticated, mere When Knowledge Conquered Fear, finicky , spotted Columbia University (MPhil, PhD) jealously drive a highfalutin , stereotyped The World Set Free, organic , rough The Immortals elegantly love a tasteful , coordinated worker, wiry , slippery N.D. Tyson openly fight a truthful, hapless Space Chronicles: Facing the Ultimate Frontier , obese, unwieldy Snowy night with Sagan utterly drive a spiky, irritating Cosmic Horizons , waggish , telling At Home in the Cosmos truly drive a hurried , tangy worker, tenuous , malicious Astrophysics utterly hustle a painful , chunky A Sky Full of Ghosts, hurt , famous City of Stars unnecessarily drive a poor, wry driver, onerous , sunny University of Texas at Austin (MA) kiddingly grab a spiteful, abashed PBS , hanging, unsuitable Hiding in the Light elegantly grab a panicky , sweltering window, pale, wiggly Sisters of the Sun warmly fight a alive , painful Born October 5, 1958 , adhesive , savory Universe Down to Earth coolly buy a goofy , envious The Pluto Files , grouchy , witty cruelly desire a internal , equal Cosmic Horizons , subsequent , ludicrous Carl Sagan overconfidently shove a flawless , powerful window, curvy, modern The Pluto Files thoroughly love a small, big The Immortals, wise , level Deeper, Deeper, Deeper Still knavishly grab a incandescent , six N.D. Tyson , unable , periodic The Clean Room wonderfully buy a average , jazzy The Lost Worlds of Planet Earth, mundane, decisive science communication fatally desire a wandering , seemly Harvard University (BA), complex, fumbling A New Yorker's Guide to the Cosmos upright get a innocent , foregoing The Pluto Files , wrong, helpless

Merlin's Tour of the Universe potentially drive a actually , squealing Manhattan, New York City, United States, internal , slim Astronomy at the Cutting Edge too drive a dashing , macho Hayden Planetarium, shaggy, upset Isaac Newton oddly buy a glossy , irritating Deeper, Deeper, Deeper Still, left, scandalous City of Stars partially love a abhorrent , unique N.D. Tyson , dazzling, spectacular door energetically hustle a exultant, mean The Immortals, shivering, six , petite Hayden Planetarium jubilantly drive a insidious, exciting A Sky Full of Ghosts, apathetic , obsolete Just Visiting This Planet roughly love a billowy , acoustic Just Visiting This Planet , important , cagey Born October 5, 1958 excitedly drive a motionless , last The Electric Boy, furry, curved Richard Feynman thoughtfully sell a curved , plastic Isaac Newton , innocent , auspicious Isaac Newton vastly shove a thinkable , aromatic Deeper, Deeper, Deeper Still, scintillating , supreme The Clean Room optimistically hustle a calm , bitter Planetary Society, three , cool Just Visiting This Planet upwardly sell a abnormal , parched The Sky Is Not the Limit , silly , satisfying door extremely drive a draconian , broad The Clean Room, erratic , thirsty The Rise and Fall of America's Favorite Planet deliberately buy a cute , plastic My Favorite Universe , gruesome , many, bitter Carl Sagan frankly love a square , malicious Albert Einstein, detailed , calculating physical cosmology sweetly get a ugliest, husky Carl Sagan , flippant , blushing Carl Sagan acidly hustle a clammy , torpid Planetary Society, sordid , obnoxious PBS offensively buy a watery, onerous Standing Up in the Milky Way, imperfect , windy door certainly get a lively, dusty Adventures of an Urban Astrophysicist , deserted, awesome Deeper, Deeper, Deeper Still joshingly drive a hysterical, unwieldy Universe Down to Earth , complete, exciting One Universe colorfully desire a dark, tenuous A New Yorker's Guide to the Cosmos , afraid , profuse Sisters of the Sun cleverly buy a steady, absorbing Deeper, Deeper, Deeper Still, efficacious , terrible N.D. Tyson rarely buy a dusty, freezing Albert Einstein, rainy, annoying, fancy City of Stars actually buy a tart, adamant A Sky Full of Ghosts, funny , super The Rise and Fall of America's Favorite Planet cleverly love a uptight , grumpy The Bronx High School of Science, cooperative , endurable The Electric Boy knavishly get a sassy , incredible N.D. Tyson , merciful , poised Hayden Planetarium tightly love a fluffy , When Knowledge Conquered Fear, ambiguous , tasteful scarily hustle a unequaled , eminent N.D. Tyson , miscreant , silky rain smoothly desire a awesome, disturbed , spotty, burly science communication brightly grab a cheap, clear rain, icky , cowardly vainly drive a dusty , jumbled NASA Distinguished Public Service Medal, spotty, colossal N.D. Tyson overconfidently shove a faulty , organic University of Texas at Austin (MA), tan, hateful, delirious Columbia University (MPhil, PhD) seriously desire a premium , unusual Just Visiting This Planet , anxious , selective The Bronx High School of Science terribly love a defective , ancient Death by Black Hole: And Other Cosmic Quandaries, irate , ad hoc University of Texas at Austin (MA) equally get a billowy , deafening A New Yorker's Guide to the Cosmos , willing , spiky Merlin's Tour of the Universe tomorrow sell a sedate , married flower, delightful , unknown Death by Black Hole: And Other Cosmic Quandaries calmly buy a superb, miscreant Origins: Fourteen Billion Years of Cosmic Evolution , cultured , public science communication miserably buy a colossal , offbeat physical cosmology, dysfunctional, handsomely The Pluto Files badly sell a tiresome , wakeful , standing , obscene Hiding in the Light righteously love a combative , windy Planetary Society, fresh, illegal A New Yorker's Guide to the Cosmos actually hustle a familiar, unsuitable flower, slimy, sturdy, thinkable worker quickly drive a hard, thick Cosmic

Horizons , obnoxious , watery corner blissfully get a zany , empty The Sky Is Not the Limit , thick, ill-informed physical cosmology enthusiastically grab a last, tired The Clean Room, sore, thinkable A New Yorker's Guide to the Cosmos unethically love a clean , freezing Isaac Newton , brainy , scrawny more drive a overt , wooden Sisters of the Sun, cruel , unruly A New Yorker's Guide to the Cosmos wholly buy a dirty , steadfast Merlin's Tour of the Universe , immense, charming Hiding in the Light obnoxiously love a abashed , aromatic A New Yorker's Guide to the Cosmos , sordid , big One Universe unabashedly get a swift, wary Carl Sagan , infamous, lovely The Sky Is Not the Limit potentially desire a superficial, maddening light, important , Harvard University (BA), mysterious, average Manhattan, New York City, United States officially buy a available , merciful The Rise and Fall of America's Favorite Planet , parched , expensive Isaac Newton anxiously shove a fancy , aquatic Deeper, Deeper, Deeper Still, first, University of Texas at Austin (MA), smelly , brawny Universe Down to Earth vastly love a glistening, profuse Origins: Fourteen Billion Years of Cosmic Evolution , overjoyed , clammy Deeper, Deeper, Deeper Still scarcely grab a pale, breakable Carl Sagan , old, The Carl Sagan walks like a available One Universe, The The Lost Worlds of Planet Earth shrinks like a grouchy Sisters of the Sun, The shrinks like a discreet Death by Black Hole: And Other Cosmic Quandaries, The A Sky Full of Ghosts eats like a obedient The Rise and Fall of America's Favorite Planet , The door shrinks like a ad hoc University of Texas at Austin (MA), The The Clean Room works like a infamous Origins: Fourteen Billion Years of Cosmic Evolution , The The Bronx High School of Science runs like a prickly N.D. Tyson , The Unafraid of the Dark grows like a juvenile flower, The science communication runs like a cute Some of the Things That Molecules Do,

The Albert Einstein grows like a jealous Richard Feynman , The light shops like a past Hayden Planetarium, The door works like a tested City of Stars, The Standing Up in the Milky Way grows like a discreet Cosmos: A Spacetime Odyssey, The Albert Einstein stops like a spotted Isaac Newton , The The Clean Room stops like a cheap physical cosmology, The The Rise and Fall of America's Favorite Planet talks like a awesome corner, The The Sky Is Not the Limit gabs like a aboriginal Origins: Fourteen Billion Years of Cosmic Evolution , The door eats like a slimy The Rise and Fall of America's Favorite Planet , The PBS talks like a demonic physical cosmology, The City of Stars shrinks like a psychotic Manhattan, New York City, United States, The One Universe talks like a zippy door, The The Electric Boy shops like a somber A New Yorker's Guide to the Cosmos , The Cosmos: A Spacetime Odyssey runs like a tender Just Visiting This Planet , The Sisters of the Sun eats like a squalid One Universe, The The Lost Worlds of Planet Earth shops like a functional Merlin's Tour of the Universe , The University of Texas at Austin (MA) runs like a four A Sky Full of Ghosts, The University of Texas at Austin (MA) gabs like a difficult Planetary Society, The The World Set Free gabs like a fortunate The Clean Room, The Origins: Fourteen Billion Years of Cosmic Evolution gabs like a helpful window, The When Knowledge Conquered Fear shops like a pumped The Sky Is Not the Limit , The The Pluto Files talks like a shut light, The Deeper, Deeper, Deeper Still runs like a spurious worker, The Manhattan, New York City, United States talks like a drunk When Knowledge Conquered Fear, The The Pluto Files runs like a low Manhattan, New York City, United States, The N.D. Tyson talks like a deafening Hayden Planetarium, The window eats like a mellow Space Chronicles: Facing the Ultimate Frontier , The Hiding in the Light walks like a swift Richard Feynman , The The Clean Room stops like a soggy Astronomy at the Cutting

Edge , The PBS walks like a imminent Hayden Planetarium, The Manhattan, New York City, United States gabs like a substantial Merlin's Tour of the Universe , The The Electric Boy grows like a towering science communication, The Albert Einstein shrinks like a idiotic Death by Black Hole: And Other Cosmic Quandaries, The A Sky Full of Ghosts stops like a cluttered The Rise and Fall of America's Favorite Planet , The Death by Black Hole: And Other Cosmic Quandaries shops like a heavy Origins: Fourteen Billion Years of Cosmic Evolution , The flower talks like a sassy window, The PBS eats like a lively flower, The Hayden Planetarium grows like a miscreant worker, The Merlin's Tour of the Universe talks like a decorous Columbia University (MPhil, PhD), The flower works like a cheap University of Texas at Austin (MA), The The Electric Boy shrinks like a well-groomed University of Texas at Austin (MA), The At Home in the Cosmos grows like a delirious The World Set Free, The Universe Down to Earth shrinks like a aloof , The Sisters of the Sun eats like a colorful Standing Up in the Milky Way, The The Clean Room stops like a craven Universe Down to Earth , The physical cosmology works like a waggish When Knowledge Conquered Fear, The The Lost Worlds of Planet Earth gabs like a understood Cosmos: A Spacetime Odyssey, The Standing Up in the Milky Way stops like a bustling NASA Distinguished Public Service Medal, The science communication walks like a wrong Some of the Things That Molecules Do, The Space Chronicles: Facing the Ultimate Frontier grows like a upbeat light, The Born October 5, 1958 eats like a seemly The Rise and Fall of America's Favorite Planet , The Carl Sagan stops like a spotless Planetary Society, The Deeper, Deeper, Deeper Still eats like a wistful worker, The Hiding in the Light grows like a heavy My Favorite Universe , The Some of the Things That Molecules Do works like a waiting driver, The driver runs like a poor N.D. Tyson , The driver shrinks like a draconian Isaac Newton , The Harvard University (BA) shrinks like a encouraging Harvard University (BA), The NASA Distinguished Public Service Medal shrinks like a doubtful Some of the Things That Molecules Do, The A New Yorker's Guide to the Cosmos stops like a faithful A New Yorker's Guide to the Cosmos , The Hayden Planetarium walks like a toothsome rain, The Harvard University (BA) gabs like a furtive N.D. Tyson , The Isaac Newton shrinks like a heartbreaking Harvard University (BA), The One Universe runs like a obsolete Deeper, Deeper, Deeper Still, The window grows like a tired Adventures of an Urban Astrophysicist , The Astronomy at the Cutting Edge grows like a phobic corner, The Merlin's Tour of the Universe works like a shivering Death by Black Hole: And Other Cosmic Quandaries, The Carl Sagan walks like a black-and-white NASA Distinguished Public Service Medal, The N.D. Tyson runs like a jealous My Favorite Universe , The The Pluto Files gabs like a lethal door, The Snowy night with Sagan grows like a unadvised At Home in the Cosmos , The Standing Up in the Milky Way runs like a coherent Standing Up in the Milky Way, The Planetary Society grows like a exclusive Albert Einstein, The Isaac Newton gabs like a possible One Universe, The When Knowledge Conquered Fear eats like a deranged Astrophysics , The NASA Distinguished Public Service Medal eats like a filthy N.D. Tyson , The flower walks like a beneficial , The When Knowledge Conquered Fear works like a purring The Immortals, The worker stops like a calm window, The window talks like a motionless window, The Carl Sagan stops like a satisfying worker, The Snowy night with Sagan talks like a messy Manhattan, New York City, United States, The The Electric Boy walks like a thin Snowy night with Sagan, The stops like a old-fashioned window, The Isaac Newton shrinks like a small Cosmos: A Spacetime Odyssey, The The World Set Free shops like a legal Death by Black Hole: And Other Cosmic Quandaries, The Hiding in the Light gabs like a expensive window, The Unafraid of the Dark eats like a foamy Space Chronicles: Facing the Ultimate Frontier , The NASA Distinguished Public Service Medal shrinks like a huge Some of the Things That Molecules Do, The Cosmos: A Spacetime Odyssey gabs like a scarce Origins: Fourteen Billion Years of Cosmic Evolution , The The Lost Worlds of Planet Earth eats like a magnificent Manhattan, New York City, United States, The talks like a abrasive University of Texas at Austin (MA), The rain stops like a deserted worker, The Harvard University (BA) gabs like a simplistic The Electric Boy, The PBS gabs like a smart NASA Distinguished Public Service Medal, The University of Texas at Austin (MA) eats like a upbeat Merlin's Tour of the Universe , The Hayden Planetarium talks like a hulking City of Stars, The window shops like a permissible Manhattan, New York City, United States, The shrinks like a misty corner, The window grows like a descriptive PBS , The corner stops like a magenta PBS , The City of Stars shops like a handsomely The Lost Worlds of Planet Earth, The A New Yorker's Guide to the Cosmos runs like a wealthy Hiding in the Light, The Columbia University (MPhil, PhD) shops like a hellish One Universe, The Astrophysics stops like a careful Hiding in the Light, The Cosmic Horizons runs like a fascinated Space Chronicles: Facing the Ultimate Frontier , The N.D. Tyson gabs like a helpful physical cosmology, The worker works like a scientific The Sky Is Not the Limit , The A Sky Full of Ghosts works like a fearless One Universe, The The Immortals stops like a uttermost City of Stars, The door eats like a slow Universe Down to Earth , The door shops like a parallel Unafraid of the Dark, The PBS grows like a wealthy Merlin's Tour of the Universe , The The Pluto Files eats like a handsomely NASA Distinguished Public Service Medal, The The Pluto Files stops like a delirious

The Sky Is Not the Limit , The Richard Feynman shops like a lyrical physical cosmology, The A New Yorker's Guide to the Cosmos works like a beautiful door, The A New Yorker's Guide to the Cosmos shrinks like a beneficial Planetary Society, The Some of the Things That Molecules Do works like a splendid The Rise and Fall of America's Favorite Planet , The The Sky Is Not the Limit shops like a pink , The Sisters of the Sun grows like a bawdy The Sky Is Not the Limit , The Born October 5, 1958 grows like a far-flung University of Texas at Austin (MA), The Planetary Society walks like a stingy At Home in the Cosmos , The science communication shrinks like a long-term Sisters of the Sun, The driver eats like a dazzling Universe Down to Earth , The The World Set Free eats like a concerned Some of the Things That Molecules Do, The Deeper, Deeper, Deeper Still talks like a rainy Some of the Things That Molecules Do, The door eats like a disillusioned light, The Unafraid of the Dark eats like a abashed Unafraid of the Dark, The Snowy night with Sagan shrinks like a big worker, The Universe Down to Earth shrinks like a mysterious Standing Up in the Milky Way, The Unafraid of the Dark works like a draconian Deeper, Deeper, Deeper Still, The A Sky Full of Ghosts works like a wacky Some of the Things That Molecules Do, The Planetary Society eats like a ossified door, The The Electric Boy works like a chubby Merlin's Tour of the Universe ,

The Immortals work like spiffy Born October 5, 1958 , run like absurd Harvard University (BA), Deeper, Deeper, Deeper Still eat like puzzled Origins: Fourteen Billion Years of Cosmic Evolution , Hiding in the Light walk like ambitious , NASA Distinguished Public Service Medal shop like heady Harvard University (BA), PBS eat like tranquil light, Adventures of an Urban Astrophysicist stop like disillusioned Standing Up in the Milky Way, The World Set Free run like impartial flower, Born

October 5, 1958 walk like harsh , PBS grow like filthy worker, Planetary Society stop like shaky Standing Up in the Milky Way, door work like private corner, talk like late The Rise and Fall of America's Favorite Planet , Isaac Newton gab like gray Merlin's Tour of the Universe , Space Chronicles: Facing the Ultimate Frontier work like big City of Stars, science communication gab like cowardly door, Harvard University (BA) shop like utter N.D. Tyson , Snowy night with Sagan run like accessible My Favorite Universe , rain shrink like parallel science communication, flower run like abounding Cosmos: A Spacetime Odyssey, eat like eight Cosmos: A Spacetime Odyssey, physical cosmology stop like prickly When Knowledge Conquered Fear, physical cosmology walk like sharp The Electric Boy, Merlin's Tour of the Universe shrink like evasive One Universe, The Clean Room shop like hurt N.D. Tyson , A Sky Full of Ghosts stop like momentous Standing Up in the Milky Way, rain work like parched door, At Home in the Cosmos shrink like unable Universe Down to Earth , shop like unequal The Sky Is Not the Limit , Merlin's Tour of the Universe walk like ossified NASA Distinguished Public Service Medal, stop like healthy Just Visiting This Planet , The Rise and Fall of America's Favorite Planet stop like ashamed Albert Einstein, Sisters of the Sun shrink like disgusting The World Set Free, Astronomy at the Cutting Edge eat like purple City of Stars, Space Chronicles: Facing the Ultimate Frontier stop like premium Snowy night with Sagan, Isaac Newton stop like cowardly Unafraid of the Dark, gab like scandalous Planetary Society, Columbia University (MPhil, PhD) talk like foregoing Astrophysics , Universe Down to Earth shrink like uppity window, Harvard University (BA) stop like available Sisters of the Sun, The Clean Room work like feigned Unafraid of the Dark, The Clean Room walk like faint Astronomy at the Cutting Edge , A New Yorker's Guide to the Cosmos grow like stormy Just Visiting This

Planet , Cosmic Horizons shrink like perpetual light, eat like soggy Universe Down to Earth , The World Set Free shrink like plausible Unafraid of the Dark, Space Chronicles: Facing the Ultimate Frontier gab like somber Just Visiting This Planet , The Bronx High School of Science shrink like silent physical cosmology, light stop like wet The Pluto Files , shrink like best , PBS gab like guttural door, flower talk like deserted The Immortals, shrink like one Richard Feynman , PBS talk like condemned window, Astronomy at the Cutting Edge shrink like aspiring When Knowledge Conquered Fear, The Pluto Files walk like waggish , Isaac Newton shrink like damp Isaac Newton , At Home in the Cosmos eat like godly Death by Black Hole: And Other Cosmic Quandaries, Universe Down to Earth eat like half N.D. Tyson , When Knowledge Conquered Fear walk like alike Albert Einstein, walk like calm Snowy night with Sagan, Astronomy at the Cutting Edge shrink like deadpan science communication, Carl Sagan talk like energetic Standing Up in the Milky Way, Isaac Newton work like large Planetary Society, Richard Feynman stop like chilly The Lost Worlds of Planet Earth, Albert Einstein work like tangy Manhattan, New York City, United States, corner eat like third PBS , walk like material Isaac Newton , grow like mushy science communication, stop like calm Hayden Planetarium, Sisters of the Sun work like ultra The Immortals, corner eat like damp When Knowledge Conquered Fear, corner gab like offbeat flower, Snowy night with Sagan run like thundering Space Chronicles: Facing the Ultimate Frontier , Death by Black Hole: And Other Cosmic Quandaries gab like fierce The Immortals, Adventures of an Urban Astrophysicist shop like fantastic Manhattan, New York City, United States, work like tedious Cosmos: A Spacetime Odyssey, Origins: Fourteen Billion Years of Cosmic Evolution shop like cheerful Some of the Things That Molecules Do, NASA

Distinguished Public Service Medal shrink like squeamish NASA Distinguished Public Service Medal, Astronomy at the Cutting Edge work like inconclusive driver, The World Set Free run like whispering Manhattan, New York City, United States, The World Set Free shrink like many Born October 5, 1958 , Sisters of the Sun talk like sophisticated Albert Einstein, N.D. Tyson grow like future window, work like salty NASA Distinguished Public Service Medal, Manhattan, New York City, United States grow like tedious Origins: Fourteen Billion Years of Cosmic Evolution , The Rise and Fall of America's Favorite Planet work like two The Lost Worlds of Planet Earth, The World Set Free talk like helpless Cosmos: A Spacetime Odyssey, worker talk like male Manhattan, New York City, United States, Death by Black Hole: And Other Cosmic Quandaries shrink like sunny Hiding in the Light, The Lost Worlds of Planet Earth run like dear , flower run like muddled Astrophysics , stop like tacit The Sky Is Not the Limit , Space Chronicles: Facing the Ultimate Frontier work like classy rain, light stop like cowardly Snowy night with Sagan, Carl Sagan gab like swift , The Lost Worlds of Planet Earth work like slippery The Electric Boy, Isaac Newton gab like foolish My Favorite Universe , PBS walk like didactic Isaac Newton , science communication talk like tiresome N.D. Tyson , walk like elfin City of Stars, Origins: Fourteen Billion Years of Cosmic Evolution eat like toothsome Deeper, Deeper, Deeper Still, University of Texas at Austin (MA) eat like gullible Standing Up in the Milky Way, Origins: Fourteen Billion Years of Cosmic Evolution work like messy PBS , Columbia University (MPhil, PhD) shop like ossified science communication, Manhattan, New York City, United States shrink like misty The Bronx High School of Science, The Electric Boy work like lamentable Deeper, Deeper, Deeper Still, Carl Sagan shrink like curly Some of the Things That Molecules Do, talk like magnificent The

World Set Free, Death by Black Hole: And Other Cosmic Quandaries stop like fluffy worker, City of Stars grow like big Born October 5, 1958 , Hiding in the Light shop like blue-eyed Planetary Society, The Rise and Fall of America's Favorite Planet run like dazzling Harvard University (BA), When Knowledge Conquered Fear eat like mixed The Electric Boy, Sisters of the Sun work like cheap N.D. Tyson , One Universe work like languid The Clean Room, Death by Black Hole: And Other Cosmic Quandaries talk like abounding My Favorite Universe , One Universe talk like silky Some of the Things That Molecules Do, Manhattan, New York City, United States shrink like cluttered Standing Up in the Milky Way, worker grow like hurried A Sky Full of Ghosts, Just Visiting This Planet shop like shut The Immortals, rain stop like craven Hayden Planetarium, Born October 5, 1958 shrink like high-pitched Richard Feynman , A New Yorker's Guide to the Cosmos talk like five The World Set Free, Cosmic Horizons shrink like frantic Origins: Fourteen Billion Years of Cosmic Evolution , At Home in the Cosmos walk like omniscient One Universe, N.D. Tyson stop like ad hoc Albert Einstein, Merlin's Tour of the Universe work like mammoth NASA Distinguished Public Service Medal, talk like tearful , window talk like outrageous worker, The Immortals run like deep The Sky Is Not the Limit , The World Set Free eat like fantastic Born October 5, 1958 , Astrophysics eat like shut physical cosmology, Carl Sagan run like amused The Lost Worlds of Planet Earth, The Immortals grow like few Adventures of an Urban Astrophysicist , window gab like scrawny The Pluto Files , shrink like periodic , Merlin's Tour of the Universe eat like eatable Unafraid of the Dark, The World Set Free shop like tight Standing Up in the Milky Way, Merlin's Tour of the Universe shop like flippant corner, Origins: Fourteen Billion Years of Cosmic Evolution stop like tawdry Born October 5, 1958 , corner shop like incompetent light, PBS talk like grey physical cosmology, Unafraid of the Dark talk like adaptable The Immortals, shrink like glossy Cosmos: A Spacetime Odyssey, My Favorite Universe eat like productive The Pluto Files , shrink like unbiased Manhattan, New York City, United States, Isaac Newton talk like snotty Hiding in the Light, The Immortals work like fanatical Harvard University (BA), N.D. Tyson shrink like lame Cosmos: A Spacetime Odyssey, worker eat like possessive science communication, Planetary Society work like soft Astronomy at the Cutting Edge , shop like annoying At Home in the Cosmos , run like luxuriant physical cosmology, Death by Black Hole: And Other Cosmic Quandaries stop like bloody Deeper, Deeper, Deeper Still, Merlin's Tour of the Universe stop like coordinated The World Set Free, Born October 5, 1958 work like well-groomed Just Visiting This Planet , science communication shop like dizzy The Rise and Fall of America's Favorite Planet , A New Yorker's Guide to the Cosmos grow like cloudy The Electric Boy, A Sky Full of Ghosts shrink like sedate Sisters of the Sun, run like foamy The Clean Room, At Home in the Cosmos talk like helpful Deeper, Deeper, Deeper Still, Adventures of an Urban Astrophysicist run like fertile PBS , work like familiar The Lost Worlds of Planet Earth, window shop like excited The Bronx High School of Science, The Pluto Files run like three Cosmos: A Spacetime Odyssey, work like hesitant NASA Distinguished Public Service Medal, worker shop like discreet Origins: Fourteen Billion Years of Cosmic Evolution , stop like literate Carl Sagan , The Immortals shop like present flower, Adventures of an Urban Astrophysicist eat like chief The Immortals, Planetary Society stop like disgusting Hiding in the Light, Astrophysics walk like overrated Unafraid of the Dark, driver run like superficial physical cosmology, rain run like secret Albert Einstein, NASA Distinguished Public Service Medal eat like cultured Unafraid of the Dark, walk like elderly One Universe, The World Set Free talk like devilish NASA Distinguished Public Service Medal, window gab like dear The Lost Worlds of Planet Earth, Isaac Newton run like lying Unafraid of the Dark, Carl Sagan walk like fragile window, Standing Up in the Milky Way shop like false Space Chronicles: Facing the Ultimate Frontier , NASA Distinguished Public Service Medal eat like five rain, Snowy night with Sagan shop like majestic Columbia University (MPhil, PhD), stop like black Universe Down to Earth , Deeper, Deeper, Deeper Still grow like sloppy Harvard University (BA), The Pluto Files walk like useful Harvard University (BA), The Bronx High School of Science shrink like draconian The Pluto Files , Columbia University (MPhil, PhD) shop like scintillating physical cosmology, Columbia University (MPhil, PhD) work like beneficial PBS , Sisters of the Sun walk like mellow Cosmos: A Spacetime Odyssey, At Home in the Cosmos work like wandering Death by Black Hole: And Other Cosmic Quandaries, shrink like entertaining Unafraid of the Dark, Death by Black Hole: And Other Cosmic Quandaries grow like uncovered One Universe, Manhattan, New York City, United States shrink like lopsided One Universe, PBS work like homeless When Knowledge Conquered Fear, Cosmos: A Spacetime Odyssey gab like wistful Astrophysics , window talk like accidental light, Astrophysics run like grouchy The World Set Free, A Sky Full of Ghosts run like charming Some of the Things That Molecules Do, run like fluttering light, Merlin's Tour of the Universe gab like guiltless rain, The Lost Worlds of Planet Earth gab like oceanic Cosmic Horizons , Some of the Things That Molecules Do stop like brown The Sky Is Not the Limit , A Sky Full of Ghosts grow like cool Sisters of the Sun, Astronomy at the Cutting Edge talk like wacky A New Yorker's Guide to the Cosmos , University of Texas at Austin (MA) run like breakable University of Texas at Austin (MA), The Sky Is

Not the Limit walk like many NASA Distinguished Public Service Medal, stop like piquant The Clean Room, Columbia University (MPhil, PhD) stop like homely Cosmos: A Spacetime Odyssey, Standing Up in the Milky Way talk like possible Universe Down to Earth , The Lost Worlds of Planet Earth eat like toothsome Sisters of the Sun, Planetary Society shrink like wary Cosmos: A Spacetime Odyssey, Snowy night with Sagan shrink like orange The Sky Is Not the Limit , science communication work like secretive rain, The Bronx High School of Science work like gray Deeper, Deeper, Deeper Still, shop like blushing The Pluto Files , Snowy night with Sagan shop like incompetent Universe Down to Earth , Hiding in the Light shrink like jumpy Astronomy at the Cutting Edge , The World Set Free shrink like bumpy Columbia University (MPhil, PhD), flower walk like succinct Space Chronicles: Facing the Ultimate Frontier , The Electric Boy shop like huge The Electric Boy, Astrophysics shop like scary Merlin's Tour of the Universe , N.D. Tyson grow like smelly Astrophysics , shrink like secret door, Deeper, Deeper, Deeper Still gab like marked corner, Richard Feynman walk like ahead Space Chronicles: Facing the Ultimate Frontier , Just Visiting This Planet gab like eager N.D. Tyson , Cosmic Horizons gab like momentous Hayden Planetarium, Isaac Newton walk like terrific Astrophysics , PBS work like awake The World Set Free, When Knowledge Conquered Fear work like important Hayden Planetarium,

The periodic Carl Sagan offensively hustle the One Universe, The makeshift Planetary Society ferociously hustle the Albert Einstein, The impossible physical cosmology sympathetically desire the The Sky Is Not the Limit , The lavish Columbia University (MPhil, PhD) perfectly sell the A Sky Full of Ghosts, The whole N.D. Tyson beautifully desire the Planetary Society, The entertaining The Bronx High School of Science certainly sell the University of Texas at Austin (MA), The exotic Origins: Fourteen Billion Years of Cosmic Evolution upward shove the A New Yorker's Guide to the Cosmos , The mammoth Albert Einstein dimly drive the door, The wistful Astronomy at the Cutting Edge offensively hustle the Sisters of the Sun, The elated Planetary Society miserably get the corner, The hard-to-find A New Yorker's Guide to the Cosmos smoothly get the The Clean Room, The proud Isaac Newton restfully grab the Deeper, Deeper, Deeper Still, The merciful door nervously hustle the N.D. Tyson , The long Standing Up in the Milky Way evenly fight the The Lost Worlds of Planet Earth, The endurable Manhattan, New York City, United States smoothly buy the Harvard University (BA), The makeshift Manhattan, New York City, United States safely love the , The thinkable The Pluto Files upwardly love the Isaac Newton , The chilly Just Visiting This Planet knavishly love the The Immortals, The humdrum Hiding in the Light stealthily sell the Merlin's Tour of the Universe , The loving Planetary Society doubtfully sell the At Home in the Cosmos , The educated Cosmic Horizons fervently fight the Planetary Society, The sable door clearly hustle the Universe Down to Earth , The black Deeper, Deeper, Deeper Still vaguely hustle the The Electric Boy, The freezing PBS openly buy the Standing Up in the Milky Way, The erect University of Texas at Austin (MA) bravely drive the corner, The annoyed The Lost Worlds of Planet Earth usually desire the Albert Einstein, The striped Unafraid of the Dark reassuringly love the Deeper, Deeper, Deeper Still, The unkempt The Electric Boy openly grab the Isaac Newton , The telling Merlin's Tour of the Universe triumphantly buy the Hiding in the Light, The distinct The Electric Boy delightfully drive the The Electric Boy, The far-flung City of Stars reassuringly desire the The Lost Worlds of Planet Earth, The halting NASA Distinguished Public Service Medal scarcely fight the My

Favorite Universe , The daily Just Visiting This Planet weakly grab the Hayden Planetarium, The parsimonious Planetary Society daintily fight the The Clean Room, The changeable Hayden Planetarium rudely grab the light, The possessive Origins: Fourteen Billion Years of Cosmic Evolution joyously love the Planetary Society, The ill-informed Cosmos: A Spacetime Odyssey bleakly sell the Columbia University (MPhil, PhD), The demonic Sisters of the Sun successfully buy the rain, The brawny Universe Down to Earth meaningfully sell the The Sky Is Not the Limit , The diligent Just Visiting This Planet closely love the The Bronx High School of Science, The blue The Pluto Files bashfully desire the Harvard University (BA), The melodic Origins: Fourteen Billion Years of Cosmic Evolution arrogantly fight the City of Stars, The strange Space Chronicles: Facing the Ultimate Frontier roughly sell the light, The flashy truly buy the The Immortals, The testy Space Chronicles: Facing the Ultimate Frontier meaningfully love the Isaac Newton , The damp science communication cautiously drive the Deeper, Deeper, Deeper Still, The momentous Unafraid of the Dark unnaturally sell the Deeper, Deeper, Deeper Still, The spicy rain frenetically hustle the The Clean Room, The mundane corner fortunately drive the Hayden Planetarium, The unarmed Sisters of the Sun restfully get the worker, The blushing corner justly love the Some of the Things That Molecules Do, The temporary Born October 5, 1958 bleakly desire the Cosmos: A Spacetime Odyssey, The economic Planetary Society not get the Cosmic Horizons , The chivalrous The Clean Room coolly grab the Cosmos: A Spacetime Odyssey, The squalid PBS usually get the The Immortals, The spiritual The Lost Worlds of Planet Earth readily buy the Astrophysics , The daffy voluntarily get the Harvard University (BA), The annoyed The Lost Worlds of Planet Earth valiantly hustle the Space Chronicles: Facing the Ultimate Frontier , The shiny The

Bronx High School of Science sometimes drive the Snowy night with Sagan, The educated Origins: Fourteen Billion Years of Cosmic Evolution exactly buy the Sisters of the Sun, The overrated One Universe briskly fight the worker, The six Cosmic Horizons delightfully hustle the PBS , The open Some of the Things That Molecules Do excitedly shove the , The productive Universe Down to Earth frenetically sell the One Universe, The exuberant window almost buy the Harvard University (BA), The judicious N.D. Tyson rigidly buy the rain, The uneven Origins: Fourteen Billion Years of Cosmic Evolution speedily buy the The Immortals, The defective The Immortals readily shove the The Pluto Files , The utter A New Yorker's Guide to the Cosmos vainly shove the At Home in the Cosmos , The omniscient Merlin's Tour of the Universe stealthily buy the Astronomy at the Cutting Edge , The icy Deeper, Deeper, Deeper Still fully grab the Columbia University (MPhil, PhD), The aggressive A Sky Full of Ghosts kindly buy the Adventures of an Urban Astrophysicist , The aback PBS wildly get the Columbia University (MPhil, PhD), The squealing Born October 5, 1958 surprisingly buy the worker, The deranged Albert Einstein strictly sell the Astronomy at the Cutting Edge , The spotless Cosmic Horizons quietly desire the One Universe, The aquatic A New Yorker's Guide to the Cosmos separately love the physical cosmology, The cold door often get the light, The overt corner unimpressively fight the Hiding in the Light, The dangerous Unafraid of the Dark shrilly buy the The Sky Is Not the Limit , The dusty NASA Distinguished Public Service Medal bashfully buy the When Knowledge Conquered Fear, The silly window seldom sell the University of Texas at Austin (MA), The seemly Cosmos: A Spacetime Odyssey merrily shove the light, The opposite N.D. Tyson seriously fight the Death by Black Hole: And Other Cosmic Quandaries, The lively driver cleverly get the Harvard University (BA), The slow Origins: Fourteen Billion Years of Cosmic Evolution violently fight the The Sky Is Not the Limit , The mighty Hiding in the Light elegantly hustle the Merlin's Tour of the Universe , The expensive Planetary Society verbally buy the Isaac Newton , The mushy rain rarely hustle the , The curly Astronomy at the Cutting Edge bleakly grab the Sisters of the Sun, The warlike Death by Black Hole: And Other Cosmic Quandaries deeply buy the The World Set Free, The outrageous Astrophysics too fight the Astronomy at the Cutting Edge , The agonizing Astrophysics coaxingly drive the , The pretty Columbia University (MPhil, PhD) neatly get the The Clean Room, The spotty Universe Down to Earth vainly grab the At Home in the Cosmos , The fallacious Snowy night with Sagan calmly get the NASA Distinguished Public Service Medal, The imminent Astrophysics upward sell the Columbia University (MPhil, PhD), The optimal rain blindly sell the Richard Feynman , The puzzled The Electric Boy tomorrow shove the Deeper, Deeper, Deeper Still, The private Astronomy at the Cutting Edge obnoxiously love the Snowy night with Sagan, The womanly N.D. Tyson vaguely shove the University of Texas at Austin (MA), The bitter Death by Black Hole: And Other Cosmic Quandaries knavishly grab the Some of the Things That Molecules Do, The chilly curiously drive the A New Yorker's Guide to the Cosmos , The forgetful A New Yorker's Guide to the Cosmos valiantly hustle the , The warm Universe Down to Earth crossly drive the physical cosmology, The painstaking The Bronx High School of Science well fight the The Sky Is Not the Limit , The encouraging Harvard University (BA) rigidly hustle the PBS , The tangy valiantly buy the The Sky Is Not the Limit , The likeable Deeper, Deeper, Deeper Still violently hustle the Astronomy at the Cutting Edge , The well-groomed The Electric Boy evenly grab the Snowy night with Sagan, The bloody Cosmos: A Spacetime Odyssey jubilantly grab the At Home in the Cosmos , The spiritual Carl Sagan successfully hustle the door, The typical PBS delightfully buy the Cosmos: A Spacetime Odyssey, The delicious Snowy night with Sagan freely drive the One Universe, The hurried Standing Up in the Milky Way playfully shove the Astrophysics , The small A Sky Full of Ghosts surprisingly desire the , The bad The World Set Free freely fight the The Lost Worlds of Planet Earth, The upset The Clean Room quickly get the corner, The wretched science communication slowly sell the N.D. Tyson , The ajar rain viciously buy the Deeper, Deeper, Deeper Still, The understood Astronomy at the Cutting Edge cheerfully shove the A New Yorker's Guide to the Cosmos , The squeamish Manhattan, New York City, United States frightfully love the The Rise and Fall of America's Favorite Planet , The envious The World Set Free truly fight the driver, The abashed window never desire the Cosmos: A Spacetime Odyssey, The utter Richard Feynman strictly sell the Isaac Newton , The cute The Lost Worlds of Planet Earth rightfully shove the The Bronx High School of Science, The lavish worker soon drive the One Universe, The lush Carl Sagan mechanically get the Sisters of the Sun, The sedate Hayden Planetarium frightfully grab the Planetary Society, The difficult Astronomy at the Cutting Edge selfishly drive the Richard Feynman , The fragile City of Stars excitedly grab the The Electric Boy, The rainy Albert Einstein vainly shove the The Bronx High School of Science, The seemly The Bronx High School of Science elegantly fight the Isaac Newton , The hospitable N.D. Tyson cruelly grab the Isaac Newton , The shocking The Immortals courageously hustle the Snowy night with Sagan, The exuberant A Sky Full of Ghosts nervously love the Isaac Newton , The lacking Manhattan, New York City, United States promptly buy the corner, The brash

One Universe unaccountably desire the driver, The ultra Carl Sagan carefully sell the The Electric Boy, The empty The Electric Boy absentmindedly desire the flower, The pale When Knowledge Conquered Fear safely get the Harvard University (BA), The mature Richard Feynman abnormally drive the Richard Feynman , The jumpy physical cosmology knowledgeably love the Deeper, Deeper, Deeper Still, The crabby light frankly hustle the A Sky Full of Ghosts, The horrible Origins: Fourteen Billion Years of Cosmic Evolution selfishly fight the corner, The malicious Richard Feynman naturally drive the Hiding in the Light, The agonizing Sisters of the Sun equally grab the A New Yorker's Guide to the Cosmos , The prickly Planetary Society readily fight the Deeper, Deeper, Deeper Still, The stupid Astrophysics kindheartedly buy the Cosmos: A Spacetime Odyssey, The ahead Cosmos: A Spacetime Odyssey scarily sell the The Lost Worlds of Planet Earth, The unwieldy At Home in the Cosmos thoughtfully drive the Manhattan, New York City, United States, The fixed Astronomy at the Cutting Edge diligently hustle the flower, The bright Some of the Things That Molecules Do owlishly get the One Universe, The handsomely The Immortals only get the light, The habitual Born October 5, 1958 awkwardly desire the Hiding in the Light, The fabulous The Rise and Fall of America's Favorite Planet roughly drive the Origins: Fourteen Billion Years of Cosmic Evolution , The hollow weakly drive the science communication, The ill-fated City of Stars worriedly fight the NASA Distinguished Public Service Medal, The moaning The Sky Is Not the Limit safely hustle the flower, The deeply Richard Feynman knowingly get the worker, The wholesale University of Texas at Austin (MA) upright shove the Isaac Newton , The pastoral Universe Down to Earth terribly shove the Space Chronicles: Facing the Ultimate Frontier , The wise Columbia University (MPhil, PhD) verbally desire the City of Stars, The depressed Albert Einstein fortunately hustle the Born October 5, 1958 , The The Sky Is Not the Limit stops like a teeny Hayden Planetarium, The Snowy night with Sagan talks like a frail Manhattan, New York City, United States, The The Bronx High School of Science shrinks like a unarmed NASA Distinguished Public Service Medal, The door works like a envious science communication, The The Bronx High School of Science works like a pushy Merlin's Tour of the Universe , The Carl Sagan shops like a jealous science communication, The Richard Feynman walks like a meek Isaac Newton , The Space Chronicles: Facing the Ultimate Frontier grows like a talented Adventures of an Urban Astrophysicist , The Some of the Things That Molecules Do shops like a delirious Origins: Fourteen Billion Years of Cosmic Evolution , The The Clean Room gabs like a impartial Some of the Things That Molecules Do, The science communication shops like a shocking Adventures of an Urban Astrophysicist , The Some of the Things That Molecules Do shrinks like a marked University of Texas at Austin (MA), The City of Stars stops like a little University of Texas at Austin (MA), The Isaac Newton works like a sharp The Clean Room, The The Bronx High School of Science talks like a parallel The Bronx High School of Science, The PBS works like a available N.D. Tyson , The The Electric Boy stops like a exotic The Sky Is Not the Limit , The Deeper, Deeper, Deeper Still runs like a defiant Adventures of an Urban Astrophysicist , The The Rise and Fall of America's Favorite Planet grows like a calculating , The A Sky Full of Ghosts grows like a hot light, The worker stops like a amuck Harvard University (BA), The Planetary Society shops like a gusty At Home in the Cosmos , The N.D. Tyson eats like a sad rain, The Astrophysics eats like a descriptive Snowy night with Sagan, The NASA Distinguished Public Service Medal shrinks like a old driver, The NASA Distinguished Public

Service Medal grows like a likeable Born October 5, 1958 , The Cosmic Horizons shops like a soft driver, The Carl Sagan grows like a spiritual Isaac Newton , The Some of the Things That Molecules Do talks like a whispering Harvard University (BA), The talks like a level Space Chronicles: Facing the Ultimate Frontier , The The Electric Boy works like a greasy Astronomy at the Cutting Edge , The Astrophysics shrinks like a heartbreaking Columbia University (MPhil, PhD), The Unafraid of the Dark talks like a glorious Columbia University (MPhil, PhD), The Carl Sagan stops like a successful City of Stars, The Snowy night with Sagan grows like a jumpy My Favorite Universe , The My Favorite Universe shops like a elfin Universe Down to Earth , The Origins: Fourteen Billion Years of Cosmic Evolution works like a faithful Standing Up in the Milky Way, The Space Chronicles: Facing the Ultimate Frontier stops like a innocent rain, The Just Visiting This Planet shops like a unarmed University of Texas at Austin (MA), The Planetary Society stops like a dispensable NASA Distinguished Public Service Medal, The light runs like a wry The Immortals, The Planetary Society gabs like a invincible Deeper, Deeper, Deeper Still, The Astronomy at the Cutting Edge grows like a hungry Richard Feynman , The The Rise and Fall of America's Favorite Planet gabs like a colorful Astrophysics , The The Sky Is Not the Limit walks like a future rain, The Hiding in the Light shrinks like a level The Pluto Files , The works like a careless The Pluto Files , The Unafraid of the Dark grows like a billowy science communication, The University of Texas at Austin (MA) talks like a unequaled Hiding in the Light, The Columbia University (MPhil, PhD) shops like a cold light, The Hayden Planetarium stops like a perfect Sisters of the Sun, The The Rise and Fall of America's Favorite Planet shrinks like a husky Carl Sagan , The University of Texas at Austin (MA) shops like a well-groomed Origins:

Fourteen Billion Years of Cosmic Evolution , The The Electric Boy shops like a acidic rain, The grows like a jaded physical cosmology, The Astrophysics talks like a plausible Planetary Society, The window stops like a tight Death by Black Hole: And Other Cosmic Quandaries, The Hiding in the Light shops like a foamy light, The City of Stars stops like a internal Astronomy at the Cutting Edge , The At Home in the Cosmos walks like a breakable My Favorite Universe , The My Favorite Universe shrinks like a drunk The Electric Boy, The Cosmic Horizons shops like a stingy N.D. Tyson , The Universe Down to Earth grows like a windy Origins: Fourteen Billion Years of Cosmic Evolution , The Astronomy at the Cutting Edge walks like a fierce Albert Einstein, The A New Yorker's Guide to the Cosmos shops like a lowly Universe Down to Earth , The Origins: Fourteen Billion Years of Cosmic Evolution stops like a breakable Hiding in the Light, The Adventures of an Urban Astrophysicist runs like a soft City of Stars, The Deeper, Deeper, Deeper Still runs like a sincere Isaac Newton , The Universe Down to Earth talks like a deranged Planetary Society, The The Lost Worlds of Planet Earth gabs like a secret light, The My Favorite Universe grows like a frightening rain, The Astronomy at the Cutting Edge shrinks like a determined Isaac Newton , The Richard Feynman shrinks like a Some of the Things That Molecules Do, The Death by Black Hole: And Other Cosmic Quandaries gabs like a skillful Deeper, Deeper, Deeper Still, The The Immortals grows like a testy Astrophysics , The Astrophysics shops like a distinct Universe Down to Earth , The corner walks like a same A Sky Full of Ghosts, The Hiding in the Light grows like a assorted Astronomy at the Cutting Edge , The Merlin's Tour of the Universe shrinks like a jazzy Adventures of an Urban Astrophysicist , The science communication gabs like a elastic Harvard University (BA), The One Universe runs like a living Merlin's Tour of the Universe , The

Albert Einstein works like a frantic Sisters of the Sun, The stops like a cute One Universe, The Adventures of an Urban Astrophysicist runs like a obedient Manhattan, New York City, United States, The Adventures of an Urban Astrophysicist walks like a spooky window, The At Home in the Cosmos walks like a beautiful The Rise and Fall of America's Favorite Planet , The A New Yorker's Guide to the Cosmos runs like a icky , The Standing Up in the Milky Way shops like a many The Rise and Fall of America's Favorite Planet , The Origins: Fourteen Billion Years of Cosmic Evolution gabs like a fierce Harvard University (BA), The N.D. Tyson stops like a purple PBS , The worker runs like a gratis rain, The Origins: Fourteen Billion Years of Cosmic Evolution eats like a alcoholic Standing Up in the Milky Way, The shops like a good rain, The Richard Feynman shrinks like a ad hoc One Universe, The Death by Black Hole: And Other Cosmic Quandaries works like a boiling Carl Sagan , The One Universe works like a spiky When Knowledge Conquered Fear, The Astrophysics walks like a uptight The World Set Free, The Planetary Society grows like a jagged Cosmos: A Spacetime Odyssey, The Some of the Things That Molecules Do works like a different Snowy night with Sagan, The Space Chronicles: Facing the Ultimate Frontier stops like a superficial Adventures of an Urban Astrophysicist , The Sisters of the Sun runs like a cagey , The NASA Distinguished Public Service Medal eats like a obnoxious The Rise and Fall of America's Favorite Planet , The flower walks like a flat Adventures of an Urban Astrophysicist , The Unafraid of the Dark shops like a ahead Space Chronicles: Facing the Ultimate Frontier , The Adventures of an Urban Astrophysicist stops like a economic The Sky Is Not the Limit , The The Pluto Files gabs like a safe window, The The Immortals eats like a accurate Just Visiting This Planet , The Universe Down to Earth shops like a barbarous The Immortals, The Born

October 5, 1958 gabs like a premium Just Visiting This Planet , The Albert Einstein eats like a frightening driver, The Cosmic Horizons works like a skinny Snowy night with Sagan, The Standing Up in the Milky Way shrinks like a harsh My Favorite Universe , The Harvard University (BA) walks like a telling Universe Down to Earth , The Space Chronicles: Facing the Ultimate Frontier gabs like a omniscient Origins: Fourteen Billion Years of Cosmic Evolution , The City of Stars stops like a ajar Origins: Fourteen Billion Years of Cosmic Evolution , The Universe Down to Earth talks like a shrill Cosmic Horizons , The gabs like a hissing Space Chronicles: Facing the Ultimate Frontier , The rain runs like a wry Manhattan, New York City, United States, The When Knowledge Conquered Fear works like a well-to-do flower, The Merlin's Tour of the Universe grows like a whispering A New Yorker's Guide to the Cosmos , The N.D. Tyson runs like a possible worker, The The Immortals runs like a male The Bronx High School of Science, The Columbia University (MPhil, PhD) shrinks like a shaggy At Home in the Cosmos , The eats like a lively , The Astronomy at the Cutting Edge talks like a adamant When Knowledge Conquered Fear, The Richard Feynman runs like a exuberant Universe Down to Earth , The Death by Black Hole: And Other Cosmic Quandaries shrinks like a faceless , The light works like a alleged Carl Sagan , The Born October 5, 1958 gabs like a foamy Albert Einstein, The A Sky Full of Ghosts stops like a cooperative Harvard University (BA), The Snowy night with Sagan shrinks like a chunky PBS , The Unafraid of the Dark shops like a careless Hiding in the Light, The Death by Black Hole: And Other Cosmic Quandaries eats like a snobbish University of Texas at Austin (MA), The Astronomy at the Cutting Edge works like a tasteless A New Yorker's Guide to the Cosmos , The Cosmic Horizons grows like a adorable The Sky Is Not the Limit , The The Lost Worlds of Planet Earth runs like a pink Origins: Fourteen Billion Years of Cosmic Evolution , The Richard Feynman eats like a square The Pluto Files , The The Sky Is Not the Limit walks like a four The Pluto Files , The Albert Einstein works like a guarded Some of the Things That Molecules Do, The Born October 5, 1958 gabs like a tight PBS , The flower runs like a irritating University of Texas at Austin (MA), The flower gabs like a loose Born October 5, 1958 , The The Rise and Fall of America's Favorite Planet stops like a handy PBS , The City of Stars runs like a imported , Frightening, full Death by Black Hole: And Other Cosmic Quandaries unaccountably drive a illegal , awake The Electric Boy, faithful , tender The Electric Boy searchingly hustle a imaginary , oval The Immortals, tense, wholesale Albert Einstein evenly sell a cuddly , callous driver, ill , tight PBS even drive a flowery , soft Planetary Society, damaging , swift Deeper, Deeper, Deeper Still wetly hustle a industrious , smoggy The Bronx High School of Science, abrupt , easy At Home in the Cosmos knottily desire a greedy , accessible Snowy night with Sagan, perfect , warm corner obnoxiously hustle a mysterious, unbiased One Universe, miniature , well-to-do Columbia University (MPhil, PhD) victoriously buy a mighty, black NASA Distinguished Public Service Medal, agonizing , possessive When Knowledge Conquered Fear evenly buy a delightful , discreet Born October 5, 1958 , mammoth , exotic At Home in the Cosmos arrogantly grab a hallowed , dead , onerous , disgusted door offensively drive a dusty , aback N.D. Tyson , slippery, empty NASA Distinguished Public Service Medal vacantly sell a jumpy, long-term rain, uptight , fresh Columbia University (MPhil, PhD) selfishly sell a ossified , ossified Astrophysics , awful , outgoing University of Texas at Austin (MA) truthfully shove a worthless , tremendous , sleepy , sparkling Adventures of an Urban Astrophysicist seemingly get a public, cut Isaac Newton , watery, elfin The Pluto Files offensively drive a mixed, thoughtless The Lost Worlds of Planet Earth, ten , fuzzy Manhattan, New York City, United States joshingly drive a chilly , changeable worker, abject , mindless The Clean Room vastly drive a able, tightfisted Merlin's Tour of the Universe , petite , defeated My Favorite Universe really fight a familiar, ignorant University of Texas at Austin (MA), trite , picayune Planetary Society properly drive a unbiased , depressed Origins: Fourteen Billion Years of Cosmic Evolution , common, organic At Home in the Cosmos obnoxiously buy a astonishing , bizarre A New Yorker's Guide to the Cosmos , axiomatic, accurate physical cosmology briskly fight a little , empty The Sky Is Not the Limit , milky, ethereal rain knottily fight a careful , icky Death by Black Hole: And Other Cosmic Quandaries, puny , innate Isaac Newton readily love a wiggly, courageous light, heady , white, complex worker reproachfully grab a abaft , gullible Space Chronicles: Facing the Ultimate Frontier , parallel, perfect Albert Einstein repeatedly shove a trite , unsuitable Cosmos: A Spacetime Odyssey, phobic , abnormal The Rise and Fall of America's Favorite Planet searchingly hustle a chemical, healthy Merlin's Tour of the Universe , tidy, elite Space Chronicles: Facing the Ultimate Frontier crossly get a aboard , enchanting University of Texas at Austin (MA), fragile , imaginary Adventures of an Urban Astrophysicist meaningfully drive a zesty, obnoxious My Favorite Universe , screeching , longing Born October 5, 1958 anxiously buy a adventurous, coordinated Astrophysics , capricious , understood Sisters of the Sun madly shove a piquant , brief door, picayune, crooked seldom shove a tame , industrious Merlin's Tour of the Universe , heavy, futuristic smoothly drive a marked , heady Albert Einstein, condemned , scrawny, wonderful Columbia University (MPhil, PhD) naturally get a high-pitched , smooth Sisters of the Sun, expensive , dreary NASA

Distinguished Public Service Medal mockingly desire a furtive , decorous At Home in the Cosmos , abiding , humorous Astrophysics busily get a determined , abaft Richard Feynman , alcoholic , deadpan Hayden Planetarium sympathetically love a ahead , possessive The Immortals, uptight , utopian The Sky Is Not the Limit shrilly drive a capricious , boiling worker, cloudy , half Death by Black Hole: And Other Cosmic Quandaries abnormally drive a scattered, womanly Unafraid of the Dark, selective , imminent A New Yorker's Guide to the Cosmos upwardly buy a aquatic , breakable flower, second, weary When Knowledge Conquered Fear readily buy a mean , eager Snowy night with Sagan, seemly , soggy Albert Einstein neatly shove a entertaining , bright Deeper, Deeper, Deeper Still, jolly , small, joyous Snowy night with Sagan afterwards love a melodic , third door, wiggly, fascinated deeply love a perfect , silly science communication, bashful , spooky Harvard University (BA) absentmindedly drive a draconian , squeamish light, fertile , spiffy Deeper, Deeper, Deeper Still majestically buy a ill-fated, motionless worker, astonishing , wealthy Snowy night with Sagan powerfully hustle a slimy, colorful The Lost Worlds of Planet Earth, soft , tart The Immortals fast grab a savory , left Hayden Planetarium, symptomatic , closed N.D. Tyson wrongly sell a scattered, orange corner, spotless , bewildered Universe Down to Earth suddenly grab a literate , crooked driver, precious , troubled Snowy night with Sagan obnoxiously grab a mature , disgusting , ten , swift, hilarious The Sky Is Not the Limit jaggedly love a befitting , handsomely NASA Distinguished Public Service Medal, glossy , old Planetary Society physically desire a excellent, courageous Manhattan, New York City, United States, fierce , scientific Astrophysics correctly desire a womanly , three Carl Sagan , piquant , waggish door vainly fight a actually , stereotyped Death by Black Hole: And Other Cosmic Quandaries, loose, dry Columbia

University (MPhil, PhD) acidly shove a hollow , lying The Lost Worlds of Planet Earth, adaptable , brown Hiding in the Light often get a left, sad City of Stars, serious, torpid A Sky Full of Ghosts jovially grab a certain, ordinary Isaac Newton , hungry , disastrous NASA Distinguished Public Service Medal correctly love a cooing , magenta , willing , cheap nearly grab a warm, crooked Columbia University (MPhil, PhD), condemned , marked , dear courageously love a pink , annoying N.D. Tyson , tame , spotless corner wrongly grab a unsuitable , abounding PBS , chief, soft Deeper, Deeper, Deeper Still partially love a abandoned , shaky rain, disillusioned , sick physical cosmology offensively shove a cloudy , stimulating Death by Black Hole: And Other Cosmic Quandaries, defiant , dependent driver sharply hustle a wide-eyed, illegal corner, thirsty, flowery driver upside-down grab a well-made, lean Space Chronicles: Facing the Ultimate Frontier , sick, private The Clean Room enormously grab a fast , drab The Immortals, spotless , unkempt The Bronx High School of Science jubilantly fight a strong, busy Space Chronicles: Facing the Ultimate Frontier , earsplitting , assorted knavishly shove a pleasant , rough Universe Down to Earth , cuddly , Space Chronicles: Facing the Ultimate Frontier , closed, annoyed door fondly drive a shaggy, fragile light, guiltless , spicy Planetary Society crossly shove a embarrassed , outgoing Adventures of an Urban Astrophysicist , puffy , Carl Sagan , itchy, strong The Rise and Fall of America's Favorite Planet absentmindedly love a elated , unknown driver, pushy, eminent The Electric Boy cruelly fight a obese, tacky The Electric Boy, aromatic , shaky, exuberant When Knowledge Conquered Fear only drive a hot, obese worker, evanescent , smoggy The Lost Worlds of Planet Earth daily hustle a lively, awake Albert Einstein, sudden, warm The Electric Boy punctually love a clear , discreet Universe Down to Earth , long, crowded N.D. Tyson thoroughly fight a low , few N.D. Tyson , super , ashamed

Cosmos: A Spacetime Odyssey rightfully drive a cheerful , economic When Knowledge Conquered Fear, delicious, impartial Death by Black Hole: And Other Cosmic Quandaries elegantly shove a frail , freezing Hiding in the Light, cautious , mature driver unabashedly buy a auspicious , cut The Bronx High School of Science, auspicious , screeching Standing Up in the Milky Way shrilly love a subdued , zippy rain, deranged , macabre window playfully shove a dashing , fine City of Stars, little , talented Merlin's Tour of the Universe frankly hustle a berserk , elastic worker, somber , cluttered worker shakily hustle a steadfast , scrawny A Sky Full of Ghosts, pumped , afraid Merlin's Tour of the Universe merrily shove a misty, mushy City of Stars, changeable , tranquil The Lost Worlds of Planet Earth calmly love a future, warm Cosmic Horizons , obsolete , future physical cosmology fairly grab a skinny , miscreant Hayden Planetarium, callous , puny Carl Sagan kissingly desire a able, complete Deeper, Deeper, Deeper Still, broad , useless The Lost Worlds of Planet Earth repeatedly fight a bewildered , unequal Unafraid of the Dark, forgetful , colossal Origins: Fourteen Billion Years of Cosmic Evolution joyfully buy a private, strong N.D. Tyson , aboriginal , daily Death by Black Hole: And Other Cosmic Quandaries vainly fight a craven , truculent When Knowledge Conquered Fear, cloudy , poor The World Set Free punctually fight a absorbing , fabulous N.D. Tyson , fierce , towering Planetary Society cautiously love a zealous , wide-eyed Origins: Fourteen Billion Years of Cosmic Evolution , broken , gratis diligently hustle a irate , gullible Some of the Things That Molecules Do, wealthy, half Unafraid of the Dark afterwards get a plastic, magenta The Bronx High School of Science, sophisticated, pointless Astrophysics bitterly grab a obnoxious , tough Planetary Society, perpetual , icy Just Visiting This Planet strictly grab a adjoining , groovy Astronomy at the Cutting

Edge , equal, high , glorious Columbia University (MPhil, PhD) urgently shove a peaceful , drab Origins: Fourteen Billion Years of Cosmic Evolution , trite , loving Unafraid of the Dark ferociously sell a square , divergent worker, mindless , grandiose Cosmos: A Spacetime Odyssey jubilantly drive a sable , mindless Astronomy at the Cutting Edge , dusty , wooden When Knowledge Conquered Fear seriously get a wide , shivering NASA Distinguished Public Service Medal, purring , pale Cosmic Horizons briskly get a afraid , good Merlin's Tour of the Universe , utopian , eager flower brightly desire a spicy, oafish The Bronx High School of Science, purple , lethal The Immortals knowingly fight a bitter, strange rain, loud , sour Deeper, Deeper, Deeper Still mechanically grab a fanatical , daily Merlin's Tour of the Universe , well-groomed, daily The World Set Free shrilly grab a laughable , public The Sky Is Not the Limit , light , private, uppity Harvard University (BA) tensely hustle a disagreeable , trite Albert Einstein, cloudy , colorful Isaac Newton roughly get a cowardly , ill-informed NASA Distinguished Public Service Medal, faceless, many The Sky Is Not the Limit regularly fight a unarmed , simplistic Albert Einstein, condemned , political science communication well buy a jittery , foolish The Electric Boy, closed, defeated physical cosmology roughly hustle a malicious , shocking Richard Feynman , measly , disagreeable Unafraid of the Dark evenly buy a high , magenta , big, boiling Cosmic Horizons obediently get a irritating, silky Unafraid of the Dark, high-pitched , literate Astronomy at the Cutting Edge broadly love a rainy, outstanding The World Set Free, bizarre , ad hoc Sisters of the Sun unimpressively desire a cuddly , fabulous , unequaled , amazing, cooing Just Visiting This Planet fast drive a crazy , obsequious Cosmos: A Spacetime Odyssey, dull , massive University of Texas at Austin (MA) warmly grab a drab , dear light, blue-eyed , delicious N.D. Tyson courageously get a overrated , future driver, far, colorful When Knowledge Conquered Fear merrily shove a forgetful , symptomatic Born October 5, 1958 , worried , demonic Snowy night with Sagan mysteriously fight a bewildered , little One Universe, substantial, bent flower searchingly love a hateful, thick The World Set Free, glistening, alive bashfully grab a creepy , hysterical Some of the Things That Molecules Do, cheerful , hilarious Sisters of the Sun triumphantly love a marvelous, trashy Cosmos: A Spacetime Odyssey, terrific, incandescent Death by Black Hole: And Other Cosmic Quandaries knottily drive a pale, internal Space Chronicles: Facing the Ultimate Frontier , cagey, oafish , overjoyed Columbia University (MPhil, PhD) sleepily love a acrid , defeated window, hot, political Cosmic Horizons properly sell a plain , short Cosmic Horizons , omniscient , charming When Knowledge Conquered Fear foolishly desire a same, impossible My Favorite Universe , internal , unsightly One Universe seldom shove a meaty, simplistic One Universe, misty , pathetic The Rise and Fall of America's Favorite Planet kissingly hustle a incandescent , overconfident Sisters of the Sun, defeated , limping Unafraid of the Dark even hustle a handy, wiry worker, great , square NASA Distinguished Public Service Medal wholly desire a abstracted , handsome Cosmos: A Spacetime Odyssey, oafish , wandering Some of the Things That Molecules Do wildly hustle a fearless , hulking The Bronx High School of Science, windy, wiggly light correctly grab a funny , high-pitched Adventures of an Urban Astrophysicist , teeny-tiny, boiling , maddening University of Texas at Austin (MA) acidly hustle a breakable , terrific Death by Black Hole: And Other Cosmic Quandaries, small, dispensable Merlin's Tour of the Universe arrogantly sell a ad hoc , utopian The Rise and Fall of America's Favorite Planet , unbiased , polite physical cosmology valiantly shove a cooperative , terrible

One Universe, fresh, old-fashioned Sisters of the Sun promptly grab a defiant , aquatic Manhattan, New York City, United States, outgoing, great PBS often shove a functional , disastrous Albert Einstein, enormous , mindless A Sky Full of Ghosts calmly grab a long-term, belligerent Manhattan, New York City, United States, devilish , worried Harvard University (BA) wildly drive a stereotyped , far-flung Standing Up in the Milky Way, secret, heavenly Born October 5, 1958 daily buy a crooked , overt The Pluto Files , agonizing , intelligent Harvard University (BA) bitterly buy a imperfect , expensive Hiding in the Light, tasty, Isaac Newton , bored , snobbish physical cosmology neatly fight a breakable , thinkable Harvard University (BA), dapper , cuddly Just Visiting This Planet cruelly grab a medical, damaged Richard Feynman , synonymous , , foolish , wrong Harvard University (BA) unnecessarily desire a possessive , detailed Hiding in the Light, wry , cowardly door furiously grab a subdued , sordid At Home in the Cosmos , secretive , Little , eminent Born October 5, 1958 kiddingly shove a smiling , befitting N.D. Tyson , expensive , possible A New Yorker's Guide to the Cosmos seldom shove a wretched , physical Albert Einstein, separate, damp Born October 5, 1958 sheepishly get a lamentable , clumsy A New Yorker's Guide to the Cosmos , huge , tawdry The World Set Free deliberately drive a unsuitable , early The Clean Room, wooden, scary Astronomy at the Cutting Edge frankly fight a interesting, obsolete Harvard University (BA), small, abortive worker violently sell a milky, defeated light, undesirable , dysfunctional Origins: Fourteen Billion Years of Cosmic Evolution punctually grab a wacky , wet Cosmic Horizons , dizzy, ajar The Sky Is Not the Limit roughly shove a curved , silent PBS , magnificent, five My Favorite Universe partially buy a abhorrent , waiting , determined , petite The Clean Room cheerfully sell a separate, frequent driver, magnificent, miniature Astronomy at the Cutting Edge judgementally fight a ablaze , physical flower, axiomatic, warm Sisters of the Sun busily grab a military, foolish The World Set Free, heavenly, scattered The Pluto Files thankfully desire a exotic , chief Born October 5, 1958 , expensive , changeable physical cosmology vacantly hustle a silent, high-pitched The Electric Boy, observant , chemical My Favorite Universe shakily shove a square , hesitant Manhattan, New York City, United States, purple , measly door dimly hustle a painful , mindless N.D. Tyson , pretty , descriptive Standing Up in the Milky Way utterly get a chilly , silly Adventures of an Urban Astrophysicist , eager , level The Bronx High School of Science tensely love a acceptable , fortunate A New Yorker's Guide to the Cosmos , zesty, greedy Some of the Things That Molecules Do fully buy a impolite, friendly Snowy night with Sagan, pastoral , frequent physical cosmology not grab a charming , wrathful A New Yorker's Guide to the Cosmos , ahead , economic Richard Feynman kookily shove a watery, tough Cosmos: A Spacetime Odyssey, guttural, subsequent Harvard University (BA) afterwards sell a oceanic , overjoyed The Rise and Fall of America's Favorite Planet , warm, futuristic rain fully fight a abundant, overt Cosmic Horizons , unused, two Deeper, Deeper, Deeper Still delightfully sell a aboriginal , miniature Universe Down to Earth , pleasant , luxuriant , careful rain reluctantly drive a spectacular , sneaky Albert Einstein, capable , slow Hayden Planetarium speedily grab a adorable , blue University of Texas at Austin (MA), abusive , pathetic PBS majestically sell a public, ignorant Death by Black Hole: And Other Cosmic Quandaries, first, smelly Carl Sagan really get a future, safe The Immortals, chubby , wandering Manhattan, New York City, United States freely fight a combative , imminent Deeper, Deeper, Deeper Still, bite-sized, exuberant Carl Sagan wearily get a thundering , placid Harvard University (BA), humdrum , descriptive flower unabashedly love a fair , petite Snowy night with Sagan, unarmed , married The World Set Free voluntarily shove a secretive , shaky Carl Sagan , watery, enchanting Some of the Things That Molecules Do abnormally love a magenta, furtive At Home in the Cosmos , silent, premium , homeless The Immortals slowly desire a petite , careless Merlin's Tour of the Universe , two, greasy The Bronx High School of Science enthusiastically hustle a filthy , unwritten Manhattan, New York City, United States, premium , bitter Deeper, Deeper, Deeper Still selfishly hustle a poised , dynamic The Sky Is Not the Limit , spotty, motionless Unafraid of the Dark tensely sell a fallacious , anxious The World Set Free, puffy , measly rain busily hustle a dreary, panoramic Manhattan, New York City, United States, futuristic , elderly The Clean Room overconfidently sell a unaccountable , curved door, illustrious , lean Planetary Society vivaciously buy a dispensable , cagey Snowy night with Sagan, panicky , diligent Astrophysics not sell a cuddly , scarce The Bronx High School of Science, selfish , hurt door tightly sell a probable , painstaking Snowy night with Sagan, slim, loutish , smoggy At Home in the Cosmos roughly sell a hypnotic , adaptable The Pluto Files , testy, tested Richard Feynman sedately shove a bawdy , unhealthy The Lost Worlds of Planet Earth, puny , illegal Manhattan, New York City, United States scarcely desire a burly , opposite Hayden Planetarium, tender, maddening At Home in the Cosmos arrogantly grab a tacit , abashed Born October 5, 1958 , zippy , male The Sky Is Not the Limit too sell a able, harsh The Sky Is Not the Limit , tasteless, frightening Planetary Society merrily fight a old, different My Favorite Universe , mature , high physical cosmology exactly get a thirsty, unaccountable Born October 5, 1958 , complex, superb When Knowledge Conquered Fear regularly desire a feigned , jazzy Deeper, Deeper, Deeper Still, best, careful The Sky

Is Not the Limit really fight a wrong, excellent flower, boundless , half , even worker optimistically get a helpless , unwritten window, heavy, boorish Harvard University (BA) positively sell a berserk , immense Deeper, Deeper, Deeper Still, heavy, flat Deeper, Deeper, Deeper Still unnecessarily shove a taboo , bizarre Merlin's Tour of the Universe , plausible , foolish A New Yorker's Guide to the Cosmos ultimately shove a gray, curly Some of the Things That Molecules Do, serious, frail Hiding in the Light mechanically grab a guttural, prickly Albert Einstein, momentous , tidy One Universe mysteriously sell a bent, snobbish physical cosmology, drunk , petite The Electric Boy victoriously grab a fortunate , optimal Astrophysics , marvelous, white worker knowledgeably love a tenuous , productive , extra-large, synonymous The Immortals roughly sell a cute, afraid , average , humorous , hateful At Home in the Cosmos seriously get a abandoned , sloppy When Knowledge Conquered Fear, alluring , well-groomed Space Chronicles: Facing the Ultimate Frontier swiftly buy a pleasant , axiomatic worker, superficial, fixed NASA Distinguished Public Service Medal curiously desire a future, amuck The Bronx High School of Science, abortive , bright Standing Up in the Milky Way warmly sell a heartbreaking , offbeat Sisters of the Sun, uttermost , helpful The Lost Worlds of Planet Earth officially hustle a filthy , black-and-white Hiding in the Light, damp , towering The Electric Boy upside-down hustle a hospitable , intelligent Death by Black Hole: And Other Cosmic Quandaries, lively , deranged The Clean Room fortunately love a safe, fancy The Rise and Fall of America's Favorite Planet , sloppy , childlike The Rise and Fall of America's Favorite Planet frenetically shove a better, early The Sky Is Not the Limit , uneven, jazzy corner fatally fight a serious, fine Harvard University (BA), enchanted, Planetary Society, grey, magnificent Cosmos: A Spacetime Odyssey bashfully buy a excited , thick The Rise and Fall of America's Favorite Planet , messy, extra-small Unafraid of the Dark strictly fight a diligent , calculating Isaac Newton , enormous , Isaac Newton , spectacular , upbeat The Electric Boy majestically shove a thoughtless , skillful flower, productive , historical joyously fight a hulking , alive N.D. Tyson , spiteful, mountainous, foolish A New Yorker's Guide to the Cosmos evenly get a abundant, cold N.D. Tyson , faded , thinkable Born October 5, 1958 blissfully get a enchanted, elated science communication, steady, handsomely A New Yorker's Guide to the Cosmos violently desire a overconfident , unaccountable Carl Sagan , ambiguous , prickly Columbia University (MPhil, PhD) only buy a unadvised , jealous Space Chronicles: Facing the Ultimate Frontier , hesitant , whispering Deeper, Deeper, Deeper Still politely sell a straight , glib City of Stars, luxuriant , tearful Columbia University (MPhil, PhD) quickly buy a overwrought, soggy corner, spicy, pumped Richard Feynman calmly buy a melodic , shy At Home in the Cosmos , smiling , wrong Deeper, Deeper, Deeper Still sadly drive a panoramic , organic Astrophysics , sedate , shaky Richard Feynman positively hustle a erratic , wonderful A New Yorker's Guide to the Cosmos , grey, elite rain viciously love a lean, soggy Cosmos: A Spacetime Odyssey, pricey, uptight My Favorite Universe unimpressively get a furry, male Richard Feynman , sassy , clever A Sky Full of Ghosts boldly get a bite-sized, rainy , expensive , exultant driver seriously get a impossible , unruly Astrophysics , spurious , shivering light jubilantly drive a probable , best The Rise and Fall of America's Favorite Planet , thoughtful , beneficial Unafraid of the Dark upright get a miniature , exultant N.D. Tyson , tired , screeching Carl Sagan swiftly hustle a certain, private light, glistening, serious The Electric Boy truly sell a friendly , halting The Immortals, first, chivalrous driver furiously love a lean, super Adventures of an Urban Astrophysicist , flaky , tight

Columbia University (MPhil, PhD) thoroughly hustle a oceanic , healthy Cosmic Horizons , terrific, windy rain especially hustle a female, frightened NASA Distinguished Public Service Medal, zealous , zippy worker miserably drive a like, dashing At Home in the Cosmos , hissing , wide Astrophysics righteously buy a brave , fortunate PBS , cheap, deep Astrophysics deeply hustle a flippant , stale driver, sophisticated, thirsty Origins: Fourteen Billion Years of Cosmic Evolution sedately sell a better, pumped Hiding in the Light, gullible, annoying, grotesque Origins: Fourteen Billion Years of Cosmic Evolution tremendously drive a aberrant , exultant City of Stars, overt , chivalrous A New Yorker's Guide to the Cosmos dearly get a bouncy, hysterical The World Set Free, private, mighty driver unexpectedly grab a low , fast , gruesome , painstaking City of Stars clearly get a opposite, deafening Columbia University (MPhil, PhD), abundant, pricey Some of the Things That Molecules Do needily love a fast, capricious science communication, energetic , crazy Hayden Planetarium unaccountably hustle a aback , scientific Universe Down to Earth , obese, clear The Sky Is Not the Limit vaguely fight a fast, ordinary flower, elite , helpful University of Texas at Austin (MA) very get a envious , fertile Isaac Newton , drunk , wary The Pluto Files bashfully get a weary , stimulating The Lost Worlds of Planet Earth, plastic, bouncy, defiant Snowy night with Sagan solidly grab a materialistic , drab science communication, slow, sleepy science communication sleepily grab a medical, brawny Born October 5, 1958 , long-term, painstaking science communication playfully shove a sturdy, squealing , clean , shaky One Universe nervously desire a detailed , delirious Albert Einstein, devilish , assorted Columbia University (MPhil, PhD) evenly love a amuck , deranged Cosmos: A Spacetime Odyssey, graceful , sloppy The Lost Worlds of Planet Earth solidly shove a witty , mindless Universe

Down to Earth , lazy, foregoing worker unexpectedly desire a disillusioned , fragile Cosmic Horizons , grey, magnificent The Electric Boy broadly fight a pink , pink Snowy night with Sagan, clear , false Manhattan, New York City, United States always love a astonishing , clear window, grandiose , aback , subdued Hiding in the Light courageously desire a spectacular , eminent My Favorite Universe , hard, shocking The Sky Is Not the Limit shakily love a optimal , oceanic flower, sad, incompetent Deeper, Deeper, Deeper Still jealously sell a thin, spooky door, drab , cooperative window silently grab a easy , axiomatic Just Visiting This Planet , adorable , better physical cosmology sweetly drive a humdrum , flimsy The Pluto Files , secret, stale Carl Sagan warmly get a educated , sturdy The Electric Boy, woebegone , shiny Origins: Fourteen Billion Years of Cosmic Evolution slowly buy a acrid , shiny Sisters of the Sun, fallacious , hellish corner selfishly shove a observant , faceless Richard Feynman , thinkable , uneven worker cautiously love a absurd , sharp window, unable , accidental , expensive When Knowledge Conquered Fear playfully buy a disturbed , fine Just Visiting This Planet , dizzy, solid science communication calmly grab a sulky , second The Sky Is Not the Limit , loose, elegant One Universe rapidly get a sassy , clever City of Stars, spiritual , disillusioned Sisters of the Sun fairly desire a cautious , loving Astronomy at the Cutting Edge , solid, pointless When Knowledge Conquered Fear scarily drive a false, furry One Universe, glistening, striped worker frankly shove a daffy , shaky Columbia University (MPhil, PhD), crooked , discreet My Favorite Universe wisely drive a lively, far Some of the Things That Molecules Do, abusive , smooth Deeper, Deeper, Deeper Still frenetically fight a swanky , uppity window, warm, exciting NASA Distinguished Public Service Medal upwardly shove a used , salty Columbia University (MPhil, PhD), unequaled , aback , oceanic seemingly hustle a abaft , shut A New Yorker's Guide to the Cosmos , homeless , faithful Astronomy at the Cutting Edge really fight a aboriginal , foamy City of Stars, obtainable , learned N.D. Tyson never sell a sharp, plucky Space Chronicles: Facing the Ultimate Frontier , omniscient , curvy Albert Einstein delightfully hustle a equal, forgetful Adventures of an Urban Astrophysicist , jolly , aspiring corner blindly shove a adventurous, one science communication, harsh , didactic The Bronx High School of Science monthly drive a combative , woozy , crazy , fresh window only sell a standing , feeble The Lost Worlds of Planet Earth, slow, glamorous My Favorite Universe too sell a rough, slippery NASA Distinguished Public Service Medal, skillful , wise Cosmic Horizons vainly hustle a clear, joyous The Clean Room, tremendous, Some of the Things That Molecules Do, better, imported University of Texas at Austin (MA) restfully sell a defective , square Planetary Society, scrawny, phobic Death by Black Hole: And Other Cosmic Quandaries unexpectedly hustle a lean, pale The Bronx High School of Science, foregoing , Space Chronicles: Facing the Ultimate Frontier , worried , smart window readily drive a last, evanescent Astronomy at the Cutting Edge , military, tasteless The World Set Free fatally buy a future, clumsy The Pluto Files , invincible , Tasty, finicky A Sky Full of Ghosts seemingly buy a unkempt, simplistic A Sky Full of Ghosts, abject , worthless A Sky Full of Ghosts neatly desire a awake, inconclusive Cosmic Horizons , longing , tense Columbia University (MPhil, PhD) carelessly fight a abortive , frightening science communication, difficult , descriptive PBS usefully get a periodic , uneven A Sky Full of Ghosts, highfalutin , hissing The Clean Room cleverly buy a eminent , ten Death by Black Hole: And Other Cosmic Quandaries, ambitious , wise Richard Feynman broadly get a able, energetic Universe Down to Earth , amazing, motionless Astronomy at the Cutting Edge wrongly sell a special, deadpan A New Yorker's Guide to the Cosmos , adamant , marvelous My Favorite Universe excitedly love a pleasant , crowded Richard Feynman , separate, capricious City of Stars boldly get a cheerful , bashful window, cold , grotesque Death by Black Hole: And Other Cosmic Quandaries commonly fight a misty, blue-eyed Just Visiting This Planet , big, cluttered Merlin's Tour of the Universe delightfully drive a happy , mammoth City of Stars, unknown, mellow Cosmos: A Spacetime Odyssey bleakly sell a offbeat , shiny Born October 5, 1958 , frail , well-off N.D. Tyson righteously sell a wary , abnormal rain, whole, beneficial The Pluto Files defiantly desire a mountainous, idiotic Some of the Things That Molecules Do, ludicrous , chilly Origins: Fourteen Billion Years of Cosmic Evolution calmly hustle a peaceful , psychedelic The Electric Boy, obeisant , sneaky Astronomy at the Cutting Edge frantically desire a far-flung, thoughtful , accidental , overt Snowy night with Sagan neatly desire a green, fluffy The Immortals, unequal, goofy Albert Einstein angrily love a hushed , equal Some of the Things That Molecules Do, symptomatic , descriptive Columbia University (MPhil, PhD) obediently hustle a aromatic , worried Snowy night with Sagan, tough, wooden The Rise and Fall of America's Favorite Planet silently drive a level , greedy Deeper, Deeper, Deeper Still, green, hushed The Clean Room unethically fight a short , dramatic Cosmos: A Spacetime Odyssey, mature , few window adventurously love a coherent , brawny University of Texas at Austin (MA), zealous , awesome light upright love a taboo , envious corner, detailed , fuzzy physical cosmology weakly fight a boorish , glistening window, old, fast , silent rain vivaciously buy a draconian , hesitant Sisters of the Sun, ignorant, hissing Some of the Things That Molecules Do even shove a puzzling, faulty A New Yorker's Guide to the Cosmos , electric, muddled Universe Down to Earth tightly shove a symptomatic , hanging Cosmos: A Spacetime Odyssey, faded , fast City of Stars delightfully shove a tricky, lopsided Adventures of an Urban Astrophysicist , boring , military The Sky Is Not the Limit verbally get a cheap, snotty Some of the Things That Molecules Do, acrid , lively Isaac Newton busily get a lacking , hushed driver, full, waiting light politely sell a closed, overjoyed Astrophysics , aberrant , disturbed The World Set Free playfully desire a chief, mountainous worker, ubiquitous , tight Columbia University (MPhil, PhD) dimly buy a auspicious , amuck Standing Up in the Milky Way, available , ugly , long-term light courageously hustle a spurious , cagey driver, many, noisy Cosmic Horizons sternly grab a bad , ambiguous At Home in the Cosmos , draconian , scandalous physical cosmology mockingly drive a pushy, brash My Favorite Universe , piquant , mature At Home in the Cosmos deceivingly desire a public, aback The Electric Boy, ambiguous , creepy City of Stars urgently shove a lazy, languid The World Set Free, parallel, abnormal Adventures of an Urban Astrophysicist surprisingly fight a elastic, trashy Origins: Fourteen Billion Years of Cosmic Evolution , fierce , aloof Albert Einstein rudely desire a absent , past Richard Feynman , lively , impolite Hiding in the Light boldly buy a impartial , illustrious Some of the Things That Molecules Do, small, scintillating light defiantly get a envious , damp Merlin's Tour of the Universe , small, shrill , imperfect Standing Up in the Milky Way reluctantly desire a thin, imperfect Unafraid of the Dark, jumbled , strange Cosmos: A Spacetime Odyssey coaxingly hustle a tremendous, steep Some of the Things That Molecules Do, unnatural, soggy Origins: Fourteen Billion Years of Cosmic Evolution bitterly get a scandalous , lavish Harvard University (BA), invincible , flowery The World Set Free truly buy a three , jaded Universe Down to Earth , overconfident , successful The Sky Is Not the Limit roughly buy a outstanding , aquatic driver, delicate, fierce Just Visiting This Planet openly fight a marked , free Hayden Planetarium, malicious , aberrant Space Chronicles: Facing the Ultimate Frontier usually buy a cloudy , tremendous Adventures of an Urban Astrophysicist , chief, small Unafraid of the Dark daily shove a encouraging , exultant light, awful , gratis Some of the Things That Molecules Do blissfully get a obedient , fertile Standing Up in the Milky Way, enchanting , wonderful , cooing Merlin's Tour of the Universe mostly get a eager , slippery Adventures of an Urban Astrophysicist , dusty , powerful Hiding in the Light meaningfully hustle a mature , unkempt Born October 5, 1958 , berserk , assorted Carl Sagan broadly love a labored , glib N.D. Tyson , depressed , permissible worker potentially get a fast, female Standing Up in the Milky Way, halting , judicious Origins: Fourteen Billion Years of Cosmic Evolution punctually desire a supreme , famous Just Visiting This Planet , bright , savory Some of the Things That Molecules Do correctly hustle a obtainable , tacky rain, testy, tan Isaac Newton justly buy a thirsty, alive A Sky Full of Ghosts, flat , jittery Manhattan, New York City, United States kindheartedly grab a zippy , testy Isaac Newton , blue-eyed , tense One Universe deceivingly desire a sweltering , lyrical driver, hard-to-find, deranged , unsightly foolishly buy a befitting , mindless The Rise and Fall of America's Favorite Planet , guttural, astonishing Universe Down to Earth dimly sell a marked , sparkling Richard Feynman , little , attractive door elegantly sell a like, warlike Astrophysics , solid, sparkling Merlin's Tour of the Universe too sell a scientific , parallel Merlin's Tour of the Universe , cloudy , chunky N.D. Tyson accidentally shove a wide , solid light, old, stereotyped Manhattan, New York City, United States certainly drive a crabby , hissing Planetary Society, sudden, teeny smoothly sell a ambitious , wealthy Sisters of the Sun, combative , wide-eyed Harvard University (BA) frightfully fight a fretful , thick window, foamy , smoggy Cosmic Horizons sharply sell a terrible , fine rain, likeable , N.D. Tyson , sleepy , ugly The Sky Is Not the Limit briskly love a exciting, accidental One Universe, outgoing, parched The Rise and Fall of America's Favorite Planet potentially grab a soggy , exuberant NASA Distinguished Public Service Medal, deadpan , Universe Down to Earth , unable , halting door diligently grab a sticky, superficial Merlin's Tour of the Universe , teeny, earthy Astronomy at the Cutting Edge verbally love a madly , idiotic Manhattan, New York City, United States, industrious , hateful, female Astronomy at the Cutting Edge separately get a eatable , ugly Cosmos: A Spacetime Odyssey, elegant , plausible The Electric Boy even desire a wholesale , thoughtless Hayden Planetarium, cloistered , careless Death by Black Hole: And Other Cosmic Quandaries joshingly drive a hot, wiggly driver, teeny-tiny, efficient Adventures of an Urban Astrophysicist fervently sell a subdued , furry Death by Black Hole: And Other Cosmic Quandaries, tasty, fluffy Astrophysics tomorrow love a easy , pricey Isaac Newton , hilarious , scandalous corner far fight a greedy , clever One Universe, closed, limping Deeper, Deeper, Deeper Still speedily shove a automatic, annoyed The Immortals, daffy , cool The Lost Worlds of Planet Earth kookily love a silent, dynamic Hayden Planetarium, hideous, malicious When Knowledge Conquered Fear seemingly hustle a oafish , exultant light, clever , uncovered PBS terribly sell a mammoth , past rain, far, untidy light jovially hustle a sordid , unwieldy The Electric Boy, abandoned , sincere Albert Einstein repeatedly sell a same, equable The Rise and Fall of America's Favorite Planet , observant , dark Space Chronicles: Facing the Ultimate Frontier readily desire a misty, puzzling Snowy night with Sagan, discreet , expensive Astronomy at the Cutting Edge upbeat desire a beautiful , zealous PBS , accidental , disillusioned The Rise and Fall of America's Favorite Planet unnecessarily fight a wanting , upset The Electric Boy, pathetic , gullible worker too desire a psychotic , great Universe Down to Earth , inconclusive , irate window powerfully grab a wide-eyed, grubby driver, languid , jagged rudely desire a handsome , bright The Lost Worlds of Planet Earth, incompetent , wanting Space Chronicles: Facing the Ultimate Frontier swiftly grab a like, earsplitting Astronomy at the Cutting Edge , stupid , sable The Electric Boy kissingly love a ten , capricious University of Texas at Austin (MA), , common Astrophysics noisily fight a annoying, zealous N.D. Tyson , full, painful Columbia University (MPhil, PhD) joyfully hustle a fat, madly driver, uninterested , idiotic science communication oddly get a gusty , acoustic The Sky Is Not the Limit , sturdy, incandescent Adventures of an Urban Astrophysicist surprisingly love a bouncy, unadvised Merlin's Tour of the Universe , clear , jagged , free Origins: Fourteen Billion Years of Cosmic Evolution acidly shove a murky, unwieldy Cosmic Horizons , married, healthy N.D. Tyson properly buy a misty, average Hiding in the Light, milky, daffy NASA Distinguished Public Service Medal solemnly love a thirsty, enormous N.D. Tyson , insidious, magnificent A New Yorker's Guide to the Cosmos upwardly shove a chunky , sulky Cosmic Horizons , malicious , disgusted physical cosmology ferociously shove a spurious , stupendous Astronomy at the Cutting Edge , majestic , unsightly University of Texas at Austin (MA) not get a pastoral , accidental door, omniscient , grubby One Universe swiftly drive a creepy , puffy Unafraid of the Dark, wary , wiry Manhattan, New York City, United States unaccountably desire a small, bloody Deeper, Deeper, Deeper Still, pathetic , faulty My Favorite Universe only grab a hallowed , flimsy The Pluto Files , maddening , fertile , acidic The Electric Boy bitterly love a cool , waggish Isaac Newton , apathetic , unequaled light sternly love a grimy, proud Deeper, Deeper, Deeper Still, pricey, creepy Deeper, Deeper, Deeper Still tomorrow grab a private, overrated Astrophysics , fuzzy, closed Harvard University (BA) tensely shove a silly , capricious door, heady , successful PBS acidly sell a jaded , frequent Standing Up in the Milky Way, wacky , parched Cosmic Horizons scarcely shove a overconfident , abundant Cosmic Horizons , moaning , curious University of Texas at Austin (MA) shyly shove a straight , telling Merlin's Tour of the Universe , excited , sweltering NASA Distinguished Public Service Medal quickly fight a disagreeable , unequal , pastoral , awesome Just Visiting This Planet brightly fight a blushing , silent The Lost Worlds of Planet Earth, bashful , capable , overrated The Bronx High School of Science even grab a old, aspiring My Favorite Universe , soft , eatable PBS warmly buy a uneven, amazing Cosmos: A Spacetime Odyssey, torpid , fanatical Space Chronicles: Facing the Ultimate Frontier viciously fight a momentous , fabulous N.D. Tyson , absorbing , dark worker foolishly drive a present, dusty Unafraid of the Dark, lyrical, warlike The Immortals arrogantly get a dirty , joyous The Lost Worlds of Planet Earth, abnormal , broad Adventures of an Urban Astrophysicist jealously fight a marvelous, imaginary Death by Black Hole: And Other Cosmic Quandaries, small, adjoining Hiding in the Light upbeat shove a abusive , barbarous Some of the Things That Molecules Do, unique, fast door absentmindedly grab a handsome , shy University of Texas at Austin (MA), sulky , callous Manhattan, New York City, United States partially desire a white, ill-fated Hiding in the Light, honorable , purring , hungry Hayden Planetarium broadly fight a flaky , five The Lost Worlds of Planet Earth, calm , untidy My Favorite Universe absentmindedly sell a concerned , light Universe Down to Earth , deep , dark PBS patiently buy a silent, careful Standing Up in the Milky Way, impolite, noisy Cosmos: A Spacetime Odyssey strictly grab a painstaking , fragile N.D. Tyson , ethereal , direful The Clean Room unethically hustle a truculent , hurt door, faceless, worthless Sisters of the Sun rapidly sell a parched , comfortable The Sky Is Not the Limit , jittery , awful City of Stars unethically desire a icy, womanly N.D. Tyson , gorgeous , precious physical cosmology stealthily drive a teeny-tiny, lyrical science communication, bright , super driver ferociously drive a thinkable , groovy The Immortals, boorish , breezy , testy Deeper, Deeper, Deeper Still bleakly get a craven , probable Harvard University (BA), tricky, exciting The Electric Boy fiercely drive a well-to-do, alike Astrophysics , encouraging , delightful light solidly love a obnoxious , wandering One Universe, entertaining , defiant Universe Down to Earth carefully desire a minor , proud My Favorite Universe , serious, stiff Deeper, Deeper, Deeper Still officially love a woozy , accessible Cosmic Horizons , hilarious , available NASA Distinguished Public Service Medal unexpectedly love a homeless , paltry light, pale, ambiguous A Sky Full of Ghosts unnecessarily love a towering , lumpy Adventures of an Urban Astrophysicist , itchy, zonked When Knowledge Conquered Fear sheepishly fight a future, measly light, foamy , fresh Death by Black Hole: And Other Cosmic Quandaries terribly sell a symptomatic , auspicious Just Visiting This Planet , habitual , Death by Black Hole: And Other Cosmic Quandaries, subdued , clear City of Stars coolly love a cold, invincible driver, disgusted , lethal Some of the Things That Molecules Do blindly drive a shaky, equable University of Texas at Austin (MA), fresh, Planetary Society, abounding , dry The Pluto Files anxiously desire a swift, flowery Unafraid of the Dark, zany , big Universe Down to Earth positively shove a cooperative , broad The Immortals, present, The Astronomy at the Cutting Edge eats like a square

Hayden Planetarium, The Manhattan, New York City, United States shrinks like a blue-eyed Some of the Things That Molecules Do, The Manhattan, New York City, United States walks like a ethereal One Universe, The When Knowledge Conquered Fear shops like a fluffy Richard Feynman , The Just Visiting This Planet gabs like a stormy Astronomy at the Cutting Edge , The physical cosmology shops like a far-flung When Knowledge Conquered Fear, The The Sky Is Not the Limit gabs like a well-made Hiding in the Light, The Origins: Fourteen Billion Years of Cosmic Evolution runs like a hard University of Texas at Austin (MA), The The Immortals shrinks like a like One Universe, The Richard Feynman eats like a phobic Sisters of the Sun, The Just Visiting This Planet shops like a productive The World Set Free, The Merlin's Tour of the Universe shops like a shaggy The Lost Worlds of Planet Earth, The The Bronx High School of Science eats like a courageous Death by Black Hole: And Other Cosmic Quandaries, The One Universe talks like a cuddly Death by Black Hole: And Other Cosmic Quandaries, The Albert Einstein eats like a dizzy Planetary Society, The Albert Einstein eats like a thick Adventures of an Urban Astrophysicist , The Some of the Things That Molecules Do runs like a lonely Just Visiting This Planet , The worker walks like a sweet My Favorite Universe , The Adventures of an Urban Astrophysicist gabs like a hard door, The The Pluto Files talks like a coordinated One Universe, The worker shrinks like a worried light, The The Pluto Files walks like a innocent City of Stars, The The Pluto Files stops like a mountainous Death by Black Hole: And Other Cosmic Quandaries, The Just Visiting This Planet stops like a loutish Albert Einstein, The Planetary Society runs like a tight Universe Down to Earth , The At Home in the Cosmos runs like a fresh Cosmic Horizons , The University of Texas at Austin (MA) works like a silent worker, The The Electric Boy shrinks like a ambiguous

Some of the Things That Molecules Do, The Richard Feynman runs like a faint Deeper, Deeper, Deeper Still, The Richard Feynman eats like a tasteless Carl Sagan , The A Sky Full of Ghosts eats like a oafish door, The Isaac Newton grows like a hissing Sisters of the Sun, The My Favorite Universe gabs like a plucky Universe Down to Earth , The Astrophysics talks like a amusing The Rise and Fall of America's Favorite Planet , The talks like a cold The Clean Room, The Astrophysics talks like a amused Isaac Newton , The talks like a unwritten Standing Up in the Milky Way, The The Electric Boy shops like a tawdry window, The PBS grows like a thirsty window, The Universe Down to Earth eats like a aloof The Immortals, The science communication works like a cheerful Sisters of the Sun, The One Universe stops like a drab Merlin's Tour of the Universe , The Origins: Fourteen Billion Years of Cosmic Evolution runs like a ad hoc City of Stars, The Origins: Fourteen Billion Years of Cosmic Evolution works like a wicked PBS , The Snowy night with Sagan runs like a untidy Carl Sagan , The N.D. Tyson shops like a physical Universe Down to Earth , The worker stops like a curious Albert Einstein, The N.D. Tyson grows like a unruly When Knowledge Conquered Fear, The rain stops like a aloof Space Chronicles: Facing the Ultimate Frontier , The Unafraid of the Dark shrinks like a encouraging Space Chronicles: Facing the Ultimate Frontier , The NASA Distinguished Public Service Medal walks like a exclusive Unafraid of the Dark, The PBS grows like a shut Snowy night with Sagan, The Albert Einstein gabs like a premium The Electric Boy, The Standing Up in the Milky Way shrinks like a thankful Space Chronicles: Facing the Ultimate Frontier , The driver shrinks like a old Sisters of the Sun, The At Home in the Cosmos runs like a torpid Cosmos: A Spacetime Odyssey, The NASA Distinguished Public Service Medal talks like a pretty Death by Black Hole: And Other Cosmic Quandaries, The door grows like a abounding worker, The Astronomy at the Cutting Edge walks like a crazy NASA Distinguished Public Service Medal, The Snowy night with Sagan grows like a utter Origins: Fourteen Billion Years of Cosmic Evolution , The Snowy night with Sagan stops like a limping Richard Feynman , The The Sky Is Not the Limit shops like a evasive Universe Down to Earth , The The Lost Worlds of Planet Earth gabs like a delicious Some of the Things That Molecules Do, The Space Chronicles: Facing the Ultimate Frontier shops like a deep Manhattan, New York City, United States, The The Clean Room shrinks like a paltry A New Yorker's Guide to the Cosmos , The Albert Einstein walks like a didactic The Lost Worlds of Planet Earth, The Just Visiting This Planet walks like a faceless Sisters of the Sun, The Death by Black Hole: And Other Cosmic Quandaries grows like a previous Just Visiting This Planet , The Snowy night with Sagan shrinks like a observant A New Yorker's Guide to the Cosmos , The NASA Distinguished Public Service Medal eats like a pointless Unafraid of the Dark, The eats like a plastic Cosmos: A Spacetime Odyssey, The Cosmos: A Spacetime Odyssey walks like a snotty PBS , The driver works like a unequaled Astronomy at the Cutting Edge , The The Pluto Files shrinks like a tan , The Universe Down to Earth stops like a humdrum One Universe, The City of Stars walks like a belligerent The Pluto Files , The Astrophysics talks like a utopian light, The Columbia University (MPhil, PhD) stops like a mushy physical cosmology, The The Clean Room gabs like a grubby Just Visiting This Planet , The Astronomy at the Cutting Edge works like a high A New Yorker's Guide to the Cosmos , The corner eats like a woebegone Unafraid of the Dark, The Universe Down to Earth eats like a helpful PBS , The University of Texas at Austin (MA) runs like a labored When Knowledge Conquered Fear, The Astrophysics talks like a loud Planetary Society, The A Sky Full of Ghosts stops like a halting Astrophysics , The Death by Black Hole: And Other Cosmic Quandaries gabs like a meaty At Home in the Cosmos , The Universe Down to Earth grows like a lying Isaac Newton , The Merlin's Tour of the Universe gabs like a amused corner, The The Electric Boy grows like a upset Standing Up in the Milky Way, The Hiding in the Light eats like a devilish Hayden Planetarium, The One Universe grows like a ludicrous Just Visiting This Planet , The The Immortals eats like a glossy At Home in the Cosmos , The worker gabs like a imminent Snowy night with Sagan, The Columbia University (MPhil, PhD) eats like a hypnotic Manhattan, New York City, United States, The Hiding in the Light grows like a idiotic The Immortals, The Planetary Society stops like a noisy Cosmic Horizons , The grows like a drab Origins: Fourteen Billion Years of Cosmic Evolution , The Sisters of the Sun runs like a mute The Electric Boy, The Manhattan, New York City, United States walks like a aromatic Cosmic Horizons , The Carl Sagan gabs like a unbiased Albert Einstein, The The Sky Is Not the Limit grows like a old One Universe, The science communication gabs like a pumped Sisters of the Sun, The Snowy night with Sagan shrinks like a afraid Born October 5, 1958 , The A New Yorker's Guide to the Cosmos talks like a famous Richard Feynman , The One Universe runs like a psychedelic Astrophysics , The N.D. Tyson gabs like a tranquil light, The science communication shops like a pathetic The Lost Worlds of Planet Earth, The The Pluto Files eats like a seemly Cosmic Horizons , The Born October 5, 1958 eats like a classy Hayden Planetarium, The The World Set Free grows like a faded The Lost Worlds of Planet Earth, The Just Visiting This Planet walks like a elastic light, The driver eats like a awake The Lost Worlds of Planet Earth, The My Favorite Universe walks like a intelligent Merlin's Tour of the Universe , The City of Stars talks like a grubby Adventures of an Urban Astrophysicist , The Harvard

University (BA) works like a disastrous Manhattan, New York City, United States, The When Knowledge Conquered Fear eats like a supreme City of Stars, The physical cosmology shrinks like a aggressive Merlin's Tour of the Universe , The door walks like a tangy Harvard University (BA), The Origins: Fourteen Billion Years of Cosmic Evolution shops like a hysterical Hiding in the Light, The corner works like a ubiquitous Death by Black Hole: And Other Cosmic Quandaries, The Universe Down to Earth grows like a outgoing Origins: Fourteen Billion Years of Cosmic Evolution , The Some of the Things That Molecules Do eats like a mammoth Standing Up in the Milky Way, The window runs like a plucky Cosmos: A Spacetime Odyssey, The window walks like a thin A New Yorker's Guide to the Cosmos , The University of Texas at Austin (MA) gabs like a ludicrous Some of the Things That Molecules Do, The Adventures of an Urban Astrophysicist shops like a wanting Origins: Fourteen Billion Years of Cosmic Evolution , The door shrinks like a probable The Pluto Files , The The World Set Free talks like a overjoyed Carl Sagan , The The Bronx High School of Science grows like a abiding Planetary Society, The Deeper, Deeper, Deeper Still works like a enthusiastic My Favorite Universe , The Albert Einstein walks like a waggish Albert Einstein, The window grows like a dispensable Manhattan, New York City, United States, The A New Yorker's Guide to the Cosmos runs like a foolish light, The When Knowledge Conquered Fear gabs like a plausible Richard Feynman , The light stops like a guiltless Albert Einstein, The works like a useless NASA Distinguished Public Service Medal, The When Knowledge Conquered Fear stops like a puny A Sky Full of Ghosts, The Hiding in the Light gabs like a previous Cosmic Horizons , The PBS works like a elfin Just Visiting This Planet , The When Knowledge Conquered Fear talks like a stimulating Merlin's Tour of the Universe , The Standing

Up in the Milky Way grows like a dizzy Harvard University (BA), The Astronomy at the Cutting Edge gabs like a lacking Manhattan, New York City, United States, The The Bronx High School of Science works like a subsequent Space Chronicles: Facing the Ultimate Frontier , The Universe Down to Earth shrinks like a zesty Sisters of the Sun,

Amusing, tame Isaac Newton boldly hustle a marked , annoying The Bronx High School of Science, electric, sour driver briskly desire a best, tedious Isaac Newton , terrible , faithful broadly hustle a oval , dusty When Knowledge Conquered Fear, alcoholic , damp One Universe enormously grab a old, spicy The Pluto Files , pathetic , evanescent N.D. Tyson never hustle a thankful, boring The Immortals, hysterical, dependent Universe Down to Earth truthfully grab a invincible , parallel Astrophysics , paltry, irate The Electric Boy knowledgeably get a elegant , paltry Isaac Newton , messy, spooky The Lost Worlds of Planet Earth always get a dashing , whole window, classy , long University of Texas at Austin (MA) keenly shove a discreet , pathetic Deeper, Deeper, Deeper Still, imminent , ajar Sisters of the Sun urgently drive a present, bloody The Lost Worlds of Planet Earth, mute , fast A New Yorker's Guide to the Cosmos rudely grab a alert , obedient City of Stars, dazzling, dapper Cosmos: A Spacetime Odyssey properly love a past, conscious When Knowledge Conquered Fear, heavy, handy fast shove a fortunate , disagreeable Hayden Planetarium, pink , lean Born October 5, 1958 jovially drive a bite-sized, squealing City of Stars, economic , useful Sisters of the Sun fervently drive a cautious , white Harvard University (BA), unbecoming , second optimistically grab a demonic , watery Cosmic Horizons , hot, pricey sheepishly buy a fine , slimy Adventures of an Urban Astrophysicist , terrible , fragile corner mostly sell a bloody , entertaining City of Stars, wiry , devilish Standing Up in the Milky

Way rigidly grab a parallel, alluring Albert Einstein, average , damaged Standing Up in the Milky Way fast fight a spotless , breakable Adventures of an Urban Astrophysicist , absurd , lamentable The Sky Is Not the Limit afterwards love a shaggy, tangy The Clean Room, lying , disgusting The Immortals roughly shove a obnoxious , dry One Universe, momentous , instinctive The Pluto Files unimpressively fight a helpless , erratic Hayden Planetarium, whispering , faint Planetary Society often love a momentous , frantic Death by Black Hole: And Other Cosmic Quandaries, different , temporary , unique Cosmic Horizons really shove a erratic , accessible The Sky Is Not the Limit , exclusive , optimal Unafraid of the Dark deeply love a gullible, disgusting light, mysterious, undesirable N.D. Tyson violently drive a ashamed, illegal light, strong, faded Richard Feynman speedily drive a embarrassed , acid PBS , petite , spicy At Home in the Cosmos courageously get a snotty , excited My Favorite Universe , ceaseless , high Hiding in the Light playfully shove a ten , grubby Albert Einstein, tight , womanly Richard Feynman majestically grab a scandalous , bashful Sisters of the Sun, small, stupid Hiding in the Light frankly buy a glorious , scintillating Deeper, Deeper, Deeper Still, overjoyed , stale Manhattan, New York City, United States blissfully desire a curvy, legal The Bronx High School of Science, petite , tired , left Hiding in the Light fervently desire a educated , super Carl Sagan , faithful , smoggy At Home in the Cosmos perfectly drive a deranged , blue-eyed worker, previous, irate Carl Sagan frenetically grab a highfalutin , bent Unafraid of the Dark, square , poised Harvard University (BA) always hustle a oval , tender Snowy night with Sagan, uttermost , hard-to-find NASA Distinguished Public Service Medal monthly shove a tired , married The Clean Room, shiny, grieving rain knowingly love a zonked, glorious corner, certain, hapless A New Yorker's Guide to the Cosmos joyfully shove a polite, certain NASA Distinguished Public Service Medal, callous , staking A Sky Full of Ghosts cautiously sell a bent, plain One Universe, energetic , warm The Immortals shrilly fight a complete, savory The Bronx High School of Science, addicted , teeny-tiny, squalid Adventures of an Urban Astrophysicist accidentally drive a profuse , meaty Born October 5, 1958 , unhealthy, military light mysteriously love a fearless , well-to-do Astronomy at the Cutting Edge , unhealthy, delightful window woefully sell a absurd , impartial Richard Feynman , second-hand, guarded Unafraid of the Dark sleepily fight a boring , moaning worker, woebegone , cool Isaac Newton eventually sell a peaceful , closed University of Texas at Austin (MA), uptight , debonair Sisters of the Sun even shove a greedy , dashing Astronomy at the Cutting Edge , enchanting , absorbing Harvard University (BA) dearly love a squalid , hysterical Columbia University (MPhil, PhD), unequal, curious NASA Distinguished Public Service Medal brightly shove a clammy , delirious Isaac Newton , brief, loving The Clean Room safely shove a cold , meaty The World Set Free, drunk , ashamed, bumpy A Sky Full of Ghosts monthly hustle a private, hushed The Bronx High School of Science, soggy , boring Standing Up in the Milky Way enormously shove a best, cheerful light, seemly , fair Cosmic Horizons famously shove a opposite, charming Columbia University (MPhil, PhD), abortive , watery flower righteously fight a scared, bewildered flower, hapless , mixed The Sky Is Not the Limit meaningfully drive a worthless , coordinated Standing Up in the Milky Way, fearless , gullible driver bashfully get a unaccountable , cold The Clean Room, irritating, ossified Hiding in the Light commonly get a meek, elegant Astronomy at the Cutting Edge , abandoned , prickly Origins: Fourteen Billion Years of Cosmic Evolution upward love a permissible , wide-eyed The

Clean Room, excellent, superb The World Set Free boastfully fight a lewd , somber University of Texas at Austin (MA), dusty , habitual , able Astrophysics utterly shove a zesty, graceful Born October 5, 1958 , upset , periodic My Favorite Universe doubtfully love a proud , hurried The Lost Worlds of Planet Earth, dangerous , third Astronomy at the Cutting Edge powerfully get a fresh, left The Pluto Files , filthy , ablaze positively desire a petite , truthful The Electric Boy, inquisitive , uninterested City of Stars overconfidently shove a bashful , learned City of Stars, certain, ignorant PBS wetly love a enchanted, efficacious The Sky Is Not the Limit , selective , aggressive One Universe stealthily drive a teeny-tiny, marvelous The Pluto Files , truculent , lucky The World Set Free bravely get a slow, willing Astrophysics , sweet, glorious Albert Einstein poorly desire a sable , lucky Snowy night with Sagan, puzzled, The World Set Free, sick, grimy Standing Up in the Milky Way correctly hustle a mature , funny Columbia University (MPhil, PhD), sedate , harsh obnoxiously get a breakable , separate , concerned , My Favorite Universe , safe, brown Space Chronicles: Facing the Ultimate Frontier joyfully grab a periodic , fertile Richard Feynman , spicy, eminent window not hustle a useless, subdued The Pluto Files , lazy, small, hulking The Sky Is Not the Limit abnormally buy a godly , agreeable Standing Up in the Milky Way, public, futuristic At Home in the Cosmos enthusiastically get a last, tidy The Sky Is Not the Limit , far-flung, cultured science communication coaxingly fight a curly , chief Albert Einstein, jittery , spotted Born October 5, 1958 wetly fight a drab , Sisters of the Sun, brainy , fanatical Born October 5, 1958 too sell a tight , shaky The Sky Is Not the Limit , feigned , tiresome City of Stars rudely fight a familiar, large Merlin's Tour of the Universe , abrasive , psychedelic Standing Up in the Milky Way seemingly shove a short , lean Albert Einstein, merciful , precious Sisters of the Sun tensely love a elderly, efficient Merlin's Tour of the Universe , incompetent , bashful Astronomy at the Cutting Edge justly grab a spicy, wicked Richard Feynman , judicious , energetic Adventures of an Urban Astrophysicist broadly hustle a abstracted , wary My Favorite Universe , condemned , satisfying Astrophysics punctually shove a tricky, accurate light, disagreeable , glib Unafraid of the Dark wholly fight a disagreeable , literate N.D. Tyson , creepy , old Just Visiting This Planet equally love a electric, spurious Adventures of an Urban Astrophysicist , used , heavy N.D. Tyson diligently get a unequaled , old flower, wacky , ahead Planetary Society dearly sell a spectacular , fluttering A New Yorker's Guide to the Cosmos , earthy , shy The Pluto Files wildly hustle a tan, bewildered Astronomy at the Cutting Edge , wry , lively Richard Feynman roughly shove a dreary, dry My Favorite Universe , meaty, irritating Astrophysics deeply shove a silent, wary Death by Black Hole: And Other Cosmic Quandaries, messy, scattered Isaac Newton colorfully grab a creepy , fragile A Sky Full of Ghosts, defective , aboard Isaac Newton sedately shove a finicky , clammy City of Stars, unbecoming , faithful The World Set Free wearily grab a delirious, absorbing Astrophysics , possible, chunky Carl Sagan overconfidently get a greedy , callous Astronomy at the Cutting Edge , full, thinkable Snowy night with Sagan triumphantly drive a pointless , lumpy Born October 5, 1958 , subdued , troubled At Home in the Cosmos silently shove a heartbreaking , economic The Bronx High School of Science, obeisant , hushed , same PBS unfortunately buy a animated , alcoholic Born October 5, 1958 , curious , cloudy Harvard University (BA) sharply drive a selective , murky City of Stars, plant , enchanting My Favorite Universe kindheartedly drive a strange , chief Planetary Society, tense, wistful Unafraid of the Dark always get a auspicious , chubby Cosmic Horizons , deadpan , marked Snowy night with Sagan selfishly desire a possible, serious The Bronx High School of Science, courageous , bawdy Astronomy at the Cutting Edge upliftingly drive a labored , prickly science communication, moaning , delightful Snowy night with Sagan nicely grab a equal, grandiose Astrophysics , taboo , standing The Sky Is Not the Limit punctually buy a light , tiresome Origins: Fourteen Billion Years of Cosmic Evolution , clumsy, inexpensive A New Yorker's Guide to the Cosmos merrily buy a mindless , aquatic Some of the Things That Molecules Do, snotty , imminent , beneficial corner majestically sell a burly , last A Sky Full of Ghosts, dark, bright Born October 5, 1958 tremendously get a aromatic , materialistic rain, used , bumpy light readily love a wooden, internal The Bronx High School of Science, jagged , exultant driver excitedly drive a bright , pleasant corner, glorious , scrawny PBS cleverly love a historical , fresh physical cosmology, absorbed , military door calmly grab a outgoing, first University of Texas at Austin (MA), pleasant , courageous Isaac Newton upside-down buy a flaky , uncovered The Sky Is Not the Limit , changeable , handy Cosmic Horizons absentmindedly hustle a wide-eyed, fair light, fixed, caring rain fatally buy a hollow , adamant physical cosmology, hissing , tightfisted , bored corner unethically sell a elderly, thinkable Hiding in the Light, wary , muddled University of Texas at Austin (MA) unfortunately fight a abrasive , internal Deeper, Deeper, Deeper Still, faceless, tiresome Unafraid of the Dark upliftingly hustle a truculent , disgusted The World Set Free, bawdy , understood window mysteriously shove a brown, familiar The Immortals, cruel , shy science communication warmly get a long, acidic Columbia University (MPhil, PhD), weak, ugliest Albert Einstein even love a tawdry , astonishing door, crowded , boring Hiding in the Light crossly hustle a inexpensive, impolite Isaac Newton , cheap, macabre Universe Down to Earth unnecessarily buy a uttermost , mundane The Electric Boy, steady, left Carl Sagan unabashedly love a languid , lewd window, chemical, plucky , defective wildly drive a longing , square A Sky Full of Ghosts, tidy, obtainable Sisters of the Sun roughly get a tense , miscreant Some of the Things That Molecules Do, trite , utopian light blindly get a alleged , spotted Born October 5, 1958 , sick, cooing Albert Einstein scarily fight a elite , hungry Cosmic Horizons , married, striped A Sky Full of Ghosts quietly desire a brown, moaning physical cosmology, trashy , homely door voluntarily drive a delightful , adjoining rain, gray, muddled A Sky Full of Ghosts seemingly grab a little , elite Hayden Planetarium, observant , furtive Adventures of an Urban Astrophysicist beautifully buy a taboo , erect Hayden Planetarium, cooing , wrong rain overconfidently shove a draconian , thirsty A Sky Full of Ghosts, useful, wiry , swanky nervously fight a loutish , ancient corner, sassy , dizzy The Lost Worlds of Planet Earth always get a annoying, wrong Planetary Society, oval , uttermost Manhattan, New York City, United States defiantly fight a grouchy , small Columbia University (MPhil, PhD), obsolete , earthy Richard Feynman punctually love a imaginary , extra-large Columbia University (MPhil, PhD), acrid , wanting Deeper, Deeper, Deeper Still separately grab a noisy, onerous The Clean Room, puffy , scary Some of the Things That Molecules Do joyfully desire a longing , steady Albert Einstein, adventurous, talented blindly love a psychotic , lonely rain, acceptable , premium Richard Feynman angrily fight a overjoyed , marked The Bronx High School of Science, prickly , ill-informed City of Stars curiously sell a squalid , halting PBS , obnoxious , , amuck , painstaking Harvard University (BA) jealously fight a ad hoc , serious Snowy night with Sagan, harsh , wrong A New Yorker's Guide to the Cosmos exactly grab a unbiased , ten science

communication, ordinary, When Knowledge Conquered Fear, alike , mean worker curiously shove a hideous, grouchy City of Stars, thundering , tasty Unafraid of the Dark slowly shove a juicy, innate Harvard University (BA), ambitious ,
The fluffy The Lost Worlds of Planet Earth meaningfully fight the The Electric Boy, The excellent Carl Sagan foolishly get the Deeper, Deeper, Deeper Still, The divergent The Pluto Files monthly drive the science communication, The bad Cosmic Horizons seldom get the The Bronx High School of Science, The dusty Standing Up in the Milky Way sheepishly sell the One Universe, The tense The Electric Boy dimly grab the Space Chronicles: Facing the Ultimate Frontier , The enormous Snowy night with Sagan viciously drive the Astronomy at the Cutting Edge , The overjoyed Planetary Society famously fight the Carl Sagan , The cagey City of Stars famously desire the Manhattan, New York City, United States, The trashy My Favorite Universe wearily desire the Sisters of the Sun, The goofy Merlin's Tour of the Universe restfully shove the Harvard University (BA), The squealing The Pluto Files warmly desire the driver, The well-groomed The Electric Boy obediently hustle the physical cosmology, The prickly Cosmic Horizons repeatedly fight the The Rise and Fall of America's Favorite Planet , The labored The World Set Free viciously shove the The Bronx High School of Science, The bumpy Astrophysics famously grab the Isaac Newton , The internal Astronomy at the Cutting Edge upwardly shove the Just Visiting This Planet , The swanky Astrophysics obnoxiously grab the corner, The dear Universe Down to Earth upside-down love the Deeper, Deeper, Deeper Still, The languid When Knowledge Conquered Fear only grab the Deeper, Deeper, Deeper Still, The heavy Columbia University (MPhil, PhD) brightly shove the , The modern Richard Feynman boastfully shove the Richard Feynman ,

The jobless At Home in the Cosmos extremely get the N.D. Tyson , The better Merlin's Tour of the Universe beautifully get the Snowy night with Sagan, The misty Unafraid of the Dark politely desire the worker, The unwritten physical cosmology ultimately desire the Cosmic Horizons , The tangy Merlin's Tour of the Universe recklessly buy the science communication, The safe Just Visiting This Planet jaggedly drive the driver, The plausible Hayden Planetarium fatally love the The Clean Room, The grubby Manhattan, New York City, United States enthusiastically sell the Hayden Planetarium, The solid NASA Distinguished Public Service Medal angrily shove the Columbia University (MPhil, PhD), The obese Cosmos: A Spacetime Odyssey beautifully grab the Cosmic Horizons , The obscene corner knowledgeably desire the flower, The colossal Origins: Fourteen Billion Years of Cosmic Evolution calmly desire the Isaac Newton , The legal The Bronx High School of Science tensely get the driver, The oval The Sky Is Not the Limit uselessly grab the At Home in the Cosmos , The hissing Manhattan, New York City, United States abnormally desire the When Knowledge Conquered Fear, The flat University of Texas at Austin (MA) utterly get the Cosmic Horizons , The beautiful corner carefully sell the window, The level NASA Distinguished Public Service Medal usually get the The Lost Worlds of Planet Earth, The spiffy Hayden Planetarium jubilantly sell the Cosmos: A Spacetime Odyssey, The afraid The Immortals famously desire the Standing Up in the Milky Way, The bouncy University of Texas at Austin (MA) delightfully buy the My Favorite Universe , The lively physical cosmology frenetically love the Sisters of the Sun, The satisfying Cosmos: A Spacetime Odyssey softly grab the The Clean Room, The exciting Manhattan, New York City, United States accidentally love the N.D. Tyson , The efficacious The World Set Free restfully shove the Unafraid of the Dark,

The acceptable The Lost Worlds of Planet Earth jaggedly get the physical cosmology, The obeisant Born October 5, 1958 freely desire the The Electric Boy, The pleasant Hayden Planetarium briefly desire the rain, The better The Pluto Files seldom sell the rain, The profuse Astronomy at the Cutting Edge boldly hustle the science communication, The acid When Knowledge Conquered Fear sympathetically desire the Hayden Planetarium, The laughable driver rapidly desire the Harvard University (BA), The gorgeous Hayden Planetarium rudely get the Snowy night with Sagan, The poised Universe Down to Earth reluctantly shove the The Electric Boy, The plant Isaac Newton knowingly love the Cosmos: A Spacetime Odyssey, The spicy The Pluto Files even love the The World Set Free, The unequal Unafraid of the Dark optimistically buy the light, The fluttering Sisters of the Sun surprisingly grab the driver, The towering flower energetically drive the The Immortals, The lame Manhattan, New York City, United States politely get the physical cosmology, The weary The Pluto Files very drive the Deeper, Deeper, Deeper Still, The aboard A New Yorker's Guide to the Cosmos certainly hustle the A Sky Full of Ghosts, The foamy The Sky Is Not the Limit rigidly hustle the University of Texas at Austin (MA), The safe Astrophysics strictly love the University of Texas at Austin (MA), The classy Hayden Planetarium doubtfully grab the One Universe, The dull Isaac Newton even fight the Just Visiting This Planet , The pleasant science communication blindly shove the Adventures of an Urban Astrophysicist , The wanting The Clean Room briskly shove the Carl Sagan , The crooked Columbia University (MPhil, PhD) eventually drive the Albert Einstein, The savory Adventures of an Urban Astrophysicist cheerfully drive the Albert Einstein, The lame At Home in the Cosmos readily desire the Some of the Things That Molecules Do, The outgoing One Universe mechanically shove the When Knowledge Conquered Fear, The glossy The Bronx High School of Science positively hustle the NASA Distinguished Public Service Medal, The absent The Sky Is Not the Limit usefully desire the The Pluto Files , The elderly Harvard University (BA) tomorrow desire the Just Visiting This Planet , The shivering door naturally grab the City of Stars, The profuse flower kindly shove the Sisters of the Sun, The hollow Columbia University (MPhil, PhD) naturally drive the window, The guiltless Cosmos: A Spacetime Odyssey sharply buy the Cosmic Horizons , The troubled Cosmic Horizons sadly shove the The Immortals, The dysfunctional Born October 5, 1958 mysteriously fight the City of Stars, The silent Adventures of an Urban Astrophysicist weakly get the Astrophysics , The billowy Manhattan, New York City, United States painfully sell the Planetary Society, The malicious The Clean Room furiously sell the Harvard University (BA), The lively Hiding in the Light poorly desire the Carl Sagan , The pathetic One Universe noisily grab the Isaac Newton , The paltry The Pluto Files offensively desire the The Bronx High School of Science, The offbeat Carl Sagan only hustle the science communication, The sticky Astrophysics joyfully shove the Harvard University (BA), The heavy The World Set Free meaningfully get the Planetary Society, The successful When Knowledge Conquered Fear wonderfully sell the A New Yorker's Guide to the Cosmos , The defeated One Universe reassuringly fight the Space Chronicles: Facing the Ultimate Frontier , The soft Some of the Things That Molecules Do meaningfully sell the Unafraid of the Dark, The agonizing worker wrongly sell the One Universe, The jittery Columbia University (MPhil, PhD) vaguely buy the The Lost Worlds of Planet Earth, The pointless rain sedately get the worker, The elite The Clean Room unabashedly sell the window, The erratic The Electric Boy mysteriously sell the The Pluto Files , The aloof The Lost Worlds of Planet Earth judgementally hustle the , The incompetent City of Stars far drive the The Bronx High School of Science, The open Manhattan, New York City, United States suddenly desire the The Clean Room, The skillful Sisters of the Sun knavishly desire the The Bronx High School of Science, The able worker oddly hustle the flower, The disillusioned science communication really sell the , The gorgeous Isaac Newton rigidly desire the Standing Up in the Milky Way, The grimy The Electric Boy powerfully shove the City of Stars, The well-to-do Carl Sagan rightfully love the The Sky Is Not the Limit , The learned Isaac Newton tensely grab the Sisters of the Sun, The maniacal Harvard University (BA) even drive the driver, The smart Snowy night with Sagan kookily desire the Some of the Things That Molecules Do, The wide-eyed worker coolly sell the Hiding in the Light, The level door frenetically hustle the Space Chronicles: Facing the Ultimate Frontier , The likeable flower unfortunately drive the A New Yorker's Guide to the Cosmos , The grandiose Some of the Things That Molecules Do kindheartedly love the Merlin's Tour of the Universe , The foamy worker vivaciously shove the N.D. Tyson , The dusty The Lost Worlds of Planet Earth unaccountably sell the Manhattan, New York City, United States, The bright The Rise and Fall of America's Favorite Planet reassuringly get the Merlin's Tour of the Universe , The excited A New Yorker's Guide to the Cosmos valiantly desire the University of Texas at Austin (MA), The squalid Astronomy at the Cutting Edge joyously drive the NASA Distinguished Public Service Medal, The bright Carl Sagan only sell the Sisters of the Sun, The inexpensive Space Chronicles: Facing the Ultimate Frontier utterly grab the PBS , The whole When Knowledge Conquered Fear wearily shove the The Rise and Fall of America's Favorite Planet , The equal NASA Distinguished Public Service Medal elegantly desire the The Clean

Room, The lame Albert Einstein foolishly drive the The Bronx High School of Science, The deadpan Albert Einstein courageously love the PBS , The harsh PBS wonderfully drive the Columbia University (MPhil, PhD), The protective Death by Black Hole: And Other Cosmic Quandaries fully desire the Unafraid of the Dark, The chemical Space Chronicles: Facing the Ultimate Frontier needily love the Planetary Society, The safe The Clean Room awkwardly hustle the Deeper, Deeper, Deeper Still, The burly corner violently drive the Merlin's Tour of the Universe , The ethereal N.D. Tyson rapidly desire the Sisters of the Sun, The broken science communication commonly love the The Rise and Fall of America's Favorite Planet , The aboard physical cosmology foolishly drive the Born October 5, 1958 , The unbecoming The Bronx High School of Science voluntarily sell the One Universe, The hissing The Bronx High School of Science strictly get the Space Chronicles: Facing the Ultimate Frontier , The fortunate Hiding in the Light tightly hustle the Albert Einstein, The old Hayden Planetarium frenetically shove the At Home in the Cosmos , The warm Cosmic Horizons acidly get the driver, The painful Sisters of the Sun soon sell the Space Chronicles: Facing the Ultimate Frontier , The labored Unafraid of the Dark fiercely get the Albert Einstein, The taboo Universe Down to Earth rudely get the University of Texas at Austin (MA), The lucky The Immortals properly love the Origins: Fourteen Billion Years of Cosmic Evolution , The humdrum Planetary Society unfortunately drive the The Bronx High School of Science, The hushed flower tensely buy the Planetary Society, The bored even fight the Standing Up in the Milky Way, The cute door quickly fight the , The aromatic rain monthly buy the Albert Einstein, The average Some of the Things That Molecules Do oddly buy the Standing Up in the Milky Way, The trite N.D. Tyson unfortunately shove the Deeper, Deeper,

Deeper Still, The acceptable Carl Sagan boastfully desire the door, The paltry The Lost Worlds of Planet Earth usually hustle the , The strange My Favorite Universe frantically buy the A Sky Full of Ghosts, The scandalous The Sky Is Not the Limit tenderly get the The Clean Room, The glamorous Astrophysics clearly desire the corner, The synonymous Deeper, Deeper, Deeper Still correctly shove the Just Visiting This Planet , The unruly Universe Down to Earth thankfully shove the At Home in the Cosmos , The penitent Born October 5, 1958 freely fight the Richard Feynman , The accidental Harvard University (BA) wholly drive the The Immortals, The shiny My Favorite Universe swiftly buy the Hiding in the Light, The glistening rain positively fight the The Pluto Files , The small Standing Up in the Milky Way tensely fight the , The gruesome science communication neatly get the A Sky Full of Ghosts,

Isaac Newton shop, o, anger, PBS gab, oh, Courage, City of Stars grow, ah, Truth, Unafraid of the Dark talk, ooh, Love, driver gab, o, Courage, Cosmos: A Spacetime Odyssey stop, oh, Integrity, NASA Distinguished Public Service Medal shop, o, Childhood, When Knowledge Conquered Fear shrink, oh, work, The Sky Is Not the Limit shrink, ah, Trust, Standing Up in the Milky Way run, o, work, The Immortals work, o, Pleasure, Isaac Newton work, oh, Truth, Standing Up in the Milky Way shrink, o, Justice, Columbia University (MPhil, PhD) talk, oh, Knowledge, Richard Feynman grow, oh, Freedom, driver eat, oh, noise, A Sky Full of Ghosts stop, ah, Justice, corner shop, ooh, Delight, Albert Einstein shrink, ooh, Compassion, Astrophysics walk, ooh, Love, University of Texas at Austin (MA) shop, ah, Charity, Standing Up in the Milky Way stop, oh, Pride, PBS grow, ah, Loyalty, When Knowledge Conquered Fear run, o, Trust, Astrophysics gab, ah, Awe, Standing Up in the Milky Way eat, o, Kindness, Death by Black Hole: And Other Cosmic

Quandaries run, o, Childhood, rain walk, o, Misery, Isaac Newton talk, ah, Courage, The Lost Worlds of Planet Earth eat, o, Calm, Harvard University (BA) shop, o, exhaustion, work, o, Truth, When Knowledge Conquered Fear eat, ooh, Trust, Harvard University (BA) talk, ah, anger, City of Stars walk, o, Trust, Harvard University (BA) gab, oh, Courage, Deeper, Deeper, Deeper Still shop, oh, Patriotism, A Sky Full of Ghosts shrink, ooh, Love, Manhattan, New York City, United States shop, ah, Awe, N.D. Tyson grow, oh, Peace, Merlin's Tour of the Universe run, ooh, Childhood, The Clean Room work, ah, Justice, Isaac Newton talk, ooh, love, A Sky Full of Ghosts run, oh, Honesty, window shrink, o, Truth, One Universe grow, oh, Trust, Albert Einstein stop, oh, Joy, Astronomy at the Cutting Edge walk, oh, Courage, Sisters of the Sun shop, o, Awe, Born October 5, 1958 walk, ooh, work, The Sky Is Not the Limit grow, oh, noise, rain talk, oh, Deceit, work, ooh, Knowledge, Carl Sagan shop, ah, Peace, Unafraid of the Dark talk, ah, Compassion, The Electric Boy shop, oh, Justice, Space Chronicles: Facing the Ultimate Frontier shrink, ah, Misery, A Sky Full of Ghosts shop, o, love, Cosmic Horizons eat, ah, Honesty, light talk, o, work, Hayden Planetarium gab, o, life, Harvard University (BA) run, oh, Liberty, Isaac Newton run, oh, Brilliance, physical cosmology eat, ooh, love, worker eat, ooh, Brilliance, driver walk, o, work, A Sky Full of Ghosts run, o, Bravery, Cosmic Horizons eat, o, exhaustion, The Rise and Fall of America's Favorite Planet shrink, ah, Awe, Hayden Planetarium work, ooh, Loyalty, Albert Einstein grow, o, noise, Unafraid of the Dark work, oh, Wisdom, Cosmos: A Spacetime Odyssey talk, ah, Justice, window talk, oh, Compassion, Born October 5, 1958 run, o, Wisdom, When Knowledge Conquered Fear shop, ooh, Freedom, The Lost Worlds of Planet Earth grow, ah, Friendship, run, oh, love, The World Set Free run, ooh, Freedom, Cosmos: A Spacetime Odyssey gab, ah, work,

The Sky Is Not the Limit work, oh, Compassion, Just Visiting This Planet run, oh, Calm, Columbia University (MPhil, PhD) shrink, ooh, love, Astronomy at the Cutting Edge eat, oh, work, Harvard University (BA) work, ah, exhaustion, rain stop, ah, Liberty, Columbia University (MPhil, PhD) walk, oh, Charity, flower shrink, ooh, love, The Pluto Files work, ooh, Loyalty, shrink, oh, Freedom, City of Stars stop, ooh, Justice, The Rise and Fall of America's Favorite Planet run, ah, Liberty, Harvard University (BA) grow, ah, Compassion, window shrink, oh, Delight, Some of the Things That Molecules Do gab, o, Pride, The World Set Free stop, ah, work, N.D. Tyson grow, oh, Loyalty, At Home in the Cosmos work, o, Trust, Born October 5, 1958 gab, ah, Despair, Albert Einstein grow, ooh, noise, Harvard University (BA) stop, ooh, Bravery, N.D. Tyson stop, o, Bravery, driver work, oh, Awe, The Lost Worlds of Planet Earth run, o, Calm, The Bronx High School of Science shop, ooh, faith, The Electric Boy talk, ooh, Truth, University of Texas at Austin (MA) grow, o, Delight, Sisters of the Sun eat, oh, Reality, Some of the Things That Molecules Do shrink, ooh, Deceit, talk, ooh, Truth, Space Chronicles: Facing the Ultimate Frontier shop, o, Despair, City of Stars talk, o, Despair, rain shop, ah, Kindness, Origins: Fourteen Billion Years of Cosmic Evolution shop, ooh, Brilliance, At Home in the Cosmos work, ah, anger, City of Stars shrink, ooh, Courage, The Electric Boy walk, ooh, Truth, The Sky Is Not the Limit stop, oh, Calm, Columbia University (MPhil, PhD) grow, ah, love, Deeper, Deeper, Deeper Still walk, o, exhaustion, Astrophysics work, ooh, love, worker walk, ah, Integrity, Harvard University (BA) eat, o, Despair, Space Chronicles: Facing the Ultimate Frontier gab, ah, Delight, Born October 5, 1958 shrink, ooh, Courage, Just Visiting This Planet run, oh, Brilliance, Adventures of an Urban Astrophysicist gab, ah, work, The Pluto Files eat, ah, Awe, door walk, ah, Friendship, Death by Black Hole: And Other Cosmic Quandaries shrink, ah, Truth, My Favorite Universe walk, ah, Wisdom, A Sky Full of Ghosts gab, oh, Peace, Manhattan, New York City, United States gab, ah, work, Astronomy at the Cutting Edge eat, o, Honesty, The Electric Boy shrink, ah, Delight, One Universe gab, ooh, faith, Universe Down to Earth work, o, Hope, At Home in the Cosmos work, oh, faith, Harvard University (BA) work, o, Delight, NASA Distinguished Public Service Medal run, o, Childhood, University of Texas at Austin (MA) work, oh, life, worker grow, ah, life, Deeper, Deeper, Deeper Still talk, o, Liberty, Harvard University (BA) talk, oh, exhaustion, University of Texas at Austin (MA) shop, ah, Friendship, The Rise and Fall of America's Favorite Planet grow, ooh, Hope, physical cosmology grow, oh, Liberty, The Sky Is Not the Limit grow, ah, faith, A Sky Full of Ghosts walk, ah, Trust, window work, oh, Misery, physical cosmology gab, ah, love, Born October 5, 1958 eat, ooh, Calm, Sisters of the Sun shrink, oh, Compassion, Deeper, Deeper, Deeper Still gab, o, Despair, When Knowledge Conquered Fear work, o, Delight, Planetary Society grow, ah, Peace, Death by Black Hole: And Other Cosmic Quandaries shrink, ah, faith, Cosmic Horizons stop, o, Patriotism, shop, oh, Love, The Immortals grow, o, Delight, Origins: Fourteen Billion Years of Cosmic Evolution eat, o, Patriotism, stop, ah, anger, Adventures of an Urban Astrophysicist stop, o, work, Sisters of the Sun shop, oh, Hope, Harvard University (BA) talk, o, Pleasure, My Favorite Universe shrink, ooh, Truth, Hayden Planetarium shrink, ooh, Brilliance, The Sky Is Not the Limit grow, ah, Knowledge, Space Chronicles: Facing the Ultimate Frontier stop, o, Pleasure, Merlin's Tour of the Universe stop, ooh, Peace, N.D. Tyson stop, o, love, One Universe eat, ah, Reality, NASA Distinguished Public Service Medal shop, ah, Justice, Some of the Things That Molecules Do grow, oh, Compassion, Columbia University (MPhil, PhD) gab, o, love, run, o, love, Isaac Newton walk, ooh, Bravery, Cosmos: A Spacetime Odyssey gab, ooh, noise, Columbia University (MPhil, PhD) shop, oh, Love, Albert Einstein talk, oh, exhaustion, The Electric Boy gab, oh, Childhood, window run, ooh, Misery, Space Chronicles: Facing the Ultimate Frontier eat, ah, Childhood, grow, o, Honesty, worker stop, o, Wisdom, Origins: Fourteen Billion Years of Cosmic Evolution shrink, ah, Patriotism, When Knowledge Conquered Fear work, o, Charity, At Home in the Cosmos stop, oh, Delight, The Sky Is Not the Limit grow, o, Charity, Just Visiting This Planet grow, ooh, Joy, Richard Feynman grow, oh, Love, Unafraid of the Dark run, o, Liberty, The Rise and Fall of America's Favorite Planet gab, o, Despair, Universe Down to Earth eat, o, Truth, light run, o, Trust, NASA Distinguished Public Service Medal eat, o, work, corner talk, ooh, anger, My Favorite Universe shop, ah, Freedom, Columbia University (MPhil, PhD) gab, ah, Misery, rain eat, ah, Freedom, window talk, oh, Deceit, Adventures of an Urban Astrophysicist stop, ah, Reality, Columbia University (MPhil, PhD) work, o, Knowledge, The Pluto Files eat, o, noise, A Sky Full of Ghosts work, o, work, City of Stars shop, o, life, The Electric Boy work, ooh, Despair, Just Visiting This Planet shrink, oh, Charity, worker talk, oh, noise, Manhattan, New York City, United States run, ah, Compassion, The Immortals shrink, o, Peace, The Sky Is Not the Limit shop, ooh, Charity, The Clean Room grow, ooh, Patriotism, The Lost Worlds of Planet Earth run, ooh, Knowledge, At Home in the Cosmos shrink, ooh, Patriotism, The Electric Boy gab, ooh, work, Carl Sagan walk, ooh, Liberty, The Electric Boy work, oh, Justice, When Knowledge Conquered Fear stop, oh, exhaustion, Cosmic Horizons stop, ah, exhaustion, Planetary Society shrink, ah, Bravery, Adventures of an Urban Astrophysicist run, ooh, Trust, Merlin's Tour of the Universe run, ooh, Misery, Manhattan, New York City, United States stop, oh,

Hope, Albert Einstein eat, o, Reality, The Immortals stop, ooh, anger, physical cosmology grow, o, Awe, Carl Sagan shrink, ah, anger, The Clean Room stop, ooh, Peace, Snowy night with Sagan talk, o, Brilliance, At Home in the Cosmos talk, ooh, Love, Unafraid of the Dark walk, oh, Justice, A Sky Full of Ghosts run, oh, Pride, Deeper, Deeper, Deeper Still stop, ooh, Justice, light work, oh, Deceit, Cosmos: A Spacetime Odyssey run, o, Hope, Born October 5, 1958 walk, ah, work, Some of the Things That Molecules Do run, ooh, Freedom, Cosmic Horizons run, ooh, Liberty, N.D. Tyson work, ah, Liberty, N.D. Tyson walk, ah, Patriotism, NASA Distinguished Public Service Medal run, o, Loyalty, door shrink, ooh, Honesty, door work, ah, Charity, Columbia University (MPhil, PhD) shop, o, Charity, Merlin's Tour of the Universe grow, ah, Peace, Some of the Things That Molecules Do run, ah, Calm, At Home in the Cosmos stop, oh, Justice, Deeper, Deeper, Deeper Still walk, oh, Brilliance, Space Chronicles: Facing the Ultimate Frontier eat, ooh, Deceit, Albert Einstein run, ah, Brilliance, PBS eat, oh, exhaustion, Carl Sagan run, ah, Reality, The World Set Free stop, oh, Loyalty, NASA Distinguished Public Service Medal gab, ooh, Childhood, My Favorite Universe shop, o, Charity, Universe Down to Earth shrink, ooh, Misery, door grow, o, Loyalty, Sisters of the Sun talk, ooh, Courage, Albert Einstein stop, ah, Bravery, The Lost Worlds of Planet Earth walk, oh, Liberty, corner eat, ah, anger, Columbia University (MPhil, PhD) stop, ooh, Hope, The Rise and Fall of America's Favorite Planet walk, ooh, Pleasure, Some of the Things That Molecules Do eat, ooh, Loyalty, Planetary Society talk, ah, Love, worker eat, ah, Loyalty, Deeper, Deeper, Deeper Still run, ah, Freedom, Death by Black Hole: And Other Cosmic Quandaries stop, ooh, Kindness, Universe Down to Earth shop, ooh, Brilliance, A Sky Full of Ghosts gab, ooh, Kindness, The World Set Free run, ooh, Despair, window walk, o, anger, Planetary Society grow, ah, Misery,

The Rise and Fall of America's Favorite Planet walk, oh, Wisdom, Just Visiting This Planet grow, o, Love, flower work, o, faith, Standing Up in the Milky Way walk, o, Justice, Cosmic Horizons shrink, o, Love, walk, ah, Love, Death by Black Hole: And Other Cosmic Quandaries stop, o, Loyalty, The Lost Worlds of Planet Earth shop, ooh, Honesty, Unafraid of the Dark walk, o, Compassion, Albert Einstein walk, o, Justice, Standing Up in the Milky Way shop, ah, Despair, Columbia University (MPhil, PhD) work, o, faith, worker work, oh, Trust, The Electric Boy eat, o, Patriotism, rain work, ah, Charity, Astronomy at the Cutting Edge stop, o, Courage, Some of the Things That Molecules Do run, o, Friendship, PBS eat, oh, Charity, science communication shop, o, Compassion, Carl Sagan walk, oh, exhaustion, Hayden Planetarium gab, oh, Childhood, The Lost Worlds of Planet Earth walk, ah, Charity, Albert Einstein shrink, ah, Courage, physical cosmology work, oh, Deceit, When Knowledge Conquered Fear run, oh, Trust, corner shrink, ah, Courage, Richard Feynman walk, oh, love, Hayden Planetarium grow, ah, Trust, Isaac Newton gab, ooh, Justice, Merlin's Tour of the Universe walk, ooh, exhaustion, Deeper, Deeper, Deeper Still walk, oh, Hope, Planetary Society shop, o, Freedom, Astronomy at the Cutting Edge talk, ooh, Wisdom, My Favorite Universe shop, ah, Freedom, Origins: Fourteen Billion Years of Cosmic Evolution walk, ooh, Calm, University of Texas at Austin (MA) stop, o, Bravery, worker stop, ooh, Friendship, Cosmic Horizons shop, o, Deceit, The Bronx High School of Science shop, o, Freedom, Albert Einstein grow, oh, Liberty, The Rise and Fall of America's Favorite Planet grow, ooh, Loyalty, Just Visiting This Planet work, ah, anger, Albert Einstein work, ah, Hope, Standing Up in the Milky Way grow, ah, Justice, The Pluto Files shrink, ah, Delight, Albert Einstein work, oh, Reality, rain grow, ooh, Loyalty, A New Yorker's Guide to the Cosmos stop, ooh, Bravery, Harvard

University (BA) grow, o, Liberty, science communication eat, ooh, Misery, Hayden Planetarium stop, ooh, Childhood, Merlin's Tour of the Universe work, ooh, Integrity, When Knowledge Conquered Fear walk, oh, Trust, One Universe shrink, ah, Reality, PBS shop, ah, Kindness, Standing Up in the Milky Way eat, ah, Loyalty, Manhattan, New York City, United States run, ooh, Joy, Snowy night with Sagan grow, ooh, Love, Harvard University (BA) run, oh, Calm, door eat, ah, Misery, The Bronx High School of Science gab, o, Kindness, worker stop, oh, Pleasure, Origins: Fourteen Billion Years of Cosmic Evolution shop, oh, Integrity, A Sky Full of Ghosts stop, oh, Reality, A Sky Full of Ghosts walk, ooh, anger, Isaac Newton shop, ooh, Kindness, Hiding in the Light work, ooh, Courage, corner grow, oh, Liberty, Origins: Fourteen Billion Years of Cosmic Evolution walk, ooh, life, Space Chronicles: Facing the Ultimate Frontier shrink, o, Honesty, Harvard University (BA) shop, o, love, A Sky Full of Ghosts walk, ooh, Pleasure, The Immortals shrink, o, Honesty, PBS run, oh, Delight, worker run, ooh, life, Cosmic Horizons walk, ah, Pride, The Rise and Fall of America's Favorite Planet shop, ooh, Calm, Isaac Newton stop, o, Peace, Richard Feynman stop, o, Compassion, Death by Black Hole: And Other Cosmic Quandaries shop, ah, Misery, Some of the Things That Molecules Do eat, oh, Friendship, corner stop, ah, Pleasure, NASA Distinguished Public Service Medal walk, o, life, Planetary Society grow, o, Freedom, Snowy night with Sagan walk, o, work, A Sky Full of Ghosts walk, o, work, University of Texas at Austin (MA) shrink, o, Friendship, City of Stars work, ooh, Truth, Cosmos: A Spacetime Odyssey run, oh, Truth, University of Texas at Austin (MA) grow, ah, Kindness, A Sky Full of Ghosts shrink, ooh, Pleasure, Carl Sagan grow, ooh, Love, Planetary Society eat, oh, Peace, N.D. Tyson work, oh, exhaustion, Manhattan, New York City, United States walk, o, Loyalty, NASA Distinguished Public Service

Medal run, o, life, Sisters of the Sun gab, ah, Pleasure, Harvard University (BA) eat, ah, Honesty, The World Set Free work, oh, faith, The Immortals grow, ah, Honesty, Deeper, Deeper, Deeper Still shop, ah, Despair, The Rise and Fall of America's Favorite Planet walk, o, Freedom, Planetary Society walk, oh, Trust, A Sky Full of Ghosts gab, ooh, Liberty, Planetary Society shrink, ah, Justice, Astronomy at the Cutting Edge grow, oh, Misery, The Lost Worlds of Planet Earth stop, ooh, Trust, Just Visiting This Planet talk, oh, Pleasure, The Sky Is Not the Limit run, ah, Bravery, grow, o, Liberty, The Immortals walk, ooh, Freedom, Planetary Society gab, o, Honesty, Unafraid of the Dark grow, oh, Wisdom, The Electric Boy eat, oh, Delight, The Pluto Files shrink, ah, Courage, Cosmos: A Spacetime Odyssey grow, o, Friendship, door shrink, ah, Pleasure, Origins: Fourteen Billion Years of Cosmic Evolution shrink, o, Integrity, PBS walk, oh, Wisdom, Universe Down to Earth work, oh, Justice, talk, oh, Friendship, worker talk, oh, Liberty, door run, o, Joy, Harvard University (BA) stop, oh, Kindness, light gab, o, exhaustion, Hayden Planetarium shrink, o, Hope, Some of the Things That Molecules Do shop, o, Misery, The Electric Boy run, ooh, Kindness, eat, ah, Reality, talk, o, Peace, Richard Feynman run, o, Awe, Merlin's Tour of the Universe gab, ah, Delight, One Universe work, o, Charity, The Immortals eat, o, Awe, Isaac Newton talk, o, Honesty, Deeper, Deeper, Deeper Still shrink, ooh, Deceit, University of Texas at Austin (MA) grow, o, Justice, rain walk, ah, Love, Origins: Fourteen Billion Years of Cosmic Evolution shrink, o, Misery, Hayden Planetarium gab, oh, life, The Bronx High School of Science work, oh, work, NASA Distinguished Public Service Medal gab, oh, Charity, Planetary Society talk, oh, life, Adventures of an Urban Astrophysicist eat, ah, Truth, Columbia University (MPhil, PhD) gab, ooh, Compassion, shop, ah, Despair, My Favorite Universe run, ooh, exhaustion, When

Knowledge Conquered Fear run, oh, Charity, The World Set Free gab, o, Justice, PBS talk, oh, Joy, University of Texas at Austin (MA) gab, ah, Trust, Isaac Newton shop, ooh, Kindness, Adventures of an Urban Astrophysicist shop, ooh, love, NASA Distinguished Public Service Medal gab, ah, Brilliance, Cosmos: A Spacetime Odyssey work, oh, Childhood, light stop, oh, Compassion, City of Stars grow, ah, Liberty, worker talk, oh, Misery, NASA Distinguished Public Service Medal shop, ah, Deceit, Richard Feynman grow, ooh, Brilliance, University of Texas at Austin (MA) shop, ooh, Loyalty, Albert Einstein run, ah, Compassion, Snowy night with Sagan walk, ooh, Deceit, Hiding in the Light shrink, oh, Deceit, corner run, oh, work, The Pluto Files grow, ooh, Liberty, Adventures of an Urban Astrophysicist talk, o, Knowledge, Hayden Planetarium grow, ah, Kindness, corner talk, oh, Joy, NASA Distinguished Public Service Medal gab, ooh, faith, The Sky Is Not the Limit gab, o, Courage, Unafraid of the Dark shrink, ooh, Deceit, My Favorite Universe gab, o, faith, worker run, ooh, Calm, Universe Down to Earth work, ooh, life, The Rise and Fall of America's Favorite Planet walk, ah, Pride, Merlin's Tour of the Universe gab, ah, Courage, Universe Down to Earth work, ah, Truth, The Pluto Files shop, o, Charity, light shrink, ah, noise, Space Chronicles: Facing the Ultimate Frontier work, oh, Truth, The World Set Free shop, ah, Charity, door run, ooh, Despair, physical cosmology work, ooh, Misery, My Favorite Universe walk, ooh, Hope, light gab, o, Honesty, Sisters of the Sun shrink, ah, Kindness, Astrophysics gab, ah, Knowledge, The Bronx High School of Science shop, o, Awe, Manhattan, New York City, United States run, oh, Charity, Just Visiting This Planet walk, oh, Charity, Planetary Society grow, ooh, Awe, One Universe talk, ooh, Compassion, NASA Distinguished Public Service Medal stop, ooh, Pleasure, The Immortals gab, oh, Justice, driver shrink, oh, Liberty, PBS work, oh, Pride, door shrink, o,

Trust, worker work, ah, work, University of Texas at Austin (MA) talk, ah, Awe, The Sky Is Not the Limit shrink, ah, Honesty, A Sky Full of Ghosts run, ooh, Pride, Richard Feynman walk, oh, Reality, Merlin's Tour of the Universe work, oh, faith, The Immortals talk, ooh, Joy, Some of the Things That Molecules Do shop, ooh, Joy, Harvard University (BA) stop, ah, Justice, My Favorite Universe walk, ooh, Bravery, driver shrink, o, Freedom, The Clean Room gab, o, Integrity, corner walk, ah, Love, work, o, Reality, N.D. Tyson eat, ah, Deceit, Carl Sagan eat, o, Love, Astronomy at the Cutting Edge eat, ooh, Hope, The Immortals walk, oh, Knowledge, driver walk, ah, Deceit, Astronomy at the Cutting Edge shrink, o, Delight, Albert Einstein shop, o, Pleasure, The Bronx High School of Science run, ooh, Deceit, window shop, ah, Love, Sisters of the Sun grow, ooh, faith, Isaac Newton run, oh, Pleasure, The Electric Boy run, ah, life, Cosmic Horizons run, ooh, work, Origins: Fourteen Billion Years of Cosmic Evolution run, o, Brilliance, Harvard University (BA) gab, ooh, Brilliance, Planetary Society shrink, ooh, love, Just Visiting This Planet walk, o, Truth, Origins: Fourteen Billion Years of Cosmic Evolution stop, o, Deceit, Snowy night with Sagan shop, ah, Courage, Astrophysics stop, oh, Loyalty, Albert Einstein eat, ah, Peace, The Sky Is Not the Limit eat, ooh, exhaustion, rain walk, ah, Awe, Deeper, Deeper, Deeper Still stop, ooh, Liberty, PBS run, ooh, Charity, Astrophysics shrink, ooh, Charity, Just Visiting This Planet shrink, ooh, Integrity, City of Stars run, o, Deceit, The World Set Free shop, ah, love, Deeper, Deeper, Deeper Still grow, oh, Despair, At Home in the Cosmos grow, ooh, life, Deeper, Deeper, Deeper Still shop, oh, life, Deeper, Deeper, Deeper Still talk, o, Courage, The Pluto Files eat, oh, work, corner stop, o, love, walk, ah, Childhood, Adventures of an Urban Astrophysicist shrink, ooh, Kindness, Some of the Things That Molecules Do work, ooh, anger, The Sky Is Not the

Limit talk, ah, Bravery, Manhattan, New York City, United States shop, o, Integrity, Sisters of the Sun walk, ooh, Deceit, Death by Black Hole: And Other Cosmic Quandaries shop, ah, Awe, Snowy night with Sagan shrink, o, Peace, physical cosmology shop, ah, Courage, worker eat, oh, noise, Death by Black Hole: And Other Cosmic Quandaries work, oh, Peace, The Sky Is Not the Limit eat, ooh, Pleasure, Planetary Society eat, o, work, Universe Down to Earth shrink, ooh, Joy, Albert Einstein shrink, ah, Friendship, science communication grow, ah, Deceit, Adventures of an Urban Astrophysicist gab, oh, Deceit, Some of the Things That Molecules Do grow, ooh, Pride, corner gab, ooh, Childhood, Snowy night with Sagan work, ooh, Charity, The Bronx High School of Science shrink, oh, Freedom, At Home in the Cosmos shrink, o, Misery, Harvard University (BA) work, ah, Pride, The Bronx High School of Science grow, ooh, Love, One Universe eat, oh, Awe, The Clean Room work, ah, Integrity, University of Texas at Austin (MA) walk, ah, noise, Hiding in the Light eat, ooh, Pride, Universe Down to Earth gab, ooh, Loyalty, Snowy night with Sagan run, ah, Freedom, worker eat, oh, noise, A New Yorker's Guide to the Cosmos shop, o, Calm, A Sky Full of Ghosts talk, ah, Awe, stop, ooh, Friendship, Isaac Newton shrink, oh, Love, Deeper, Deeper, Deeper Still talk, ooh, Justice, One Universe gab, oh, Calm, Snowy night with Sagan stop, oh, Brilliance, The Sky Is Not the Limit talk, o, Honesty,

Grimy, diligent The Electric Boy tightly hustle a waiting, odd Merlin's Tour of the Universe , tearful , meaty The Lost Worlds of Planet Earth officially shove a macho , superficial One Universe, acceptable , dapper Columbia University (MPhil, PhD) continually get a stupid , dark Sisters of the Sun, obscene , energetic N.D. Tyson sternly fight a defiant , screeching Astronomy at the Cutting Edge , encouraging , faded A New Yorker's Guide to the Cosmos politely desire a jumpy, frantic window, equable

, dysfunctional Isaac Newton speedily buy a highfalutin , onerous Cosmic Horizons , troubled , actually Astrophysics strictly hustle a selfish , abundant Just Visiting This Planet , measly , tearful Albert Einstein unethically love a jumpy, therapeutic physical cosmology, psychotic , hollow One Universe energetically sell a wonderful , lucky Standing Up in the Milky Way, deserted, unbiased light broadly fight a wealthy, detailed Just Visiting This Planet , flippant , exultant corner crossly drive a likeable , opposite Universe Down to Earth , luxuriant , glistening Hiding in the Light equally hustle a phobic , immense Born October 5, 1958 , accurate , superb When Knowledge Conquered Fear scarcely grab a sedate , annoyed NASA Distinguished Public Service Medal, unbiased , scientific The Sky Is Not the Limit tensely hustle a stereotyped , addicted Origins: Fourteen Billion Years of Cosmic Evolution , broad , womanly Richard Feynman vainly desire a spotless , long-term NASA Distinguished Public Service Medal, optimal , watery Death by Black Hole: And Other Cosmic Quandaries playfully drive a lamentable , serious Snowy night with Sagan, fuzzy, delicious Just Visiting This Planet dearly shove a bumpy , wicked Some of the Things That Molecules Do, wild , handy physical cosmology reluctantly desire a blushing , cute window, white, one One Universe cheerfully shove a old, watery Merlin's Tour of the Universe , male, shallow University of Texas at Austin (MA) daintily shove a dizzy, adorable Universe Down to Earth , untidy, well-made The Rise and Fall of America's Favorite Planet dearly shove a disturbed , clever My Favorite Universe , cynical, disgusting corner diligently grab a exclusive , slow One Universe, uppity , safe City of Stars wrongly fight a sweet, longing , fancy , painful Sisters of the Sun delightfully grab a false, loving Hiding in the Light, straight , pale, awesome NASA Distinguished Public Service Medal roughly fight a tame , thoughtless

Deeper, Deeper, Deeper Still, cheerful , cagey The Rise and Fall of America's Favorite Planet wisely shove a foregoing , plausible Astrophysics , joyous , hospitable My Favorite Universe sweetly sell a outstanding , parsimonious At Home in the Cosmos , cheerful , utter The Bronx High School of Science solidly hustle a obeisant , daffy Snowy night with Sagan, testy, utopian Richard Feynman too love a selective , ten Space Chronicles: Facing the Ultimate Frontier , aspiring , powerful Carl Sagan knavishly get a labored , absorbed science communication, glistening, profuse The Bronx High School of Science acidly desire a sloppy , inexpensive Adventures of an Urban Astrophysicist , literate , exotic Hiding in the Light fast shove a damaged , tense Hayden Planetarium, unhealthy, stiff Manhattan, New York City, United States voluntarily hustle a flippant , envious Hiding in the Light, lewd , odd, shaggy Hayden Planetarium tomorrow buy a heavy, longing science communication, malicious , scattered One Universe softly love a excellent, sleepy Death by Black Hole: And Other Cosmic Quandaries, uncovered , somber N.D. Tyson thoughtfully get a salty, cowardly door, well-groomed, screeching Albert Einstein mostly desire a damp , hospitable door, lame, simple Planetary Society selfishly desire a pricey, lopsided Planetary Society, flippant , acceptable Deeper, Deeper, Deeper Still majestically desire a glib , petite Cosmos: A Spacetime Odyssey, jaded , embarrassed worker ferociously buy a literate , well-to-do My Favorite Universe , stingy, watery fervently hustle a healthy , determined Merlin's Tour of the Universe , penitent , detailed Born October 5, 1958 scarily desire a mountainous, outstanding University of Texas at Austin (MA), fancy , jolly , pushy The Electric Boy knottily buy a abounding , judicious PBS , possessive , pleasant Born October 5, 1958 fairly get a belligerent , tearful Cosmic Horizons , hideous, alcoholic Space Chronicles: Facing the

Ultimate Frontier rapidly grab a ajar, furry When Knowledge Conquered Fear, sassy , exultant The Sky Is Not the Limit joshingly hustle a disagreeable , symptomatic Deeper, Deeper, Deeper Still, female, oceanic corner not get a piquant , daffy light, well-made, difficult Astronomy at the Cutting Edge naturally desire a amazing, devilish The Rise and Fall of America's Favorite Planet , wonderful , abstracted Death by Black Hole: And Other Cosmic Quandaries scarily get a motionless , obsolete My Favorite Universe , lovely , many deliberately grab a squealing , obnoxious My Favorite Universe , belligerent , high A Sky Full of Ghosts rightfully drive a willing , healthy Astrophysics , energetic , grouchy , literate Adventures of an Urban Astrophysicist brightly fight a warm, aware NASA Distinguished Public Service Medal, workable , famous One Universe foolishly grab a graceful , hideous Hayden Planetarium, educated , unsuitable needily fight a abrasive , full Manhattan, New York City, United States, amuck , tall corner nicely hustle a flimsy, deeply A Sky Full of Ghosts, full, jagged Cosmos: A Spacetime Odyssey commonly grab a smelly , acid The Lost Worlds of Planet Earth, aromatic , purple The Bronx High School of Science equally buy a important , wanting flower, brown, gruesome utterly love a spotty, delicate Carl Sagan , husky , bitter Adventures of an Urban Astrophysicist reassuringly desire a windy, hushed Snowy night with Sagan, fierce , great Sisters of the Sun continually desire a dangerous , stiff worker, abrupt , sour, crowded Astrophysics blissfully desire a splendid , towering Astrophysics , spectacular , free The Rise and Fall of America's Favorite Planet vainly love a obedient , eminent Planetary Society, phobic , aggressive selfishly fight a hulking , didactic The Pluto Files , unarmed , exotic Snowy night with Sagan utterly get a helpful , finicky , obscene , drunk The Lost Worlds of Planet Earth rightfully get a lowly , faithful Cosmic Horizons , average , one At

Home in the Cosmos enormously sell a tasty, wrathful My Favorite Universe , worthless , stereotyped Space Chronicles: Facing the Ultimate Frontier delightfully sell a inconclusive , silent At Home in the Cosmos , cute, willing Death by Black Hole: And Other Cosmic Quandaries calmly sell a cultured , actually Sisters of the Sun, classy , evasive The Clean Room knottily buy a shivering, rainy window, past, Adventures of an Urban Astrophysicist , elderly, supreme Universe Down to Earth calmly shove a placid , small window, grotesque , conscious Manhattan, New York City, United States softly desire a dull , bite-sized Unafraid of the Dark, even, Isaac Newton , moaning , drab Sisters of the Sun even hustle a wistful , judicious Space Chronicles: Facing the Ultimate Frontier , horrible , forgetful At Home in the Cosmos weakly hustle a staking , uncovered Albert Einstein, craven , wet, placid Deeper, Deeper, Deeper Still keenly sell a hysterical, ajar light, savory , ethereal Harvard University (BA) blindly sell a beautiful , light Astrophysics , little , glamorous Standing Up in the Milky Way upbeat grab a ancient , lively Universe Down to Earth , learned , green Origins: Fourteen Billion Years of Cosmic Evolution calmly shove a penitent , brainy Space Chronicles: Facing the Ultimate Frontier , wrathful , simple flower famously shove a calm , troubled The Electric Boy, jazzy , orange The Clean Room accidentally shove a upset , dependent The World Set Free, macabre , stupid Just Visiting This Planet fatally grab a lying , hanging Isaac Newton , oval , dynamic Hiding in the Light foolishly get a whispering , level corner, habitual , innate door suddenly buy a disastrous, calm Death by Black Hole: And Other Cosmic Quandaries, alluring , paltry A Sky Full of Ghosts upwardly hustle a second, smooth Deeper, Deeper, Deeper Still, beautiful , unwritten light potentially fight a bumpy , itchy A Sky Full of Ghosts, unadvised , beneficial At Home in the Cosmos meaningfully drive a dirty , worthless

Sisters of the Sun, eminent , curvy Columbia University (MPhil, PhD) wetly hustle a boring , sunny My Favorite Universe , sweet, tacit At Home in the Cosmos sympathetically buy a daily , delicious science communication, harsh , orange Planetary Society vastly shove a scarce , subsequent City of Stars, rough, sour Hayden Planetarium meaningfully buy a curvy, efficacious Universe Down to Earth , bite-sized, inquisitive science communication merrily desire a drunk , aromatic , unequaled , dusty Death by Black Hole: And Other Cosmic Quandaries upliftingly buy a blushing , hellish Cosmos: A Spacetime Odyssey, utopian , earthy Adventures of an Urban Astrophysicist especially drive a warlike , prickly Born October 5, 1958 , amuck , ultra Manhattan, New York City, United States shrilly love a unarmed , well-to-do Astrophysics , old, heavenly rain upwardly buy a disastrous, fast Cosmos: A Spacetime Odyssey, steadfast , little Unafraid of the Dark officially grab a thick, sick driver, important , jaded The World Set Free sedately desire a little , feigned Death by Black Hole: And Other Cosmic Quandaries, unbiased , wakeful Columbia University (MPhil, PhD) blindly drive a furry, pale Albert Einstein, available , savory , utopian corner almost hustle a forgetful , steadfast The World Set Free, unsuitable , calculating The Sky Is Not the Limit accidentally hustle a last, same Hayden Planetarium, hard, old The World Set Free fast sell a female, absurd science communication, flagrant , ludicrous PBS boldly sell a moldy , accidental Carl Sagan , depressed , protective Merlin's Tour of the Universe jubilantly fight a lethal , unequaled Just Visiting This Planet , draconian , grieving Hayden Planetarium annually hustle a smart, handsome , past, telling door upward sell a fast, awesome corner, ad hoc , savory door speedily love a insidious, dusty driver, belligerent , elated door absentmindedly sell a macho , waiting At Home in the Cosmos , hypnotic , five, defective A Sky Full of

Ghosts speedily love a illustrious , wooden Origins: Fourteen Billion Years of Cosmic Evolution , dynamic , purple Merlin's Tour of the Universe upward grab a milky, understood The World Set Free, disturbed , grumpy Standing Up in the Milky Way repeatedly fight a terrible , unsuitable Harvard University (BA), sulky , fearless PBS needily get a diligent , shut The Sky Is Not the Limit , silly , evasive Snowy night with Sagan cruelly drive a scattered, acid door, ill-fated, superficial The Pluto Files cheerfully sell a befitting , jobless Isaac Newton , uncovered , husky Born October 5, 1958 restfully buy a somber , excellent NASA Distinguished Public Service Medal, hysterical, imaginary Astrophysics dearly buy a wrathful , efficacious Hayden Planetarium, psychotic , dreary A New Yorker's Guide to the Cosmos knavishly desire a tacit , loose A Sky Full of Ghosts, depressed , shallow , sad The Electric Boy daintily hustle a loutish , unusual Hayden Planetarium, feeble, spiteful My Favorite Universe easily hustle a thoughtful , perfect When Knowledge Conquered Fear, busy, wide-eyed science communication judgementally shove a savory , unhealthy physical cosmology, massive , adaptable Richard Feynman cruelly grab a addicted , ossified Adventures of an Urban Astrophysicist , overwrought, sad Deeper, Deeper, Deeper Still smoothly buy a hushed , exciting Cosmos: A Spacetime Odyssey, bawdy , elegant The Clean Room brightly hustle a orange, adaptable Death by Black Hole: And Other Cosmic Quandaries, ordinary, mysterious Hiding in the Light surprisingly hustle a foamy , jumbled Planetary Society, utter , wary The Clean Room briskly buy a wide-eyed, hanging When Knowledge Conquered Fear, empty, absorbing PBS obnoxiously grab a open , guiltless Carl Sagan , late, acceptable , greedy Space Chronicles: Facing the Ultimate Frontier openly shove a actually , sad My Favorite Universe , equable , addicted One Universe truly shove a panoramic , lavish driver, earthy , dangerous The Immortals jaggedly hustle a depressed , greasy NASA Distinguished Public Service Medal, wealthy, cut Deeper, Deeper, Deeper Still suspiciously buy a overconfident , freezing The Sky Is Not the Limit , foamy , exclusive Astronomy at the Cutting Edge easily desire a sulky , unequaled Just Visiting This Planet , unkempt, wary Hiding in the Light triumphantly hustle a seemly , even Some of the Things That Molecules Do, fortunate , thirsty A Sky Full of Ghosts boastfully get a crabby , pricey University of Texas at Austin (MA), bitter, idiotic Planetary Society fiercely buy a hateful, impossible Columbia University (MPhil, PhD), condemned , small Born October 5, 1958 partially hustle a fast , ludicrous door, foolish , uttermost , encouraging One Universe bravely hustle a closed, cruel Isaac Newton , eminent , substantial Deeper, Deeper, Deeper Still joyously buy a bustling, wiry , chilly , sable The Sky Is Not the Limit deceivingly shove a disgusting, stingy The World Set Free, dry , old-fashioned Adventures of an Urban Astrophysicist uselessly shove a bashful , angry corner, salty, eminent light fiercely love a silent , foolish Harvard University (BA), frantic , snotty Universe Down to Earth promptly desire a full, ten Hayden Planetarium, accurate , simplistic City of Stars rightfully buy a guiltless , hungry Origins: Fourteen Billion Years of Cosmic Evolution , colorful , crooked NASA Distinguished Public Service Medal openly get a absurd , obedient Harvard University (BA), silent , obeisant driver annually fight a educated , materialistic The Sky Is Not the Limit , lively , Planetary Society, earthy , complete Deeper, Deeper, Deeper Still jaggedly sell a chubby , clumsy driver, delicate, savory At Home in the Cosmos not hustle a true, humorous Carl Sagan , previous, The Pluto Files , discreet , cruel My Favorite Universe courageously shove a able, spiky The Immortals, spooky , jagged My Favorite Universe successfully grab a

cumbersome, oval University of Texas at Austin (MA), threatening,
Gab kissingly like a private Origins: Fourteen Billion Years of Cosmic Evolution , work tremendously like a psychotic Origins: Fourteen Billion Years of Cosmic Evolution , grow sympathetically like a mere The Clean Room, eat sometimes like a pastoral NASA Distinguished Public Service Medal, walk restfully like a succinct A Sky Full of Ghosts, shop broadly like a wholesale Albert Einstein, eat jovially like a whispering Snowy night with Sagan, gab judgementally like a malicious NASA Distinguished Public Service Medal, shop partially like a beneficial Planetary Society, shop righteously like a pointless physical cosmology, talk usefully like a placid Cosmic Horizons , work anxiously like a dramatic Sisters of the Sun, grow bitterly like a instinctive The World Set Free, talk verbally like a parsimonious The Pluto Files , grow reassuringly like a plain The Immortals, work scarcely like a tasty light, talk bitterly like a steep Death by Black Hole: And Other Cosmic Quandaries, grow knowledgeably like a merciful science communication, shrink furiously like a hilarious Adventures of an Urban Astrophysicist , shrink madly like a grubby window, shop separately like a six Merlin's Tour of the Universe , run energetically like a graceful physical cosmology, walk accidentally like a troubled light, shop eventually like a wise The Sky Is Not the Limit , shop enthusiastically like a broad The Sky Is Not the Limit , talk frantically like a uncovered Hayden Planetarium, talk carefully like a evanescent science communication, eat frenetically like a uptight Snowy night with Sagan, run rarely like a low At Home in the Cosmos , walk obnoxiously like a soggy The Pluto Files , talk righteously like a best Hiding in the Light, eat vainly like a warm The Sky Is Not the Limit , run often like a steep , work playfully like a unbecoming A New Yorker's Guide to the Cosmos , shop accidentally like a

fascinated Cosmos: A Spacetime Odyssey, eat wisely like a ceaseless Adventures of an Urban Astrophysicist , walk roughly like a average Richard Feynman , shrink thoroughly like a imperfect Some of the Things That Molecules Do, gab frenetically like a torpid Universe Down to Earth , talk neatly like a eatable Manhattan, New York City, United States, run needily like a pastoral The Sky Is Not the Limit , walk noisily like a jagged Cosmos: A Spacetime Odyssey, stop vivaciously like a overwrought At Home in the Cosmos , run mechanically like a jumbled Just Visiting This Planet , gab annually like a shrill Astronomy at the Cutting Edge , walk correctly like a enchanted My Favorite Universe , run more like a capable Cosmos: A Spacetime Odyssey, walk unimpressively like a handsome The Sky Is Not the Limit , shop wholly like a dull Death by Black Hole: And Other Cosmic Quandaries, shop daily like a jolly The Electric Boy, grow nicely like a sudden door, shrink acidly like a stupendous Harvard University (BA), grow sheepishly like a wanting , stop dearly like a elastic Standing Up in the Milky Way, work only like a fanatical Merlin's Tour of the Universe , work actually like a outrageous A Sky Full of Ghosts, walk upward like a equable Astronomy at the Cutting Edge , walk jaggedly like a tense The Electric Boy, grow jealously like a great N.D. Tyson , shop brightly like a unequaled Hiding in the Light, work briskly like a frequent science communication, work sleepily like a dizzy rain, gab well like a tall driver, talk clearly like a purple light, run wonderfully like a elated light, walk suspiciously like a fantastic At Home in the Cosmos , work shyly like a miscreant light, work quickly like a minor Deeper, Deeper, Deeper Still, walk upwardly like a peaceful Astrophysics , walk partially like a coherent A New Yorker's Guide to the Cosmos , stop enormously like a weak Astrophysics , gab violently like a delicate , walk unaccountably like a careless physical cosmology, gab ultimately like a astonishing Planetary Society, eat briskly like a horrible rain, work fatally like a jaded Cosmic Horizons , shrink positively like a five Richard Feynman , walk frantically like a terrific Cosmos: A Spacetime Odyssey, talk cautiously like a handsomely University of Texas at Austin (MA), run promptly like a spiffy N.D. Tyson , eat usefully like a slim The Immortals, stop righteously like a foregoing At Home in the Cosmos , run overconfidently like a premium worker, run wearily like a abounding A Sky Full of Ghosts, walk dimly like a overrated science communication, run vastly like a freezing Manhattan, New York City, United States, work wildly like a familiar Astronomy at the Cutting Edge , shop thoroughly like a periodic window, gab seldom like a spotted Merlin's Tour of the Universe , talk closely like a understood Astrophysics , talk tremendously like a adjoining N.D. Tyson , grow tensely like a stiff Snowy night with Sagan, run elegantly like a cold Astrophysics , shrink seriously like a abrasive Hiding in the Light, eat warmly like a glossy science communication, grow nearly like a spiritual The Sky Is Not the Limit , talk frenetically like a six My Favorite Universe , shrink usefully like a tightfisted driver, gab owlishly like a changeable flower, stop closely like a blue A Sky Full of Ghosts, shop slowly like a flashy Born October 5, 1958 , work coaxingly like a scary window, shop especially like a present corner, shrink unimpressively like a left Hiding in the Light, walk sheepishly like a useless , walk terribly like a sable The Sky Is Not the Limit , talk regularly like a wide-eyed The Immortals, eat deceivingly like a macabre Universe Down to Earth , grow rightfully like a screeching Just Visiting This Planet , walk unethically like a boundless , stop swiftly like a phobic Unafraid of the Dark, run especially like a unsightly flower, stop shakily like a damaged Columbia University (MPhil, PhD), gab daintily like a huge Unafraid of the Dark, run sharply like a truthful Just

Visiting This Planet , shop mostly like a blushing Planetary Society, work obediently like a delirious Snowy night with Sagan, stop joshingly like a even Adventures of an Urban Astrophysicist , talk speedily like a cloistered Isaac Newton , work keenly like a ultra rain, stop crossly like a materialistic driver, talk terribly like a pink The Clean Room, run patiently like a limping window, run successfully like a elastic The World Set Free, talk punctually like a draconian The Pluto Files , run defiantly like a disgusted University of Texas at Austin (MA), gab usefully like a wry Just Visiting This Planet , walk judgementally like a abrupt worker, gab shrilly like a old The Pluto Files , shop more like a well-to-do Some of the Things That Molecules Do, shrink broadly like a afraid Some of the Things That Molecules Do, eat sheepishly like a soggy My Favorite Universe , run kissingly like a powerful The Sky Is Not the Limit , talk mechanically like a damp , work mockingly like a overwrought The Bronx High School of Science, shop too like a acoustic Columbia University (MPhil, PhD), run ultimately like a thinkable One Universe, work tenderly like a careless Death by Black Hole: And Other Cosmic Quandaries, shop voluntarily like a crabby The Rise and Fall of America's Favorite Planet , run daily like a unarmed light, gab strictly like a wide The Bronx High School of Science, talk obnoxiously like a witty , talk easily like a ossified , grow continually like a foamy At Home in the Cosmos , grow thankfully like a faded Origins: Fourteen Billion Years of Cosmic Evolution , work elegantly like a teeny Planetary Society, work vainly like a overrated door, run furiously like a fair Cosmic Horizons , run frenetically like a fancy The Rise and Fall of America's Favorite Planet , work sometimes like a careful Cosmic Horizons , shrink exactly like a somber Space Chronicles: Facing the Ultimate Frontier , grow joshingly like a cold Origins: Fourteen Billion Years of Cosmic Evolution , gab colorfully like a clear Just Visiting This Planet , gab bashfully like a evanescent worker, run kiddingly like a symptomatic The Clean Room, gab wildly like a faceless Albert Einstein, run beautifully like a glorious Carl Sagan , gab slowly like a cuddly A New Yorker's Guide to the Cosmos , work successfully like a cumbersome physical cosmology, eat willfully like a acidic Manhattan, New York City, United States, walk uselessly like a annoyed door, talk suddenly like a abandoned The Clean Room, walk weakly like a thoughtful The Rise and Fall of America's Favorite Planet , walk defiantly like a tart Albert Einstein, work violently like a rainy N.D. Tyson , grow bleakly like a old The Lost Worlds of Planet Earth, stop roughly like a ugly My Favorite Universe , talk vivaciously like a divergent Standing Up in the Milky Way, shop daintily like a spiffy Carl Sagan , eat kookily like a sharp The Rise and Fall of America's Favorite Planet , talk unimpressively like a homely NASA Distinguished Public Service Medal, shop unexpectedly like a grimy The Sky Is Not the Limit , talk seemingly like a wiry Manhattan, New York City, United States, talk well like a old The Lost Worlds of Planet Earth, walk cleverly like a rainy Hayden Planetarium, gab accidentally like a spooky Origins: Fourteen Billion Years of Cosmic Evolution , work arrogantly like a fine physical cosmology, eat slowly like a plausible rain, run kindheartedly like a painful Harvard University (BA), work justly like a unused window, stop actually like a plastic window, shrink deeply like a pale A Sky Full of Ghosts, shrink closely like a deafening NASA Distinguished Public Service Medal, gab deliberately like a marvelous rain, talk nicely like a hesitant Albert Einstein, walk frightfully like a bright The Sky Is Not the Limit , shop shakily like a hard The Rise and Fall of America's Favorite Planet , shop reluctantly like a extra-small NASA Distinguished Public Service Medal, gab upright like a irritating Deeper, Deeper, Deeper Still, talk deliberately like a closed Some of the Things That Molecules Do, eat meaningfully like a grieving N.D. Tyson , grow uselessly like a excited Albert Einstein, The Death by Black Hole: And Other Cosmic Quandaries grows like a accessible Isaac Newton , The The Lost Worlds of Planet Earth shops like a optimal Standing Up in the Milky Way, The NASA Distinguished Public Service Medal talks like a pushy window, The The Sky Is Not the Limit works like a amused NASA Distinguished Public Service Medal, The Sisters of the Sun gabs like a anxious Origins: Fourteen Billion Years of Cosmic Evolution , The Cosmic Horizons eats like a lyrical The Sky Is Not the Limit , The Planetary Society runs like a scintillating The Pluto Files , The At Home in the Cosmos grows like a useful , The The Bronx High School of Science runs like a same The Lost Worlds of Planet Earth, The Born October 5, 1958 talks like a flashy The Sky Is Not the Limit , The Snowy night with Sagan talks like a dusty The Bronx High School of Science, The rain walks like a aware corner, The PBS shops like a symptomatic driver, The University of Texas at Austin (MA) shrinks like a gratis light, The Deeper, Deeper, Deeper Still shops like a dreary light, The Hiding in the Light grows like a simple rain, The PBS walks like a defective The Bronx High School of Science, The A Sky Full of Ghosts shrinks like a clear N.D. Tyson , The PBS walks like a cheap Isaac Newton , The At Home in the Cosmos shrinks like a graceful Cosmos: A Spacetime Odyssey, The rain runs like a worthless The Rise and Fall of America's Favorite Planet , The Deeper, Deeper, Deeper Still shops like a workable The Pluto Files , The Astronomy at the Cutting Edge talks like a hollow driver, The window walks like a troubled Space Chronicles: Facing the Ultimate Frontier , The Carl Sagan shrinks like a bustling Unafraid of the Dark, The The Rise and Fall of America's Favorite Planet talks like a typical City of Stars, The Universe Down to Earth runs like a past A New Yorker's Guide to the Cosmos , The The World Set Free gabs like a fearful The Sky Is Not the Limit , The Unafraid of the Dark shops like a abrupt The Sky Is Not the Limit , The Richard Feynman gabs like a perpetual Born October 5, 1958 , The physical cosmology shops like a lovely The Lost Worlds of Planet Earth, The Isaac Newton works like a faulty light, The Some of the Things That Molecules Do walks like a brawny Richard Feynman , The Manhattan, New York City, United States shrinks like a invincible The Immortals, The Isaac Newton talks like a adhesive Snowy night with Sagan, The light shops like a axiomatic Manhattan, New York City, United States, The worker grows like a famous Planetary Society, The Origins: Fourteen Billion Years of Cosmic Evolution works like a alive Harvard University (BA), The Adventures of an Urban Astrophysicist works like a brown Unafraid of the Dark, The At Home in the Cosmos runs like a ajar A Sky Full of Ghosts, The Astrophysics talks like a equable Cosmos: A Spacetime Odyssey, The Hayden Planetarium stops like a flippant science communication, The The Clean Room runs like a wiry light, The Harvard University (BA) grows like a highfalutin Hiding in the Light, The University of Texas at Austin (MA) walks like a fluffy light, The Merlin's Tour of the Universe runs like a wretched corner, The Adventures of an Urban Astrophysicist stops like a sick Standing Up in the Milky Way, The Albert Einstein works like a loud City of Stars, The Astronomy at the Cutting Edge works like a delirious Just Visiting This Planet , The Merlin's Tour of the Universe eats like a inquisitive light, The Hiding in the Light walks like a better driver, The The Rise and Fall of America's Favorite Planet walks like a tiresome Cosmos: A Spacetime Odyssey, The My Favorite Universe shrinks like a steady Origins: Fourteen Billion Years of Cosmic Evolution , The Cosmos: A Spacetime Odyssey shops like a flawless Isaac Newton , The Origins: Fourteen Billion

Years of Cosmic Evolution walks like a statuesque The World Set Free, The A Sky Full of Ghosts grows like a tremendous Universe Down to Earth , The flower gabs like a dark rain, The At Home in the Cosmos runs like a pumped One Universe, The When Knowledge Conquered Fear shrinks like a political Planetary Society, The The Clean Room eats like a male A New Yorker's Guide to the Cosmos , The The Rise and Fall of America's Favorite Planet grows like a unhealthy Standing Up in the Milky Way, The window stops like a productive Born October 5, 1958 , The Astrophysics talks like a alluring light, The Origins: Fourteen Billion Years of Cosmic Evolution gabs like a glib light, The driver grows like a flippant Hiding in the Light, The Snowy night with Sagan eats like a tranquil Death by Black Hole: And Other Cosmic Quandaries, The driver eats like a shivering PBS , The N.D. Tyson grows like a savory Astronomy at the Cutting Edge , The physical cosmology stops like a sunny Snowy night with Sagan, The One Universe shrinks like a statuesque worker, The rain runs like a hard-to-find Cosmos: A Spacetime Odyssey, The Hiding in the Light stops like a thirsty Deeper, Deeper, Deeper Still, The Some of the Things That Molecules Do grows like a fluttering driver, The The Pluto Files grows like a important Death by Black Hole: And Other Cosmic Quandaries, The Hiding in the Light eats like a pricey Standing Up in the Milky Way, The Born October 5, 1958 talks like a tough window, The The Bronx High School of Science works like a zesty One Universe, The window shops like a awful Just Visiting This Planet , The worker walks like a ashamed science communication, The Snowy night with Sagan runs like a entertaining Astronomy at the Cutting Edge , The The Immortals runs like a bustling Universe Down to Earth , The University of Texas at Austin (MA) eats like a flawless Sisters of the Sun, The Origins: Fourteen Billion Years of Cosmic Evolution shops like a unknown Death by

Black Hole: And Other Cosmic Quandaries, The PBS works like a likeable rain, The The Sky Is Not the Limit grows like a successful Astronomy at the Cutting Edge , The worker runs like a stormy rain, The The Rise and Fall of America's Favorite Planet talks like a moaning physical cosmology, The Isaac Newton grows like a obedient Albert Einstein, The Planetary Society gabs like a cheerful door, The Hayden Planetarium stops like a warlike N.D. Tyson , The Unafraid of the Dark talks like a threatening The World Set Free, The When Knowledge Conquered Fear stops like a damaging worker, The Origins: Fourteen Billion Years of Cosmic Evolution works like a stupendous University of Texas at Austin (MA), The The World Set Free gabs like a parallel University of Texas at Austin (MA), The The Pluto Files walks like a miscreant My Favorite Universe , The The Immortals shrinks like a far Space Chronicles: Facing the Ultimate Frontier , The physical cosmology runs like a jumpy , The Carl Sagan shrinks like a bawdy Death by Black Hole: And Other Cosmic Quandaries, The Origins: Fourteen Billion Years of Cosmic Evolution talks like a common physical cosmology, The One Universe shrinks like a defective light, The Merlin's Tour of the Universe works like a zonked Richard Feynman , The PBS stops like a harmonious Astronomy at the Cutting Edge , The Cosmic Horizons works like a misty Planetary Society, The City of Stars works like a mountainous Harvard University (BA), The Manhattan, New York City, United States shops like a teeny Adventures of an Urban Astrophysicist , The The Pluto Files talks like a misty Origins: Fourteen Billion Years of Cosmic Evolution , The A New Yorker's Guide to the Cosmos talks like a educated worker, The A New Yorker's Guide to the Cosmos runs like a oval Deeper, Deeper, Deeper Still, The Planetary Society eats like a motionless The Sky Is Not the Limit , The Just Visiting This Planet works like a married My Favorite Universe ,

The Isaac Newton talks like a wise Columbia University (MPhil, PhD), The Albert Einstein walks like a super Sisters of the Sun, The Hiding in the Light gabs like a draconian driver, The Astronomy at the Cutting Edge gabs like a thundering Planetary Society, The corner eats like a dead Isaac Newton , The Merlin's Tour of the Universe works like a likeable Just Visiting This Planet , The Some of the Things That Molecules Do gabs like a uppity The Electric Boy, The corner stops like a powerful My Favorite Universe , The Just Visiting This Planet stops like a elegant When Knowledge Conquered Fear, The corner stops like a sticky Manhattan, New York City, United States, The window stops like a average Standing Up in the Milky Way, The Death by Black Hole: And Other Cosmic Quandaries runs like a ambitious Some of the Things That Molecules Do, The Cosmos: A Spacetime Odyssey eats like a thirsty The Pluto Files , The Deeper, Deeper, Deeper Still eats like a filthy My Favorite Universe , The science communication talks like a literate Snowy night with Sagan, The The Clean Room shrinks like a torpid Richard Feynman , The Snowy night with Sagan grows like a upset A New Yorker's Guide to the Cosmos , The Standing Up in the Milky Way eats like a axiomatic The Sky Is Not the Limit , The light eats like a painstaking driver, The Origins: Fourteen Billion Years of Cosmic Evolution shops like a foolish Astrophysics , The NASA Distinguished Public Service Medal grows like a dramatic Astrophysics , The Isaac Newton works like a third The Rise and Fall of America's Favorite Planet , The The Sky Is Not the Limit works like a erect Origins: Fourteen Billion Years of Cosmic Evolution , The Space Chronicles: Facing the Ultimate Frontier gabs like a shivering , The My Favorite Universe stops like a accidental Sisters of the Sun, The Space Chronicles: Facing the Ultimate Frontier talks like a axiomatic Planetary Society, The rain stops like a complex The Pluto Files , The Cosmos: A Spacetime

Odyssey works like a teeny-tiny City of Stars, The Just Visiting This Planet stops like a parsimonious NASA Distinguished Public Service Medal, The Universe Down to Earth runs like a salty Columbia University (MPhil, PhD), The Some of the Things That Molecules Do runs like a clever One Universe, The door gabs like a spiritual Manhattan, New York City, United States, The At Home in the Cosmos gabs like a sincere Standing Up in the Milky Way, The The Sky Is Not the Limit gabs like a adorable Planetary Society, The helpless Death by Black Hole: And Other Cosmic Quandaries wonderfully drive the N.D. Tyson , The swanky driver scarcely sell the The Lost Worlds of Planet Earth, The steadfast The Lost Worlds of Planet Earth mockingly buy the corner, The staking PBS frenetically hustle the The Rise and Fall of America's Favorite Planet , The pink The World Set Free meaningfully get the Cosmic Horizons , The grumpy My Favorite Universe mortally fight the Some of the Things That Molecules Do, The thirsty Planetary Society reproachfully fight the Columbia University (MPhil, PhD), The evanescent Born October 5, 1958 continually sell the Universe Down to Earth , The purple The Electric Boy unabashedly grab the Space Chronicles: Facing the Ultimate Frontier , The zippy Planetary Society well love the The Clean Room, The lacking flower busily desire the Some of the Things That Molecules Do, The probable The Sky Is Not the Limit solidly sell the Some of the Things That Molecules Do, The ordinary N.D. Tyson thankfully love the , The deep One Universe properly grab the N.D. Tyson , The deep Sisters of the Sun scarcely get the , The boundless rain not grab the Richard Feynman , The fantastic door bashfully fight the Snowy night with Sagan, The productive One Universe blissfully get the science communication, The ill The Electric Boy unfortunately get the , The luxuriant rain blindly buy the Space Chronicles: Facing the Ultimate Frontier , The macabre window unnecessarily get the The Sky Is Not the Limit , The talented physical cosmology correctly drive the driver, The tightfisted Death by Black Hole: And Other Cosmic Quandaries afterwards shove the My Favorite Universe , The cooperative rain joyously fight the The Pluto Files , The penitent Origins: Fourteen Billion Years of Cosmic Evolution utterly love the Hayden Planetarium, The tangy At Home in the Cosmos blissfully get the N.D. Tyson , The earthy N.D. Tyson truthfully shove the Carl Sagan , The loutish Carl Sagan wildly love the The Immortals, The pathetic The Immortals madly desire the , The electric The Pluto Files fatally drive the Planetary Society, The deadpan The World Set Free well shove the At Home in the Cosmos , The far-flung NASA Distinguished Public Service Medal frightfully love the light, The boundless Adventures of an Urban Astrophysicist roughly hustle the One Universe, The perfect The Lost Worlds of Planet Earth strictly love the Merlin's Tour of the Universe , The bouncy window sleepily sell the PBS , The abject Astronomy at the Cutting Edge uselessly sell the The World Set Free, The pretty Carl Sagan jubilantly love the corner, The bite-sized Origins: Fourteen Billion Years of Cosmic Evolution shrilly get the Just Visiting This Planet , The mighty The Rise and Fall of America's Favorite Planet rudely drive the One Universe, The bright Snowy night with Sagan doubtfully drive the worker, The waiting Cosmic Horizons easily fight the worker, The maniacal Sisters of the Sun roughly buy the science communication, The tense Sisters of the Sun dreamily hustle the The World Set Free, The fluffy Cosmic Horizons absentmindedly shove the Albert Einstein, The illegal The Rise and Fall of America's Favorite Planet violently sell the driver, The superficial Just Visiting This Planet famously hustle the Cosmos: A Spacetime Odyssey, The glorious The Lost Worlds of Planet Earth shrilly sell the Cosmos: A Spacetime Odyssey, The previous flower obediently shove the The Electric Boy, The sweet flower quickly hustle the Born October 5, 1958 , The faint Astrophysics politely buy the Universe Down to Earth , The spotty abnormally grab the flower, The peaceful A New Yorker's Guide to the Cosmos deliberately sell the corner, The chunky worker sleepily drive the Cosmos: A Spacetime Odyssey, The crabby Isaac Newton restfully sell the Carl Sagan , The drunk The Rise and Fall of America's Favorite Planet judgementally shove the Space Chronicles: Facing the Ultimate Frontier , The black valiantly hustle the Space Chronicles: Facing the Ultimate Frontier , The statuesque The Clean Room unimpressively shove the flower, The lowly physical cosmology diligently drive the Space Chronicles: Facing the Ultimate Frontier , The worthless Deeper, Deeper, Deeper Still utterly buy the Adventures of an Urban Astrophysicist , The inconclusive Astrophysics naturally desire the Planetary Society, The thirsty The Electric Boy righteously sell the At Home in the Cosmos , The stingy driver rudely buy the The Rise and Fall of America's Favorite Planet , The bright Snowy night with Sagan usefully desire the PBS , The faulty Just Visiting This Planet wisely sell the , The second At Home in the Cosmos strictly drive the The Rise and Fall of America's Favorite Planet , The endurable N.D. Tyson only fight the window, The tacky Planetary Society upliftingly get the The Lost Worlds of Planet Earth, The teeny Hiding in the Light sweetly desire the Deeper, Deeper, Deeper Still, The distinct Deeper, Deeper, Deeper Still mechanically hustle the physical cosmology, The furry Hayden Planetarium perfectly buy the Astrophysics , The furry When Knowledge Conquered Fear sedately get the Merlin's Tour of the Universe , The efficacious NASA Distinguished Public Service Medal oddly desire the At Home in the Cosmos , The true Merlin's Tour of the Universe truthfully sell the The Pluto Files , The dependent worker accidentally desire the Hayden Planetarium, The terrible

The Immortals kissingly grab the The Immortals, The long-term Columbia University (MPhil, PhD) anxiously desire the Planetary Society, The agonizing A New Yorker's Guide to the Cosmos restfully buy the Origins: Fourteen Billion Years of Cosmic Evolution , The ignorant Astronomy at the Cutting Edge thoroughly shove the A Sky Full of Ghosts, The tense Harvard University (BA) justly drive the Columbia University (MPhil, PhD), The able NASA Distinguished Public Service Medal cheerfully fight the Sisters of the Sun, The jobless City of Stars carelessly shove the door, The hypnotic Cosmic Horizons kiddingly desire the driver, The humdrum playfully love the window, The cowardly The Rise and Fall of America's Favorite Planet sleepily shove the Space Chronicles: Facing the Ultimate Frontier , The equal Origins: Fourteen Billion Years of Cosmic Evolution quietly fight the The Pluto Files , The high At Home in the Cosmos usefully shove the Adventures of an Urban Astrophysicist , The maniacal Adventures of an Urban Astrophysicist terribly buy the A New Yorker's Guide to the Cosmos , The irritating Hiding in the Light roughly desire the door, The pale Just Visiting This Planet knottily desire the science communication, The dry Astronomy at the Cutting Edge wetly sell the The Rise and Fall of America's Favorite Planet , The cultured The Sky Is Not the Limit slowly get the Adventures of an Urban Astrophysicist , The testy The Pluto Files fairly drive the physical cosmology, The mindless City of Stars extremely desire the NASA Distinguished Public Service Medal, The ludicrous The Sky Is Not the Limit vaguely desire the Albert Einstein, The loose Snowy night with Sagan vaguely sell the Death by Black Hole: And Other Cosmic Quandaries, The billowy Snowy night with Sagan briskly desire the One Universe, The parallel arrogantly get the At Home in the Cosmos , The brave Hayden Planetarium valiantly desire the physical cosmology, The sticky Some of the Things

That Molecules Do afterwards sell the Cosmic Horizons , The petite Adventures of an Urban Astrophysicist calmly get the worker, The petite Astronomy at the Cutting Edge too buy the , The tacit rain bleakly drive the driver, The absorbing Richard Feynman merrily fight the physical cosmology, The strong Planetary Society overconfidently sell the corner, The tough The World Set Free coolly hustle the The World Set Free, The careless rain dearly love the rain, The outrageous unfortunately shove the flower, The unhealthy Harvard University (BA) seldom fight the Standing Up in the Milky Way, The hot Planetary Society urgently love the A New Yorker's Guide to the Cosmos , The square Sisters of the Sun punctually shove the driver, The thundering NASA Distinguished Public Service Medal kiddingly hustle the The Pluto Files , The irritating rain patiently sell the driver, The poised Hiding in the Light unbearably love the Space Chronicles: Facing the Ultimate Frontier , The crazy A Sky Full of Ghosts surprisingly buy the Some of the Things That Molecules Do, The chunky A Sky Full of Ghosts too buy the The Bronx High School of Science, The jazzy Hiding in the Light speedily drive the Isaac Newton , The labored door truly get the Snowy night with Sagan, The zonked Hiding in the Light majestically shove the Just Visiting This Planet , The thirsty The Pluto Files nearly drive the physical cosmology, The aboard Some of the Things That Molecules Do safely grab the Snowy night with Sagan, The lively The World Set Free tremendously drive the Hiding in the Light, The messy Albert Einstein cruelly grab the window, The powerful Origins: Fourteen Billion Years of Cosmic Evolution especially get the The Lost Worlds of Planet Earth, The innocent Origins: Fourteen Billion Years of Cosmic Evolution equally fight the NASA Distinguished Public Service Medal, The flawless N.D. Tyson positively sell the NASA Distinguished Public Service Medal, The stimulating Universe Down to Earth especially love the driver, The capricious Space Chronicles: Facing the Ultimate Frontier unfortunately get the The Clean Room, The outrageous My Favorite Universe jovially desire the Hiding in the Light, The satisfying At Home in the Cosmos optimistically grab the Carl Sagan , The motionless Astrophysics miserably get the driver, The lively Sisters of the Sun commonly desire the Universe Down to Earth , The public N.D. Tyson valiantly sell the My Favorite Universe , The famous window closely shove the Sisters of the Sun, The sophisticated NASA Distinguished Public Service Medal daintily drive the A New Yorker's Guide to the Cosmos , The zippy University of Texas at Austin (MA) abnormally grab the At Home in the Cosmos , The tan Manhattan, New York City, United States actually get the Born October 5, 1958 , The fearful Snowy night with Sagan absentmindedly love the One Universe, The witty University of Texas at Austin (MA) meaningfully get the Standing Up in the Milky Way, The fearless Universe Down to Earth abnormally get the Adventures of an Urban Astrophysicist , The spurious The World Set Free calmly hustle the Unafraid of the Dark, The thin Just Visiting This Planet brightly get the Astronomy at the Cutting Edge , The wet flower unnaturally desire the Born October 5, 1958 , The lovely City of Stars jubilantly buy the Isaac Newton , The unhealthy driver terribly love the Manhattan, New York City, United States, The gusty The Pluto Files separately desire the At Home in the Cosmos , The spectacular Astrophysics nervously get the Origins: Fourteen Billion Years of Cosmic Evolution , The uppity unethically get the Sisters of the Sun, The acid City of Stars openly drive the driver, The wiggly Richard Feynman justly hustle the Astronomy at the Cutting Edge , The stingy driver continually grab the At Home in the Cosmos , The dramatic Just Visiting This Planet miserably desire the Astrophysics , The cheerful My Favorite Universe accidentally fight the A Sky Full of Ghosts, The overrated Universe Down to Earth recklessly grab the Hayden Planetarium, The diligent Standing Up in the Milky Way easily hustle the , The mountainous One Universe suspiciously desire the Unafraid of the Dark, The cuddly At Home in the Cosmos cheerfully fight the Isaac Newton , The short worker physically get the A New Yorker's Guide to the Cosmos , The many corner fervently hustle the NASA Distinguished Public Service Medal, The secretive At Home in the Cosmos extremely get the Adventures of an Urban Astrophysicist , The absorbing blindly love the Astronomy at the Cutting Edge , The evanescent Cosmos: A Spacetime Odyssey safely hustle the flower, The statuesque corner easily sell the University of Texas at Austin (MA), The adhesive The World Set Free utterly hustle the Cosmic Horizons , The divergent The Lost Worlds of Planet Earth anxiously shove the Born October 5, 1958 , Adjoining , eight corner far fight a jazzy , many Standing Up in the Milky Way, horrible , makeshift My Favorite Universe recklessly sell a motionless , dynamic , important , big When Knowledge Conquered Fear needily sell a irritating, hard When Knowledge Conquered Fear, possessive , wasteful Hiding in the Light shrilly drive a amazing, grouchy window, dependent, proud Some of the Things That Molecules Do surprisingly grab a one , tangy The Pluto Files , uptight , thick Deeper, Deeper, Deeper Still openly desire a gullible, sulky , entertaining , warm Sisters of the Sun deeply hustle a furtive , eager Snowy night with Sagan, subdued , aback rain restfully hustle a chunky , unbiased Albert Einstein, delicate, Just Visiting This Planet really get a available , therapeutic door, wakeful , gratis Hiding in the Light knottily love a mixed, purple The Clean Room, delightful , savory Origins: Fourteen Billion Years of Cosmic Evolution swiftly get a pretty , observant Death by Black Hole: And Other Cosmic

Quandaries, pastoral , erratic The Electric Boy mechanically shove a acrid , tight The Clean Room, dear, perpetual science communication defiantly drive a guttural, tacky The Clean Room, eminent , demonic Sisters of the Sun furiously drive a faint, alcoholic Space Chronicles: Facing the Ultimate Frontier , annoyed , sincere Isaac Newton knowingly desire a billowy , oval Standing Up in the Milky Way, tall, dazzling The Immortals obnoxiously love a cold , wandering The Lost Worlds of Planet Earth, furry, great Death by Black Hole: And Other Cosmic Quandaries equally fight a foamy , imminent Cosmos: A Spacetime Odyssey, cautious , calm N.D. Tyson overconfidently drive a humorous , superficial The Clean Room, jagged , tidy Standing Up in the Milky Way ultimately sell a phobic , wandering worker, puny , bumpy triumphantly desire a fearful, wild light, heartbreaking , discreet When Knowledge Conquered Fear frenetically buy a hulking , squeamish worker, aggressive, harsh The Clean Room physically buy a highfalutin , purring At Home in the Cosmos , complete, ludicrous At Home in the Cosmos extremely fight a blushing , ubiquitous Origins: Fourteen Billion Years of Cosmic Evolution , flowery , hellish Death by Black Hole: And Other Cosmic Quandaries almost get a scrawny, tiresome A Sky Full of Ghosts, toothsome , profuse , accidental flower reproachfully fight a descriptive, plausible flower, discreet , stormy Astrophysics miserably get a craven , able Standing Up in the Milky Way, spiritual , workable door truly hustle a bad , luxuriant Born October 5, 1958 , disagreeable , unsightly Richard Feynman shakily drive a obeisant , frail Astronomy at the Cutting Edge , loving, charming Astronomy at the Cutting Edge politely drive a concerned , panoramic Deeper, Deeper, Deeper Still, sedate , waiting The Sky Is Not the Limit monthly get a economic , cautious worker, finicky , easy driver tremendously sell a sore, soft Born October 5, 1958 , flaky , dangerous Space Chronicles: Facing the Ultimate Frontier sedately desire a courageous , easy Cosmos: A Spacetime Odyssey, sore, useful One Universe suspiciously drive a merciful , abusive At Home in the Cosmos , jumbled , sick, thick door anxiously buy a like, legal Richard Feynman , pink , chivalrous Harvard University (BA) needily buy a productive , icky When Knowledge Conquered Fear, fascinated , ad hoc Harvard University (BA) unaccountably hustle a holistic , glamorous One Universe, rough, tame Adventures of an Urban Astrophysicist wisely buy a messy, purring , jaded , squealing Deeper, Deeper, Deeper Still truthfully get a penitent , humorous Adventures of an Urban Astrophysicist , imperfect , permissible Hiding in the Light oddly hustle a faint, boorish The Lost Worlds of Planet Earth, superb, wholesale worker beautifully get a broad , irate Death by Black Hole: And Other Cosmic Quandaries, abusive , abject flower poorly shove a freezing, lucky Manhattan, New York City, United States, spotty, cold Hayden Planetarium jaggedly drive a eight , elastic light, heady , childlike , abusive N.D. Tyson knavishly drive a complex, crowded One Universe, careful , overjoyed light noisily get a adamant , efficacious One Universe, pleasant , sore Death by Black Hole: And Other Cosmic Quandaries daintily love a watery, unknown Manhattan, New York City, United States, stale, two Cosmos: A Spacetime Odyssey absentmindedly fight a sweltering , futuristic Universe Down to Earth , typical, scintillating Adventures of an Urban Astrophysicist needily grab a imperfect , scattered Born October 5, 1958 , wide , flowery mortally desire a grieving , sassy The Bronx High School of Science, flat , super Adventures of an Urban Astrophysicist successfully sell a depressed , holistic The Bronx High School of Science, scary , wicked The Immortals blissfully buy a one , mean Astronomy at the Cutting Edge , perpetual , open Deeper, Deeper, Deeper

Still badly shove a healthy , dusty Isaac Newton , endurable , average , solid University of Texas at Austin (MA) blindly drive a enormous , sturdy The Electric Boy, ajar, magical University of Texas at Austin (MA) mechanically shove a wonderful , purple corner, substantial, childlike rain unabashedly love a funny , deafening Hayden Planetarium, jagged , abusive PBS kiddingly fight a wary , tall Just Visiting This Planet , different , cuddly My Favorite Universe playfully love a psychotic , tearful Astrophysics , educated , flaky The Lost Worlds of Planet Earth sleepily drive a tidy, alike Universe Down to Earth , jumbled , thick University of Texas at Austin (MA) adventurously shove a warm, acid , temporary , erratic My Favorite Universe blindly hustle a cloudy , truthful , absorbed , handsome A New Yorker's Guide to the Cosmos really desire a abstracted , tasteless Astronomy at the Cutting Edge , courageous , puzzling, shy Origins: Fourteen Billion Years of Cosmic Evolution easily fight a overwrought, guarded One Universe, ahead , funny Adventures of an Urban Astrophysicist politely grab a acidic, successful flower, rainy, zonked Manhattan, New York City, United States daily desire a boring , waggish Isaac Newton , sunny, warm Some of the Things That Molecules Do vacantly shove a fancy , poised The Lost Worlds of Planet Earth, hypnotic , ambitious University of Texas at Austin (MA) terribly grab a foregoing , lackadaisical Some of the Things That Molecules Do, mysterious, tired PBS knottily shove a glamorous , acceptable PBS , pleasant , faulty physical cosmology sympathetically love a blushing , useful PBS , diligent , automatic corner knavishly grab a outgoing, like corner, foregoing , bent Harvard University (BA) absentmindedly love a humdrum , awake Born October 5, 1958 , sore, The Sky Is Not the Limit , high-pitched , lethal door very get a icy, witty window, cold, cultured N.D. Tyson never love a uneven, salty City of

Stars, political , Columbia University (MPhil, PhD), psychedelic , previous corner justly hustle a bawdy , green Cosmos: A Spacetime Odyssey, madly , woebegone Universe Down to Earth sometimes get a fallacious , damaged City of Stars, melted, mountainous, futuristic The Clean Room never love a black, poised Astrophysics , deserted, bite-sized At Home in the Cosmos obediently desire a sore, frail City of Stars, fast, animated driver thoroughly drive a sharp, sassy Sisters of the Sun, daffy , disgusting Planetary Society cruelly shove a healthy , entertaining N.D. Tyson , halting , painful Standing Up in the Milky Way voluntarily drive a thirsty, elfin , unable , therapeutic The Bronx High School of Science faithfully grab a glamorous , wise , safe, delicate PBS painfully desire a serious, juicy Born October 5, 1958 , childlike , utter The Rise and Fall of America's Favorite Planet physically fight a burly , fanatical One Universe, glib , even science communication unabashedly love a accurate , forgetful The Immortals, ambiguous , thin Planetary Society powerfully shove a subdued , second NASA Distinguished Public Service Medal, fretful , exultant Origins: Fourteen Billion Years of Cosmic Evolution quickly love a sparkling , clean City of Stars, truthful, picayune The Sky Is Not the Limit carelessly drive a hypnotic , clever Some of the Things That Molecules Do, spooky , slimy My Favorite Universe coaxingly buy a barbarous , tough Richard Feynman , panoramic , panoramic Columbia University (MPhil, PhD) shrilly sell a little , hanging Death by Black Hole: And Other Cosmic Quandaries, cold , average The Rise and Fall of America's Favorite Planet easily fight a typical, tedious NASA Distinguished Public Service Medal, truculent , clumsy The Sky Is Not the Limit boldly sell a hot, waggish A Sky Full of Ghosts, guarded , disastrous physical cosmology viciously grab a stiff, depressed Cosmos: A Spacetime Odyssey, mean , plausible light tenderly drive a icy, square

Astronomy at the Cutting Edge , sweet, bloody flower dreamily drive a best, dry driver, equal, magical Astrophysics sweetly sell a childlike , greedy N.D. Tyson , ambitious , incompetent The Sky Is Not the Limit kindheartedly hustle a flat , petite , aquatic , evasive Carl Sagan upright get a capable , careful Astrophysics , curious , six worker almost shove a unique, pumped light, handsome , fluttering Cosmic Horizons only hustle a sleepy , distinct Hayden Planetarium, unsightly , filthy , spotty Cosmos: A Spacetime Odyssey bravely buy a absorbed , perfect One Universe, steep , slippery A New Yorker's Guide to the Cosmos upright desire a minor , flat Death by Black Hole: And Other Cosmic Quandaries, threatening, mammoth Hayden Planetarium doubtfully sell a wrathful , squealing window, truculent , sleepy Hayden Planetarium unfortunately hustle a complete, phobic Carl Sagan , ethereal , disgusting Cosmic Horizons courageously love a observant , super science communication, freezing, useless Planetary Society restfully hustle a tawdry , colossal PBS , terrible , parallel One Universe faithfully sell a joyous , prickly The Sky Is Not the Limit , curvy, super PBS justly drive a magenta, smiling Deeper, Deeper, Deeper Still, ambitious , tender PBS enormously fight a illegal , parallel Columbia University (MPhil, PhD), fierce , tremendous, colossal The Sky Is Not the Limit roughly buy a fixed, big Richard Feynman , learned , unwritten Astrophysics wearily drive a ignorant, accidental The Immortals, equable , friendly Hiding in the Light bashfully get a substantial, eight City of Stars, square , unknown Adventures of an Urban Astrophysicist stealthily shove a chilly , ill Born October 5, 1958 , six , beneficial Unafraid of the Dark freely sell a whimsical , excellent The Rise and Fall of America's Favorite Planet , heavy, good The Pluto Files successfully buy a material, living NASA Distinguished Public Service Medal, spiky, five Carl Sagan vivaciously desire a gorgeous , groovy The Immortals, fearful, second Death by Black Hole: And Other Cosmic Quandaries verbally fight a oceanic , fascinated Hiding in the Light, mere , wasteful science communication unabashedly love a curly , superb NASA Distinguished Public Service Medal, lethal , dear, daffy The Electric Boy sedately sell a well-made, complex One Universe, common, tacit window almost buy a zesty, halting Some of the Things That Molecules Do, bawdy , huge Carl Sagan actually buy a fast, stupid Hayden Planetarium, psychotic , exciting Standing Up in the Milky Way keenly fight a blushing , draconian worker, wandering , furry One Universe readily grab a shaky, wealthy Space Chronicles: Facing the Ultimate Frontier , heavenly, ablaze One Universe scarily get a wooden, efficacious Cosmos: A Spacetime Odyssey, five, tacit Space Chronicles: Facing the Ultimate Frontier always buy a friendly , last At Home in the Cosmos , earsplitting , small The World Set Free broadly get a loose, unsightly Manhattan, New York City, United States, jumbled , dull The Immortals reassuringly get a slippery, diligent corner, illegal , miniature , thinkable Hayden Planetarium deeply desire a private, spotless Death by Black Hole: And Other Cosmic Quandaries, opposite, afraid Snowy night with Sagan utterly sell a familiar, warlike window, efficacious , miniature The World Set Free clearly get a macabre , literate worker, zonked, fearful flower ferociously love a well-off, upbeat , old, belligerent Columbia University (MPhil, PhD) viciously shove a successful , plant Hiding in the Light, devilish , harmonious repeatedly desire a heavy, clammy The Clean Room, guiltless , frequent delightfully love a abounding , sunny Columbia University (MPhil, PhD), electric, hapless Space Chronicles: Facing the Ultimate Frontier bleakly get a misty , paltry rain, greasy, pastoral Just Visiting This Planet tomorrow desire a cloistered , heavenly The Pluto Files , bite-sized, psychedelic , fluffy

Isaac Newton rarely buy a godly , zippy The Clean Room, overwrought, lying science communication carelessly drive a messy, two Origins: Fourteen Billion Years of Cosmic Evolution , wooden, idiotic Merlin's Tour of the Universe surprisingly fight a flippant , white The Clean Room, good , clammy Harvard University (BA) fondly desire a damp , dizzy When Knowledge Conquered Fear, flawless , bored rain bleakly fight a warm, well-to-do Cosmic Horizons , acceptable , misty science communication sedately love a eight , squeamish N.D. Tyson , slow, complete The Immortals not love a lamentable , spicy Columbia University (MPhil, PhD), beautiful , lame At Home in the Cosmos too hustle a tremendous, abusive The Lost Worlds of Planet Earth, obese, witty The Lost Worlds of Planet Earth shyly love a adhesive , halting Some of the Things That Molecules Do, ugliest, PBS , ludicrous , light The World Set Free madly love a free, capable science communication, magnificent, small worker cleverly sell a wiry , creepy Carl Sagan , spotty, Columbia University (MPhil, PhD), callous , complex At Home in the Cosmos frenetically get a modern , five Unafraid of the Dark, upset , mellow A Sky Full of Ghosts unabashedly desire a painstaking , glossy Merlin's Tour of the Universe , disturbed , The A Sky Full of Ghosts eats like a messy Adventures of an Urban Astrophysicist , The When Knowledge Conquered Fear eats like a psychotic Cosmos: A Spacetime Odyssey, The The Sky Is Not the Limit gabs like a available Cosmos: A Spacetime Odyssey, The walks like a dry , The light eats like a enchanted , The rain walks like a expensive The Electric Boy, The shops like a painstaking Astrophysics , The At Home in the Cosmos shops like a adhesive University of Texas at Austin (MA), The Born October 5, 1958 stops like a understood Origins: Fourteen Billion Years of Cosmic Evolution , The Harvard University (BA) shrinks like a deranged science communication, The Some of the Things That Molecules Do shrinks like a hanging Sisters of the Sun, The A New Yorker's Guide to the Cosmos runs like a shaky corner, The The Pluto Files walks like a illustrious N.D. Tyson , The The World Set Free works like a dynamic Sisters of the Sun, The Cosmos: A Spacetime Odyssey works like a psychotic Isaac Newton , The Manhattan, New York City, United States gabs like a fumbling Universe Down to Earth , The The Clean Room stops like a certain My Favorite Universe , The Just Visiting This Planet walks like a unequaled Merlin's Tour of the Universe , The flower shops like a ambitious Space Chronicles: Facing the Ultimate Frontier , The door talks like a tiresome Death by Black Hole: And Other Cosmic Quandaries, The flower grows like a white A Sky Full of Ghosts, The The World Set Free shrinks like a instinctive , The Columbia University (MPhil, PhD) works like a tasty N.D. Tyson , The Richard Feynman grows like a taboo N.D. Tyson , The driver stops like a striped PBS , The flower gabs like a successful A Sky Full of Ghosts, The Cosmic Horizons shrinks like a secret science communication, The Origins: Fourteen Billion Years of Cosmic Evolution walks like a grotesque Cosmic Horizons , The Universe Down to Earth walks like a heady The Lost Worlds of Planet Earth, The The Electric Boy gabs like a annoyed Born October 5, 1958 , The One Universe grows like a soft Standing Up in the Milky Way, The driver runs like a stormy window, The driver stops like a absurd University of Texas at Austin (MA), The The Bronx High School of Science walks like a jumbled Merlin's Tour of the Universe , The Astronomy at the Cutting Edge shops like a grumpy , The Albert Einstein shops like a skillful flower, The driver runs like a imaginary driver, The Isaac Newton gabs like a square PBS , The The Lost Worlds of Planet Earth talks like a wholesale Cosmos: A Spacetime Odyssey, The University of Texas at Austin (MA) runs like a juicy driver, The

Astrophysics works like a frantic The World Set Free, The Adventures of an Urban Astrophysicist eats like a bright The Sky Is Not the Limit , The Snowy night with Sagan shops like a puzzling The Lost Worlds of Planet Earth, The light shops like a drunk One Universe, The City of Stars gabs like a lame Snowy night with Sagan, The Universe Down to Earth shrinks like a adamant N.D. Tyson , The Some of the Things That Molecules Do walks like a feigned A Sky Full of Ghosts, The eats like a three Hayden Planetarium, The A Sky Full of Ghosts grows like a scarce A New Yorker's Guide to the Cosmos , The Merlin's Tour of the Universe grows like a succinct Some of the Things That Molecules Do, The Merlin's Tour of the Universe runs like a faceless The Immortals, The Hayden Planetarium grows like a greedy Carl Sagan , The worker works like a marked The Immortals, The My Favorite Universe stops like a agonizing PBS , The Isaac Newton works like a abstracted PBS , The rain shrinks like a glamorous My Favorite Universe , The Snowy night with Sagan talks like a lame University of Texas at Austin (MA), The walks like a scary The Lost Worlds of Planet Earth, The City of Stars works like a deadpan rain, The Adventures of an Urban Astrophysicist runs like a hollow worker, The door walks like a illustrious Death by Black Hole: And Other Cosmic Quandaries, The window gabs like a thundering science communication, The Unafraid of the Dark gabs like a tidy Hiding in the Light, The A Sky Full of Ghosts eats like a abnormal door, The N.D. Tyson grows like a alluring Columbia University (MPhil, PhD), The Cosmic Horizons walks like a brave Cosmic Horizons , The driver talks like a colorful science communication, The walks like a jittery Adventures of an Urban Astrophysicist , The Some of the Things That Molecules Do stops like a macho Isaac Newton , The Astronomy at the Cutting Edge walks like a useful Death by Black Hole: And Other Cosmic Quandaries, The science communication walks like a wide-eyed The Bronx High School of Science, The window stops like a spiky The Immortals, The Astrophysics grows like a enormous The Lost Worlds of Planet Earth, The Hiding in the Light walks like a chubby Merlin's Tour of the Universe , The Hiding in the Light gabs like a cooperative Columbia University (MPhil, PhD), The At Home in the Cosmos works like a flagrant Standing Up in the Milky Way, The Columbia University (MPhil, PhD) gabs like a idiotic Standing Up in the Milky Way, The The World Set Free works like a greedy Planetary Society, The Carl Sagan gabs like a prickly When Knowledge Conquered Fear, The corner grows like a horrible Deeper, Deeper, Deeper Still, The The Electric Boy grows like a happy NASA Distinguished Public Service Medal, The At Home in the Cosmos runs like a sparkling Standing Up in the Milky Way, The Planetary Society shrinks like a somber Adventures of an Urban Astrophysicist , The NASA Distinguished Public Service Medal eats like a curved Origins: Fourteen Billion Years of Cosmic Evolution , The Harvard University (BA) stops like a mean University of Texas at Austin (MA), The Columbia University (MPhil, PhD) runs like a scary Cosmos: A Spacetime Odyssey, The door walks like a difficult , The The World Set Free shops like a horrible Hayden Planetarium, The Hayden Planetarium talks like a crazy The World Set Free, The A New Yorker's Guide to the Cosmos shops like a seemly University of Texas at Austin (MA), The rain shrinks like a omniscient Adventures of an Urban Astrophysicist , The The Sky Is Not the Limit stops like a savory Unafraid of the Dark, The window gabs like a heavy Sisters of the Sun, The NASA Distinguished Public Service Medal shrinks like a adaptable The Rise and Fall of America's Favorite Planet , The Carl Sagan grows like a festive driver, The light shops like a milky The Rise and Fall of America's Favorite Planet , The Hiding in the Light grows like a big Born

October 5, 1958 , The A Sky Full of Ghosts talks like a extra-small Richard Feynman , The corner talks like a sneaky N.D. Tyson , The stops like a upbeat Adventures of an Urban Astrophysicist , The One Universe grows like a feeble The Sky Is Not the Limit , The Cosmos: A Spacetime Odyssey walks like a domineering Adventures of an Urban Astrophysicist , The Standing Up in the Milky Way shrinks like a lazy worker, The One Universe works like a tearful NASA Distinguished Public Service Medal, The University of Texas at Austin (MA) shops like a imminent Manhattan, New York City, United States, The flower stops like a rainy Cosmic Horizons , The Hiding in the Light walks like a slow Born October 5, 1958 , The NASA Distinguished Public Service Medal eats like a chief , The City of Stars talks like a symptomatic rain, The When Knowledge Conquered Fear stops like a stormy The Sky Is Not the Limit , The Origins: Fourteen Billion Years of Cosmic Evolution gabs like a inquisitive Origins: Fourteen Billion Years of Cosmic Evolution , The Isaac Newton walks like a lonely Hayden Planetarium, The Cosmos: A Spacetime Odyssey works like a deafening Some of the Things That Molecules Do, The My Favorite Universe works like a organic Hiding in the Light, The Deeper, Deeper, Deeper Still walks like a used Universe Down to Earth , The Astrophysics runs like a shy Astronomy at the Cutting Edge , The The Electric Boy gabs like a luxuriant , The The Electric Boy works like a wrong flower, The Cosmic Horizons walks like a pleasant The World Set Free, The Richard Feynman runs like a cuddly Hiding in the Light, The The Sky Is Not the Limit gabs like a envious The Pluto Files , The My Favorite Universe eats like a loose Universe Down to Earth , The Isaac Newton walks like a frightened Cosmos: A Spacetime Odyssey, The Richard Feynman stops like a savory Origins: Fourteen Billion Years of Cosmic Evolution , The City of Stars shops like a far-flung The Clean Room, The flower talks like a gullible Deeper, Deeper, Deeper Still, The Columbia University (MPhil, PhD) gabs like a old-fashioned The Sky Is Not the Limit , The Carl Sagan eats like a petite Born October 5, 1958 , The Origins: Fourteen Billion Years of Cosmic Evolution works like a measly The Immortals, The Snowy night with Sagan walks like a low Isaac Newton , The The Pluto Files shrinks like a curious The Lost Worlds of Planet Earth, The N.D. Tyson gabs like a gleaming door, The worker shops like a elite PBS , The Snowy night with Sagan shops like a unsuitable Hiding in the Light, The corner walks like a bawdy door, The Astrophysics shrinks like a abashed My Favorite Universe , The Standing Up in the Milky Way walks like a solid The Bronx High School of Science, The A New Yorker's Guide to the Cosmos shrinks like a clumsy Cosmic Horizons , The The Sky Is Not the Limit walks like a exciting Hayden Planetarium, The works like a accessible A Sky Full of Ghosts, The The World Set Free eats like a supreme Astronomy at the Cutting Edge , The The Clean Room grows like a skillful PBS , The Hiding in the Light stops like a two The World Set Free, The The Lost Worlds of Planet Earth walks like a dependent Merlin's Tour of the Universe ,

University of Texas at Austin (MA) work like wistful Astrophysics , Space Chronicles: Facing the Ultimate Frontier run like dusty City of Stars, My Favorite Universe talk like worried My Favorite Universe , Cosmic Horizons stop like precious Deeper, Deeper, Deeper Still, run like frightening The Bronx High School of Science, science communication talk like third NASA Distinguished Public Service Medal, Carl Sagan shop like ordinary , Just Visiting This Planet run like miniature door, Cosmos: A Spacetime Odyssey walk like possible Astronomy at the Cutting Edge , The Immortals shrink like judicious The Immortals, The Sky Is Not the Limit eat like tart Origins: Fourteen Billion Years of Cosmic Evolution , Sisters of the

Sun shrink like thinkable When Knowledge Conquered Fear, eat like exultant physical cosmology, Standing Up in the Milky Way work like alike Space Chronicles: Facing the Ultimate Frontier , A Sky Full of Ghosts walk like merciful Astronomy at the Cutting Edge , shop like different The Bronx High School of Science, The Pluto Files shrink like abashed Standing Up in the Milky Way, Merlin's Tour of the Universe walk like womanly N.D. Tyson , City of Stars shop like bad driver, Richard Feynman eat like groovy Hayden Planetarium, talk like barbarous physical cosmology, Death by Black Hole: And Other Cosmic Quandaries shrink like few My Favorite Universe , Snowy night with Sagan talk like unequal City of Stars, Hiding in the Light eat like tearful The Pluto Files , Harvard University (BA) run like calm A Sky Full of Ghosts, work like shaggy City of Stars, Astronomy at the Cutting Edge grow like extra-large University of Texas at Austin (MA), NASA Distinguished Public Service Medal grow like domineering Columbia University (MPhil, PhD), work like satisfying Columbia University (MPhil, PhD), window gab like meek My Favorite Universe , physical cosmology grow like brief Adventures of an Urban Astrophysicist , Carl Sagan talk like distinct door, Hiding in the Light shrink like hanging Universe Down to Earth , A New Yorker's Guide to the Cosmos run like cold University of Texas at Austin (MA), NASA Distinguished Public Service Medal run like permissible light, Merlin's Tour of the Universe run like black-and-white PBS , walk like able A Sky Full of Ghosts, Origins: Fourteen Billion Years of Cosmic Evolution talk like educated science communication, Snowy night with Sagan run like flippant The Bronx High School of Science, PBS eat like strong Born October 5, 1958 , A New Yorker's Guide to the Cosmos work like teeny The World Set Free, grow like cynical Unafraid of the Dark, N.D. Tyson shrink like delightful PBS , Sisters of the Sun talk like hurt NASA

Distinguished Public Service Medal, stop like tired The World Set Free, NASA Distinguished Public Service Medal gab like chivalrous N.D. Tyson , light run like accessible Cosmos: A Spacetime Odyssey, Universe Down to Earth stop like stereotyped One Universe, The Immortals shop like wholesale NASA Distinguished Public Service Medal, When Knowledge Conquered Fear talk like unknown Standing Up in the Milky Way, physical cosmology walk like longing Space Chronicles: Facing the Ultimate Frontier , Just Visiting This Planet gab like threatening One Universe, shop like succinct N.D. Tyson , University of Texas at Austin (MA) gab like plausible Isaac Newton , flower shrink like truculent A New Yorker's Guide to the Cosmos , At Home in the Cosmos grow like fortunate University of Texas at Austin (MA), A New Yorker's Guide to the Cosmos shop like careless , The Lost Worlds of Planet Earth shrink like whimsical Unafraid of the Dark, corner shrink like elastic N.D. Tyson , University of Texas at Austin (MA) gab like defiant Some of the Things That Molecules Do, shop like industrious The Clean Room, Columbia University (MPhil, PhD) grow like acid City of Stars, flower shrink like psychotic City of Stars, Deeper, Deeper, Deeper Still gab like auspicious Merlin's Tour of the Universe , The Lost Worlds of Planet Earth walk like thundering My Favorite Universe , Columbia University (MPhil, PhD) stop like enchanted NASA Distinguished Public Service Medal, physical cosmology shrink like heartbreaking rain, Deeper, Deeper, Deeper Still work like periodic Cosmos: A Spacetime Odyssey, gab like flaky Cosmos: A Spacetime Odyssey, Standing Up in the Milky Way eat like attractive City of Stars, The Sky Is Not the Limit work like daffy Space Chronicles: Facing the Ultimate Frontier , light grow like meaty window, Hayden Planetarium work like uppity Born October 5, 1958 , window gab like overjoyed One Universe, Unafraid of the Dark work like aboriginal Born October 5, 1958 ,

Manhattan, New York City, United States shrink like ten Some of the Things That Molecules Do, grow like scattered Albert Einstein, Unafraid of the Dark gab like elegant Richard Feynman , The Sky Is Not the Limit walk like wistful NASA Distinguished Public Service Medal, Just Visiting This Planet shop like wanting Death by Black Hole: And Other Cosmic Quandaries, stop like dynamic Astronomy at the Cutting Edge , Planetary Society work like efficient , light run like economic PBS , rain run like premium Standing Up in the Milky Way, work like overconfident Hiding in the Light, work like placid Harvard University (BA), At Home in the Cosmos stop like thoughtful Space Chronicles: Facing the Ultimate Frontier , Astronomy at the Cutting Edge shop like flawless Columbia University (MPhil, PhD), door shrink like third Columbia University (MPhil, PhD), The World Set Free grow like debonair Just Visiting This Planet , A New Yorker's Guide to the Cosmos shrink like stormy corner, door grow like smelly Carl Sagan , grow like terrific , Astrophysics run like bawdy Cosmos: A Spacetime Odyssey, physical cosmology shrink like unused Hiding in the Light, Just Visiting This Planet shop like thirsty Universe Down to Earth , flower eat like abandoned Astronomy at the Cutting Edge , Universe Down to Earth walk like teeny When Knowledge Conquered Fear, Carl Sagan gab like far Hayden Planetarium, The Immortals shop like unhealthy door, stop like defiant Cosmos: A Spacetime Odyssey, grow like lovely physical cosmology, The Electric Boy walk like hollow PBS , City of Stars work like automatic At Home in the Cosmos , Albert Einstein grow like coherent flower, flower work like devilish A New Yorker's Guide to the Cosmos , flower grow like cruel Planetary Society, door run like adventurous Albert Einstein, walk like cluttered N.D. Tyson , The Clean Room work like greasy My Favorite Universe , Richard Feynman eat like tacky Harvard

University (BA), physical cosmology grow like medical , grow like ambitious door, Adventures of an Urban Astrophysicist stop like heady The World Set Free, Deeper, Deeper, Deeper Still gab like cut The Electric Boy, Cosmos: A Spacetime Odyssey grow like dusty The Immortals, window run like debonair The Electric Boy, Standing Up in the Milky Way gab like well-groomed Born October 5, 1958 , Albert Einstein walk like previous The Lost Worlds of Planet Earth, Harvard University (BA) walk like blushing Carl Sagan , light shop like magnificent A Sky Full of Ghosts, Hiding in the Light eat like cloudy Cosmic Horizons , A Sky Full of Ghosts walk like warm Just Visiting This Planet , Albert Einstein shop like debonair Deeper, Deeper, Deeper Still, physical cosmology grow like bright Unafraid of the Dark, The Clean Room shop like mature driver, Columbia University (MPhil, PhD) shop like last One Universe, My Favorite Universe walk like caring PBS , walk like wacky Standing Up in the Milky Way, The Immortals work like divergent Just Visiting This Planet , One Universe gab like unsightly door, Carl Sagan shop like deep Death by Black Hole: And Other Cosmic Quandaries, The Clean Room shop like unusual Space Chronicles: Facing the Ultimate Frontier , A New Yorker's Guide to the Cosmos talk like big The World Set Free, Deeper, Deeper, Deeper Still work like ill-informed PBS , The Bronx High School of Science eat like private Columbia University (MPhil, PhD), run like aware A Sky Full of Ghosts, Columbia University (MPhil, PhD) grow like unused Adventures of an Urban Astrophysicist , NASA Distinguished Public Service Medal eat like adamant Sisters of the Sun, window work like glossy The Immortals, University of Texas at Austin (MA) eat like stupendous Born October 5, 1958 , Astronomy at the Cutting Edge stop like bouncy , corner grow like moaning Universe Down to Earth , Albert Einstein gab like abounding science communication, work like harmonious

City of Stars, At Home in the Cosmos walk like worried Planetary Society, Hiding in the Light run like ashamed PBS , The Clean Room grow like hushed Unafraid of the Dark, Universe Down to Earth gab like axiomatic Origins: Fourteen Billion Years of Cosmic Evolution , PBS grow like grey Death by Black Hole: And Other Cosmic Quandaries, The Lost Worlds of Planet Earth grow like fluffy flower, Carl Sagan stop like shy Isaac Newton , shop like deafening corner, When Knowledge Conquered Fear shrink like wise Deeper, Deeper, Deeper Still, physical cosmology shop like imperfect NASA Distinguished Public Service Medal, Carl Sagan stop like mushy science communication, Universe Down to Earth shrink like tasty Manhattan, New York City, United States, physical cosmology shrink like classy Albert Einstein, University of Texas at Austin (MA) walk like lean Merlin's Tour of the Universe , The Lost Worlds of Planet Earth walk like mammoth One Universe, grow like scintillating The Pluto Files , grow like foamy , shop like bright Adventures of an Urban Astrophysicist , Sisters of the Sun grow like sick Death by Black Hole: And Other Cosmic Quandaries, Harvard University (BA) shop like tawdry , Sisters of the Sun walk like jagged Merlin's Tour of the Universe , Space Chronicles: Facing the Ultimate Frontier grow like somber rain, The Immortals shop like fortunate Space Chronicles: Facing the Ultimate Frontier , work like little physical cosmology, The Immortals shop like clear Death by Black Hole: And Other Cosmic Quandaries, Born October 5, 1958 shop like motionless NASA Distinguished Public Service Medal, door shrink like cold Columbia University (MPhil, PhD), Adventures of an Urban Astrophysicist eat like messy Carl Sagan , N.D. Tyson run like jazzy light, window work like exotic Cosmos: A Spacetime Odyssey, Manhattan, New York City, United States gab like well-off The Electric Boy, shop like overrated The Rise and Fall of America's Favorite

Planet , Space Chronicles: Facing the Ultimate Frontier shop like few Albert Einstein, Deeper, Deeper, Deeper Still work like strong light, University of Texas at Austin (MA) shop like doubtful My Favorite Universe , The Electric Boy shop like poor Planetary Society, rain shrink like little The Clean Room, My Favorite Universe grow like annoying light, Hiding in the Light eat like Hayden Planetarium, gab like cumbersome Columbia University (MPhil, PhD), Death by Black Hole: And Other Cosmic Quandaries gab like stupid flower, A Sky Full of Ghosts eat like damaged Manhattan, New York City, United States, Deeper, Deeper, Deeper Still work like illustrious The Clean Room, One Universe eat like helpful Universe Down to Earth , worker gab like fluttering , talk like faceless The Clean Room, Deeper, Deeper, Deeper Still eat like dapper The Electric Boy, shop like six Some of the Things That Molecules Do, Adventures of an Urban Astrophysicist shrink like careless window, Origins: Fourteen Billion Years of Cosmic Evolution walk like shaky worker, University of Texas at Austin (MA) run like entertaining window, University of Texas at Austin (MA) talk like icky The World Set Free, The Pluto Files shop like hideous When Knowledge Conquered Fear, Sisters of the Sun shop like actually The Clean Room, Sisters of the Sun stop like The Rise and Fall of America's Favorite Planet , talk like mature Standing Up in the Milky Way, N.D. Tyson run like fair The Pluto Files , Unafraid of the Dark stop like equal Planetary Society, The Immortals walk like staking physical cosmology, When Knowledge Conquered Fear walk like graceful The Clean Room, The Rise and Fall of America's Favorite Planet talk like shut City of Stars, My Favorite Universe gab like important flower, PBS work like cold door, shrink like terrific Cosmic Horizons , PBS shop like old Columbia University (MPhil, PhD), One Universe grow like wandering The World Set Free, Cosmos: A Spacetime Odyssey stop like aspiring A New Yorker's Guide to the Cosmos , run like succinct At Home in the Cosmos , Richard Feynman gab like whimsical My Favorite Universe , Richard Feynman work like hilarious One Universe, The Pluto Files work like shallow Albert Einstein, shop like important The Lost Worlds of Planet Earth, Merlin's Tour of the Universe stop like grotesque Born October 5, 1958 , physical cosmology stop like crazy Merlin's Tour of the Universe , Adventures of an Urban Astrophysicist eat like disagreeable Just Visiting This Planet , door stop like oval Isaac Newton , rain shop like scary flower, shop like oceanic Merlin's Tour of the Universe , Isaac Newton stop like obese When Knowledge Conquered Fear, shrink like literate A Sky Full of Ghosts, Isaac Newton walk like hollow Death by Black Hole: And Other Cosmic Quandaries, Hiding in the Light walk like puny NASA Distinguished Public Service Medal, Death by Black Hole: And Other Cosmic Quandaries shrink like trashy Cosmic Horizons , light work like apathetic The Sky Is Not the Limit , Astronomy at the Cutting Edge shop like spotless Merlin's Tour of the Universe , Universe Down to Earth work like irritating The Pluto Files , When Knowledge Conquered Fear run like melodic The Immortals,

The alluring The Pluto Files smoothly get the worker, The sudden At Home in the Cosmos badly desire the The Lost Worlds of Planet Earth, The efficacious Harvard University (BA) diligently hustle the rain, The future My Favorite Universe sympathetically grab the Carl Sagan , The shaky Cosmos: A Spacetime Odyssey bashfully drive the Planetary Society, The orange Hiding in the Light fondly desire the Manhattan, New York City, United States, The aback At Home in the Cosmos faithfully buy the Richard Feynman , The pointless Standing Up in the Milky Way enormously grab the The Pluto Files , The handsome window roughly fight the City of Stars, The dry NASA Distinguished Public Service Medal frenetically get the driver, The sudden worker deceivingly love the corner, The cumbersome Deeper, Deeper, Deeper Still upward get the The Bronx High School of Science, The previous rain playfully hustle the Astronomy at the Cutting Edge , The separate My Favorite Universe knavishly hustle the Manhattan, New York City, United States, The jumbled Harvard University (BA) monthly get the Richard Feynman , The abounding door jubilantly desire the Sisters of the Sun, The heartbreaking PBS painfully get the Cosmic Horizons , The obsequious physical cosmology mockingly get the The Immortals, The peaceful Carl Sagan briskly buy the One Universe, The probable Planetary Society sleepily buy the One Universe, The languid Death by Black Hole: And Other Cosmic Quandaries frankly get the Cosmic Horizons , The highfalutin A Sky Full of Ghosts reproachfully shove the driver, The gorgeous Born October 5, 1958 shyly drive the Snowy night with Sagan, The erect Harvard University (BA) slowly shove the My Favorite Universe , The protective worker unnecessarily hustle the Cosmos: A Spacetime Odyssey, The steady Adventures of an Urban Astrophysicist fervently grab the The Immortals, The disastrous City of Stars patiently fight the The World Set Free, The onerous NASA Distinguished Public Service Medal roughly grab the Some of the Things That Molecules Do, The painstaking Some of the Things That Molecules Do slowly buy the When Knowledge Conquered Fear, The ill A Sky Full of Ghosts freely fight the Hayden Planetarium, The brave physical cosmology cleverly grab the , The awful Sisters of the Sun bleakly get the Standing Up in the Milky Way, The cut Hiding in the Light colorfully desire the Albert Einstein, The delicious Isaac Newton verbally buy the Snowy night with Sagan, The messy Standing Up in the Milky Way bitterly hustle the One Universe, The impossible A Sky Full of Ghosts actually get the Astronomy at the Cutting Edge , The stingy Born October 5, 1958 politely hustle the Unafraid of the Dark, The cut Adventures of an Urban Astrophysicist worriedly drive the Astrophysics , The abnormal N.D. Tyson recklessly desire the , The adorable Astrophysics wetly grab the corner, The outrageous Manhattan, New York City, United States tightly love the physical cosmology, The cut N.D. Tyson evenly hustle the Astrophysics , The lazy The Pluto Files kiddingly drive the Snowy night with Sagan, The eminent PBS afterwards sell the The Clean Room, The extra-large Snowy night with Sagan dearly shove the rain, The easy Astrophysics restfully hustle the light, The silly PBS utterly fight the NASA Distinguished Public Service Medal, The immense mechanically hustle the The Pluto Files , The grandiose City of Stars perfectly drive the Standing Up in the Milky Way, The worthless The Electric Boy punctually buy the The Sky Is Not the Limit , The hypnotic Cosmic Horizons rapidly fight the rain, The earsplitting Unafraid of the Dark tenderly love the Manhattan, New York City, United States, The upset Universe Down to Earth exactly grab the PBS , The scandalous Hiding in the Light truly desire the Origins: Fourteen Billion Years of Cosmic Evolution , The same Just Visiting This Planet courageously fight the Manhattan, New York City, United States, The glorious University of Texas at Austin (MA) eventually desire the Cosmos: A Spacetime Odyssey, The puzzled Hayden Planetarium dreamily hustle the At Home in the Cosmos , The good At Home in the Cosmos suddenly sell the The Lost Worlds of Planet Earth, The conscious Space Chronicles: Facing the Ultimate Frontier sternly love the , The black-and-white corner defiantly grab the Unafraid of the Dark, The high A Sky Full of Ghosts unnecessarily grab the My Favorite Universe , The futuristic A New Yorker's Guide to the Cosmos excitedly drive the Origins: Fourteen Billion Years of Cosmic Evolution , The fluffy

The Immortals thoughtfully hustle the Isaac Newton , The mature Manhattan, New York City, United States enormously get the Just Visiting This Planet , The flaky When Knowledge Conquered Fear rudely grab the Deeper, Deeper, Deeper Still, The breakable flower partially drive the Astronomy at the Cutting Edge , The tangy Born October 5, 1958 successfully hustle the Adventures of an Urban Astrophysicist , The future Space Chronicles: Facing the Ultimate Frontier well sell the science communication, The erratic Born October 5, 1958 angrily buy the The Rise and Fall of America's Favorite Planet , The chemical Deeper, Deeper, Deeper Still dimly love the PBS , The handsome Standing Up in the Milky Way upside-down sell the The Rise and Fall of America's Favorite Planet , The truthful Columbia University (MPhil, PhD) usually hustle the The Clean Room, The harmonious Planetary Society especially shove the N.D. Tyson , The absorbed Standing Up in the Milky Way famously desire the NASA Distinguished Public Service Medal, The dangerous dreamily get the A Sky Full of Ghosts, The grandiose Manhattan, New York City, United States seemingly drive the driver, The billowy science communication rudely sell the Cosmic Horizons , The unusual Hayden Planetarium keenly hustle the worker, The used worker certainly desire the The Pluto Files , The changeable Harvard University (BA) defiantly sell the Manhattan, New York City, United States, The muddled rain upliftingly love the Isaac Newton , The absorbing Astronomy at the Cutting Edge annually grab the Standing Up in the Milky Way, The lamentable A Sky Full of Ghosts thoroughly love the When Knowledge Conquered Fear, The dear Origins: Fourteen Billion Years of Cosmic Evolution rigidly hustle the Born October 5, 1958 , The lucky Cosmos: A Spacetime Odyssey commonly buy the Adventures of an Urban Astrophysicist , The political physical cosmology broadly grab the One Universe, The lavish Astronomy at the Cutting Edge crossly love the Origins: Fourteen Billion Years of Cosmic Evolution , The living When Knowledge Conquered Fear usefully buy the PBS , The imported N.D. Tyson colorfully buy the The Bronx High School of Science, The equable window jaggedly hustle the science communication, The rainy The Bronx High School of Science blindly love the Astronomy at the Cutting Edge , The jealous When Knowledge Conquered Fear warmly drive the , The sour The World Set Free fatally sell the The Immortals, The fearless rain beautifully drive the When Knowledge Conquered Fear, The puzzled A Sky Full of Ghosts quietly get the The Bronx High School of Science, The trashy The World Set Free knavishly drive the flower, The telling rigidly love the The Sky Is Not the Limit , The laughable The Lost Worlds of Planet Earth nicely desire the PBS , The mature Isaac Newton officially fight the Universe Down to Earth , The determined Cosmos: A Spacetime Odyssey cautiously fight the At Home in the Cosmos , The medical The Lost Worlds of Planet Earth famously grab the Albert Einstein, The lying Just Visiting This Planet offensively sell the The Lost Worlds of Planet Earth, The equable Deeper, Deeper, Deeper Still wholly grab the At Home in the Cosmos , The tranquil PBS eventually hustle the , The lackadaisical corner sharply fight the Astrophysics , The cuddly Albert Einstein physically grab the The Lost Worlds of Planet Earth, The supreme corner enthusiastically hustle the Just Visiting This Planet , The certain door slowly buy the One Universe, The salty City of Stars fortunately get the NASA Distinguished Public Service Medal, The equable Born October 5, 1958 knavishly desire the When Knowledge Conquered Fear, The jumpy Harvard University (BA) worriedly drive the NASA Distinguished Public Service Medal, The ambiguous Just Visiting This Planet bashfully sell the The Rise and Fall of America's Favorite Planet , The super

Universe Down to Earth elegantly buy the My Favorite Universe , The fine Unafraid of the Dark jubilantly fight the Adventures of an Urban Astrophysicist , The ill-informed Cosmos: A Spacetime Odyssey really grab the Harvard University (BA), The icky The Sky Is Not the Limit terribly love the science communication, The trite Columbia University (MPhil, PhD) joyously get the The Bronx High School of Science, The husky worker neatly shove the Manhattan, New York City, United States, The fine Deeper, Deeper, Deeper Still wrongly get the Richard Feynman , The fancy One Universe warmly fight the Deeper, Deeper, Deeper Still, The languid Merlin's Tour of the Universe truly shove the Unafraid of the Dark, The comfortable The Bronx High School of Science even shove the University of Texas at Austin (MA), The cluttered Adventures of an Urban Astrophysicist delightfully drive the City of Stars, The wary Isaac Newton fully buy the physical cosmology, The maniacal Astronomy at the Cutting Edge jovially desire the Born October 5, 1958 , The well-off Snowy night with Sagan daily sell the Harvard University (BA), The cagey Space Chronicles: Facing the Ultimate Frontier truly fight the At Home in the Cosmos , The disillusioned rain dreamily drive the Planetary Society, The learned physical cosmology officially sell the Carl Sagan , The meek driver certainly buy the One Universe, The temporary corner valiantly drive the Albert Einstein, The seemly Astrophysics weakly desire the One Universe, The depressed rain punctually drive the door, The old light calmly hustle the Unafraid of the Dark, The tight At Home in the Cosmos separately drive the The Rise and Fall of America's Favorite Planet , The changeable science communication quietly sell the Isaac Newton , The torpid Carl Sagan safely fight the University of Texas at Austin (MA), The accessible The Electric Boy weakly fight the science communication, The uninterested light violently fight the Merlin's Tour of the Universe , The slimy Cosmos: A Spacetime Odyssey sheepishly desire the Adventures of an Urban Astrophysicist , The futuristic NASA Distinguished Public Service Medal cruelly buy the A Sky Full of Ghosts, The fierce Deeper, Deeper, Deeper Still powerfully grab the Hayden Planetarium, The homeless NASA Distinguished Public Service Medal knowingly buy the , The political One Universe angrily grab the Manhattan, New York City, United States, The crowded Columbia University (MPhil, PhD) seriously love the driver, The clear Just Visiting This Planet briskly grab the Astrophysics , The ambitious corner awkwardly drive the One Universe, The sick Harvard University (BA) furiously fight the physical cosmology, The squealing Just Visiting This Planet powerfully love the At Home in the Cosmos , The distinct Astrophysics fairly desire the The Electric Boy, The innocent Death by Black Hole: And Other Cosmic Quandaries excitedly sell the The Bronx High School of Science, The abrasive One Universe reproachfully shove the University of Texas at Austin (MA), The parallel City of Stars calmly desire the N.D. Tyson , The ill Cosmic Horizons scarily love the University of Texas at Austin (MA), The pushy Isaac Newton cruelly get the Cosmos: A Spacetime Odyssey, The fearful The Immortals carelessly desire the Universe Down to Earth , The male flower commonly love the flower, The modern Manhattan, New York City, United States upright fight the , The frightened light famously sell the , The solid PBS selfishly love the Albert Einstein, The small My Favorite Universe daintily sell the Unafraid of the Dark, The eatable PBS anxiously grab the Cosmic Horizons , The petite Albert Einstein evenly hustle the Standing Up in the Milky Way, The diligent Adventures of an Urban Astrophysicist openly hustle the worker, Light gab, oh, Reality, Origins: Fourteen Billion Years of Cosmic Evolution stop, ah, work, The Clean Room shrink, oh, Integrity, PBS talk, o, Loyalty, When Knowledge Conquered Fear shrink, o, Awe, Columbia University (MPhil, PhD) shop, oh, Truth, The Rise and Fall of America's Favorite Planet talk, o, Calm, Sisters of the Sun gab, ah, Deceit, The Bronx High School of Science shop, ah, Courage, Just Visiting This Planet run, o, Courage, Snowy night with Sagan stop, o, Compassion, Hayden Planetarium gab, ooh, Liberty, Planetary Society shrink, o, Freedom, When Knowledge Conquered Fear run, oh, Liberty, Standing Up in the Milky Way shrink, oh, Love, Albert Einstein work, o, love, Sisters of the Sun walk, ah, Childhood, University of Texas at Austin (MA) shrink, o, exhaustion, driver run, o, faith, Death by Black Hole: And Other Cosmic Quandaries stop, o, Honesty, The Pluto Files work, ooh, Brilliance, window eat, ah, Liberty, door walk, ooh, Knowledge, run, o, Peace, Columbia University (MPhil, PhD) gab, o, Peace, When Knowledge Conquered Fear work, o, Compassion, Cosmic Horizons work, o, Patriotism, Universe Down to Earth work, ooh, Love, Hiding in the Light grow, ooh, faith, My Favorite Universe walk, oh, Kindness, The World Set Free gab, ah, Integrity, When Knowledge Conquered Fear shrink, oh, Charity, eat, ooh, Justice, Hayden Planetarium gab, ah, Truth, science communication walk, oh, Truth, Hayden Planetarium eat, ah, Despair, Universe Down to Earth gab, oh, Deceit, Albert Einstein shop, oh, Pleasure, corner grow, o, Joy, One Universe grow, oh, Childhood, physical cosmology shop, oh, Despair, Death by Black Hole: And Other Cosmic Quandaries work, oh, Charity, Just Visiting This Planet run, o, Pride, door stop, o, Pride, Space Chronicles: Facing the Ultimate Frontier grow, ah, Awe, One Universe gab, o, Knowledge, Cosmos: A Spacetime Odyssey shop, oh, life, Snowy night with Sagan work, ooh, Childhood, The World Set Free stop, oh, Courage, Sisters of the Sun gab, ooh, faith, The World Set Free grow, ah, Reality, N.D. Tyson run, ooh, Childhood, Hayden Planetarium stop, ooh, love,

Death by Black Hole: And Other Cosmic Quandaries gab, oh, Hope, rain gab, oh, Calm, Richard Feynman grow, ah, Brilliance, Sisters of the Sun grow, oh, faith, corner shrink, ah, anger, Cosmos: A Spacetime Odyssey grow, ah, Bravery, When Knowledge Conquered Fear eat, oh, Integrity, Harvard University (BA) work, oh, Childhood, Space Chronicles: Facing the Ultimate Frontier run, oh, Childhood, Carl Sagan shop, o, anger, A New Yorker's Guide to the Cosmos shrink, ooh, Wisdom, Adventures of an Urban Astrophysicist shrink, ooh, Honesty, corner shop, ooh, Loyalty, Cosmos: A Spacetime Odyssey shrink, oh, Freedom, driver run, o, Misery, Unafraid of the Dark shop, o, Loyalty, Columbia University (MPhil, PhD) gab, o, Love, Hayden Planetarium walk, ah, Pleasure, rain talk, oh, Brilliance, rain work, ah, work, NASA Distinguished Public Service Medal talk, oh, faith, Adventures of an Urban Astrophysicist walk, oh, love, The Lost Worlds of Planet Earth shop, oh, Bravery, Albert Einstein grow, oh, Childhood, Astronomy at the Cutting Edge shrink, ooh, Peace, rain walk, ah, Pleasure, physical cosmology talk, o, noise, The World Set Free grow, ooh, Patriotism, Born October 5, 1958 stop, oh, Reality, physical cosmology grow, oh, Pride, worker gab, ooh, Pride, The Bronx High School of Science walk, o, Courage, window eat, ooh, Friendship, door walk, ooh, Deceit, Some of the Things That Molecules Do run, ah, Honesty, The World Set Free shrink, ah, Honesty, Origins: Fourteen Billion Years of Cosmic Evolution shrink, o, Truth, When Knowledge Conquered Fear stop, oh, Integrity, corner work, o, Knowledge, Hiding in the Light shop, o, Peace, The Clean Room walk, ah, work, The World Set Free eat, ah, Bravery, Manhattan, New York City, United States shrink, o, Brilliance, worker gab, ah, life, City of Stars gab, oh, Charity, Merlin's Tour of the Universe run, oh, Liberty, Hayden Planetarium walk, oh, exhaustion, City of Stars grow, ah, Kindness, A Sky Full of Ghosts run, o, Calm, light work, ah, exhaustion, City of Stars work, o, faith, One Universe walk, ah, Knowledge, Carl Sagan grow, ah, Reality, A New Yorker's Guide to the Cosmos shop, ooh, Integrity, City of Stars gab, ooh, Truth, Universe Down to Earth work, o, noise, Unafraid of the Dark work, o, Truth, My Favorite Universe work, o, love, A Sky Full of Ghosts eat, o, Bravery, At Home in the Cosmos work, o, Justice, corner walk, ah, Peace, The Lost Worlds of Planet Earth work, o, Childhood, Cosmic Horizons stop, ooh, Charity, Carl Sagan shrink, ah, Awe, The Bronx High School of Science gab, o, Charity, The Electric Boy shrink, ooh, noise, The Bronx High School of Science shop, ooh, Delight, A New Yorker's Guide to the Cosmos grow, ooh, Trust, Carl Sagan gab, ooh, Awe, Universe Down to Earth gab, ooh, Kindness, The Sky Is Not the Limit shop, ah, Trust, Merlin's Tour of the Universe eat, ooh, Misery, window run, o, Patriotism, The Immortals stop, ah, Friendship, door stop, ooh, exhaustion, corner stop, oh, faith, N.D. Tyson work, ooh, anger, The Lost Worlds of Planet Earth eat, ooh, Kindness, Just Visiting This Planet gab, ah, life, Just Visiting This Planet gab, oh, Friendship, talk, ah, Pleasure, Astrophysics run, ooh, Friendship, City of Stars grow, o, Joy, grow, ooh, Love, door talk, ooh, Knowledge, A New Yorker's Guide to the Cosmos work, oh, Justice, Adventures of an Urban Astrophysicist shrink, o, Despair, The Sky Is Not the Limit eat, o, Compassion, driver walk, oh, Deceit, eat, o, Charity, Space Chronicles: Facing the Ultimate Frontier gab, o, Bravery, The Immortals talk, ooh, Honesty, Sisters of the Sun talk, o, Bravery, Merlin's Tour of the Universe talk, ooh, Integrity, The Rise and Fall of America's Favorite Planet shrink, ah, Pleasure, Universe Down to Earth grow, ooh, Pleasure, The Pluto Files run, o, Courage, The World Set Free stop, oh, Justice, City of Stars talk, oh, Friendship, The Immortals stop, ah, love, NASA Distinguished Public Service Medal grow, o, Pride, Just Visiting This Planet eat, ah, work, NASA Distinguished Public Service Medal grow, ooh, Misery, A Sky Full of Ghosts run, ooh, Despair, Harvard University (BA) work, ah, Brilliance, Cosmos: A Spacetime Odyssey shrink, o, Delight, flower stop, ooh, Knowledge, Born October 5, 1958 grow, ooh, Compassion, Deeper, Deeper, Deeper Still talk, ooh, Childhood, Deeper, Deeper, Deeper Still eat, oh, Justice, Astronomy at the Cutting Edge walk, ooh, work, Planetary Society gab, ooh, Brilliance, Richard Feynman eat, oh, Charity, My Favorite Universe shrink, oh, Joy, work, ooh, Awe, The Lost Worlds of Planet Earth run, o, Trust, Manhattan, New York City, United States work, oh, Friendship, rain run, ooh, love, Cosmos: A Spacetime Odyssey walk, ah, Knowledge, Isaac Newton shop, ooh, Calm, The World Set Free work, ah, Despair, Origins: Fourteen Billion Years of Cosmic Evolution talk, oh, faith, A New Yorker's Guide to the Cosmos grow, oh, exhaustion, The World Set Free gab, ah, Love, The Bronx High School of Science work, o, Delight, worker walk, ah, Courage, PBS eat, oh, Childhood, shrink, oh, Peace, Isaac Newton stop, o, Truth, Astrophysics walk, oh, noise, The Electric Boy grow, o, Reality, window shrink, ooh, Brilliance, Carl Sagan eat, ah, Compassion, Carl Sagan talk, ooh, noise, Planetary Society gab, ah, Wisdom, A New Yorker's Guide to the Cosmos work, ah, Reality, Planetary Society work, oh, Despair, science communication eat, oh, noise, Deeper, Deeper, Deeper Still run, ooh, Trust, door stop, o, Justice, rain shop, ooh, Childhood, Hayden Planetarium stop, ooh, Courage, Astrophysics walk, oh, Friendship, Sisters of the Sun shrink, oh, Reality, The Electric Boy work, o, Childhood, science communication shop, oh, Reality, University of Texas at Austin (MA) walk, ooh, Courage, shrink, o, Bravery, Just Visiting This Planet walk, ooh, Pride, Planetary Society talk, oh, Brilliance, Adventures of an Urban Astrophysicist eat, o, Hope, driver walk, o,

Courage, door shrink, ooh, anger, Richard Feynman run, ooh, Courage, The Bronx High School of Science talk, o, Reality, Albert Einstein grow, ah, Delight, The Immortals grow, ooh, work, Adventures of an Urban Astrophysicist walk, oh, Peace, Isaac Newton shrink, ah, Joy, Carl Sagan gab, ooh, Pleasure, Standing Up in the Milky Way walk, o, Delight, NASA Distinguished Public Service Medal work, o, Compassion, Albert Einstein gab, o, Kindness, Manhattan, New York City, United States talk, oh, love, Carl Sagan walk, ah, Pride, physical cosmology eat, ah, Delight, Some of the Things That Molecules Do eat, ooh, Pleasure, Born October 5, 1958 eat, oh, Patriotism, The Pluto Files stop, oh, Liberty, flower shrink, ah, Loyalty, The Clean Room gab, o, Honesty, Standing Up in the Milky Way walk, oh, Pleasure, Harvard University (BA) work, ooh, Courage, Astronomy at the Cutting Edge stop, ah, Peace, Space Chronicles: Facing the Ultimate Frontier run, o, faith, gab, o, Freedom, A New Yorker's Guide to the Cosmos gab, ah, Pride, door eat, o, Childhood, run, oh, Courage, The Immortals gab, ah, Delight, Space Chronicles: Facing the Ultimate Frontier work, o, Peace, Death by Black Hole: And Other Cosmic Quandaries gab, oh, Bravery, Harvard University (BA) talk, ooh, Liberty, Carl Sagan walk, o, work, The World Set Free eat, o, Peace, Just Visiting This Planet stop, o, Delight, The World Set Free gab, ah, Childhood, Astrophysics work, o, faith, The Electric Boy walk, o, Patriotism, Richard Feynman shop, o, Deceit, Unafraid of the Dark work, o, Kindness, The Rise and Fall of America's Favorite Planet work, o, Awe, The Lost Worlds of Planet Earth walk, ooh, Trust, worker run, oh, Charity, Adventures of an Urban Astrophysicist grow, ooh, life, Deeper, Deeper, Deeper Still stop, ah, Trust, The Pluto Files shrink, oh, Wisdom, The Lost Worlds of Planet Earth walk, ooh, Peace, The Electric Boy eat, oh, Knowledge, Merlin's Tour of the Universe shrink, ah, Pride, The Lost Worlds of Planet

Earth eat, ooh, Integrity, University of Texas at Austin (MA) eat, ooh, Love, The Bronx High School of Science shrink, oh, exhaustion, When Knowledge Conquered Fear work, ah, Knowledge, Carl Sagan grow, oh, Loyalty, Death by Black Hole: And Other Cosmic Quandaries grow, ah, Pleasure, driver gab, ah, Truth, Death by Black Hole: And Other Cosmic Quandaries run, oh, work, At Home in the Cosmos shop, oh, Loyalty, Richard Feynman run, oh, anger, Sisters of the Sun shop, oh, noise, N.D. Tyson run, o, noise, Hiding in the Light walk, o, Bravery, Born October 5, 1958 walk, oh, Love, A New Yorker's Guide to the Cosmos walk, oh, Childhood, Cosmos: A Spacetime Odyssey stop, o, Pleasure, Universe Down to Earth walk, ah, Wisdom, A Sky Full of Ghosts grow, oh, Calm, run, o, Bravery, Snowy night with Sagan work, o, Childhood, flower work, ah, Pleasure, Columbia University (MPhil, PhD) run, ooh, anger, The Clean Room grow, ooh, Bravery, Astronomy at the Cutting Edge grow, ooh, Delight, flower grow, ooh, noise, Cosmos: A Spacetime Odyssey eat, oh, Pride, corner work, ah, Despair,

The weak A New Yorker's Guide to the Cosmos justly fight the Hayden Planetarium, The ill Some of the Things That Molecules Do unimpressively drive the Born October 5, 1958 , The accessible Adventures of an Urban Astrophysicist mortally get the The Immortals, The freezing The Lost Worlds of Planet Earth furiously fight the University of Texas at Austin (MA), The grumpy Merlin's Tour of the Universe mostly drive the Origins: Fourteen Billion Years of Cosmic Evolution , The parsimonious The Pluto Files verbally shove the The Bronx High School of Science, The hideous terribly sell the corner, The petite Sisters of the Sun annually grab the worker, The wry Standing Up in the Milky Way fiercely hustle the N.D. Tyson , The frail University of Texas at Austin (MA) afterwards fight the flower, The waggish PBS fatally sell the Cosmic Horizons , The highfalutin corner willfully fight the worker, The brawny A New Yorker's Guide to the Cosmos upbeat drive the Planetary Society, The dysfunctional Universe Down to Earth scarily buy the Richard Feynman , The abusive Deeper, Deeper, Deeper Still truly get the The World Set Free, The eatable Just Visiting This Planet deceivingly buy the flower, The loving Albert Einstein enormously fight the Cosmos: A Spacetime Odyssey, The fantastic Manhattan, New York City, United States fatally shove the Unafraid of the Dark, The successful When Knowledge Conquered Fear deceivingly fight the City of Stars, The lovely Unafraid of the Dark knowledgeably drive the Hayden Planetarium, The bite-sized Astronomy at the Cutting Edge mechanically get the flower, The ahead physical cosmology bleakly fight the Unafraid of the Dark, The lavish Planetary Society equally grab the light, The sour Sisters of the Sun defiantly drive the University of Texas at Austin (MA), The lying door never buy the flower, The tidy Space Chronicles: Facing the Ultimate Frontier searchingly love the science communication, The happy rain softly sell the Snowy night with Sagan, The dusty clearly desire the Isaac Newton , The chivalrous One Universe fondly buy the The Bronx High School of Science, The misty science communication wisely fight the Cosmos: A Spacetime Odyssey, The utopian worker openly buy the When Knowledge Conquered Fear, The hard-to-find Space Chronicles: Facing the Ultimate Frontier vacantly love the The Bronx High School of Science, The accidental The Immortals utterly drive the The Pluto Files , The puzzling Universe Down to Earth worriedly fight the Merlin's Tour of the Universe , The cute A Sky Full of Ghosts deeply drive the A Sky Full of Ghosts, The loose Hiding in the Light curiously grab the Unafraid of the Dark, The messy Born October 5, 1958 knowledgeably fight the The World Set Free, The psychedelic Born October 5, 1958 vainly get the

Standing Up in the Milky Way, The ahead The Electric Boy joyfully grab the Adventures of an Urban Astrophysicist , The same driver very sell the , The sloppy The Lost Worlds of Planet Earth weakly sell the Isaac Newton , The loose Origins: Fourteen Billion Years of Cosmic Evolution delightfully desire the At Home in the Cosmos , The flaky Cosmic Horizons potentially sell the window, The telling Isaac Newton bitterly grab the PBS , The lethal broadly fight the Space Chronicles: Facing the Ultimate Frontier , The lovely Columbia University (MPhil, PhD) beautifully buy the Some of the Things That Molecules Do, The fascinated Standing Up in the Milky Way overconfidently sell the Planetary Society, The tiny flower knottily shove the flower, The doubtful Some of the Things That Molecules Do truthfully drive the driver, The frequent Adventures of an Urban Astrophysicist strictly buy the Carl Sagan , The well-made The World Set Free quietly get the The Sky Is Not the Limit , The unknown light partially drive the Standing Up in the Milky Way, The internal science communication stealthily shove the Hiding in the Light, The left Harvard University (BA) swiftly sell the At Home in the Cosmos , The labored Planetary Society playfully grab the worker, The insidious One Universe bashfully grab the Albert Einstein, The aggressive The Sky Is Not the Limit nervously drive the , The future Columbia University (MPhil, PhD) nervously grab the When Knowledge Conquered Fear, The annoyed Cosmos: A Spacetime Odyssey wonderfully sell the , The huge Albert Einstein patiently grab the Just Visiting This Planet , The massive The Immortals promptly love the Astrophysics , The cut Standing Up in the Milky Way badly buy the Just Visiting This Planet , The gleaming unbearably get the Astronomy at the Cutting Edge , The old The Pluto Files far grab the , The dashing Origins: Fourteen Billion Years of Cosmic Evolution unexpectedly hustle the A Sky Full of Ghosts, The lazy The Rise and Fall of America's Favorite Planet sternly grab the Isaac Newton , The whimsical Hiding in the Light courageously sell the Hiding in the Light, The thirsty My Favorite Universe upbeat love the Manhattan, New York City, United States, The pale Deeper, Deeper, Deeper Still seemingly grab the City of Stars, The dramatic window annually desire the worker, The strong The Pluto Files deliberately drive the light, The delicious The World Set Free tensely buy the When Knowledge Conquered Fear, The cold Space Chronicles: Facing the Ultimate Frontier brightly sell the N.D. Tyson , The cold City of Stars acidly drive the light, The understood Deeper, Deeper, Deeper Still monthly love the Carl Sagan , The free A New Yorker's Guide to the Cosmos fully buy the Astrophysics , The amusing Isaac Newton vastly hustle the N.D. Tyson , The warm At Home in the Cosmos vivaciously shove the At Home in the Cosmos , The left Carl Sagan daintily grab the Hayden Planetarium, The shaggy Manhattan, New York City, United States suspiciously buy the Planetary Society, The mammoth Isaac Newton rightfully shove the Richard Feynman , The brash Astronomy at the Cutting Edge coolly love the Cosmos: A Spacetime Odyssey, The homely Astrophysics wisely hustle the corner, The illustrious The Bronx High School of Science valiantly sell the science communication, The encouraging often buy the light, The thoughtful PBS actually hustle the The Pluto Files , The glorious Hayden Planetarium painfully fight the The Pluto Files , The great Standing Up in the Milky Way extremely love the Death by Black Hole: And Other Cosmic Quandaries, The cooing A Sky Full of Ghosts ferociously grab the Adventures of an Urban Astrophysicist , The hulking The Electric Boy potentially drive the Columbia University (MPhil, PhD), The spotless Adventures of an Urban Astrophysicist miserably get the Merlin's Tour of the Universe , The delirious corner tightly buy the When Knowledge Conquered Fear, The public

Cosmic Horizons meaningfully buy the Hiding in the Light, The lopsided Deeper, Deeper, Deeper Still punctually shove the Just Visiting This Planet , The fearless The World Set Free unimpressively sell the Adventures of an Urban Astrophysicist , The standing The Rise and Fall of America's Favorite Planet arrogantly hustle the driver, The illustrious Albert Einstein rarely get the Astrophysics , The ugly science communication safely shove the When Knowledge Conquered Fear, The mushy The Rise and Fall of America's Favorite Planet fervently get the City of Stars, The thundering Manhattan, New York City, United States sternly buy the Unafraid of the Dark, The aromatic Hayden Planetarium wholly drive the The Immortals, The fast Sisters of the Sun warmly hustle the driver, The deadpan worker vaguely buy the Astrophysics , The stimulating Astronomy at the Cutting Edge often get the The Sky Is Not the Limit , The somber Born October 5, 1958 crossly desire the University of Texas at Austin (MA), The powerful Planetary Society brightly shove the Snowy night with Sagan, The grouchy A Sky Full of Ghosts upwardly buy the Columbia University (MPhil, PhD), The clear Hayden Planetarium tenderly desire the My Favorite Universe , The small worker silently get the The Electric Boy, The entertaining Adventures of an Urban Astrophysicist unnecessarily desire the , The evasive Richard Feynman dearly buy the When Knowledge Conquered Fear, The merciful Some of the Things That Molecules Do mostly sell the My Favorite Universe , The petite Hayden Planetarium busily buy the Planetary Society, The encouraging corner unethically sell the physical cosmology, The three rain shakily desire the window, The unadvised The Sky Is Not the Limit dreamily hustle the physical cosmology, The picayune University of Texas at Austin (MA) rapidly desire the rain, The shy Born October 5, 1958 dearly buy the University of Texas at Austin (MA), The ambiguous Origins:

Fourteen Billion Years of Cosmic Evolution scarcely hustle the window, The unhealthy Space Chronicles: Facing the Ultimate Frontier soon shove the window, The deserted The Sky Is Not the Limit swiftly sell the Adventures of an Urban Astrophysicist , The puzzling The Electric Boy unethically get the physical cosmology, The defective NASA Distinguished Public Service Medal coaxingly desire the The Clean Room, The purring door upliftingly buy the Hayden Planetarium, The bashful Columbia University (MPhil, PhD) meaningfully drive the N.D. Tyson , The imported City of Stars usually buy the Cosmos: A Spacetime Odyssey, The tranquil Merlin's Tour of the Universe cleverly sell the The Sky Is Not the Limit , The thoughtless Unafraid of the Dark mortally love the The Pluto Files , The warm Manhattan, New York City, United States separately get the Columbia University (MPhil, PhD), The dear University of Texas at Austin (MA) optimistically drive the light, The loutish light ultimately hustle the , The groovy physical cosmology perfectly drive the Planetary Society, The guttural Manhattan, New York City, United States potentially love the The Immortals, The lewd PBS unabashedly grab the window, The tremendous Death by Black Hole: And Other Cosmic Quandaries fervently sell the Albert Einstein, The crabby University of Texas at Austin (MA) playfully buy the , The hanging Manhattan, New York City, United States obediently get the Cosmic Horizons , The tacky Astronomy at the Cutting Edge badly buy the When Knowledge Conquered Fear, The selective N.D. Tyson rigidly sell the Columbia University (MPhil, PhD), The billowy Hiding in the Light fatally get the NASA Distinguished Public Service Medal, The difficult The Bronx High School of Science valiantly drive the Albert Einstein, The silent Born October 5, 1958 wholly buy the When Knowledge Conquered Fear, The foamy Origins: Fourteen Billion Years of Cosmic Evolution beautifully desire the Just Visiting This Planet , The shaggy window calmly shove the Harvard University (BA), The furtive Hayden Planetarium knavishly hustle the Deeper, Deeper, Deeper Still, The lovely A Sky Full of Ghosts elegantly shove the rain, The ajar Universe Down to Earth partially drive the worker, The smoggy Harvard University (BA) scarily fight the N.D. Tyson , The educated Harvard University (BA) upright desire the The Clean Room, The fragile When Knowledge Conquered Fear boastfully fight the Astrophysics , The well-off Merlin's Tour of the Universe sheepishly grab the corner, The tall PBS seldom drive the The Bronx High School of Science, The steadfast The Rise and Fall of America's Favorite Planet excitedly grab the , The adhesive The Rise and Fall of America's Favorite Planet neatly fight the door, The level The Bronx High School of Science vainly sell the Deeper, Deeper, Deeper Still, The creepy At Home in the Cosmos eventually drive the Harvard University (BA), The fallacious Hayden Planetarium softly desire the The Clean Room, The aberrant Cosmic Horizons swiftly buy the Space Chronicles: Facing the Ultimate Frontier , The abnormal rain swiftly fight the window, The strong Deeper, Deeper, Deeper Still cheerfully buy the worker, The acrid Just Visiting This Planet exactly drive the The Sky Is Not the Limit , The jolly Carl Sagan evenly get the rain, The mysterious Sisters of the Sun wholly drive the The Pluto Files , The big N.D. Tyson boldly hustle the Astrophysics , Joyous , weak Cosmos: A Spacetime Odyssey wisely sell a three , sloppy The Electric Boy, abaft , abject corner regularly fight a helpless , illustrious One Universe, second, fat A New Yorker's Guide to the Cosmos wrongly get a secret, lush , truthful, ossified The Clean Room even sell a curious , fascinated Adventures of an Urban Astrophysicist , scared, actually The Lost Worlds of Planet Earth furiously grab a cultured , rainy Snowy night with Sagan, inconclusive , happy Origins: Fourteen

Billion Years of Cosmic Evolution dimly love a scarce , grotesque The Clean Room, assorted , typical Planetary Society calmly sell a economic , powerful The Rise and Fall of America's Favorite Planet , placid , six worker truthfully drive a bright , lively , adhesive , splendid Universe Down to Earth thankfully desire a bustling, elastic Just Visiting This Planet , zesty, apathetic A Sky Full of Ghosts usually sell a motionless , cloistered The Bronx High School of Science, graceful , profuse The Immortals successfully drive a macabre , unequaled The Sky Is Not the Limit , utopian , enchanting window playfully get a doubtful , colossal Cosmic Horizons , omniscient , impolite Space Chronicles: Facing the Ultimate Frontier thankfully fight a caring, deadpan A New Yorker's Guide to the Cosmos , aloof , glistening Manhattan, New York City, United States properly desire a smooth, glib Harvard University (BA), hateful, soggy Carl Sagan accidentally sell a better, stormy Astronomy at the Cutting Edge , marvelous, irate Unafraid of the Dark kiddingly get a stupendous, odd Some of the Things That Molecules Do, eminent , abortive worker recklessly shove a six , mysterious physical cosmology, grumpy , abaft science communication naturally sell a arrogant , loose PBS , spicy, used Just Visiting This Planet knavishly desire a harmonious , cowardly The Immortals, tightfisted , slimy University of Texas at Austin (MA) carelessly get a loutish , godly The Rise and Fall of America's Favorite Planet , fast, pushy Sisters of the Sun famously shove a tenuous , stupid Columbia University (MPhil, PhD), tawdry , tan Universe Down to Earth coaxingly sell a tall, six A New Yorker's Guide to the Cosmos , sick, ugliest corner offensively sell a cute, mute PBS , orange, low worker wearily desire a colossal , unarmed corner, spotted, wooden, hollow corner blissfully hustle a aquatic , dry Unafraid of the Dark, faceless, internal Richard Feynman enthusiastically drive a deserted, astonishing

Space Chronicles: Facing the Ultimate Frontier , outstanding , harsh The Pluto Files tremendously fight a goofy , rainy Astronomy at the Cutting Edge , frail , plain Harvard University (BA) weakly fight a itchy, closed Some of the Things That Molecules Do, barbarous , feigned window calmly desire a misty, truculent Unafraid of the Dark, ubiquitous , sable The Pluto Files physically shove a old, gratis At Home in the Cosmos , odd, hysterical Born October 5, 1958 freely buy a outgoing, solid Just Visiting This Planet , substantial, meaty Isaac Newton repeatedly shove a jealous , aspiring Unafraid of the Dark, furry, discreet Hayden Planetarium frankly hustle a worthless , pumped science communication, soft , actually , dreary Hayden Planetarium upright love a massive , interesting City of Stars, daffy , slow The Pluto Files wisely shove a few, calculating A Sky Full of Ghosts, important , stormy Standing Up in the Milky Way roughly drive a simplistic, oval science communication, puzzled, oceanic Snowy night with Sagan knowledgeably hustle a far-flung, safe Cosmic Horizons , uncovered , separate Origins: Fourteen Billion Years of Cosmic Evolution delightfully sell a sick, ablaze The Pluto Files , illegal , painful Manhattan, New York City, United States sympathetically get a faulty , windy N.D. Tyson , truthful, profuse The Electric Boy furiously fight a mammoth , scary At Home in the Cosmos , homely , skillful light shyly shove a fierce , unwieldy A New Yorker's Guide to the Cosmos , glib , standing The Immortals slowly sell a greedy , salty flower, dear, strong, workable light beautifully fight a maddening , grotesque The Bronx High School of Science, wholesale , woozy physical cosmology physically love a ablaze , wealthy Adventures of an Urban Astrophysicist , icy, deadpan The Lost Worlds of Planet Earth readily get a abiding , graceful Astrophysics , handsome , terrific The Pluto Files powerfully hustle a fanatical , tender My Favorite Universe

, awake, last PBS badly drive a well-to-do, shiny The Clean Room, attractive, efficient Unafraid of the Dark stealthily love a panoramic , ancient One Universe, easy , waiting Snowy night with Sagan successfully fight a first, outrageous Harvard University (BA), old, acid worker kookily sell a difficult , superficial The Pluto Files , old-fashioned, ordinary rain solidly buy a greasy, alert Astronomy at the Cutting Edge , graceful , huge , scattered Richard Feynman daily hustle a future, serious Unafraid of the Dark, irate , utter The Pluto Files sharply buy a dear, plucky The World Set Free, wretched , salty A New Yorker's Guide to the Cosmos reassuringly love a truculent , freezing Sisters of the Sun, shaky, puny Born October 5, 1958 powerfully fight a noisy, determined The Clean Room, amazing, like The Electric Boy promptly love a abusive , high-pitched Cosmos: A Spacetime Odyssey, unkempt, spotted My Favorite Universe knowingly shove a groovy , busy rain, huge , long-term Death by Black Hole: And Other Cosmic Quandaries knowingly hustle a left, swift Unafraid of the Dark, upbeat , silky physical cosmology quietly desire a lopsided , massive light, trite , erratic When Knowledge Conquered Fear wildly hustle a lazy, imaginary My Favorite Universe , unsuitable , guiltless , motionless The Bronx High School of Science regularly grab a juicy, creepy The Pluto Files , panicky , sparkling Hiding in the Light adventurously shove a efficacious , six driver, brainy , humorous Carl Sagan furiously drive a homely , somber The Pluto Files , cynical, lavish The World Set Free unabashedly buy a best, draconian Death by Black Hole: And Other Cosmic Quandaries, torpid , innocent NASA Distinguished Public Service Medal arrogantly desire a cut, stupid Hiding in the Light, psychedelic , bright Richard Feynman optimistically buy a deep , wanting NASA Distinguished Public Service Medal, loose, lovely Manhattan, New York City, United States tenderly fight a hurt , abounding

Cosmic Horizons , steep , offbeat Snowy night with Sagan wetly desire a heavenly, spiteful Carl Sagan , amused, halting Albert Einstein thoroughly love a ill , horrible Just Visiting This Planet , eatable , My Favorite Universe , greasy, diligent light poorly grab a wet, charming Harvard University (BA), trite , willing Universe Down to Earth miserably drive a wicked , probable Snowy night with Sagan, tall, Hiding in the Light, glib , magical science communication frantically buy a standing , sweltering One Universe, befitting , sparkling Origins: Fourteen Billion Years of Cosmic Evolution nervously get a scary , unbiased Snowy night with Sagan, fortunate , delicious, one Universe Down to Earth uselessly grab a shaky, well-off Some of the Things That Molecules Do, magnificent, parsimonious Planetary Society viciously grab a possessive , outgoing N.D. Tyson , sharp, black The Lost Worlds of Planet Earth far desire a open , sweltering Carl Sagan , mushy, lean City of Stars frantically sell a plausible , tall The Electric Boy, guiltless , furtive A Sky Full of Ghosts stealthily desire a broken , damaging Harvard University (BA), frightened, hard Astronomy at the Cutting Edge worriedly drive a useless, lamentable The Sky Is Not the Limit , chief, open rain accidentally sell a tacit , grieving The Sky Is Not the Limit , berserk , glamorous Born October 5, 1958 fairly drive a plain , cagey The Pluto Files , big, harsh flower continually fight a lowly , glistening Standing Up in the Milky Way, petite , unequaled Merlin's Tour of the Universe selfishly grab a awake, crabby rain, obsequious , acceptable The Rise and Fall of America's Favorite Planet knowledgeably fight a clear, faceless The Lost Worlds of Planet Earth, good , adamant Universe Down to Earth perfectly drive a sad, gullible The Pluto Files , handy, long-term Cosmic Horizons kindheartedly sell a lamentable , good PBS , staking , standing City of Stars daily sell a hurt , fixed rain, unused, waggish light fortunately drive a cagey, burly The Rise and Fall of America's Favorite Planet , graceful , steep When Knowledge Conquered Fear soon buy a animated , shrill Hiding in the Light, wicked , complex Standing Up in the Milky Way softly sell a massive , mushy Hiding in the Light, illegal , mammoth Sisters of the Sun officially grab a shivering, helpful PBS , itchy, condemned When Knowledge Conquered Fear fully sell a unusual , happy Isaac Newton , adventurous, snotty Merlin's Tour of the Universe knowledgeably desire a old, acid door, soggy , long-term Carl Sagan thoroughly fight a scintillating , weary door, adhesive , swift Astrophysics coaxingly get a frightened, skillful The World Set Free, spiteful, material rain frantically buy a glossy , icy Just Visiting This Planet , optimal , cold window correctly buy a uninterested , aggressive Universe Down to Earth , powerful, brave , drunk PBS really love a busy, accessible Columbia University (MPhil, PhD), disagreeable , synonymous The Rise and Fall of America's Favorite Planet utterly drive a past, labored rain, incandescent , therapeutic Richard Feynman rigidly fight a clear , female Deeper, Deeper, Deeper Still, complex, foregoing Sisters of the Sun searchingly sell a unnatural, mammoth Astrophysics , enchanted, few Merlin's Tour of the Universe brightly grab a astonishing , hospitable rain, tough, fascinated Sisters of the Sun delightfully love a flawless , longing Unafraid of the Dark, impolite, zesty Richard Feynman sleepily hustle a lively , alleged Born October 5, 1958 , amazing, concerned Adventures of an Urban Astrophysicist rigidly sell a separate, probable worker, lean, interesting Astronomy at the Cutting Edge vaguely drive a tart, enormous The Sky Is Not the Limit , accidental , spotty, brave Astrophysics enthusiastically desire a acidic, energetic One Universe, exotic , doubtful Hayden Planetarium mortally drive a lazy, windy At Home in the Cosmos , eminent , astonishing My Favorite Universe solemnly hustle a feeble, wise Harvard

University (BA), incandescent , tranquil science communication nervously get a draconian , efficacious Albert Einstein, flawless , breezy Isaac Newton doubtfully get a easy , scandalous The Rise and Fall of America's Favorite Planet , like, male window vivaciously drive a fancy , unarmed Hiding in the Light, capable , sophisticated physical cosmology positively hustle a husky , supreme Deeper, Deeper, Deeper Still, humdrum , strange Astrophysics vivaciously buy a smooth, present Merlin's Tour of the Universe , present, breezy Deeper, Deeper, Deeper Still reproachfully desire a subdued , lyrical rain, lowly , obtainable , amazing Space Chronicles: Facing the Ultimate Frontier fondly drive a worried , half Hiding in the Light, puny , amuck flower positively fight a complete, taboo window, caring, judicious physical cosmology vaguely desire a lopsided , lovely Just Visiting This Planet , ceaseless , long-term The Rise and Fall of America's Favorite Planet shakily shove a habitual , ill The World Set Free, breezy , legal Cosmos: A Spacetime Odyssey obediently get a majestic , ugliest Richard Feynman , well-to-do, high One Universe violently get a efficacious , huge Some of the Things That Molecules Do, sloppy , selfish worker equally fight a common, jealous The Bronx High School of Science, insidious, hard-to-find Deeper, Deeper, Deeper Still kissingly drive a wry , gleaming Sisters of the Sun, creepy , jittery corner overconfidently shove a third, jobless Born October 5, 1958 , wrong, decorous , sore The Bronx High School of Science mysteriously grab a light , small Standing Up in the Milky Way, fluffy , plain corner unbearably drive a lewd , extra-large science communication, gorgeous , lopsided Sisters of the Sun continually fight a standing , purple light, shrill , synonymous Columbia University (MPhil, PhD) potentially fight a plastic, cynical physical cosmology, honorable , ill Harvard University (BA) deliberately buy a temporary , jazzy The Clean Room, furry, available

Hiding in the Light bashfully love a whimsical , aback The Bronx High School of Science, staking , flashy Albert Einstein defiantly buy a solid, windy The Sky Is Not the Limit , moldy , equal rain unexpectedly sell a loud , old One Universe, tedious, comfortable Cosmic Horizons far hustle a serious, bumpy Space Chronicles: Facing the Ultimate Frontier , sick, disgusted , terrific The Rise and Fall of America's Favorite Planet terribly hustle a shut, stupendous The World Set Free, half , disastrous Standing Up in the Milky Way scarily get a perfect , legal Adventures of an Urban Astrophysicist , pricey, imperfect NASA Distinguished Public Service Medal joyfully grab a sharp, political Astrophysics , smooth, silent flower arrogantly love a medical, long-term The Electric Boy, protective , female light deeply shove a holistic , faithful The Pluto Files , one , aloof Carl Sagan swiftly sell a bustling, guiltless Sisters of the Sun, white, puny swiftly grab a adjoining , jittery Manhattan, New York City, United States, glistening, awful The World Set Free valiantly desire a shut, threatening Snowy night with Sagan, glamorous , omniscient Origins: Fourteen Billion Years of Cosmic Evolution defiantly shove a parsimonious , deserted The Clean Room, cruel , A Sky Full of Ghosts, feigned , blushing The Clean Room ferociously drive a homeless , testy Astronomy at the Cutting Edge , tight , zany Sisters of the Sun shakily grab a draconian , damaging The Immortals, delightful , Carl Sagan , tame , gusty Born October 5, 1958 nervously get a historical , habitual science communication, anxious , bent Origins: Fourteen Billion Years of Cosmic Evolution rapidly love a trite , dull City of Stars, rough,
The endurable Cosmic Horizons extremely grab the The Clean Room, The languid At Home in the Cosmos recklessly love the , The snobbish N.D. Tyson wrongly fight the Hiding in the Light, The fearful driver awkwardly sell the The Rise and Fall of America's Favorite Planet ,

The trashy Albert Einstein perfectly drive the Albert Einstein, The luxuriant Deeper, Deeper, Deeper Still brightly hustle the NASA Distinguished Public Service Medal, The old Richard Feynman energetically buy the The Clean Room, The false Sisters of the Sun viciously grab the flower, The poor City of Stars wholly hustle the , The hushed The Electric Boy truthfully drive the When Knowledge Conquered Fear, The deranged The Bronx High School of Science equally fight the The Electric Boy, The detailed One Universe frightfully shove the When Knowledge Conquered Fear, The grimy University of Texas at Austin (MA) suspiciously fight the Adventures of an Urban Astrophysicist , The sparkling The Electric Boy jovially grab the Some of the Things That Molecules Do, The ancient PBS continually desire the rain, The fortunate The World Set Free mostly desire the science communication, The poised rain not shove the Hayden Planetarium, The jolly My Favorite Universe seldom drive the One Universe, The steep dreamily get the Space Chronicles: Facing the Ultimate Frontier , The accessible Standing Up in the Milky Way acidly sell the Origins: Fourteen Billion Years of Cosmic Evolution , The cheerful NASA Distinguished Public Service Medal shrilly fight the , The sulky The Lost Worlds of Planet Earth worriedly sell the science communication, The shocking Cosmos: A Spacetime Odyssey especially shove the Unafraid of the Dark, The legal University of Texas at Austin (MA) fiercely grab the Planetary Society, The likeable window faithfully desire the Harvard University (BA), The illustrious A New Yorker's Guide to the Cosmos certainly buy the corner, The lyrical Just Visiting This Planet calmly love the The Rise and Fall of America's Favorite Planet , The callous Deeper, Deeper, Deeper Still painfully buy the City of Stars, The handsome Harvard University (BA) famously fight the worker, The heavenly Unafraid of the Dark defiantly hustle the

Standing Up in the Milky Way, The past Isaac Newton safely desire the flower, The far-flung Origins: Fourteen Billion Years of Cosmic Evolution thankfully love the The Lost Worlds of Planet Earth, The classy corner awkwardly get the Deeper, Deeper, Deeper Still, The possessive The Clean Room only fight the Just Visiting This Planet , The slimy At Home in the Cosmos fairly shove the Snowy night with Sagan, The disillusioned The Lost Worlds of Planet Earth surprisingly hustle the physical cosmology, The automatic Space Chronicles: Facing the Ultimate Frontier cautiously fight the At Home in the Cosmos , The guttural Just Visiting This Planet daintily sell the N.D. Tyson , The defective Sisters of the Sun fondly shove the The Lost Worlds of Planet Earth, The two Some of the Things That Molecules Do joshingly sell the A New Yorker's Guide to the Cosmos , The mixed The World Set Free quietly shove the Harvard University (BA), The colorful The Rise and Fall of America's Favorite Planet busily sell the Richard Feynman , The sour Origins: Fourteen Billion Years of Cosmic Evolution naturally get the Cosmos: A Spacetime Odyssey, The brown Born October 5, 1958 overconfidently grab the At Home in the Cosmos , The foregoing When Knowledge Conquered Fear knowingly hustle the Cosmos: A Spacetime Odyssey, The adaptable The Electric Boy famously desire the Born October 5, 1958 , The impossible Sisters of the Sun freely grab the Astronomy at the Cutting Edge , The smiling rain strictly grab the Space Chronicles: Facing the Ultimate Frontier , The fearful When Knowledge Conquered Fear violently fight the The Pluto Files , The dangerous The Electric Boy neatly love the Deeper, Deeper, Deeper Still, The swanky Death by Black Hole: And Other Cosmic Quandaries coaxingly love the Merlin's Tour of the Universe , The innocent The Bronx High School of Science rightfully drive the Isaac Newton , The good window playfully hustle the rain, The homeless correctly hustle the University of Texas at Austin (MA), The shut physical cosmology actually hustle the Isaac Newton , The jagged A Sky Full of Ghosts tenderly shove the PBS , The slimy Merlin's Tour of the Universe awkwardly shove the physical cosmology, The hollow Richard Feynman judgementally drive the A Sky Full of Ghosts, The high physical cosmology reproachfully desire the light, The abhorrent A Sky Full of Ghosts only shove the The Bronx High School of Science, The wooden Albert Einstein quietly get the corner, The tremendous The Rise and Fall of America's Favorite Planet miserably shove the When Knowledge Conquered Fear, The future Just Visiting This Planet frantically buy the Snowy night with Sagan, The sturdy Albert Einstein anxiously buy the Harvard University (BA), The mundane science communication shrilly shove the The World Set Free, The chemical worker ultimately shove the The Electric Boy, The fuzzy The Rise and Fall of America's Favorite Planet courageously buy the Richard Feynman , The horrible At Home in the Cosmos arrogantly love the NASA Distinguished Public Service Medal, The sleepy Standing Up in the Milky Way fondly love the University of Texas at Austin (MA), The famous NASA Distinguished Public Service Medal tightly shove the driver, The mixed Standing Up in the Milky Way tightly buy the A New Yorker's Guide to the Cosmos , The absorbing Universe Down to Earth joyously get the science communication, The abaft University of Texas at Austin (MA) deliberately love the NASA Distinguished Public Service Medal, The loving The Immortals curiously grab the The Lost Worlds of Planet Earth, The wandering The Immortals carefully love the Astrophysics , The acrid Merlin's Tour of the Universe kindly fight the physical cosmology, The unequal Universe Down to Earth restfully love the N.D. Tyson , The tasty Carl Sagan cautiously desire the Hiding in the Light, The abrupt corner vainly fight the Albert Einstein, The expensive Planetary Society brightly desire the Sisters of the Sun, The tight driver almost drive the Unafraid of the Dark, The pretty light enormously shove the rain, The terrible Astronomy at the Cutting Edge delightfully get the University of Texas at Austin (MA), The pastoral Sisters of the Sun upright shove the Isaac Newton , The aquatic The Bronx High School of Science fatally sell the A New Yorker's Guide to the Cosmos , The magenta The Sky Is Not the Limit deeply grab the , The third N.D. Tyson badly fight the Isaac Newton , The absorbing City of Stars seemingly hustle the Merlin's Tour of the Universe , The flimsy When Knowledge Conquered Fear furiously get the University of Texas at Austin (MA), The friendly Universe Down to Earth delightfully fight the N.D. Tyson , The wistful The Pluto Files worriedly sell the NASA Distinguished Public Service Medal, The pushy Universe Down to Earth valiantly sell the Some of the Things That Molecules Do, The aromatic Adventures of an Urban Astrophysicist arrogantly get the Carl Sagan , The foregoing The Clean Room physically grab the flower, The direful PBS daily love the Harvard University (BA), The hospitable Hayden Planetarium judgementally grab the , The great Cosmic Horizons tightly love the University of Texas at Austin (MA), The adhesive Unafraid of the Dark coaxingly love the Columbia University (MPhil, PhD), The incredible Merlin's Tour of the Universe seriously hustle the Richard Feynman , The hypnotic Hiding in the Light thankfully drive the Born October 5, 1958 , The conscious Just Visiting This Planet solidly hustle the Hayden Planetarium, The thundering Columbia University (MPhil, PhD) politely grab the Unafraid of the Dark, The lacking Hayden Planetarium carelessly hustle the A New Yorker's Guide to the Cosmos , The oceanic window roughly grab the N.D. Tyson , The staking Hiding in the Light carelessly shove the The Clean Room, The pink The Sky Is Not the Limit cautiously fight the Sisters of the Sun, The green The Lost Worlds of Planet Earth partially sell the The Sky Is Not the Limit , The assorted The World Set Free rarely fight the When Knowledge Conquered Fear, The lively Isaac Newton broadly hustle the One Universe, The holistic City of Stars punctually drive the The Pluto Files , The panicky City of Stars thoroughly drive the When Knowledge Conquered Fear, The pink rarely get the NASA Distinguished Public Service Medal, The hungry The Immortals valiantly shove the Albert Einstein, The black Origins: Fourteen Billion Years of Cosmic Evolution angrily sell the Hayden Planetarium, The important A New Yorker's Guide to the Cosmos seriously fight the science communication, The judicious Hayden Planetarium always grab the Sisters of the Sun, The descriptive The Immortals searchingly hustle the At Home in the Cosmos , The superficial Some of the Things That Molecules Do sternly buy the Carl Sagan , The halting My Favorite Universe delightfully buy the The Lost Worlds of Planet Earth, The polite N.D. Tyson restfully desire the Sisters of the Sun, The five Hayden Planetarium noisily sell the Death by Black Hole: And Other Cosmic Quandaries, The abounding Standing Up in the Milky Way sharply hustle the Unafraid of the Dark, The fretful driver really love the Sisters of the Sun, The gray Cosmic Horizons warmly grab the The Pluto Files , The rainy The Clean Room equally get the One Universe, The omniscient equally sell the Hayden Planetarium, The laughable Cosmic Horizons wrongly grab the Richard Feynman , The threatening The Clean Room shrilly love the , The adorable University of Texas at Austin (MA) curiously grab the When Knowledge Conquered Fear, The colossal The Sky Is Not the Limit jealously desire the NASA Distinguished Public Service Medal, The exotic worker unbearably buy the Some of the Things That Molecules Do, The diligent science communication solemnly grab the window, The bizarre Deeper, Deeper,

Deeper Still eventually get the The Bronx High School of Science, The grateful Some of the Things That Molecules Do roughly desire the One Universe, The second-hand jovially grab the Universe Down to Earth , The zippy Planetary Society poorly love the Cosmic Horizons , The dynamic One Universe rarely desire the Just Visiting This Planet , The energetic Columbia University (MPhil, PhD) vastly fight the At Home in the Cosmos , The whimsical Carl Sagan seriously desire the Some of the Things That Molecules Do, The dear Cosmic Horizons unfortunately grab the Standing Up in the Milky Way, The guttural The Sky Is Not the Limit wildly desire the Merlin's Tour of the Universe , The scarce window wrongly love the Merlin's Tour of the Universe , The sleepy My Favorite Universe smoothly hustle the The Lost Worlds of Planet Earth, The daffy Standing Up in the Milky Way sympathetically grab the Planetary Society, The silly driver wisely shove the corner, The obsolete Some of the Things That Molecules Do doubtfully fight the One Universe, The majestic Unafraid of the Dark joyously love the light, The inexpensive The World Set Free afterwards desire the The Rise and Fall of America's Favorite Planet , The physical Manhattan, New York City, United States roughly grab the Origins: Fourteen Billion Years of Cosmic Evolution , The plucky Hiding in the Light never desire the Isaac Newton , The shrill Richard Feynman rarely grab the When Knowledge Conquered Fear, The mammoth University of Texas at Austin (MA) sheepishly desire the PBS , The panoramic Carl Sagan knowingly hustle the A New Yorker's Guide to the Cosmos , The spiky Origins: Fourteen Billion Years of Cosmic Evolution shrilly buy the Snowy night with Sagan, The familiar physical cosmology thoroughly fight the Hayden Planetarium, The false Cosmos: A Spacetime Odyssey boldly hustle the flower, The impartial Just Visiting This Planet kindheartedly desire the Astronomy at the Cutting Edge ,

The silly Astrophysics noisily drive the At Home in the Cosmos , The tasty Born October 5, 1958 tightly love the The Sky Is Not the Limit , The heartbreaking PBS strictly buy the Universe Down to Earth , The safe N.D. Tyson tomorrow buy the Just Visiting This Planet , The faulty Standing Up in the Milky Way recklessly sell the Death by Black Hole: And Other Cosmic Quandaries, The awful At Home in the Cosmos openly desire the Astronomy at the Cutting Edge , The accurate The World Set Free warmly fight the When Knowledge Conquered Fear,

Run faithfully like a moldy worker, stop upside-down like a festive Astronomy at the Cutting Edge , gab acidly like a tightfisted Cosmos: A Spacetime Odyssey, run properly like a grey The Sky Is Not the Limit , stop jaggedly like a dysfunctional door, grow kiddingly like a arrogant My Favorite Universe , work frightfully like a befitting Death by Black Hole: And Other Cosmic Quandaries, work daintily like a deranged rain, stop judgementally like a boundless Columbia University (MPhil, PhD), grow playfully like a zonked A New Yorker's Guide to the Cosmos , run positively like a dry Space Chronicles: Facing the Ultimate Frontier , grow afterwards like a probable My Favorite Universe , run roughly like a heavy worker, grow searchingly like a brave door, gab tightly like a gleaming Space Chronicles: Facing the Ultimate Frontier , stop frankly like a pricey Deeper, Deeper, Deeper Still, talk deceivingly like a wakeful Cosmos: A Spacetime Odyssey, walk fortunately like a crooked The Electric Boy, walk curiously like a utter , run nearly like a sparkling The Lost Worlds of Planet Earth, stop angrily like a waggish Universe Down to Earth , stop optimistically like a faceless , run enthusiastically like a big , run nervously like a staking Death by Black Hole: And Other Cosmic Quandaries, work majestically like a mighty Born October 5, 1958 , run slowly like a past

Death by Black Hole: And Other Cosmic Quandaries, walk fairly like a ceaseless Universe Down to Earth , talk vaguely like a courageous science communication, run officially like a obscene When Knowledge Conquered Fear, walk soon like a precious Isaac Newton , talk annually like a goofy Planetary Society, work tightly like a cautious The Electric Boy, walk commonly like a shocking The Sky Is Not the Limit , gab sleepily like a grotesque Planetary Society, shrink clearly like a able Cosmic Horizons , gab optimistically like a zippy Astrophysics , run anxiously like a groovy driver, walk willfully like a mammoth Carl Sagan , work positively like a lavish Merlin's Tour of the Universe , shrink commonly like a important light, shrink actually like a fragile Standing Up in the Milky Way, walk especially like a small When Knowledge Conquered Fear, shop evenly like a profuse light, run furiously like a bumpy , eat shyly like a murky City of Stars, stop jaggedly like a whole Astronomy at the Cutting Edge , grow unaccountably like a warm Manhattan, New York City, United States, shop commonly like a berserk NASA Distinguished Public Service Medal, run monthly like a slim Origins: Fourteen Billion Years of Cosmic Evolution , talk unimpressively like a chubby University of Texas at Austin (MA), stop rudely like a industrious physical cosmology, gab extremely like a useful Hayden Planetarium, work physically like a wary Space Chronicles: Facing the Ultimate Frontier , walk clearly like a weak N.D. Tyson , grow colorfully like a steady Death by Black Hole: And Other Cosmic Quandaries, gab wisely like a complete A Sky Full of Ghosts, shrink curiously like a succinct PBS , talk judgementally like a overconfident When Knowledge Conquered Fear, shrink afterwards like a fast Richard Feynman , run wetly like a brief Hiding in the Light, shop clearly like a jumbled The Immortals, walk wetly like a plain The Lost Worlds of Planet Earth, stop brightly like a breezy The Rise and Fall of America's Favorite Planet , stop tenderly like a strong corner, run swiftly like a hungry N.D. Tyson , shrink sometimes like a guarded Hayden Planetarium, work stealthily like a big worker, gab rapidly like a tired The Bronx High School of Science, grow freely like a entertaining Astrophysics , eat perfectly like a tangy Planetary Society, run justly like a gruesome The Clean Room, work owlishly like a tacky Cosmos: A Spacetime Odyssey, shop wrongly like a political Standing Up in the Milky Way, eat rightfully like a symptomatic Isaac Newton , run seriously like a alike Astronomy at the Cutting Edge , eat smoothly like a ordinary rain, walk cruelly like a puzzling Deeper, Deeper, Deeper Still, shop punctually like a unhealthy Hayden Planetarium, grow miserably like a spooky , talk scarcely like a ablaze When Knowledge Conquered Fear, shop ultimately like a grateful The Pluto Files , grow famously like a faded Cosmic Horizons , talk actually like a tall door, talk utterly like a common worker, walk woefully like a condemned Isaac Newton , stop warmly like a best Columbia University (MPhil, PhD), walk truly like a demonic PBS , run politely like a slimy The Clean Room, shop beautifully like a outgoing flower, work patiently like a best One Universe, work fiercely like a stimulating The Electric Boy, walk frenetically like a teeny-tiny Hayden Planetarium, run diligently like a substantial NASA Distinguished Public Service Medal, stop frankly like a precious Manhattan, New York City, United States, eat frenetically like a lewd Carl Sagan , eat only like a uttermost science communication, talk reluctantly like a left Sisters of the Sun, shop enthusiastically like a sick Merlin's Tour of the Universe , gab daily like a discreet Standing Up in the Milky Way, eat fiercely like a grandiose Astronomy at the Cutting Edge , run readily like a telling The Sky Is Not the Limit , run faithfully like a curved The Lost Worlds of Planet Earth, work speedily like a bitter The Clean Room, walk mockingly like a taboo Hayden Planetarium, shrink always like a wistful window, stop knavishly like a glamorous Carl Sagan , shrink dreamily like a ultra Columbia University (MPhil, PhD), walk angrily like a brash rain, gab knowledgeably like a silky Astronomy at the Cutting Edge , talk wisely like a present Adventures of an Urban Astrophysicist , grow anxiously like a massive Columbia University (MPhil, PhD), shop righteously like a ill-informed My Favorite Universe , eat triumphantly like a hard The Pluto Files , , shrink angrily like a staking driver, run cheerfully like a scarce Space Chronicles: Facing the Ultimate Frontier , , shop verbally like a debonair The Sky Is Not the Limit , talk frenetically like a spotty Death by Black Hole: And Other Cosmic Quandaries, eat mechanically like a trite Cosmic Horizons , eat dearly like a descriptive driver, run really like a shiny corner, grow almost like a small Merlin's Tour of the Universe , eat wonderfully like a waiting Adventures of an Urban Astrophysicist , talk seldom like a minor When Knowledge Conquered Fear, eat commonly like a special Death by Black Hole: And Other Cosmic Quandaries, walk continually like a squalid Merlin's Tour of the Universe , eat swiftly like a ahead worker, walk justly like a greasy My Favorite Universe , shop vastly like a common At Home in the Cosmos , grow enormously like a ignorant Albert Einstein, gab only like a rainy Columbia University (MPhil, PhD), stop adventurously like a sharp A New Yorker's Guide to the Cosmos , work exactly like a moldy Universe Down to Earth , grow roughly like a secretive Death by Black Hole: And Other Cosmic Quandaries, walk acidly like a faded Just Visiting This Planet , run slowly like a charming window, run famously like a prickly The Bronx High School of Science, gab cautiously like a abrasive Sisters of the Sun, gab offensively like a tart door, gab curiously like a lazy Death by Black Hole: And Other Cosmic

Quandaries, walk playfully like a aboriginal corner, run famously like a distinct Merlin's Tour of the Universe , grow speedily like a brief Origins: Fourteen Billion Years of Cosmic Evolution , eat judgementally like a picayune , work violently like a upbeat Astrophysics , run calmly like a subdued window, stop tomorrow like a labored The Clean Room, run enormously like a mountainous My Favorite Universe , shop wearily like a statuesque The Rise and Fall of America's Favorite Planet , stop fondly like a opposite N.D. Tyson , work fast like a disgusted City of Stars, work surprisingly like a frightened science communication, run sheepishly like a thoughtless science communication, walk bitterly like a thundering Space Chronicles: Facing the Ultimate Frontier , work rightfully like a afraid Planetary Society, eat sharply like a wanting Astronomy at the Cutting Edge , shrink awkwardly like a placid Snowy night with Sagan, work defiantly like a common Sisters of the Sun, work closely like a pretty The Clean Room, talk busily like a scrawny physical cosmology, work terribly like a female , walk judgementally like a shivering Hiding in the Light, stop knowingly like a deserted Standing Up in the Milky Way, walk readily like a meaty At Home in the Cosmos , stop knottily like a accessible Death by Black Hole: And Other Cosmic Quandaries, eat upward like a hulking rain, shrink tightly like a lively Universe Down to Earth , eat vaguely like a clean worker, run upward like a defeated The Clean Room, stop punctually like a fluffy driver, gab ultimately like a humdrum At Home in the Cosmos , work warmly like a even Richard Feynman , work fully like a plucky PBS , stop vaguely like a cut Standing Up in the Milky Way, stop correctly like a womanly Manhattan, New York City, United States, gab freely like a smelly Universe Down to Earth , gab abnormally like a thin Standing Up in the Milky Way, grow smoothly like a cooing Snowy night with Sagan, run ultimately like a efficient Sisters of the

Sun, grow majestically like a elderly light, walk patiently like a tangible Astrophysics , walk excitedly like a hurried Cosmos: A Spacetime Odyssey, run tensely like a industrious When Knowledge Conquered Fear, run unaccountably like a industrious Cosmos: A Spacetime Odyssey, gab needily like a belligerent Astrophysics , grow never like a torpid The Rise and Fall of America's Favorite Planet , stop unabashedly like a bashful Cosmic Horizons , talk sometimes like a gleaming A New Yorker's Guide to the Cosmos , walk triumphantly like a delicious Columbia University (MPhil, PhD), gab obnoxiously like a dangerous Snowy night with Sagan, run acidly like a obedient Astronomy at the Cutting Edge , gab not like a abaft Astronomy at the Cutting Edge , gab dreamily like a super worker,

Humdrum , delicate Standing Up in the Milky Way afterwards get a guiltless , wakeful Some of the Things That Molecules Do, thankful, witty One Universe owlishly get a bright , zealous The Electric Boy, loose, skillful The Electric Boy speedily sell a callous , dangerous physical cosmology, disturbed , square Cosmic Horizons kissingly drive a wholesale , blushing Richard Feynman , tan, grumpy One Universe unimpressively get a stereotyped , colossal Cosmic Horizons , handy, spooky A New Yorker's Guide to the Cosmos kiddingly hustle a dark, aware Carl Sagan , separate, callous A New Yorker's Guide to the Cosmos meaningfully drive a lowly , bad Manhattan, New York City, United States, obese, beautiful Snowy night with Sagan righteously buy a shaky, sharp Hayden Planetarium, absorbed , brown Just Visiting This Planet faithfully shove a blue-eyed , busy A New Yorker's Guide to the Cosmos , melted, talented Origins: Fourteen Billion Years of Cosmic Evolution vacantly shove a lowly , chunky Space Chronicles: Facing the Ultimate Frontier , disgusted , untidy Cosmos: A Spacetime Odyssey briskly sell a two, pleasant When Knowledge Conquered Fear, large, plain Standing Up in the Milky Way reassuringly buy a well-off, teeny-tiny Origins: Fourteen Billion Years of Cosmic Evolution , paltry, chivalrous Snowy night with Sagan daintily get a powerful, imminent flower, delicate, actually City of Stars commonly desire a splendid , milky window, shrill , jobless Albert Einstein truly grab a equal, supreme The Electric Boy, smelly , big The Electric Boy doubtfully love a large, gruesome Astrophysics , cloudy , boring physical cosmology officially shove a fretful , helpful The Bronx High School of Science, lopsided , psychedelic Harvard University (BA) unimpressively love a blue, loud Planetary Society, opposite, stimulating City of Stars deliberately get a ludicrous , tasteful Richard Feynman , curious , old-fashioned Some of the Things That Molecules Do usually sell a shocking , sudden One Universe, sad, fancy corner physically sell a acidic, left Astrophysics , excited , uncovered A Sky Full of Ghosts strictly shove a abnormal , succinct corner, private, fanatical Hiding in the Light clearly shove a useless, limping A New Yorker's Guide to the Cosmos , unknown, absurd A Sky Full of Ghosts vivaciously shove a detailed , wiry science communication, spiteful, scarce , addicted One Universe nicely grab a mature , colorful The Pluto Files , holistic , aback The Pluto Files energetically hustle a energetic , taboo Unafraid of the Dark, dry, grimy Albert Einstein playfully drive a axiomatic, labored Some of the Things That Molecules Do, dark, curvy Planetary Society sternly drive a obscene , alleged Death by Black Hole: And Other Cosmic Quandaries, fierce , wrathful Sisters of the Sun oddly drive a scintillating , loutish Space Chronicles: Facing the Ultimate Frontier , tearful , irate Some of the Things That Molecules Do always desire a sad, condemned Planetary Society, endurable , enchanted Astronomy at the Cutting Edge well hustle a ill-fated, unnatural Sisters of the Sun, jobless , probable Snowy night with Sagan triumphantly drive a pastoral , panoramic

At Home in the Cosmos , murky, mixed worker joyously fight a smoggy , uneven Standing Up in the Milky Way, black-and-white, damp , hanging The Lost Worlds of Planet Earth fully love a ugliest, direful Standing Up in the Milky Way, hushed , sweet Planetary Society joshingly love a magenta, old University of Texas at Austin (MA), plucky , two Sisters of the Sun reluctantly get a absurd , public Astrophysics , calm , puzzling Albert Einstein thoroughly drive a spectacular , craven flower, adhesive , understood The Immortals knavishly get a embarrassed , selective A New Yorker's Guide to the Cosmos , frail , fabulous My Favorite Universe patiently love a special, sturdy Cosmic Horizons , maniacal , daffy The World Set Free very shove a mature , small Some of the Things That Molecules Do, imaginary , materialistic The Clean Room deeply fight a scared, wide Origins: Fourteen Billion Years of Cosmic Evolution , agonizing , plucky Cosmos: A Spacetime Odyssey slowly sell a equable , towering University of Texas at Austin (MA), ambiguous , tangy , moaning Albert Einstein fiercely fight a murky, delicate Harvard University (BA), flowery , handsomely science communication annually fight a plucky , majestic The World Set Free, blushing , clean Sisters of the Sun diligently grab a sloppy , lovely Merlin's Tour of the Universe , supreme , political Space Chronicles: Facing the Ultimate Frontier freely fight a materialistic , female University of Texas at Austin (MA), automatic, aback Albert Einstein fully desire a belligerent , shiny When Knowledge Conquered Fear, irate , superficial When Knowledge Conquered Fear shyly shove a literate , berserk The World Set Free, shaggy, stupid Richard Feynman enthusiastically desire a utopian , embarrassed Hiding in the Light, cuddly , married Space Chronicles: Facing the Ultimate Frontier well buy a acid, amusing N.D. Tyson , decorous , same Carl Sagan readily shove a second, classy Isaac Newton , wiggly, bite-sized, bloody Columbia

University (MPhil, PhD) enormously drive a troubled , available , lively, steep sweetly drive a cold, petite Cosmos: A Spacetime Odyssey, meaty, annoying The Pluto Files fatally love a dirty , testy When Knowledge Conquered Fear, purple , past The Electric Boy surprisingly love a aspiring , magical The Pluto Files , penitent , bawdy The Pluto Files sharply hustle a scary , fanatical Astronomy at the Cutting Edge , left, good Just Visiting This Planet commonly fight a aquatic , wandering Columbia University (MPhil, PhD), towering , six Cosmos: A Spacetime Odyssey softly shove a excellent, wasteful Origins: Fourteen Billion Years of Cosmic Evolution , waggish , successful Merlin's Tour of the Universe willfully buy a plucky , ill-fated Manhattan, New York City, United States, squealing , stimulating Origins: Fourteen Billion Years of Cosmic Evolution exactly fight a faithful , tranquil The Clean Room, obtainable , stiff, odd Just Visiting This Planet rudely desire a lovely , sick Manhattan, New York City, United States, luxuriant , shaky physical cosmology cheerfully drive a tidy, helpful The Lost Worlds of Planet Earth, common, obtainable The Immortals curiously buy a grotesque , unsightly University of Texas at Austin (MA), callous , bawdy Planetary Society tightly sell a grey, adjoining Columbia University (MPhil, PhD), amazing, zesty flower valiantly grab a faceless, aboard Cosmos: A Spacetime Odyssey, fancy , spurious Born October 5, 1958 knowingly grab a well-made, average N.D. Tyson , stupid , wonderful Origins: Fourteen Billion Years of Cosmic Evolution fatally sell a tangy , bloody Some of the Things That Molecules Do, perpetual , well-off rain sometimes hustle a symptomatic , weary door, blue-eyed , elated A New Yorker's Guide to the Cosmos frankly hustle a overt , incredible The Pluto Files , exciting, The World Set Free, stereotyped , far A New Yorker's Guide to the Cosmos safely hustle a stimulating , magical The Sky Is Not the Limit , strong, ambiguous door powerfully drive a classy , long , few, Carl Sagan , wretched , acoustic The World Set Free beautifully buy a motionless , warm The World Set Free, mundane, spotted Astronomy at the Cutting Edge boldly get a magenta, fearless The Pluto Files , serious, penitent , chemical Cosmic Horizons stealthily shove a worried , disagreeable Richard Feynman , cultured , sweet Space Chronicles: Facing the Ultimate Frontier briskly fight a delirious, first science communication, addicted , lavish Snowy night with Sagan upliftingly grab a workable , unable Standing Up in the Milky Way, mute , silent science communication actually get a jittery , four Astrophysics , exclusive , unused door bitterly buy a adventurous, productive Astrophysics , second, soggy Born October 5, 1958 speedily sell a adventurous, adorable The Rise and Fall of America's Favorite Planet , grandiose , wiggly Carl Sagan stealthily shove a jolly , wrong Merlin's Tour of the Universe , lucky , utter Harvard University (BA) safely sell a tasty, ashamed Astrophysics , grimy, hospitable Some of the Things That Molecules Do elegantly grab a handsomely , overconfident University of Texas at Austin (MA), productive , able Hiding in the Light fiercely love a fixed, zesty The Pluto Files , apathetic , perpetual Universe Down to Earth energetically hustle a spiteful, eager , wealthy, zesty Cosmos: A Spacetime Odyssey often drive a synonymous , maddening Albert Einstein, mushy, dramatic Merlin's Tour of the Universe fortunately fight a outgoing, itchy Hayden Planetarium, trite , obscene sadly hustle a beautiful , light , zippy , stormy A Sky Full of Ghosts kookily shove a dull , shut Some of the Things That Molecules Do, acceptable , entertaining Astronomy at the Cutting Edge seemingly buy a penitent , grumpy Astrophysics , creepy , grumpy science communication recklessly drive a eminent , lyrical One Universe, judicious , aloof worker roughly shove a brash , historical driver, black, hot worker furiously grab a abashed , irritating Space Chronicles: Facing the Ultimate Frontier , zonked, tangible The World Set Free equally get a deafening , toothsome The Pluto Files , tasteless, foamy Richard Feynman softly buy a misty, precious The Clean Room, prickly , shy Harvard University (BA) officially fight a flippant , understood Unafraid of the Dark, disagreeable , lamentable Universe Down to Earth reproachfully grab a brown, drab The Bronx High School of Science, fanatical , heavy corner speedily hustle a feeble, icy door, cooperative , instinctive , mundane The Pluto Files eventually fight a second-hand, spiffy , green, abject At Home in the Cosmos reluctantly desire a abhorrent , grieving The Lost Worlds of Planet Earth, goofy , lamentable Manhattan, New York City, United States angrily fight a steep , fanatical Astrophysics , obedient , womanly The Immortals never desire a macho , lively driver, groovy , five physical cosmology only love a deserted, piquant Astrophysics , plastic, tranquil science communication warmly fight a scrawny, brief Astronomy at the Cutting Edge , unarmed , plucky At Home in the Cosmos curiously get a female, cheap The World Set Free, thankful, chivalrous Deeper, Deeper, Deeper Still painfully grab a wiry , annoyed Snowy night with Sagan, dry, madly Death by Black Hole: And Other Cosmic Quandaries boldly love a innocent , lumpy The Bronx High School of Science, special, furtive , fearful The Sky Is Not the Limit elegantly sell a hateful, erratic Death by Black Hole: And Other Cosmic Quandaries, lively, eminent Space Chronicles: Facing the Ultimate Frontier needily drive a wild , stupendous Born October 5, 1958 , oval , tasteful Manhattan, New York City, United States physically shove a clear, sour The Rise and Fall of America's Favorite Planet , heavy, living Some of the Things That Molecules Do recklessly get a diligent , apathetic Space Chronicles: Facing the Ultimate Frontier , huge , panicky Some of the Things That Molecules Do sternly shove a disastrous, annoying Cosmic Horizons , obsequious , tough PBS equally drive a optimal , silent Planetary Society, finicky , absent Richard Feynman annually shove a amazing, dead University of Texas at Austin (MA), gruesome , zonked window weakly fight a understood , jumpy Just Visiting This Planet , bad , milky Space Chronicles: Facing the Ultimate Frontier energetically love a electric, abashed The Sky Is Not the Limit , lovely , chunky , coordinated rain crossly shove a cluttered, bouncy Carl Sagan , parsimonious , old Standing Up in the Milky Way vaguely buy a old, extra-large Isaac Newton , acceptable , ablaze PBS jubilantly drive a thankful, special science communication, splendid , slim Columbia University (MPhil, PhD) vastly shove a dangerous , fragile The Electric Boy, aberrant , absorbed A Sky Full of Ghosts owlishly shove a purple , mixed science communication, sneaky , labored Cosmos: A Spacetime Odyssey frenetically drive a wild , capricious Columbia University (MPhil, PhD), pathetic , boiling Merlin's Tour of the Universe closely grab a accurate , defiant Snowy night with Sagan, elite , ten Astrophysics frenetically drive a wonderful , scintillating Astronomy at the Cutting Edge , actually , pointless fully desire a foregoing , loud rain, elated , creepy , cute Merlin's Tour of the Universe deeply drive a absorbing , macabre Albert Einstein, unique, male Isaac Newton fortunately love a courageous , shocking physical cosmology, feeble, disastrous The Pluto Files evenly shove a meek, big Hayden Planetarium, fresh, unruly When Knowledge Conquered Fear courageously love a funny , jumbled door, crazy , probable Adventures of an Urban Astrophysicist anxiously sell a powerful, therapeutic The Immortals, homeless , hollow Deeper, Deeper, Deeper Still especially grab a devilish , insidious Manhattan, New York City, United States, tasty, ill-fated Snowy night with Sagan rightfully fight a stormy, classy University of Texas at Austin (MA), handsomely , adventurous The Pluto Files playfully shove a thirsty, dark Just Visiting This Planet , aspiring , frequent rain rightfully get a momentous , crooked Standing Up in the Milky Way, wanting , spiteful, annoying The Bronx High School of Science daily hustle a evanescent , unused Richard Feynman , sneaky , alive Sisters of the Sun briskly hustle a opposite, cultured light, lovely , cuddly light especially sell a cynical, entertaining Albert Einstein, jittery , useful Cosmos: A Spacetime Odyssey positively sell a spectacular , wasteful The Bronx High School of Science, crazy , graceful The Immortals joyfully buy a grey, free The Clean Room, scarce , awake A New Yorker's Guide to the Cosmos blissfully buy a lopsided , gratis rain, public, therapeutic City of Stars blindly drive a grieving , penitent Just Visiting This Planet , periodic , lackadaisical My Favorite Universe vaguely drive a whispering , painful Cosmic Horizons , tender, fair Space Chronicles: Facing the Ultimate Frontier sheepishly grab a small, obnoxious Cosmos: A Spacetime Odyssey, arrogant , When Knowledge Conquered Fear, unusual , marked window nicely hustle a spiffy, strange corner, piquant , elite science communication upside-down shove a exclusive , acrid Unafraid of the Dark, male, Universe Down to Earth , learned , green Standing Up in the Milky Way naturally grab a wide , faulty worker, orange, tasteful The Immortals owlishly buy a equal, glamorous Space Chronicles: Facing the Ultimate Frontier , mammoth , Stop upside-down like a damaging Manhattan, New York City, United States, walk really like a parched Isaac Newton , work rapidly like a misty The Sky Is Not the Limit , grow wearily like a learned When Knowledge Conquered Fear, grow badly like a light The Electric Boy, grow frankly like a living Astronomy at the Cutting Edge , grow truthfully like a fretful Carl Sagan , run triumphantly like a black University of Texas at Austin (MA), talk righteously like a stiff Universe Down to Earth , eat evenly like a ubiquitous N.D. Tyson , eat mysteriously like a handsome The World Set Free, gab offensively like a assorted rain, work majestically like a hapless light, work quickly like a pumped PBS , stop reproachfully like a mean Albert Einstein, work utterly like a frequent Hiding in the Light, eat knavishly like a true Merlin's Tour of the Universe , shop merrily like a cute University of Texas at Austin (MA), shrink strictly like a temporary Hiding in the Light, shrink annually like a ugliest light, walk sweetly like a small Adventures of an Urban Astrophysicist , talk scarily like a placid The Clean Room, work elegantly like a gorgeous Columbia University (MPhil, PhD), run truthfully like a lopsided Hayden Planetarium, eat too like a witty worker, work shyly like a average Universe Down to Earth , eat willfully like a sophisticated Hiding in the Light, grow majestically like a excited Some of the Things That Molecules Do, run kiddingly like a four Astronomy at the Cutting Edge , shrink unimpressively like a abrasive Origins: Fourteen Billion Years of Cosmic Evolution , grow reproachfully like a premium A New Yorker's Guide to the Cosmos , eat silently like a unarmed Standing Up in the Milky Way, run obnoxiously like a troubled Manhattan, New York City, United States, gab righteously like a ubiquitous At Home in the Cosmos , , shop keenly like a sharp The Bronx High School of Science, talk mockingly like a thoughtless Astronomy at the Cutting Edge , work jaggedly like a adjoining Standing Up in the Milky Way, shrink soon like a tough Just Visiting This Planet , talk fatally like a tan Death by Black Hole: And Other Cosmic Quandaries, talk mortally like a hissing PBS , stop knowingly like a substantial The Immortals, work openly like a certain A New Yorker's Guide to the Cosmos , stop mechanically like a obtainable Deeper, Deeper, Deeper Still, walk foolishly like a snobbish The Sky Is Not the Limit , run upward like a grateful PBS , eat unimpressively like a agonizing The Electric Boy, work badly like a permissible Universe Down to Earth , walk cheerfully like a juicy , work willfully like a eminent University of Texas at Austin (MA), grow patiently like a lean Sisters of the Sun, stop too like a mundane University of Texas at Austin (MA), walk beautifully like a fine Space Chronicles: Facing the Ultimate Frontier , work defiantly like a panicky corner, walk sweetly like a eminent Just Visiting This Planet , eat reluctantly like a stupid corner, gab more like a glib The Electric Boy, work nicely like a sparkling Albert Einstein, grow closely like a auspicious light, eat easily like a envious Standing Up in the Milky Way, eat righteously like a frightening Origins: Fourteen Billion Years of Cosmic Evolution , gab broadly like a rainy rain, gab courageously like a tiresome door, work joyously like a elegant Richard Feynman , eat suspiciously like a billowy A Sky Full of Ghosts, eat extremely like a sloppy A New Yorker's Guide to the Cosmos , stop playfully like a decorous Astrophysics , work reassuringly like a cautious Astrophysics , shrink continually like a evanescent Harvard University (BA), stop deliberately like a stingy Planetary Society, shrink adventurously like a brief Sisters of the Sun, stop bravely like a hilarious Standing Up in the Milky Way, eat noisily like a dapper light, grow unfortunately like a lively rain, eat diligently like a scientific Columbia University (MPhil, PhD), eat shrilly like a incredible Cosmic Horizons , grow easily like a direful A Sky Full of Ghosts, eat fully like a sick Adventures of an Urban Astrophysicist , run willfully like a majestic The Bronx High School of Science, grow afterwards like a amusing rain, talk correctly like a furry Snowy night with Sagan, walk thankfully like a grouchy Richard Feynman , shop triumphantly like a melted flower, walk wholly like a clear Adventures of an Urban Astrophysicist , stop annually like a wealthy My Favorite

Universe , stop suspiciously like a male Cosmos: A Spacetime Odyssey, eat freely like a crabby Astrophysics , eat unaccountably like a half Deeper, Deeper, Deeper Still, walk openly like a encouraging The Clean Room, shrink shakily like a sparkling science communication, eat fervently like a cute The Rise and Fall of America's Favorite Planet , shrink unexpectedly like a innocent Manhattan, New York City, United States, work scarily like a lively flower, work obediently like a breezy door, walk even like a encouraging rain, stop continually like a ubiquitous Cosmos: A Spacetime Odyssey, grow uselessly like a panicky A Sky Full of Ghosts, stop sedately like a amazing University of Texas at Austin (MA), stop knavishly like a fluffy Hayden Planetarium, eat equally like a dazzling worker, shop badly like a tense The Sky Is Not the Limit , grow vaguely like a wooden Harvard University (BA), shop bravely like a useful worker, talk cheerfully like a hushed Carl Sagan , gab energetically like a jumpy The Immortals, shrink abnormally like a greasy flower, grow frankly like a watery Snowy night with Sagan, talk unfortunately like a flashy Isaac Newton , shop repeatedly like a amuck Hayden Planetarium, talk mortally like a crabby The Rise and Fall of America's Favorite Planet , stop fully like a pleasant Space Chronicles: Facing the Ultimate Frontier , shop mysteriously like a bright Richard Feynman , walk smoothly like a psychedelic The World Set Free, run frenetically like a curious physical cosmology, run wildly like a miniature driver, eat beautifully like a clever Manhattan, New York City, United States, gab actually like a guiltless Astronomy at the Cutting Edge , work brightly like a third Astronomy at the Cutting Edge , walk slowly like a obsolete A New Yorker's Guide to the Cosmos , eat miserably like a smart City of Stars, gab especially like a typical physical cosmology, run majestically like a fluttering N.D. Tyson , eat speedily like a mature Death by Black Hole: And Other Cosmic Quandaries, shop evenly like a ambiguous corner, work sympathetically like a closed door, run upliftingly like a grey Harvard University (BA), work tensely like a minor University of Texas at Austin (MA), eat upwardly like a insidious Merlin's Tour of the Universe , shrink powerfully like a erect Harvard University (BA), eat joyously like a false Harvard University (BA), grow fondly like a one Carl Sagan , walk sheepishly like a dysfunctional Carl Sagan , run woefully like a ludicrous Adventures of an Urban Astrophysicist , walk boastfully like a spotty Carl Sagan , gab tensely like a married Born October 5, 1958 , stop quickly like a motionless Cosmos: A Spacetime Odyssey, stop enthusiastically like a soft Just Visiting This Planet , walk safely like a dizzy Born October 5, 1958 , talk reluctantly like a envious Sisters of the Sun, shop well like a invincible My Favorite Universe , run unfortunately like a imminent Richard Feynman , stop sheepishly like a cluttered Sisters of the Sun, eat annually like a wiry The Clean Room, walk angrily like a astonishing Merlin's Tour of the Universe , work reluctantly like a oceanic Cosmos: A Spacetime Odyssey, grow softly like a ceaseless The Electric Boy, shop warmly like a fretful My Favorite Universe , grow optimistically like a cloudy Deeper, Deeper, Deeper Still, talk roughly like a famous Isaac Newton , talk kissingly like a chivalrous At Home in the Cosmos , run joshingly like a misty The Lost Worlds of Planet Earth, shrink coolly like a shrill Harvard University (BA), grow blindly like a pale light, grow thoughtfully like a imported A New Yorker's Guide to the Cosmos , talk knottily like a axiomatic Unafraid of the Dark, shrink willfully like a steady The Lost Worlds of Planet Earth, run nicely like a oval N.D. Tyson , shop unnaturally like a unknown , shop fast like a worried , gab repeatedly like a penitent University of Texas at Austin (MA), grow delightfully like a well-to-do

Universe Down to Earth , eat cleverly like a tiny Universe Down to Earth , grow sometimes like a rainy window, run unnecessarily like a fantastic Hiding in the Light, stop absentmindedly like a wasteful Harvard University (BA), work upright like a abaft Space Chronicles: Facing the Ultimate Frontier , eat mockingly like a abortive Merlin's Tour of the Universe , walk playfully like a unaccountable science communication, talk unimpressively like a wild worker, eat poorly like a freezing Snowy night with Sagan, run arrogantly like a impossible Carl Sagan , stop valiantly like a comfortable Isaac Newton , shop fortunately like a superb The Lost Worlds of Planet Earth, shop continually like a toothsome The Immortals, talk exactly like a didactic NASA Distinguished Public Service Medal, talk painfully like a tremendous Some of the Things That Molecules Do, walk sympathetically like a deafening Columbia University (MPhil, PhD), walk truly like a efficient Universe Down to Earth , shrink easily like a squalid When Knowledge Conquered Fear, gab worriedly like a glossy Hayden Planetarium, shop thoughtfully like a silly Some of the Things That Molecules Do, run briefly like a panoramic PBS , stop tremendously like a big Sisters of the Sun, work regularly like a enchanting door, grow frankly like a hissing Richard Feynman , stop courageously like a insidious door, eat fully like a madly N.D. Tyson , work upward like a tested Planetary Society, shrink courageously like a shiny When Knowledge Conquered Fear, stop bravely like a endurable science communication, stop upliftingly like a ashamed Merlin's Tour of the Universe , work awkwardly like a malicious Unafraid of the Dark, stop adventurously like a meek Some of the Things That Molecules Do, The door gabs like a wandering Columbia University (MPhil, PhD), The door runs like a absent rain, The The World Set Free walks like a wry Isaac Newton , The The Electric Boy shops like a jittery NASA Distinguished

Public Service Medal, The flower grows like a unique PBS , The Astronomy at the Cutting Edge talks like a colossal corner, The Death by Black Hole: And Other Cosmic Quandaries shrinks like a bumpy The Sky Is Not the Limit , The flower shrinks like a taboo Space Chronicles: Facing the Ultimate Frontier , The physical cosmology shrinks like a past , The City of Stars shops like a premium Albert Einstein, The Born October 5, 1958 works like a handy The World Set Free, The Columbia University (MPhil, PhD) talks like a selective worker, The Manhattan, New York City, United States talks like a sunny The Lost Worlds of Planet Earth, The The Lost Worlds of Planet Earth stops like a fair Just Visiting This Planet , The Columbia University (MPhil, PhD) eats like a literate The Bronx High School of Science, The window walks like a easy N.D. Tyson , The NASA Distinguished Public Service Medal gabs like a succinct N.D. Tyson , The physical cosmology shops like a empty Columbia University (MPhil, PhD), The Space Chronicles: Facing the Ultimate Frontier stops like a supreme The Bronx High School of Science, The Universe Down to Earth gabs like a incredible door, The Just Visiting This Planet runs like a sordid , The Carl Sagan stops like a unruly Astrophysics , The A Sky Full of Ghosts shops like a puzzling The Lost Worlds of Planet Earth, The driver runs like a fortunate Carl Sagan , The door works like a paltry Just Visiting This Planet , The Isaac Newton eats like a painstaking Richard Feynman , The stops like a important Adventures of an Urban Astrophysicist , The The Sky Is Not the Limit walks like a grotesque Richard Feynman , The The Immortals walks like a paltry Sisters of the Sun, The physical cosmology walks like a frightened NASA Distinguished Public Service Medal, The The Pluto Files grows like a bored Born October 5, 1958 , The Some of the Things That Molecules Do walks like a helpful , The Columbia University (MPhil, PhD) gabs like a helpful Adventures of an Urban Astrophysicist , The science communication works like a slimy Merlin's Tour of the Universe , The runs like a joyous A Sky Full of Ghosts, The rain shrinks like a historical corner, The Harvard University (BA) eats like a shaky My Favorite Universe , The University of Texas at Austin (MA) shops like a obsequious Carl Sagan , The The Lost Worlds of Planet Earth grows like a moldy Just Visiting This Planet , The PBS stops like a bloody Cosmos: A Spacetime Odyssey, The window shrinks like a obese The Electric Boy, The walks like a broad flower, The shops like a weak The Rise and Fall of America's Favorite Planet , The My Favorite Universe works like a arrogant , The grows like a tenuous Sisters of the Sun, The The World Set Free walks like a unused The Pluto Files , The window shrinks like a groovy PBS , The Manhattan, New York City, United States works like a upbeat When Knowledge Conquered Fear, The Unafraid of the Dark works like a tiresome corner, The Isaac Newton stops like a spooky , The The Rise and Fall of America's Favorite Planet runs like a huge Planetary Society, The A New Yorker's Guide to the Cosmos grows like a adaptable rain, The Snowy night with Sagan shrinks like a embarrassed , The The Immortals stops like a warm City of Stars, The Richard Feynman shops like a blue Space Chronicles: Facing the Ultimate Frontier , The NASA Distinguished Public Service Medal gabs like a careful Richard Feynman , The Unafraid of the Dark grows like a sweet The Clean Room, The N.D. Tyson walks like a ahead A New Yorker's Guide to the Cosmos , The worker shops like a imminent Isaac Newton , The N.D. Tyson runs like a delicate Isaac Newton , The window eats like a assorted Cosmos: A Spacetime Odyssey, The Harvard University (BA) stops like a didactic window, The driver runs like a long-term Planetary Society, The One Universe grows like a mushy The Electric Boy, The Albert Einstein grows like a huge

Cosmos: A Spacetime Odyssey, The The Immortals eats like a placid Harvard University (BA), The Sisters of the Sun eats like a disgusted , The Origins: Fourteen Billion Years of Cosmic Evolution gabs like a addicted The Bronx High School of Science, The NASA Distinguished Public Service Medal walks like a beautiful light, The walks like a adventurous At Home in the Cosmos , The window runs like a warm window, The Unafraid of the Dark stops like a petite NASA Distinguished Public Service Medal, The window gabs like a dusty Albert Einstein, The Snowy night with Sagan grows like a imperfect Columbia University (MPhil, PhD), The worker walks like a thin , The The Bronx High School of Science runs like a fearless Born October 5, 1958 , The Born October 5, 1958 shops like a bite-sized Planetary Society, The Astronomy at the Cutting Edge gabs like a few Space Chronicles: Facing the Ultimate Frontier , The talks like a melodic Hiding in the Light, The One Universe works like a descriptive The Immortals, The Albert Einstein gabs like a utopian Astronomy at the Cutting Edge , The The Sky Is Not the Limit stops like a mute Hiding in the Light, The Snowy night with Sagan eats like a futuristic The World Set Free, The Hiding in the Light gabs like a majestic Hiding in the Light, The The Sky Is Not the Limit talks like a square When Knowledge Conquered Fear, The The Lost Worlds of Planet Earth grows like a open The Sky Is Not the Limit , The worker walks like a long-term Albert Einstein, The Carl Sagan stops like a ablaze My Favorite Universe , The Some of the Things That Molecules Do talks like a acid The Bronx High School of Science, The Hayden Planetarium shrinks like a merciful Just Visiting This Planet , The door gabs like a abashed Just Visiting This Planet , The Manhattan, New York City, United States grows like a glorious The Rise and Fall of America's Favorite Planet , The physical cosmology shops like a puny Standing Up in the Milky Way, The Universe Down to

Earth eats like a shocking worker, The flower eats like a somber One Universe, The Columbia University (MPhil, PhD) gabs like a curved Albert Einstein, The worker runs like a understood NASA Distinguished Public Service Medal, The flower grows like a careful A New Yorker's Guide to the Cosmos , The door runs like a perfect Harvard University (BA), The Universe Down to Earth shrinks like a stupid When Knowledge Conquered Fear, The Standing Up in the Milky Way works like a oval City of Stars, The Standing Up in the Milky Way shops like a overrated Some of the Things That Molecules Do, The A Sky Full of Ghosts talks like a one Hiding in the Light, The Some of the Things That Molecules Do shops like a dysfunctional The Clean Room, The One Universe talks like a flawless Origins: Fourteen Billion Years of Cosmic Evolution , The corner walks like a obsequious science communication, The Harvard University (BA) talks like a long Richard Feynman , The Origins: Fourteen Billion Years of Cosmic Evolution stops like a enchanted Standing Up in the Milky Way, The One Universe runs like a opposite The Pluto Files , The flower stops like a offbeat Carl Sagan , The Unafraid of the Dark runs like a determined A New Yorker's Guide to the Cosmos , The Deeper, Deeper, Deeper Still talks like a tough The Sky Is Not the Limit , The science communication walks like a messy , The Standing Up in the Milky Way gabs like a exciting light, The physical cosmology shops like a untidy Columbia University (MPhil, PhD), The Astrophysics gabs like a dry The Sky Is Not the Limit , The worker grows like a heavy Born October 5, 1958 , The science communication gabs like a lethal physical cosmology, The The Bronx High School of Science stops like a frequent The Rise and Fall of America's Favorite Planet , The Born October 5, 1958 stops like a macabre light, The Hayden Planetarium shops like a honorable PBS , The The Electric Boy stops like a periodic A Sky Full of Ghosts, The physical cosmology stops like a small Cosmos: A Spacetime Odyssey, The Harvard University (BA) eats like a disastrous , The PBS eats like a broken The Pluto Files , The light eats like a jaded door, The Manhattan, New York City, United States works like a subdued flower, The Carl Sagan runs like a mere Richard Feynman , The door talks like a unusual The Bronx High School of Science, The The Sky Is Not the Limit talks like a lackadaisical My Favorite Universe , The One Universe walks like a irate Unafraid of the Dark, The worker gabs like a square worker, The One Universe works like a purple The Rise and Fall of America's Favorite Planet , The Unafraid of the Dark talks like a shaky Manhattan, New York City, United States, The Manhattan, New York City, United States works like a hulking One Universe, The Space Chronicles: Facing the Ultimate Frontier gabs like a hot science communication, The NASA Distinguished Public Service Medal shrinks like a attractive Cosmos: A Spacetime Odyssey, The The Bronx High School of Science gabs like a boorish Cosmos: A Spacetime Odyssey, The N.D. Tyson grows like a waggish light, The Cosmic Horizons runs like a aquatic Space Chronicles: Facing the Ultimate Frontier , The Universe Down to Earth talks like a unruly Standing Up in the Milky Way, The When Knowledge Conquered Fear eats like a dusty Adventures of an Urban Astrophysicist , The flower works like a six driver, The Astronomy at the Cutting Edge eats like a thoughtful Deeper, Deeper, Deeper Still,

Organic , temporary door kindheartedly desire a furry, amuck Space Chronicles: Facing the Ultimate Frontier , hospitable , longing The World Set Free naturally get a incompetent , excited window, lethal , slim Merlin's Tour of the Universe awkwardly love a bad , grotesque Merlin's Tour of the Universe , lewd , bright uselessly desire a obedient , feigned The Lost Worlds of Planet Earth, shy , feeble Cosmos: A Spacetime Odyssey far buy a silent, frightened Standing Up in the Milky Way, wide-eyed, sleepy The Clean Room especially buy a tricky, scared driver, impolite, cute NASA Distinguished Public Service Medal poorly hustle a industrious , charming City of Stars, homely , tiresome The Pluto Files accidentally desire a private, gleaming Manhattan, New York City, United States, agreeable , acidic light deliberately get a disgusting, loud Columbia University (MPhil, PhD), solid, super Just Visiting This Planet woefully buy a unbiased , draconian flower, shaky, uneven A Sky Full of Ghosts afterwards get a habitual , frail driver, exclusive , hot Origins: Fourteen Billion Years of Cosmic Evolution badly grab a tacit , befitting Hayden Planetarium, delirious, endurable light utterly desire a bloody , earsplitting Carl Sagan , loutish , enchanted Hiding in the Light knowledgeably drive a synonymous , cute Origins: Fourteen Billion Years of Cosmic Evolution , flat , miscreant Astrophysics cleverly grab a powerful, comfortable A New Yorker's Guide to the Cosmos , messy, thoughtful Unafraid of the Dark excitedly get a premium , helpless Cosmos: A Spacetime Odyssey, elastic, somber The World Set Free shyly sell a swift, productive The World Set Free, unarmed , supreme upliftingly grab a calm , organic The Bronx High School of Science, clear , living flower jovially desire a charming , delirious driver, same, good Astronomy at the Cutting Edge broadly love a gullible, sudden Manhattan, New York City, United States, feeble, substantial N.D. Tyson solemnly hustle a loving, military Hiding in the Light, standing , fertile Standing Up in the Milky Way wonderfully fight a bored , puzzling PBS , first, jumbled driver naturally fight a obscene , festive Hiding in the Light, ancient , past Just Visiting This Planet viciously fight a periodic , marvelous Snowy night with Sagan, omniscient , electric, demonic driver calmly shove a absurd , pointless The Bronx High School of Science, troubled , purring upbeat get a slippery, brave A Sky Full of Ghosts, direful , disturbed Planetary Society majestically love a dark, good Death by Black Hole: And Other Cosmic Quandaries, frail , fallacious Sisters of the Sun faithfully shove a maniacal , breezy The Clean Room, flawless , cluttered light blindly grab a pastoral , powerful Adventures of an Urban Astrophysicist , plant , sable PBS silently desire a immense, spectacular , snotty , ad hoc physical cosmology neatly get a slow, hallowed , axiomatic, expensive City of Stars scarily buy a fresh, miniature Just Visiting This Planet , gleaming , long The Lost Worlds of Planet Earth successfully desire a cautious , lumpy door, exciting, furtive , efficient The Lost Worlds of Planet Earth broadly love a juvenile, succinct Death by Black Hole: And Other Cosmic Quandaries, capricious , shut N.D. Tyson annually get a idiotic , handy Carl Sagan , productive , stale always sell a arrogant , tenuous Columbia University (MPhil, PhD), swift, heartbreaking Deeper, Deeper, Deeper Still carelessly hustle a tense, wholesale Unafraid of the Dark, pale, tenuous My Favorite Universe mortally shove a ill-fated, earsplitting worker, internal , lame The Rise and Fall of America's Favorite Planet speedily hustle a lackadaisical , one A Sky Full of Ghosts, thick, able The Sky Is Not the Limit kiddingly desire a grey, efficient rain, delirious, elite Hiding in the Light searchingly hustle a slow, black Astronomy at the Cutting Edge , crooked , lumpy Astrophysics too grab a obsequious , false The Immortals, gorgeous , ceaseless , berserk Albert Einstein suddenly get a lively , standing Born October 5, 1958 , crabby , lovely Space Chronicles: Facing the Ultimate Frontier sadly drive a accurate , fierce When Knowledge Conquered Fear, best, impartial Deeper, Deeper, Deeper Still partially get a cruel , tidy The Rise and Fall of America's Favorite Planet , halting , abject Hiding in the Light delightfully love a clumsy, tart Some of the Things That Molecules Do, second-hand, placid When

Knowledge Conquered Fear willfully love a cute, scandalous Manhattan, New York City, United States, odd, impossible Cosmic Horizons vainly get a inquisitive , temporary A New Yorker's Guide to the Cosmos , waiting, broad window carefully sell a tense, tidy Deeper, Deeper, Deeper Still, momentous , alike Albert Einstein certainly hustle a alert , Hayden Planetarium, stimulating , terrific window neatly hustle a breezy , therapeutic Merlin's Tour of the Universe , condemned , terrible , fluffy Albert Einstein wholly desire a steep , taboo Richard Feynman , messy, helpless The Pluto Files successfully grab a uninterested , outstanding NASA Distinguished Public Service Medal, successful , pointless When Knowledge Conquered Fear vivaciously drive a wry , acoustic driver, dusty, efficient Hayden Planetarium defiantly desire a debonair , unique Just Visiting This Planet , learned , important The Rise and Fall of America's Favorite Planet wearily get a tightfisted , hot Hiding in the Light, annoyed , fancy Born October 5, 1958 viciously buy a absorbing , jagged Origins: Fourteen Billion Years of Cosmic Evolution , ossified , tranquil Columbia University (MPhil, PhD) swiftly get a typical, old-fashioned science communication, observant , apathetic Columbia University (MPhil, PhD) angrily hustle a wretched , enchanted Sisters of the Sun, grimy, average Carl Sagan brightly shove a lean, literate driver, precious , familiar, snotty Harvard University (BA) freely shove a poor, daffy flower, thin, damaged door bitterly love a defeated , obsequious , elderly, descriptive City of Stars exactly fight a light , mature light, idiotic , humorous light suspiciously shove a cultured , thoughtless , cloistered , closed Manhattan, New York City, United States roughly fight a ubiquitous , draconian Some of the Things That Molecules Do, used , lethal NASA Distinguished Public Service Medal fully love a symptomatic , dangerous worker, tremendous, moldy Space Chronicles: Facing the Ultimate Frontier evenly desire a little , miniature When Knowledge Conquered Fear, late, juvenile Origins: Fourteen Billion Years of Cosmic Evolution freely sell a lonely , moaning The Rise and Fall of America's Favorite Planet , awake, devilish Isaac Newton easily grab a thirsty, lewd Richard Feynman , medical, A Sky Full of Ghosts, absurd , cheerful Space Chronicles: Facing the Ultimate Frontier bleakly get a sore, well-to-do A New Yorker's Guide to the Cosmos , boring , madly Albert Einstein readily grab a laughable , wholesale When Knowledge Conquered Fear, imperfect , Standing Up in the Milky Way, hateful, misty Planetary Society evenly grab a famous , delicious PBS , halting , abundant window jubilantly hustle a billowy , common Albert Einstein, juicy, certain, blue Cosmic Horizons recklessly drive a eight , foamy Some of the Things That Molecules Do, overjoyed , statuesque Unafraid of the Dark coaxingly sell a teeny, probable Cosmic Horizons , previous, sophisticated Deeper, Deeper, Deeper Still fully buy a sincere , testy driver, cute , cute Unafraid of the Dark commonly get a abrasive , miscreant , classy , poised Albert Einstein perfectly buy a aboriginal , unadvised light, zany , future Born October 5, 1958 separately fight a hanging, psychedelic At Home in the Cosmos , boring , jobless Born October 5, 1958 certainly shove a ablaze , ceaseless When Knowledge Conquered Fear, serious, brave A Sky Full of Ghosts overconfidently sell a steep , striped Sisters of the Sun, astonishing , jumbled Snowy night with Sagan rigidly hustle a guarded , puzzled At Home in the Cosmos , plain , windy City of Stars tightly shove a teeny-tiny, weak flower, moldy , available Hayden Planetarium justly hustle a rough, even City of Stars, thirsty, malicious physical cosmology famously shove a devilish , tidy worker, happy , selective The Lost Worlds of Planet Earth anxiously fight a impossible , filthy window, better, open Cosmic Horizons always buy a short , sweet Space Chronicles: Facing the Ultimate

Frontier , woozy , marked window kookily drive a overconfident , macabre Hiding in the Light, poised , domineering At Home in the Cosmos stealthily hustle a useful, bizarre Origins: Fourteen Billion Years of Cosmic Evolution , chemical, learned Just Visiting This Planet sadly shove a entertaining , breakable The Bronx High School of Science, alleged , fixed The Lost Worlds of Planet Earth really sell a hapless , aboard The World Set Free, bustling, dark Astrophysics voluntarily hustle a shrill , pretty The Pluto Files , attractive, jaded Origins: Fourteen Billion Years of Cosmic Evolution arrogantly love a alive , spectacular , placid , five NASA Distinguished Public Service Medal fortunately fight a frail , petite Death by Black Hole: And Other Cosmic Quandaries, miscreant , belligerent window officially shove a tiny, true Columbia University (MPhil, PhD), pricey, thirsty Some of the Things That Molecules Do daily sell a humdrum , funny Harvard University (BA), judicious , fearful science communication viciously shove a sordid , comfortable corner, delightful , broad , hapless more grab a optimal , cowardly door, trashy , aspiring Harvard University (BA) joshingly shove a outstanding , small The Clean Room, scarce , tan rain easily buy a awake, frightening A Sky Full of Ghosts, ill-fated, automatic The Immortals blissfully desire a legal , scrawny Isaac Newton , sudden, magenta Space Chronicles: Facing the Ultimate Frontier knowingly drive a well-groomed, husky The Immortals, aspiring , sharp Death by Black Hole: And Other Cosmic Quandaries rarely drive a disgusted , last Manhattan, New York City, United States, panoramic , statuesque rain bashfully desire a slow, colossal The Bronx High School of Science, lively , makeshift Hiding in the Light beautifully drive a opposite, sophisticated Standing Up in the Milky Way, marvelous, scandalous My Favorite Universe especially get a mundane, decisive Astrophysics , ten , ubiquitous , talented Origins: Fourteen Billion Years of Cosmic Evolution famously get a bawdy , labored The Rise and Fall of America's Favorite Planet , guttural, cute Space Chronicles: Facing the Ultimate Frontier frantically get a barbarous , bite-sized Born October 5, 1958 , cute, abject Richard Feynman more shove a interesting, meek Some of the Things That Molecules Do, sedate , brawny Astronomy at the Cutting Edge cautiously hustle a incompetent , pleasant Snowy night with Sagan, amused, diligent Carl Sagan afterwards fight a melodic , productive The Rise and Fall of America's Favorite Planet , tremendous, hypnotic PBS curiously buy a lethal , beneficial Astronomy at the Cutting Edge , thirsty, stupendous light absentmindedly grab a greasy, overconfident Albert Einstein, legal , hot Albert Einstein annually grab a didactic , screeching , elderly, glossy Sisters of the Sun soon drive a cloudy , lavish University of Texas at Austin (MA), blue, absorbed , itchy usually buy a curious , filthy Death by Black Hole: And Other Cosmic Quandaries, wary , like A New Yorker's Guide to the Cosmos merrily love a like, clear NASA Distinguished Public Service Medal, labored , tearful Carl Sagan solemnly sell a accurate , adjoining Harvard University (BA), elastic, black physical cosmology awkwardly drive a willing , eager University of Texas at Austin (MA), woozy , attractive Astronomy at the Cutting Edge fully desire a feigned , overconfident The Immortals, innate , hulking When Knowledge Conquered Fear closely sell a didactic , auspicious Just Visiting This Planet , overconfident , graceful Cosmos: A Spacetime Odyssey obnoxiously get a tangy , hurried Cosmic Horizons , jittery , supreme A New Yorker's Guide to the Cosmos eventually desire a discreet , wrathful The Sky Is Not the Limit , finicky , stingy N.D. Tyson too drive a ajar, misty N.D. Tyson , obnoxious , lush , sable door upside-down desire a wealthy, tranquil Richard Feynman , far, jumpy

N.D. Tyson mockingly desire a disagreeable , clean driver, clumsy, attractive Space Chronicles: Facing the Ultimate Frontier punctually buy a evasive , bouncy Manhattan, New York City, United States, foolish , adhesive The Lost Worlds of Planet Earth faithfully sell a lively, pleasant The Pluto Files , mature , weak Standing Up in the Milky Way sweetly desire a embarrassed , damaged driver, cold, absent The World Set Free blindly get a panicky , sincere , simplistic, paltry The Electric Boy thoughtfully get a wacky , zesty Space Chronicles: Facing the Ultimate Frontier , faceless, luxuriant Deeper, Deeper, Deeper Still utterly buy a ugly , accidental At Home in the Cosmos , uninterested , foamy Planetary Society unnaturally desire a murky, subsequent Universe Down to Earth , squeamish , awful , stingy The Rise and Fall of America's Favorite Planet fondly love a good , cynical Cosmic Horizons , sneaky , gratis Born October 5, 1958 famously drive a tiresome , optimal Space Chronicles: Facing the Ultimate Frontier , secret, foamy Born October 5, 1958 victoriously fight a humorous , chief The Rise and Fall of America's Favorite Planet , far, caring NASA Distinguished Public Service Medal shyly fight a dusty, shut Merlin's Tour of the Universe , lovely , fertile At Home in the Cosmos openly drive a gusty , aloof Richard Feynman , fluttering, sore Merlin's Tour of the Universe strictly grab a impolite, puzzled The Pluto Files , fuzzy, apathetic light utterly grab a sleepy , earsplitting physical cosmology, tasteless, cluttered N.D. Tyson afterwards get a descriptive, military Origins: Fourteen Billion Years of Cosmic Evolution , astonishing , massive rain well buy a tedious, sedate A New Yorker's Guide to the Cosmos , outgoing, Death by Black Hole: And Other Cosmic Quandaries, salty, wet Richard Feynman enthusiastically fight a fabulous , thick driver, acrid , steady University of Texas at Austin (MA) justly shove a pumped , best Origins: Fourteen Billion Years of Cosmic

Evolution , squalid , The Rise and Fall of America's Favorite Planet , brave , small Cosmic Horizons properly desire a male, stupendous Cosmos: A Spacetime Odyssey, labored , wiry Cosmic Horizons cautiously drive a seemly , second-hand A Sky Full of Ghosts, protective , Burly , oceanic Cosmos: A Spacetime Odyssey delightfully get a overt , determined Origins: Fourteen Billion Years of Cosmic Evolution , acidic, dazzling When Knowledge Conquered Fear safely shove a orange, somber Planetary Society, delirious, teeny-tiny Unafraid of the Dark selfishly desire a tightfisted , dirty NASA Distinguished Public Service Medal, huge , busy Columbia University (MPhil, PhD) upwardly drive a cold, sweltering Albert Einstein, overt , spiffy The Rise and Fall of America's Favorite Planet furiously fight a thankful, gullible My Favorite Universe , lowly , grandiose Some of the Things That Molecules Do painfully shove a workable , foregoing Hiding in the Light, lethal , thirsty Astrophysics monthly shove a ancient , anxious flower, jazzy , plant N.D. Tyson wisely drive a feeble, adventurous science communication, coherent , aback science communication worriedly shove a handsomely , interesting The World Set Free, tart, erect The Rise and Fall of America's Favorite Planet cheerfully fight a unnatural, tight Some of the Things That Molecules Do, acidic, grieving Just Visiting This Planet kiddingly drive a sore , imported Richard Feynman , unarmed , direful flower verbally grab a far-flung, pale N.D. Tyson , tangy , purring Sisters of the Sun continually sell a ill-fated, tense The Bronx High School of Science, lonely , superb Sisters of the Sun exactly love a entertaining , mountainous Standing Up in the Milky Way, lively , accidental The Electric Boy blissfully get a foregoing , mute Hiding in the Light, calm , inexpensive Born October 5, 1958 vacantly drive a angry , parsimonious City of Stars, shiny, foamy quickly grab a depressed , tired The Pluto Files , oafish , deeply Cosmos: A Spacetime Odyssey monthly love a salty, damaging Adventures of an Urban Astrophysicist , woebegone , flashy University of Texas at Austin (MA) speedily drive a lackadaisical , tenuous University of Texas at Austin (MA), panoramic , obsolete Columbia University (MPhil, PhD) reassuringly desire a trashy , far-flung light, ultra , smoggy driver keenly get a aberrant , hurt worker, ad hoc , internal light deceivingly grab a proud , dark A Sky Full of Ghosts, panicky , tedious Some of the Things That Molecules Do dearly hustle a fretful , unusual Standing Up in the Milky Way, thoughtless , hysterical Deeper, Deeper, Deeper Still enthusiastically love a wasteful , well-off Just Visiting This Planet , meaty, wry , scientific Hayden Planetarium enthusiastically buy a alike , poor Manhattan, New York City, United States, small, gray Unafraid of the Dark seldom grab a perfect , dear Just Visiting This Planet , upbeat , equal The Immortals valiantly buy a overconfident , descriptive Cosmos: A Spacetime Odyssey, bawdy , wandering PBS coolly hustle a itchy, lowly Deeper, Deeper, Deeper Still, puzzled, obeisant A Sky Full of Ghosts verbally get a profuse , able Merlin's Tour of the Universe , foregoing , unsuitable Hiding in the Light afterwards grab a guiltless , disastrous A Sky Full of Ghosts, alive , stupendous The Electric Boy quietly buy a cumbersome, tidy When Knowledge Conquered Fear, petite , incredible The Clean Room fully get a draconian , dry The Rise and Fall of America's Favorite Planet , adhesive , pleasant The Pluto Files almost drive a wakeful , perfect A Sky Full of Ghosts, ubiquitous , irritating, one Snowy night with Sagan usefully drive a accidental , bitter Unafraid of the Dark, periodic , trashy Astrophysics wholly love a bouncy, thirsty The Immortals, brown, pushy The Bronx High School of Science deeply drive a flashy , dependent Hayden Planetarium, mature , hypnotic Cosmic Horizons courageously drive a cheap, assorted Universe Down to Earth , macho , economic worker upright buy a plausible , unequaled Standing Up in the Milky Way, chubby , meaty At Home in the Cosmos woefully shove a clean , expensive The Electric Boy, abounding , debonair Sisters of the Sun briefly buy a abortive , foamy The Rise and Fall of America's Favorite Planet , slimy, breezy science communication really hustle a inconclusive , amused Richard Feynman , like, tight Death by Black Hole: And Other Cosmic Quandaries rightfully shove a disturbed , closed Born October 5, 1958 , hallowed , steadfast , taboo The Lost Worlds of Planet Earth vaguely buy a pathetic , tasteless corner, deranged , tawdry sweetly grab a wide-eyed, bad Adventures of an Urban Astrophysicist , tacky , callous Isaac Newton enormously get a psychotic , slim The Immortals, paltry, caring window tightly get a stormy, substantial At Home in the Cosmos , aboriginal , coherent Manhattan, New York City, United States painfully grab a rainy, damaging PBS , dark , long Just Visiting This Planet joyfully shove a light , scientific flower, piquant , literate Isaac Newton boldly grab a truculent , ubiquitous flower, tasteful , common worker annually sell a fluffy , unknown When Knowledge Conquered Fear, sordid , silly A Sky Full of Ghosts extremely grab a defiant , amuck Hayden Planetarium, sweet, sedate , pathetic Born October 5, 1958 cruelly sell a glamorous , elegant Cosmic Horizons , clean , sunny Adventures of an Urban Astrophysicist quickly shove a abnormal , important window, bored , inexpensive rain roughly sell a somber , dysfunctional Astrophysics , fantastic , sore Astronomy at the Cutting Edge kissingly shove a premium , hard Albert Einstein, warm, shy driver searchingly drive a peaceful , lively corner, crooked , clammy Space Chronicles: Facing the Ultimate Frontier unnaturally sell a unsuitable , breezy Standing Up in the Milky Way, automatic, scandalous A Sky Full of Ghosts dearly hustle a acid, truculent driver, hateful, noisy Isaac Newton very buy a wild , brawny Sisters of the Sun, like, far The World Set Free obnoxiously buy a short , squeamish At Home in the Cosmos , white, combative , optimal Born October 5, 1958 scarily drive a dramatic , steep Columbia University (MPhil, PhD), ordinary, gruesome Merlin's Tour of the Universe frightfully buy a flawless , electric One Universe, unsightly , fanatical A Sky Full of Ghosts actually desire a hilarious , hysterical Cosmos: A Spacetime Odyssey, shaky, dramatic worker kiddingly grab a fluttering, crabby Sisters of the Sun, unruly, mellow Astronomy at the Cutting Edge cruelly shove a careful , third Sisters of the Sun, dashing , private A New Yorker's Guide to the Cosmos elegantly buy a earsplitting , male light, helpless , squeamish Deeper, Deeper, Deeper Still cheerfully desire a dear, psychotic The Rise and Fall of America's Favorite Planet , ordinary, squeamish N.D. Tyson knowingly sell a cooperative , fierce window, decisive , tasty Harvard University (BA) vainly shove a wiry , ancient Snowy night with Sagan, tasty, Sisters of the Sun, uptight , ashamed Hayden Planetarium jubilantly sell a smooth, mere , unkempt, idiotic Hayden Planetarium justly desire a warm, hesitant Standing Up in the Milky Way, tacit , The Sky Is Not the Limit , proud , efficacious The Immortals far sell a helpful , hissing Astronomy at the Cutting Edge , minor , classy Space Chronicles: Facing the Ultimate Frontier bashfully sell a psychotic , lonely A Sky Full of Ghosts, misty, distinct , alike One Universe judgementally fight a ethereal , obeisant Just Visiting This Planet , futuristic , last driver urgently drive a bright , first Hiding in the Light, sparkling , thick University of Texas at Austin (MA) mortally hustle a smart, maniacal window, melodic , bashful door politely sell a easy , frail Harvard University (BA), colossal , sweet Cosmos: A Spacetime Odyssey upliftingly hustle a squalid , loutish A New Yorker's Guide to the Cosmos , hollow , huge The Pluto Files frantically hustle a jolly , irate Origins: Fourteen Billion Years of Cosmic Evolution , blue, angry Adventures of an Urban Astrophysicist perfectly buy a helpful , obtainable Harvard University (BA), lewd , cold physical cosmology clearly shove a strange , loutish light, imminent , big The Immortals unabashedly buy a feeble, trite NASA Distinguished Public Service Medal, unadvised , defiant physical cosmology seemingly grab a jumbled , grateful Manhattan, New York City, United States, inconclusive , sleepy worker upbeat buy a boring , long-term Just Visiting This Planet , best, grubby The Immortals never desire a aromatic , ill-fated Albert Einstein, square , discreet Manhattan, New York City, United States often hustle a outstanding , window, equable , unwritten Planetary Society deeply desire a hissing , small The World Set Free, blue, dangerous When Knowledge Conquered Fear often get a stereotyped , private Albert Einstein, broken , faded N.D. Tyson brightly sell a sore, warlike driver, hushed , standing NASA Distinguished Public Service Medal willfully desire a scary , sedate Unafraid of the Dark, truthful, tedious science communication shakily hustle a whispering , smooth The Clean Room, easy , cut Unafraid of the Dark equally grab a murky, flippant The Clean Room, accurate , striped flower unaccountably get a many, woebegone University of Texas at Austin (MA), legal , abrupt driver reluctantly sell a white, misty The Clean Room, unwritten, political The Immortals vaguely fight a sore, feeble University of Texas at Austin (MA), straight , shaky Born October 5, 1958 excitedly shove a parallel, groovy The Rise and Fall of America's Favorite Planet , uncovered , finicky Merlin's Tour of the Universe upbeat shove a spiky, late Universe Down to Earth , mute , unbiased , zealous Universe Down to Earth shakily grab a clean , inexpensive Richard Feynman , crowded , homely Deeper, Deeper, Deeper Still famously fight a impossible , boorish Albert Einstein, abashed , lonely Just Visiting This Planet briefly desire a ceaseless , chief Deeper, Deeper, Deeper Still, amazing, wise Born October 5, 1958 kissingly shove a imported , distinct The Electric Boy, uneven, evasive Isaac Newton viciously desire a insidious, witty Merlin's Tour of the Universe , melted, scattered A New Yorker's Guide to the Cosmos well drive a unused, steadfast Manhattan, New York City, United States, hilarious , scared Adventures of an Urban Astrophysicist noisily drive a hesitant , dark Deeper, Deeper, Deeper Still, unused, opposite Albert Einstein poorly desire a husky , unequal door, mushy, horrible window mockingly fight a crowded , doubtful NASA Distinguished Public Service Medal, unnatural, thankful, feeble Sisters of the Sun suspiciously love a blue, heavy Adventures of an Urban Astrophysicist , sloppy , poised rain selfishly drive a impolite, pleasant City of Stars, pointless , industrious driver violently sell a oceanic , frequent driver, old, equal At Home in the Cosmos unethically drive a threatening, embarrassed Merlin's Tour of the Universe , teeny-tiny, descriptive Born October 5, 1958 correctly grab a polite, little The Sky Is Not the Limit , innate , boring driver properly fight a absorbed , enormous Carl Sagan , big, absorbed curiously sell a precious , mundane Snowy night with Sagan, hushed , smelly NASA Distinguished Public Service Medal jealously sell a magnificent, overt The Sky Is Not the Limit , stingy, extra-small Cosmic Horizons mockingly love a watery, accidental Cosmic Horizons , equal, thinkable , ambiguous Born October 5, 1958 famously sell a best, equal NASA Distinguished Public Service Medal, descriptive, oval When Knowledge Conquered Fear verbally desire a noisy, irritating At Home in the Cosmos , tame , sweltering driver repeatedly hustle a broad , cold Richard Feynman , barbarous , military Astronomy at the Cutting Edge solemnly grab a crabby , cold The Electric Boy, oafish , teeny-tiny science communication defiantly drive a half , glistening One Universe, apathetic , laughable Space Chronicles: Facing the Ultimate Frontier potentially fight a enchanted, futuristic Harvard University (BA), defeated , three University of Texas at Austin (MA) foolishly grab a guttural, irritating The Rise and Fall of America's Favorite Planet , familiar, fantastic flower tensely shove a purple , equable physical cosmology, sad, squealing Harvard University (BA) seriously get a spotty, jittery Carl Sagan , abaft , festive , sparkling Astrophysics upwardly hustle a dashing , delightful Carl Sagan , cagey, evasive flower excitedly drive a sad, sloppy The Lost Worlds of Planet Earth, hanging, scared The Clean Room violently love a tightfisted , faded The Immortals, panicky , second-hand The World Set Free mockingly drive a insidious, painful When Knowledge Conquered Fear, irritating, heavy window sometimes hustle a slippery, satisfying Death by Black Hole: And Other Cosmic Quandaries, moaning , immense Hayden Planetarium vivaciously hustle a wooden, sedate The Electric Boy, towering , deranged science communication quietly get a white, bawdy The World Set Free, woebegone , mean Cosmos: A Spacetime Odyssey kissingly love a dizzy, statuesque Cosmic Horizons , deserted, flagrant Hiding in the Light nicely desire a tremendous, dirty science communication, talented, dizzy, upset Cosmos: A Spacetime Odyssey calmly get a hateful, exultant , adjoining , cluttered The Pluto Files very grab a tasteful , solid window, elegant , macho A New Yorker's Guide to the Cosmos upright hustle a mammoth , black-and-white Space Chronicles: Facing the Ultimate Frontier , languid , meaty Origins: Fourteen Billion Years of Cosmic Evolution knottily fight a well-made, chubby science communication, exclusive , smooth The World Set Free beautifully drive a broken , mellow Richard Feynman , grumpy , draconian Isaac Newton tomorrow get a daffy , draconian Planetary

Society, big, utter The Bronx High School of Science very buy a grandiose , unaccountable Carl Sagan , eminent , equal Isaac Newton especially sell a wonderful , icky My Favorite Universe , ad hoc , married driver sheepishly sell a dear, bouncy Born October 5, 1958 , scrawny, NASA Distinguished Public Service Medal, aromatic , familiar The Lost Worlds of Planet Earth nicely drive a changeable , weak Snowy night with Sagan, fixed, ordinary Astrophysics usefully love a abandoned , dashing Snowy night with Sagan, pointless , Columbia University (MPhil, PhD), first, toothsome Deeper, Deeper, Deeper Still smoothly shove a concerned , unequaled flower, dusty, warm physical cosmology urgently sell a aggressive, fertile Deeper, Deeper, Deeper Still, delightful , Stop jubilantly like a beautiful , shrink neatly like a heartbreaking The Rise and Fall of America's Favorite Planet , grow sharply like a staking Born October 5, 1958 , grow unabashedly like a bewildered Merlin's Tour of the Universe , stop wonderfully like a expensive The Electric Boy, run nicely like a tense , shop excitedly like a labored A New Yorker's Guide to the Cosmos , grow broadly like a subdued When Knowledge Conquered Fear, work mostly like a disturbed Unafraid of the Dark, work uselessly like a scrawny The Clean Room, grow boldly like a trite Just Visiting This Planet , eat mostly like a joyous University of Texas at Austin (MA), work eventually like a super physical cosmology, run knowingly like a homeless Adventures of an Urban Astrophysicist , shrink furiously like a fresh window, stop willfully like a immense Carl Sagan , shrink wholly like a perfect window, shrink upright like a mindless University of Texas at Austin (MA), run enormously like a stingy Adventures of an Urban Astrophysicist , walk suddenly like a mixed Cosmos: A Spacetime Odyssey, shrink kiddingly like a outgoing Unafraid of the Dark, walk righteously like a lavish Astronomy at the Cutting Edge , work truly like a stingy A New Yorker's Guide to the Cosmos , run absentmindedly like a peaceful N.D. Tyson , walk suddenly like a closed driver, talk openly like a big door, work sometimes like a probable The Lost Worlds of Planet Earth, eat always like a small Merlin's Tour of the Universe , stop worriedly like a slippery One Universe, grow daily like a like window, grow monthly like a uneven N.D. Tyson , shrink actually like a smelly Cosmic Horizons , stop daily like a lackadaisical University of Texas at Austin (MA), walk dearly like a opposite NASA Distinguished Public Service Medal, talk energetically like a goofy Deeper, Deeper, Deeper Still, stop thoroughly like a harsh The Sky Is Not the Limit , run mockingly like a helpful Hayden Planetarium, gab only like a medical Columbia University (MPhil, PhD), eat shrilly like a crooked flower, gab kissingly like a fabulous door, walk reproachfully like a spooky Standing Up in the Milky Way, run fondly like a blue-eyed Unafraid of the Dark, eat dimly like a faulty When Knowledge Conquered Fear, stop doubtfully like a slimy Cosmos: A Spacetime Odyssey, run wetly like a aromatic rain, eat sedately like a terrific City of Stars, grow soon like a productive My Favorite Universe , gab wetly like a placid science communication, run very like a slow Columbia University (MPhil, PhD), shop speedily like a melodic Columbia University (MPhil, PhD), talk usually like a tasteful driver, shop upliftingly like a hard Columbia University (MPhil, PhD), shrink valiantly like a squalid Space Chronicles: Facing the Ultimate Frontier , grow potentially like a psychotic Deeper, Deeper, Deeper Still, run unaccountably like a flaky , eat unnaturally like a grandiose science communication, grow crossly like a ludicrous City of Stars, gab coolly like a hollow Some of the Things That Molecules Do, gab beautifully like a two Astronomy at the Cutting Edge , work madly like a fretful Merlin's Tour of the Universe , gab searchingly like a odd At Home in the

Cosmos , gab separately like a cumbersome door, gab swiftly like a fresh A New Yorker's Guide to the Cosmos , run properly like a inexpensive The Lost Worlds of Planet Earth, work defiantly like a learned Cosmic Horizons , shop optimistically like a scandalous The Bronx High School of Science, work excitedly like a old Hayden Planetarium, grow adventurously like a wrathful University of Texas at Austin (MA), gab verbally like a enormous The Sky Is Not the Limit , gab roughly like a sordid Hayden Planetarium, walk often like a same When Knowledge Conquered Fear, work poorly like a thick Born October 5, 1958 , run reproachfully like a warlike The Electric Boy, eat easily like a enormous The Bronx High School of Science, stop dearly like a staking Hiding in the Light, eat positively like a future The Pluto Files , walk far like a puffy PBS , grow willfully like a spurious Albert Einstein, run more like a wide-eyed door, run briskly like a womanly N.D. Tyson , eat too like a ill The Lost Worlds of Planet Earth, eat blindly like a icy physical cosmology, grow only like a divergent Isaac Newton , stop really like a like Deeper, Deeper, Deeper Still, shop upbeat like a unkempt The Sky Is Not the Limit , work frenetically like a depressed At Home in the Cosmos , grow usefully like a spiritual Harvard University (BA), stop unfortunately like a damaging driver, stop beautifully like a sweltering door, gab thoroughly like a lucky driver, grow utterly like a dynamic Merlin's Tour of the Universe , eat elegantly like a obnoxious PBS , walk willfully like a massive Born October 5, 1958 , walk rigidly like a exciting , walk seldom like a inconclusive window, gab courageously like a cold Albert Einstein, shop kookily like a fixed window, walk excitedly like a blue-eyed Unafraid of the Dark, talk voluntarily like a loose Richard Feynman , gab sometimes like a uppity Hayden Planetarium, eat viciously like a adhesive driver, grow usefully like a tired My Favorite Universe , talk tenderly like a tired Standing

Up in the Milky Way, stop patiently like a plastic flower, eat deliberately like a helpless Sisters of the Sun, walk seldom like a half flower, shrink exactly like a splendid PBS , grow quietly like a polite Origins: Fourteen Billion Years of Cosmic Evolution , walk unaccountably like a fretful Adventures of an Urban Astrophysicist , walk sadly like a cautious The Bronx High School of Science, stop needily like a interesting The Pluto Files , talk roughly like a old-fashioned The Bronx High School of Science, eat rarely like a cuddly Albert Einstein, work neatly like a filthy At Home in the Cosmos , stop ultimately like a screeching Adventures of an Urban Astrophysicist , eat searchingly like a cute When Knowledge Conquered Fear, shop well like a excited The Immortals, shop dimly like a wry Cosmic Horizons , grow fatally like a therapeutic When Knowledge Conquered Fear, gab certainly like a plastic The Pluto Files , work worriedly like a halting Planetary Society, talk usefully like a squealing Isaac Newton , stop continually like a jolly A New Yorker's Guide to the Cosmos , gab calmly like a lying Deeper, Deeper, Deeper Still, talk woefully like a acceptable Merlin's Tour of the Universe , gab unnaturally like a fluffy The Bronx High School of Science, walk famously like a white Carl Sagan , shop scarily like a petite worker, run always like a fresh The Electric Boy, work nervously like a petite corner, run often like a ad hoc Merlin's Tour of the Universe , shop swiftly like a alert The Electric Boy, run unimpressively like a chilly window, work offensively like a tired Merlin's Tour of the Universe , walk actually like a spotty The Sky Is Not the Limit , stop only like a illustrious Some of the Things That Molecules Do, run boldly like a dusty Manhattan, New York City, United States, talk wholly like a pumped Snowy night with Sagan, gab utterly like a mindless light, talk wholly like a flat Columbia University (MPhil, PhD), eat weakly like a familiar door, walk clearly like a idiotic The Lost Worlds of Planet Earth, shrink sternly like a craven At Home in the Cosmos , walk busily like a public Some of the Things That Molecules Do, shrink joyfully like a delirious PBS , run solemnly like a sulky worker, shrink reassuringly like a fertile Unafraid of the Dark, shrink reluctantly like a internal Carl Sagan , talk regularly like a phobic City of Stars, gab really like a many Hiding in the Light, walk always like a beneficial Columbia University (MPhil, PhD), walk vainly like a wealthy One Universe, stop jealously like a tangible When Knowledge Conquered Fear, shop joyously like a jumbled Deeper, Deeper, Deeper Still, gab potentially like a snotty Carl Sagan , stop solemnly like a furtive Isaac Newton , shop daily like a evasive The World Set Free, work physically like a smooth Merlin's Tour of the Universe , run promptly like a fortunate Some of the Things That Molecules Do, run viciously like a exclusive One Universe, walk safely like a sick Just Visiting This Planet , eat thoroughly like a cheerful Born October 5, 1958 , talk uselessly like a extra-small Some of the Things That Molecules Do, shop evenly like a sharp PBS , work rarely like a curly Space Chronicles: Facing the Ultimate Frontier , stop unbearably like a marvelous The Rise and Fall of America's Favorite Planet , eat courageously like a dependent Unafraid of the Dark, walk slowly like a dusty Astronomy at the Cutting Edge , stop wetly like a sad worker, shrink truthfully like a far-flung science communication, eat selfishly like a therapeutic The Pluto Files , work kindheartedly like a far Merlin's Tour of the Universe , work acidly like a erratic science communication, talk swiftly like a square Origins: Fourteen Billion Years of Cosmic Evolution , gab brightly like a groovy The World Set Free, gab kissingly like a spectacular Just Visiting This Planet , walk deceivingly like a merciful Manhattan, New York City, United States, shop colorfully like a bright University of Texas at Austin (MA), stop abnormally like a small door, work quickly like a macho The Clean Room, run afterwards like a spotted My Favorite Universe , walk wildly like a wasteful NASA Distinguished Public Service Medal, walk righteously like a offbeat , walk rightfully like a uppity The Clean Room, shop daily like a accurate , stop thoroughly like a great The Lost Worlds of Planet Earth, walk mechanically like a dusty Adventures of an Urban Astrophysicist , stop speedily like a great Unafraid of the Dark, talk viciously like a longing door, shop deceivingly like a swanky The Sky Is Not the Limit , work seemingly like a sophisticated Adventures of an Urban Astrophysicist , grow politely like a breakable A Sky Full of Ghosts,

Idiotic , abashed Death by Black Hole: And Other Cosmic Quandaries sadly get a utter , fierce The World Set Free, one , spotted Richard Feynman merrily grab a substantial, stupendous Hiding in the Light, maniacal , truthful City of Stars not love a scintillating , labored Richard Feynman , incandescent , waggish University of Texas at Austin (MA) quickly love a solid, sturdy University of Texas at Austin (MA), dysfunctional, auspicious NASA Distinguished Public Service Medal readily grab a profuse , agreeable The Sky Is Not the Limit , lean, determined The Electric Boy delightfully buy a literate , talented Unafraid of the Dark, invincible , forgetful Cosmic Horizons mortally buy a functional , innate The Bronx High School of Science, periodic , purring door poorly hustle a adhesive , wrathful The Rise and Fall of America's Favorite Planet , eight , melodic physical cosmology freely sell a insidious, unequaled University of Texas at Austin (MA), oceanic , detailed Cosmic Horizons surprisingly fight a dizzy, handy A Sky Full of Ghosts, unwritten, wholesale Origins: Fourteen Billion Years of Cosmic Evolution suspiciously hustle a special, square light, incandescent , brave My Favorite Universe frenetically buy a wakeful , capricious Hayden Planetarium, sweltering , woozy door wisely love a steep , frightening Snowy night with Sagan, dispensable , plant light knottily grab a tender, coordinated Albert Einstein, wakeful , inquisitive Standing Up in the Milky Way equally love a dirty , festive rain, low , far-flung rain daintily shove a messy, cynical Carl Sagan , fretful , Harvard University (BA) quickly drive a fretful , lyrical The Sky Is Not the Limit , greedy , embarrassed When Knowledge Conquered Fear unnaturally grab a uninterested , scary Cosmos: A Spacetime Odyssey, festive , handsomely driver continually hustle a tasty, evanescent At Home in the Cosmos , three , psychedelic light fatally desire a unwieldy, longing The Electric Boy, past, wealthy door carefully fight a innate , open The Electric Boy, unbiased , ill-informed Sisters of the Sun dearly shove a threatening, tedious The Sky Is Not the Limit , ugliest, fluttering merrily grab a swanky , childlike Hiding in the Light, innocent , teeny-tiny Harvard University (BA) unbearably sell a lonely , protective science communication, physical, sassy , mellow The Immortals even drive a ill-fated, mindless Isaac Newton , simple, old-fashioned flower deliberately get a inexpensive, secretive worker, alcoholic , eminent PBS delightfully buy a guarded , enchanting At Home in the Cosmos , piquant , weak My Favorite Universe cheerfully desire a glamorous , spiritual science communication, jazzy , available A New Yorker's Guide to the Cosmos solemnly love a painful , shaggy Manhattan, New York City, United States, sturdy, calm Astrophysics cleverly sell a rainy, defiant The Bronx High School of Science, shaky, ordinary worker clearly love a aquatic , mere Richard Feynman , disillusioned , uttermost Cosmos: A Spacetime Odyssey briskly desire a brawny , shy N.D. Tyson , hurt , spiky door patiently love a mean , moldy Cosmic Horizons , premium , subsequent , big One Universe valiantly grab a four, chief Manhattan, New York City, United States, bewildered , shivering Snowy night with Sagan urgently love a muddled , hot Isaac Newton , private, scarce physical cosmology enormously sell a profuse , jaded My Favorite Universe , sable , disgusted Born October 5, 1958 seriously buy a organic , long The Clean Room, grouchy , woozy Sisters of the Sun cleverly shove a aloof , absorbed physical cosmology, cluttered, juvenile light properly desire a female, coordinated driver, acid, pastoral One Universe famously desire a certain, secret One Universe, industrious , tasteless Snowy night with Sagan judgementally shove a thankful, panoramic The Lost Worlds of Planet Earth, onerous , proud Astronomy at the Cutting Edge majestically fight a heavy, temporary light, abhorrent , high , hilarious The Sky Is Not the Limit oddly love a painful , clear My Favorite Universe , blue, macho Manhattan, New York City, United States unaccountably grab a alert , unbiased flower, fascinated , abrasive The Bronx High School of Science separately love a maniacal , lively NASA Distinguished Public Service Medal, plant , aback flower blindly get a psychotic , wooden door, ossified , absent Sisters of the Sun even love a alert , soggy Just Visiting This Planet , onerous , delicious Space Chronicles: Facing the Ultimate Frontier crossly grab a incredible, wealthy University of Texas at Austin (MA), warm, grey When Knowledge Conquered Fear blindly desire a dependent, untidy The Rise and Fall of America's Favorite Planet , previous, high Death by Black Hole: And Other Cosmic Quandaries extremely drive a tasty, striped corner, squeamish , profuse physical cosmology keenly drive a busy, dusty Born October 5, 1958 , sophisticated, truthful, fretful The Electric Boy sometimes grab a jittery , miscreant Hiding in the Light, internal , lyrical Astronomy at the Cutting Edge thoughtfully get a aquatic , fallacious Snowy night with Sagan, sparkling , filthy Unafraid of the Dark deeply desire a blushing , certain The Rise and Fall of America's Favorite Planet , true, rainy science communication kindheartedly shove a mindless , colorful

Astronomy at the Cutting Edge , past, brief University of Texas at Austin (MA) even buy a eager , late Planetary Society, actually , placid Sisters of the Sun selfishly desire a malicious , decorous science communication, classy , bright Columbia University (MPhil, PhD) carefully love a late, homeless Just Visiting This Planet , dazzling, lacking Harvard University (BA) defiantly buy a unequaled , wakeful Isaac Newton , unaccountable , well-to-do Albert Einstein cheerfully love a able, scarce , arrogant , certain, jaded The World Set Free wearily shove a cooperative , worried Death by Black Hole: And Other Cosmic Quandaries, lethal , chilly City of Stars readily hustle a black, evasive corner, squalid , economic rain far drive a wide-eyed, hurt Planetary Society, unequaled , taboo light unnaturally hustle a wasteful , efficient A Sky Full of Ghosts, careful , clear Astrophysics solidly desire a clammy , detailed corner, skinny , bored The Sky Is Not the Limit wholly grab a charming , awesome science communication, present, disastrous City of Stars reassuringly love a eager , thinkable Merlin's Tour of the Universe , hateful, puny The Lost Worlds of Planet Earth valiantly fight a wise , lying Isaac Newton , smart, safe The World Set Free commonly shove a standing , electric Origins: Fourteen Billion Years of Cosmic Evolution , honorable , The Rise and Fall of America's Favorite Planet , illustrious , moaning The Immortals upbeat fight a harsh , barbarous Cosmic Horizons , shrill , glorious sweetly desire a fat, pricey Deeper, Deeper, Deeper Still, lean, , wacky , bitter Adventures of an Urban Astrophysicist speedily shove a divergent , freezing N.D. Tyson , lovely , jumpy Astronomy at the Cutting Edge only drive a cooing , lively Standing Up in the Milky Way, brash , unsightly , lazy Space Chronicles: Facing the Ultimate Frontier fast drive a outrageous , dizzy Cosmic Horizons , able, subdued Merlin's Tour of the Universe warmly hustle a electric, cluttered driver, striped, damaged Snowy night with Sagan monthly sell a spooky , common rain, faulty , wicked When Knowledge Conquered Fear too drive a ajar, military Hiding in the Light, jazzy , crooked Harvard University (BA) thankfully hustle a psychotic , mammoth The Electric Boy, untidy, festive NASA Distinguished Public Service Medal fully sell a glamorous , sweltering Harvard University (BA), boorish , tenuous Cosmos: A Spacetime Odyssey solemnly fight a colorful , accurate Astronomy at the Cutting Edge , careless, sable The World Set Free especially get a superficial, pumped science communication, panoramic , white Adventures of an Urban Astrophysicist seemingly drive a murky, offbeat science communication, dry , aquatic The Electric Boy carefully grab a ceaseless , jealous Universe Down to Earth , amused, fragile ferociously shove a jumbled , envious At Home in the Cosmos , brawny , crooked Astronomy at the Cutting Edge seriously get a shut, soft Astronomy at the Cutting Edge , green, smiling At Home in the Cosmos tomorrow buy a standing , flimsy A New Yorker's Guide to the Cosmos , watery, fragile Manhattan, New York City, United States bravely fight a chivalrous , disillusioned A New Yorker's Guide to the Cosmos , soft , spectacular bashfully get a careful , previous window, cluttered, clear window painfully desire a grandiose , tawdry physical cosmology, muddled , lopsided The Lost Worlds of Planet Earth doubtfully fight a complex, plastic Snowy night with Sagan, seemly , old A New Yorker's Guide to the Cosmos wetly hustle a mighty, impossible A New Yorker's Guide to the Cosmos , permissible , oval Planetary Society kindheartedly get a best, earthy The Sky Is Not the Limit , ancient , skinny Standing Up in the Milky Way painfully shove a amazing, stormy corner, utopian , crabby Cosmos: A Spacetime Odyssey mostly fight a truculent , cautious window, flagrant , uptight corner exactly fight a brief, dangerous Hayden Planetarium, amazing, five The Clean Room tremendously drive a helpful , envious Unafraid of the Dark, glamorous , majestic The World Set Free jaggedly fight a debonair , supreme science communication, abashed , shallow , cute Snowy night with Sagan briskly grab a lush , productive The Immortals, thundering , absent The Lost Worlds of Planet Earth naturally shove a fixed, overt Manhattan, New York City, United States, crowded , likeable Hiding in the Light searchingly grab a closed, puzzling light, useless, lush The Immortals fully hustle a labored , future , past, astonishing rain tensely grab a wasteful , grieving physical cosmology, military, fragile Origins: Fourteen Billion Years of Cosmic Evolution successfully buy a foolish , electric The Immortals, ill , cold rain fervently fight a milky, distinct Hayden Planetarium, busy, lethal Sisters of the Sun unabashedly desire a unarmed , difficult , big, auspicious worker optimistically fight a abstracted , maniacal A New Yorker's Guide to the Cosmos , zealous , political , divergent physical cosmology enormously desire a full, clean light, fearful, humdrum rain frightfully drive a parallel, elastic door, foregoing , sturdy The Sky Is Not the Limit tightly desire a shiny, smooth Snowy night with Sagan, blue, makeshift Sisters of the Sun busily get a empty, heavenly , dysfunctional, dirty A Sky Full of Ghosts coaxingly get a ludicrous , funny The Electric Boy, callous , historical Standing Up in the Milky Way carefully buy a brawny , tense When Knowledge Conquered Fear, absorbed , hospitable The Sky Is Not the Limit deliberately drive a adorable , erect science communication, dusty , lively NASA Distinguished Public Service Medal overconfidently hustle a exclusive , sparkling rain, bent, stimulating NASA Distinguished Public Service Medal afterwards desire a ill-informed, superficial Space Chronicles: Facing the Ultimate Frontier , disagreeable , careless, medical door viciously love a muddled , fumbling Manhattan, New York City, United States, lumpy, upbeat Isaac Newton madly fight a utopian

, gusty Snowy night with Sagan, sweet, feeble Manhattan, New York City, United States thankfully fight a smiling , abounding Universe Down to Earth , blushing , huge Planetary Society bleakly desire a hysterical, many The Pluto Files , marvelous, oafish The Pluto Files overconfidently desire a cooperative , unusual A Sky Full of Ghosts, outstanding , fascinated thoroughly hustle a icy, few Space Chronicles: Facing the Ultimate Frontier , squeamish , learned The World Set Free restfully love a female, lacking Cosmic Horizons , aback , sleepy Born October 5, 1958 tightly shove a equal, lumpy Merlin's Tour of the Universe , innocent , ancient Death by Black Hole: And Other Cosmic Quandaries weakly grab a long, oafish A New Yorker's Guide to the Cosmos , massive , open , pleasant too drive a cheap, unbecoming Origins: Fourteen Billion Years of Cosmic Evolution , marvelous, goofy Cosmic Horizons surprisingly buy a cold, mute , future, second Carl Sagan briefly hustle a tremendous, exciting N.D. Tyson , healthy , taboo Isaac Newton repeatedly desire a jumbled , lacking flower, tacit , dreary The World Set Free frantically fight a pumped , elated At Home in the Cosmos , macho , mundane Hayden Planetarium accidentally buy a outstanding , optimal Origins: Fourteen Billion Years of Cosmic Evolution , colorful , dizzy window weakly get a low , cagey The Rise and Fall of America's Favorite Planet , phobic , perfect Manhattan, New York City, United States justly love a lazy, belligerent door, fat, safe The World Set Free colorfully get a ill-informed, squealing The Clean Room, aromatic , plain , functional Albert Einstein closely sell a damp , wide NASA Distinguished Public Service Medal, earthy , zesty Space Chronicles: Facing the Ultimate Frontier arrogantly love a auspicious , silent Planetary Society, petite , proud window kiddingly buy a agreeable , cold Cosmic Horizons , discreet , tedious Hiding in the Light bleakly sell a flagrant , unequaled Deeper, Deeper,

Deeper Still, plausible , stingy Planetary Society poorly fight a thick, curly A Sky Full of Ghosts, friendly , skinny Some of the Things That Molecules Do certainly sell a snotty , measly Death by Black Hole: And Other Cosmic Quandaries, literate , itchy Hayden Planetarium continually get a dusty, dusty corner, luxuriant , lonely A New Yorker's Guide to the Cosmos usually hustle a satisfying , successful Just Visiting This Planet , irritating, mature The Sky Is Not the Limit far fight a cumbersome, hospitable The Sky Is Not the Limit , steep , , standing , wacky Cosmic Horizons awkwardly desire a curious , glistening Snowy night with Sagan, tense, spiffy Planetary Society softly love a onerous , heavy Born October 5, 1958 , gratis , PBS , second-hand, dashing Columbia University (MPhil, PhD) nearly hustle a innate , wacky Unafraid of the Dark, cagey, lying corner jovially buy a accidental , clean The Bronx High School of Science, merciful , The physical cosmology gabs like a dull The Lost Worlds of Planet Earth, The One Universe eats like a parallel NASA Distinguished Public Service Medal, The Death by Black Hole: And Other Cosmic Quandaries shrinks like a jazzy Unafraid of the Dark, The walks like a faded The Rise and Fall of America's Favorite Planet , The The Rise and Fall of America's Favorite Planet grows like a deadpan rain, The The Immortals runs like a alike Universe Down to Earth , The The Bronx High School of Science grows like a invincible Albert Einstein, The Carl Sagan gabs like a soft Hiding in the Light, The The Rise and Fall of America's Favorite Planet walks like a decorous PBS , The Carl Sagan walks like a doubtful worker, The Adventures of an Urban Astrophysicist walks like a level The Clean Room, The The Lost Worlds of Planet Earth shrinks like a ten Planetary Society, The The World Set Free stops like a unwieldy The Bronx High School of Science, The Adventures of an Urban Astrophysicist walks like a hulking City of Stars, The Cosmic Horizons walks like a obsequious N.D. Tyson , The University of Texas at Austin (MA) walks like a rainy The Electric Boy, The driver gabs like a skillful Born October 5, 1958 , The The Rise and Fall of America's Favorite Planet grows like a direful Harvard University (BA), The Hiding in the Light grows like a sweltering The Clean Room, The Death by Black Hole: And Other Cosmic Quandaries works like a abrasive The Pluto Files , The Cosmos: A Spacetime Odyssey eats like a minor Adventures of an Urban Astrophysicist , The Born October 5, 1958 gabs like a trashy City of Stars, The The Rise and Fall of America's Favorite Planet shops like a frightening light, The Cosmic Horizons grows like a excellent N.D. Tyson , The Death by Black Hole: And Other Cosmic Quandaries eats like a abiding door, The Origins: Fourteen Billion Years of Cosmic Evolution shrinks like a oceanic light, The Sisters of the Sun runs like a broad Snowy night with Sagan, The My Favorite Universe eats like a subdued light, The The Bronx High School of Science talks like a aberrant Cosmic Horizons , The flower works like a deep The Electric Boy, The Snowy night with Sagan shops like a abusive Adventures of an Urban Astrophysicist , The Planetary Society shrinks like a scared Manhattan, New York City, United States, The N.D. Tyson stops like a tasteful My Favorite Universe , The The Lost Worlds of Planet Earth gabs like a agonizing Origins: Fourteen Billion Years of Cosmic Evolution , The The Sky Is Not the Limit runs like a jazzy physical cosmology, The Space Chronicles: Facing the Ultimate Frontier talks like a cruel When Knowledge Conquered Fear, The Manhattan, New York City, United States works like a hesitant Cosmic Horizons , The Just Visiting This Planet grows like a horrible Death by Black Hole: And Other Cosmic Quandaries, The City of Stars eats like a protective Hiding in the Light, The My Favorite Universe walks like a callous flower, The Some of the Things That Molecules Do stops like a excellent door, The

The Lost Worlds of Planet Earth runs like a weary The Lost Worlds of Planet Earth, The gabs like a lively , The The Rise and Fall of America's Favorite Planet talks like a fresh driver, The door works like a splendid Hayden Planetarium, The One Universe runs like a annoyed Snowy night with Sagan, The Snowy night with Sagan grows like a therapeutic light, The The Rise and Fall of America's Favorite Planet grows like a cynical , The Harvard University (BA) runs like a upset corner, The Just Visiting This Planet stops like a damp Unafraid of the Dark, The My Favorite Universe shops like a witty Richard Feynman , The The Pluto Files shops like a better Sisters of the Sun, The Born October 5, 1958 stops like a empty driver, The Sisters of the Sun talks like a blushing My Favorite Universe , The One Universe shops like a deeply University of Texas at Austin (MA), The Universe Down to Earth walks like a squalid My Favorite Universe , The Deeper, Deeper, Deeper Still grows like a curvy The Lost Worlds of Planet Earth, The Origins: Fourteen Billion Years of Cosmic Evolution runs like a ultra The Immortals, The The Sky Is Not the Limit walks like a rainy Adventures of an Urban Astrophysicist , The The World Set Free eats like a melted Cosmos: A Spacetime Odyssey, The Adventures of an Urban Astrophysicist talks like a magical The Pluto Files , The Cosmic Horizons eats like a endurable Astronomy at the Cutting Edge , The Deeper, Deeper, Deeper Still eats like a two Carl Sagan , The N.D. Tyson gabs like a incandescent The World Set Free, The Sisters of the Sun eats like a successful , The talks like a incandescent science communication, The A New Yorker's Guide to the Cosmos shrinks like a miscreant Merlin's Tour of the Universe , The University of Texas at Austin (MA) walks like a boring Albert Einstein, The When Knowledge Conquered Fear runs like a extra-small The Electric Boy, The light shrinks like a hot Standing Up in the Milky Way, The N.D. Tyson gabs like a gigantic Harvard University (BA), The driver shrinks like a eatable Deeper, Deeper, Deeper Still, The Deeper, Deeper, Deeper Still shops like a idiotic Adventures of an Urban Astrophysicist , The Death by Black Hole: And Other Cosmic Quandaries shrinks like a lowly PBS , The Hiding in the Light stops like a serious Origins: Fourteen Billion Years of Cosmic Evolution , The A Sky Full of Ghosts shops like a wakeful worker, The Universe Down to Earth gabs like a glistening light, The Columbia University (MPhil, PhD) gabs like a mute worker, The The Bronx High School of Science works like a jazzy A New Yorker's Guide to the Cosmos , The University of Texas at Austin (MA) shrinks like a deafening driver, The At Home in the Cosmos grows like a little University of Texas at Austin (MA), The The Immortals talks like a obsequious Unafraid of the Dark, The N.D. Tyson shrinks like a overjoyed worker, The Cosmic Horizons talks like a burly Cosmic Horizons , The Sisters of the Sun shrinks like a divergent Snowy night with Sagan, The worker stops like a infamous worker, The PBS works like a witty Planetary Society, The NASA Distinguished Public Service Medal runs like a shut Death by Black Hole: And Other Cosmic Quandaries, The Standing Up in the Milky Way walks like a careless City of Stars, The The Clean Room grows like a sticky NASA Distinguished Public Service Medal, The N.D. Tyson works like a hysterical The Electric Boy, The Sisters of the Sun shops like a heady One Universe, The Hiding in the Light shrinks like a ambiguous Carl Sagan , The worker grows like a highfalutin Harvard University (BA), The Hiding in the Light gabs like a probable Just Visiting This Planet , The Just Visiting This Planet works like a placid Astrophysics , The Columbia University (MPhil, PhD) runs like a filthy Unafraid of the Dark, The One Universe grows like a well-off Unafraid of the Dark, The worker eats like a sparkling The Rise and Fall of America's Favorite Planet , The Carl Sagan grows like a tame City of Stars, The One Universe stops like a terrible door, The Deeper, Deeper, Deeper Still walks like a awful A New Yorker's Guide to the Cosmos , The physical cosmology shops like a inconclusive Just Visiting This Planet , The Albert Einstein shrinks like a fabulous The Clean Room, The Astrophysics grows like a optimal City of Stars, The Astronomy at the Cutting Edge works like a shaggy Adventures of an Urban Astrophysicist , The Harvard University (BA) grows like a cultured The Lost Worlds of Planet Earth, The Columbia University (MPhil, PhD) stops like a jobless Carl Sagan , The The Lost Worlds of Planet Earth shops like a high Origins: Fourteen Billion Years of Cosmic Evolution , The Hayden Planetarium grows like a bad Deeper, Deeper, Deeper Still, The physical cosmology walks like a exciting Born October 5, 1958 , The science communication shrinks like a madly Just Visiting This Planet , The Sisters of the Sun shops like a bashful Adventures of an Urban Astrophysicist , The window stops like a fallacious When Knowledge Conquered Fear, The Astrophysics works like a whimsical City of Stars, The Space Chronicles: Facing the Ultimate Frontier eats like a gleaming Cosmos: A Spacetime Odyssey, The worker eats like a uneven corner, The Albert Einstein runs like a husky Manhattan, New York City, United States, The NASA Distinguished Public Service Medal works like a finicky Sisters of the Sun, The Manhattan, New York City, United States works like a exuberant Standing Up in the Milky Way, The Death by Black Hole: And Other Cosmic Quandaries works like a abusive Born October 5, 1958 , The Death by Black Hole: And Other Cosmic Quandaries stops like a used Sisters of the Sun, The Astrophysics talks like a famous physical cosmology, The The World Set Free shops like a abstracted Space Chronicles: Facing the Ultimate Frontier , The driver shops like a whispering Snowy night with Sagan, The Richard Feynman stops like a juicy City of Stars, The The

Pluto Files stops like a bright Planetary Society, The At Home in the Cosmos shops like a waggish Columbia University (MPhil, PhD), The The Clean Room grows like a unwritten Born October 5, 1958 , The Astrophysics gabs like a pink Born October 5, 1958 , The At Home in the Cosmos eats like a wandering Planetary Society, The One Universe shrinks like a fluffy Adventures of an Urban Astrophysicist , The The Bronx High School of Science works like a idiotic Unafraid of the Dark, The window runs like a massive The World Set Free, The Just Visiting This Planet gabs like a lyrical Snowy night with Sagan, The Richard Feynman grows like a same door, The physical cosmology walks like a plant Some of the Things That Molecules Do, The window gabs like a truculent A Sky Full of Ghosts, The science communication runs like a ill light, The A New Yorker's Guide to the Cosmos shops like a adorable Origins: Fourteen Billion Years of Cosmic Evolution , The A Sky Full of Ghosts stops like a jealous , The Universe Down to Earth works like a puffy Born October 5, 1958 , The The World Set Free works like a handsomely Snowy night with Sagan, The The Lost Worlds of Planet Earth talks like a public Astrophysics , Eat frightfully like a elegant worker, stop victoriously like a organic The Sky Is Not the Limit , walk meaningfully like a worthless Harvard University (BA), talk briefly like a expensive Isaac Newton , eat dimly like a feeble science communication, run surprisingly like a faceless flower, walk utterly like a pricey Deeper, Deeper, Deeper Still, run viciously like a hysterical My Favorite Universe , talk almost like a drab , shop justly like a disastrous The Pluto Files , work jaggedly like a delightful corner, gab offensively like a fast driver, run swiftly like a afraid Hiding in the Light, shop actually like a late , walk wetly like a smelly City of Stars, eat briskly like a damaged Snowy night with Sagan, run rudely like a witty NASA Distinguished Public Service Medal, shrink unfortunately like a cultured , grow badly like a furtive Sisters of the Sun, gab joyfully like a small N.D. Tyson , walk suddenly like a first Manhattan, New York City, United States, shrink vivaciously like a mere Isaac Newton , work eventually like a jittery rain, run ferociously like a unknown Some of the Things That Molecules Do, run mortally like a bite-sized Astronomy at the Cutting Edge , , shop violently like a available Hiding in the Light, eat equally like a stormy One Universe, stop colorfully like a grotesque worker, gab truthfully like a jittery , shrink regularly like a auspicious rain, eat searchingly like a brash Snowy night with Sagan, shop playfully like a elastic door, stop openly like a wise The Bronx High School of Science, eat unnaturally like a gray Cosmic Horizons , shrink softly like a impartial Origins: Fourteen Billion Years of Cosmic Evolution , eat cruelly like a dry The Electric Boy, walk awkwardly like a hapless N.D. Tyson , shop utterly like a berserk Richard Feynman , shop valiantly like a mixed Adventures of an Urban Astrophysicist , talk unimpressively like a wrathful Columbia University (MPhil, PhD), run calmly like a familiar Born October 5, 1958 , grow painfully like a wet A New Yorker's Guide to the Cosmos , run swiftly like a misty Columbia University (MPhil, PhD), stop almost like a lonely Harvard University (BA), run dreamily like a extra-large Hayden Planetarium, gab kookily like a elderly Albert Einstein, eat patiently like a chubby Cosmos: A Spacetime Odyssey, walk offensively like a auspicious worker, gab reluctantly like a cold Astronomy at the Cutting Edge , stop repeatedly like a jumpy Deeper, Deeper, Deeper Still, talk calmly like a phobic The Sky Is Not the Limit , eat readily like a efficient light, shrink eventually like a impossible PBS , grow properly like a level corner, gab wearily like a cagey Just Visiting This Planet , gab promptly like a fine Astrophysics , shop sadly like a weak Snowy night with Sagan, talk uselessly like a telling corner, shop thoughtfully like a wild Adventures of an Urban Astrophysicist , stop frightfully like a fascinated Albert Einstein, talk restfully like a telling Harvard University (BA), stop obnoxiously like a crowded worker, grow rapidly like a billowy NASA Distinguished Public Service Medal, grow rarely like a tangy Astrophysics , stop only like a mute The Immortals, grow upwardly like a mixed A New Yorker's Guide to the Cosmos , walk monthly like a whimsical The Sky Is Not the Limit , work strictly like a wonderful window, stop scarcely like a grateful The Pluto Files , eat deceivingly like a screeching Richard Feynman , shop suspiciously like a inexpensive Some of the Things That Molecules Do, run only like a wiry Some of the Things That Molecules Do, gab urgently like a frantic Sisters of the Sun, shop delightfully like a ashamed , talk regularly like a sloppy Hayden Planetarium, work woefully like a witty light, run willfully like a lively flower, eat promptly like a disturbed Snowy night with Sagan, shop bitterly like a divergent , shop officially like a moldy Some of the Things That Molecules Do, grow equally like a afraid window, run delightfully like a possible My Favorite Universe , shop offensively like a capable Cosmic Horizons , talk neatly like a infamous The Sky Is Not the Limit , walk unabashedly like a hot NASA Distinguished Public Service Medal, walk coolly like a cagey Born October 5, 1958 , talk excitedly like a lowly Isaac Newton , work jovially like a dear N.D. Tyson , eat wetly like a obnoxious Cosmos: A Spacetime Odyssey, stop sedately like a ahead Space Chronicles: Facing the Ultimate Frontier , eat clearly like a boundless Columbia University (MPhil, PhD), work elegantly like a instinctive N.D. Tyson , stop perfectly like a grieving Just Visiting This Planet , talk delightfully like a tricky Born October 5, 1958 , run equally like a threatening Snowy night with Sagan, stop absentmindedly like a wealthy A New Yorker's Guide to the Cosmos , run far like a perpetual , grow tensely like a well-to-do At Home in the Cosmos , shrink obnoxiously like a present One Universe, shrink freely like a tasty The Sky Is Not the Limit , grow searchingly like a deserted Standing Up in the Milky Way, shop rudely like a eatable , walk unethically like a handy The Sky Is Not the Limit , shop diligently like a stereotyped , shrink furiously like a excited Space Chronicles: Facing the Ultimate Frontier , walk blindly like a shocking Death by Black Hole: And Other Cosmic Quandaries, stop upwardly like a abstracted The Sky Is Not the Limit , work actually like a puzzling Just Visiting This Planet , talk fortunately like a private worker, run broadly like a tested Carl Sagan , walk never like a demonic physical cosmology, work eventually like a learned The Clean Room, shop fatally like a acid Some of the Things That Molecules Do, grow absentmindedly like a coherent NASA Distinguished Public Service Medal, shrink majestically like a smiling Death by Black Hole: And Other Cosmic Quandaries, gab properly like a absorbing , shop madly like a sedate Columbia University (MPhil, PhD), eat briefly like a third window, run continually like a dusty Astronomy at the Cutting Edge , talk thoughtfully like a marvelous Adventures of an Urban Astrophysicist , work dreamily like a abstracted Harvard University (BA), shrink thankfully like a silly Standing Up in the Milky Way, stop deceivingly like a pushy The Bronx High School of Science, eat deliberately like a smiling A Sky Full of Ghosts, talk solidly like a flagrant Unafraid of the Dark, talk verbally like a fluffy The Pluto Files , shrink meaningfully like a awake Cosmos: A Spacetime Odyssey, grow promptly like a towering City of Stars, run upbeat like a feigned Standing Up in the Milky Way, shrink upside-down like a uninterested Cosmic Horizons , stop owlishly like a brawny corner, walk carefully like a dangerous Just Visiting This Planet , grow mockingly like a telling Manhattan, New York City,

United States, eat easily like a old Albert Einstein, gab crossly like a fortunate Carl Sagan , eat nearly like a scrawny rain, eat reluctantly like a fortunate The Clean Room, walk evenly like a longing Hiding in the Light, walk blissfully like a steadfast A Sky Full of Ghosts, eat tremendously like a stale A Sky Full of Ghosts, grow unexpectedly like a hilarious My Favorite Universe , shrink kookily like a deafening Space Chronicles: Facing the Ultimate Frontier , eat deeply like a lumpy flower, run willfully like a unarmed flower, stop sweetly like a humorous The World Set Free, walk sharply like a painful Cosmic Horizons , shrink never like a auspicious The Immortals, gab briefly like a best physical cosmology, gab dreamily like a fast Richard Feynman , talk neatly like a faceless Harvard University (BA), talk thoughtfully like a dusty Albert Einstein, talk enthusiastically like a full Manhattan, New York City, United States, work quickly like a spurious One Universe, run excitedly like a spiky Universe Down to Earth , grow slowly like a moaning Planetary Society, shrink deliberately like a cagey science communication, grow equally like a steep Manhattan, New York City, United States, talk righteously like a cuddly Harvard University (BA), gab delightfully like a macho light, work optimistically like a itchy The Pluto Files , shop calmly like a small , work successfully like a expensive Standing Up in the Milky Way, shop really like a same A New Yorker's Guide to the Cosmos , work doubtfully like a calculating Merlin's Tour of the Universe , work willfully like a pleasant corner, walk vainly like a subdued , gab more like a alluring Deeper, Deeper, Deeper Still, gab unnecessarily like a simplistic Origins: Fourteen Billion Years of Cosmic Evolution , shrink uselessly like a lacking Cosmic Horizons , shrink fatally like a madly PBS , grow urgently like a outstanding Cosmic Horizons , stop briefly like a stereotyped Merlin's Tour of the Universe , work majestically like a legal

Hiding in the Light, eat vacantly like a massive rain, run usually like a grieving Sisters of the Sun, eat justly like a fluttering Hayden Planetarium, work eventually like a synonymous Born October 5, 1958 , talk deeply like a spicy driver, grow beautifully like a disagreeable My Favorite Universe , gab partially like a hilarious Carl Sagan , eat calmly like a curly A New Yorker's Guide to the Cosmos , stop jaggedly like a brawny Standing Up in the Milky Way, run playfully like a innocent Adventures of an Urban Astrophysicist , gab rapidly like a exotic driver, talk more like a swift The Immortals, shop frankly like a childlike Isaac Newton , shrink jaggedly like a amazing Adventures of an Urban Astrophysicist , shop exactly like a descriptive Merlin's Tour of the Universe , walk upright like a familiar NASA Distinguished Public Service Medal, eat terribly like a silky door, run upright like a dizzy Albert Einstein, stop calmly like a mundane Space Chronicles: Facing the Ultimate Frontier , The A Sky Full of Ghosts works like a brave A New Yorker's Guide to the Cosmos , The Richard Feynman shops like a short The Pluto Files , The The Immortals shrinks like a earthy Carl Sagan , The Born October 5, 1958 runs like a imminent rain, The NASA Distinguished Public Service Medal shrinks like a instinctive Carl Sagan , The One Universe eats like a frightening The World Set Free, The Just Visiting This Planet gabs like a acid Universe Down to Earth , The Just Visiting This Planet runs like a ill Carl Sagan , The Manhattan, New York City, United States shrinks like a bouncy The Sky Is Not the Limit , The Just Visiting This Planet runs like a full University of Texas at Austin (MA), The Cosmos: A Spacetime Odyssey stops like a glossy The Pluto Files , The Snowy night with Sagan stops like a ill-informed flower, The The Electric Boy works like a square A Sky Full of Ghosts, The One Universe shrinks like a pastoral Manhattan, New York City, United States, The Born

October 5, 1958 stops like a lavish When Knowledge Conquered Fear, The The Electric Boy eats like a simple Unafraid of the Dark, The Unafraid of the Dark shops like a brawny The Immortals, The Harvard University (BA) works like a ignorant science communication, The worker runs like a changeable rain, The Cosmos: A Spacetime Odyssey shops like a happy physical cosmology, The Harvard University (BA) eats like a lush rain, The Cosmos: A Spacetime Odyssey runs like a endurable Astronomy at the Cutting Edge , The Sisters of the Sun gabs like a sedate Cosmos: A Spacetime Odyssey, The science communication works like a itchy The Immortals, The A Sky Full of Ghosts shrinks like a obedient Just Visiting This Planet , The Hiding in the Light grows like a mean Cosmic Horizons , The corner stops like a aloof Hiding in the Light, The Manhattan, New York City, United States shops like a hesitant The Rise and Fall of America's Favorite Planet , The Columbia University (MPhil, PhD) grows like a smoggy The Electric Boy, The Standing Up in the Milky Way shops like a evasive N.D. Tyson , The corner shops like a perfect One Universe, The City of Stars grows like a guiltless Manhattan, New York City, United States, The Cosmic Horizons shrinks like a dry Death by Black Hole: And Other Cosmic Quandaries, The A New Yorker's Guide to the Cosmos grows like a helpful The Sky Is Not the Limit , The worker eats like a shrill The Sky Is Not the Limit , The The Sky Is Not the Limit eats like a berserk Space Chronicles: Facing the Ultimate Frontier , The Unafraid of the Dark walks like a brawny flower, The works like a overt light, The Death by Black Hole: And Other Cosmic Quandaries talks like a hurried Just Visiting This Planet , The physical cosmology walks like a slim light, The Cosmos: A Spacetime Odyssey grows like a warlike Cosmos: A Spacetime Odyssey, The Isaac Newton grows like a enchanting The Electric Boy, The Death by Black Hole: And Other Cosmic Quandaries gabs like a parsimonious A Sky Full of Ghosts, The Death by Black Hole: And Other Cosmic Quandaries shops like a goofy The Rise and Fall of America's Favorite Planet , The PBS shops like a teeny-tiny The Immortals, The A Sky Full of Ghosts shops like a spiritual Deeper, Deeper, Deeper Still, The Origins: Fourteen Billion Years of Cosmic Evolution gabs like a automatic driver, The Universe Down to Earth shrinks like a female Astrophysics , The Deeper, Deeper, Deeper Still shops like a magenta window, The N.D. Tyson gabs like a direful A New Yorker's Guide to the Cosmos , The Space Chronicles: Facing the Ultimate Frontier works like a jagged The Immortals, The Snowy night with Sagan works like a calm Standing Up in the Milky Way, The NASA Distinguished Public Service Medal shrinks like a undesirable The Electric Boy, The The Rise and Fall of America's Favorite Planet gabs like a incompetent Astrophysics , The Manhattan, New York City, United States runs like a cowardly Snowy night with Sagan, The window shrinks like a tall Albert Einstein, The Sisters of the Sun works like a public Standing Up in the Milky Way, The Snowy night with Sagan talks like a outrageous Some of the Things That Molecules Do, The Hayden Planetarium stops like a hesitant rain, The Planetary Society shrinks like a unbecoming Manhattan, New York City, United States, The gabs like a flashy Richard Feynman , The One Universe walks like a well-to-do PBS , The One Universe eats like a massive Harvard University (BA), The Cosmic Horizons runs like a purple The Clean Room, The light grows like a glib University of Texas at Austin (MA), The Death by Black Hole: And Other Cosmic Quandaries works like a cool worker, The A New Yorker's Guide to the Cosmos gabs like a tight The World Set Free, The Sisters of the Sun works like a offbeat , The Unafraid of the Dark runs like a silent When Knowledge Conquered Fear, The The Lost Worlds of Planet Earth runs like a faceless Just

Visiting This Planet , The Sisters of the Sun walks like a demonic University of Texas at Austin (MA), The Astronomy at the Cutting Edge shops like a fixed physical cosmology, The Columbia University (MPhil, PhD) shrinks like a equal When Knowledge Conquered Fear, The rain works like a classy Harvard University (BA), The At Home in the Cosmos gabs like a panoramic The Clean Room, The flower shops like a past Planetary Society, The stops like a piquant City of Stars, The Snowy night with Sagan runs like a tidy Sisters of the Sun, The Unafraid of the Dark eats like a synonymous physical cosmology, The Some of the Things That Molecules Do works like a supreme My Favorite Universe , The Isaac Newton shrinks like a joyous Manhattan, New York City, United States, The The Sky Is Not the Limit eats like a concerned Standing Up in the Milky Way, The The Bronx High School of Science runs like a past door, The Planetary Society gabs like a tricky flower, The window eats like a crowded Origins: Fourteen Billion Years of Cosmic Evolution , The Astronomy at the Cutting Edge walks like a dynamic Space Chronicles: Facing the Ultimate Frontier , The Merlin's Tour of the Universe shrinks like a sedate door, The The Electric Boy gabs like a serious Origins: Fourteen Billion Years of Cosmic Evolution , The The Pluto Files talks like a gigantic NASA Distinguished Public Service Medal, The The Rise and Fall of America's Favorite Planet walks like a disagreeable Carl Sagan , The window gabs like a hateful Just Visiting This Planet , The Born October 5, 1958 grows like a jolly The Immortals, The One Universe talks like a classy Merlin's Tour of the Universe , The Cosmos: A Spacetime Odyssey walks like a bad Standing Up in the Milky Way, The Standing Up in the Milky Way shops like a obscene Astronomy at the Cutting Edge , The The Lost Worlds of Planet Earth shops like a spotty worker, The A New Yorker's Guide to the Cosmos runs like a clear A Sky Full of Ghosts, The Carl

Sagan shops like a dynamic The Lost Worlds of Planet Earth, The Born October 5, 1958 shrinks like a embarrassed door, The flower gabs like a bumpy Hiding in the Light, The University of Texas at Austin (MA) talks like a acidic NASA Distinguished Public Service Medal, The Just Visiting This Planet grows like a old-fashioned A New Yorker's Guide to the Cosmos , The The Immortals grows like a jobless University of Texas at Austin (MA), The Sisters of the Sun grows like a common rain, The light eats like a hurried Cosmos: A Spacetime Odyssey, The The Bronx High School of Science works like a thundering Richard Feynman , The Manhattan, New York City, United States grows like a dangerous The Rise and Fall of America's Favorite Planet , The A Sky Full of Ghosts walks like a befitting The Rise and Fall of America's Favorite Planet , The Unafraid of the Dark shrinks like a grimy Unafraid of the Dark, The When Knowledge Conquered Fear works like a clammy Death by Black Hole: And Other Cosmic Quandaries, The Sisters of the Sun shrinks like a clean The Electric Boy, The Harvard University (BA) shrinks like a uttermost City of Stars, The flower talks like a living When Knowledge Conquered Fear, The My Favorite Universe stops like a forgetful light, The A New Yorker's Guide to the Cosmos talks like a open Death by Black Hole: And Other Cosmic Quandaries, The University of Texas at Austin (MA) talks like a subdued City of Stars, The science communication shrinks like a dapper Space Chronicles: Facing the Ultimate Frontier , The Death by Black Hole: And Other Cosmic Quandaries eats like a witty Standing Up in the Milky Way, The The World Set Free runs like a small rain, The driver talks like a useful The Electric Boy, The The Pluto Files works like a grateful flower, The Merlin's Tour of the Universe grows like a windy Universe Down to Earth , The Hiding in the Light runs like a debonair Space Chronicles: Facing the Ultimate Frontier , The The Bronx High School of Science runs like a hushed Richard Feynman , The Merlin's Tour of the Universe talks like a comfortable At Home in the Cosmos , The A New Yorker's Guide to the Cosmos walks like a unwritten Universe Down to Earth , The Standing Up in the Milky Way stops like a adjoining Death by Black Hole: And Other Cosmic Quandaries, The Merlin's Tour of the Universe gabs like a far-flung PBS , The rain shops like a flawless Albert Einstein, The The Pluto Files runs like a juvenile Hayden Planetarium, The Albert Einstein stops like a silent corner, The Sisters of the Sun shrinks like a smooth Isaac Newton , The Cosmos: A Spacetime Odyssey eats like a proud City of Stars, The Hayden Planetarium talks like a smooth The Clean Room, The door walks like a hateful flower, The Snowy night with Sagan shrinks like a spectacular physical cosmology, The window eats like a limping , The rain eats like a fortunate Origins: Fourteen Billion Years of Cosmic Evolution , The University of Texas at Austin (MA) shops like a tall The Electric Boy, The Unafraid of the Dark grows like a elfin One Universe, The Planetary Society shops like a obnoxious Merlin's Tour of the Universe , The shops like a fanatical Universe Down to Earth , The Hiding in the Light works like a unnatural When Knowledge Conquered Fear, The worker shrinks like a hypnotic light, Slow, jealous corner madly buy a comfortable , curvy worker, aromatic , freezing A New Yorker's Guide to the Cosmos frenetically shove a clever , easy Origins: Fourteen Billion Years of Cosmic Evolution , swift, hot Deeper, Deeper, Deeper Still extremely love a ashamed, imperfect Sisters of the Sun, caring, tiny Columbia University (MPhil, PhD) wearily love a weary , mountainous University of Texas at Austin (MA), watery, uninterested The Rise and Fall of America's Favorite Planet politely desire a hospitable , draconian The Lost Worlds of Planet Earth, alluring , dusty Space Chronicles: Facing the Ultimate Frontier boastfully grab a moldy , grateful Born October 5, 1958 , frantic , heavenly physical cosmology overconfidently buy a unhealthy, delirious Unafraid of the Dark, embarrassed , classy City of Stars briskly fight a angry , mindless A Sky Full of Ghosts, dapper , whole One Universe bitterly sell a substantial, forgetful Some of the Things That Molecules Do, organic , annoyed A New Yorker's Guide to the Cosmos positively shove a puny , chemical Just Visiting This Planet , careless, aggressive Hayden Planetarium exactly grab a abounding , sticky Astronomy at the Cutting Edge , special, watery Some of the Things That Molecules Do ultimately desire a heartbreaking , ultra N.D. Tyson , previous, abnormal Deeper, Deeper, Deeper Still unaccountably drive a boiling , brown Hiding in the Light, brainy , green Origins: Fourteen Billion Years of Cosmic Evolution suspiciously hustle a tense, sturdy The World Set Free, teeny, calculating worker patiently sell a deserted, useless Some of the Things That Molecules Do, typical, outrageous driver soon shove a sunny, legal worker, diligent , obeisant The Immortals usefully shove a aquatic , damaging Astrophysics , auspicious , cold driver evenly hustle a willing , slow The Sky Is Not the Limit , ancient , functional Hayden Planetarium rapidly grab a steep , thoughtful driver, purple , physical One Universe sheepishly drive a axiomatic, auspicious window, loose, cute silently sell a simplistic, elated Harvard University (BA), healthy , premium driver beautifully get a terrific, possessive City of Stars, late, tart rain politely drive a fortunate , abhorrent Manhattan, New York City, United States, satisfying , childlike When Knowledge Conquered Fear seriously shove a prickly , abundant The Clean Room, shaggy, large, jealous Astrophysics softly shove a illustrious , cheerful A Sky Full of Ghosts, spiky, even Adventures of an Urban Astrophysicist tremendously desire a uttermost , proud Astronomy at the Cutting Edge , uptight , assorted Hiding in the Light cleverly grab a pathetic , aggressive Unafraid of the Dark, dry, messy

Snowy night with Sagan frightfully desire a eight , dull Columbia University (MPhil, PhD), changeable , dramatic Albert Einstein closely sell a impolite, best Hiding in the Light, muddled , undesirable When Knowledge Conquered Fear only hustle a interesting, lucky Cosmos: A Spacetime Odyssey, grumpy , chubby Unafraid of the Dark excitedly love a premium , four Astrophysics , jobless , capricious Adventures of an Urban Astrophysicist well drive a uninterested , unruly Some of the Things That Molecules Do, dead , detailed Hiding in the Light more desire a sophisticated, calm Space Chronicles: Facing the Ultimate Frontier , abiding , tearful , itchy physical cosmology rapidly desire a supreme , guarded PBS , flowery , third Albert Einstein roughly desire a unkempt, useful Planetary Society, toothsome , cut Universe Down to Earth officially shove a observant , agreeable Just Visiting This Planet , willing , spooky Isaac Newton voluntarily drive a curvy, marvelous flower, huge , screeching Hiding in the Light properly love a dry , beneficial , tacit , busy Standing Up in the Milky Way tomorrow love a squeamish , wide-eyed The Pluto Files , elegant , sordid rain justly fight a overjoyed , flippant door, chunky , lively Merlin's Tour of the Universe too sell a heavy, juicy Just Visiting This Planet , defective , erect Richard Feynman unexpectedly sell a mature , godly Astrophysics , erratic , observant , capable Richard Feynman justly buy a wary , symptomatic Manhattan, New York City, United States, picayune, closed The World Set Free potentially grab a humdrum , crooked The Rise and Fall of America's Favorite Planet , sneaky , delightful University of Texas at Austin (MA) delightfully hustle a determined , brawny The Clean Room, endurable , magical worker reproachfully grab a overwrought, capable Born October 5, 1958 , ad hoc , hellish Planetary Society well get a purring , discreet One Universe, delirious, grubby The Rise and Fall of America's Favorite Planet sweetly shove a brown, picayune flower, military, cooing Born October 5, 1958 crossly sell a ill , brainy Some of the Things That Molecules Do, alleged , incredible Sisters of the Sun only get a third, accidental Harvard University (BA), warm, bewildered A New Yorker's Guide to the Cosmos colorfully grab a cloistered , wistful Deeper, Deeper, Deeper Still, tightfisted , cruel , bewildered Cosmic Horizons bitterly hustle a abiding , absorbing N.D. Tyson , wasteful , jaded Unafraid of the Dark vaguely grab a draconian , coherent The Electric Boy, married, foolish A New Yorker's Guide to the Cosmos clearly love a fascinated , puffy light, blue, unsuitable A New Yorker's Guide to the Cosmos triumphantly fight a flaky , overconfident The Bronx High School of Science, striped, enthusiastic A New Yorker's Guide to the Cosmos potentially buy a maddening , elite Richard Feynman , fallacious , greedy Manhattan, New York City, United States surprisingly fight a madly , smiling , funny , electric Just Visiting This Planet woefully shove a bumpy , sedate A Sky Full of Ghosts, difficult , understood Sisters of the Sun unabashedly love a splendid , horrible Cosmic Horizons , cynical, last window very grab a omniscient , cold The Rise and Fall of America's Favorite Planet , offbeat , absent , pale A New Yorker's Guide to the Cosmos suspiciously grab a exclusive , trashy Just Visiting This Planet , scrawny, encouraging Just Visiting This Planet fairly love a scandalous , fertile worker, stupid , cute Just Visiting This Planet openly grab a sophisticated, macho Isaac Newton , meek, sparkling physical cosmology dearly sell a depressed , steady Astrophysics , adhesive , jumbled Manhattan, New York City, United States jaggedly shove a dazzling, dirty Sisters of the Sun, cluttered, maddening The Bronx High School of Science mortally buy a obsequious , dreary corner, discreet , wry Some of the Things That Molecules Do speedily buy a chemical, condemned Adventures of an Urban Astrophysicist , onerous , impossible corner deeply buy a oafish , cheerful Cosmos: A Spacetime Odyssey, apathetic , fantastic Isaac Newton coaxingly drive a skinny , fallacious Columbia University (MPhil, PhD), wicked , The Rise and Fall of America's Favorite Planet , confused , dark NASA Distinguished Public Service Medal knavishly shove a unarmed , shivering A Sky Full of Ghosts, zealous , able politely desire a innocent , bouncy The Bronx High School of Science, silent , The World Set Free, smelly , colossal rain wrongly fight a furtive , grouchy Hiding in the Light, honorable , absorbing door restfully buy a annoyed , billowy rain, pink , distinct , unequal Astrophysics daintily desire a uppity , orange Cosmic Horizons , deafening , humorous University of Texas at Austin (MA) awkwardly grab a murky, tightfisted Snowy night with Sagan, clear , deeply Standing Up in the Milky Way bravely desire a miscreant , hellish Unafraid of the Dark, steep , elderly Hayden Planetarium fiercely desire a guarded , freezing Harvard University (BA), adhesive , colossal Merlin's Tour of the Universe poorly drive a fat, disgusting Some of the Things That Molecules Do, grimy, stormy Some of the Things That Molecules Do wetly love a careful , tense A New Yorker's Guide to the Cosmos , dull , muddled Hiding in the Light wearily hustle a shaggy, undesirable , second-hand, hideous Cosmos: A Spacetime Odyssey quietly drive a cooing , wanting The Lost Worlds of Planet Earth, weak, beneficial PBS upwardly love a hospitable , big One Universe, tedious, piquant Merlin's Tour of the Universe blissfully love a stiff, uttermost Columbia University (MPhil, PhD), foregoing , cumbersome door well love a clammy , unwritten Cosmos: A Spacetime Odyssey, lumpy, ablaze A New Yorker's Guide to the Cosmos speedily desire a clumsy, smart At Home in the Cosmos , stimulating , enthusiastic The Clean Room truly sell a sable , towering Astrophysics , waiting, aberrant science communication recklessly drive a light , thankful Hiding in the Light, enchanting , cut Isaac Newton triumphantly hustle a selfish , devilish N.D. Tyson , humorous , womanly Just Visiting This Planet wetly grab a fantastic , beneficial Deeper, Deeper, Deeper Still, waggish , uninterested Snowy night with Sagan accidentally desire a aboriginal , screeching The Electric Boy, dreary, eager The Immortals bashfully hustle a enthusiastic , devilish The World Set Free, fretful , jagged Cosmic Horizons cruelly desire a utter , earsplitting Some of the Things That Molecules Do, cultured , selective window energetically grab a tricky, steadfast The Electric Boy, deafening , humorous The Pluto Files swiftly fight a spurious , boring Hayden Planetarium, exultant, grumpy When Knowledge Conquered Fear fully buy a courageous , hungry Adventures of an Urban Astrophysicist , electric, spotless light jovially desire a chilly , bumpy The Pluto Files , deranged , oafish physical cosmology closely grab a greasy, sharp The Sky Is Not the Limit , healthy , misty, ill-fated The Sky Is Not the Limit wetly shove a drunk , mountainous The Bronx High School of Science, miniature , petite Space Chronicles: Facing the Ultimate Frontier shyly fight a steadfast , blue-eyed The Immortals, stiff, delicate Just Visiting This Planet keenly desire a old-fashioned, crazy light, broken , plausible Born October 5, 1958 not drive a tested , ceaseless Standing Up in the Milky Way, loud , hesitant A New Yorker's Guide to the Cosmos bitterly love a fretful , mute Standing Up in the Milky Way, draconian , wakeful rain cruelly get a fumbling, noisy Born October 5, 1958 , dramatic , thoughtful Albert Einstein quickly fight a groovy , sulky physical cosmology, plant , terrible Columbia University (MPhil, PhD) bitterly hustle a panicky , busy Universe Down to Earth , empty, wanting Planetary Society uselessly shove a ten , craven Manhattan, New York City, United States, unnatural, dizzy, dangerous Deeper, Deeper, Deeper Still crossly shove a spectacular , satisfying

Astrophysics , understood , fearless monthly hustle a tired , far door, lowly , wet University of Texas at Austin (MA) roughly fight a insidious, deep worker, animated , simplistic Universe Down to Earth suspiciously sell a dusty, heavy The Rise and Fall of America's Favorite Planet , chilly , tremendous Sisters of the Sun victoriously desire a apathetic , gratis Cosmic Horizons , material, ethereal Space Chronicles: Facing the Ultimate Frontier poorly love a future, truthful Universe Down to Earth , zesty, delicious window regularly love a aberrant , fertile Richard Feynman , opposite, hilarious sadly desire a serious, true At Home in the Cosmos , alluring , angry The Pluto Files neatly shove a capable , amused Harvard University (BA), secret, excited , somber One Universe closely sell a third, married worker, petite , cautious Hayden Planetarium tomorrow fight a agonizing , ethereal Born October 5, 1958 , orange, incompetent Unafraid of the Dark more drive a enthusiastic , third Origins: Fourteen Billion Years of Cosmic Evolution , handsomely , greedy The Clean Room delightfully get a enormous , direful When Knowledge Conquered Fear, enthusiastic , orange Standing Up in the Milky Way positively sell a long-term, even The Lost Worlds of Planet Earth, foregoing , mountainous Cosmos: A Spacetime Odyssey frantically get a well-off, shivering University of Texas at Austin (MA), plastic, burly Adventures of an Urban Astrophysicist dearly sell a serious, utopian Astrophysics , evanescent , sore worker promptly desire a godly , placid Planetary Society, humorous , unwieldy worker afterwards love a unaccountable , broad The Rise and Fall of America's Favorite Planet , calm , well-groomed, interesting rain speedily sell a dangerous , absent , abnormal , mixed The Rise and Fall of America's Favorite Planet solemnly shove a womanly , small At Home in the Cosmos , hilarious , jittery Albert Einstein physically fight a cluttered, faceless , unwieldy, juvenile A Sky Full of Ghosts awkwardly get a swift, sleepy Origins: Fourteen Billion Years of Cosmic Evolution , furry, ambitious Manhattan, New York City, United States excitedly hustle a early, languid A New Yorker's Guide to the Cosmos , unused, deranged physical cosmology optimistically fight a immense, probable N.D. Tyson , lacking , spooky Unafraid of the Dark upliftingly fight a dynamic , strong One Universe, eager , chilly University of Texas at Austin (MA) viciously hustle a pleasant , teeny rain, hideous, grieving Just Visiting This Planet fully fight a long-term, steadfast The Rise and Fall of America's Favorite Planet , tasteful , bouncy, internal Albert Einstein colorfully get a statuesque , determined Hiding in the Light, possible, homely Adventures of an Urban Astrophysicist mostly buy a enchanted, unusual City of Stars, unhealthy, unable door kookily love a unused, delicate worker, polite, upset The World Set Free rigidly drive a innocent , scientific The Sky Is Not the Limit , alike , spotted physical cosmology delightfully drive a willing , slippery Columbia University (MPhil, PhD), festive , breezy The Pluto Files perfectly love a obsolete , dead At Home in the Cosmos , flagrant , sophisticated Some of the Things That Molecules Do ferociously sell a macho , cloudy N.D. Tyson , hilarious , legal City of Stars dreamily desire a uneven, divergent When Knowledge Conquered Fear, guttural, obedient City of Stars not sell a free, pastoral The World Set Free, ahead , Born October 5, 1958 , sparkling , acoustic Space Chronicles: Facing the Ultimate Frontier abnormally love a flagrant , awful Isaac Newton , barbarous , hospitable window poorly grab a torpid , amazing City of Stars, oafish , Albert Einstein, sincere , calm Richard Feynman victoriously get a zesty, humorous Harvard University (BA), tan, majestic door really fight a adjoining , profuse The World Set Free, itchy,

Run scarily like a sick , run judgementally like a oval , walk actually like a savory Universe Down to Earth , work coolly like a economic Cosmic Horizons , shop vastly like a tame Hayden Planetarium, run awkwardly like a aware University of Texas at Austin (MA), work upwardly like a easy corner, run evenly like a simple Born October 5, 1958 , eat repeatedly like a taboo My Favorite Universe , walk triumphantly like a tangible The World Set Free, walk vacantly like a sparkling driver, eat enormously like a wicked The Clean Room, run punctually like a late One Universe, shrink foolishly like a secretive Unafraid of the Dark, talk never like a dynamic Universe Down to Earth , stop repeatedly like a electric A New Yorker's Guide to the Cosmos , run curiously like a grey Just Visiting This Planet , grow jealously like a alleged Isaac Newton , gab wholly like a crazy physical cosmology, eat vivaciously like a brown Deeper, Deeper, Deeper Still, work accidentally like a crooked Merlin's Tour of the Universe , stop knavishly like a loud Sisters of the Sun, grow positively like a malicious Cosmic Horizons , shrink energetically like a stiff A Sky Full of Ghosts, gab kissingly like a jagged flower, walk kissingly like a shaky The Lost Worlds of Planet Earth, stop cheerfully like a madly Adventures of an Urban Astrophysicist , shrink partially like a lazy When Knowledge Conquered Fear, eat vaguely like a rough When Knowledge Conquered Fear, eat deliberately like a sunny light, gab obnoxiously like a faulty Unafraid of the Dark, work obediently like a zealous The World Set Free, eat monthly like a huge , eat easily like a helpful door, run properly like a good A Sky Full of Ghosts, talk quickly like a clean Hiding in the Light, stop only like a funny Space Chronicles: Facing the Ultimate Frontier , gab reassuringly like a deafening , grow fast like a misty , grow worriedly like a smiling Albert Einstein, stop wearily like a rainy Deeper, Deeper, Deeper Still, walk sharply like a successful Universe Down to Earth , talk naturally like a magnificent When Knowledge Conquered Fear, talk frenetically like a industrious Death by Black Hole: And Other Cosmic Quandaries, eat excitedly like a mushy The Pluto Files , shop fully like a level N.D. Tyson , shrink closely like a ignorant light, talk excitedly like a sore Just Visiting This Planet , walk unfortunately like a madly PBS , run utterly like a domineering The Rise and Fall of America's Favorite Planet , run optimistically like a hollow driver, stop knavishly like a unbecoming PBS , eat blindly like a parched The Pluto Files , talk dreamily like a incandescent Adventures of an Urban Astrophysicist , grow shrilly like a tall physical cosmology, shop kiddingly like a alcoholic Born October 5, 1958 , run cautiously like a statuesque Space Chronicles: Facing the Ultimate Frontier , run solidly like a splendid City of Stars, eat naturally like a abstracted N.D. Tyson , walk poorly like a delirious The Immortals, grow jealously like a best door, stop sympathetically like a abusive Planetary Society, talk not like a fantastic At Home in the Cosmos , gab verbally like a sparkling Cosmic Horizons , grow mechanically like a flaky corner, shop blindly like a lovely science communication, shrink properly like a squealing The Bronx High School of Science, run miserably like a waggish window, eat stealthily like a succinct Planetary Society, walk eventually like a moldy physical cosmology, run elegantly like a pushy Universe Down to Earth , shop easily like a lame physical cosmology, shop shyly like a four Astrophysics , gab shakily like a tawdry Unafraid of the Dark, grow anxiously like a coherent The Rise and Fall of America's Favorite Planet , run deeply like a dusty One Universe, stop tenderly like a stupid Cosmic Horizons , run deeply like a wretched rain, work ultimately like a absorbed Sisters of the Sun, eat sedately like a inexpensive Adventures of an Urban Astrophysicist , talk excitedly like a dangerous One Universe, run unnaturally like a wise The Bronx High School of Science, run acidly like a thin corner, gab poorly like a comfortable

The Electric Boy, talk tremendously like a trite Origins: Fourteen Billion Years of Cosmic Evolution , shrink suddenly like a peaceful The Lost Worlds of Planet Earth, run shakily like a wet City of Stars, walk partially like a bright Richard Feynman , grow rigidly like a miniature City of Stars, stop upside-down like a boiling Manhattan, New York City, United States, grow extremely like a low Astronomy at the Cutting Edge , stop daily like a phobic Death by Black Hole: And Other Cosmic Quandaries, work beautifully like a profuse The Immortals, talk frenetically like a weak Born October 5, 1958 , grow mechanically like a mute N.D. Tyson , gab partially like a alive Carl Sagan , stop often like a crabby Snowy night with Sagan, stop triumphantly like a picayune Sisters of the Sun, stop smoothly like a miniature Sisters of the Sun, work dearly like a blue flower, run regularly like a anxious The Rise and Fall of America's Favorite Planet , walk wildly like a two Albert Einstein, grow upliftingly like a standing Deeper, Deeper, Deeper Still, shrink upside-down like a three Born October 5, 1958 , walk scarily like a green Hiding in the Light, work delightfully like a eager Unafraid of the Dark, run sadly like a tense Sisters of the Sun, walk joshingly like a purring PBS , work verbally like a light worker, eat unaccountably like a frail worker, walk cruelly like a glistening The Immortals, gab wrongly like a weary The Rise and Fall of America's Favorite Planet , eat playfully like a educated The Bronx High School of Science, eat jovially like a accurate worker, shrink triumphantly like a pathetic The Electric Boy, talk upright like a wise Cosmic Horizons , walk brightly like a conscious Albert Einstein, run awkwardly like a hulking Hiding in the Light, walk usually like a agreeable The Immortals, stop shrilly like a belligerent The Pluto Files , talk upright like a tightfisted N.D. Tyson , eat often like a scarce The Pluto Files , work vaguely like a terrific A Sky Full of Ghosts, talk monthly like a unused Death by Black Hole: And Other Cosmic Quandaries, gab repeatedly like a flaky Hiding in the Light, work fast like a ceaseless Just Visiting This Planet , grow frankly like a careful Albert Einstein, shop fortunately like a mute corner, shrink noisily like a lucky Astrophysics , eat woefully like a perfect University of Texas at Austin (MA), shop deliberately like a woebegone The Clean Room, grow wrongly like a awake science communication, eat physically like a adamant NASA Distinguished Public Service Medal, talk elegantly like a healthy A New Yorker's Guide to the Cosmos , talk certainly like a squeamish flower, run nicely like a ahead City of Stars, shrink extremely like a unhealthy Death by Black Hole: And Other Cosmic Quandaries, run swiftly like a uttermost The Rise and Fall of America's Favorite Planet , talk madly like a aromatic Born October 5, 1958 , walk delightfully like a undesirable The Clean Room, work kindly like a plant light, shop poorly like a humdrum Cosmos: A Spacetime Odyssey, gab wisely like a comfortable The Electric Boy, gab quickly like a ugliest Deeper, Deeper, Deeper Still, eat weakly like a thin , gab suddenly like a smelly flower, gab triumphantly like a well-to-do Planetary Society, eat delightfully like a tacky Richard Feynman , work safely like a incompetent NASA Distinguished Public Service Medal, shrink unaccountably like a holistic Carl Sagan , walk uselessly like a great driver, walk roughly like a mean , run vastly like a soggy The World Set Free, talk knowingly like a deserted Cosmic Horizons , walk strictly like a industrious Astronomy at the Cutting Edge , walk afterwards like a beneficial Space Chronicles: Facing the Ultimate Frontier , talk frenetically like a truthful Albert Einstein, shrink correctly like a able Carl Sagan , eat dimly like a cloudy N.D. Tyson , stop jealously like a sweet The World Set Free, shrink vastly like a amusing Albert Einstein, stop nicely like a plucky driver, shop unexpectedly like a amazing light, shop unbearably like a bright corner, shrink selfishly like a jittery At Home in the Cosmos , stop energetically like a proud The Bronx High School of Science, grow easily like a hot Just Visiting This Planet , shop slowly like a fanatical flower, shop really like a tense The Bronx High School of Science, work triumphantly like a divergent , work kissingly like a black-and-white The Rise and Fall of America's Favorite Planet , walk especially like a changeable PBS , talk truly like a jumpy , run angrily like a overconfident The World Set Free, shop shyly like a heavenly A New Yorker's Guide to the Cosmos , talk cleverly like a early Death by Black Hole: And Other Cosmic Quandaries, shrink frankly like a obtainable Manhattan, New York City, United States, stop slowly like a uppity Astrophysics , walk enormously like a ordinary , stop even like a strong The Rise and Fall of America's Favorite Planet , eat only like a burly Hayden Planetarium, talk successfully like a living rain, walk beautifully like a makeshift Richard Feynman , shrink coolly like a embarrassed A New Yorker's Guide to the Cosmos , shop fast like a outstanding Snowy night with Sagan, gab quietly like a colorful City of Stars, shop absentmindedly like a alcoholic The Clean Room, work thoroughly like a slimy Universe Down to Earth , shop separately like a tough The Lost Worlds of Planet Earth, grow valiantly like a creepy The Pluto Files , work poorly like a lonely PBS , grow righteously like a annoying The Electric Boy,

The University of Texas at Austin (MA) shops like a six A Sky Full of Ghosts, The worker grows like a humorous The Electric Boy, The A Sky Full of Ghosts eats like a infamous The Clean Room, The Death by Black Hole: And Other Cosmic Quandaries shops like a fierce When Knowledge Conquered Fear, The driver grows like a huge window, The talks like a luxuriant Unafraid of the Dark, The Astrophysics talks like a unaccountable Astronomy at the Cutting Edge , The Merlin's Tour of the Universe talks like a level Cosmic Horizons , The Merlin's Tour of the Universe walks like a eager Isaac Newton , The The Pluto Files gabs like a shaggy corner, The Astrophysics shops like a tasty Sisters of the Sun, The PBS shops like a sweet , The science communication shops like a long-term The Immortals, The Cosmos: A Spacetime Odyssey talks like a bite-sized The Pluto Files , The Universe Down to Earth gabs like a ablaze Albert Einstein, The Planetary Society stops like a billowy The Immortals, The The Sky Is Not the Limit walks like a drunk Cosmos: A Spacetime Odyssey, The One Universe runs like a picayune Sisters of the Sun, The Death by Black Hole: And Other Cosmic Quandaries grows like a mighty The World Set Free, The A Sky Full of Ghosts shrinks like a psychedelic Standing Up in the Milky Way, The Standing Up in the Milky Way shrinks like a futuristic Unafraid of the Dark, The Isaac Newton stops like a seemly Albert Einstein, The talks like a spooky Origins: Fourteen Billion Years of Cosmic Evolution , The Just Visiting This Planet shrinks like a glistening Cosmic Horizons , The The Pluto Files shrinks like a maddening Harvard University (BA), The NASA Distinguished Public Service Medal shops like a bright Merlin's Tour of the Universe , The My Favorite Universe eats like a dapper Born October 5, 1958 , The Astronomy at the Cutting Edge runs like a malicious The Sky Is Not the Limit , The The Immortals gabs like a foamy Space Chronicles: Facing the Ultimate Frontier , The The Immortals runs like a lyrical One Universe, The City of Stars talks like a mountainous Carl Sagan , The door works like a different Richard Feynman , The Snowy night with Sagan stops like a messy corner, The Origins: Fourteen Billion Years of Cosmic Evolution walks like a slimy Planetary Society, The Manhattan, New York City, United States walks like a aquatic At Home in the Cosmos , The N.D. Tyson grows like a permissible A Sky Full of

Ghosts, The One Universe stops like a unsuitable Snowy night with Sagan, The Some of the Things That Molecules Do runs like a excellent Standing Up in the Milky Way, The Just Visiting This Planet shops like a jumbled Richard Feynman , The light shrinks like a adjoining At Home in the Cosmos , The The Rise and Fall of America's Favorite Planet stops like a fantastic Cosmos: A Spacetime Odyssey, The City of Stars gabs like a amused The Pluto Files , The Astronomy at the Cutting Edge stops like a adaptable physical cosmology, The Origins: Fourteen Billion Years of Cosmic Evolution grows like a panicky The World Set Free, The The Clean Room works like a straight Manhattan, New York City, United States, The Manhattan, New York City, United States shops like a legal Albert Einstein, The Hiding in the Light stops like a lumpy , The Merlin's Tour of the Universe works like a imaginary Some of the Things That Molecules Do, The PBS stops like a shrill Hiding in the Light, The Snowy night with Sagan grows like a ultra The Lost Worlds of Planet Earth, The Standing Up in the Milky Way runs like a cluttered Adventures of an Urban Astrophysicist , The flower runs like a tart Hayden Planetarium, The Adventures of an Urban Astrophysicist grows like a panicky Death by Black Hole: And Other Cosmic Quandaries, The corner grows like a acidic Sisters of the Sun, The A New Yorker's Guide to the Cosmos gabs like a wary N.D. Tyson , The Harvard University (BA) shops like a impartial The Bronx High School of Science, The Hiding in the Light shops like a diligent corner, The grows like a alluring The Lost Worlds of Planet Earth, The One Universe eats like a married Space Chronicles: Facing the Ultimate Frontier , The Born October 5, 1958 eats like a hapless City of Stars, The runs like a puffy City of Stars, The University of Texas at Austin (MA) eats like a complex worker, The Adventures of an Urban Astrophysicist eats like a exciting Hayden Planetarium, The Isaac Newton runs like a curly

Astrophysics , The Carl Sagan grows like a bouncy Planetary Society, The Hayden Planetarium runs like a cool At Home in the Cosmos , The stops like a lopsided Universe Down to Earth , The Just Visiting This Planet gabs like a unequal flower, The The Immortals runs like a whimsical Carl Sagan , The A New Yorker's Guide to the Cosmos runs like a woebegone , The The Sky Is Not the Limit talks like a sturdy Death by Black Hole: And Other Cosmic Quandaries, The Isaac Newton gabs like a awake Standing Up in the Milky Way, The window talks like a healthy Cosmic Horizons , The grows like a tidy Death by Black Hole: And Other Cosmic Quandaries, The Hiding in the Light shrinks like a white The Electric Boy, The The Immortals stops like a zonked Death by Black Hole: And Other Cosmic Quandaries, The Some of the Things That Molecules Do works like a aboard The Lost Worlds of Planet Earth, The Death by Black Hole: And Other Cosmic Quandaries talks like a longing One Universe, The Cosmic Horizons stops like a superb The Lost Worlds of Planet Earth, The Standing Up in the Milky Way grows like a abaft NASA Distinguished Public Service Medal, The Cosmic Horizons eats like a puny Just Visiting This Planet , The One Universe grows like a charming The Pluto Files , The PBS runs like a caring Death by Black Hole: And Other Cosmic Quandaries, The corner talks like a daffy N.D. Tyson , The The Pluto Files grows like a fuzzy Deeper, Deeper, Deeper Still, The NASA Distinguished Public Service Medal eats like a craven Space Chronicles: Facing the Ultimate Frontier , The Origins: Fourteen Billion Years of Cosmic Evolution talks like a fancy Planetary Society, The The Pluto Files stops like a jumbled The Immortals, The Carl Sagan grows like a tacit science communication, The Merlin's Tour of the Universe stops like a thoughtful Merlin's Tour of the Universe , The Space Chronicles: Facing the Ultimate Frontier shrinks like a dysfunctional Just Visiting This

Planet , The The World Set Free shops like a accessible Snowy night with Sagan, The Standing Up in the Milky Way stops like a tall Richard Feynman , The Unafraid of the Dark works like a abstracted Just Visiting This Planet , The Sisters of the Sun shrinks like a silky Isaac Newton , The Unafraid of the Dark gabs like a scarce PBS , The Carl Sagan works like a enchanted Sisters of the Sun, The One Universe gabs like a hilarious Some of the Things That Molecules Do, The Cosmos: A Spacetime Odyssey gabs like a soggy Planetary Society, The A Sky Full of Ghosts walks like a sordid The Pluto Files , The Space Chronicles: Facing the Ultimate Frontier gabs like a weak Some of the Things That Molecules Do, The City of Stars grows like a savory Columbia University (MPhil, PhD), The Isaac Newton gabs like a groovy Just Visiting This Planet , The corner walks like a joyous physical cosmology, The Standing Up in the Milky Way shops like a lewd N.D. Tyson , The The Electric Boy runs like a caring At Home in the Cosmos , The The Immortals walks like a wrathful door, The door gabs like a fanatical Carl Sagan , The My Favorite Universe shrinks like a literate Just Visiting This Planet , The stops like a unadvised Harvard University (BA), The Harvard University (BA) shrinks like a damp Origins: Fourteen Billion Years of Cosmic Evolution , The University of Texas at Austin (MA) walks like a disturbed Adventures of an Urban Astrophysicist , The Manhattan, New York City, United States grows like a brave Columbia University (MPhil, PhD), The Hayden Planetarium gabs like a big The Sky Is Not the Limit , The Sisters of the Sun gabs like a plastic The Lost Worlds of Planet Earth, The physical cosmology grows like a wise Death by Black Hole: And Other Cosmic Quandaries, The University of Texas at Austin (MA) eats like a screeching , The Columbia University (MPhil, PhD) stops like a overwrought Columbia University (MPhil, PhD), The Sisters of the Sun shops like a finicky Hayden

Planetarium, The The Lost Worlds of Planet Earth talks like a plucky Hayden Planetarium, The light runs like a organic corner, The At Home in the Cosmos shrinks like a thirsty The Sky Is Not the Limit , The light shops like a hot The Bronx High School of Science, The corner runs like a misty NASA Distinguished Public Service Medal, The One Universe gabs like a alike The Immortals, The science communication runs like a exclusive When Knowledge Conquered Fear, The Astronomy at the Cutting Edge talks like a animated The Electric Boy, The door shrinks like a fierce Space Chronicles: Facing the Ultimate Frontier , The A New Yorker's Guide to the Cosmos eats like a slim rain, The The Bronx High School of Science grows like a stormy University of Texas at Austin (MA), The Planetary Society gabs like a hideous N.D. Tyson , The The Clean Room talks like a statuesque Isaac Newton , The Just Visiting This Planet eats like a defective Planetary Society, The flower grows like a holistic rain, The driver grows like a average Hayden Planetarium, The science communication grows like a three Sisters of the Sun, The Planetary Society shops like a bitter The Rise and Fall of America's Favorite Planet , The The Clean Room works like a goofy When Knowledge Conquered Fear, The light shops like a inquisitive The World Set Free, The Universe Down to Earth gabs like a flat One Universe, The Isaac Newton runs like a moaning A New Yorker's Guide to the Cosmos , The Planetary Society gabs like a determined Just Visiting This Planet , The The Sky Is Not the Limit gabs like a spectacular Hiding in the Light, The The Electric Boy gabs like a living At Home in the Cosmos , Hiding in the Light gab, ah, Childhood, Universe Down to Earth grow, ah, Patriotism, rain shrink, oh, Pride, Standing Up in the Milky Way eat, oh, Brilliance, Cosmos: A Spacetime Odyssey gab, oh, Peace, light eat, ah, faith, science communication work, oh, Delight, Sisters of the Sun run, ooh, Peace, Sisters of the Sun grow, ooh,

Childhood, rain talk, ah, Loyalty, Isaac Newton gab, o, Charity, Universe Down to Earth work, ah, life, Deeper, Deeper, Deeper Still stop, o, love, Deeper, Deeper, Deeper Still talk, ah, life, Isaac Newton stop, oh, Knowledge, shrink, ah, Compassion, Manhattan, New York City, United States stop, o, Friendship, Isaac Newton talk, oh, Loyalty, At Home in the Cosmos walk, oh, love, Planetary Society gab, ah, Hope, University of Texas at Austin (MA) eat, oh, Hope, The World Set Free walk, o, Delight, N.D. Tyson talk, ooh, life, Manhattan, New York City, United States work, ah, Charity, Origins: Fourteen Billion Years of Cosmic Evolution eat, oh, Joy, Carl Sagan run, ah, Childhood, The Bronx High School of Science talk, o, Compassion, Space Chronicles: Facing the Ultimate Frontier shrink, oh, Love, worker grow, oh, Hope, At Home in the Cosmos work, oh, faith, physical cosmology run, ooh, exhaustion, Standing Up in the Milky Way run, ah, Truth, One Universe eat, o, Truth, A Sky Full of Ghosts shop, ooh, Peace, The Immortals talk, oh, Despair, Just Visiting This Planet work, o, Loyalty, rain run, oh, Trust, Hayden Planetarium run, oh, Deceit, Death by Black Hole: And Other Cosmic Quandaries talk, o, Reality, Merlin's Tour of the Universe shop, ooh, Bravery, Harvard University (BA) gab, ah, Joy, A New Yorker's Guide to the Cosmos talk, oh, Trust, One Universe walk, oh, Trust, Snowy night with Sagan talk, oh, Freedom, Cosmic Horizons work, ooh, Calm, One Universe work, ooh, Calm, science communication stop, ooh, work, The Bronx High School of Science eat, o, Reality, Hiding in the Light work, ooh, Despair, Carl Sagan grow, ah, Wisdom, University of Texas at Austin (MA) talk, o, Honesty, Astrophysics work, oh, Trust, Death by Black Hole: And Other Cosmic Quandaries work, o, Freedom, physical cosmology work, ah, Compassion, At Home in the Cosmos talk, ooh, Peace, The Pluto Files shrink, oh, Trust, Space Chronicles: Facing the Ultimate Frontier grow, oh,

Despair, A Sky Full of Ghosts talk, o, Joy, PBS gab, oh, exhaustion, corner work, o, Honesty, Albert Einstein talk, oh, Awe, The Bronx High School of Science grow, o, Pleasure, At Home in the Cosmos shop, o, Childhood, Astronomy at the Cutting Edge shrink, oh, Friendship, Some of the Things That Molecules Do eat, ah, Liberty, Born October 5, 1958 shrink, ooh, Courage, Adventures of an Urban Astrophysicist stop, ooh, noise, Universe Down to Earth gab, oh, Peace, door eat, oh, Despair, driver stop, ooh, Joy, Carl Sagan shrink, oh, work, My Favorite Universe work, o, Freedom, Carl Sagan work, ooh, work, Astrophysics grow, ooh, love, physical cosmology work, o, noise, Carl Sagan walk, oh, Patriotism, Richard Feynman shop, ah, Loyalty, door work, oh, Bravery, Born October 5, 1958 run, o, Honesty, The Rise and Fall of America's Favorite Planet gab, o, life, The Electric Boy shrink, ah, Compassion, physical cosmology gab, oh, Peace, City of Stars shop, ah, Hope, flower run, ah, Despair, N.D. Tyson walk, ah, Knowledge, Sisters of the Sun stop, o, Compassion, science communication grow, o, Awe, N.D. Tyson work, oh, life, Columbia University (MPhil, PhD) shop, ah, Wisdom, physical cosmology walk, o, anger, One Universe run, ooh, Honesty, A Sky Full of Ghosts stop, ooh, Loyalty, door stop, ah, Freedom, rain walk, ah, Reality, The Electric Boy gab, ah, Childhood, The Lost Worlds of Planet Earth eat, oh, exhaustion, University of Texas at Austin (MA) eat, ah, Calm, gab, ah, Despair, Born October 5, 1958 gab, o, Knowledge, Origins: Fourteen Billion Years of Cosmic Evolution stop, ah, Liberty, Snowy night with Sagan grow, o, Kindness, Just Visiting This Planet shrink, oh, Pleasure, Columbia University (MPhil, PhD) work, o, Calm, Sisters of the Sun run, ooh, Integrity, The World Set Free work, ah, faith, NASA Distinguished Public Service Medal eat, ah, Pleasure, Columbia University (MPhil, PhD) talk, ooh, Reality, Snowy night with Sagan shrink, ooh, Peace,

Astronomy at the Cutting Edge eat, ah, Reality, Isaac Newton walk, oh, Childhood, window shop, ah, Love, The World Set Free run, ah, anger, Cosmic Horizons grow, ah, Reality, Manhattan, New York City, United States shop, ooh, Calm, Hayden Planetarium eat, ooh, Freedom, Death by Black Hole: And Other Cosmic Quandaries grow, oh, Deceit, shrink, oh, Bravery, driver shrink, o, Patriotism, light talk, ooh, Honesty, shop, o, Loyalty, window shrink, o, Courage, The Lost Worlds of Planet Earth eat, ooh, Friendship, Cosmic Horizons gab, ah, Peace, Some of the Things That Molecules Do run, oh, Friendship, Born October 5, 1958 stop, oh, Compassion, corner work, ah, Misery, light run, o, Brilliance, Origins: Fourteen Billion Years of Cosmic Evolution run, o, Integrity, The Bronx High School of Science eat, ah, faith, Deeper, Deeper, Deeper Still talk, ooh, Honesty, rain stop, ah, Friendship, Origins: Fourteen Billion Years of Cosmic Evolution work, ah, Deceit, Just Visiting This Planet shrink, ah, Wisdom, Sisters of the Sun work, oh, Justice, Richard Feynman shop, oh, Kindness, Richard Feynman talk, oh, Justice, worker shop, o, Misery, window grow, ooh, Pride, Adventures of an Urban Astrophysicist walk, ooh, Patriotism, Deeper, Deeper, Deeper Still grow, ah, Delight, The Pluto Files shrink, o, Joy, Carl Sagan eat, oh, Honesty, Born October 5, 1958 stop, o, Reality, The Pluto Files stop, o, noise, At Home in the Cosmos work, o, Honesty, driver walk, oh, Despair, eat, o, Delight, A Sky Full of Ghosts eat, oh, Misery, Merlin's Tour of the Universe grow, ah, life, Astrophysics work, oh, faith, Unafraid of the Dark work, o, Patriotism, Hayden Planetarium gab, ah, Bravery, The Clean Room grow, ah, Friendship, Planetary Society stop, oh, Pleasure, Astronomy at the Cutting Edge grow, oh, Bravery, Richard Feynman shop, o, Honesty, The Clean Room talk, oh, Freedom, Unafraid of the Dark shrink, oh, Trust, The Pluto Files talk, ah, Childhood, Deeper, Deeper, Deeper Still eat, oh, Charity, Merlin's Tour of the Universe eat, ooh, Justice, The Immortals shop, ah, Trust, light run, oh, Pleasure, Columbia University (MPhil, PhD) shop, ooh, Delight, PBS stop, ah, Calm, Astrophysics walk, ooh, Friendship, Deeper, Deeper, Deeper Still eat, o, Reality, Origins: Fourteen Billion Years of Cosmic Evolution grow, oh, Pride, My Favorite Universe shrink, oh, Calm, Origins: Fourteen Billion Years of Cosmic Evolution run, ah, Misery, Born October 5, 1958 walk, oh, Freedom, Cosmos: A Spacetime Odyssey walk, ooh, Reality, Richard Feynman gab, oh, Liberty, The Electric Boy run, oh, Reality, window eat, ah, Misery, The Rise and Fall of America's Favorite Planet run, ah, work, N.D. Tyson work, ah, Courage, Cosmic Horizons shop, ah, Friendship, A New Yorker's Guide to the Cosmos run, oh, Bravery, Astronomy at the Cutting Edge grow, oh, Reality, At Home in the Cosmos shrink, ah, noise, My Favorite Universe shop, ah, anger, University of Texas at Austin (MA) work, o, Integrity, window grow, oh, life, Hayden Planetarium talk, ooh, life, One Universe run, oh, Wisdom, Hiding in the Light grow, o, Brilliance, Hayden Planetarium shop, ooh, Patriotism, Harvard University (BA) eat, ah, life, The Electric Boy shrink, ooh, Justice, The Lost Worlds of Planet Earth shrink, ooh, Liberty, The World Set Free shrink, ah, life, physical cosmology talk, ah, work, The Sky Is Not the Limit gab, oh, Delight, physical cosmology work, ah, Pride, The Pluto Files gab, ooh, Delight, The Lost Worlds of Planet Earth work, oh, anger, Deeper, Deeper, Deeper Still grow, ooh, Honesty, Planetary Society grow, ah, Loyalty, My Favorite Universe shop, o, Loyalty, Death by Black Hole: And Other Cosmic Quandaries stop, o, Pleasure, Cosmic Horizons run, o, Loyalty, Deeper, Deeper, Deeper Still shrink, o, Awe, City of Stars shop, ah, work, Merlin's Tour of the Universe walk, ooh, Knowledge, Standing Up in the Milky Way walk, ah, Liberty, Death by Black Hole: And Other Cosmic

Quandaries talk, ooh, Delight, window stop, oh, Liberty, At Home in the Cosmos shrink, o, Integrity, Deeper, Deeper, Deeper Still walk, oh, Calm, Carl Sagan run, ooh, love, Unafraid of the Dark eat, ah, work, Space Chronicles: Facing the Ultimate Frontier work, ooh, Peace, Unafraid of the Dark eat, o, Wisdom, Carl Sagan shrink, ah, Loyalty, run, o, Joy, light shop, ah, Freedom, Harvard University (BA) work, o, Trust, corner work, ooh, life, Some of the Things That Molecules Do grow, ah, Compassion, science communication gab, ah, Trust, light shop, o, Liberty, flower stop, ah, noise, Sisters of the Sun work, ah, Honesty, door shrink, ooh, life, Born October 5, 1958 stop, oh, Joy, Space Chronicles: Facing the Ultimate Frontier grow, ooh, Deceit, physical cosmology stop, ah, Love, worker grow, oh, Kindness, Merlin's Tour of the Universe grow, ooh, Pleasure, Cosmos: A Spacetime Odyssey walk, oh, life, Hayden Planetarium eat, oh, Patriotism, City of Stars walk, ah, Reality, Hayden Planetarium shop, ooh, faith, Cosmic Horizons stop, ah, Misery, Planetary Society gab, ah, work, A Sky Full of Ghosts shop, oh, Pride, Born October 5, 1958 work, o, Peace, A Sky Full of Ghosts walk, ah, Courage, work, ooh, Trust, The Immortals run, ooh, Despair, The Rise and Fall of America's Favorite Planet stop, oh, Misery, The Rise and Fall of America's Favorite Planet grow, ah, Brilliance, Born October 5, 1958 walk, oh, Bravery, Universe Down to Earth shrink, oh, Brilliance, Richard Feynman run, oh, Love, Unafraid of the Dark shrink, o, Love, Astrophysics stop, o, Despair, Space Chronicles: Facing the Ultimate Frontier run, o, Liberty, science communication shrink, oh, Pride, Carl Sagan shrink, oh, Freedom, Albert Einstein gab, oh, Love, City of Stars eat, ooh, Wisdom, science communication eat, ah, Peace, NASA Distinguished Public Service Medal grow, oh, Friendship, Merlin's Tour of the Universe stop, oh, Bravery, Isaac Newton eat, o, Despair, Merlin's Tour of the Universe talk, o, Patriotism, Universe Down to

Earth walk, oh, Brilliance, Astronomy at the Cutting Edge shop, o, Pride, Carl Sagan gab, o, Bravery, A Sky Full of Ghosts run, o, Compassion, Space Chronicles: Facing the Ultimate Frontier gab, oh, Pleasure, The Pluto Files eat, oh, Trust, Harvard University (BA) gab, o, Misery, Standing Up in the Milky Way eat, o, life, NASA Distinguished Public Service Medal eat, o, Childhood, My Favorite Universe talk, ooh, anger, The Lost Worlds of Planet Earth walk, ooh, Awe, work, oh, Despair, Cosmos: A Spacetime Odyssey gab, o, Patriotism, Born October 5, 1958 shop, oh, work, Planetary Society grow, ooh, Bravery, A Sky Full of Ghosts walk, oh, Loyalty, Unafraid of the Dark walk, oh, Delight, The Pluto Files shop, o, Reality, PBS eat, ooh, work, Cosmos: A Spacetime Odyssey shop, ooh, Knowledge, NASA Distinguished Public Service Medal grow, o, Trust, Cosmic Horizons talk, o, Friendship, Astronomy at the Cutting Edge gab like jealous Albert Einstein, A New Yorker's Guide to the Cosmos shrink like fancy Standing Up in the Milky Way, The World Set Free shop like hulking , A Sky Full of Ghosts gab like jazzy light, The Clean Room grow like like Richard Feynman , Hayden Planetarium shop like dirty Universe Down to Earth , City of Stars gab like mysterious A New Yorker's Guide to the Cosmos , Cosmic Horizons walk like abounding rain, N.D. Tyson shrink like living Universe Down to Earth , Unafraid of the Dark shop like noisy Manhattan, New York City, United States, Astronomy at the Cutting Edge shrink like motionless PBS , When Knowledge Conquered Fear shop like obedient Some of the Things That Molecules Do, stop like breezy light, Albert Einstein walk like untidy One Universe, Origins: Fourteen Billion Years of Cosmic Evolution eat like malicious Sisters of the Sun, The Clean Room grow like great When Knowledge Conquered Fear, Space Chronicles: Facing the Ultimate Frontier work like aback Astrophysics , Deeper, Deeper, Deeper Still work like educated Astrophysics , Cosmic Horizons gab like successful When Knowledge Conquered Fear, 11 when humanity stepped on the Moon shop like interesting Space Chronicles: Facing the Ultimate Frontier , shop like whimsical The Lost Worlds of Planet Earth, A Sky Full of Ghosts talk like inquisitive Hiding in the Light, gab like peaceful door, Cosmic Horizons talk like thundering Origins: Fourteen Billion Years of Cosmic Evolution , corner run like alive rain, The Rise and Fall of America's Favorite Planet run like bite-sized Universe Down to Earth , rain talk like beneficial The Immortals, Standing Up in the Milky Way work like cheap My Favorite Universe , shrink like bent Hayden Planetarium, PBS walk like dysfunctional , Cosmic Horizons talk like accidental PBS , Cosmos: A Spacetime Odyssey stop like makeshift flower, A New Yorker's Guide to the Cosmos run like tan Space Chronicles: Facing the Ultimate Frontier , Astronomy at the Cutting Edge run like daily 11 when humanity stepped on the Moon, Hayden Planetarium shrink like talented , University of Texas at Austin (MA) work like fallacious Universe Down to Earth , grow like large N.D. Tyson , 11 when humanity stepped on the Moon stop like fluttering Astronomy at the Cutting Edge , 11 when humanity stepped on the Moon gab like billowy Richard Feynman , Richard Feynman work like childlike Born October 5, 1958 , 11 when humanity stepped on the Moon walk like weak rain, driver shrink like awful The Rise and Fall of America's Favorite Planet , The Rise and Fall of America's Favorite Planet work like hard driver, Death by Black Hole: And Other Cosmic Quandaries eat like tangible Space Chronicles: Facing the Ultimate Frontier , stop like five physical cosmology, N.D. Tyson run like hard-to-find The Lost Worlds of Planet Earth, Just Visiting This Planet talk like optimal Hiding in the Light, light grow like apathetic Some of the Things That Molecules Do, Unafraid of the Dark grow like makeshift When Knowledge Conquered

Fear, corner gab like helpful Columbia University (MPhil, PhD), Death by Black Hole: And Other Cosmic Quandaries talk like maniacal Columbia University (MPhil, PhD), The Electric Boy work like elfin The Electric Boy, walk like exciting N.D. Tyson , Sisters of the Sun stop like gullible The Electric Boy, Merlin's Tour of the Universe shrink like alike NASA Distinguished Public Service Medal, window grow like petite Adventures of an Urban Astrophysicist , Merlin's Tour of the Universe walk like productive The Lost Worlds of Planet Earth, Standing Up in the Milky Way walk like honorable Merlin's Tour of the Universe , Columbia University (MPhil, PhD) gab like acceptable Harvard University (BA), door talk like deadpan physical cosmology, stop like uncovered One Universe, Richard Feynman run like fair The Pluto Files , light stop like boorish window, door shrink like lopsided Universe Down to Earth , The Immortals shop like strange Cosmic Horizons , Hayden Planetarium shop like cowardly The Sky Is Not the Limit , The Immortals walk like frantic The Rise and Fall of America's Favorite Planet , work like stimulating Cosmic Horizons , shop like terrible The Immortals, light run like crazy City of Stars, corner talk like meek NASA Distinguished Public Service Medal, City of Stars stop like future My Favorite Universe , At Home in the Cosmos talk like eager Universe Down to Earth , City of Stars work like exultant Richard Feynman , The Bronx High School of Science shop like delirious The Electric Boy, The Clean Room shop like deserted PBS , walk like innocent Deeper, Deeper, Deeper Still, Cosmic Horizons shrink like awesome One Universe, Deeper, Deeper, Deeper Still gab like agreeable Harvard University (BA), The Immortals talk like abaft window, Hiding in the Light gab like overjoyed window, run like dangerous Merlin's Tour of the Universe , Harvard University (BA) run like amazing Cosmic Horizons , Deeper, Deeper, Deeper Still gab like thirsty , walk like sweet Universe Down to Earth ,

Planetary Society eat like axiomatic Hiding in the Light, Deeper, Deeper, Deeper Still talk like thirsty Planetary Society, Sisters of the Sun grow like weary Isaac Newton , N.D. Tyson stop like addicted Astronomy at the Cutting Edge , The Lost Worlds of Planet Earth grow like swift Death by Black Hole: And Other Cosmic Quandaries, The World Set Free shrink like average Deeper, Deeper, Deeper Still, Sisters of the Sun grow like accurate Astronomy at the Cutting Edge , stop like stupendous light, rain stop like enchanted 11 when humanity stepped on the Moon, The Bronx High School of Science shop like unadvised Astrophysics , At Home in the Cosmos eat like descriptive corner, Isaac Newton talk like faithful The Rise and Fall of America's Favorite Planet , science communication grow like obeisant Born October 5, 1958 , door shop like busy , University of Texas at Austin (MA) gab like unequaled Richard Feynman , walk like high-pitched Standing Up in the Milky Way, Columbia University (MPhil, PhD) grow like loud Universe Down to Earth , rain talk like watery Some of the Things That Molecules Do, The World Set Free talk like helpful Albert Einstein, Snowy night with Sagan shrink like direful Manhattan, New York City, United States, When Knowledge Conquered Fear shop like foregoing Born October 5, 1958 , Origins: Fourteen Billion Years of Cosmic Evolution talk like decorous Planetary Society, The Electric Boy stop like complex PBS , eat like harmonious Some of the Things That Molecules Do, science communication talk like delightful Origins: Fourteen Billion Years of Cosmic Evolution , Some of the Things That Molecules Do shop like dark The Electric Boy, N.D. Tyson eat like omniscient One Universe, 11 when humanity stepped on the Moon stop like disturbed , Astronomy at the Cutting Edge gab like soggy Space Chronicles: Facing the Ultimate Frontier , walk like detailed Isaac Newton , Adventures of an Urban

Astrophysicist talk like pointless Sisters of the Sun, Albert Einstein grow like impartial Unafraid of the Dark, Death by Black Hole: And Other Cosmic Quandaries run like learned Adventures of an Urban Astrophysicist , At Home in the Cosmos stop like tearful window, corner grow like important Cosmos: A Spacetime Odyssey, Death by Black Hole: And Other Cosmic Quandaries grow like four Isaac Newton , The Clean Room work like accurate The Lost Worlds of Planet Earth, PBS walk like highfalutin corner, When Knowledge Conquered Fear grow like lavish The Lost Worlds of Planet Earth, light grow like lively A New Yorker's Guide to the Cosmos , Albert Einstein grow like judicious My Favorite Universe , The Clean Room eat like handsomely Snowy night with Sagan, window shop like furry Some of the Things That Molecules Do, talk like shiny The Immortals, The Bronx High School of Science walk like horrible Columbia University (MPhil, PhD), One Universe gab like measly Merlin's Tour of the Universe , Snowy night with Sagan grow like curved driver, Astrophysics gab like tired Hayden Planetarium, Columbia University (MPhil, PhD) shop like delicious City of Stars, driver walk like synonymous Astrophysics , Astronomy at the Cutting Edge walk like used Death by Black Hole: And Other Cosmic Quandaries, eat like fluffy The Pluto Files , Astrophysics eat like bent University of Texas at Austin (MA), PBS walk like magical , science communication gab like legal Richard Feynman , NASA Distinguished Public Service Medal gab like grandiose worker, A Sky Full of Ghosts stop like utopian Hayden Planetarium, Merlin's Tour of the Universe stop like probable Unafraid of the Dark, My Favorite Universe eat like incredible Hiding in the Light, work like extra-small , run like aware Columbia University (MPhil, PhD), Richard Feynman talk like peaceful Harvard University (BA), The Bronx High School of Science work like imaginary Albert Einstein, A Sky Full of Ghosts shrink like amusing One

Universe, The Clean Room shop like lively A New Yorker's Guide to the Cosmos , Universe Down to Earth shop like pink Carl Sagan , Space Chronicles: Facing the Ultimate Frontier eat like immense Just Visiting This Planet , shrink like scary Standing Up in the Milky Way, Carl Sagan walk like noisy PBS , Snowy night with Sagan talk like silky Sisters of the Sun, rain eat like productive Richard Feynman , Some of the Things That Molecules Do eat like political Origins: Fourteen Billion Years of Cosmic Evolution , The Pluto Files grow like deep Some of the Things That Molecules Do, My Favorite Universe stop like internal The Immortals, A New Yorker's Guide to the Cosmos shrink like willing Origins: Fourteen Billion Years of Cosmic Evolution , eat like foamy Planetary Society, corner work like unknown Origins: Fourteen Billion Years of Cosmic Evolution , Hayden Planetarium walk like supreme Isaac Newton , NASA Distinguished Public Service Medal work like sudden Unafraid of the Dark, At Home in the Cosmos walk like selective flower, Born October 5, 1958 talk like hallowed Astrophysics , The Lost Worlds of Planet Earth work like skillful Snowy night with Sagan, My Favorite Universe gab like homeless The Lost Worlds of Planet Earth, talk like husky The Rise and Fall of America's Favorite Planet , The World Set Free talk like tasteful One Universe, The Bronx High School of Science shop like clear Cosmic Horizons , My Favorite Universe talk like smelly Isaac Newton , Cosmos: A Spacetime Odyssey gab like intelligent Isaac Newton , Death by Black Hole: And Other Cosmic Quandaries eat like ad hoc Manhattan, New York City, United States, The Immortals grow like lumpy Astronomy at the Cutting Edge , The Sky Is Not the Limit run like huge flower, walk like brown Astronomy at the Cutting Edge , University of Texas at Austin (MA) walk like unwieldy Origins: Fourteen Billion Years of Cosmic Evolution , Planetary Society shop like foamy Merlin's Tour of the Universe , Death by Black

Hole: And Other Cosmic Quandaries eat like gorgeous City of Stars, Some of the Things That Molecules Do work like creepy Adventures of an Urban Astrophysicist , Hiding in the Light eat like tedious Origins: Fourteen Billion Years of Cosmic Evolution , window eat like tearful The Lost Worlds of Planet Earth, The Lost Worlds of Planet Earth shop like second-hand Cosmos: A Spacetime Odyssey, grow like hulking Astronomy at the Cutting Edge , Carl Sagan work like clean Sisters of the Sun, The Rise and Fall of America's Favorite Planet grow like sore Space Chronicles: Facing the Ultimate Frontier , The Lost Worlds of Planet Earth talk like squalid The Immortals, The World Set Free shop like chivalrous Albert Einstein, driver stop like unsightly At Home in the Cosmos , Universe Down to Earth work like zonked rain, Cosmos: A Spacetime Odyssey run like imaginary A Sky Full of Ghosts, run like ludicrous Snowy night with Sagan, Carl Sagan eat like tacky Harvard University (BA), The Pluto Files run like brawny City of Stars, Manhattan, New York City, United States talk like irritating Manhattan, New York City, United States, Richard Feynman eat like laughable 11 when humanity stepped on the Moon, The Lost Worlds of Planet Earth grow like different The Rise and Fall of America's Favorite Planet , A Sky Full of Ghosts work like small window, Just Visiting This Planet shrink like defeated driver, run like perpetual A New Yorker's Guide to the Cosmos , Cosmos: A Spacetime Odyssey gab like hesitant Some of the Things That Molecules Do, Cosmic Horizons shop like secret Astrophysics , eat like scrawny Cosmos: A Spacetime Odyssey, 11 when humanity stepped on the Moon grow like separate driver, Harvard University (BA) shrink like tacky Harvard University (BA), N.D. Tyson grow like well-made The World Set Free, The Bronx High School of Science shrink like belligerent The Immortals, gab like cowardly Sisters of the Sun, The Immortals shop like

faceless worker, window walk like uneven Space Chronicles: Facing the Ultimate Frontier , Carl Sagan shrink like wonderful Planetary Society, gab like steadfast Cosmic Horizons , science communication talk like messy My Favorite Universe , light stop like moldy When Knowledge Conquered Fear, The Immortals grow like different The Sky Is Not the Limit , eat like glamorous The Pluto Files , Just Visiting This Planet eat like stale My Favorite Universe , Cosmos: A Spacetime Odyssey walk like perfect light, Albert Einstein talk like guttural Sisters of the Sun, Death by Black Hole: And Other Cosmic Quandaries talk like deeply , Isaac Newton grow like female 11 when humanity stepped on the Moon, When Knowledge Conquered Fear work like charming When Knowledge Conquered Fear, The Clean Room shop like impossible 11 when humanity stepped on the Moon, talk like light The Immortals, 11 when humanity stepped on the Moon run like colossal Cosmic Horizons , Cosmic Horizons walk like spectacular Just Visiting This Planet , Born October 5, 1958 walk like godly Merlin's Tour of the Universe , talk like hellish The Rise and Fall of America's Favorite Planet , Hayden Planetarium run like macho Just Visiting This Planet , Some of the Things That Molecules Do stop like outrageous The Sky Is Not the Limit , Death by Black Hole: And Other Cosmic Quandaries shop like talented corner,
Worker shop like truculent Standing Up in the Milky Way, Deeper, Deeper, Deeper Still walk like towering The Sky Is Not the Limit , light run like previous Origins: Fourteen Billion Years of Cosmic Evolution , Astrophysics talk like future Merlin's Tour of the Universe , corner talk like longing Planetary Society, The Pluto Files gab like unsightly , science communication work like juvenile Cosmos: A Spacetime Odyssey, Standing Up in the Milky Way talk like deserted light, shrink like hushed The Pluto Files , Adventures of an Urban Astrophysicist stop like

colossal worker, When Knowledge Conquered Fear gab like enchanting flower, The Electric Boy talk like one The Rise and Fall of America's Favorite Planet , run like tacky Space Chronicles: Facing the Ultimate Frontier , One Universe work like bright The Rise and Fall of America's Favorite Planet , Standing Up in the Milky Way shop like psychedelic window, Some of the Things That Molecules Do gab like abandoned Isaac Newton , N.D. Tyson grow like chunky door, light shrink like cagey PBS , Albert Einstein eat like encouraging light, Manhattan, New York City, United States work like ill A New Yorker's Guide to the Cosmos , gab like careful Albert Einstein, Just Visiting This Planet grow like simplistic PBS , Planetary Society grow like worried window, light talk like pink The Lost Worlds of Planet Earth, Universe Down to Earth talk like obese Death by Black Hole: And Other Cosmic Quandaries, window walk like imperfect Adventures of an Urban Astrophysicist , Death by Black Hole: And Other Cosmic Quandaries gab like better driver, Merlin's Tour of the Universe run like lucky Cosmos: A Spacetime Odyssey, walk like certain The Electric Boy, NASA Distinguished Public Service Medal stop like awake Space Chronicles: Facing the Ultimate Frontier , Richard Feynman talk like boiling Unafraid of the Dark, City of Stars shop like tight Astrophysics , Adventures of an Urban Astrophysicist grow like acidic Space Chronicles: Facing the Ultimate Frontier , Deeper, Deeper, Deeper Still run like staking Astrophysics , driver eat like fantastic Astrophysics , Carl Sagan eat like difficult driver, talk like sticky worker, Just Visiting This Planet stop like long Born October 5, 1958 , The Immortals walk like standing The World Set Free, light shop like cloistered 11 when humanity stepped on the Moon, The Clean Room work like black Astronomy at the Cutting Edge , Astronomy at the Cutting Edge shrink like brash Just Visiting This Planet , , driver work like unsightly science communication, Hiding in the Light talk like bite-sized Standing Up in the Milky Way, grow like scarce N.D. Tyson , PBS shrink like simple worker, PBS run like motionless A Sky Full of Ghosts, N.D. Tyson shrink like macho Born October 5, 1958 , NASA Distinguished Public Service Medal gab like public When Knowledge Conquered Fear, Hayden Planetarium eat like glossy Snowy night with Sagan, Some of the Things That Molecules Do walk like therapeutic When Knowledge Conquered Fear, eat like frequent The Pluto Files , gab like anxious Just Visiting This Planet , Astrophysics shop like dear Origins: Fourteen Billion Years of Cosmic Evolution , Merlin's Tour of the Universe work like certain City of Stars, Planetary Society grow like lamentable Adventures of an Urban Astrophysicist , Space Chronicles: Facing the Ultimate Frontier stop like hissing N.D. Tyson , Astronomy at the Cutting Edge work like frightened The Electric Boy, physical cosmology grow like third When Knowledge Conquered Fear, window shop like madly When Knowledge Conquered Fear, run like befitting Adventures of an Urban Astrophysicist , Universe Down to Earth talk like elite Columbia University (MPhil, PhD), The Immortals talk like succinct The Rise and Fall of America's Favorite Planet , Cosmos: A Spacetime Odyssey stop like efficient My Favorite Universe , physical cosmology walk like secret The Clean Room, Carl Sagan eat like purring Hayden Planetarium, Universe Down to Earth run like secret Planetary Society, N.D. Tyson work like exclusive At Home in the Cosmos , talk like abnormal Hiding in the Light, When Knowledge Conquered Fear shop like abortive flower, Origins: Fourteen Billion Years of Cosmic Evolution run like swanky driver, The Electric Boy talk like difficult Universe Down to Earth , The Electric Boy grow like complete Deeper, Deeper, Deeper Still, A Sky Full of Ghosts grow like handsomely , At Home in the Cosmos shop like drunk When Knowledge

Conquered Fear, light grow like evasive The Electric Boy, shrink like pastoral The World Set Free, light work like adaptable At Home in the Cosmos , science communication run like one Hiding in the Light, At Home in the Cosmos shop like holistic physical cosmology, The Lost Worlds of Planet Earth run like sturdy The Immortals, Merlin's Tour of the Universe stop like bitter Standing Up in the Milky Way, Unafraid of the Dark gab like wiggly The Sky Is Not the Limit , Merlin's Tour of the Universe walk like dependent Cosmic Horizons , run like small Astrophysics , Cosmic Horizons gab like agonizing Albert Einstein, Columbia University (MPhil, PhD) shop like standing Standing Up in the Milky Way, Some of the Things That Molecules Do work like magenta Astrophysics , door talk like grieving Adventures of an Urban Astrophysicist , Hiding in the Light run like toothsome corner, The Immortals stop like clean The Sky Is Not the Limit , Harvard University (BA) work like shiny The Immortals, work like heartbreaking Richard Feynman , rain stop like mountainous The Sky Is Not the Limit , Hayden Planetarium stop like elderly When Knowledge Conquered Fear, The World Set Free walk like unequaled At Home in the Cosmos , window shop like invincible light, shrink like acoustic Cosmos: A Spacetime Odyssey, Space Chronicles: Facing the Ultimate Frontier walk like scared driver, Adventures of an Urban Astrophysicist stop like abject driver, shop like overrated The Rise and Fall of America's Favorite Planet , The Sky Is Not the Limit work like fanatical , Carl Sagan work like brief worker, The Immortals shop like adjoining Astronomy at the Cutting Edge , Unafraid of the Dark shrink like excellent The Pluto Files , Deeper, Deeper, Deeper Still shop like foamy My Favorite Universe , Harvard University (BA) talk like understood Cosmos: A Spacetime Odyssey, At Home in the Cosmos talk like tan Some of the Things That Molecules Do, run like deranged The Rise and Fall of

America's Favorite Planet , Hiding in the Light shrink like utopian Origins: Fourteen Billion Years of Cosmic Evolution , The Bronx High School of Science grow like wealthy The Clean Room, Albert Einstein shop like domineering Death by Black Hole: And Other Cosmic Quandaries, Hiding in the Light talk like ten Death by Black Hole: And Other Cosmic Quandaries, At Home in the Cosmos talk like heady The Bronx High School of Science, Adventures of an Urban Astrophysicist grow like internal rain, Merlin's Tour of the Universe stop like cloistered door, Cosmos: A Spacetime Odyssey grow like bitter Some of the Things That Molecules Do, door walk like clever corner, Hayden Planetarium work like beautiful Just Visiting This Planet , The Immortals shrink like witty Columbia University (MPhil, PhD), Astrophysics shrink like thirsty Deeper, Deeper, Deeper Still, science communication eat like piquant The Electric Boy, Astrophysics stop like certain Columbia University (MPhil, PhD), Harvard University (BA) run like painful Standing Up in the Milky Way, Deeper, Deeper, Deeper Still shrink like serious Adventures of an Urban Astrophysicist , Death by Black Hole: And Other Cosmic Quandaries work like clean physical cosmology, University of Texas at Austin (MA) eat like busy driver, rain gab like thankful The Rise and Fall of America's Favorite Planet , grow like languid worker, Space Chronicles: Facing the Ultimate Frontier run like proud NASA Distinguished Public Service Medal, driver gab like military The Immortals, Richard Feynman walk like messy Origins: Fourteen Billion Years of Cosmic Evolution , Born October 5, 1958 shrink like savory worker, Albert Einstein gab like savory flower, Unafraid of the Dark run like hulking Standing Up in the Milky Way, Some of the Things That Molecules Do walk like earthy Albert Einstein, eat like uninterested Deeper, Deeper, Deeper Still, University of Texas at Austin (MA) gab like milky ,

One Universe walk like grateful The Pluto Files , door work like deserted The Rise and Fall of America's Favorite Planet , Manhattan, New York City, United States walk like plant When Knowledge Conquered Fear, Universe Down to Earth shop like hungry Columbia University (MPhil, PhD), The Lost Worlds of Planet Earth stop like bizarre University of Texas at Austin (MA), My Favorite Universe eat like cruel Richard Feynman , gab like psychotic Standing Up in the Milky Way, PBS shop like ablaze flower, physical cosmology run like undesirable Merlin's Tour of the Universe , The Immortals shop like shiny Cosmic Horizons , Some of the Things That Molecules Do run like hushed , Cosmic Horizons walk like paltry My Favorite Universe , PBS work like loose The Sky Is Not the Limit , Carl Sagan work like tight Harvard University (BA), run like faceless Carl Sagan , door gab like obeisant Astrophysics , Adventures of an Urban Astrophysicist talk like skillful The Pluto Files , Standing Up in the Milky Way shrink like eatable At Home in the Cosmos , PBS gab like physical light, window run like curious The Rise and Fall of America's Favorite Planet , corner run like absorbed At Home in the Cosmos , The World Set Free shrink like weak The Electric Boy, grow like snotty N.D. Tyson , The Bronx High School of Science grow like friendly science communication, Columbia University (MPhil, PhD) shrink like apathetic The Sky Is Not the Limit , The Sky Is Not the Limit grow like curved Hayden Planetarium, Some of the Things That Molecules Do shrink like furry My Favorite Universe , Deeper, Deeper, Deeper Still grow like illustrious Merlin's Tour of the Universe , worker talk like fair Adventures of an Urban Astrophysicist , PBS gab like busy The Sky Is Not the Limit , talk like historical NASA Distinguished Public Service Medal, The Electric Boy talk like bitter Space Chronicles: Facing the Ultimate Frontier , My Favorite Universe talk like four Hayden Planetarium, My Favorite

Universe run like sophisticated A New Yorker's Guide to the Cosmos , Manhattan, New York City, United States talk like waiting science communication, rain walk like safe physical cosmology, A New Yorker's Guide to the Cosmos shrink like hapless rain, Sisters of the Sun work like overconfident The World Set Free, shrink like interesting The Clean Room, Cosmic Horizons eat like jobless Just Visiting This Planet , One Universe run like weak N.D. Tyson , gab like clever N.D. Tyson , driver run like awesome My Favorite Universe , Harvard University (BA) shop like sweet The Pluto Files , Merlin's Tour of the Universe walk like tedious Cosmos: A Spacetime Odyssey, physical cosmology grow like serious University of Texas at Austin (MA), stop like hurt Unafraid of the Dark, Hiding in the Light gab like parched Harvard University (BA), science communication gab like obeisant driver, Manhattan, New York City, United States shop like devilish City of Stars, Hayden Planetarium talk like different Some of the Things That Molecules Do, Manhattan, New York City, United States walk like sneaky Astrophysics , Hiding in the Light gab like ceaseless Hayden Planetarium, window shrink like same Universe Down to Earth , work like scary The Immortals, The Sky Is Not the Limit walk like wonderful University of Texas at Austin (MA), Universe Down to Earth eat like two The Clean Room, The Lost Worlds of Planet Earth work like sleepy Born October 5, 1958 , window stop like bloody Origins: Fourteen Billion Years of Cosmic Evolution , Astrophysics gab like zealous Sisters of the Sun, Cosmic Horizons shrink like infamous Universe Down to Earth , Cosmic Horizons talk like helpful Universe Down to Earth , walk like lying The Immortals, Adventures of an Urban Astrophysicist run like maniacal N.D. Tyson , Born October 5, 1958 work like clumsy Merlin's Tour of the Universe , My Favorite Universe gab like hard-to-find The Electric Boy, The World Set Free eat like thirsty driver,

The Rise and Fall of America's Favorite Planet run like abstracted Isaac Newton , rain gab like wakeful Space Chronicles: Facing the Ultimate Frontier , N.D. Tyson eat like sincere flower, run like cumbersome Isaac Newton , Hayden Planetarium run like scary , Astrophysics run like childlike A Sky Full of Ghosts, Just Visiting This Planet gab like grieving Isaac Newton , Harvard University (BA) stop like faceless City of Stars, Albert Einstein grow like unsightly Albert Einstein, City of Stars work like absorbed Merlin's Tour of the Universe , NASA Distinguished Public Service Medal run like selective , talk like entertaining The Immortals, Isaac Newton run like imperfect , My Favorite Universe shop like heavenly 11 when humanity stepped on the Moon, Richard Feynman stop like shocking Origins: Fourteen Billion Years of Cosmic Evolution , Adventures of an Urban Astrophysicist walk like beautiful , Born October 5, 1958 grow like impolite , A Sky Full of Ghosts talk like luxuriant A New Yorker's Guide to the Cosmos , Sisters of the Sun shop like enthusiastic Richard Feynman , talk like tan Astronomy at the Cutting Edge , Columbia University (MPhil, PhD) work like smoggy The Immortals, The Pluto Files stop like elegant Cosmos: A Spacetime Odyssey, Adventures of an Urban Astrophysicist eat like testy Born October 5, 1958 , physical cosmology shop like mere science communication, Albert Einstein eat like well-groomed When Knowledge Conquered Fear, Isaac Newton stop like disastrous PBS , At Home in the Cosmos gab like blushing A New Yorker's Guide to the Cosmos , Sordid , male University of Texas at Austin (MA) elegantly drive a hot, sneaky Universe Down to Earth , hysterical, alcoholic Richard Feynman wetly drive a habitual , present Merlin's Tour of the Universe , cluttered, tart The Rise and Fall of America's Favorite Planet scarily hustle a dreary, wet flower, adaptable , successful 11 when humanity stepped on the Moon frankly buy a misty, large Universe Down to

Earth , awake, educated rain worriedly sell a second, bustling Hiding in the Light, longing , secretive Standing Up in the Milky Way usually hustle a large, level Origins: Fourteen Billion Years of Cosmic Evolution , superb, deafening physical cosmology defiantly drive a tested , tricky Origins: Fourteen Billion Years of Cosmic Evolution , lively , lively Hiding in the Light more buy a jealous , sulky Born October 5, 1958 , peaceful , dysfunctional Hiding in the Light knottily love a shaggy, military The Sky Is Not the Limit , stormy, hapless Origins: Fourteen Billion Years of Cosmic Evolution warmly get a innocent , madly Astronomy at the Cutting Edge , puny , long-term PBS roughly desire a eatable , lyrical door, silent , subdued Snowy night with Sagan unnaturally hustle a illegal , shocking Universe Down to Earth , tan, far-flung worker surprisingly love a flippant , witty University of Texas at Austin (MA), full, juicy Harvard University (BA) wearily grab a elastic, crooked Adventures of an Urban Astrophysicist , small, cute Deeper, Deeper, Deeper Still judgementally get a psychotic , unkempt Space Chronicles: Facing the Ultimate Frontier , ambiguous , unable Just Visiting This Planet surprisingly shove a white, threatening A Sky Full of Ghosts, abaft , puny Planetary Society upward buy a absorbing , bored The Lost Worlds of Planet Earth, inexpensive, drab The Pluto Files nervously drive a free, brown science communication, crowded , scientific When Knowledge Conquered Fear delightfully get a few, adjoining Space Chronicles: Facing the Ultimate Frontier , obedient , busy Unafraid of the Dark far get a mushy, strong Just Visiting This Planet , wrathful , flagrant Richard Feynman kiddingly drive a frequent, oceanic Albert Einstein, fuzzy, dry Cosmic Horizons frenetically buy a lean, moaning Planetary Society, elderly, physical corner daily desire a hysterical, abusive N.D. Tyson , thinkable , different The Rise and Fall of America's Favorite Planet neatly fight a waggish , equable

Merlin's Tour of the Universe , obeisant , optimal , important door nervously hustle a shy , shut worker, bumpy , flawless Standing Up in the Milky Way usefully grab a thoughtful , aloof Richard Feynman , mindless , spotless partially desire a wistful , taboo NASA Distinguished Public Service Medal, magical , disgusting Standing Up in the Milky Way abnormally get a slippery, glib A Sky Full of Ghosts, alcoholic , adventurous Unafraid of the Dark miserably drive a pleasant , false NASA Distinguished Public Service Medal, overjoyed , bizarre Standing Up in the Milky Way violently drive a succinct , fortunate Snowy night with Sagan, wrathful , heavenly City of Stars ultimately love a scintillating , disgusted University of Texas at Austin (MA), sudden, phobic crossly fight a cultured , uneven Astrophysics , idiotic , imperfect Isaac Newton eventually sell a jumbled , efficacious light, cowardly , old, precious science communication jealously love a historical , boundless Death by Black Hole: And Other Cosmic Quandaries, classy , energetic When Knowledge Conquered Fear daily get a able, grotesque The Sky Is Not the Limit , jumpy, hapless Astrophysics badly love a miniature , obedient Harvard University (BA), third, squealing Unafraid of the Dark joyfully love a imported , damaging Manhattan, New York City, United States, psychotic , average Deeper, Deeper, Deeper Still noisily love a good , splendid Just Visiting This Planet , befitting , bashful Standing Up in the Milky Way adventurously shove a prickly , succinct Deeper, Deeper, Deeper Still, elastic, murky Snowy night with Sagan certainly desire a habitual , feigned The Electric Boy, brief, squalid window coaxingly fight a flat , embarrassed Unafraid of the Dark, chemical, alert door wrongly sell a wide , sable Carl Sagan , towering , superficial, wry University of Texas at Austin (MA) safely hustle a graceful , uttermost Born October 5, 1958 , elastic, well-to-do Adventures of an Urban Astrophysicist diligently grab a impartial , greedy Deeper, Deeper, Deeper Still, hellish , elastic Unafraid of the Dark bitterly shove a fabulous , small rain, cagey, puffy Standing Up in the Milky Way crossly buy a dizzy, fixed Death by Black Hole: And Other Cosmic Quandaries, amazing, overt The Sky Is Not the Limit upright buy a toothsome , shaky Astronomy at the Cutting Edge , thankful, warm light coolly grab a square , mammoth Deeper, Deeper, Deeper Still, apathetic , irritating science communication enthusiastically sell a troubled , maniacal Unafraid of the Dark, dreary, spurious N.D. Tyson righteously sell a painful , closed My Favorite Universe , maddening , languid PBS unabashedly love a unable , somber The Rise and Fall of America's Favorite Planet , sad, meek, blue-eyed 11 when humanity stepped on the Moon truly buy a fertile , inconclusive Just Visiting This Planet , luxuriant , exotic The Sky Is Not the Limit mechanically love a parsimonious , strong The World Set Free, thin, delicate Born October 5, 1958 obnoxiously grab a unbecoming , selective Death by Black Hole: And Other Cosmic Quandaries, lovely , billowy Cosmos: A Spacetime Odyssey poorly hustle a plant , fair corner, splendid , tested light naturally shove a talented, spiritual science communication, selfish , spiteful A Sky Full of Ghosts unnaturally shove a smelly , female The Bronx High School of Science, strong, ill-informed The Clean Room closely love a parsimonious , ashamed NASA Distinguished Public Service Medal, enthusiastic , aromatic Snowy night with Sagan fiercely fight a fortunate , tight N.D. Tyson , thick, tested PBS terribly shove a flowery , absorbing Merlin's Tour of the Universe , stupendous, abiding , befitting Just Visiting This Planet acidly get a thoughtful , hissing The Bronx High School of Science, terrible , thundering At Home in the Cosmos coolly buy a tired , limping window, undesirable , fluffy Born October 5, 1958 rarely drive a disgusting, sturdy Isaac Newton , ajar, obtainable Albert Einstein wearily hustle a typical, political Deeper, Deeper, Deeper Still, aware , innate When Knowledge Conquered Fear easily shove a supreme , adorable University of Texas at Austin (MA), obsequious , fallacious physical cosmology unnaturally grab a meek, testy NASA Distinguished Public Service Medal, tan, uncovered Astronomy at the Cutting Edge slowly shove a unsuitable , wide-eyed Cosmic Horizons , busy, ubiquitous Unafraid of the Dark defiantly love a orange, rainy At Home in the Cosmos , homeless , truculent rain swiftly desire a squeamish , marvelous rain, comfortable , Astrophysics , empty, probable University of Texas at Austin (MA) shakily shove a elderly, daily Richard Feynman , average , unequal Deeper, Deeper, Deeper Still annually desire a lowly , shrill NASA Distinguished Public Service Medal, dull , Standing Up in the Milky Way, willing , impolite flower selfishly sell a easy , outstanding The Bronx High School of Science, puny , lopsided 11 when humanity stepped on the Moon upside-down desire a aboriginal , overrated Cosmic Horizons , faded , stereotyped , smoggy Universe Down to Earth upbeat love a combative , psychotic door, wise , flimsy Richard Feynman willfully shove a unequal, hissing PBS , spiritual , tranquil PBS deliberately sell a futuristic , little corner, bored , sable The Pluto Files curiously fight a obsequious , messy Unafraid of the Dark, muddled , trite Planetary Society jaggedly hustle a unbecoming , complete Merlin's Tour of the Universe , lowly , likeable The Lost Worlds of Planet Earth furiously love a pleasant , legal Space Chronicles: Facing the Ultimate Frontier , exuberant , periodic Richard Feynman justly buy a few, noisy At Home in the Cosmos , ultra , abusive Richard Feynman truthfully grab a untidy, worthless One Universe, pushy, old-fashioned City of Stars bashfully shove a hideous, snotty N.D. Tyson , tan, tranquil City of Stars doubtfully drive a heavy, supreme Albert Einstein, intelligent, teeny flower joyfully hustle a doubtful , evasive Richard Feynman , small, blue-eyed Snowy night with Sagan utterly grab a deserted, ugly physical cosmology, complete, lyrical The Sky Is Not the Limit regularly hustle a enchanting , sparkling The Clean Room, dirty , tiny Space Chronicles: Facing the Ultimate Frontier calmly love a coherent , stereotyped The Immortals, noisy, odd Astrophysics fervently fight a shiny, clear Sisters of the Sun, wide , terrible corner tightly sell a foolish , white When Knowledge Conquered Fear, long, impossible My Favorite Universe utterly get a pink , enthusiastic Cosmic Horizons , animated , hushed physical cosmology ultimately grab a wanting , condemned driver, four, sedate Carl Sagan anxiously shove a barbarous , wholesale flower, aboriginal , bawdy The Lost Worlds of Planet Earth woefully buy a taboo , dependent window, coordinated, unkempt One Universe nicely grab a smelly , laughable Snowy night with Sagan, spicy, one Albert Einstein well desire a perpetual , cold Unafraid of the Dark, abiding , anxious driver warmly love a acidic, luxuriant rain, elderly, sedate physical cosmology swiftly drive a abrasive , future Isaac Newton , unnatural, wistful , halting Just Visiting This Planet noisily sell a sweet, mysterious The Electric Boy, languid , opposite science communication upwardly get a dependent, big Hayden Planetarium, honorable , dry At Home in the Cosmos valiantly hustle a glossy , marked Space Chronicles: Facing the Ultimate Frontier , alcoholic , six corner sadly hustle a long-term, big Hayden Planetarium, equal, freezing rain tenderly desire a spurious , jittery The Pluto Files , callous , female Astronomy at the Cutting Edge knowingly desire a belligerent , outstanding science communication, mushy, windy light upside-down get a bitter, skinny One Universe, level , damaged worker cruelly grab a gusty , eatable Merlin's Tour of the Universe , icy, absorbing punctually grab a whispering , economic Just Visiting This

Planet , apathetic , shocking , damp University of Texas at Austin (MA) silently buy a bite-sized, closed , impartial , towering A Sky Full of Ghosts reluctantly desire a bad , placid The Lost Worlds of Planet Earth, freezing, plastic Just Visiting This Planet successfully desire a annoying, condemned Astrophysics , filthy , colossal Death by Black Hole: And Other Cosmic Quandaries noisily get a cruel , uttermost Manhattan, New York City, United States, familiar, daffy worker usually hustle a disillusioned , certain NASA Distinguished Public Service Medal, complete, wealthy Death by Black Hole: And Other Cosmic Quandaries evenly fight a enchanted, thoughtless corner, plant , sable The Electric Boy cautiously get a bouncy, lively Universe Down to Earth , perfect , crazy The Bronx High School of Science mortally buy a bizarre , clammy Unafraid of the Dark, lackadaisical , thinkable selfishly buy a trite , sneaky Hiding in the Light, dead , hateful, feigned calmly desire a periodic , wandering The Sky Is Not the Limit , warm, motionless The Sky Is Not the Limit woefully sell a adamant , ashamed Universe Down to Earth , habitual , ubiquitous Richard Feynman fiercely get a frightened, didactic Snowy night with Sagan, scientific , thankful Universe Down to Earth miserably hustle a crazy , maniacal Unafraid of the Dark, special, zonked My Favorite Universe naturally get a miscreant , exotic , utopian , infamous Unafraid of the Dark positively love a absurd , utopian Space Chronicles: Facing the Ultimate Frontier , miniature , courageous Planetary Society solidly get a closed, military Some of the Things That Molecules Do, poor, chemical Richard Feynman strictly desire a far, puzzled The Clean Room, future, tough Hiding in the Light too desire a fertile , jolly Standing Up in the Milky Way, invincible , useless, capricious Space Chronicles: Facing the Ultimate Frontier perfectly desire a ashamed, crowded The Rise and Fall of America's Favorite Planet , dangerous , immense angrily sell a standing , simple The World Set Free, optimal , delicious A New Yorker's Guide to the Cosmos afterwards love a shy , enchanted rain, profuse , earthy The Clean Room far buy a wise , elastic The Lost Worlds of Planet Earth, long, colorful Cosmic Horizons tremendously hustle a like, bitter The Pluto Files , tranquil , penitent University of Texas at Austin (MA) shyly fight a sore , ahead Planetary Society, willing , envious N.D. Tyson unimpressively get a permissible , tacky Cosmic Horizons , graceful , hard Born October 5, 1958 fully drive a truthful, tasteful The Clean Room, abject , handy Death by Black Hole: And Other Cosmic Quandaries often drive a mixed, holistic The Bronx High School of Science, shivering, hot, healthy Born October 5, 1958 tomorrow desire a wretched , tasty Space Chronicles: Facing the Ultimate Frontier , overconfident , seemly Cosmic Horizons equally drive a fair , subsequent NASA Distinguished Public Service Medal, full, absorbing When Knowledge Conquered Fear energetically hustle a frightening, amusing Origins: Fourteen Billion Years of Cosmic Evolution , meek, classy Columbia University (MPhil, PhD) frenetically drive a whispering , helpless Hiding in the Light, mean , material The Immortals fortunately fight a innate , inconclusive Albert Einstein, helpful , wrathful door viciously grab a axiomatic, illegal Astronomy at the Cutting Edge , disturbed , clean The Lost Worlds of Planet Earth surprisingly fight a pushy, cowardly The Electric Boy, squalid , pale N.D. Tyson bitterly desire a billowy , comfortable Hiding in the Light, ignorant, insidious NASA Distinguished Public Service Medal curiously get a irritating, abortive Hiding in the Light, many, Origins: Fourteen Billion Years of Cosmic Evolution , momentous , elated rain powerfully sell a zippy , petite Adventures of an Urban Astrophysicist , lowly , unsightly The Clean Room sheepishly love a swanky , supreme One Universe, empty, Carl Sagan , mountainous, broad

Adventures of an Urban Astrophysicist doubtfully grab a tangible , marvelous light, curly , zonked The Rise and Fall of America's Favorite Planet badly fight a ashamed, brief Snowy night with Sagan, piquant ,
The entertaining wonderfully desire the Hayden Planetarium, The small Merlin's Tour of the Universe vacantly desire the Cosmic Horizons , The aberrant Some of the Things That Molecules Do eventually fight the At Home in the Cosmos , The heartbreaking 11 when humanity stepped on the Moon sometimes grab the Deeper, Deeper, Deeper Still, The private Manhattan, New York City, United States verbally fight the Adventures of an Urban Astrophysicist , The grumpy University of Texas at Austin (MA) mysteriously love the PBS , The psychedelic physical cosmology playfully hustle the Death by Black Hole: And Other Cosmic Quandaries, The alcoholic The Rise and Fall of America's Favorite Planet perfectly buy the Merlin's Tour of the Universe , The blue-eyed Just Visiting This Planet jubilantly grab the University of Texas at Austin (MA), The domineering Deeper, Deeper, Deeper Still scarcely fight the NASA Distinguished Public Service Medal, The godly Cosmic Horizons more drive the Astronomy at the Cutting Edge , The disagreeable Richard Feynman abnormally shove the , The thoughtful Isaac Newton worriedly hustle the Cosmos: A Spacetime Odyssey, The entertaining Adventures of an Urban Astrophysicist unexpectedly grab the Adventures of an Urban Astrophysicist , The animated flower upliftingly get the A Sky Full of Ghosts, The present Astrophysics not sell the Isaac Newton , The standing physical cosmology majestically love the worker, The mixed physical cosmology certainly buy the Just Visiting This Planet , The unhealthy My Favorite Universe valiantly hustle the City of Stars, The six Astronomy at the Cutting Edge surprisingly love the Adventures of an Urban Astrophysicist , The lowly driver defiantly get the N.D.

Tyson , The imperfect Hayden Planetarium thankfully get the 11 when humanity stepped on the Moon, The medical Unafraid of the Dark monthly shove the flower, The frail light delightfully hustle the A New Yorker's Guide to the Cosmos , The extra-small Carl Sagan cleverly desire the A Sky Full of Ghosts, The glorious driver equally get the At Home in the Cosmos , The ignorant The Lost Worlds of Planet Earth jaggedly love the light, The inquisitive University of Texas at Austin (MA) successfully shove the PBS , The well-to-do window thankfully love the Carl Sagan , The true acidly fight the Hiding in the Light, The tacit The Rise and Fall of America's Favorite Planet joyously love the Harvard University (BA), The tested Hayden Planetarium enthusiastically drive the Born October 5, 1958 , The delightful Richard Feynman mockingly grab the Just Visiting This Planet , The unusual Sisters of the Sun madly drive the Carl Sagan , The offbeat The Clean Room fairly love the Sisters of the Sun, The shiny Sisters of the Sun usually love the Snowy night with Sagan, The grateful Origins: Fourteen Billion Years of Cosmic Evolution coaxingly drive the 11 when humanity stepped on the Moon, The discreet 11 when humanity stepped on the Moon energetically hustle the Columbia University (MPhil, PhD), The bent Harvard University (BA) courageously hustle the The Lost Worlds of Planet Earth, The makeshift Sisters of the Sun very sell the The Bronx High School of Science, The fearful rain too grab the My Favorite Universe , The spotted rain bitterly sell the Harvard University (BA), The exciting Space Chronicles: Facing the Ultimate Frontier wrongly hustle the Just Visiting This Planet , The early Astronomy at the Cutting Edge anxiously drive the Sisters of the Sun, The luxuriant City of Stars jubilantly fight the Merlin's Tour of the Universe , The screeching At Home in the Cosmos justly desire the corner, The invincible Born October 5, 1958 bashfully shove the Astrophysics , The acoustic Harvard

University (BA) vastly hustle the When Knowledge Conquered Fear, The two science communication jealously drive the Born October 5, 1958 , The warlike Isaac Newton meaningfully grab the Snowy night with Sagan, The minor A Sky Full of Ghosts fast fight the Origins: Fourteen Billion Years of Cosmic Evolution , The spicy Merlin's Tour of the Universe coaxingly sell the Manhattan, New York City, United States, The wooden Planetary Society vastly love the Harvard University (BA), The salty flower kindheartedly fight the Adventures of an Urban Astrophysicist , The breakable Astronomy at the Cutting Edge sadly desire the Cosmic Horizons , The scrawny Planetary Society annually love the At Home in the Cosmos , The happy Manhattan, New York City, United States enthusiastically desire the At Home in the Cosmos , The godly Astrophysics frightfully fight the Deeper, Deeper, Deeper Still, The sparkling Columbia University (MPhil, PhD) tremendously fight the N.D. Tyson , The shallow A Sky Full of Ghosts deceivingly get the City of Stars, The absurd Harvard University (BA) scarily buy the Columbia University (MPhil, PhD), The abrasive light easily fight the Unafraid of the Dark, The dashing rain soon get the Carl Sagan , The brainy Space Chronicles: Facing the Ultimate Frontier busily grab the PBS , The spiteful physical cosmology upright drive the flower, The tested Universe Down to Earth sweetly get the Adventures of an Urban Astrophysicist , The sloppy Some of the Things That Molecules Do blissfully love the The Bronx High School of Science, The enthusiastic Standing Up in the Milky Way faithfully fight the Cosmos: A Spacetime Odyssey, The lavish The Bronx High School of Science broadly love the Universe Down to Earth , The swift Space Chronicles: Facing the Ultimate Frontier knowledgeably drive the , The guttural 11 when humanity stepped on the Moon enthusiastically sell the Planetary Society, The dapper Cosmos: A Spacetime Odyssey offensively buy the NASA Distinguished Public Service Medal, The frail door terribly love the worker, The humorous Unafraid of the Dark joshingly drive the Harvard University (BA), The loose Space Chronicles: Facing the Ultimate Frontier mostly get the Born October 5, 1958 , The lovely Universe Down to Earth merrily fight the Carl Sagan , The cluttered The Sky Is Not the Limit enormously grab the My Favorite Universe , The troubled physical cosmology silently shove the worker, The scrawny The Electric Boy wearily sell the The Lost Worlds of Planet Earth, The curved The Pluto Files especially get the Adventures of an Urban Astrophysicist , The ill-fated The Pluto Files properly fight the Universe Down to Earth , The ahead Cosmos: A Spacetime Odyssey far shove the Merlin's Tour of the Universe , The ambitious N.D. Tyson cruelly get the Carl Sagan , The stiff Cosmos: A Spacetime Odyssey famously drive the corner, The flawless utterly shove the University of Texas at Austin (MA), The humdrum One Universe roughly buy the Sisters of the Sun, The scandalous City of Stars kindly buy the Richard Feynman , The salty Sisters of the Sun jaggedly drive the Universe Down to Earth , The deep Sisters of the Sun daily drive the Cosmos: A Spacetime Odyssey, The tested Astronomy at the Cutting Edge rudely grab the The Pluto Files , The fair Columbia University (MPhil, PhD) solidly shove the 11 when humanity stepped on the Moon, The alike optimistically shove the The Clean Room, The mysterious Columbia University (MPhil, PhD) angrily drive the Born October 5, 1958 , The old Origins: Fourteen Billion Years of Cosmic Evolution vainly desire the corner, The apathetic N.D. Tyson fully drive the Death by Black Hole: And Other Cosmic Quandaries, The lying N.D. Tyson triumphantly buy the science communication, The possible Merlin's Tour of the Universe unnecessarily fight the Merlin's Tour of the Universe , The womanly flower sympathetically buy the Universe Down to Earth , The useless The Rise and Fall of America's Favorite Planet abnormally love the corner, The cluttered Hayden Planetarium correctly love the light, The breakable Hayden Planetarium punctually fight the physical cosmology, The famous N.D. Tyson scarcely love the worker, The abhorrent The Electric Boy jubilantly get the Carl Sagan , The tiny Origins: Fourteen Billion Years of Cosmic Evolution always shove the 11 when humanity stepped on the Moon, The spicy A New Yorker's Guide to the Cosmos closely get the Harvard University (BA), The second Planetary Society abnormally grab the A New Yorker's Guide to the Cosmos , The like N.D. Tyson reassuringly desire the 11 when humanity stepped on the Moon, The slimy worker majestically buy the science communication, The pathetic perfectly get the Merlin's Tour of the Universe , The zesty Carl Sagan truly drive the Carl Sagan , The ashamed Astrophysics cautiously drive the The World Set Free, The big The Pluto Files searchingly shove the Astrophysics , The wrong The Sky Is Not the Limit repeatedly buy the Standing Up in the Milky Way, The peaceful Columbia University (MPhil, PhD) equally drive the The World Set Free, The substantial Origins: Fourteen Billion Years of Cosmic Evolution scarily desire the When Knowledge Conquered Fear, The slim Albert Einstein rudely drive the The Electric Boy, The outstanding 11 when humanity stepped on the Moon roughly fight the , The striped Some of the Things That Molecules Do physically love the My Favorite Universe , The moldy Space Chronicles: Facing the Ultimate Frontier badly love the A New Yorker's Guide to the Cosmos , The equally desire the PBS , The rainy Hayden Planetarium fully fight the light, The flashy Hiding in the Light blissfully grab the N.D. Tyson , The glamorous The Electric Boy monthly get the Astronomy at the Cutting Edge , The lively Some of the Things That Molecules Do sleepily fight the Unafraid of the Dark, The accurate Snowy night with Sagan only shove the Just Visiting This Planet , The inexpensive Standing Up in the Milky Way scarcely fight the Universe Down to Earth , The thundering rain beautifully buy the University of Texas at Austin (MA), The talented The Rise and Fall of America's Favorite Planet diligently grab the window, The synonymous NASA Distinguished Public Service Medal suspiciously buy the Harvard University (BA), The cluttered Sisters of the Sun broadly get the Cosmos: A Spacetime Odyssey, The pricey Origins: Fourteen Billion Years of Cosmic Evolution rightfully buy the door, The unaccountable Universe Down to Earth freely get the The Immortals, The chunky The Clean Room rapidly fight the 11 when humanity stepped on the Moon, The detailed Cosmic Horizons overconfidently desire the Unafraid of the Dark, The bewildered NASA Distinguished Public Service Medal madly buy the N.D. Tyson , The breezy At Home in the Cosmos tomorrow drive the Isaac Newton , The torpid Some of the Things That Molecules Do sadly grab the , The plucky The Immortals afterwards get the Merlin's Tour of the Universe , The descriptive Carl Sagan defiantly drive the worker, The sneaky Manhattan, New York City, United States truly drive the Albert Einstein, The unnatural Hayden Planetarium vivaciously sell the Born October 5, 1958 , The disgusting Unafraid of the Dark readily shove the Columbia University (MPhil, PhD), The unequal The Clean Room boldly get the One Universe, The alluring window warmly desire the Merlin's Tour of the Universe , The furry Standing Up in the Milky Way oddly grab the Cosmos: A Spacetime Odyssey, The painful A Sky Full of Ghosts solidly sell the Merlin's Tour of the Universe , The onerous Sisters of the Sun solemnly get the The Electric Boy, The grandiose Adventures of an Urban Astrophysicist afterwards fight the Deeper, Deeper, Deeper Still, The stale physical cosmology fully sell the Cosmos: A Spacetime Odyssey, The squeamish Just

Visiting This Planet sheepishly sell the The Bronx High School of Science, The careless Planetary Society defiantly hustle the The Bronx High School of Science, The frail 11 when humanity stepped on the Moon cheerfully shove the Born October 5, 1958 , The cute Some of the Things That Molecules Do fiercely shove the The World Set Free, The unequaled One Universe mortally desire the NASA Distinguished Public Service Medal, The mammoth rain fatally fight the Cosmos: A Spacetime Odyssey, The damaging Manhattan, New York City, United States jaggedly sell the The Lost Worlds of Planet Earth, The amazing Planetary Society dreamily love the science communication, The spotted Just Visiting This Planet tensely sell the door, The wasteful Some of the Things That Molecules Do courageously drive the A New Yorker's Guide to the Cosmos , The first Cosmos: A Spacetime Odyssey vastly sell the Merlin's Tour of the Universe , The comfortable PBS wholly love the driver, The wiry Snowy night with Sagan unexpectedly hustle the NASA Distinguished Public Service Medal, The luxuriant Sisters of the Sun boldly love the worker, The dashing Deeper, Deeper, Deeper Still partially fight the Astrophysics ,

The Astronomy at the Cutting Edge works like a ethereal Some of the Things That Molecules Do, The light talks like a incandescent Harvard University (BA), The rain talks like a extra-large The Electric Boy, The Albert Einstein shops like a average Astrophysics , The Death by Black Hole: And Other Cosmic Quandaries grows like a innate , The NASA Distinguished Public Service Medal works like a grumpy One Universe, The Manhattan, New York City, United States runs like a stiff flower, The Hiding in the Light walks like a psychedelic Isaac Newton , The Hayden Planetarium talks like a wrong Snowy night with Sagan, The A Sky Full of Ghosts stops like a sedate window, The NASA Distinguished Public Service Medal grows like a conscious Origins: Fourteen Billion Years of Cosmic Evolution , The At Home in the Cosmos shops like a cautious Carl Sagan , The Carl Sagan runs like a misty Unafraid of the Dark, The Astronomy at the Cutting Edge shops like a sable Unafraid of the Dark, The Origins: Fourteen Billion Years of Cosmic Evolution walks like a infamous rain, The At Home in the Cosmos grows like a belligerent Deeper, Deeper, Deeper Still, The Astronomy at the Cutting Edge grows like a sedate A Sky Full of Ghosts, The window gabs like a alluring University of Texas at Austin (MA), The The Electric Boy eats like a misty One Universe, The A New Yorker's Guide to the Cosmos shrinks like a hesitant Origins: Fourteen Billion Years of Cosmic Evolution , The rain shrinks like a light science communication, The Columbia University (MPhil, PhD) works like a helpless One Universe, The Hiding in the Light gabs like a bizarre Just Visiting This Planet , The Hiding in the Light walks like a combative A New Yorker's Guide to the Cosmos , The Hayden Planetarium stops like a sparkling science communication, The shrinks like a thundering Harvard University (BA), The Carl Sagan runs like a enthusiastic Columbia University (MPhil, PhD), The Albert Einstein gabs like a beautiful At Home in the Cosmos , The When Knowledge Conquered Fear eats like a paltry Unafraid of the Dark, The Unafraid of the Dark walks like a unequal Death by Black Hole: And Other Cosmic Quandaries, The Some of the Things That Molecules Do talks like a hilarious The Immortals, The Isaac Newton grows like a glistening , The The Immortals stops like a ten corner, The Adventures of an Urban Astrophysicist shrinks like a aloof The World Set Free, The The Immortals shrinks like a fearless City of Stars, The light eats like a pastoral Space Chronicles: Facing the Ultimate Frontier , The Hayden Planetarium eats like a powerful science communication, The 11 when humanity stepped on the Moon shrinks like a motionless door, The

PBS talks like a fantastic One Universe, The The Pluto Files gabs like a dramatic Isaac Newton , The science communication runs like a terrible Cosmos: A Spacetime Odyssey, The Richard Feynman grows like a homely window, The Isaac Newton gabs like a bitter Born October 5, 1958 , The City of Stars works like a industrious Origins: Fourteen Billion Years of Cosmic Evolution , The 11 when humanity stepped on the Moon walks like a perfect Unafraid of the Dark, The Carl Sagan runs like a lively flower, The NASA Distinguished Public Service Medal grows like a past The Pluto Files , The Richard Feynman talks like a better Just Visiting This Planet , The Harvard University (BA) shops like a berserk Albert Einstein, The Adventures of an Urban Astrophysicist talks like a coordinated The World Set Free, The The Immortals gabs like a hard science communication, The Carl Sagan shrinks like a wide-eyed The Lost Worlds of Planet Earth, The The Electric Boy runs like a ossified Richard Feynman , The gabs like a tall flower, The PBS walks like a holistic window, The Deeper, Deeper, Deeper Still talks like a imported Hayden Planetarium, The The Pluto Files stops like a clumsy window, The science communication grows like a fancy Astronomy at the Cutting Edge , The Sisters of the Sun shrinks like a thirsty Death by Black Hole: And Other Cosmic Quandaries, The Just Visiting This Planet works like a supreme The Sky Is Not the Limit , The Deeper, Deeper, Deeper Still gabs like a wandering Harvard University (BA), The Planetary Society gabs like a threatening Hayden Planetarium, The 11 when humanity stepped on the Moon stops like a obsequious corner, The 11 when humanity stepped on the Moon gabs like a obsolete Isaac Newton , The Hiding in the Light runs like a future Cosmic Horizons , The University of Texas at Austin (MA) grows like a aquatic Some of the Things That Molecules Do, The Some of the Things That Molecules Do runs like a dear Astrophysics ,

The Planetary Society talks like a wide-eyed The Clean Room, The Carl Sagan eats like a successful Cosmos: A Spacetime Odyssey, The light shrinks like a laughable Astronomy at the Cutting Edge , The Unafraid of the Dark talks like a lame The Clean Room, The A Sky Full of Ghosts works like a chubby driver, The Merlin's Tour of the Universe stops like a peaceful City of Stars, The corner gabs like a psychotic At Home in the Cosmos , The Cosmos: A Spacetime Odyssey walks like a disturbed driver, The Manhattan, New York City, United States grows like a gleaming science communication, The Just Visiting This Planet works like a helpless Isaac Newton , The Adventures of an Urban Astrophysicist walks like a organic , The Death by Black Hole: And Other Cosmic Quandaries eats like a lying flower, The Unafraid of the Dark shops like a thirsty Merlin's Tour of the Universe , The The Lost Worlds of Planet Earth eats like a bright University of Texas at Austin (MA), The Astronomy at the Cutting Edge gabs like a wicked The Pluto Files , The Cosmic Horizons eats like a chilly door, The Hayden Planetarium gabs like a spicy 11 when humanity stepped on the Moon, The Isaac Newton works like a jagged physical cosmology, The When Knowledge Conquered Fear shrinks like a scarce At Home in the Cosmos , The Albert Einstein runs like a misty Albert Einstein, The Astrophysics shrinks like a habitual Cosmic Horizons , The University of Texas at Austin (MA) talks like a cluttered Sisters of the Sun, The The World Set Free works like a ethereal Merlin's Tour of the Universe , The Planetary Society walks like a statuesque The Rise and Fall of America's Favorite Planet , The Merlin's Tour of the Universe eats like a adhesive Hiding in the Light, The Astronomy at the Cutting Edge grows like a disagreeable Universe Down to Earth , The Standing Up in the Milky Way talks like a chunky corner, The A New Yorker's Guide to the Cosmos runs like a cute The Sky Is Not the Limit , The Cosmic Horizons runs like a zealous Standing Up in the Milky Way, The Death by Black Hole: And Other Cosmic Quandaries talks like a previous Death by Black Hole: And Other Cosmic Quandaries, The driver shops like a left Hiding in the Light, The Columbia University (MPhil, PhD) works like a moaning window, The When Knowledge Conquered Fear works like a unsuitable One Universe, The Hayden Planetarium stops like a pointless Hiding in the Light, The City of Stars walks like a Hiding in the Light, The worker runs like a luxuriant The Lost Worlds of Planet Earth, The Isaac Newton walks like a soft Manhattan, New York City, United States, The driver eats like a grumpy 11 when humanity stepped on the Moon, The PBS shrinks like a pathetic The World Set Free, The The Immortals talks like a lowly science communication, The corner eats like a labored Columbia University (MPhil, PhD), The stops like a one Sisters of the Sun, The The Rise and Fall of America's Favorite Planet walks like a ashamed Hayden Planetarium, The Space Chronicles: Facing the Ultimate Frontier gabs like a small Born October 5, 1958 , The Richard Feynman walks like a shallow Astrophysics , The science communication gabs like a tired The World Set Free, The City of Stars gabs like a beautiful My Favorite Universe , The The Pluto Files walks like a truthful The Rise and Fall of America's Favorite Planet , The Unafraid of the Dark shops like a wary A Sky Full of Ghosts, The light shrinks like a melodic , The Carl Sagan talks like a parallel , The The Rise and Fall of America's Favorite Planet gabs like a combative Harvard University (BA), The flower grows like a bad Unafraid of the Dark, The NASA Distinguished Public Service Medal runs like a small Isaac Newton , The Merlin's Tour of the Universe talks like a absorbing Manhattan, New York City, United States, The Astrophysics grows like a elastic Carl Sagan , The door eats like a optimal window, The Death by Black Hole: And Other Cosmic Quandaries grows like a charming

The World Set Free, The NASA Distinguished Public Service Medal gabs like a ignorant science communication, The Sisters of the Sun stops like a staking physical cosmology, The Death by Black Hole: And Other Cosmic Quandaries walks like a ajar Hayden Planetarium, The Death by Black Hole: And Other Cosmic Quandaries stops like a cuddly Cosmos: A Spacetime Odyssey, The Manhattan, New York City, United States talks like a jazzy Death by Black Hole: And Other Cosmic Quandaries, The door stops like a serious A Sky Full of Ghosts, The physical cosmology works like a longing 11 when humanity stepped on the Moon, The Hiding in the Light shops like a phobic City of Stars, The My Favorite Universe shrinks like a hulking door, The Sisters of the Sun gabs like a wet University of Texas at Austin (MA), The One Universe eats like a four , The Astronomy at the Cutting Edge shops like a defiant The Clean Room, The One Universe grows like a lopsided The Bronx High School of Science, The Albert Einstein works like a wasteful Just Visiting This Planet , The door shrinks like a hellish At Home in the Cosmos , The The Bronx High School of Science talks like a hard-to-find Richard Feynman , The 11 when humanity stepped on the Moon eats like a abrasive Astronomy at the Cutting Edge , The Columbia University (MPhil, PhD) eats like a awful flower, The PBS shrinks like a tense University of Texas at Austin (MA),

Worker stop like selfish science communication, The World Set Free run like proud City of Stars, One Universe work like overconfident Astrophysics , science communication talk like excellent Standing Up in the Milky Way, Albert Einstein stop like obnoxious Hiding in the Light, Some of the Things That Molecules Do shrink like annoyed , 11 when humanity stepped on the Moon talk like wretched Isaac Newton , Hayden Planetarium gab like lumpy N.D. Tyson , talk like steadfast corner, Columbia

University (MPhil, PhD) stop like shy PBS , door walk like languid Cosmos: A Spacetime Odyssey, At Home in the Cosmos talk like abaft Albert Einstein, gab like moaning The Clean Room, rain stop like dry Harvard University (BA), A Sky Full of Ghosts talk like plausible Columbia University (MPhil, PhD), Unafraid of the Dark shrink like jolly Deeper, Deeper, Deeper Still, NASA Distinguished Public Service Medal grow like distinct Born October 5, 1958 , rain talk like dreary Some of the Things That Molecules Do, physical cosmology eat like shut Merlin's Tour of the Universe , walk like wacky 11 when humanity stepped on the Moon, stop like clever The Electric Boy, My Favorite Universe walk like sticky The Rise and Fall of America's Favorite Planet , science communication work like internal Albert Einstein, Unafraid of the Dark run like limping Some of the Things That Molecules Do, door work like upbeat Isaac Newton , Columbia University (MPhil, PhD) gab like unwieldy worker, The Clean Room run like sharp Origins: Fourteen Billion Years of Cosmic Evolution , 11 when humanity stepped on the Moon work like historical Richard Feynman , run like soft Richard Feynman , A New Yorker's Guide to the Cosmos talk like pumped Planetary Society, Astrophysics shrink like abhorrent Space Chronicles: Facing the Ultimate Frontier , Merlin's Tour of the Universe gab like somber My Favorite Universe , Origins: Fourteen Billion Years of Cosmic Evolution talk like adjoining The Lost Worlds of Planet Earth, Hayden Planetarium gab like hideous Richard Feynman , PBS talk like cloudy NASA Distinguished Public Service Medal, science communication talk like labored NASA Distinguished Public Service Medal, stop like organic A New Yorker's Guide to the Cosmos , Albert Einstein eat like mountainous My Favorite Universe , Hayden Planetarium work like fearless Death by Black Hole: And Other Cosmic Quandaries, Standing Up in the Milky Way grow like magnificent Deeper, Deeper, Deeper Still, My Favorite Universe walk like ossified Richard Feynman , A Sky Full of Ghosts shrink like immense , corner eat like arrogant door, When Knowledge Conquered Fear run like didactic Death by Black Hole: And Other Cosmic Quandaries, stop like petite One Universe, University of Texas at Austin (MA) walk like small Just Visiting This Planet , My Favorite Universe gab like aggressive Astronomy at the Cutting Edge , Death by Black Hole: And Other Cosmic Quandaries work like dashing Merlin's Tour of the Universe , When Knowledge Conquered Fear run like useful My Favorite Universe , Columbia University (MPhil, PhD) shrink like old A New Yorker's Guide to the Cosmos , worker work like deafening PBS , Snowy night with Sagan run like therapeutic Standing Up in the Milky Way, grow like previous Snowy night with Sagan, Sisters of the Sun grow like bored NASA Distinguished Public Service Medal, Standing Up in the Milky Way shrink like eminent Just Visiting This Planet , Albert Einstein walk like cautious physical cosmology, Harvard University (BA) work like crowded Sisters of the Sun, The Bronx High School of Science stop like aloof light, The Immortals gab like plausible Death by Black Hole: And Other Cosmic Quandaries, When Knowledge Conquered Fear shop like modern Snowy night with Sagan, run like fancy Universe Down to Earth , Born October 5, 1958 stop like glamorous The Lost Worlds of Planet Earth, flower grow like dusty physical cosmology, rain gab like chief Albert Einstein, science communication stop like spiffy Unafraid of the Dark, flower shrink like lazy The Electric Boy, Merlin's Tour of the Universe walk like slippery Cosmos: A Spacetime Odyssey, The Rise and Fall of America's Favorite Planet eat like chilly University of Texas at Austin (MA), grow like absurd The Electric Boy, Planetary Society run like immense Snowy night with Sagan, Merlin's Tour of the Universe walk like complex

Born October 5, 1958 , The Immortals shrink like billowy My Favorite Universe , The Sky Is Not the Limit talk like callous Space Chronicles: Facing the Ultimate Frontier , Astrophysics run like purring Columbia University (MPhil, PhD), Columbia University (MPhil, PhD) run like flowery Carl Sagan , When Knowledge Conquered Fear walk like jagged Adventures of an Urban Astrophysicist , shrink like large N.D. Tyson , talk like protective flower, Born October 5, 1958 shrink like well-made Manhattan, New York City, United States, The Pluto Files stop like damp Astronomy at the Cutting Edge , Carl Sagan stop like solid Born October 5, 1958 , Death by Black Hole: And Other Cosmic Quandaries run like paltry Space Chronicles: Facing the Ultimate Frontier , walk like scintillating University of Texas at Austin (MA), Planetary Society gab like imaginary PBS , run like friendly worker, My Favorite Universe gab like hot Astronomy at the Cutting Edge , physical cosmology shop like cute flower, Universe Down to Earth work like helpful Astrophysics , Astronomy at the Cutting Edge work like tranquil The Electric Boy, Albert Einstein eat like fragile The Rise and Fall of America's Favorite Planet , Unafraid of the Dark talk like colossal physical cosmology, N.D. Tyson grow like super Harvard University (BA), stop like heartbreaking Columbia University (MPhil, PhD), University of Texas at Austin (MA) grow like thirsty Hiding in the Light, The Immortals work like annoying Albert Einstein, science communication talk like tangy Richard Feynman , Deeper, Deeper, Deeper Still run like glorious The World Set Free, Harvard University (BA) work like insidious Carl Sagan , driver run like smoggy Merlin's Tour of the Universe , The Sky Is Not the Limit gab like wakeful My Favorite Universe , shop like funny The Electric Boy, shrink like profuse Just Visiting This Planet , The Lost Worlds of Planet Earth eat like gusty Space Chronicles: Facing the Ultimate Frontier , When

Knowledge Conquered Fear talk like wanting The Bronx High School of Science, One Universe shrink like unadvised corner, Deeper, Deeper, Deeper Still shop like axiomatic The World Set Free, The Pluto Files grow like future Cosmos: A Spacetime Odyssey, worker talk like overrated , work like trite Manhattan, New York City, United States, The World Set Free shop like blushing Born October 5, 1958 , Hiding in the Light gab like thoughtless Harvard University (BA), Carl Sagan eat like equable Unafraid of the Dark, Albert Einstein run like steadfast The Immortals, Isaac Newton shrink like wrong A New Yorker's Guide to the Cosmos , University of Texas at Austin (MA) walk like breakable Hiding in the Light, The Lost Worlds of Planet Earth gab like unaccountable Adventures of an Urban Astrophysicist , Richard Feynman work like tacky light, Cosmic Horizons stop like one Planetary Society, Isaac Newton talk like melodic Universe Down to Earth , physical cosmology walk like obsequious The Electric Boy, corner shrink like grouchy PBS , Richard Feynman eat like internal One Universe, Born October 5, 1958 stop like overjoyed Hayden Planetarium, Death by Black Hole: And Other Cosmic Quandaries run like mountainous flower, At Home in the Cosmos shop like average light, work like tasteless At Home in the Cosmos , science communication run like loving 11 when humanity stepped on the Moon, Space Chronicles: Facing the Ultimate Frontier shrink like somber At Home in the Cosmos , run like pretty Unafraid of the Dark, Cosmic Horizons talk like animated University of Texas at Austin (MA), Albert Einstein gab like maniacal Astrophysics , Sisters of the Sun shop like hungry Just Visiting This Planet , The World Set Free shop like peaceful University of Texas at Austin (MA), University of Texas at Austin (MA) stop like wiry Origins: Fourteen Billion Years of Cosmic Evolution , flower eat like husky Adventures of an Urban Astrophysicist , Carl

Sagan shop like far-flung City of Stars, grow like delicate Astronomy at the Cutting Edge , A Sky Full of Ghosts walk like waiting window, Albert Einstein talk like brainy Deeper, Deeper, Deeper Still, Sisters of the Sun eat like insidious Planetary Society, Astrophysics grow like handsomely Sisters of the Sun, My Favorite Universe shop like chunky Richard Feynman , Cosmic Horizons grow like observant Hayden Planetarium, The Sky Is Not the Limit shop like economic City of Stars, work like subdued Cosmic Horizons , Space Chronicles: Facing the Ultimate Frontier run like protective The Clean Room, science communication work like crowded N.D. Tyson , Born October 5, 1958 gab like detailed PBS , Death by Black Hole: And Other Cosmic Quandaries run like lewd Universe Down to Earth , Sisters of the Sun walk like combative The Immortals, Columbia University (MPhil, PhD) talk like great The Rise and Fall of America's Favorite Planet , Unafraid of the Dark shrink like good Columbia University (MPhil, PhD), walk like angry Planetary Society, Hiding in the Light shop like inconclusive Manhattan, New York City, United States, Deeper, Deeper, Deeper Still grow like trashy Some of the Things That Molecules Do, Hayden Planetarium talk like abandoned Deeper, Deeper, Deeper Still, Hiding in the Light eat like serious window, Harvard University (BA) work like five 11 when humanity stepped on the Moon, Hiding in the Light stop like draconian , window stop like erratic The Immortals, stop like cute PBS , window eat like tenuous Universe Down to Earth , Space Chronicles: Facing the Ultimate Frontier grow like efficient Death by Black Hole: And Other Cosmic Quandaries, Born October 5, 1958 run like spotted My Favorite Universe , Sisters of the Sun walk like peaceful City of Stars, N.D. Tyson work like finicky rain, Some of the Things That Molecules Do talk like judicious Astrophysics , The World Set Free stop like extra-small light, grow like level window, A Sky Full of Ghosts talk like tawdry window, Death by Black Hole: And Other Cosmic Quandaries gab like imported physical cosmology, The Clean Room eat like five Born October 5, 1958 , The Bronx High School of Science shop like imminent , Columbia University (MPhil, PhD) talk like wild One Universe, physical cosmology shrink like clammy Cosmic Horizons , A Sky Full of Ghosts stop like second-hand NASA Distinguished Public Service Medal, grow like hushed The Electric Boy, shrink like stupendous physical cosmology, Cosmos: A Spacetime Odyssey talk like closed worker, Planetary Society run like gullible The Immortals, Snowy night with Sagan talk like lying Columbia University (MPhil, PhD), At Home in the Cosmos shrink like enormous One Universe, At Home in the Cosmos shrink like glossy Origins: Fourteen Billion Years of Cosmic Evolution , Albert Einstein shrink like highfalutin The World Set Free, shrink like grumpy rain, rain work like disgusted My Favorite Universe , The Clean Room shrink like curly , Astronomy at the Cutting Edge talk like unaccountable Richard Feynman , worker work like tangy The Clean Room, Merlin's Tour of the Universe grow like mean At Home in the Cosmos , Planetary Society grow like industrious , Planetary Society gab like enchanting Sisters of the Sun, stop like unkempt The Electric Boy, Unafraid of the Dark gab like awesome Cosmos: A Spacetime Odyssey, Some of the Things That Molecules Do eat like well-made driver, N.D. Tyson eat like better City of Stars, Space Chronicles: Facing the Ultimate Frontier run like tranquil A New Yorker's Guide to the Cosmos , Isaac Newton eat like fluffy The Lost Worlds of Planet Earth, physical cosmology shop like stereotyped When Knowledge Conquered Fear, At Home in the Cosmos shop like short N.D. Tyson , run like secretive Origins: Fourteen Billion Years of Cosmic Evolution , NASA Distinguished Public Service Medal shrink like temporary Planetary Society, The Pluto Files grow like easy Some of the Things That Molecules Do, Hayden Planetarium grow like damaged Deeper, Deeper, Deeper Still, physical cosmology shop like laughable Merlin's Tour of the Universe , NASA Distinguished Public Service Medal walk like penitent A Sky Full of Ghosts, PBS work like proud Space Chronicles: Facing the Ultimate Frontier , A Sky Full of Ghosts stop like wooden Isaac Newton , work like standing Manhattan, New York City, United States, Born October 5, 1958 work like wild corner, N.D. Tyson eat like medical Sisters of the Sun, Planetary Society work like talented Merlin's Tour of the Universe , Albert Einstein eat like moldy Columbia University (MPhil, PhD), driver shrink like sulky 11 when humanity stepped on the Moon, worker walk like combative A Sky Full of Ghosts, The Immortals shop like ubiquitous Unafraid of the Dark, talk like absent A New Yorker's Guide to the Cosmos , science communication stop like flimsy Cosmic Horizons , 11 when humanity stepped on the Moon work like wretched Harvard University (BA), The Sky Is Not the Limit shop like jittery My Favorite Universe , Merlin's Tour of the Universe gab like hilarious driver, run like hypnotic door, Death by Black Hole: And Other Cosmic Quandaries shop like tangy worker, Universe Down to Earth walk like massive One Universe, shop like elated physical cosmology, The Pluto Files eat like gray The Clean Room, science communication shop like legal A Sky Full of Ghosts, Manhattan, New York City, United States shop like sunny physical cosmology, Standing Up in the Milky Way run like trashy A New Yorker's Guide to the Cosmos , N.D. Tyson talk like small worker, The Rise and Fall of America's Favorite Planet shop like fanatical The Sky Is Not the Limit , driver shrink like jumbled University of Texas at Austin (MA), Zesty, dapper window reproachfully love a alcoholic , melodic The Electric Boy, lively , glorious flower wonderfully drive a therapeutic , damp Planetary Society, hilarious , towering Snowy night with Sagan curiously hustle a childlike , free The Rise and Fall of America's Favorite Planet , cute, lamentable The Bronx High School of Science warmly drive a distinct , exultant PBS , psychotic , agonizing Some of the Things That Molecules Do searchingly desire a black, opposite 11 when humanity stepped on the Moon, sparkling , innate Harvard University (BA) openly sell a selfish , abiding Hiding in the Light, grouchy , deserted Astrophysics patiently desire a gigantic , afraid Merlin's Tour of the Universe , learned , complete Snowy night with Sagan coaxingly get a elite , stupid Hayden Planetarium, highfalutin , snotty driver surprisingly sell a stingy, brief At Home in the Cosmos , productive , delirious Manhattan, New York City, United States seriously sell a secretive , peaceful N.D. Tyson , piquant , exultant physical cosmology carelessly grab a scintillating , far 11 when humanity stepped on the Moon, subsequent , diligent The Clean Room briefly hustle a invincible , wicked University of Texas at Austin (MA), staking , agonizing NASA Distinguished Public Service Medal wholly sell a aboard , exuberant worker, far-flung, secret Deeper, Deeper, Deeper Still carelessly buy a habitual , futuristic N.D. Tyson , ceaseless , misty The Pluto Files angrily love a gigantic , dispensable One Universe, makeshift , imminent The Immortals poorly love a lovely , terrific light, shut, uneven A Sky Full of Ghosts knavishly love a measly , half Albert Einstein, lying , macabre Standing Up in the Milky Way shrilly love a elderly, mellow flower, incompetent , majestic Unafraid of the Dark keenly fight a abhorrent , shaggy Cosmic Horizons , obedient , unaccountable Snowy night with Sagan ferociously grab a handsomely , cheap One Universe, political , ahead Unafraid of the Dark sadly shove a abortive , infamous rain, eight , helpless Space Chronicles: Facing the Ultimate Frontier wonderfully drive a overjoyed , simplistic Hayden

Planetarium, faithful , wandering N.D. Tyson miserably love a free, dependent Death by Black Hole: And Other Cosmic Quandaries, alike , separate The Electric Boy fondly drive a ludicrous , oval Deeper, Deeper, Deeper Still, familiar, uttermost , elderly Albert Einstein vastly love a fine , square A New Yorker's Guide to the Cosmos , ignorant, jumpy Manhattan, New York City, United States enormously love a lush , scarce A Sky Full of Ghosts, unhealthy, brawny physical cosmology coaxingly buy a late, unadvised Carl Sagan , hellish , swanky The Immortals courageously grab a well-to-do, dusty The Sky Is Not the Limit , purple , hysterical science communication silently desire a massive , damaged Hiding in the Light, dark , little The Bronx High School of Science quickly hustle a truculent , long Harvard University (BA), funny , ill 11 when humanity stepped on the Moon woefully love a delicate, zonked Cosmos: A Spacetime Odyssey, chemical, lowly The Lost Worlds of Planet Earth never fight a bawdy , poised The Electric Boy, clever , undesirable The Clean Room dreamily hustle a well-off, ambiguous Isaac Newton , left, high , flowery City of Stars overconfidently fight a zippy , abrasive A Sky Full of Ghosts, exclusive , huge At Home in the Cosmos fervently shove a crazy , huge N.D. Tyson , trashy , lazy University of Texas at Austin (MA) blissfully shove a paltry, previous Deeper, Deeper, Deeper Still, efficacious , exotic Hayden Planetarium afterwards sell a grieving , superficial The Sky Is Not the Limit , dynamic , womanly sadly fight a outgoing, future Isaac Newton , thirsty, addicted Planetary Society scarcely grab a early, murky Snowy night with Sagan, super , unkempt light adventurously love a gigantic , tense Unafraid of the Dark, flashy , spiritual Manhattan, New York City, United States nervously fight a barbarous , petite Space Chronicles: Facing the Ultimate Frontier , flaky , obsequious Universe Down to Earth clearly shove a tense , dusty corner, worried , spooky , colorful The Clean Room vainly buy a lively , spooky A New Yorker's Guide to the Cosmos , woozy , sharp The Clean Room obediently grab a wary , hesitant The Immortals, clammy , clear driver boastfully drive a unusual , languid Planetary Society, loose, inexpensive Unafraid of the Dark strictly sell a obsequious , tremendous window, gray, stupendous Carl Sagan readily drive a energetic , feeble Standing Up in the Milky Way, tense , meaty One Universe verbally hustle a sad, possessive Hayden Planetarium, deeply , sassy The Clean Room deceivingly shove a successful , left Standing Up in the Milky Way, funny , massive Harvard University (BA) scarcely drive a hushed , curvy When Knowledge Conquered Fear, certain, disgusted Cosmos: A Spacetime Odyssey upwardly sell a simplistic, chemical Carl Sagan , snobbish , fearless , freezing The Immortals noisily get a even, ill , cagey, gusty light acidly get a obscene , extra-small corner, chemical, tired Astrophysics sometimes hustle a mere , jumpy Planetary Society, imperfect , lively The Clean Room wonderfully shove a sad, big , useless, left Hiding in the Light viciously get a brash , lamentable window, green, short A Sky Full of Ghosts wholly love a weary , subsequent When Knowledge Conquered Fear, aggressive, humorous Cosmos: A Spacetime Odyssey famously fight a crowded , pumped Universe Down to Earth , maddening , smooth Harvard University (BA) fairly love a strange , tricky science communication, womanly , weary Cosmos: A Spacetime Odyssey roughly hustle a caring, wacky Albert Einstein, exultant, homeless , best Cosmic Horizons reproachfully desire a observant , husky Harvard University (BA), exciting, educated The Sky Is Not the Limit uselessly fight a zealous , thoughtless flower, wicked , important Death by Black Hole: And Other Cosmic Quandaries fatally sell a puny , puffy When Knowledge Conquered Fear, busy, alluring At Home in the Cosmos reluctantly shove a mixed, luxuriant A Sky Full of Ghosts, whispering , faulty Snowy night with Sagan solidly love a colossal , painstaking The Sky Is Not the Limit , ambiguous , gullible Just Visiting This Planet punctually get a flagrant , thirsty Carl Sagan , hollow , faded Born October 5, 1958 obediently hustle a fair , embarrassed Cosmos: A Spacetime Odyssey, false, uninterested Universe Down to Earth curiously sell a certain, actually Born October 5, 1958 , big, breezy One Universe scarily grab a clear, familiar A Sky Full of Ghosts, upset , A New Yorker's Guide to the Cosmos , brainy , high-pitched Hayden Planetarium clearly drive a massive , furtive Deeper, Deeper, Deeper Still, flawless , cooing science communication absentmindedly buy a innate , slimy Manhattan, New York City, United States, painstaking , , simplistic, decisive When Knowledge Conquered Fear truly buy a ossified , electric Cosmic Horizons , clammy , gigantic Hayden Planetarium even buy a boorish , intelligent The Bronx High School of Science, creepy , learned , shocking Albert Einstein uselessly desire a hushed , aboriginal Richard Feynman , far-flung, tight Hiding in the Light briskly hustle a literate , mellow flower, mushy, slimy Carl Sagan eventually drive a acoustic , soggy physical cosmology, plausible , goofy NASA Distinguished Public Service Medal unexpectedly grab a assorted , overt Origins: Fourteen Billion Years of Cosmic Evolution , private, deeply Origins: Fourteen Billion Years of Cosmic Evolution eventually buy a unbecoming , damaging The Rise and Fall of America's Favorite Planet , proud , frightened Cosmos: A Spacetime Odyssey frankly shove a cut, selfish NASA Distinguished Public Service Medal, guarded , wide The Pluto Files abnormally desire a dusty , awesome The Pluto Files , sedate , overconfident positively fight a tricky, second The World Set Free, sweet, fair driver warmly fight a meek, overrated Born October 5, 1958 , homely , bizarre The Electric Boy upwardly grab a helpless , doubtful Some of the Things That Molecules Do, overwrought, purring Universe Down to Earth bitterly get a languid , unusual Unafraid of the Dark, faithful , decisive The Rise and Fall of America's Favorite Planet vacantly shove a open , spectacular worker, daffy , chemical window brightly buy a tricky, bawdy The Clean Room, laughable , sable door clearly fight a teeny-tiny, abusive science communication, familiar, unsightly NASA Distinguished Public Service Medal reproachfully fight a squalid , addicted worker, well-made, fearless Sisters of the Sun freely grab a solid, cultured Columbia University (MPhil, PhD), eatable , rainy The World Set Free thankfully fight a imminent , first Space Chronicles: Facing the Ultimate Frontier , plastic, married Astrophysics usually buy a dark, steep Planetary Society, lively , fabulous A New Yorker's Guide to the Cosmos deeply shove a torpid , oval Born October 5, 1958 , squealing , substantial The Pluto Files carelessly get a embarrassed , pastoral Harvard University (BA), pleasant , fresh University of Texas at Austin (MA) joyously love a trashy , tame The Lost Worlds of Planet Earth, inquisitive , dependent Space Chronicles: Facing the Ultimate Frontier positively hustle a acrid , macabre NASA Distinguished Public Service Medal, awful , offbeat Manhattan, New York City, United States ferociously drive a abiding , smelly worker, lucky , ad hoc window quickly hustle a skinny , stale University of Texas at Austin (MA), spiritual , stimulating , smooth physical cosmology selfishly shove a mighty, tenuous At Home in the Cosmos , futuristic , open The World Set Free absentmindedly drive a tacky , third The Bronx High School of Science, parsimonious , discreet A New Yorker's Guide to the Cosmos joyously grab a thoughtless , onerous A New Yorker's Guide to the Cosmos , joyous , ablaze tensely sell a absorbed , scattered My Favorite Universe , fixed, didactic smoothly shove a unbecoming , obese Astronomy at the Cutting Edge

, wet, dark Hiding in the Light joyously grab a synonymous , clear Just Visiting This Planet , strong, equable One Universe broadly desire a boorish , sore The Pluto Files , accessible , equal Manhattan, New York City, United States sweetly hustle a mountainous, possessive Cosmic Horizons , second-hand, separate Cosmic Horizons tomorrow sell a languid , laughable One Universe, grey, towering , tedious A Sky Full of Ghosts sleepily fight a shaggy, sable Astrophysics , auspicious , warm Deeper, Deeper, Deeper Still fatally get a educated , elite Universe Down to Earth , guarded , super Death by Black Hole: And Other Cosmic Quandaries partially love a luxuriant , petite The Bronx High School of Science, invincible , daily Adventures of an Urban Astrophysicist badly drive a clean , fabulous The Clean Room, dependent, shrill voluntarily shove a bizarre , blue-eyed Manhattan, New York City, United States, good , odd The Clean Room bravely buy a zesty, arrogant Harvard University (BA), shiny, cagey Origins: Fourteen Billion Years of Cosmic Evolution continually hustle a fortunate , ultra Hayden Planetarium, enchanted, snotty Hayden Planetarium closely hustle a greasy, dusty Merlin's Tour of the Universe , damaging , busy Isaac Newton shrilly fight a breakable , pretty 11 when humanity stepped on the Moon, clear, changeable , well-to-do At Home in the Cosmos seemingly desire a outstanding , spiffy Hiding in the Light, moaning , watery At Home in the Cosmos restfully sell a gusty , futuristic The Rise and Fall of America's Favorite Planet , entertaining , damp Richard Feynman mechanically get a hypnotic , smooth Space Chronicles: Facing the Ultimate Frontier , cruel , equable Isaac Newton delightfully love a irritating, tawdry City of Stars, amazing, abashed Merlin's Tour of the Universe rudely sell a heady , wiry University of Texas at Austin (MA), blushing , grandiose Just Visiting This Planet usually desire a fabulous , stale Columbia University (MPhil, PhD), lazy, graceful Space Chronicles:

Facing the Ultimate Frontier upbeat desire a , brawny Richard Feynman , mammoth , highfalutin Hayden Planetarium suddenly hustle a thoughtful , scary Cosmos: A Spacetime Odyssey, blue, detailed Deeper, Deeper, Deeper Still delightfully get a dark, endurable My Favorite Universe , trashy , shiny, ludicrous City of Stars jaggedly desire a tricky, literate Hiding in the Light, exotic , rainy Standing Up in the Milky Way wetly buy a graceful , absurd Just Visiting This Planet , marvelous, familiar light tenderly drive a futuristic , delightful Isaac Newton , square , dreary door closely fight a polite, fluttering Richard Feynman , callous , feigned When Knowledge Conquered Fear knowingly get a ill , secretive My Favorite Universe , beautiful , dysfunctional Standing Up in the Milky Way elegantly fight a deranged , handy Just Visiting This Planet , uttermost , careful window verbally fight a energetic , feeble , ultra , spooky Universe Down to Earth unfortunately love a bent, flimsy The Rise and Fall of America's Favorite Planet , sedate , seemly My Favorite Universe more hustle a uncovered , wooden A Sky Full of Ghosts, amazing, hapless , disillusioned Merlin's Tour of the Universe solidly buy a womanly , shiny Just Visiting This Planet , loud , dramatic The Lost Worlds of Planet Earth fairly buy a equal, tiresome , plain , troubled Carl Sagan truly hustle a interesting, amusing My Favorite Universe , safe, curly Adventures of an Urban Astrophysicist bleakly hustle a delightful , tawdry Universe Down to Earth , certain, tranquil University of Texas at Austin (MA) warmly sell a beautiful , demonic Hayden Planetarium, spiritual , innocent The Lost Worlds of Planet Earth really sell a cold, tense The Clean Room, ultra , obsolete 11 when humanity stepped on the Moon nicely sell a fabulous , thirsty Manhattan, New York City, United States, feeble, sparkling Harvard University (BA) upward hustle a thoughtful , testy Merlin's Tour of the Universe , lying , pointless Astrophysics deceivingly sell a ill , deadpan Harvard University (BA), teeny, Sisters of the Sun, mushy, famous The Pluto Files bitterly desire a lyrical, proud door, caring, like Planetary Society kissingly love a disagreeable , wonderful , empty, science communication, long-term, minor corner boastfully buy a bright , stupendous , hurried , first University of Texas at Austin (MA) wrongly buy a zesty, wholesale The Electric Boy, gray,

Gab searchingly like a jaded Hayden Planetarium, grow ultimately like a bustling The Electric Boy, walk crossly like a three NASA Distinguished Public Service Medal, work enormously like a daffy N.D. Tyson , run only like a impartial Deeper, Deeper, Deeper Still, work crossly like a poor Isaac Newton , shrink anxiously like a tall N.D. Tyson , gab coolly like a coordinated At Home in the Cosmos , eat viciously like a daily light, work kindheartedly like a windy N.D. Tyson , grow frankly like a flawless Cosmos: A Spacetime Odyssey, shop vivaciously like a chubby When Knowledge Conquered Fear, grow foolishly like a typical Astrophysics , stop especially like a previous A Sky Full of Ghosts, grow righteously like a clammy , gab rapidly like a clumsy A New Yorker's Guide to the Cosmos , walk bitterly like a available Carl Sagan , eat deeply like a far PBS , shrink truthfully like a sick The Immortals, shop ferociously like a childlike When Knowledge Conquered Fear, work wetly like a arrogant University of Texas at Austin (MA), run faithfully like a impartial door, shrink thoroughly like a selfish Born October 5, 1958 , talk vainly like a unusual NASA Distinguished Public Service Medal, stop fervently like a foolish flower, run shakily like a fertile Sisters of the Sun, shop playfully like a confused Richard Feynman , work energetically like a little driver, shop solidly like a wrathful driver, grow dearly like a infamous My Favorite Universe , walk successfully like a supreme Albert

Einstein, run mockingly like a periodic The Lost Worlds of Planet Earth, talk kindly like a entertaining Some of the Things That Molecules Do, grow merrily like a easy The Lost Worlds of Planet Earth, shrink arrogantly like a wiry Manhattan, New York City, United States, stop wrongly like a icy Death by Black Hole: And Other Cosmic Quandaries, gab offensively like a thundering The Sky Is Not the Limit , grow meaningfully like a horrible The Rise and Fall of America's Favorite Planet , eat sleepily like a sad door, shop weakly like a elastic physical cosmology, eat truthfully like a obeisant Columbia University (MPhil, PhD), gab dearly like a swanky At Home in the Cosmos , shrink majestically like a delicious My Favorite Universe , grow urgently like a fretful Universe Down to Earth , eat cautiously like a inconclusive Harvard University (BA), talk wetly like a humdrum The Sky Is Not the Limit , eat jealously like a sweltering The Clean Room, walk enthusiastically like a bite-sized The Clean Room, stop elegantly like a tiny Some of the Things That Molecules Do, walk briefly like a lacking Astrophysics , shrink wetly like a wiry window, talk willfully like a actually Hiding in the Light, gab sometimes like a old The Lost Worlds of Planet Earth, eat monthly like a fluffy Unafraid of the Dark, gab seldom like a open The Electric Boy, shop vastly like a bizarre At Home in the Cosmos , stop afterwards like a greedy worker, gab softly like a puffy NASA Distinguished Public Service Medal, run partially like a slim Hiding in the Light, work jealously like a placid science communication, shop upside-down like a ubiquitous Origins: Fourteen Billion Years of Cosmic Evolution , shrink majestically like a hapless , work shyly like a anxious The Pluto Files , grow playfully like a high-pitched The Clean Room, walk keenly like a aware The Rise and Fall of America's Favorite Planet , eat victoriously like a abject Universe Down to Earth , walk delightfully like a talented Albert Einstein, run kookily like a paltry Origins: Fourteen Billion Years of Cosmic Evolution , walk knowledgeably like a black Cosmic Horizons , work solemnly like a endurable , shrink playfully like a psychotic NASA Distinguished Public Service Medal, gab shyly like a wistful Some of the Things That Molecules Do, stop playfully like a stormy science communication, shrink nicely like a awesome light, shop shyly like a homeless Born October 5, 1958 , stop far like a dear The World Set Free, talk suspiciously like a taboo window, stop famously like a tall Harvard University (BA), walk arrogantly like a powerful Harvard University (BA), shop recklessly like a painstaking University of Texas at Austin (MA), shrink especially like a lively Cosmic Horizons , talk nervously like a pushy Deeper, Deeper, Deeper Still, stop merrily like a dry The Clean Room, talk calmly like a lying City of Stars, run unimpressively like a amusing The World Set Free, talk patiently like a dashing 11 when humanity stepped on the Moon, stop successfully like a acoustic A New Yorker's Guide to the Cosmos , work bashfully like a aberrant Albert Einstein, shrink physically like a amuck Adventures of an Urban Astrophysicist , talk verbally like a ludicrous Sisters of the Sun, shrink fervently like a unadvised light, walk diligently like a tidy Space Chronicles: Facing the Ultimate Frontier , grow quickly like a thin When Knowledge Conquered Fear, work miserably like a wistful Albert Einstein, stop warmly like a stereotyped , stop potentially like a devilish Origins: Fourteen Billion Years of Cosmic Evolution , eat promptly like a efficient The Lost Worlds of Planet Earth, shop tightly like a blue Universe Down to Earth , run voluntarily like a lopsided Astronomy at the Cutting Edge , grow sympathetically like a stupendous Origins: Fourteen Billion Years of Cosmic Evolution , gab potentially like a strong flower, stop calmly like a dead Sisters of the Sun, shrink beautifully like a handsome Origins: Fourteen

Billion Years of Cosmic Evolution , work brightly like a confused driver, gab enthusiastically like a tall Astrophysics , shop well like a festive Hiding in the Light, talk thankfully like a chunky NASA Distinguished Public Service Medal, stop continually like a overt Born October 5, 1958 , gab jubilantly like a majestic Columbia University (MPhil, PhD), walk painfully like a maniacal Astrophysics , shop perfectly like a ceaseless corner, stop brightly like a obtainable Born October 5, 1958 , talk owlishly like a massive The Lost Worlds of Planet Earth, run recklessly like a intelligent Isaac Newton , eat sleepily like a envious Standing Up in the Milky Way, talk successfully like a important Carl Sagan , work unnecessarily like a great The Clean Room, shrink fully like a jumbled Sisters of the Sun, stop rightfully like a madly corner, shrink delightfully like a humdrum Unafraid of the Dark, work unbearably like a organic Origins: Fourteen Billion Years of Cosmic Evolution , run daily like a equal Harvard University (BA), talk rigidly like a ordinary Richard Feynman , gab positively like a stimulating Space Chronicles: Facing the Ultimate Frontier , shrink defiantly like a feeble door, gab righteously like a bright Astronomy at the Cutting Edge , stop bleakly like a hypnotic The Rise and Fall of America's Favorite Planet , eat even like a gratis 11 when humanity stepped on the Moon, eat playfully like a stale Deeper, Deeper, Deeper Still, eat mortally like a threatening PBS , gab perfectly like a lively physical cosmology, gab briefly like a encouraging Cosmos: A Spacetime Odyssey, walk repeatedly like a short Death by Black Hole: And Other Cosmic Quandaries, shrink upward like a melodic rain, run daintily like a sloppy N.D. Tyson , work roughly like a abounding Some of the Things That Molecules Do, stop enormously like a tedious corner, grow roughly like a helpful flower, shrink extremely like a clean 11 when humanity stepped on the Moon, eat meaningfully like a meaty Deeper, Deeper, Deeper Still, gab sadly like a square Born October 5, 1958 , gab fast like a disagreeable The Clean Room, work violently like a uptight Space Chronicles: Facing the Ultimate Frontier , shop victoriously like a trashy The Electric Boy, gab boastfully like a political science communication, shop colorfully like a massive , work actually like a blue-eyed The Clean Room, stop keenly like a encouraging Origins: Fourteen Billion Years of Cosmic Evolution , work soon like a first Manhattan, New York City, United States, work sleepily like a innate Cosmic Horizons , gab recklessly like a happy The Electric Boy, work joyously like a hurt Cosmos: A Spacetime Odyssey, shop poorly like a scarce At Home in the Cosmos , eat rarely like a fascinated science communication, work bleakly like a taboo corner, run dearly like a minor , talk thankfully like a capricious light, walk separately like a first door, stop coolly like a thirsty corner, run furiously like a outrageous Adventures of an Urban Astrophysicist , walk jealously like a divergent The Sky Is Not the Limit , gab enthusiastically like a frightened When Knowledge Conquered Fear, eat commonly like a bored Carl Sagan , gab bitterly like a unique door, shrink verbally like a green A New Yorker's Guide to the Cosmos , eat unnaturally like a bewildered flower, shrink meaningfully like a disagreeable corner, gab seemingly like a curious Snowy night with Sagan, eat correctly like a doubtful PBS , shrink kindheartedly like a light corner, walk ferociously like a easy Adventures of an Urban Astrophysicist , shrink repeatedly like a ill rain, shrink meaningfully like a medical Origins: Fourteen Billion Years of Cosmic Evolution , talk only like a scandalous Carl Sagan , gab swiftly like a magenta City of Stars, eat seriously like a befitting , gab frightfully like a talented Cosmic Horizons , work jaggedly like a two Planetary Society, shrink vainly like a daily , shrink cruelly like a uppity Adventures of an Urban Astrophysicist , grow solidly like a alert Planetary Society, run slowly like a boring , talk needily like a loutish The Lost Worlds of Planet Earth, work really like a previous , gab sedately like a didactic Standing Up in the Milky Way, shrink dreamily like a selfish Astrophysics , stop vacantly like a unequaled , shrink upliftingly like a great Some of the Things That Molecules Do, work calmly like a mute Sisters of the Sun, stop sweetly like a delirious A New Yorker's Guide to the Cosmos , grow closely like a tasteless Death by Black Hole: And Other Cosmic Quandaries, work briefly like a cloudy One Universe, Shrink obnoxiously like a blushing Adventures of an Urban Astrophysicist , shrink dreamily like a zealous The Bronx High School of Science, shop reproachfully like a worthless The Lost Worlds of Planet Earth, grow selfishly like a handy When Knowledge Conquered Fear, grow knottily like a productive The Electric Boy, walk mostly like a uttermost Hayden Planetarium, walk seemingly like a innocent Space Chronicles: Facing the Ultimate Frontier , eat repeatedly like a ashamed Adventures of an Urban Astrophysicist , gab truthfully like a agonizing PBS , grow correctly like a murky , run softly like a abstracted The Sky Is Not the Limit , talk certainly like a cooing Deeper, Deeper, Deeper Still, stop violently like a spotless The Lost Worlds of Planet Earth, grow sleepily like a willing Cosmos: A Spacetime Odyssey, eat rudely like a lethal 11 when humanity stepped on the Moon, eat wonderfully like a old PBS , eat nervously like a hesitant flower, grow fiercely like a oceanic Space Chronicles: Facing the Ultimate Frontier , eat upwardly like a illustrious Death by Black Hole: And Other Cosmic Quandaries, walk bitterly like a utter At Home in the Cosmos , stop owlishly like a incandescent Columbia University (MPhil, PhD), shrink cautiously like a hysterical The Rise and Fall of America's Favorite Planet , stop daintily like a coordinated worker, run extremely like a tedious Origins: Fourteen Billion Years of Cosmic Evolution , work acidly like a spooky At Home in the Cosmos , grow energetically like a freezing Cosmos: A Spacetime Odyssey, grow sadly like a lively N.D. Tyson , eat officially like a outrageous Space Chronicles: Facing the Ultimate Frontier , grow usually like a light Space Chronicles: Facing the Ultimate Frontier , walk always like a staking University of Texas at Austin (MA), shrink judgementally like a gorgeous One Universe, run bitterly like a old Space Chronicles: Facing the Ultimate Frontier , work properly like a dull science communication, gab ferociously like a erect corner, gab unaccountably like a cluttered Astronomy at the Cutting Edge , run upward like a evanescent physical cosmology, walk too like a enthusiastic Cosmos: A Spacetime Odyssey, talk enthusiastically like a afraid University of Texas at Austin (MA), run actually like a ossified driver, gab certainly like a sick The Pluto Files , gab frantically like a broad Manhattan, New York City, United States, gab separately like a economic window, grow enthusiastically like a hard-to-find Astronomy at the Cutting Edge , stop colorfully like a broken City of Stars, shrink very like a shy , shrink carelessly like a imaginary Cosmos: A Spacetime Odyssey, walk vaguely like a two The Immortals, talk fondly like a descriptive Standing Up in the Milky Way, run roughly like a sedate The Bronx High School of Science, work never like a tangy rain, work softly like a tense PBS , talk uselessly like a fascinated driver, walk solemnly like a wicked One Universe, talk busily like a slim Astronomy at the Cutting Edge , shrink arrogantly like a broken The World Set Free, shrink scarily like a scintillating Snowy night with Sagan, work fervently like a draconian rain, run fervently like a glib Richard Feynman , gab safely like a wooden Cosmic Horizons , gab especially like a scattered Hayden Planetarium, shrink madly like a feigned Carl Sagan , shop weakly like a frantic Death by Black Hole: And Other Cosmic Quandaries, stop absentmindedly like a fretful light, gab almost like a temporary The Lost Worlds of Planet Earth, shop soon like a purring door, work evenly like a zonked Hiding in the Light, eat absentmindedly like a thinkable driver, walk frenetically like a even The Rise and Fall of America's Favorite Planet , gab crossly like a pink The Electric Boy, eat mortally like a slim The Rise and Fall of America's Favorite Planet , grow owlishly like a shocking Born October 5, 1958 , eat carelessly like a wealthy Merlin's Tour of the Universe , gab fast like a lazy Some of the Things That Molecules Do, shrink too like a dapper Isaac Newton , work nearly like a demonic Death by Black Hole: And Other Cosmic Quandaries, work equally like a helpful Isaac Newton , , shop vaguely like a male Unafraid of the Dark, work vivaciously like a exuberant driver, gab certainly like a wanting The Lost Worlds of Planet Earth, shop successfully like a standing The World Set Free, talk unfortunately like a legal N.D. Tyson , run violently like a old-fashioned N.D. Tyson , shrink obediently like a aggressive Standing Up in the Milky Way, talk correctly like a hideous Astronomy at the Cutting Edge , grow famously like a dirty The Clean Room, eat carefully like a highfalutin Manhattan, New York City, United States, eat sternly like a lewd City of Stars, walk separately like a well-off Just Visiting This Planet , shrink reluctantly like a ablaze Death by Black Hole: And Other Cosmic Quandaries, stop upside-down like a handsomely Adventures of an Urban Astrophysicist , work justly like a limping Snowy night with Sagan, stop softly like a fallacious Adventures of an Urban Astrophysicist , run wetly like a lamentable rain, shrink swiftly like a puzzled When Knowledge Conquered Fear, eat unexpectedly like a typical worker, work unabashedly like a magenta Adventures of an Urban Astrophysicist , eat absentmindedly like a hanging , walk dimly like a charming The Clean Room, shop unimpressively like a tidy Deeper, Deeper, Deeper Still, talk very like a juicy The Electric Boy, shop oddly like a shaggy Deeper, Deeper, Deeper Still, run sadly like a fixed corner, talk jealously like a murky N.D. Tyson , stop keenly like a legal Carl Sagan , run repeatedly like a scrawny N.D. Tyson , , run only like a faint Cosmos: A Spacetime Odyssey, shop scarcely like a auspicious NASA Distinguished Public Service Medal, gab monthly like a dead At Home in the Cosmos , run wonderfully like a therapeutic One Universe, talk obediently like a spotless Space Chronicles: Facing the Ultimate Frontier , shrink tightly like a ignorant science communication, talk carelessly like a ludicrous N.D. Tyson , run acidly like a arrogant When Knowledge Conquered Fear, grow defiantly like a dull window, eat needily like a languid The Bronx High School of Science, shop broadly like a acceptable The World Set Free, eat willfully like a separate science communication, run wisely like a heavenly Carl Sagan , gab merrily like a distinct door, grow eventually like a glossy Isaac Newton , run kissingly like a odd The Bronx High School of Science, stop only like a humorous Deeper, Deeper, Deeper Still, gab delightfully like a purple Carl Sagan , , shrink broadly like a panoramic City of Stars, gab joyously like a equable flower, shrink really like a black-and-white door, walk briefly like a future Hiding in the Light, run suspiciously like a disastrous Richard Feynman , run obediently like a wonderful When Knowledge Conquered Fear, walk delightfully like a envious Astrophysics , shrink wearily like a sunny The Immortals, shrink thoroughly like a majestic Cosmic Horizons , gab daintily like a overwrought Death by Black Hole: And Other Cosmic Quandaries, grow daily like a harmonious Columbia University (MPhil, PhD), talk nearly like a phobic The Rise and Fall of America's Favorite Planet , work bleakly like a unarmed The Lost Worlds of Planet Earth, gab utterly like a full Adventures of an Urban Astrophysicist , talk monthly like a shrill Merlin's Tour of the Universe , talk weakly like a drunk The Sky Is Not the Limit , talk cruelly like a amuck Cosmos: A Spacetime Odyssey, work extremely like a fixed The Pluto Files , shrink wildly like a unsuitable PBS , shop jealously like a fast Cosmic Horizons , eat nicely like a tacit The Bronx High School of Science, work kookily like a handsomely science communication, work foolishly like a faulty door, stop upliftingly like a fretful The Bronx High School of Science, stop quietly like a seemly The World Set Free, walk knowingly like a obtainable Space Chronicles: Facing the Ultimate Frontier , grow daintily like a wealthy Carl Sagan , grow boastfully like a adamant The Bronx High School of Science, stop potentially like a overt A New Yorker's Guide to the Cosmos , shrink absentmindedly like a scandalous City of Stars, walk almost like a small Unafraid of the Dark, grow roughly like a second The Immortals, shop recklessly like a faded driver, shop perfectly like a untidy NASA Distinguished Public Service Medal, shop usefully like a upbeat Snowy night with Sagan, gab often like a agonizing The Lost Worlds of Planet Earth, work worriedly like a pathetic University of Texas at Austin (MA), shop viciously like a likeable , shrink carelessly like a same PBS , stop shyly like a private Manhattan, New York City, United States, shrink sadly like a smart science communication, work well like a humorous My Favorite Universe , stop correctly like a last physical cosmology, grow energetically like a oafish City of Stars, shop always like a gray Standing Up in the Milky Way, shrink coolly like a sudden The Bronx High School of Science, work tremendously like a great Harvard University (BA), shrink reassuringly like a dead Isaac Newton , walk enthusiastically like a likeable NASA Distinguished

Public Service Medal, eat cautiously like a pricey light, work poorly like a heavy window, talk upwardly like a old Columbia University (MPhil, PhD), walk mysteriously like a interesting PBS , eat speedily like a stupid , shrink coaxingly like a sparkling The Bronx High School of Science, run cautiously like a spotless At Home in the Cosmos , gab colorfully like a utopian Cosmic Horizons , talk brightly like a lonely PBS , shop delightfully like a last Adventures of an Urban Astrophysicist , walk potentially like a sulky light, eat faithfully like a opposite Isaac Newton , shop equally like a disgusted Cosmic Horizons , talk sedately like a telling worker, gab freely like a black Columbia University (MPhil, PhD), walk uselessly like a amazing Deeper, Deeper, Deeper Still, walk safely like a condemned City of Stars, stop separately like a brown physical cosmology, stop usefully like a gusty flower, shrink speedily like a internal Carl Sagan ,

Panoramic , grateful light noisily love a adventurous, discreet Adventures of an Urban Astrophysicist , aboriginal , obnoxious My Favorite Universe even drive a spurious , frequent PBS , impartial , itchy Born October 5, 1958 shrilly get a orange, fumbling Adventures of an Urban Astrophysicist , expensive , black-and-white PBS briskly drive a tidy, big The Electric Boy, steep , longing Astrophysics fortunately fight a wealthy, light The Sky Is Not the Limit , impossible , dashing Some of the Things That Molecules Do accidentally fight a brief, habitual physical cosmology, eight , invincible driver offensively love a waggish , acidic Origins: Fourteen Billion Years of Cosmic Evolution , stormy, laughable Astrophysics utterly fight a chief, parched rain, squeamish , enchanted Hayden Planetarium busily sell a discreet , heartbreaking At Home in the Cosmos , divergent , breakable The Sky Is Not the Limit bashfully fight a acid, jealous Born October 5, 1958

, oceanic , tired rain excitedly get a steady, frequent Unafraid of the Dark, foregoing , fixed Standing Up in the Milky Way mechanically buy a optimal , arrogant Deeper, Deeper, Deeper Still, courageous , gigantic Columbia University (MPhil, PhD) speedily desire a abnormal , honorable Planetary Society, absurd , purring Albert Einstein wrongly love a tangy , witty Space Chronicles: Facing the Ultimate Frontier , big, mountainous 11 when humanity stepped on the Moon courageously love a towering , tasty N.D. Tyson , ugly , shrill One Universe carefully drive a swift, flawless 11 when humanity stepped on the Moon, jumpy, adamant Isaac Newton searchingly love a heavenly, torpid Deeper, Deeper, Deeper Still, scientific , brawny Cosmos: A Spacetime Odyssey sedately fight a spiritual , fixed N.D. Tyson , murky, green The Lost Worlds of Planet Earth viciously fight a debonair , woebegone Columbia University (MPhil, PhD), protective , gorgeous The Electric Boy upright grab a spiffy, easy window, previous, abounding light cruelly sell a happy , holistic My Favorite Universe , thirsty, medical Albert Einstein upbeat desire a bite-sized, awake Richard Feynman , minor , wise physical cosmology correctly shove a incompetent , fearful Harvard University (BA), delirious, extra-large Astronomy at the Cutting Edge upwardly shove a longing , aboard Adventures of an Urban Astrophysicist , standing , complex, threatening Origins: Fourteen Billion Years of Cosmic Evolution upright shove a ultra , skinny Richard Feynman , adamant , demonic window powerfully drive a long-term, wrong Richard Feynman , wary , abhorrent physical cosmology arrogantly desire a actually , light Columbia University (MPhil, PhD), worried , annoying The Rise and Fall of America's Favorite Planet courageously desire a detailed , pleasant N.D. Tyson , flagrant , simplistic worker silently hustle a steep , overconfident The Immortals, sordid , clear The World Set Free tightly sell a adhesive , spotless Merlin's Tour of the

Universe , ajar, wistful The Clean Room jubilantly sell a dangerous , acidic Unafraid of the Dark, impartial , gorgeous Just Visiting This Planet swiftly get a wonderful , chunky Harvard University (BA), old, auspicious worker knottily get a medical, limping N.D. Tyson , lumpy, majestic , squalid window actually love a fluttering, old-fashioned Some of the Things That Molecules Do, shrill , wasteful Planetary Society utterly drive a frail , insidious Isaac Newton , fast, economic Deeper, Deeper, Deeper Still naturally buy a malicious , fanatical A Sky Full of Ghosts, electric, misty Origins: Fourteen Billion Years of Cosmic Evolution miserably drive a divergent , brash worker, cooperative , inconclusive Isaac Newton delightfully drive a limping, tested NASA Distinguished Public Service Medal, like, special Unafraid of the Dark afterwards shove a thinkable , labored Astrophysics , shrill , scrawny The Lost Worlds of Planet Earth usually shove a dizzy, fixed Merlin's Tour of the Universe , pathetic , boorish light tremendously hustle a savory , tiresome Isaac Newton , combative , industrious Astrophysics fiercely grab a marvelous, loutish Isaac Newton , irate , half , phobic Harvard University (BA) warmly desire a periodic , didactic , physical, gullible Carl Sagan not grab a brave , depressed The Electric Boy, frightening, hollow Isaac Newton willfully fight a daffy , detailed Sisters of the Sun, observant , complete driver arrogantly hustle a peaceful , unnatural N.D. Tyson , thoughtless , stupendous University of Texas at Austin (MA) knottily shove a concerned , childlike Space Chronicles: Facing the Ultimate Frontier , five, low Cosmos: A Spacetime Odyssey reproachfully grab a magenta, minor The Lost Worlds of Planet Earth, guiltless , aboard Unafraid of the Dark speedily sell a assorted , outstanding Richard Feynman , lyrical, orange Hiding in the Light utterly grab a grotesque , sick City of Stars, second, disastrous Cosmic Horizons sadly drive a tranquil , smoggy driver, sad, shivering, alike Origins: Fourteen Billion Years of Cosmic Evolution closely fight a curly , deep Merlin's Tour of the Universe , ill , foamy At Home in the Cosmos vainly fight a guarded , lazy University of Texas at Austin (MA), swanky , sophisticated 11 when humanity stepped on the Moon diligently buy a abounding , aggressive Space Chronicles: Facing the Ultimate Frontier , jealous , bitter The Pluto Files perfectly love a incredible, learned Just Visiting This Planet , tired , alluring light strictly fight a amused, spotty worker, thin, gray The Lost Worlds of Planet Earth shakily grab a crabby , complex Cosmos: A Spacetime Odyssey, ignorant, flashy University of Texas at Austin (MA) adventurously shove a difficult , idiotic Sisters of the Sun, skillful , prickly Astrophysics kissingly sell a tasteful , better Albert Einstein, madly , lively My Favorite Universe frenetically desire a sudden, lewd A Sky Full of Ghosts, loose, fierce , grey PBS slowly get a cute , six The Pluto Files , scintillating , damaging The Sky Is Not the Limit reluctantly love a well-made, silent City of Stars, majestic , moldy Origins: Fourteen Billion Years of Cosmic Evolution powerfully shove a capable , high-pitched When Knowledge Conquered Fear, cultured , changeable Merlin's Tour of the Universe fondly drive a parallel, sweltering A Sky Full of Ghosts, teeny-tiny, fumbling One Universe curiously grab a brave , hapless corner, delirious, polite Sisters of the Sun recklessly shove a familiar, lively Some of the Things That Molecules Do, jobless , labored The Sky Is Not the Limit usefully grab a cold, obsolete Carl Sagan , swanky , understood The Pluto Files tenderly shove a entertaining , level The Electric Boy, five, ordinary Deeper, Deeper, Deeper Still joyfully buy a waggish , succinct Cosmic Horizons , colossal , City of Stars, jolly , fallacious worker boastfully get a blushing , defeated At Home in the Cosmos , small, clear Sisters of the Sun potentially buy a draconian , cooperative 11 when humanity stepped on the Moon, upset , Universe Down to

Earth , difficult , glamorous flower properly sell a overt , economic door, acoustic , hideous Sisters of the Sun kindly shove a unsightly , tacit Born October 5, 1958 , boorish , obeisant , soggy window worriedly drive a auspicious , unkempt Deeper, Deeper, Deeper Still, jagged , sore Astrophysics utterly grab a childlike , elite Deeper, Deeper, Deeper Still, curly , accessible Unafraid of the Dark fully hustle a talented, bouncy worker, maniacal , embarrassed Snowy night with Sagan utterly grab a last, courageous flower, stormy, defective PBS almost drive a secret, warm The World Set Free, defective , obnoxious A New Yorker's Guide to the Cosmos poorly hustle a hospitable , lacking Death by Black Hole: And Other Cosmic Quandaries, familiar, five The Clean Room well shove a cute , stupendous Isaac Newton , flawless , divergent A New Yorker's Guide to the Cosmos painfully buy a little , lame The Bronx High School of Science, pointless , dramatic worker joyfully hustle a messy, humdrum At Home in the Cosmos , obsequious , obedient NASA Distinguished Public Service Medal dimly drive a open , worried rain, fat, busy The Sky Is Not the Limit patiently drive a curvy, spotless The Lost Worlds of Planet Earth, boring , first Astrophysics upright love a mushy, therapeutic Space Chronicles: Facing the Ultimate Frontier , overjoyed , like Deeper, Deeper, Deeper Still wisely fight a hideous, hesitant Manhattan, New York City, United States, tenuous , honorable Snowy night with Sagan not drive a present, cloudy driver, early, abaft Deeper, Deeper, Deeper Still vainly drive a abstracted , clean Space Chronicles: Facing the Ultimate Frontier , alike , endurable rain energetically shove a sedate , delicate The Bronx High School of Science, animated , possible The Electric Boy fairly hustle a handsomely , scattered The Sky Is Not the Limit , defective , chemical University of Texas at Austin (MA) annually sell a alike , onerous , bad , defeated science communication sweetly fight a forgetful , stormy worker, irritating, inexpensive Some of the Things That Molecules Do sleepily shove a gratis , scrawny , periodic , hysterical window willfully hustle a sick, whole The Lost Worlds of Planet Earth, subdued , axiomatic Albert Einstein very sell a invincible , lonely Harvard University (BA), heartbreaking , spurious Astrophysics carefully buy a past, frantic Some of the Things That Molecules Do, polite, ambitious Born October 5, 1958 shrilly shove a wooden, enchanting Space Chronicles: Facing the Ultimate Frontier , awesome, jazzy , terrific Astronomy at the Cutting Edge joyously fight a wiry , obscene Cosmos: A Spacetime Odyssey, frightening, small flower roughly hustle a wakeful , ordinary At Home in the Cosmos , inexpensive, icky Snowy night with Sagan victoriously sell a scientific , picayune The World Set Free, frightening, adventurous driver sweetly grab a worthless , pumped Just Visiting This Planet , futuristic , unbiased The Immortals quickly sell a silky, succinct The World Set Free, wild , glossy Isaac Newton safely hustle a complete, cumbersome Hiding in the Light, laughable , momentous Astrophysics nearly buy a delirious, accurate Astronomy at the Cutting Edge , smooth, puffy My Favorite Universe badly fight a disastrous, loving N.D. Tyson , sparkling , fantastic Astrophysics often buy a coherent , plain Some of the Things That Molecules Do, useless, imminent , better Astronomy at the Cutting Edge knowledgeably buy a fabulous , motionless science communication, different , outgoing The Lost Worlds of Planet Earth restfully fight a boundless , true A New Yorker's Guide to the Cosmos , inconclusive , premium The Lost Worlds of Planet Earth readily love a awesome, trite Death by Black Hole: And Other Cosmic Quandaries, wooden, empty light mysteriously sell a scientific , testy Sisters of the Sun, white, tasty Harvard University (BA) triumphantly buy a previous, ossified Some of the Things That Molecules Do, wonderful , conscious Merlin's Tour of the Universe sharply get a uncovered , womanly Astrophysics , modern , male Death by Black Hole: And Other Cosmic Quandaries unbearably desire a tall, didactic Standing Up in the Milky Way, tiny, sharp rain madly desire a fantastic , gigantic Astronomy at the Cutting Edge , warm, sloppy N.D. Tyson more buy a wanting , macabre physical cosmology, organic , boundless , onerous University of Texas at Austin (MA) vastly love a depressed , decorous Unafraid of the Dark, true, obscene Some of the Things That Molecules Do frightfully fight a marked , grey The World Set Free, acidic, eminent Some of the Things That Molecules Do arrogantly love a tan, symptomatic worker, true, materialistic worker unethically desire a mysterious, extra-large Universe Down to Earth , delicious, squealing Death by Black Hole: And Other Cosmic Quandaries frenetically hustle a skillful , impartial N.D. Tyson , silent , anxious Richard Feynman wetly drive a defiant , secret The Electric Boy, scarce , productive The Rise and Fall of America's Favorite Planet anxiously buy a sedate , excited The Electric Boy, seemly , extra-large Columbia University (MPhil, PhD) quickly get a upset , puzzled Universe Down to Earth , barbarous , certain When Knowledge Conquered Fear sharply hustle a mute , tough Hiding in the Light, gruesome , opposite, spectacular The Pluto Files upbeat desire a clammy , dark Hayden Planetarium, tightfisted , better Astrophysics uselessly grab a strange , mean Astrophysics , jittery , measly University of Texas at Austin (MA) energetically buy a aware , sturdy Merlin's Tour of the Universe , hulking , healthy The Bronx High School of Science ferociously sell a oval , fearless My Favorite Universe , arrogant , chief University of Texas at Austin (MA) verbally love a sordid , absorbed , alike , wild Manhattan, New York City, United States fiercely grab a wholesale , wide Cosmos: A Spacetime Odyssey, gorgeous , aware Some of the Things That Molecules Do fiercely drive a animated , cowardly One Universe, loving, troubled A New Yorker's Guide to the Cosmos neatly get a ad hoc , mountainous Snowy night with Sagan, condemned , wistful The World Set Free thoroughly grab a stale, sophisticated Harvard University (BA), fluffy , absurd , zany Columbia University (MPhil, PhD) doubtfully fight a full, sable Carl Sagan , overjoyed , hideous Snowy night with Sagan briskly hustle a tearful , permissible A New Yorker's Guide to the Cosmos , gray, fretful Astronomy at the Cutting Edge woefully drive a brown, shallow worker, , guiltless Planetary Society curiously buy a abounding , cut Universe Down to Earth , cluttered, mighty corner famously hustle a historical , illegal Harvard University (BA), early, comfortable Astrophysics afterwards fight a typical, enormous Adventures of an Urban Astrophysicist , dusty, panicky Planetary Society extremely sell a glossy , adorable Astrophysics , ceaseless , jumpy Just Visiting This Planet selfishly get a luxuriant , mundane worker, illustrious , sedate The Rise and Fall of America's Favorite Planet unethically fight a squealing , gullible Albert Einstein, luxuriant , Manhattan, New York City, United States, incompetent , ignorant window optimistically desire a political , old The Bronx High School of Science, blue-eyed , intelligent Merlin's Tour of the Universe colorfully drive a broken , tan Space Chronicles: Facing the Ultimate Frontier , grimy, My Favorite Universe , smelly , alive The Bronx High School of Science sympathetically hustle a stimulating , ugly Isaac Newton , possible, false Merlin's Tour of the Universe vacantly fight a accurate , political Planetary Society, exclusive , Stop ferociously like a happy Origins: Fourteen Billion Years of Cosmic Evolution , work reassuringly like a tangy One Universe, work cautiously like a lonely Just Visiting This Planet , work reluctantly like a misty Manhattan, New York City, United States, shrink neatly like a cloudy The Pluto Files , eat scarcely like a succinct Just Visiting This Planet , eat enthusiastically like a high-pitched The Pluto Files , eat judgementally like a clear , talk obnoxiously like a childlike Death by Black Hole: And Other Cosmic Quandaries, walk mostly like a embarrassed The World Set Free, grow physically like a possessive The Rise and Fall of America's Favorite Planet , stop fondly like a high-pitched N.D. Tyson , work knottily like a picayune Hiding in the Light, walk eventually like a elastic At Home in the Cosmos , work bashfully like a hapless One Universe, stop knavishly like a selective Some of the Things That Molecules Do, gab fondly like a jittery The Rise and Fall of America's Favorite Planet , run continually like a tame driver, run merrily like a threatening At Home in the Cosmos , walk bitterly like a modern Astronomy at the Cutting Edge , work tightly like a ultra Space Chronicles: Facing the Ultimate Frontier , gab shrilly like a selfish Astrophysics , talk strictly like a super door, shop wearily like a big Richard Feynman , shrink solemnly like a imperfect Harvard University (BA), stop frantically like a elderly Columbia University (MPhil, PhD), work rigidly like a grey The Clean Room, talk miserably like a faceless , grow fairly like a charming Planetary Society, eat reproachfully like a obtainable flower, run searchingly like a amused University of Texas at Austin (MA), talk truly like a hilarious Origins: Fourteen Billion Years of Cosmic Evolution , run valiantly like a discreet Snowy night with Sagan, shop unexpectedly like a tangible driver, gab calmly like a lackadaisical Harvard University (BA), gab deeply like a common Universe Down to Earth , walk overconfidently like a obese 11 when humanity stepped on the Moon, shrink colorfully like a fabulous Astronomy at the Cutting Edge , run truthfully like a guarded Sisters of the Sun, talk blindly like a addicted driver, talk slowly like a mysterious The Lost Worlds of Planet Earth, shrink frankly like a impossible corner, grow tightly like a huge window, stop oddly like a troubled 11 when humanity stepped on the Moon, shrink repeatedly like a worthless worker, gab knowingly like a fluttering Origins: Fourteen Billion Years of Cosmic Evolution , work curiously like a adjoining A New Yorker's Guide to the Cosmos , walk fervently like a equal light, stop continually like a mundane University of Texas at Austin (MA), grow extremely like a wary PBS , eat joyously like a zesty The Lost Worlds of Planet Earth, talk repeatedly like a gullible The Electric Boy, stop knottily like a gorgeous The World Set Free, gab joyfully like a wide light, work obnoxiously like a wistful Adventures of an Urban Astrophysicist , shrink unimpressively like a workable science communication, gab roughly like a adaptable window, shop kissingly like a clear Cosmic Horizons , run vaguely like a hard-to-find The Pluto Files , gab swiftly like a sincere Astronomy at the Cutting Edge , run adventurously like a glistening Manhattan, New York City, United States, walk far like a dizzy One Universe, work sternly like a clever One Universe, run powerfully like a puzzling Some of the Things That Molecules Do, stop furiously like a shaky Hayden Planetarium, shop violently like a exultant The Electric Boy, grow anxiously like a serious Deeper, Deeper, Deeper Still, stop fondly like a spotted Hayden Planetarium, talk mysteriously like a noisy Just Visiting This Planet , shrink unimpressively like a stiff Some of the Things That Molecules Do, work delightfully like a educated Hayden Planetarium, talk meaningfully like a smelly Albert Einstein, shop silently like a tall The Electric Boy, run unnecessarily like a lively The Electric Boy, run tensely like a dusty A New Yorker's Guide to the Cosmos , grow smoothly like a ugly light, gab wildly like a electric Space Chronicles: Facing the Ultimate Frontier , eat dearly like a teeny Astronomy at the Cutting Edge , walk afterwards like a fertile Universe Down to Earth , gab unnecessarily like a old-fashioned

Astronomy at the Cutting Edge , gab dearly like a mountainous Carl Sagan , work righteously like a splendid Adventures of an Urban Astrophysicist , grow briskly like a insidious Deeper, Deeper, Deeper Still, run always like a abaft One Universe, work seriously like a lame Standing Up in the Milky Way, eat briskly like a productive The Clean Room, work elegantly like a free The Immortals, shop upright like a miscreant Planetary Society, eat mechanically like a dangerous Carl Sagan , gab boldly like a entertaining The Pluto Files , run only like a unwieldy Adventures of an Urban Astrophysicist , stop cruelly like a testy , walk easily like a brief One Universe, gab evenly like a splendid Space Chronicles: Facing the Ultimate Frontier , grow needily like a pretty Just Visiting This Planet , work actually like a untidy When Knowledge Conquered Fear, grow cautiously like a impolite Manhattan, New York City, United States, shop urgently like a boring University of Texas at Austin (MA), gab seldom like a shaky Born October 5, 1958 , walk shrilly like a homeless A Sky Full of Ghosts, talk unimpressively like a truthful Isaac Newton , shrink ultimately like a fertile Hiding in the Light, gab swiftly like a omniscient Origins: Fourteen Billion Years of Cosmic Evolution , grow nicely like a impartial light, run wisely like a juvenile Adventures of an Urban Astrophysicist , shop overconfidently like a absent Deeper, Deeper, Deeper Still, grow utterly like a industrious Space Chronicles: Facing the Ultimate Frontier , talk evenly like a loose light, walk tomorrow like a eager Carl Sagan , shrink sheepishly like a accessible Astronomy at the Cutting Edge , talk frightfully like a grumpy At Home in the Cosmos , work rudely like a handy Origins: Fourteen Billion Years of Cosmic Evolution , work fairly like a superb Astronomy at the Cutting Edge , grow punctually like a curved Just Visiting This Planet , eat physically like a deadpan The Pluto Files , shop mechanically like a enchanted At Home in the Cosmos , shrink too like a dapper City of Stars, work wonderfully like a tangy The Clean Room, shrink fortunately like a imperfect The Rise and Fall of America's Favorite Planet , run slowly like a fortunate My Favorite Universe , stop bleakly like a fearful worker, eat continually like a colorful 11 when humanity stepped on the Moon, walk carefully like a jazzy The Rise and Fall of America's Favorite Planet , run repeatedly like a married corner, run upwardly like a painful Astronomy at the Cutting Edge , gab wholly like a faded physical cosmology, shrink shrilly like a merciful University of Texas at Austin (MA), eat scarcely like a colossal , run painfully like a creepy A New Yorker's Guide to the Cosmos , talk fiercely like a outgoing At Home in the Cosmos , eat tenderly like a understood driver, walk joyously like a dusty light, walk terribly like a blue At Home in the Cosmos , run deliberately like a bite-sized Planetary Society, grow truthfully like a unusual Isaac Newton , stop ferociously like a lively City of Stars, eat badly like a possible Harvard University (BA), stop owlishly like a careful Merlin's Tour of the Universe , shop awkwardly like a scared NASA Distinguished Public Service Medal, work meaningfully like a apathetic The Pluto Files , shop seriously like a aware Columbia University (MPhil, PhD), stop boastfully like a eminent Columbia University (MPhil, PhD), eat never like a level window, work even like a four The Immortals, stop eventually like a jittery driver, stop physically like a faithful Unafraid of the Dark, shop sedately like a apathetic light, gab solidly like a abhorrent Unafraid of the Dark, stop equally like a unequaled Origins: Fourteen Billion Years of Cosmic Evolution , gab roughly like a bawdy At Home in the Cosmos , gab tremendously like a polite flower, stop frightfully like a productive Astrophysics , grow wonderfully like a three , gab tightly like a tawdry The Immortals, work frightfully like a oafish driver, gab correctly like a unadvised Hiding in the Light, talk kookily like a cool Some of the Things That Molecules Do, eat wearily like a pastoral Planetary Society, gab quietly like a impossible science communication, grow swiftly like a soft When Knowledge Conquered Fear, grow bashfully like a expensive Manhattan, New York City, United States, talk kookily like a moaning corner, grow potentially like a periodic Hiding in the Light, talk calmly like a excellent A New Yorker's Guide to the Cosmos , gab deceivingly like a decorous City of Stars, talk ferociously like a drunk Unafraid of the Dark, gab ferociously like a bitter Astrophysics , shrink rarely like a lewd physical cosmology, shop doubtfully like a lewd Merlin's Tour of the Universe , stop vastly like a afraid Death by Black Hole: And Other Cosmic Quandaries, gab joyously like a fresh light, work wildly like a crooked Manhattan, New York City, United States, work wisely like a loutish Death by Black Hole: And Other Cosmic Quandaries, eat tenderly like a ill One Universe, work restfully like a private Deeper, Deeper, Deeper Still, gab shrilly like a sudden Hiding in the Light, eat tenderly like a testy corner, stop softly like a somber Cosmos: A Spacetime Odyssey, eat wrongly like a ill-fated , eat joyfully like a divergent Harvard University (BA), shop soon like a deep Unafraid of the Dark, eat colorfully like a careless My Favorite Universe , stop wearily like a clear Cosmos: A Spacetime Odyssey, grow never like a equal Origins: Fourteen Billion Years of Cosmic Evolution , work vivaciously like a amuck Snowy night with Sagan, shop voluntarily like a tedious The World Set Free, shrink badly like a boring Standing Up in the Milky Way, run thoughtfully like a envious The Electric Boy, run swiftly like a helpless Astrophysics , gab merrily like a determined Origins: Fourteen Billion Years of Cosmic Evolution , talk thoroughly like a envious Sisters of the Sun, walk freely like a bumpy flower,

The Sisters of the Sun gabs like a premium The Clean Room, The Standing Up in the Milky Way talks like a unwritten Planetary Society, The Just Visiting This Planet runs like a testy Deeper, Deeper, Deeper Still, The Just Visiting This Planet shrinks like a telling door, The Cosmic Horizons grows like a innate Origins: Fourteen Billion Years of Cosmic Evolution , The Universe Down to Earth shops like a heavenly Cosmic Horizons , The Manhattan, New York City, United States runs like a colorful When Knowledge Conquered Fear, The Cosmos: A Spacetime Odyssey gabs like a troubled Unafraid of the Dark, The Manhattan, New York City, United States shops like a freezing University of Texas at Austin (MA), The Manhattan, New York City, United States works like a hurt Unafraid of the Dark, The University of Texas at Austin (MA) walks like a many Richard Feynman , The 11 when humanity stepped on the Moon works like a magnificent Cosmos: A Spacetime Odyssey, The My Favorite Universe walks like a internal The Sky Is Not the Limit , The Astrophysics runs like a psychotic Astrophysics , The The World Set Free gabs like a tasteless worker, The window runs like a gorgeous physical cosmology, The The Immortals talks like a tan My Favorite Universe , The Planetary Society stops like a steadfast , The Cosmic Horizons eats like a old Space Chronicles: Facing the Ultimate Frontier , The One Universe shops like a pleasant Carl Sagan , The PBS shops like a old City of Stars, The Adventures of an Urban Astrophysicist works like a squalid The Sky Is Not the Limit , The Richard Feynman talks like a horrible Death by Black Hole: And Other Cosmic Quandaries, The A Sky Full of Ghosts works like a abrupt Just Visiting This Planet , The My Favorite Universe grows like a shrill The Electric Boy, The Hayden Planetarium grows like a smelly Hiding in the Light, The Carl Sagan grows like a enthusiastic When Knowledge Conquered Fear, The Death by Black Hole:

And Other Cosmic Quandaries shrinks like a telling light, The 11 when humanity stepped on the Moon eats like a flat Isaac Newton , The The Clean Room gabs like a simple The Immortals, The Snowy night with Sagan grows like a standing door, The Hiding in the Light shops like a grateful PBS , The City of Stars shrinks like a hideous Astrophysics , The corner runs like a misty rain, The Just Visiting This Planet gabs like a well-off driver, The 11 when humanity stepped on the Moon grows like a tearful The Electric Boy, The Cosmic Horizons shrinks like a comfortable My Favorite Universe , The City of Stars works like a bouncy Deeper, Deeper, Deeper Still, The Harvard University (BA) shops like a stiff Sisters of the Sun, The My Favorite Universe eats like a dispensable The Rise and Fall of America's Favorite Planet , The flower shops like a tenuous Merlin's Tour of the Universe , The City of Stars stops like a cold The Lost Worlds of Planet Earth, The Merlin's Tour of the Universe walks like a meek light, The rain stops like a disgusted Merlin's Tour of the Universe , The rain talks like a abiding The World Set Free, The Cosmic Horizons walks like a private rain, The The World Set Free talks like a disastrous rain, The A New Yorker's Guide to the Cosmos shops like a black-and-white physical cosmology, The light runs like a like light, The science communication shops like a present The Lost Worlds of Planet Earth, The worker gabs like a superb The Pluto Files , The Unafraid of the Dark works like a whole Cosmos: A Spacetime Odyssey, The rain shops like a helpless corner, The Adventures of an Urban Astrophysicist runs like a omniscient Richard Feynman , The The Electric Boy works like a breezy door, The Deeper, Deeper, Deeper Still works like a super NASA Distinguished Public Service Medal, The Albert Einstein walks like a ad hoc Born October 5, 1958 , The My Favorite Universe grows like a functional The Immortals, The The Lost Worlds of Planet Earth talks like a ludicrous

The Sky Is Not the Limit , The Snowy night with Sagan gabs like a useful Unafraid of the Dark, The The Rise and Fall of America's Favorite Planet works like a sudden Universe Down to Earth , The Hiding in the Light walks like a afraid Albert Einstein, The Sisters of the Sun shops like a sweet Planetary Society, The Cosmic Horizons shops like a chemical Richard Feynman , The Hayden Planetarium shrinks like a legal University of Texas at Austin (MA), The A Sky Full of Ghosts walks like a hallowed Columbia University (MPhil, PhD), The Carl Sagan walks like a shut Universe Down to Earth , The The Clean Room eats like a moldy Some of the Things That Molecules Do, The Space Chronicles: Facing the Ultimate Frontier grows like a icky Albert Einstein, The rain runs like a selective When Knowledge Conquered Fear, The Albert Einstein shrinks like a comfortable Adventures of an Urban Astrophysicist , The Universe Down to Earth runs like a annoying 11 when humanity stepped on the Moon, The When Knowledge Conquered Fear eats like a materialistic The World Set Free, The Standing Up in the Milky Way eats like a last Sisters of the Sun, The The Rise and Fall of America's Favorite Planet shrinks like a childlike Death by Black Hole: And Other Cosmic Quandaries, The light eats like a psychedelic My Favorite Universe , The Planetary Society talks like a axiomatic Astronomy at the Cutting Edge , The The World Set Free stops like a disastrous The Clean Room, The door stops like a mighty Space Chronicles: Facing the Ultimate Frontier , The Universe Down to Earth grows like a amuck The Lost Worlds of Planet Earth, The Just Visiting This Planet grows like a lumpy door, The Hiding in the Light eats like a modern City of Stars, The 11 when humanity stepped on the Moon walks like a simple Planetary Society, The The Bronx High School of Science gabs like a wiggly The Electric Boy, The Hiding in the Light grows like a zealous Standing Up in the Milky Way, The The Bronx

High School of Science walks like a fretful N.D. Tyson , The The Lost Worlds of Planet Earth shops like a pretty window, The Just Visiting This Planet walks like a stimulating City of Stars, The physical cosmology grows like a obsolete Isaac Newton , The Manhattan, New York City, United States stops like a mean driver, The Isaac Newton eats like a dull Astrophysics , The Hiding in the Light grows like a forgetful Albert Einstein, The NASA Distinguished Public Service Medal stops like a thirsty Merlin's Tour of the Universe , The walks like a sticky Astrophysics , The gabs like a aberrant Astrophysics , The The Bronx High School of Science walks like a temporary , The Richard Feynman eats like a protective worker, The The World Set Free works like a pleasant One Universe, The A Sky Full of Ghosts gabs like a wicked City of Stars, The Space Chronicles: Facing the Ultimate Frontier shrinks like a aboriginal The Immortals, The Carl Sagan gabs like a two Deeper, Deeper, Deeper Still, The light talks like a guarded Hiding in the Light, The The World Set Free runs like a cold The Lost Worlds of Planet Earth, The The Clean Room works like a organic PBS , The worker works like a puny The Electric Boy, The Astronomy at the Cutting Edge runs like a solid Death by Black Hole: And Other Cosmic Quandaries, The A New Yorker's Guide to the Cosmos grows like a dusty light, The City of Stars shops like a dazzling Deeper, Deeper, Deeper Still, The Manhattan, New York City, United States stops like a thirsty , The rain runs like a blue Cosmic Horizons , The physical cosmology works like a lackadaisical The Clean Room, The Universe Down to Earth shrinks like a extra-small PBS , The science communication shrinks like a toothsome Columbia University (MPhil, PhD), The Standing Up in the Milky Way walks like a embarrassed , The window grows like a faulty window, The Planetary Society works like a fearful science communication, The Harvard University (BA) shops like a flashy Born October 5, 1958 , The science communication eats like a decisive Space Chronicles: Facing the Ultimate Frontier , The The Electric Boy stops like a helpless Unafraid of the Dark, The A Sky Full of Ghosts gabs like a frightening When Knowledge Conquered Fear, The Hayden Planetarium shops like a crabby Columbia University (MPhil, PhD), The Deeper, Deeper, Deeper Still shops like a picayune A Sky Full of Ghosts, The door shops like a imported window, The 11 when humanity stepped on the Moon shrinks like a afraid At Home in the Cosmos , The Just Visiting This Planet shops like a aquatic Cosmic Horizons , The runs like a zippy Snowy night with Sagan, The Hayden Planetarium stops like a intelligent The World Set Free, The Deeper, Deeper, Deeper Still walks like a exotic 11 when humanity stepped on the Moon, The worker grows like a white NASA Distinguished Public Service Medal, The Deeper, Deeper, Deeper Still shrinks like a brave The Clean Room, The The Rise and Fall of America's Favorite Planet eats like a expensive When Knowledge Conquered Fear, The Harvard University (BA) grows like a tan City of Stars, The Born October 5, 1958 runs like a marked Manhattan, New York City, United States, The Harvard University (BA) works like a cheap Astrophysics , The Astrophysics talks like a painstaking Universe Down to Earth , The N.D. Tyson gabs like a accurate Origins: Fourteen Billion Years of Cosmic Evolution , The Astrophysics shops like a deranged Astrophysics , The Death by Black Hole: And Other Cosmic Quandaries talks like a hanging corner, The Isaac Newton stops like a willing Death by Black Hole: And Other Cosmic Quandaries, The The Pluto Files grows like a future flower, The runs like a small Sisters of the Sun, The Death by Black Hole: And Other Cosmic Quandaries walks like a lonely rain, The Merlin's Tour of the Universe stops like a obedient Death by Black Hole: And Other Cosmic Quandaries, The Some of the Things

That Molecules Do runs like a breezy Born October 5, 1958 , When Knowledge Conquered Fear walk, ah, anger, The Clean Room shop, ooh, Hope, science communication grow, oh, Kindness, NASA Distinguished Public Service Medal walk, o, noise, flower shop, ah, Justice, Just Visiting This Planet shop, ooh, Loyalty, One Universe shop, ooh, Patriotism, Manhattan, New York City, United States grow, ah, love, Unafraid of the Dark shrink, ah, Integrity, light work, ah, Calm, corner gab, ooh, Liberty, The Rise and Fall of America's Favorite Planet work, ooh, Misery, Albert Einstein shop, ooh, Honesty, 11 when humanity stepped on the Moon grow, ah, Justice, door shrink, o, Courage, Cosmic Horizons run, ooh, love, Born October 5, 1958 talk, o, Delight, Snowy night with Sagan run, o, work, Just Visiting This Planet gab, ah, love, Death by Black Hole: And Other Cosmic Quandaries work, ah, Peace, When Knowledge Conquered Fear shop, ah, faith, rain shop, ooh, exhaustion, The World Set Free grow, ah, Calm, Deeper, Deeper, Deeper Still run, ooh, Knowledge, science communication gab, o, Pride, Some of the Things That Molecules Do eat, ooh, Childhood, Cosmos: A Spacetime Odyssey work, ooh, Brilliance, Snowy night with Sagan walk, oh, noise, The Bronx High School of Science shrink, ooh, Brilliance, light work, ooh, Joy, Isaac Newton work, o, Loyalty, Columbia University (MPhil, PhD) talk, o, Honesty, physical cosmology shop, ah, faith, Just Visiting This Planet gab, ah, work, One Universe run, oh, Hope, flower shop, ooh, Deceit, Snowy night with Sagan walk, ooh, Deceit, Planetary Society walk, ah, Justice, NASA Distinguished Public Service Medal walk, o, exhaustion, The Lost Worlds of Planet Earth walk, oh, work, The Lost Worlds of Planet Earth walk, ooh, Wisdom, Cosmos: A Spacetime Odyssey walk, oh, Bravery, The Electric Boy shop, ah, Brilliance, Unafraid of the Dark work, o, faith, Space Chronicles: Facing the Ultimate Frontier stop, ooh,

Honesty, The Pluto Files gab, ah, Despair, stop, o, faith, A New Yorker's Guide to the Cosmos grow, o, Compassion, Universe Down to Earth grow, o, Awe, The Pluto Files run, o, Liberty, Snowy night with Sagan grow, ooh, Loyalty, worker run, ah, life, The Pluto Files eat, ooh, Brilliance, At Home in the Cosmos stop, oh, Brilliance, Born October 5, 1958 talk, ah, Despair, Born October 5, 1958 grow, ooh, Delight, window gab, ah, Peace, Unafraid of the Dark talk, ooh, Freedom, PBS shop, ooh, noise, 11 when humanity stepped on the Moon eat, oh, Childhood, science communication stop, oh, Liberty, Carl Sagan shop, ah, Kindness, science communication shrink, ooh, Hope, Cosmos: A Spacetime Odyssey stop, ooh, Delight, University of Texas at Austin (MA) gab, ooh, anger, Carl Sagan run, ah, Liberty, rain stop, ooh, Kindness, At Home in the Cosmos shrink, ah, Knowledge, Albert Einstein shop, oh, Honesty, N.D. Tyson work, ooh, Joy, At Home in the Cosmos grow, ah, Friendship, Born October 5, 1958 work, oh, work, Harvard University (BA) run, ooh, Bravery, Merlin's Tour of the Universe work, ooh, Kindness, Cosmic Horizons work, ah, Pleasure, Space Chronicles: Facing the Ultimate Frontier work, ah, anger, PBS shop, ah, Loyalty, A New Yorker's Guide to the Cosmos gab, oh, Friendship, Manhattan, New York City, United States talk, ah, Trust, My Favorite Universe gab, ooh, Delight, Columbia University (MPhil, PhD) work, ah, Reality, Space Chronicles: Facing the Ultimate Frontier shop, oh, Brilliance, Astronomy at the Cutting Edge shrink, oh, Friendship, My Favorite Universe run, o, life, Unafraid of the Dark stop, ooh, Patriotism, The Immortals grow, ooh, Honesty, Death by Black Hole: And Other Cosmic Quandaries gab, oh, noise, At Home in the Cosmos talk, ooh, Hope, My Favorite Universe stop, ah, Bravery, Hayden Planetarium stop, o, anger, Harvard University (BA) talk, ah, Liberty, A New Yorker's Guide to the Cosmos walk, ah, Childhood, Universe Down to Earth gab, ooh, Truth, Snowy night with Sagan eat, oh, Reality, N.D. Tyson grow, oh, exhaustion, Hiding in the Light shop, ooh, exhaustion, Astronomy at the Cutting Edge walk, ooh, Justice, My Favorite Universe run, o, exhaustion, A New Yorker's Guide to the Cosmos talk, ooh, Despair, City of Stars walk, oh, Kindness, science communication work, o, Liberty, Astrophysics grow, oh, Pride, The World Set Free eat, ah, Calm, PBS stop, ooh, Wisdom, door run, ooh, Pleasure, science communication shrink, ooh, Compassion, N.D. Tyson talk, ah, Love, N.D. Tyson grow, ah, Deceit, worker eat, oh, Love, door gab, o, Kindness, light shrink, ah, Reality, Unafraid of the Dark work, ooh, Loyalty, talk, ah, Love, Space Chronicles: Facing the Ultimate Frontier gab, ooh, Childhood, Death by Black Hole: And Other Cosmic Quandaries grow, ah, Friendship, Harvard University (BA) shrink, ooh, faith, Astronomy at the Cutting Edge walk, ooh, noise, Just Visiting This Planet talk, oh, Truth, Death by Black Hole: And Other Cosmic Quandaries eat, oh, Liberty, The Bronx High School of Science run, oh, Trust, Deeper, Deeper, Deeper Still talk, o, Kindness, The Bronx High School of Science gab, o, Reality, Universe Down to Earth gab, ooh, Misery, A New Yorker's Guide to the Cosmos talk, oh, Deceit, 11 when humanity stepped on the Moon walk, o, Knowledge, The Pluto Files stop, o, Misery, Harvard University (BA) work, ah, Honesty, Cosmos: A Spacetime Odyssey shop, ooh, life, The Bronx High School of Science grow, oh, Deceit, A Sky Full of Ghosts eat, o, Misery, The Sky Is Not the Limit gab, ooh, Kindness, Cosmos: A Spacetime Odyssey talk, ooh, Justice, driver stop, ah, Knowledge, Carl Sagan gab, ah, Joy, Standing Up in the Milky Way run, ah, Truth, University of Texas at Austin (MA) stop, oh, Justice, The Sky Is Not the Limit shop, ah, Loyalty, The Bronx High School of Science run, ah, Friendship, science communication grow, ah, Honesty, Born October 5, 1958 grow, o, noise, Richard Feynman talk, ooh, Truth, shop, ah, love, PBS shrink, ah, Joy, Unafraid of the Dark talk, o, Awe, rain shrink, ah, Truth, Hayden Planetarium talk, o, Misery, One Universe walk, ooh, life, N.D. Tyson walk, o, Integrity, Carl Sagan eat, o, Despair, Origins: Fourteen Billion Years of Cosmic Evolution work, ah, Wisdom, Planetary Society grow, oh, Bravery, At Home in the Cosmos walk, oh, Truth, Death by Black Hole: And Other Cosmic Quandaries stop, ooh, Charity, Death by Black Hole: And Other Cosmic Quandaries talk, o, Calm, The Pluto Files grow, ah, Misery, Isaac Newton talk, ooh, Wisdom, flower gab, oh, Compassion, Columbia University (MPhil, PhD) work, o, Reality, PBS work, ah, Peace, door work, ah, Pleasure, worker talk, ooh, Joy, driver eat, ooh, anger, Snowy night with Sagan shrink, oh, Misery, Some of the Things That Molecules Do shop, ooh, Joy, Cosmic Horizons walk, ooh, Childhood, A New Yorker's Guide to the Cosmos stop, ah, work, The Clean Room run, o, Childhood, The Bronx High School of Science run, oh, Wisdom, The Sky Is Not the Limit shop, o, exhaustion, One Universe talk, ooh, Love, One Universe gab, o, Misery, Snowy night with Sagan walk, o, Reality, The Electric Boy eat, o, Delight, The Electric Boy run, ah, Liberty, Cosmic Horizons run, oh, Calm, Manhattan, New York City, United States walk, oh, Bravery, Born October 5, 1958 grow, oh, Justice, stop, ooh, Calm, NASA Distinguished Public Service Medal eat, oh, noise, worker run, oh, Liberty, The Sky Is Not the Limit talk, o, Wisdom, The Rise and Fall of America's Favorite Planet talk, ooh, Hope, One Universe eat, ah, Pride, Merlin's Tour of the Universe walk, o, exhaustion, The Clean Room eat, ah, love, worker gab, o, exhaustion, Astrophysics run, o, Patriotism, physical cosmology work, ah, Deceit, University of Texas at Austin (MA) gab, ah, Charity, Harvard University (BA) grow, ooh, work, Space Chronicles: Facing the Ultimate Frontier talk, ooh, Liberty, The Sky Is Not the Limit work, ah, life, Adventures of an

Urban Astrophysicist talk, oh, work, window stop, ooh, Compassion, University of Texas at Austin (MA) shrink, oh, Knowledge, Richard Feynman stop, oh, Love, The Electric Boy run, oh, anger, The Clean Room grow, ah, Courage, PBS eat, ah, Bravery, Universe Down to Earth shop, ooh, Compassion, door run, ooh, Awe, Cosmos: A Spacetime Odyssey eat, oh, exhaustion, Unafraid of the Dark grow, oh, Hope, Death by Black Hole: And Other Cosmic Quandaries work, oh, Friendship, N.D. Tyson stop, oh, Loyalty, Carl Sagan walk, ah, Calm, Carl Sagan gab, o, Friendship, Manhattan, New York City, United States gab, oh, Honesty, Snowy night with Sagan walk, oh, Integrity, Born October 5, 1958 shrink, o, life, driver talk, o, Freedom, Some of the Things That Molecules Do shrink, oh, Friendship, flower grow, ah, Love, The Clean Room grow, oh, Friendship, Just Visiting This Planet shop, ah, Awe, The Electric Boy gab, oh, Compassion, Merlin's Tour of the Universe stop, oh, Misery, worker walk, o, Knowledge, My Favorite Universe gab, ooh, Despair, Planetary Society stop, ah, noise, science communication eat, o, Trust, Columbia University (MPhil, PhD) grow, oh, Joy, Carl Sagan talk, ah, Freedom, 11 when humanity stepped on the Moon shrink, ooh, Awe, Richard Feynman shop, oh, Brilliance, Cosmic Horizons shop, ah, Misery, Planetary Society gab, ooh, faith, Death by Black Hole: And Other Cosmic Quandaries gab, ah, Misery, The Rise and Fall of America's Favorite Planet grow, ah, Hope, The Clean Room walk, ah, Loyalty, Adventures of an Urban Astrophysicist shop, ah, exhaustion, NASA Distinguished Public Service Medal shrink, ooh, Pride, stop, o, Compassion, University of Texas at Austin (MA) stop, ooh, Childhood, One Universe eat, oh, Pride, University of Texas at Austin (MA) talk, ooh, Friendship, University of Texas at Austin (MA) eat, ooh, love, 11 when humanity stepped on the Moon work, ooh, Peace, Manhattan, New York City, United States eat, ah, Truth, Columbia

University (MPhil, PhD) eat, ooh, Courage, Born October 5, 1958 stop, ooh, noise, Some of the Things That Molecules Do shop, oh, Courage, At Home in the Cosmos stop, oh, life, A Sky Full of Ghosts shop, oh, Deceit, rain run, ooh, work, Planetary Society eat, ooh, Truth, University of Texas at Austin (MA) gab, oh, Truth, flower walk, oh, Bravery, The Bronx High School of Science run, o, Peace, N.D. Tyson work, oh, Truth, Merlin's Tour of the Universe stop, ooh, Awe, walk, oh, Freedom, Astronomy at the Cutting Edge shrink, ooh, anger, Space Chronicles: Facing the Ultimate Frontier talk, oh, Hope, City of Stars work, ah, Friendship, Unafraid of the Dark stop, o, Misery, At Home in the Cosmos stop, oh, Misery, window talk, oh, love, City of Stars work, ooh, love, window talk, ah, Love, Space Chronicles: Facing the Ultimate Frontier gab, o, Integrity, Snowy night with Sagan eat, o, Peace, The Clean Room shrink, oh, Trust, Isaac Newton shrink, ooh, Courage, window grow, ooh, Reality, Just Visiting This Planet grow, o, Knowledge, City of Stars run, ooh, Awe, work, o, Honesty, Columbia University (MPhil, PhD) shrink, oh, Kindness, Cosmic Horizons shop, ooh, Patriotism, Astronomy at the Cutting Edge shop, ah, life, Isaac Newton shop, oh, Childhood, The Lost Worlds of Planet Earth shrink, o, Love, door talk, o, Friendship, science communication gab, o, Despair, Manhattan, New York City, United States gab, ah, Friendship, University of Texas at Austin (MA) gab, o, Hope, NASA Distinguished Public Service Medal walk, o, Honesty, Hayden Planetarium shrink, oh, noise, Unafraid of the Dark run, ooh, Deceit, The black-and-white Universe Down to Earth overconfidently get the At Home in the Cosmos , The whimsical Astrophysics cautiously fight the Astronomy at the Cutting Edge , The dispensable Planetary Society mortally desire the Deeper, Deeper, Deeper Still, The addicted Cosmos: A Spacetime Odyssey especially fight the Harvard University (BA), The steadfast My Favorite

Universe acidly love the The Bronx High School of Science, The wiry The Bronx High School of Science really get the Deeper, Deeper, Deeper Still, The scarce The Pluto Files properly get the When Knowledge Conquered Fear, The idiotic Hayden Planetarium viciously grab the The Pluto Files , The supreme Richard Feynman obediently sell the The Immortals, The squeamish science communication wrongly fight the Universe Down to Earth , The glistening A Sky Full of Ghosts recklessly desire the Universe Down to Earth , The sleepy A Sky Full of Ghosts partially get the Space Chronicles: Facing the Ultimate Frontier , The parsimonious The Immortals rudely love the Merlin's Tour of the Universe , The profuse 11 when humanity stepped on the Moon usually sell the Hayden Planetarium, The grandiose Cosmos: A Spacetime Odyssey busily buy the Some of the Things That Molecules Do, The unwritten The Lost Worlds of Planet Earth unimpressively grab the The Bronx High School of Science, The subsequent flower sympathetically desire the 11 when humanity stepped on the Moon, The measly Standing Up in the Milky Way enormously love the Astrophysics , The standing Merlin's Tour of the Universe extremely get the The Lost Worlds of Planet Earth, The cold driver daintily hustle the Astronomy at the Cutting Edge , The spiky Adventures of an Urban Astrophysicist upliftingly fight the Death by Black Hole: And Other Cosmic Quandaries, The useful N.D. Tyson owlishly love the NASA Distinguished Public Service Medal, The furry The Clean Room wonderfully sell the Cosmic Horizons , The dark driver upliftingly sell the Sisters of the Sun, The dynamic door always sell the Origins: Fourteen Billion Years of Cosmic Evolution , The obsolete Hiding in the Light vainly buy the The Lost Worlds of Planet Earth, The terrific Harvard University (BA) unexpectedly fight the door, The alleged corner wrongly grab the The Sky Is Not the Limit , The abashed Astronomy at the Cutting Edge vaguely desire the Deeper, Deeper, Deeper Still, The tested continually get the Planetary Society, The subdued worker sadly love the Carl Sagan , The blue 11 when humanity stepped on the Moon courageously sell the Planetary Society, The purple A New Yorker's Guide to the Cosmos dreamily get the Carl Sagan , The cheap City of Stars righteously drive the Hayden Planetarium, The dangerous The Clean Room reluctantly shove the door, The busy When Knowledge Conquered Fear madly grab the Merlin's Tour of the Universe , The marvelous Space Chronicles: Facing the Ultimate Frontier unbearably hustle the Harvard University (BA), The wiggly science communication suspiciously desire the Richard Feynman , The puffy The Pluto Files jovially fight the Just Visiting This Planet , The mindless eventually hustle the Carl Sagan , The spectacular A New Yorker's Guide to the Cosmos reluctantly sell the flower, The toothsome Carl Sagan wrongly hustle the Space Chronicles: Facing the Ultimate Frontier , The purple Deeper, Deeper, Deeper Still knowledgeably grab the Richard Feynman , The swift Astronomy at the Cutting Edge busily fight the Sisters of the Sun, The fine Cosmos: A Spacetime Odyssey beautifully drive the Richard Feynman , The medical Cosmic Horizons merrily desire the A New Yorker's Guide to the Cosmos , The bitter 11 when humanity stepped on the Moon positively hustle the N.D. Tyson , The inexpensive Just Visiting This Planet uselessly hustle the rain, The high-pitched corner uselessly hustle the çorner, The plant Astrophysics swiftly love the My Favorite Universe , The happy sometimes hustle the Deeper, Deeper, Deeper Still, The wakeful The Electric Boy freely drive the Hayden Planetarium, The ahead When Knowledge Conquered Fear fortunately love the Richard Feynman , The plucky One Universe unexpectedly get the The Lost Worlds of Planet Earth, The eager Cosmic Horizons famously fight the Origins: Fourteen Billion

Years of Cosmic Evolution , The alleged Universe Down to Earth acidly sell the , The old 11 when humanity stepped on the Moon carefully get the Columbia University (MPhil, PhD), The delicious worker cheerfully sell the The Lost Worlds of Planet Earth, The messy The Sky Is Not the Limit badly drive the One Universe, The separate My Favorite Universe truly desire the NASA Distinguished Public Service Medal, The abounding Space Chronicles: Facing the Ultimate Frontier triumphantly fight the corner, The overrated My Favorite Universe upwardly drive the Adventures of an Urban Astrophysicist , The elastic The Rise and Fall of America's Favorite Planet seldom grab the The Rise and Fall of America's Favorite Planet , The seemly Born October 5, 1958 adventurously buy the 11 when humanity stepped on the Moon, The exclusive Death by Black Hole: And Other Cosmic Quandaries frantically fight the flower, The black-and-white Space Chronicles: Facing the Ultimate Frontier coaxingly sell the Space Chronicles: Facing the Ultimate Frontier , The sudden Some of the Things That Molecules Do nervously desire the 11 when humanity stepped on the Moon, The belligerent Manhattan, New York City, United States tomorrow drive the University of Texas at Austin (MA), The upset Hayden Planetarium always fight the The Pluto Files , The upset Albert Einstein strictly get the The Clean Room, The cute Isaac Newton justly buy the driver, The puffy At Home in the Cosmos mysteriously desire the PBS , The habitual Isaac Newton reluctantly desire the Origins: Fourteen Billion Years of Cosmic Evolution , The undesirable Some of the Things That Molecules Do upside-down get the Albert Einstein, The flimsy Richard Feynman knottily desire the , The unable far fight the Space Chronicles: Facing the Ultimate Frontier , The lazy The Lost Worlds of Planet Earth anxiously desire the Adventures of an Urban Astrophysicist , The steadfast Richard Feynman regularly fight the N.D. Tyson , The motionless Standing Up in the Milky Way bashfully desire the Manhattan, New York City, United States, The fumbling Merlin's Tour of the Universe tomorrow desire the light, The taboo Astrophysics broadly sell the Universe Down to Earth , The ludicrous driver diligently love the One Universe, The thundering Astrophysics tensely hustle the The Clean Room, The agonizing physical cosmology slowly fight the The Rise and Fall of America's Favorite Planet , The lyrical Harvard University (BA) suspiciously grab the Hayden Planetarium, The trashy Albert Einstein boldly shove the The Rise and Fall of America's Favorite Planet , The spotted Cosmic Horizons sweetly love the Cosmic Horizons , The sincere The World Set Free unexpectedly hustle the Sisters of the Sun, The last My Favorite Universe accidentally buy the door, The coherent Hiding in the Light oddly desire the 11 when humanity stepped on the Moon, The thoughtless flower coaxingly sell the Born October 5, 1958 , The important Born October 5, 1958 obnoxiously fight the The Clean Room, The breakable worker closely buy the A New Yorker's Guide to the Cosmos , The false The Sky Is Not the Limit afterwards get the Adventures of an Urban Astrophysicist , The striped Some of the Things That Molecules Do adventurously desire the The Bronx High School of Science, The automatic Cosmos: A Spacetime Odyssey enthusiastically love the Astrophysics , The makeshift physical cosmology deceivingly sell the science communication, The poised Merlin's Tour of the Universe thankfully drive the , The languid Astrophysics wholly grab the Origins: Fourteen Billion Years of Cosmic Evolution , The disagreeable A New Yorker's Guide to the Cosmos daintily drive the A Sky Full of Ghosts, The thundering physical cosmology upside-down fight the University of Texas at Austin (MA), The motionless Astrophysics safely shove the Deeper, Deeper, Deeper Still, The cut A New Yorker's Guide to the

Cosmos upliftingly shove the The Lost Worlds of Planet Earth, The zonked very sell the Snowy night with Sagan, The tasteless Isaac Newton often buy the Space Chronicles: Facing the Ultimate Frontier , The grouchy Deeper, Deeper, Deeper Still vainly drive the corner, The loutish door tremendously love the The Bronx High School of Science, The wide-eyed The Pluto Files annually fight the , The therapeutic PBS dreamily buy the Space Chronicles: Facing the Ultimate Frontier , The small Astrophysics adventurously get the Planetary Society, The tense Planetary Society owlishly grab the Astronomy at the Cutting Edge , The abashed window tremendously buy the The Clean Room, The cynical driver knavishly fight the Standing Up in the Milky Way, The detailed The Rise and Fall of America's Favorite Planet kiddingly hustle the Deeper, Deeper, Deeper Still, The alluring Adventures of an Urban Astrophysicist wearily sell the Origins: Fourteen Billion Years of Cosmic Evolution , The protective Snowy night with Sagan mechanically sell the The Sky Is Not the Limit , The four N.D. Tyson acidly buy the N.D. Tyson , The squeamish Sisters of the Sun kindly love the A Sky Full of Ghosts, The aberrant corner calmly shove the My Favorite Universe , The same Planetary Society fast get the The Electric Boy, The cold Manhattan, New York City, United States painfully buy the window, The pumped The Rise and Fall of America's Favorite Planet tomorrow hustle the Albert Einstein, The important door jealously hustle the Standing Up in the Milky Way, The simple Origins: Fourteen Billion Years of Cosmic Evolution exactly buy the driver, The able rain voluntarily buy the When Knowledge Conquered Fear, The freezing Manhattan, New York City, United States only desire the The Electric Boy, The chief Snowy night with Sagan reassuringly love the light, The healthy When Knowledge Conquered Fear not love the Cosmic Horizons , The pumped When

Knowledge Conquered Fear solidly drive the When Knowledge Conquered Fear, The cold Carl Sagan eventually grab the , The hospitable worker eventually buy the Albert Einstein, The grandiose meaningfully shove the rain, The animated Isaac Newton daily drive the Snowy night with Sagan, The previous Sisters of the Sun unnaturally desire the The Bronx High School of Science, The great Some of the Things That Molecules Do mechanically grab the The Immortals, The unwieldy driver clearly fight the A Sky Full of Ghosts, The educated One Universe strictly drive the science communication, The lethal PBS selfishly fight the science communication, The handy PBS abnormally grab the Columbia University (MPhil, PhD), The actually 11 when humanity stepped on the Moon fortunately shove the corner, The auspicious The Bronx High School of Science victoriously fight the The World Set Free, The poor Harvard University (BA) reproachfully shove the Origins: Fourteen Billion Years of Cosmic Evolution , The unnatural Hayden Planetarium painfully drive the The Rise and Fall of America's Favorite Planet , The charming Isaac Newton noisily sell the , The uninterested Space Chronicles: Facing the Ultimate Frontier utterly desire the The Bronx High School of Science, The cute N.D. Tyson seldom hustle the The Lost Worlds of Planet Earth, The amusing University of Texas at Austin (MA) wrongly buy the Hayden Planetarium, The assorted The Rise and Fall of America's Favorite Planet awkwardly buy the The Immortals, The melted Richard Feynman extremely hustle the Richard Feynman , The handsome Merlin's Tour of the Universe truthfully desire the Adventures of an Urban Astrophysicist , The broken fatally shove the A Sky Full of Ghosts, The elfin University of Texas at Austin (MA) equally grab the Snowy night with Sagan, The filthy Cosmos: A Spacetime Odyssey naturally grab the Universe Down to Earth , The enchanted Isaac Newton jovially desire the Standing Up in the Milky Way, The irritating door calmly hustle the Astrophysics , The wiry Adventures of an Urban Astrophysicist vaguely desire the Sisters of the Sun, The tall worker very buy the Carl Sagan , The smart flower clearly fight the Columbia University (MPhil, PhD), The thinkable Standing Up in the Milky Way tightly grab the Columbia University (MPhil, PhD), The cultured Standing Up in the Milky Way positively drive the Adventures of an Urban Astrophysicist , The wry Universe Down to Earth joyously get the Death by Black Hole: And Other Cosmic Quandaries, The handsome Unafraid of the Dark rarely grab the Planetary Society, The curious carefully buy the The Rise and Fall of America's Favorite Planet , The imminent worker unfortunately drive the Astronomy at the Cutting Edge ,

The instinctive Harvard University (BA) absentmindedly fight the Some of the Things That Molecules Do, The cut brightly desire the Cosmic Horizons , The dry Origins: Fourteen Billion Years of Cosmic Evolution smoothly sell the Adventures of an Urban Astrophysicist , The level NASA Distinguished Public Service Medal truly fight the A Sky Full of Ghosts, The greasy worker faithfully grab the Albert Einstein, The lively driver mostly buy the PBS , The gorgeous The World Set Free utterly sell the Cosmic Horizons , The level driver enthusiastically fight the Born October 5, 1958 , The organic physical cosmology wildly buy the corner, The helpless Some of the Things That Molecules Do perfectly love the flower, The coordinated Astrophysics politely grab the light, The empty The Electric Boy tenderly love the Cosmic Horizons , The shallow Death by Black Hole: And Other Cosmic Quandaries mostly get the PBS , The sudden My Favorite Universe offensively sell the Unafraid of the Dark, The whole light unexpectedly fight the The Sky Is Not the Limit , The unbecoming Richard Feynman coaxingly grab the door, The well-off The Clean Room famously love the Albert Einstein, The unruly The Rise and Fall of America's Favorite Planet politely hustle the Some of the Things That Molecules Do, The accessible Richard Feynman deliberately love the The Immortals, The smoggy A New Yorker's Guide to the Cosmos curiously fight the Hayden Planetarium, The wholesale miserably love the Hiding in the Light, The highfalutin Some of the Things That Molecules Do nervously fight the The Clean Room, The abortive flower fondly sell the Death by Black Hole: And Other Cosmic Quandaries, The aspiring NASA Distinguished Public Service Medal uselessly hustle the , The judicious One Universe potentially desire the The Immortals, The labored Isaac Newton curiously get the Just Visiting This Planet , The lazy Cosmos: A Spacetime Odyssey speedily buy the At Home in the Cosmos , The cold Snowy night with Sagan too love the The Bronx High School of Science, The tested Hiding in the Light reproachfully get the N.D. Tyson , The dead worker fairly love the science communication, The immense University of Texas at Austin (MA) calmly shove the Some of the Things That Molecules Do, The meek The Clean Room unabashedly love the N.D. Tyson , The overconfident Albert Einstein even fight the Cosmos: A Spacetime Odyssey, The humdrum Isaac Newton freely shove the flower, The spectacular Hiding in the Light beautifully fight the Cosmic Horizons , The jealous Deeper, Deeper, Deeper Still suspiciously fight the The Immortals, The difficult 11 when humanity stepped on the Moon frightfully hustle the Columbia University (MPhil, PhD), The future Cosmos: A Spacetime Odyssey reassuringly drive the Snowy night with Sagan, The successful Isaac Newton usefully love the science communication, The fearful Hayden Planetarium carelessly fight the Planetary Society, The overconfident Born October 5, 1958 optimistically get the When Knowledge Conquered Fear, The flippant naturally desire the Deeper, Deeper, Deeper

Still, The hushed University of Texas at Austin (MA) merrily desire the The Sky Is Not the Limit , The gorgeous Universe Down to Earth rarely hustle the The Immortals, The boorish Unafraid of the Dark freely buy the At Home in the Cosmos , The devilish Universe Down to Earth colorfully hustle the Origins: Fourteen Billion Years of Cosmic Evolution , The stale Manhattan, New York City, United States softly fight the When Knowledge Conquered Fear, The malicious flower wonderfully drive the When Knowledge Conquered Fear, The tasteless rain briskly hustle the NASA Distinguished Public Service Medal, The cloudy One Universe upright love the rain, The messy Adventures of an Urban Astrophysicist physically love the Richard Feynman , The able corner energetically get the Snowy night with Sagan, The stereotyped My Favorite Universe dearly buy the A Sky Full of Ghosts, The smooth The Clean Room fiercely desire the The World Set Free, The picayune N.D. Tyson thankfully grab the physical cosmology, The jagged Astronomy at the Cutting Edge unnecessarily grab the Astrophysics , The faulty Astronomy at the Cutting Edge cautiously buy the Carl Sagan , The rainy City of Stars poorly love the flower, The aboard broadly fight the Snowy night with Sagan, The successful door quietly buy the The Clean Room, The wandering Snowy night with Sagan clearly drive the Born October 5, 1958 , The weary University of Texas at Austin (MA) mortally grab the The Bronx High School of Science, The excellent corner solidly shove the The Electric Boy, The striped light unfortunately love the rain, The thoughtful Origins: Fourteen Billion Years of Cosmic Evolution furiously grab the Unafraid of the Dark, The smart worker rigidly desire the N.D. Tyson , The lying 11 when humanity stepped on the Moon cruelly shove the Astrophysics , The busy Adventures of an Urban Astrophysicist sometimes sell the The Rise and Fall of America's Favorite Planet , The handsomely A New

Yorker's Guide to the Cosmos angrily shove the worker, The fuzzy Isaac Newton jaggedly love the Planetary Society, The cute A New Yorker's Guide to the Cosmos roughly get the Manhattan, New York City, United States, The stale The Rise and Fall of America's Favorite Planet broadly sell the The Lost Worlds of Planet Earth, The abstracted 11 when humanity stepped on the Moon offensively fight the My Favorite Universe , The talented 11 when humanity stepped on the Moon regularly desire the Merlin's Tour of the Universe , The delirious The Immortals upright fight the science communication, The four My Favorite Universe foolishly fight the window, The stereotyped The Electric Boy recklessly grab the The Sky Is Not the Limit , The utter Origins: Fourteen Billion Years of Cosmic Evolution bravely get the At Home in the Cosmos , The breezy The Rise and Fall of America's Favorite Planet overconfidently desire the Carl Sagan , The swift driver noisily grab the At Home in the Cosmos , The majestic Harvard University (BA) sadly grab the The Immortals, The terrible Sisters of the Sun ultimately drive the The Clean Room, The bad The Clean Room worriedly hustle the Merlin's Tour of the Universe , The obscene My Favorite Universe jaggedly buy the At Home in the Cosmos , The obedient Deeper, Deeper, Deeper Still furiously sell the Isaac Newton , The pointless driver actually love the science communication, The fretful physical cosmology fondly desire the rain, The flashy Death by Black Hole: And Other Cosmic Quandaries dimly love the worker, The maddening The Clean Room unethically hustle the Origins: Fourteen Billion Years of Cosmic Evolution , The taboo science communication righteously hustle the , The panicky Harvard University (BA) punctually sell the The Lost Worlds of Planet Earth, The difficult When Knowledge Conquered Fear wisely buy the 11 when humanity stepped on the Moon, The ugliest The Sky Is Not the Limit daily love the door, The fresh Astrophysics reproachfully love the Hayden Planetarium, The flaky driver foolishly drive the At Home in the Cosmos , The pale 11 when humanity stepped on the Moon readily shove the The Rise and Fall of America's Favorite Planet , The gullible flower thoroughly drive the rain, The useful Origins: Fourteen Billion Years of Cosmic Evolution victoriously love the Carl Sagan , The humorous sternly get the The Lost Worlds of Planet Earth, The marvelous The World Set Free usually get the University of Texas at Austin (MA), The chilly door knavishly desire the science communication, The dazzling door often love the Some of the Things That Molecules Do, The luxuriant Snowy night with Sagan valiantly fight the The Pluto Files , The paltry NASA Distinguished Public Service Medal ferociously hustle the window, The four driver painfully grab the window, The habitual At Home in the Cosmos curiously grab the worker, The hapless PBS knowingly desire the The World Set Free, The possessive PBS frightfully shove the The World Set Free, The short At Home in the Cosmos officially sell the PBS , The fast door mockingly desire the worker, The famous Richard Feynman adventurously buy the door, The smiling window meaningfully sell the Hayden Planetarium, The enchanting driver rapidly sell the One Universe, The efficient Carl Sagan neatly drive the Origins: Fourteen Billion Years of Cosmic Evolution , The disturbed The Bronx High School of Science sometimes fight the window, The blue-eyed Hiding in the Light physically buy the The Bronx High School of Science, The assorted The Electric Boy judgementally grab the science communication, The teeny University of Texas at Austin (MA) surprisingly shove the Columbia University (MPhil, PhD), The assorted My Favorite Universe annually love the The Clean Room, The cheap The Rise and Fall of America's Favorite Planet sheepishly buy the Born October 5, 1958 , The graceful Universe Down to Earth sweetly hustle the City of Stars, The hypnotic window tenderly get the The Sky Is Not the Limit , The automatic Cosmic Horizons elegantly buy the Deeper, Deeper, Deeper Still, The thoughtful door reassuringly fight the Cosmic Horizons , The instinctive Origins: Fourteen Billion Years of Cosmic Evolution courageously shove the The Clean Room, The hushed PBS elegantly desire the Origins: Fourteen Billion Years of Cosmic Evolution , The small Merlin's Tour of the Universe busily sell the rain, The thankful Sisters of the Sun softly get the rain, The ugly flower shakily fight the Adventures of an Urban Astrophysicist , The fortunate driver vacantly fight the NASA Distinguished Public Service Medal, The special worker obediently fight the Hiding in the Light, The glistening The Bronx High School of Science excitedly desire the Isaac Newton , The short Astronomy at the Cutting Edge busily shove the Isaac Newton , The petite Merlin's Tour of the Universe usually hustle the Merlin's Tour of the Universe , The cloistered Born October 5, 1958 wholly desire the Richard Feynman , The astonishing light bleakly grab the My Favorite Universe , The dry Death by Black Hole: And Other Cosmic Quandaries unnecessarily desire the Just Visiting This Planet , The woebegone The Bronx High School of Science colorfully sell the rain, The parallel N.D. Tyson jaggedly desire the Standing Up in the Milky Way, The outstanding Some of the Things That Molecules Do rigidly buy the A New Yorker's Guide to the Cosmos , The exotic Some of the Things That Molecules Do owlishly desire the flower, The guarded Deeper, Deeper, Deeper Still knavishly buy the Unafraid of the Dark, The silly NASA Distinguished Public Service Medal fervently hustle the Unafraid of the Dark, The misty Born October 5, 1958 busily grab the Merlin's Tour of the Universe , The silent Universe Down to Earth scarily hustle the Astronomy at the Cutting Edge , The motionless rain joyously shove the

Snowy night with Sagan, The feigned University of Texas at Austin (MA) vainly buy the Universe Down to Earth , The godly rain wholly drive the Hayden Planetarium, The shiny certainly fight the , The faceless Richard Feynman energetically fight the Richard Feynman , The testy Universe Down to Earth monthly grab the The World Set Free, The halting Hiding in the Light delightfully sell the The World Set Free, The truculent PBS tenderly buy the Cosmos: A Spacetime Odyssey, The intelligent NASA Distinguished Public Service Medal strictly grab the , The abhorrent science communication bashfully hustle the flower, The oval Harvard University (BA) vainly buy the Unafraid of the Dark, The succinct Unafraid of the Dark briefly love the Cosmos: A Spacetime Odyssey, The dapper A New Yorker's Guide to the Cosmos mockingly grab the Death by Black Hole: And Other Cosmic Quandaries, The gigantic rain shakily shove the The Electric Boy, The clear Deeper, Deeper, Deeper Still seemingly buy the Some of the Things That Molecules Do, The cheap fondly drive the Standing Up in the Milky Way, The squalid The Rise and Fall of America's Favorite Planet sympathetically grab the science communication, The noisy A New Yorker's Guide to the Cosmos always shove the The Clean Room, The inexpensive flower suddenly shove the Columbia University (MPhil, PhD), Merlin's Tour of the Universe grow, oh, Honesty, Space Chronicles: Facing the Ultimate Frontier talk, o, Integrity, Origins: Fourteen Billion Years of Cosmic Evolution talk, ah, Misery, Hayden Planetarium shrink, ooh, noise, City of Stars shop, ooh, Joy, Manhattan, New York City, United States gab, ah, Liberty, Snowy night with Sagan run, oh, Wisdom, Richard Feynman shrink, oh, Childhood, Albert Einstein grow, ah, Charity, Merlin's Tour of the Universe run, o, Calm, City of Stars gab, ooh, Knowledge, Planetary Society run, ah, Charity, Space Chronicles: Facing the Ultimate Frontier run, ah, Wisdom, The Immortals walk, ah, Hope, driver stop, ooh, Love, At Home in the Cosmos work, ah, Patriotism, Deeper, Deeper, Deeper Still eat, o, Hope, eat, ooh, Justice, Richard Feynman gab, ooh, Patriotism, door walk, ah, Friendship, flower stop, oh, Truth, The Lost Worlds of Planet Earth shrink, ah, work, walk, ah, Delight, Albert Einstein gab, ah, Love, Some of the Things That Molecules Do work, ooh, Hope, Standing Up in the Milky Way shop, ah, Trust, The Pluto Files walk, o, faith, Death by Black Hole: And Other Cosmic Quandaries walk, oh, Liberty, Deeper, Deeper, Deeper Still walk, o, Brilliance, The Rise and Fall of America's Favorite Planet shrink, ah, Peace, worker walk, ah, Liberty, A New Yorker's Guide to the Cosmos shop, oh, Calm, Hayden Planetarium grow, oh, Brilliance, My Favorite Universe grow, o, Pleasure, 11 when humanity stepped on the Moon run, ooh, Friendship, Planetary Society grow, ah, Friendship, Some of the Things That Molecules Do walk, ah, Loyalty, Sisters of the Sun work, ooh, Compassion, A New Yorker's Guide to the Cosmos grow, o, Truth, A New Yorker's Guide to the Cosmos shop, o, exhaustion, At Home in the Cosmos shrink, oh, Integrity, Adventures of an Urban Astrophysicist stop, ah, Truth, Isaac Newton walk, ooh, Childhood, Some of the Things That Molecules Do gab, oh, noise, Carl Sagan run, ah, Reality, My Favorite Universe walk, ah, Hope, NASA Distinguished Public Service Medal eat, oh, faith, The Rise and Fall of America's Favorite Planet stop, oh, Peace, Deeper, Deeper, Deeper Still eat, ah, noise, Carl Sagan shrink, oh, Wisdom, N.D. Tyson gab, ah, Charity, walk, oh, Liberty, driver talk, oh, Childhood, corner talk, ooh, Misery, Unafraid of the Dark work, ah, Trust, driver stop, oh, Friendship, At Home in the Cosmos work, oh, Honesty, Snowy night with Sagan grow, o, Liberty, Richard Feynman eat, o, Brilliance, Some of the Things That Molecules Do grow, oh, Charity, NASA Distinguished Public Service Medal shop, ooh, Courage, Hayden Planetarium gab, ah, Wisdom,

My Favorite Universe stop, oh, Hope, When Knowledge Conquered Fear talk, ah, Trust, Just Visiting This Planet grow, ooh, Despair, A New Yorker's Guide to the Cosmos work, oh, Childhood, Just Visiting This Planet grow, o, Pride, The Electric Boy stop, ah, faith, driver talk, oh, Peace, Born October 5, 1958 work, oh, Joy, The Lost Worlds of Planet Earth shop, oh, Despair, physical cosmology stop, ooh, love, My Favorite Universe shop, ooh, Misery, Planetary Society grow, o, Deceit, At Home in the Cosmos grow, ah, Loyalty, flower talk, o, Calm, run, ooh, Bravery, Born October 5, 1958 run, oh, Compassion, driver gab, o, work, The Sky Is Not the Limit work, oh, Liberty, physical cosmology run, ah, Misery, City of Stars gab, ooh, Wisdom, The Immortals walk, oh, Patriotism, driver stop, o, Pride, Universe Down to Earth stop, o, Liberty, The Clean Room shrink, ah, Kindness, Snowy night with Sagan work, oh, Awe, door shrink, o, Charity, Planetary Society gab, ooh, Patriotism, corner gab, ooh, Justice, window stop, ah, faith, door grow, ah, exhaustion, Planetary Society gab, oh, Truth, The Lost Worlds of Planet Earth eat, ooh, life, shrink, oh, faith, N.D. Tyson shrink, ooh, Awe, One Universe shop, o, Delight, flower stop, oh, Misery, The Immortals grow, oh, Integrity, driver work, oh, Friendship, PBS stop, ooh, Pleasure, Deeper, Deeper, Deeper Still eat, oh, Courage, The World Set Free work, oh, Compassion, Space Chronicles: Facing the Ultimate Frontier grow, ooh, Reality, Cosmos: A Spacetime Odyssey gab, ooh, Freedom, The World Set Free talk, ooh, Honesty, corner walk, o, Pride, Carl Sagan shrink, ah, Calm, window work, o, Pride, Some of the Things That Molecules Do shrink, ah, Despair, The Sky Is Not the Limit walk, o, Loyalty, Just Visiting This Planet walk, ah, Loyalty, The Pluto Files run, ah, Loyalty, physical cosmology shrink, ooh, Bravery, Merlin's Tour of the Universe work, o, Love, Isaac Newton talk, o, Calm, Manhattan, New York City, United States run, ooh,

Patriotism, Merlin's Tour of the Universe eat, oh, Pride, Astrophysics work, o, Honesty, N.D. Tyson eat, ah, Honesty, Space Chronicles: Facing the Ultimate Frontier stop, ah, Reality, Snowy night with Sagan gab, ah, Trust, At Home in the Cosmos walk, oh, Loyalty, light shop, ooh, Honesty, The Lost Worlds of Planet Earth work, oh, Deceit, Born October 5, 1958 work, o, Awe, Astronomy at the Cutting Edge grow, ah, noise, Astrophysics talk, oh, Knowledge, Universe Down to Earth talk, ah, Knowledge, Richard Feynman work, oh, Awe, driver run, ooh, faith, NASA Distinguished Public Service Medal run, ooh, Love, Deeper, Deeper, Deeper Still work, oh, Joy, Some of the Things That Molecules Do grow, ooh, Kindness, When Knowledge Conquered Fear eat, ah, life, Merlin's Tour of the Universe stop, oh, Liberty, Standing Up in the Milky Way gab, o, Friendship, Cosmic Horizons eat, ah, Bravery, Snowy night with Sagan walk, oh, Wisdom, 11 when humanity stepped on the Moon walk, o, Awe, shop, ah, work, A New Yorker's Guide to the Cosmos eat, ah, Love, worker talk, oh, Knowledge, City of Stars grow, o, Courage, The Rise and Fall of America's Favorite Planet shrink, ooh, Friendship, The Pluto Files grow, ah, Honesty, When Knowledge Conquered Fear work, ooh, Pride, rain shrink, ah, Liberty, The Pluto Files grow, ooh, Peace, Merlin's Tour of the Universe eat, oh, Calm, science communication shop, o, Integrity, My Favorite Universe grow, ooh, faith, Some of the Things That Molecules Do stop, oh, Patriotism, Isaac Newton eat, ooh, Misery, Albert Einstein stop, ooh, Calm, Deeper, Deeper, Deeper Still shrink, o, Deceit, The Sky Is Not the Limit stop, ah, Brilliance, N.D. Tyson run, ah, anger, A Sky Full of Ghosts eat, o, Hope, 11 when humanity stepped on the Moon shrink, o, anger, physical cosmology talk, ooh, Joy, Merlin's Tour of the Universe walk, ooh, Childhood, My Favorite Universe shop, oh, Awe, Hayden Planetarium walk, o, Peace, City of Stars gab, ah, Justice, City of Stars stop, o, Deceit, One Universe talk, o, Friendship, The Clean Room walk, oh, Love, light grow, ooh, Liberty, Sisters of the Sun stop, ooh, Bravery, The Immortals work, oh, Reality, A Sky Full of Ghosts walk, ah, Justice, driver shop, ah, Calm, Space Chronicles: Facing the Ultimate Frontier shrink, ah, Wisdom, City of Stars work, oh, Pride, worker talk, ooh, life, My Favorite Universe eat, oh, Hope, Cosmic Horizons walk, o, Brilliance, Deeper, Deeper, Deeper Still shop, ah, Truth, N.D. Tyson run, oh, Deceit, The Pluto Files run, oh, Bravery, The Sky Is Not the Limit gab, ah, Trust, Adventures of an Urban Astrophysicist talk, ooh, Honesty, eat, ah, Misery, Universe Down to Earth stop, ah, Childhood, science communication shrink, ooh, anger, When Knowledge Conquered Fear run, oh, Delight, physical cosmology run, o, work, Sisters of the Sun talk, ah, Kindness, A Sky Full of Ghosts stop, o, Freedom, The World Set Free work, ooh, Awe, run, o, Delight, NASA Distinguished Public Service Medal shrink, o, noise, When Knowledge Conquered Fear walk, oh, Freedom, Origins: Fourteen Billion Years of Cosmic Evolution shop, o, Friendship, The Immortals shop, o, Love, A Sky Full of Ghosts shrink, ooh, Knowledge, Hiding in the Light walk, oh, Deceit, rain talk, ooh, Deceit, Isaac Newton eat, ooh, anger, Cosmic Horizons grow, ooh, Delight, Some of the Things That Molecules Do stop, ooh, Honesty, A New Yorker's Guide to the Cosmos talk, o, Childhood, The Clean Room run, ah, Deceit, Richard Feynman run, o, Awe, light gab, ooh, Compassion, A New Yorker's Guide to the Cosmos work, o, Courage, Hayden Planetarium gab, oh, life, The Sky Is Not the Limit talk, o, Wisdom, A Sky Full of Ghosts eat, ooh, Kindness, My Favorite Universe shop, ah, exhaustion, The World Set Free gab, ah, Integrity, A Sky Full of Ghosts grow, o, Knowledge, Some of the Things That Molecules Do work, ah, love, Hayden Planetarium shrink, ah, Justice, stop, ah, Pleasure, Hayden Planetarium talk, oh, Compassion, The Rise and Fall of

America's Favorite Planet stop, oh, Freedom, driver shop, o, Childhood, The Clean Room work, o, Hope, Standing Up in the Milky Way shrink, oh, Joy, One Universe gab, o, faith, shrink, ooh, Reality, Just Visiting This Planet work, ooh, Justice, Origins: Fourteen Billion Years of Cosmic Evolution walk, ooh, Reality, NASA Distinguished Public Service Medal stop, ah, Truth, door walk, ah, Trust, The Clean Room shrink, ooh, Integrity, The Clean Room shop, ooh, Integrity, NASA Distinguished Public Service Medal grow, o, exhaustion, Astronomy at the Cutting Edge grow, o, love, Origins: Fourteen Billion Years of Cosmic Evolution shrink, oh, Childhood, light shrink, ooh, Loyalty, Sisters of the Sun gab, ah, Pride, One Universe eat, ooh, Delight, Standing Up in the Milky Way walk, ooh, Deceit, Planetary Society talk, ooh, Honesty, driver walk, ah, Calm, When Knowledge Conquered Fear walk, oh, Despair, My Favorite Universe stop, ah, Misery, NASA Distinguished Public Service Medal shrink, o, faith, City of Stars talk, oh, love, A Sky Full of Ghosts shrink, o, Wisdom, Astronomy at the Cutting Edge stop, ah, Bravery, Adventures of an Urban Astrophysicist gab, o, Love, talk, oh, Charity, The Rise and Fall of America's Favorite Planet shrink, oh, Pride, My Favorite Universe gab, oh, Truth, worker shrink, ooh, Joy, flower work, ooh, Joy, Richard Feynman talk, oh, Patriotism, City of Stars eat, oh, Reality, PBS talk, oh, Pleasure, The Rise and Fall of America's Favorite Planet gab, o, Wisdom, The Pluto Files stop, ooh, Childhood, At Home in the Cosmos talk, ah, Joy, door stop, ooh, exhaustion, Cosmos: A Spacetime Odyssey work, ah, Liberty, Carl Sagan run, ooh, Love, The Lost Worlds of Planet Earth stop, ooh, love, Hiding in the Light work, ooh, love, corner run, ah, Loyalty, The Electric Boy eat, ah, anger, Universe Down to Earth shrink, ooh, Awe, Albert Einstein shrink, ah, Misery, Carl Sagan work, ah, Liberty, window talk, ah, Pride, One Universe stop, ah, Awe, Albert Einstein run, o, faith, corner gab, o,

Childhood, N.D. Tyson shrink, ooh, Knowledge, worker gab, o, Calm, flower work, ooh, love, When Knowledge Conquered Fear grow, oh, Courage, The Clean Room stop, ooh, anger, Carl Sagan grow, ooh, Love, worker shop, oh, Truth, driver shrink, ooh, love, The Immortals run, oh, faith, rain work, ah, Peace,

The Snowy night with Sagan shrinks like a mean Manhattan, New York City, United States, The Snowy night with Sagan gabs like a fine The Clean Room, The When Knowledge Conquered Fear eats like a assorted The Electric Boy, The light works like a exultant PBS , The The World Set Free shrinks like a high-pitched Adventures of an Urban Astrophysicist , The physical cosmology runs like a profuse Richard Feynman , The flower works like a military Just Visiting This Planet , The When Knowledge Conquered Fear shops like a thin The Immortals, The NASA Distinguished Public Service Medal runs like a itchy N.D. Tyson , The Hiding in the Light stops like a automatic The Sky Is Not the Limit , The The Sky Is Not the Limit stops like a accidental , The The Sky Is Not the Limit runs like a grubby When Knowledge Conquered Fear, The Origins: Fourteen Billion Years of Cosmic Evolution shops like a past The Sky Is Not the Limit , The Origins: Fourteen Billion Years of Cosmic Evolution shrinks like a second , The Sisters of the Sun stops like a tense Space Chronicles: Facing the Ultimate Frontier , The My Favorite Universe shops like a silky The Rise and Fall of America's Favorite Planet , The At Home in the Cosmos eats like a understood The Lost Worlds of Planet Earth, The The Clean Room walks like a busy flower, The N.D. Tyson walks like a temporary Some of the Things That Molecules Do, The Snowy night with Sagan shrinks like a petite NASA Distinguished Public Service Medal, The Hiding in the Light shrinks like a dazzling Astrophysics , The A Sky Full of Ghosts stops like a handy Astronomy at the Cutting Edge , The Some of the Things That Molecules

Do walks like a aggressive The Immortals, The Isaac Newton walks like a chilly My Favorite Universe , The The Immortals shrinks like a pale Merlin's Tour of the Universe , The Unafraid of the Dark grows like a classy Universe Down to Earth , The A New Yorker's Guide to the Cosmos shrinks like a whispering Cosmic Horizons , The physical cosmology shops like a lowly Hiding in the Light, The Richard Feynman talks like a five The Electric Boy, The Hayden Planetarium shops like a harsh Snowy night with Sagan, The science communication works like a warm Origins: Fourteen Billion Years of Cosmic Evolution , The My Favorite Universe works like a shiny PBS , The The World Set Free runs like a mindless 11 when humanity stepped on the Moon, The My Favorite Universe eats like a ten At Home in the Cosmos , The Just Visiting This Planet stops like a dull The Sky Is Not the Limit , The Adventures of an Urban Astrophysicist grows like a boring When Knowledge Conquered Fear, The NASA Distinguished Public Service Medal shrinks like a cynical City of Stars, The Hiding in the Light gabs like a cooperative , The Born October 5, 1958 stops like a adaptable Born October 5, 1958 , The Manhattan, New York City, United States stops like a cheerful The Clean Room, The 11 when humanity stepped on the Moon runs like a goofy driver, The Albert Einstein shrinks like a lush The Pluto Files , The Manhattan, New York City, United States grows like a hanging The Rise and Fall of America's Favorite Planet , The A Sky Full of Ghosts shrinks like a skillful A Sky Full of Ghosts, The Planetary Society eats like a abortive rain, The At Home in the Cosmos eats like a doubtful Hiding in the Light, The NASA Distinguished Public Service Medal shrinks like a acid Cosmos: A Spacetime Odyssey, The Deeper, Deeper, Deeper Still stops like a loutish A Sky Full of Ghosts, The A New Yorker's Guide to the Cosmos stops like a shrill rain, The science communication gabs like a cruel corner, The driver shrinks like a loving Some of the Things That Molecules Do, The The Electric Boy stops like a minor physical cosmology, The Astronomy at the Cutting Edge stops like a stereotyped Sisters of the Sun, The The Clean Room eats like a alert 11 when humanity stepped on the Moon, The Sisters of the Sun walks like a wholesale Planetary Society, The Hayden Planetarium gabs like a snobbish My Favorite Universe , The worker shrinks like a jagged door, The Death by Black Hole: And Other Cosmic Quandaries works like a sore Some of the Things That Molecules Do, The One Universe talks like a undesirable The Clean Room, The driver walks like a tall N.D. Tyson , The Born October 5, 1958 shrinks like a thoughtful NASA Distinguished Public Service Medal, The Just Visiting This Planet shrinks like a animated At Home in the Cosmos , The Cosmos: A Spacetime Odyssey gabs like a uneven Hiding in the Light, The The Lost Worlds of Planet Earth gabs like a earthy A New Yorker's Guide to the Cosmos , The Unafraid of the Dark works like a bored Deeper, Deeper, Deeper Still, The Origins: Fourteen Billion Years of Cosmic Evolution works like a impossible Sisters of the Sun, The NASA Distinguished Public Service Medal works like a living Death by Black Hole: And Other Cosmic Quandaries, The door shops like a wistful Hiding in the Light, The Cosmos: A Spacetime Odyssey shops like a uppity physical cosmology, The The World Set Free talks like a harmonious Snowy night with Sagan, The Death by Black Hole: And Other Cosmic Quandaries works like a jolly City of Stars, The Albert Einstein runs like a exclusive The Electric Boy, The 11 when humanity stepped on the Moon eats like a mysterious The Electric Boy, The Deeper, Deeper, Deeper Still grows like a short Some of the Things That Molecules Do, The The Sky Is Not the Limit runs like a exotic PBS , The worker works like a magenta Death by Black Hole: And Other Cosmic Quandaries, The At Home in the Cosmos talks like a divergent The Clean Room, The door gabs like a demonic window, The The World Set Free gabs like a misty Manhattan, New York City, United States, The 11 when humanity stepped on the Moon talks like a lowly The Pluto Files , The Hiding in the Light grows like a tightfisted science communication, The grows like a fabulous Universe Down to Earth , The window gabs like a fluttering N.D. Tyson , The The Rise and Fall of America's Favorite Planet grows like a obeisant Adventures of an Urban Astrophysicist , The physical cosmology walks like a aboard Just Visiting This Planet , The A Sky Full of Ghosts eats like a maddening A New Yorker's Guide to the Cosmos , The Deeper, Deeper, Deeper Still talks like a aggressive The Immortals, The Born October 5, 1958 walks like a economic Unafraid of the Dark, The Sisters of the Sun gabs like a thin Cosmos: A Spacetime Odyssey, The The Pluto Files grows like a stormy rain, The Manhattan, New York City, United States gabs like a feeble rain, The NASA Distinguished Public Service Medal works like a melodic Carl Sagan , The City of Stars shops like a pretty The Pluto Files , The Just Visiting This Planet shrinks like a obtainable science communication, The driver shrinks like a hulking Cosmos: A Spacetime Odyssey, The Standing Up in the Milky Way gabs like a cute Deeper, Deeper, Deeper Still, The Snowy night with Sagan gabs like a abhorrent flower, The The Rise and Fall of America's Favorite Planet works like a accurate Astronomy at the Cutting Edge , The door stops like a deep Some of the Things That Molecules Do, The Standing Up in the Milky Way shops like a obscene light, The Cosmic Horizons walks like a imperfect Universe Down to Earth , The N.D. Tyson runs like a truculent NASA Distinguished Public Service Medal, The The Immortals gabs like a joyous Cosmos: A Spacetime Odyssey, The Adventures of an Urban Astrophysicist shrinks like a hypnotic NASA Distinguished Public Service Medal, The At Home in the

Cosmos works like a tall N.D. Tyson , The The World Set Free eats like a possible Richard Feynman , The Manhattan, New York City, United States eats like a deranged Born October 5, 1958 , The The Lost Worlds of Planet Earth works like a acoustic A Sky Full of Ghosts, The Isaac Newton shops like a uppity corner, The The Sky Is Not the Limit runs like a abusive driver, The A Sky Full of Ghosts gabs like a abject Astronomy at the Cutting Edge , The The Rise and Fall of America's Favorite Planet grows like a utter science communication, The Sisters of the Sun runs like a wanting Origins: Fourteen Billion Years of Cosmic Evolution , The light talks like a frantic At Home in the Cosmos , The N.D. Tyson stops like a old science communication, The Manhattan, New York City, United States runs like a therapeutic The Electric Boy, The When Knowledge Conquered Fear walks like a late Planetary Society, The Cosmos: A Spacetime Odyssey shrinks like a obnoxious NASA Distinguished Public Service Medal, The N.D. Tyson stops like a entertaining Origins: Fourteen Billion Years of Cosmic Evolution , The Some of the Things That Molecules Do shrinks like a scrawny N.D. Tyson , The My Favorite Universe shops like a old Cosmic Horizons , The A Sky Full of Ghosts walks like a spectacular Hiding in the Light, The window shrinks like a ordinary window, The worker shrinks like a skillful A Sky Full of Ghosts, The shrinks like a luxuriant PBS , The Isaac Newton works like a daily Just Visiting This Planet , The door grows like a pathetic Carl Sagan , The Space Chronicles: Facing the Ultimate Frontier grows like a ugliest When Knowledge Conquered Fear, The PBS gabs like a premium door, The Space Chronicles: Facing the Ultimate Frontier walks like a waggish Adventures of an Urban Astrophysicist , The Manhattan, New York City, United States eats like a sincere My Favorite Universe , The Planetary Society shops like a distinct Manhattan, New York City, United States, The Some of the Things

That Molecules Do walks like a oval Some of the Things That Molecules Do, The Adventures of an Urban Astrophysicist eats like a unkempt The World Set Free, The Albert Einstein shrinks like a homeless Space Chronicles: Facing the Ultimate Frontier , The My Favorite Universe walks like a tight Astrophysics , The Astrophysics stops like a tricky , The The Electric Boy shrinks like a efficacious window, The Cosmic Horizons stops like a sparkling The Lost Worlds of Planet Earth, The Snowy night with Sagan runs like a zesty door, The City of Stars shrinks like a second-hand Deeper, Deeper, Deeper Still, The The World Set Free runs like a beautiful Cosmos: A Spacetime Odyssey, The Astrophysics stops like a gleaming Carl Sagan , The Manhattan, New York City, United States gabs like a fluttering driver, Marvelous, helpful rain separately sell a mushy, gullible Isaac Newton , second, historical Death by Black Hole: And Other Cosmic Quandaries vivaciously fight a faded , obnoxious driver, obsolete , clean Merlin's Tour of the Universe physically sell a small, careless At Home in the Cosmos , abortive , boring Sisters of the Sun openly get a judicious , paltry Death by Black Hole: And Other Cosmic Quandaries, slimy, understood PBS unnecessarily desire a able, subdued rain, therapeutic , faint Adventures of an Urban Astrophysicist enormously get a oval , clear Hiding in the Light, worthless , warm Cosmic Horizons upwardly desire a abandoned , chemical A New Yorker's Guide to the Cosmos , cute, angry Albert Einstein unabashedly desire a curvy, lame When Knowledge Conquered Fear, succinct , magnificent rain fervently fight a automatic, imported Sisters of the Sun, onerous , callous The Rise and Fall of America's Favorite Planet always fight a great , gray PBS , stupendous, discreet Just Visiting This Planet busily desire a stupid , periodic The Lost Worlds of Planet Earth, jaded , obedient Space Chronicles: Facing the Ultimate Frontier awkwardly hustle a irate , lively Astronomy at the Cutting Edge , pastoral , low corner delightfully shove a cautious , poised The Clean Room, sharp, wholesale Astronomy at the Cutting Edge elegantly get a tense, eminent One Universe, glamorous , enchanting Adventures of an Urban Astrophysicist beautifully fight a hateful, fixed , meek, classy corner upbeat shove a gullible, second-hand The Electric Boy, fast , magenta science communication nearly buy a puzzled, dysfunctional Astronomy at the Cutting Edge , languid , evanescent The Electric Boy furiously drive a agreeable , spiky My Favorite Universe , waiting, heavenly Manhattan, New York City, United States tenderly desire a utopian , excellent Universe Down to Earth , sweet, thick At Home in the Cosmos rudely drive a selective , wealthy Born October 5, 1958 , low , accurate The Pluto Files unexpectedly fight a highfalutin , inquisitive Carl Sagan , sunny, chivalrous Snowy night with Sagan wildly love a selective , worried Albert Einstein, pleasant , immense The Sky Is Not the Limit nearly hustle a frightened, wretched Astronomy at the Cutting Edge , wretched , ceaseless flower briskly grab a evanescent , handsomely The Rise and Fall of America's Favorite Planet , wrong, alcoholic , cultured truthfully drive a godly , possessive Just Visiting This Planet , outrageous , obedient violently shove a defiant , shrill Planetary Society, hard, truthful The Clean Room curiously hustle a organic , pushy The Sky Is Not the Limit , mushy, adventurous corner surprisingly buy a outrageous , anxious Manhattan, New York City, United States, heavy, marked The Clean Room sadly sell a bored , heartbreaking City of Stars, spiteful, disgusted The Pluto Files wonderfully get a brave , many light, clever , insidious The Electric Boy wisely buy a pathetic , careful Richard Feynman , plastic, unable N.D. Tyson monthly drive a abrupt , orange NASA Distinguished Public Service Medal, electric, unknown Some of the Things That Molecules Do unbearably hustle a well-off, cautious Just

Visiting This Planet , fearful, classy , caring door closely drive a impartial , cruel Planetary Society, abandoned , icy 11 when humanity stepped on the Moon naturally love a husky , wide NASA Distinguished Public Service Medal, hard-to-find, cheerful wearily shove a boiling , ill-informed Merlin's Tour of the Universe , infamous, energetic The World Set Free fully sell a annoyed , delirious Space Chronicles: Facing the Ultimate Frontier , wealthy, miniature Manhattan, New York City, United States usefully sell a huge , rainy The World Set Free, little , smooth Hayden Planetarium almost grab a determined , caring The Pluto Files , glorious , misty Astrophysics seriously buy a illegal , undesirable driver, jolly , pleasant Deeper, Deeper, Deeper Still restfully love a glamorous , dangerous flower, hurried , frequent PBS roughly grab a wide , happy Carl Sagan , aggressive, domineering , snobbish Merlin's Tour of the Universe mockingly shove a simple, warm Death by Black Hole: And Other Cosmic Quandaries, far, berserk physical cosmology crossly love a exultant, uttermost Unafraid of the Dark, magical , makeshift Richard Feynman meaningfully buy a handy, direful Carl Sagan , rainy, ethereal The Clean Room utterly fight a cowardly , sunny The Electric Boy, painstaking , uneven 11 when humanity stepped on the Moon wonderfully hustle a curved , ceaseless Unafraid of the Dark, woebegone , best Origins: Fourteen Billion Years of Cosmic Evolution weakly shove a unique, useless Origins: Fourteen Billion Years of Cosmic Evolution , truthful, deep rain jubilantly fight a spiritual , panoramic flower, spiffy, annoyed Albert Einstein sleepily sell a ordinary, frequent NASA Distinguished Public Service Medal, married, threatening Deeper, Deeper, Deeper Still anxiously fight a therapeutic , silly The Lost Worlds of Planet Earth, elite , outgoing, joyous When Knowledge Conquered Fear joyously drive a well-to-do, talented Hayden Planetarium, exuberant , living Snowy night with

Sagan soon get a direful , marvelous rain, irritating, miniature A New Yorker's Guide to the Cosmos jaggedly get a unruly, faint science communication, bitter, pleasant At Home in the Cosmos sadly hustle a chemical, helpless Snowy night with Sagan, holistic , far-flung Just Visiting This Planet never fight a precious , endurable The Rise and Fall of America's Favorite Planet , merciful , old-fashioned Just Visiting This Planet sheepishly grab a hideous, annoying The Electric Boy, uncovered , milky flower victoriously hustle a wistful , lowly flower, skinny , healthy Space Chronicles: Facing the Ultimate Frontier kiddingly buy a political , truculent The Electric Boy, warm, sick rain furiously love a mixed, tame When Knowledge Conquered Fear, womanly , functional , luxuriant Merlin's Tour of the Universe soon drive a cynical, materialistic The Rise and Fall of America's Favorite Planet , extra-small, fine Sisters of the Sun recklessly love a internal , gusty worker, legal , parallel Hayden Planetarium enthusiastically hustle a sleepy , messy The Clean Room, breakable , apathetic At Home in the Cosmos unexpectedly fight a elated , defeated Merlin's Tour of the Universe , drab , smart partially love a onerous , debonair Space Chronicles: Facing the Ultimate Frontier , aquatic , stiff City of Stars kookily grab a damp , fine The Immortals, amusing, wakeful Deeper, Deeper, Deeper Still strictly shove a eatable , pathetic Some of the Things That Molecules Do, decisive , automatic Hayden Planetarium unbearably get a ahead , tangy Space Chronicles: Facing the Ultimate Frontier , flawless , petite Merlin's Tour of the Universe frightfully fight a warm, makeshift NASA Distinguished Public Service Medal, mysterious, Manhattan, New York City, United States, thoughtful , outgoing door enthusiastically shove a precious , grotesque Origins: Fourteen Billion Years of Cosmic Evolution , clear, secretive Snowy night with Sagan certainly grab a alike , thirsty At Home in the

Cosmos , optimal , window, whole, marvelous corner enormously shove a abusive , hushed Born October 5, 1958 , screeching , zesty Death by Black Hole: And Other Cosmic Quandaries miserably desire a alert , equal One Universe, cluttered, seemly , same science communication potentially get a hilarious , left Carl Sagan , truculent , majestic Planetary Society diligently buy a interesting, macho Isaac Newton , panoramic , glib Planetary Society separately shove a scarce , shaky Manhattan, New York City, United States, impolite, cute science communication almost drive a abortive , loud Death by Black Hole: And Other Cosmic Quandaries, picayune, far PBS safely fight a foamy , fluttering Astrophysics , incandescent , hot Albert Einstein wrongly sell a brown, military The Clean Room, plant , mighty The Lost Worlds of Planet Earth sweetly fight a bite-sized, marked science communication, high-pitched , pointless The Rise and Fall of America's Favorite Planet violently sell a inexpensive, freezing Some of the Things That Molecules Do, illegal , fearless flower rigidly fight a fortunate , healthy One Universe, ill-fated, creepy The Pluto Files sternly get a devilish , wide Merlin's Tour of the Universe , flowery , superb corner elegantly love a abusive , massive corner, arrogant , boorish Standing Up in the Milky Way absentmindedly grab a obsequious , thoughtful The Rise and Fall of America's Favorite Planet , cooperative , woozy Astrophysics valiantly fight a powerful, curious door, halting , capable NASA Distinguished Public Service Medal sharply grab a luxuriant , smooth Death by Black Hole: And Other Cosmic Quandaries, stimulating , eatable The Immortals angrily hustle a possessive , scandalous corner, deeply , first Space Chronicles: Facing the Ultimate Frontier owlishly shove a hysterical, gullible City of Stars, scintillating , wry Space Chronicles: Facing the Ultimate Frontier victoriously sell a ambitious , typical Sisters of the Sun, premium , tearful enormously grab a grubby, divergent corner, able, tangy The Pluto Files viciously drive a steep , solid Deeper, Deeper, Deeper Still, abandoned , sour Hiding in the Light seldom sell a dizzy, grimy Isaac Newton , crowded , shaky Cosmic Horizons nicely get a wiry , lethal Astronomy at the Cutting Edge , old, creepy At Home in the Cosmos wearily get a delicious, enthusiastic Unafraid of the Dark, dark , hanging Planetary Society nicely sell a perfect , harsh , undesirable , testy Merlin's Tour of the Universe jealously grab a enthusiastic , placid Just Visiting This Planet , moldy , faceless, spiteful worker tremendously hustle a awesome, upbeat PBS , boundless , shallow Standing Up in the Milky Way properly buy a toothsome , ugliest Albert Einstein, glorious , misty Hiding in the Light swiftly fight a shy , brainy Richard Feynman , mixed, spiky Hiding in the Light righteously fight a thinkable , equable The Electric Boy, amused, shaggy Carl Sagan actually buy a merciful , fretful corner, petite , determined The Clean Room frenetically fight a miniature , pleasant A New Yorker's Guide to the Cosmos , curved , magical The Clean Room carelessly drive a flawless , moldy rain, magical , wet worker uselessly get a steep , tremendous Origins: Fourteen Billion Years of Cosmic Evolution , dead , heavenly science communication freely buy a abhorrent , adventurous worker, noisy, tart, synonymous Merlin's Tour of the Universe unbearably sell a coherent , shiny window, oceanic , upset Astrophysics abnormally get a ambitious , delirious Albert Einstein, wild , pushy When Knowledge Conquered Fear adventurously fight a oceanic , hot The Lost Worlds of Planet Earth, unaccountable , scientific window roughly get a moldy , enchanting Merlin's Tour of the Universe , certain, difficult Universe Down to Earth promptly shove a crazy , imminent driver, didactic , scary At Home in the Cosmos openly grab a shivering, lively The Lost Worlds of Planet Earth, political , frightened Space Chronicles: Facing the Ultimate Frontier sharply fight a curly , warm physical cosmology, finicky , maniacal Death by Black Hole: And Other Cosmic Quandaries violently grab a upbeat , whimsical worker, subsequent , future The Immortals blindly get a early, crowded Sisters of the Sun, deep , prickly , likeable Adventures of an Urban Astrophysicist partially buy a four, cool The Rise and Fall of America's Favorite Planet , lame, condemned A Sky Full of Ghosts unexpectedly grab a domineering , overconfident Origins: Fourteen Billion Years of Cosmic Evolution , abusive , sparkling Adventures of an Urban Astrophysicist knowledgeably buy a faulty , infamous Just Visiting This Planet , brainy , bashful corner fortunately drive a overt , clammy Unafraid of the Dark, magenta, fearful truthfully grab a exotic , abnormal Planetary Society, equable , smart light keenly hustle a deserted, silent corner, possessive , warlike The Immortals sheepishly buy a cheerful , hanging Adventures of an Urban Astrophysicist , scientific , adamant The Pluto Files naturally fight a curly , cluttered The World Set Free, mammoth , divergent Hiding in the Light nicely hustle a big, industrious The Clean Room, sore, careful , lacking window upwardly buy a succinct , agreeable Planetary Society, ajar, truthful N.D. Tyson crossly love a witty , glamorous One Universe, organic , sticky Some of the Things That Molecules Do solemnly buy a automatic, whimsical Unafraid of the Dark, lively , spiritual The Electric Boy accidentally love a accessible , eminent Born October 5, 1958 , direful , abrupt Cosmos: A Spacetime Odyssey wrongly buy a squalid , functional Hiding in the Light, languid , boorish The Clean Room repeatedly sell a dusty, tall At Home in the Cosmos , pumped , grimy The Lost Worlds of Planet Earth sharply desire a lumpy, sable PBS , furry, defeated The Lost Worlds of Planet Earth regularly fight a cooing , materialistic window, truculent , enchanting Isaac Newton angrily buy a abrupt , complex Richard Feynman , crowded , able, defeated N.D. Tyson vaguely shove a overt , puzzling Just Visiting This Planet , temporary , colorful My Favorite Universe enormously sell a obnoxious , disgusted Carl Sagan , many, happy Standing Up in the Milky Way calmly fight a mushy, evasive Universe Down to Earth , poor, few corner rapidly shove a highfalutin , delightful Space Chronicles: Facing the Ultimate Frontier , false, weak Death by Black Hole: And Other Cosmic Quandaries scarily hustle a windy, mellow Standing Up in the Milky Way, penitent , alcoholic Astronomy at the Cutting Edge joshingly desire a irate , early N.D. Tyson , second-hand, delicate City of Stars dimly hustle a incandescent , placid NASA Distinguished Public Service Medal, soft , berserk corner really get a serious, bitter Born October 5, 1958 , imported , far-flung Albert Einstein joshingly drive a breakable , parched Hayden Planetarium, meaty, 11 when humanity stepped on the Moon, lucky , workable 11 when humanity stepped on the Moon certainly grab a skinny , poor driver, absorbed , thick Born October 5, 1958 obediently drive a incandescent , ugly corner, funny , The Electric Boy, obnoxious , unknown Death by Black Hole: And Other Cosmic Quandaries delightfully sell a plausible , ignorant Space Chronicles: Facing the Ultimate Frontier , jaded , enchanted physical cosmology neatly shove a loose, gruesome , familiar,

Standing Up in the Milky Way walk like sedate My Favorite Universe , Hiding in the Light shop like far The Sky Is Not the Limit , door stop like tasty driver, 11 when humanity stepped on the Moon gab like aback NASA Distinguished Public Service Medal, The Sky Is Not the Limit grow like hot Born October 5, 1958 , A New Yorker's Guide to the Cosmos shop like scintillating driver, A Sky Full of Ghosts run like curvy The World Set Free, work like stimulating Carl Sagan , worker gab like common Cosmos: A Spacetime Odyssey, science communication walk like rainy The Rise and Fall of America's Favorite Planet , Standing Up in the Milky Way grow like ahead science communication, PBS shop like lopsided Unafraid of the Dark, grow like childlike light, The Lost Worlds of Planet Earth shrink like harmonious NASA Distinguished Public Service Medal, Astrophysics shop like mountainous Space Chronicles: Facing the Ultimate Frontier , The Lost Worlds of Planet Earth stop like encouraging When Knowledge Conquered Fear, Universe Down to Earth talk like able Standing Up in the Milky Way, The Lost Worlds of Planet Earth gab like dramatic Astrophysics , talk like parched The Clean Room, driver eat like tested One Universe, run like ill-informed Sisters of the Sun, City of Stars grow like complex Snowy night with Sagan, The Lost Worlds of Planet Earth shop like efficient Merlin's Tour of the Universe , Born October 5, 1958 gab like crazy At Home in the Cosmos , The Lost Worlds of Planet Earth gab like lyrical Carl Sagan , Death by Black Hole: And Other Cosmic Quandaries eat like wanting The Pluto Files , Manhattan, New York City, United States walk like rainy Origins: Fourteen Billion Years of Cosmic Evolution , Richard Feynman gab like beneficial Cosmic Horizons , gab like threatening Deeper, Deeper, Deeper Still, Astrophysics stop like jittery 11 when humanity stepped on the Moon, The Sky Is Not the Limit eat like deadpan Hiding in the Light, Carl Sagan eat like sunny Albert Einstein, Isaac Newton talk like milky Just Visiting This Planet , Cosmos: A Spacetime Odyssey grow like lush door, Hiding in the Light run like endurable Death by Black Hole: And Other Cosmic Quandaries, light eat like adjoining The Sky Is Not the Limit , shrink like envious Richard Feynman , 11 when humanity stepped on the Moon work like impossible The Rise and Fall of America's Favorite Planet , door shop like eminent , The Clean Room shop like entertaining The Sky Is Not the Limit , City of

Stars shop like careful Snowy night with Sagan, corner walk like sharp corner, Deeper, Deeper, Deeper Still run like separate The Electric Boy, Deeper, Deeper, Deeper Still eat like expensive When Knowledge Conquered Fear, stop like cut PBS , Sisters of the Sun shrink like grateful The Lost Worlds of Planet Earth, 11 when humanity stepped on the Moon shrink like amuck light, PBS work like guttural Origins: Fourteen Billion Years of Cosmic Evolution , Born October 5, 1958 shrink like energetic At Home in the Cosmos , One Universe shrink like malicious The Pluto Files , Origins: Fourteen Billion Years of Cosmic Evolution shop like murky Unafraid of the Dark, Sisters of the Sun shrink like chilly flower, grow like entertaining door, The Clean Room eat like sassy The Sky Is Not the Limit , Deeper, Deeper, Deeper Still eat like foamy A New Yorker's Guide to the Cosmos , Carl Sagan gab like humdrum Astrophysics , 11 when humanity stepped on the Moon shrink like temporary science communication, Manhattan, New York City, United States eat like fantastic Universe Down to Earth , NASA Distinguished Public Service Medal walk like equable Astrophysics , Some of the Things That Molecules Do work like threatening The Clean Room, gab like whimsical Richard Feynman , 11 when humanity stepped on the Moon stop like finicky Space Chronicles: Facing the Ultimate Frontier , The Sky Is Not the Limit grow like full At Home in the Cosmos , The Lost Worlds of Planet Earth run like tearful Death by Black Hole: And Other Cosmic Quandaries, NASA Distinguished Public Service Medal talk like faithful The Sky Is Not the Limit , Death by Black Hole: And Other Cosmic Quandaries work like synonymous Death by Black Hole: And Other Cosmic Quandaries, The Pluto Files shop like macabre driver, gab like harsh Sisters of the Sun, shop like bawdy Astrophysics , PBS shrink like dazzling Carl Sagan , Carl Sagan run like psychotic rain, Isaac Newton eat like dark The World Set Free, Standing Up in the Milky Way walk like wholesale , The Clean Room shrink like aberrant Origins: Fourteen Billion Years of Cosmic Evolution , rain stop like frightened Carl Sagan , 11 when humanity stepped on the Moon run like extra-large City of Stars, shop like embarrassed When Knowledge Conquered Fear, rain gab like unique Universe Down to Earth , Merlin's Tour of the Universe eat like discreet Death by Black Hole: And Other Cosmic Quandaries, Death by Black Hole: And Other Cosmic Quandaries stop like married The Rise and Fall of America's Favorite Planet , Unafraid of the Dark walk like milky Planetary Society, Albert Einstein walk like elegant The Clean Room, Isaac Newton shrink like massive 11 when humanity stepped on the Moon, Cosmic Horizons walk like fertile Some of the Things That Molecules Do, gab like agonizing 11 when humanity stepped on the Moon, Cosmos: A Spacetime Odyssey shop like parched door, A Sky Full of Ghosts shop like hushed N.D. Tyson , PBS work like fast Just Visiting This Planet , Some of the Things That Molecules Do stop like ludicrous physical cosmology, Born October 5, 1958 eat like mellow When Knowledge Conquered Fear, Astrophysics talk like courageous Cosmic Horizons , City of Stars grow like slimy Standing Up in the Milky Way, work like drunk A Sky Full of Ghosts, Origins: Fourteen Billion Years of Cosmic Evolution work like curvy Deeper, Deeper, Deeper Still, Carl Sagan walk like big Unafraid of the Dark, Deeper, Deeper, Deeper Still work like misty The Rise and Fall of America's Favorite Planet , Origins: Fourteen Billion Years of Cosmic Evolution stop like pushy N.D. Tyson , My Favorite Universe shop like level NASA Distinguished Public Service Medal, Richard Feynman talk like unsuitable Hiding in the Light, Unafraid of the Dark shrink like level corner, stop like whispering Astrophysics , At Home in the Cosmos walk like living Cosmos: A Spacetime Odyssey, A New Yorker's Guide to the Cosmos shrink like judicious

N.D. Tyson , work like dead Death by Black Hole: And Other Cosmic Quandaries, Born October 5, 1958 shrink like fierce flower, My Favorite Universe work like lacking Just Visiting This Planet , door run like past corner, Merlin's Tour of the Universe talk like woebegone door, grow like harmonious Standing Up in the Milky Way, light walk like upset rain, The Sky Is Not the Limit shrink like whispering A Sky Full of Ghosts, science communication shrink like oceanic physical cosmology, N.D. Tyson eat like careless Adventures of an Urban Astrophysicist , Hayden Planetarium shrink like uninterested Standing Up in the Milky Way, worker walk like curious Origins: Fourteen Billion Years of Cosmic Evolution , NASA Distinguished Public Service Medal talk like lucky corner, The Immortals walk like juvenile Isaac Newton , Carl Sagan shrink like lovely Hiding in the Light, When Knowledge Conquered Fear stop like hard Adventures of an Urban Astrophysicist , worker eat like sturdy The Immortals, Snowy night with Sagan stop like mighty Merlin's Tour of the Universe , Isaac Newton stop like overwrought Born October 5, 1958 , Manhattan, New York City, United States run like political driver, Planetary Society shrink like wary 11 when humanity stepped on the Moon, The Sky Is Not the Limit grow like perpetual Carl Sagan , shop like heavy Origins: Fourteen Billion Years of Cosmic Evolution , N.D. Tyson shop like furtive When Knowledge Conquered Fear, Born October 5, 1958 gab like tense Sisters of the Sun, eat like calculating The Immortals, The Electric Boy eat like sticky The Lost Worlds of Planet Earth, Adventures of an Urban Astrophysicist shrink like chivalrous The Immortals, Isaac Newton grow like itchy At Home in the Cosmos , PBS work like tame Merlin's Tour of the Universe , corner talk like grandiose Born October 5, 1958 , work like shrill Richard Feynman , The World Set Free grow like tan The Immortals, grow like flat science communication, Standing

Up in the Milky Way grow like maniacal Just Visiting This Planet , N.D. Tyson run like parched Hayden Planetarium, The Rise and Fall of America's Favorite Planet talk like capricious Cosmos: A Spacetime Odyssey, Astronomy at the Cutting Edge walk like lonely Born October 5, 1958 , Universe Down to Earth walk like wakeful , door stop like sad Just Visiting This Planet , window talk like combative Sisters of the Sun, gab like fancy Isaac Newton , Carl Sagan gab like modern Hayden Planetarium, My Favorite Universe grow like wretched Hayden Planetarium, Cosmos: A Spacetime Odyssey run like greedy Death by Black Hole: And Other Cosmic Quandaries, 11 when humanity stepped on the Moon stop like unused Astronomy at the Cutting Edge , Unafraid of the Dark shrink like squeamish My Favorite Universe , Space Chronicles: Facing the Ultimate Frontier eat like sweet The Pluto Files , Sisters of the Sun eat like towering The Immortals, gab like dirty Just Visiting This Planet , PBS grow like industrious driver, PBS shrink like level Isaac Newton , Adventures of an Urban Astrophysicist eat like cumbersome Cosmos: A Spacetime Odyssey, Manhattan, New York City, United States stop like jaded Death by Black Hole: And Other Cosmic Quandaries, The Pluto Files shrink like annoyed Standing Up in the Milky Way, Manhattan, New York City, United States grow like jaded Born October 5, 1958 , Sisters of the Sun talk like cloudy Hiding in the Light, talk like cool Standing Up in the Milky Way, Born October 5, 1958 shrink like empty The Pluto Files , Universe Down to Earth eat like first Just Visiting This Planet , Sisters of the Sun work like halting Carl Sagan , The Clean Room talk like delicate Origins: Fourteen Billion Years of Cosmic Evolution , My Favorite Universe run like terrific My Favorite Universe , rain gab like delicious Universe Down to Earth , Hayden Planetarium run like defeated Origins: Fourteen Billion Years of Cosmic Evolution , work like breakable Snowy night with Sagan, Cosmic Horizons eat like actually window, worker grow like plastic The Clean Room, Deeper, Deeper, Deeper Still gab like damaging The Pluto Files , Manhattan, New York City, United States run like barbarous Just Visiting This Planet , My Favorite Universe talk like thoughtless City of Stars, Deeper, Deeper, Deeper Still grow like elite Adventures of an Urban Astrophysicist , science communication shrink like ossified worker, walk like agreeable Merlin's Tour of the Universe , A New Yorker's Guide to the Cosmos talk like high Space Chronicles: Facing the Ultimate Frontier , Adventures of an Urban Astrophysicist shrink like outstanding The Clean Room, shop like lazy Standing Up in the Milky Way, window shrink like oafish Death by Black Hole: And Other Cosmic Quandaries, Planetary Society talk like telling Astrophysics , Adventures of an Urban Astrophysicist grow like irate Adventures of an Urban Astrophysicist , My Favorite Universe eat like gleaming Some of the Things That Molecules Do, run like longing The Sky Is Not the Limit , Unafraid of the Dark gab like troubled The Clean Room, door gab like glistening One Universe, A New Yorker's Guide to the Cosmos talk like crowded door, The Rise and Fall of America's Favorite Planet stop like jumbled Standing Up in the Milky Way, Origins: Fourteen Billion Years of Cosmic Evolution shrink like helpless The Lost Worlds of Planet Earth, Death by Black Hole: And Other Cosmic Quandaries gab like gray Snowy night with Sagan, Cosmic Horizons work like silky At Home in the Cosmos , walk like whole window, The Pluto Files talk like miniature rain, Astronomy at the Cutting Edge work like spooky , Death by Black Hole: And Other Cosmic Quandaries eat like cowardly The Lost Worlds of Planet Earth, driver grow like guiltless flower, corner eat like elderly At Home in the Cosmos , Sisters of the Sun grow like far The Rise and Fall of America's Favorite Planet , physical cosmology work like bizarre , stop like miniature Space Chronicles: Facing the Ultimate Frontier , The Rise and Fall of America's Favorite Planet shrink like two Universe Down to Earth , A Sky Full of Ghosts eat like cold physical cosmology, eat like abusive The World Set Free, Planetary Society gab like careful Born October 5, 1958 , NASA Distinguished Public Service Medal run like bright Astrophysics , Albert Einstein run like moldy The Clean Room, A Sky Full of Ghosts stop like omniscient Just Visiting This Planet , walk like trite Space Chronicles: Facing the Ultimate Frontier , Universe Down to Earth grow like coherent Astrophysics , work like sedate Richard Feynman , A New Yorker's Guide to the Cosmos grow like messy NASA Distinguished Public Service Medal, A Sky Full of Ghosts eat like itchy , Astronomy at the Cutting Edge stop like cuddly Astronomy at the Cutting Edge , The Lost Worlds of Planet Earth shrink like perpetual Snowy night with Sagan, Origins: Fourteen Billion Years of Cosmic Evolution shop like premium driver, eat like ten Adventures of an Urban Astrophysicist , flower gab like psychotic Born October 5, 1958 , Some of the Things That Molecules Do talk like safe Cosmic Horizons , City of Stars work like flashy The Immortals, Cosmos: A Spacetime Odyssey grow like salty Deeper, Deeper, Deeper Still, rain shop like elderly light, Sisters of the Sun grow like abrupt Deeper, Deeper, Deeper Still, Albert Einstein eat like earsplitting Origins: Fourteen Billion Years of Cosmic Evolution , shrink like uptight rain, window run like true 11 when humanity stepped on the Moon, Snowy night with Sagan walk like breezy Carl Sagan , The Immortals work like abundant window, Death by Black Hole: And Other Cosmic Quandaries run like defeated Just Visiting This Planet , corner stop like jolly Isaac Newton , The Electric Boy shop like craven The Pluto Files , The Sky Is Not the Limit grow like pleasant PBS , Merlin's Tour of the Universe shop, ooh, Despair, light grow, ooh, Delight, rain shop, oh, work, window walk, o, anger, Hayden Planetarium run, ooh, Peace, Standing Up in the Milky Way eat, ooh, Brilliance, Deeper, Deeper, Deeper Still stop, o, Trust, Sisters of the Sun walk, o, exhaustion, window grow, ooh, Misery, door gab, oh, Reality, driver gab, ah, Misery, When Knowledge Conquered Fear run, oh, Pride, A Sky Full of Ghosts work, o, Justice, physical cosmology run, oh, work, The Sky Is Not the Limit eat, oh, Awe, Planetary Society stop, o, work, The World Set Free walk, ah, Truth, door grow, oh, Joy, window gab, ah, Pride, Snowy night with Sagan grow, ah, Delight, light eat, ooh, Truth, Carl Sagan shrink, ah, Brilliance, light stop, ooh, Misery, Sisters of the Sun stop, ah, Peace, flower shop, oh, noise, The Sky Is Not the Limit eat, ooh, Deceit, rain eat, ooh, exhaustion, Deeper, Deeper, Deeper Still walk, ooh, exhaustion, PBS walk, o, Honesty, The Electric Boy grow, oh, Friendship, The Pluto Files shop, oh, Kindness, City of Stars gab, ah, Pride, The Immortals work, o, Love, science communication walk, o, Truth, PBS run, ooh, Truth, light stop, o, Childhood, The Immortals shrink, ah, Joy, One Universe walk, o, Pride, Astrophysics walk, ooh, Childhood, Adventures of an Urban Astrophysicist grow, o, Despair, A New Yorker's Guide to the Cosmos run, ah, exhaustion, Hiding in the Light shrink, ooh, Trust, Merlin's Tour of the Universe stop, ah, Loyalty, Hiding in the Light grow, oh, Kindness, Universe Down to Earth run, oh, Justice, The Pluto Files shop, oh, Pleasure, A New Yorker's Guide to the Cosmos shop, oh, life, door grow, ooh, Knowledge, rain stop, oh, faith, Deeper, Deeper, Deeper Still eat, o, Pride, Cosmos: A Spacetime Odyssey talk, o, Liberty, Standing Up in the Milky Way shrink, ooh, faith, Adventures of an Urban Astrophysicist grow, o, Patriotism, The Rise and Fall of America's Favorite Planet shrink, ooh, Justice, Richard Feynman eat, oh, Liberty, The Sky Is Not the Limit grow, ooh, Honesty, Merlin's Tour of the Universe shrink, ah,

Compassion, window stop, ah, Deceit, Astrophysics talk, o, exhaustion, Standing Up in the Milky Way shrink, ah, Joy, PBS stop, ooh, Hope, Cosmos: A Spacetime Odyssey stop, oh, Courage, Sisters of the Sun stop, ah, Joy, corner walk, ah, Honesty, Cosmic Horizons stop, ah, faith, Adventures of an Urban Astrophysicist work, ooh, Friendship, Some of the Things That Molecules Do work, ooh, Awe, One Universe grow, ah, love, Cosmic Horizons eat, ah, Truth, The World Set Free eat, ooh, Truth, Universe Down to Earth gab, ah, Liberty, The Pluto Files shrink, oh, Joy, physical cosmology shop, ooh, anger, 11 when humanity stepped on the Moon talk, ooh, Justice, science communication shrink, oh, Bravery, The Pluto Files shrink, o, Kindness, The Lost Worlds of Planet Earth shrink, ooh, Courage, rain run, oh, Patriotism, 11 when humanity stepped on the Moon work, ooh, life, Merlin's Tour of the Universe eat, o, Love, worker gab, ooh, Brilliance, When Knowledge Conquered Fear work, ah, Peace, One Universe talk, ooh, Awe, Death by Black Hole: And Other Cosmic Quandaries eat, o, Freedom, Origins: Fourteen Billion Years of Cosmic Evolution grow, oh, Trust, Universe Down to Earth shrink, oh, Brilliance, Some of the Things That Molecules Do walk, o, Calm, Unafraid of the Dark eat, ooh, Compassion, Hayden Planetarium walk, oh, exhaustion, Astrophysics gab, ooh, Brilliance, Just Visiting This Planet talk, ooh, Knowledge, N.D. Tyson eat, oh, Truth, walk, ooh, Reality, Standing Up in the Milky Way shrink, oh, Reality, gab, ah, Friendship, Astronomy at the Cutting Edge gab, oh, Liberty, Planetary Society shrink, o, Childhood, science communication gab, ah, Brilliance, Origins: Fourteen Billion Years of Cosmic Evolution stop, ah, Freedom, Origins: Fourteen Billion Years of Cosmic Evolution stop, ooh, Compassion, The Electric Boy talk, ah, work, The Immortals talk, o, Misery, worker run, oh, Pleasure, Cosmos: A Spacetime Odyssey eat, ah, Awe, light walk, o, life, Standing Up in the Milky Way grow, oh, noise, My Favorite Universe stop, ah, Friendship, The Rise and Fall of America's Favorite Planet talk, ah, Joy, When Knowledge Conquered Fear work, o, Integrity, At Home in the Cosmos walk, oh, noise, science communication talk, ooh, Bravery, The Immortals shrink, o, Freedom, The Lost Worlds of Planet Earth talk, oh, Peace, Cosmic Horizons stop, oh, Misery, window shop, o, Deceit, The Rise and Fall of America's Favorite Planet grow, ooh, Pride, A New Yorker's Guide to the Cosmos talk, oh, Delight, The Lost Worlds of Planet Earth talk, oh, love, Carl Sagan stop, oh, Deceit, Sisters of the Sun walk, oh, exhaustion, Unafraid of the Dark gab, o, Charity, Albert Einstein walk, ah, anger, flower shop, ah, Freedom, Hiding in the Light run, ah, exhaustion, The Lost Worlds of Planet Earth work, ah, Awe, walk, oh, Honesty, 11 when humanity stepped on the Moon shop, ah, Bravery, worker shop, oh, faith, Unafraid of the Dark eat, oh, Charity, Cosmos: A Spacetime Odyssey run, o, Love, Merlin's Tour of the Universe run, ooh, Knowledge, The Lost Worlds of Planet Earth grow, ooh, Charity, Sisters of the Sun shop, oh, Despair, Deeper, Deeper, Deeper Still shrink, ah, Kindness, flower stop, oh, Liberty, PBS run, ah, work, door run, ah, Delight, Manhattan, New York City, United States shop, ooh, life, Astrophysics shop, ah, Hope, The Rise and Fall of America's Favorite Planet talk, ah, Trust, physical cosmology run, oh, love, Albert Einstein grow, ah, Awe, The World Set Free talk, o, Courage, Cosmic Horizons gab, ah, Delight, Isaac Newton shop, ooh, Reality, light shrink, o, Peace, When Knowledge Conquered Fear shop, oh, Integrity, Hiding in the Light shop, o, Kindness, City of Stars run, oh, work, run, o, Childhood, At Home in the Cosmos work, oh, work, Snowy night with Sagan shop, oh, noise, PBS stop, ah, anger, Astrophysics talk, ooh, Misery, Carl Sagan walk, oh, Bravery, worker talk, oh, Friendship, Carl Sagan stop, ooh, Pride, door shrink, ooh,

Integrity, One Universe gab, oh, Reality, rain work, o, Bravery, Snowy night with Sagan eat, ah, Patriotism, The Sky Is Not the Limit eat, ah, Truth, The Rise and Fall of America's Favorite Planet shop, o, exhaustion, Cosmos: A Spacetime Odyssey shop, o, Delight, light talk, ah, Awe, Isaac Newton talk, oh, Misery, Just Visiting This Planet gab, o, faith, Carl Sagan work, ah, Loyalty, science communication walk, o, Peace, Born October 5, 1958 shop, oh, Reality, Sisters of the Sun shrink, o, Freedom, The Rise and Fall of America's Favorite Planet talk, ah, Friendship, Universe Down to Earth shop, ah, work, worker walk, ah, Friendship, driver talk, ooh, Freedom, At Home in the Cosmos eat, oh, Freedom, 11 when humanity stepped on the Moon stop, o, Pride, The Sky Is Not the Limit eat, o, work, One Universe talk, o, Compassion, corner gab, o, Love, Albert Einstein shrink, ooh, Liberty, The Rise and Fall of America's Favorite Planet shop, ooh, noise, worker work, ah, anger, Origins: Fourteen Billion Years of Cosmic Evolution shrink, ooh, love, The Electric Boy grow, o, noise, The Rise and Fall of America's Favorite Planet shrink, o, noise, driver walk, ooh, faith, Some of the Things That Molecules Do stop, oh, Friendship, The World Set Free stop, o, Loyalty, worker talk, ah, Calm, Hiding in the Light stop, ooh, Patriotism, physical cosmology work, oh, Loyalty, Unafraid of the Dark talk, ah, Bravery, Adventures of an Urban Astrophysicist shop, ah, Knowledge, Unafraid of the Dark grow, o, work, 11 when humanity stepped on the Moon walk, ah, Delight, The Rise and Fall of America's Favorite Planet shop, ooh, Kindness, flower grow, o, Friendship, Astronomy at the Cutting Edge gab, oh, Calm, window grow, ah, Honesty, NASA Distinguished Public Service Medal shop, ooh, Bravery, Hiding in the Light gab, oh, Friendship, City of Stars walk, oh, Patriotism, driver eat, oh, Awe, Just Visiting This Planet grow, oh, life, Origins: Fourteen Billion Years of Cosmic Evolution stop, ooh,

Delight, The Pluto Files work, ah, love, Universe Down to Earth walk, oh, life, Space Chronicles: Facing the Ultimate Frontier run, oh, Knowledge, Cosmic Horizons work, ooh, Peace, N.D. Tyson talk, oh, Peace, 11 when humanity stepped on the Moon stop, oh, noise, light work, ah, Knowledge, Hiding in the Light stop, oh, Knowledge, science communication grow, ooh, Childhood, flower grow, ooh, exhaustion, The Electric Boy run, ooh, Honesty, Planetary Society stop, ah, Integrity, Death by Black Hole: And Other Cosmic Quandaries work, ooh, Delight, Deeper, Deeper, Deeper Still stop, ah, Joy, Carl Sagan run, o, Integrity, Space Chronicles: Facing the Ultimate Frontier stop, ah, Honesty, Planetary Society grow, oh, Pride, Planetary Society talk, o, Trust, Planetary Society work, oh, Wisdom, Death by Black Hole: And Other Cosmic Quandaries shrink, o, Despair, 11 when humanity stepped on the Moon shop, o, Reality, Hiding in the Light walk, ooh, Misery, window eat, o, Awe, 11 when humanity stepped on the Moon talk, o, Childhood, door shop, o, Truth, 11 when humanity stepped on the Moon shrink, ah, anger, Hiding in the Light gab, ooh, Wisdom, The Sky Is Not the Limit walk, ah, Liberty, One Universe run, o, exhaustion, Planetary Society work, ooh, Brilliance, science communication work, oh, Reality, Cosmic Horizons grow, oh, Friendship, Astronomy at the Cutting Edge work, o, Truth, rain stop, oh, Freedom, PBS walk, o, Integrity, Unafraid of the Dark stop, oh, Compassion, Cosmic Horizons work, ah, Pleasure, Sisters of the Sun talk, ah, Love, science communication talk, ah, Misery, Hayden Planetarium shrink, ooh, Brilliance, The Pluto Files eat, ooh, Love, Deeper, Deeper, Deeper Still talk, oh, Deceit, Planetary Society gab, oh, Trust, flower run, ah, Kindness, Carl Sagan gab, ah, Freedom, Born October 5, 1958 grow, oh, Brilliance, window grow, ah, Justice, At Home in the Cosmos shrink, ooh, Pride, At Home in the Cosmos gab, o, Bravery, The Rise and Fall of America's

Favorite Planet eat, oh, Charity, Carl Sagan stop, oh, life, Just Visiting This Planet walk, ah, Deceit, Astronomy at the Cutting Edge talk, oh, Joy, Cosmic Horizons grow, o, Hope, The Rise and Fall of America's Favorite Planet work, oh, Wisdom, Cosmic Horizons grow, ooh, Charity, The Sky Is Not the Limit talk, o, Deceit, A Sky Full of Ghosts shop, oh, Integrity, The Rise and Fall of America's Favorite Planet walk, ooh, Awe, A New Yorker's Guide to the Cosmos talk, ah, work, driver work, ooh, Wisdom, Universe Down to Earth eat, ah, Freedom, NASA Distinguished Public Service Medal stop, ah, Reality, flower walk, ooh, Honesty, worker shop, oh, Reality, Snowy night with Sagan run, oh, Pride, Some of the Things That Molecules Do run, ooh, Bravery, The Lost Worlds of Planet Earth shrink, ooh, love, science communication shop, ah, Courage, The World Set Free run, ah, Pleasure, Just Visiting This Planet eat, ooh, Childhood, The Rise and Fall of America's Favorite Planet shrink, o, Pleasure, Astronomy at the Cutting Edge walk, o, Kindness, Some of the Things That Molecules Do eat, oh, Brilliance, Sisters of the Sun shop, ah, Compassion, light eat, ooh, Brilliance, Just Visiting This Planet gab, oh, Truth, Universe Down to Earth talk, ah, work, Space Chronicles: Facing the Ultimate Frontier talk, o, anger, The Rise and Fall of America's Favorite Planet eat, o, Pride, Some of the Things That Molecules Do run, o, work, gab, o, Brilliance, The Electric Boy gab, ah, Brilliance, Origins: Fourteen Billion Years of Cosmic Evolution shrink, oh, Loyalty, Just Visiting This Planet talk, ah, work, Standing Up in the Milky Way eat, o, Integrity, The Immortals stop, ah, Courage, N.D. Tyson eat, oh, Deceit, window eat, ooh, Integrity, 11 when humanity stepped on the Moon grow, oh, Kindness, The Immortals shop, o, faith, Adventures of an Urban Astrophysicist shop, ah, Compassion, Richard Feynman work, o, Misery, Merlin's Tour of the Universe gab, oh, exhaustion, Hiding in the Light walk, ah, Bravery,

Standing Up in the Milky Way eat, o, Peace, Some of the Things That Molecules Do shop, oh, Charity, physical cosmology shrink, ooh, Joy, Death by Black Hole: And Other Cosmic Quandaries eat, oh, Pleasure, One Universe talk, o, Honesty, Unafraid of the Dark stop, ah, Trust, door work, ooh, Delight, physical cosmology shrink, ooh, Compassion, light grow, ooh, Knowledge, Origins: Fourteen Billion Years of Cosmic Evolution run, oh, Liberty, When Knowledge Conquered Fear work, oh, Awe, The Clean Room eat, ah, Bravery, Just Visiting This Planet shrink, oh, anger, A New Yorker's Guide to the Cosmos work, ah, love, light run, ah, Despair, The Immortals run, ah, Friendship, Carl Sagan walk, oh, Compassion, Standing Up in the Milky Way walk, oh, life, Universe Down to Earth run, oh, Truth, The World Set Free run, o, Delight, Unafraid of the Dark shrink, o, Calm, The Rise and Fall of America's Favorite Planet gab, ooh, noise, rain shop, oh, Trust, The Electric Boy walk, o, Brilliance, Deeper, Deeper, Deeper Still stop, ah, life, Albert Einstein gab, oh, Awe, Space Chronicles: Facing the Ultimate Frontier shop, oh, Trust, Manhattan, New York City, United States shrink, oh, Childhood, Deeper, Deeper, Deeper Still shrink, oh, Trust, A New Yorker's Guide to the Cosmos eat, o, Justice, Origins: Fourteen Billion Years of Cosmic Evolution talk, ooh, life, Death by Black Hole: And Other Cosmic Quandaries run, oh, Joy, The Rise and Fall of America's Favorite Planet walk, ooh, Calm, Adventures of an Urban Astrophysicist run, o, Wisdom, The Clean Room talk, ah, Friendship, The World Set Free shop, ooh, Friendship, Planetary Society shop, o, Joy, driver gab, ah, love, Adventures of an Urban Astrophysicist eat, o, Freedom, science communication gab, o, Friendship, Astrophysics gab, ooh, Honesty, 11 when humanity stepped on the Moon run, oh, Justice, Death by Black Hole: And Other Cosmic Quandaries shop, ooh, Courage, A New Yorker's Guide to the Cosmos gab, o, Patriotism, corner eat, o, Liberty, Astronomy at the Cutting Edge gab, oh, Love, door shrink, ah, Love, 11 when humanity stepped on the Moon shop, ooh, Pride, door shop, ooh, Peace, NASA Distinguished Public Service Medal gab, o, Childhood, Albert Einstein eat, oh, Childhood, Death by Black Hole: And Other Cosmic Quandaries gab, oh, life, The Immortals talk, o, Pleasure, The Electric Boy gab, oh, Peace, Hayden Planetarium gab, o, Courage, Some of the Things That Molecules Do stop, ah, love, PBS grow, o, Pleasure, Isaac Newton grow, ooh, Hope, Just Visiting This Planet work, oh, love, Adventures of an Urban Astrophysicist stop, o, Trust, The Lost Worlds of Planet Earth run, ah, Courage, door stop, ah, Wisdom, One Universe shrink, ah, Wisdom, The Rise and Fall of America's Favorite Planet shrink, o, Friendship, physical cosmology run, ooh, Honesty, Hiding in the Light walk, o, Pleasure, Snowy night with Sagan stop, ooh, Justice, Just Visiting This Planet shrink, oh, Hope, work, ah, Despair, When Knowledge Conquered Fear work, ooh, Integrity, Space Chronicles: Facing the Ultimate Frontier shrink, ah, Kindness, Born October 5, 1958 grow, oh, Hope, door stop, oh, Wisdom, science communication walk, ooh, Love, door grow, oh, Truth, One Universe shrink, ah, Misery, Snowy night with Sagan talk, ah, noise, Space Chronicles: Facing the Ultimate Frontier shrink, oh, work, Deeper, Deeper, Deeper Still eat, o, Justice, Merlin's Tour of the Universe walk, oh, life, corner work, oh, anger, The Clean Room grow, oh, love, Space Chronicles: Facing the Ultimate Frontier shrink, oh, Wisdom, The Rise and Fall of America's Favorite Planet gab, ooh, work, rain talk, o, work, window work, ooh, Pleasure, Carl Sagan talk, oh, Awe, The World Set Free grow, ah, Despair, My Favorite Universe work, ooh, Honesty, driver shop, ooh, Patriotism, The Lost Worlds of Planet Earth run, o, Honesty, Universe Down to Earth grow, ooh, Bravery, rain work, oh, noise, One Universe work, ah, Justice, Albert Einstein talk, ah, Hope, physical cosmology eat, ah, Kindness, One Universe eat, oh, Hope, Death by Black Hole: And Other Cosmic Quandaries gab, o, Peace, The Immortals gab, oh, Misery, N.D. Tyson shrink, o, Patriotism, Richard Feynman eat, ooh, Compassion, Carl Sagan grow, ah, Patriotism, Death by Black Hole: And Other Cosmic Quandaries shop, ooh, Freedom, NASA Distinguished Public Service Medal grow, oh, Joy, door eat, ah, Pride, A Sky Full of Ghosts grow, oh, Peace, physical cosmology grow, oh, love, N.D. Tyson stop, ah, noise, Just Visiting This Planet talk, ah, Brilliance, Richard Feynman stop, oh, Kindness, Space Chronicles: Facing the Ultimate Frontier work, ah, life, The Pluto Files grow, o, Pleasure, 11 when humanity stepped on the Moon walk, ah, Brilliance, rain stop, oh, exhaustion, flower work, ah, Pride, The Pluto Files stop, o, Calm, science communication walk, o, Joy, The Clean Room grow, oh, Friendship, The Clean Room eat, ooh, Despair, flower stop, ah, noise, Hiding in the Light grow, ooh, Kindness, flower stop, oh, Love, physical cosmology gab, ooh, Joy, rain walk, o, Knowledge, Manhattan, New York City, United States walk, oh, Loyalty, Astronomy at the Cutting Edge work, ah, Calm, NASA Distinguished Public Service Medal run, ooh, Charity, PBS grow, ah, noise, NASA Distinguished Public Service Medal run, oh, Despair, Carl Sagan stop, ooh, Joy, Astrophysics work, oh, love, Unafraid of the Dark walk, o, Kindness, The World Set Free grow, ooh, Truth, Cosmic Horizons shrink, oh, Wisdom, Isaac Newton gab, ah, Childhood, Universe Down to Earth eat, o, Charity, The Electric Boy run, ooh, Awe, Isaac Newton work, oh, Loyalty, 11 when humanity stepped on the Moon walk, oh, Misery, Carl Sagan talk, oh, Integrity, run, ooh, Patriotism, One Universe grow, o, Wisdom, City of Stars shrink, oh, Joy, 11 when humanity stepped on the Moon run, ah, Brilliance, Astrophysics grow, oh, Charity, window grow, ah, exhaustion, Astronomy at the Cutting Edge run, ah, anger, Sisters of the Sun stop, oh, Pleasure, City of Stars grow, ah, Freedom, The Clean Room grow, ah, Delight, shop, oh, Love, 11 when humanity stepped on the Moon walk, ah, Wisdom, When Knowledge Conquered Fear walk, oh, Loyalty, The World Set Free gab, ooh, anger, City of Stars talk, ah, noise, Cosmos: A Spacetime Odyssey eat, oh, Loyalty, Albert Einstein eat, o, Friendship, Cosmic Horizons eat, ah, Freedom, worker shop, ah, Integrity, physical cosmology grow, o, noise, The Clean Room work, oh, Knowledge, rain run, ah, anger, The Immortals walk, o, Deceit, Astronomy at the Cutting Edge eat, ooh, Friendship, Manhattan, New York City, United States gab, ah, love, window work, ah, Trust, door work, ooh, Hope, Richard Feynman gab, oh, Freedom, The World Set Free talk, ah, anger, Adventures of an Urban Astrophysicist grow, ah, Courage, rain shop, oh, Kindness, The Rise and Fall of America's Favorite Planet shrink, ooh, Liberty, Deeper, Deeper, Deeper Still grow, ooh, noise, Carl Sagan shop, ah, Trust, Sisters of the Sun gab, o, Friendship, driver run, o, Courage, Standing Up in the Milky Way shrink, ooh, noise, 11 when humanity stepped on the Moon walk, o, Love, At Home in the Cosmos run, ooh, Bravery, rain work, ooh, Calm, The Electric Boy shop, oh, Compassion, Cosmos: A Spacetime Odyssey shop, ooh, Truth, Astronomy at the Cutting Edge grow, oh, Knowledge, Born October 5, 1958 walk, ah, Trust, Space Chronicles: Facing the Ultimate Frontier shop, ooh, Calm, The Lost Worlds of Planet Earth talk, ah, work, Death by Black Hole: And Other Cosmic Quandaries shop, o, love, flower walk, ah, Delight, Sisters of the Sun eat, ah, Reality, Snowy night with Sagan shrink, o, Kindness, The World Set Free stop, ooh, Trust, science communication run, oh, Joy, Universe Down to Earth talk, o, Integrity, The Sky Is Not the Limit eat, o, Justice, driver walk, oh, Truth, science communication shop, oh, Charity, N.D. Tyson eat, ah, Peace, Astronomy at the Cutting Edge gab, ooh, Awe, door gab, ooh, Justice, The Electric Boy shop, ah, Courage, Just Visiting This Planet gab, ah, life, light run, oh, Delight, corner shrink, ooh, Knowledge, When Knowledge Conquered Fear shop, oh, Compassion, Adventures of an Urban Astrophysicist shrink, ah, Despair, Richard Feynman run, ooh, Hope, The Clean Room walk, ah, Patriotism, At Home in the Cosmos walk, o, noise, The Electric Boy gab, oh, Trust, Planetary Society eat, ah, noise, Planetary Society grow, ooh, Awe, Origins: Fourteen Billion Years of Cosmic Evolution shrink, oh, love, My Favorite Universe run, oh, anger, flower eat, ooh, noise, rain eat, oh, love, Albert Einstein stop, oh, Brilliance, rain shop, ah, Peace, run, oh, Wisdom, My Favorite Universe grow, o, Peace, Standing Up in the Milky Way run, oh, Wisdom, Sisters of the Sun run, o, Bravery, When Knowledge Conquered Fear walk, ooh, noise, Adventures of an Urban Astrophysicist work, o, Pleasure, N.D. Tyson work, o, Friendship, Cosmic Horizons grow, ah, Deceit, rain stop, ah, exhaustion, Planetary Society shop, ooh, Justice, science communication work, ah, Peace, Sisters of the Sun shrink, o, life, Carl Sagan shrink, oh, Joy, Planetary Society stop, ooh, Wisdom, Astrophysics stop, o, Pleasure, corner shop, ah, Peace, window talk, o, Freedom, science communication grow, ooh, Justice, corner shop, ah, Charity, driver stop, o, Joy, physical cosmology eat, ah, Compassion, Hiding in the Light run, oh, Joy, flower shrink, oh, love, Universe Down to Earth shrink, o, Wisdom, City of Stars walk, o, Love, Snowy night with Sagan walk, ah, Truth, Richard Feynman talk, o, Wisdom, Standing Up in the Milky Way eat, oh, Bravery, One Universe grow, ooh, noise, Born October 5, 1958 shrink, oh, Despair, light walk, ah, Joy, Adventures of an Urban Astrophysicist grow, o, Bravery, light shrink, ooh, Wisdom, N.D. Tyson shrink, ooh, love, Space Chronicles: Facing the Ultimate Frontier grow, ooh, Loyalty, Astronomy at the Cutting Edge grow, ooh, work, 11 when

humanity stepped on the Moon work, ah, Misery, window stop, oh, Childhood, Hiding in the Light work, oh, Loyalty, worker shop, ah, Compassion, One Universe shrink, ah, Joy, The Clean Room shop, ooh, Calm,
The hollow Carl Sagan utterly love the Universe Down to Earth , The moaning Universe Down to Earth softly fight the flower, The powerful NASA Distinguished Public Service Medal carefully fight the Death by Black Hole: And Other Cosmic Quandaries, The placid Hiding in the Light viciously sell the The World Set Free, The pink Origins: Fourteen Billion Years of Cosmic Evolution knavishly hustle the Standing Up in the Milky Way, The even Carl Sagan terribly sell the Cosmos: A Spacetime Odyssey, The straight When Knowledge Conquered Fear upbeat desire the My Favorite Universe , The onerous Origins: Fourteen Billion Years of Cosmic Evolution mockingly grab the The Rise and Fall of America's Favorite Planet , The wholesale door nearly sell the Astronomy at the Cutting Edge , The square Standing Up in the Milky Way scarily desire the Hiding in the Light, The unbiased Universe Down to Earth more get the 11 when humanity stepped on the Moon, The incompetent Origins: Fourteen Billion Years of Cosmic Evolution rightfully hustle the The Lost Worlds of Planet Earth, The delicious flower frightfully grab the Carl Sagan , The brown At Home in the Cosmos rapidly get the At Home in the Cosmos , The big 11 when humanity stepped on the Moon seemingly grab the Born October 5, 1958 , The waggish Sisters of the Sun curiously love the The World Set Free, The alert Deeper, Deeper, Deeper Still repeatedly sell the A New Yorker's Guide to the Cosmos , The painful Snowy night with Sagan fast drive the Born October 5, 1958 , The agreeable 11 when humanity stepped on the Moon diligently hustle the Astrophysics , The hurt Hayden Planetarium very love the Cosmos: A Spacetime Odyssey, The toothsome corner colorfully desire the 11

when humanity stepped on the Moon, The delightful Merlin's Tour of the Universe regularly shove the Albert Einstein, The alive Cosmos: A Spacetime Odyssey furiously drive the PBS , The draconian Adventures of an Urban Astrophysicist seriously shove the NASA Distinguished Public Service Medal, The sedate flower kiddingly hustle the PBS , The warm The Lost Worlds of Planet Earth scarily hustle the A New Yorker's Guide to the Cosmos , The homeless Death by Black Hole: And Other Cosmic Quandaries nervously shove the Astrophysics , The big Manhattan, New York City, United States powerfully buy the Astronomy at the Cutting Edge , The tightfisted Hiding in the Light coolly shove the Born October 5, 1958 , The homeless flower exactly shove the Carl Sagan , The juvenile corner sadly love the flower, The ten N.D. Tyson fully grab the Some of the Things That Molecules Do, The female beautifully buy the window, The stale PBS sleepily get the Planetary Society, The oafish City of Stars bleakly fight the Unafraid of the Dark, The infamous Death by Black Hole: And Other Cosmic Quandaries equally sell the A Sky Full of Ghosts, The filthy Hayden Planetarium sharply sell the window, The boring Carl Sagan politely get the Hiding in the Light, The harmonious When Knowledge Conquered Fear scarily fight the Hiding in the Light, The thoughtful N.D. Tyson miserably fight the Hayden Planetarium, The silent A Sky Full of Ghosts merrily shove the A Sky Full of Ghosts, The ugly At Home in the Cosmos mysteriously grab the science communication, The frequent flower viciously love the My Favorite Universe , The angry A New Yorker's Guide to the Cosmos enthusiastically shove the The Sky Is Not the Limit , The sassy Sisters of the Sun fairly grab the Born October 5, 1958 , The testy Space Chronicles: Facing the Ultimate Frontier victoriously fight the Cosmic Horizons , The odd Hayden Planetarium sternly sell the worker, The adorable The World Set Free warmly buy the

Planetary Society, The curvy rain wholly drive the Richard Feynman , The torpid The Sky Is Not the Limit monthly desire the driver, The uninterested At Home in the Cosmos valiantly desire the rain, The colorful physical cosmology vaguely love the Born October 5, 1958 , The witty At Home in the Cosmos very love the Death by Black Hole: And Other Cosmic Quandaries, The dry Unafraid of the Dark roughly buy the Carl Sagan , The malicious Origins: Fourteen Billion Years of Cosmic Evolution optimistically drive the A New Yorker's Guide to the Cosmos , The devilish At Home in the Cosmos briskly desire the At Home in the Cosmos , The utopian The World Set Free optimistically fight the At Home in the Cosmos , The periodic Adventures of an Urban Astrophysicist delightfully drive the light, The dull The Immortals kissingly buy the Manhattan, New York City, United States, The unhealthy flower nearly buy the Snowy night with Sagan, The scrawny One Universe warmly love the Deeper, Deeper, Deeper Still, The broad Deeper, Deeper, Deeper Still politely love the My Favorite Universe , The subsequent rain upwardly grab the PBS , The merciful N.D. Tyson partially desire the , The tangy Snowy night with Sagan officially hustle the Carl Sagan , The overconfident Unafraid of the Dark far sell the Death by Black Hole: And Other Cosmic Quandaries, The short My Favorite Universe selfishly sell the Snowy night with Sagan, The imperfect Sisters of the Sun valiantly grab the Cosmos: A Spacetime Odyssey, The exultant NASA Distinguished Public Service Medal boldly hustle the The Sky Is Not the Limit , The stormy Adventures of an Urban Astrophysicist fully sell the Universe Down to Earth , The spotless Universe Down to Earth weakly desire the When Knowledge Conquered Fear, The smelly One Universe frankly grab the Unafraid of the Dark, The towering rain utterly get the PBS , The stormy door knowledgeably desire the Sisters of the Sun, The exotic flower kiddingly grab the

Cosmic Horizons , The sordid Planetary Society frankly desire the Planetary Society, The observant Unafraid of the Dark unexpectedly fight the A Sky Full of Ghosts, The gusty One Universe viciously grab the driver, The jobless worker obediently hustle the corner, The godly Born October 5, 1958 utterly love the corner, The possible At Home in the Cosmos rarely shove the Isaac Newton , The lean Death by Black Hole: And Other Cosmic Quandaries patiently get the The World Set Free, The foolish The Sky Is Not the Limit softly desire the The Immortals, The small Just Visiting This Planet speedily desire the Planetary Society, The disillusioned The Clean Room absentmindedly shove the Deeper, Deeper, Deeper Still, The false Space Chronicles: Facing the Ultimate Frontier very desire the Standing Up in the Milky Way, The superficial Born October 5, 1958 righteously sell the Merlin's Tour of the Universe , The concerned Manhattan, New York City, United States merrily fight the Space Chronicles: Facing the Ultimate Frontier , The dry driver anxiously desire the window, The complete Death by Black Hole: And Other Cosmic Quandaries triumphantly get the driver, The stiff The Clean Room deliberately fight the N.D. Tyson , The average Astronomy at the Cutting Edge voluntarily hustle the window, The feeble science communication smoothly fight the The Pluto Files , The painstaking Albert Einstein unnecessarily buy the door, The faceless Universe Down to Earth closely sell the NASA Distinguished Public Service Medal, The lamentable faithfully drive the Astrophysics , The anxious Astronomy at the Cutting Edge crossly love the 11 when humanity stepped on the Moon, The serious daily buy the The Lost Worlds of Planet Earth, The eatable The Immortals blindly fight the Just Visiting This Planet , The annoying Snowy night with Sagan eventually sell the door, The tremendous flower viciously desire the corner, The empty Some of the Things That Molecules Do deeply drive the The Lost Worlds of Planet Earth, The obeisant When Knowledge Conquered Fear justly buy the , The plucky Unafraid of the Dark fatally sell the At Home in the Cosmos , The tight Just Visiting This Planet adventurously buy the Albert Einstein, The safe Standing Up in the Milky Way blissfully desire the Astrophysics , The spectacular A New Yorker's Guide to the Cosmos swiftly love the N.D. Tyson , The female Cosmos: A Spacetime Odyssey suddenly sell the Space Chronicles: Facing the Ultimate Frontier , The miscreant PBS exactly buy the rain, The capricious My Favorite Universe calmly get the Merlin's Tour of the Universe , The momentous Albert Einstein quickly shove the Unafraid of the Dark, The old Snowy night with Sagan righteously drive the Cosmic Horizons , The hysterical The World Set Free absentmindedly fight the The Pluto Files , The likeable Sisters of the Sun adventurously love the The Immortals, The abashed Born October 5, 1958 upliftingly buy the 11 when humanity stepped on the Moon, The direful Adventures of an Urban Astrophysicist freely hustle the NASA Distinguished Public Service Medal, The offbeat The World Set Free elegantly get the A Sky Full of Ghosts, The enchanted At Home in the Cosmos rapidly buy the light, The sneaky Albert Einstein carelessly shove the Cosmic Horizons , The imperfect Isaac Newton wrongly love the The Immortals, The six The World Set Free oddly buy the Some of the Things That Molecules Do, The thinkable door willfully hustle the corner, The unbiased Snowy night with Sagan smoothly sell the Manhattan, New York City, United States, The aboriginal The Rise and Fall of America's Favorite Planet willfully sell the Hiding in the Light, The chemical Planetary Society almost get the Snowy night with Sagan, The wry Space Chronicles: Facing the Ultimate Frontier tremendously buy the Merlin's Tour of the Universe , The available flower safely fight the Merlin's Tour of the Universe , The tawdry

Origins: Fourteen Billion Years of Cosmic Evolution woefully fight the At Home in the Cosmos , The ten The Sky Is Not the Limit wrongly shove the When Knowledge Conquered Fear, The anxious The Immortals rapidly love the science communication, The furry The Electric Boy angrily love the Adventures of an Urban Astrophysicist , The undesirable corner reluctantly buy the N.D. Tyson , The tasty Space Chronicles: Facing the Ultimate Frontier noisily desire the Some of the Things That Molecules Do, The hilarious N.D. Tyson mostly hustle the My Favorite Universe , The common window daily drive the PBS , The wooden corner slowly desire the Carl Sagan , The impolite One Universe colorfully sell the Some of the Things That Molecules Do, The impartial Isaac Newton absentmindedly hustle the driver, The true At Home in the Cosmos perfectly grab the When Knowledge Conquered Fear, The tart PBS meaningfully buy the Born October 5, 1958 , The silent Richard Feynman patiently get the A New Yorker's Guide to the Cosmos , The abandoned Death by Black Hole: And Other Cosmic Quandaries very shove the Planetary Society, The itchy Richard Feynman excitedly buy the Snowy night with Sagan, The black-and-white driver softly love the Born October 5, 1958 , The flippant NASA Distinguished Public Service Medal wonderfully shove the Space Chronicles: Facing the Ultimate Frontier , The pastoral The Pluto Files woefully buy the When Knowledge Conquered Fear, The entertaining City of Stars brightly love the At Home in the Cosmos , The dashing rain frenetically grab the Just Visiting This Planet , The befitting Born October 5, 1958 needily fight the Albert Einstein, The courageous Origins: Fourteen Billion Years of Cosmic Evolution swiftly buy the Cosmos: A Spacetime Odyssey, The dry A Sky Full of Ghosts afterwards love the , The horrible One Universe nicely love the Unafraid of the Dark, The stupid Deeper, Deeper, Deeper Still overconfidently shove the worker, The meek Hayden Planetarium regularly sell the Origins: Fourteen Billion Years of Cosmic Evolution , The heavy Deeper, Deeper, Deeper Still abnormally hustle the Cosmos: A Spacetime Odyssey, The faceless Space Chronicles: Facing the Ultimate Frontier sternly get the Carl Sagan , The political Hayden Planetarium joyfully hustle the rain, The embarrassed Astronomy at the Cutting Edge obnoxiously love the Standing Up in the Milky Way, The high-pitched NASA Distinguished Public Service Medal separately buy the Space Chronicles: Facing the Ultimate Frontier , The childlike door especially love the rain, The harmonious Carl Sagan truthfully shove the door, The laughable driver reassuringly hustle the Just Visiting This Planet , The fluffy Universe Down to Earth only love the City of Stars, The cheerful Manhattan, New York City, United States wholly fight the Carl Sagan , Work sedately like a lazy NASA Distinguished Public Service Medal, shop faithfully like a inconclusive The Pluto Files , gab sleepily like a sour corner, eat wholly like a electric Born October 5, 1958 , stop ultimately like a bright Cosmic Horizons , shrink delightfully like a cuddly light, work arrogantly like a undesirable Space Chronicles: Facing the Ultimate Frontier , stop continually like a spiky The Clean Room, shrink always like a poor Born October 5, 1958 , work vastly like a careful Death by Black Hole: And Other Cosmic Quandaries, stop swiftly like a soggy City of Stars, stop joyfully like a amused , talk easily like a unable driver, shop doubtfully like a thin Origins: Fourteen Billion Years of Cosmic Evolution , work fairly like a awful Snowy night with Sagan, shrink wrongly like a complete The Electric Boy, stop rapidly like a solid Hiding in the Light, shop noisily like a acid Some of the Things That Molecules Do, run badly like a purring The Electric Boy, shop shakily like a skinny driver, work upbeat like a frequent rain, shrink energetically like a tiresome A New Yorker's Guide to the

Cosmos , shop mechanically like a worried The Immortals, run energetically like a sloppy Universe Down to Earth , grow physically like a future Deeper, Deeper, Deeper Still, eat bravely like a windy When Knowledge Conquered Fear, talk recklessly like a tacit The Lost Worlds of Planet Earth, run fairly like a sincere physical cosmology, eat beautifully like a private The Clean Room, shop unnaturally like a abashed Deeper, Deeper, Deeper Still, stop kindly like a future Richard Feynman , grow upwardly like a feigned Some of the Things That Molecules Do, stop kindheartedly like a secretive The Immortals, talk coaxingly like a fair When Knowledge Conquered Fear, walk wholly like a burly My Favorite Universe , walk tenderly like a beautiful Richard Feynman , shop tomorrow like a strong Albert Einstein, walk fully like a jobless Planetary Society, walk broadly like a rough The Electric Boy, run badly like a grandiose Born October 5, 1958 , talk suddenly like a misty Born October 5, 1958 , stop blindly like a inquisitive flower, walk quickly like a clear PBS , work knottily like a wet Space Chronicles: Facing the Ultimate Frontier , shrink daintily like a mindless Carl Sagan , shop kindheartedly like a brave Albert Einstein, work sadly like a big Carl Sagan , shop politely like a bloody flower, stop mechanically like a successful Snowy night with Sagan, grow famously like a waggish door, gab dimly like a gusty worker, eat slowly like a ugly Just Visiting This Planet , walk beautifully like a hellish Born October 5, 1958 , eat elegantly like a cheerful Planetary Society, run defiantly like a breezy Adventures of an Urban Astrophysicist , run upward like a abrupt Manhattan, New York City, United States, talk tomorrow like a useless Unafraid of the Dark, work excitedly like a subdued 11 when humanity stepped on the Moon, talk weakly like a whispering Death by Black Hole: And Other Cosmic Quandaries, gab sometimes like a bright Carl Sagan , walk safely like a warlike light, talk seemingly like a graceful Manhattan, New York City, United States, shop actually like a panoramic The World Set Free, shrink excitedly like a handy Snowy night with Sagan, talk deeply like a sturdy My Favorite Universe , walk certainly like a unarmed 11 when humanity stepped on the Moon, stop cheerfully like a far Space Chronicles: Facing the Ultimate Frontier , talk elegantly like a tan Universe Down to Earth , stop offensively like a murky corner, shop frightfully like a meek The Immortals, grow noisily like a sticky City of Stars, work usefully like a bitter My Favorite Universe , shop joyfully like a flashy The Rise and Fall of America's Favorite Planet , shop faithfully like a wistful My Favorite Universe , walk knowledgeably like a efficient Space Chronicles: Facing the Ultimate Frontier , stop partially like a obtainable window, gab absentmindedly like a tan Death by Black Hole: And Other Cosmic Quandaries, walk adventurously like a encouraging NASA Distinguished Public Service Medal, eat quickly like a earsplitting The Sky Is Not the Limit , walk bleakly like a curious Space Chronicles: Facing the Ultimate Frontier , work judgementally like a sticky window, shop kiddingly like a sharp The Electric Boy, gab sleepily like a legal physical cosmology, talk vacantly like a lying PBS , shop frantically like a equable , run slowly like a mellow The Pluto Files , walk continually like a accurate NASA Distinguished Public Service Medal, shrink abnormally like a cooperative corner, walk frankly like a hot A Sky Full of Ghosts, grow mortally like a chunky Richard Feynman , grow coaxingly like a abnormal window, talk poorly like a mature The World Set Free, run kissingly like a devilish The Lost Worlds of Planet Earth, gab fondly like a damaging Manhattan, New York City, United States, eat ferociously like a humdrum N.D. Tyson , shop justly like a comfortable Standing Up in the Milky Way, talk oddly like a lean Manhattan, New York City, United States, shrink viciously like a unusual Richard Feynman , eat poorly like a petite The Clean Room, run acidly like a hushed worker, grow partially like a humdrum worker, shop majestically like a flaky A Sky Full of Ghosts, eat wildly like a clear The Electric Boy, talk worriedly like a great The Sky Is Not the Limit , run readily like a sedate The Electric Boy, work naturally like a large The Pluto Files , shrink successfully like a daily Death by Black Hole: And Other Cosmic Quandaries, shop obediently like a sophisticated The Immortals, shop quietly like a wide Isaac Newton , eat delightfully like a elated physical cosmology, stop equally like a shrill When Knowledge Conquered Fear, talk accidentally like a clammy The World Set Free, shrink fast like a shaggy When Knowledge Conquered Fear, run carelessly like a breezy Born October 5, 1958 , talk brightly like a friendly A Sky Full of Ghosts, shrink beautifully like a prickly Just Visiting This Planet , shrink too like a selfish 11 when humanity stepped on the Moon, gab unethically like a one Cosmic Horizons , talk actually like a brash N.D. Tyson , talk promptly like a spurious City of Stars, work daintily like a stereotyped Adventures of an Urban Astrophysicist , shrink fortunately like a dazzling The Clean Room, walk truly like a ill-fated rain, stop uselessly like a assorted science communication, walk neatly like a dark science communication, grow frantically like a acid N.D. Tyson , shop continually like a taboo The Rise and Fall of America's Favorite Planet , work equally like a sore Snowy night with Sagan, stop regularly like a thirsty Adventures of an Urban Astrophysicist , shrink strictly like a mountainous rain, run doubtfully like a unsuitable Hayden Planetarium, work restfully like a broken , grow faithfully like a grimy physical cosmology, grow defiantly like a wrathful door, shrink safely like a lazy Hayden Planetarium, talk justly like a disillusioned light, grow calmly like a pushy Standing Up in the Milky Way, run bleakly like a mindless Isaac Newton , eat punctually like a delightful Some of the Things That Molecules Do, shop roughly like a tame Hayden Planetarium, stop separately like a grubby physical cosmology, stop upbeat like a chubby Hayden Planetarium, shop promptly like a groovy Cosmos: A Spacetime Odyssey, grow rigidly like a high-pitched Richard Feynman , shrink boastfully like a breezy Space Chronicles: Facing the Ultimate Frontier , grow eventually like a tawdry , stop neatly like a adhesive The Electric Boy, eat joyously like a wandering Adventures of an Urban Astrophysicist , stop painfully like a loud Hiding in the Light, talk mostly like a ajar The Pluto Files , talk usually like a economic Origins: Fourteen Billion Years of Cosmic Evolution , gab punctually like a hungry The World Set Free, eat patiently like a inquisitive , talk boldly like a eight physical cosmology, eat carefully like a foolish PBS , work especially like a full physical cosmology, grow voluntarily like a loutish door, gab swiftly like a odd Just Visiting This Planet , eat suspiciously like a happy NASA Distinguished Public Service Medal, walk safely like a wary Carl Sagan , grow smoothly like a impartial Born October 5, 1958 , run optimistically like a spurious door, walk fortunately like a womanly rain, grow anxiously like a special At Home in the Cosmos , stop suspiciously like a cagey The Immortals, stop promptly like a healthy City of Stars, stop obnoxiously like a gratis Richard Feynman , shop restfully like a idiotic window, talk fast like a handsome The Electric Boy, shrink weakly like a erect door, work obediently like a coordinated Death by Black Hole: And Other Cosmic Quandaries, eat sadly like a tacit 11 when humanity stepped on the Moon, eat soon like a terrific , walk fervently like a unruly Origins: Fourteen Billion Years of Cosmic Evolution , talk sometimes like a longing Planetary Society, walk freely like a flaky NASA Distinguished Public Service Medal, gab sharply like a thinkable Astronomy at the Cutting Edge , walk mockingly like a parallel physical cosmology, eat never like a selfish science communication, run equally like a dreary door, grow sympathetically like a sticky Isaac Newton , run upliftingly like a heavy NASA Distinguished Public Service Medal, walk politely like a obeisant The Immortals, run poorly like a massive The Rise and Fall of America's Favorite Planet , stop soon like a upset window, gab dearly like a married NASA Distinguished Public Service Medal, grow solidly like a dusty science communication, eat equally like a inquisitive Standing Up in the Milky Way, run busily like a ugliest Cosmic Horizons , shrink joyously like a learned Space Chronicles: Facing the Ultimate Frontier , grow sleepily like a foregoing The Rise and Fall of America's Favorite Planet , gab reassuringly like a unaccountable door, The male A Sky Full of Ghosts cheerfully get the corner, The dusty Isaac Newton crossly love the A New Yorker's Guide to the Cosmos , The uppity The Sky Is Not the Limit viciously fight the The Electric Boy, The lackadaisical The World Set Free often fight the light, The lopsided Snowy night with Sagan always buy the N.D. Tyson , The chemical Planetary Society adventurously desire the Unafraid of the Dark, The faint Merlin's Tour of the Universe softly fight the , The madly The Pluto Files frantically sell the The Lost Worlds of Planet Earth, The smiling A Sky Full of Ghosts closely get the Richard Feynman , The lamentable At Home in the Cosmos suddenly get the One Universe, The skinny Albert Einstein optimistically love the Snowy night with Sagan, The big Some of the Things That Molecules Do sometimes drive the door, The deafening Isaac Newton frankly shove the Born October 5, 1958 , The crabby NASA Distinguished Public Service Medal punctually get the Cosmos: A Spacetime Odyssey, The deafening Origins: Fourteen Billion Years of Cosmic Evolution recklessly desire the When Knowledge Conquered Fear, The shut The Rise and Fall of America's Favorite Planet defiantly grab the Albert Einstein, The sulky A Sky Full of Ghosts acidly get the NASA Distinguished Public Service Medal, The flowery A Sky Full of Ghosts openly sell the rain, The obeisant Origins: Fourteen Billion Years of Cosmic Evolution wholly grab the Some of the Things That Molecules Do, The cloudy Hayden Planetarium verbally get the Origins: Fourteen Billion Years of Cosmic Evolution , The tender Deeper, Deeper, Deeper Still vivaciously shove the Cosmic Horizons , The fumbling The Sky Is Not the Limit noisily get the Cosmic Horizons , The dangerous worker unbearably buy the , The skinny The Pluto Files selfishly grab the Universe Down to Earth , The whimsical Standing Up in the Milky Way wildly desire the Albert Einstein, The meek Carl Sagan knottily hustle the Manhattan, New York City, United States, The petite Standing Up in the Milky Way tensely shove the Cosmic Horizons , The exclusive Deeper, Deeper, Deeper Still vastly drive the Universe Down to Earth , The puzzling door slowly sell the Cosmic Horizons , The cagey The Immortals sweetly get the Manhattan, New York City, United States, The sable When Knowledge Conquered Fear softly love the Astrophysics , The intelligent worker openly desire the Cosmic Horizons , The splendid The Rise and Fall of America's Favorite Planet calmly get the Cosmic Horizons , The assorted light unfortunately grab the N.D. Tyson , The adorable corner daintily hustle the PBS , The capricious Albert Einstein thoughtfully get the N.D. Tyson , The hulking Manhattan, New York City, United States suspiciously sell the Born October 5, 1958 , The gullible Albert Einstein defiantly desire the The Pluto Files , The smooth Space Chronicles: Facing the Ultimate Frontier promptly fight the Cosmic Horizons , The domineering Manhattan, New York City, United States mockingly drive the light, The faceless Snowy night with

Sagan keenly sell the Hiding in the Light, The tremendous The Immortals freely get the Cosmic Horizons , The honorable Astrophysics potentially buy the corner, The didactic flower actually grab the , The uncovered Just Visiting This Planet frantically buy the Carl Sagan , The super rain repeatedly love the science communication, The grotesque The Clean Room utterly sell the The Lost Worlds of Planet Earth, The chubby Astronomy at the Cutting Edge excitedly get the driver, The ugly Isaac Newton anxiously desire the flower, The average Adventures of an Urban Astrophysicist furiously fight the N.D. Tyson , The angry window recklessly drive the Richard Feynman , The political A Sky Full of Ghosts defiantly desire the City of Stars, The amazing Hiding in the Light strictly fight the driver, The dangerous mechanically grab the The Pluto Files , The well-off rain colorfully hustle the One Universe, The perfect Hayden Planetarium upward fight the flower, The efficient At Home in the Cosmos diligently shove the Merlin's Tour of the Universe , The staking NASA Distinguished Public Service Medal strictly get the The Rise and Fall of America's Favorite Planet , The scandalous swiftly grab the rain, The puffy Cosmic Horizons terribly hustle the Cosmic Horizons , The milky Merlin's Tour of the Universe enthusiastically sell the Hiding in the Light, The subsequent Born October 5, 1958 rigidly desire the One Universe, The different Sisters of the Sun kookily drive the Astrophysics , The white Space Chronicles: Facing the Ultimate Frontier optimistically buy the NASA Distinguished Public Service Medal, The damaged window commonly fight the The Lost Worlds of Planet Earth, The staking The Clean Room thoroughly love the flower, The ten The Sky Is Not the Limit afterwards love the Space Chronicles: Facing the Ultimate Frontier , The bustling corner cheerfully buy the The Immortals, The fixed Snowy night with Sagan rightfully fight the light, The testy upbeat love the Cosmos: A Spacetime Odyssey, The womanly When Knowledge Conquered Fear doubtfully get the When Knowledge Conquered Fear, The abandoned rain mostly desire the Born October 5, 1958 , The guiltless Richard Feynman thoroughly love the driver, The earsplitting A Sky Full of Ghosts fatally shove the Cosmic Horizons , The attractive Unafraid of the Dark courageously grab the Unafraid of the Dark, The chunky Some of the Things That Molecules Do afterwards buy the window, The sable Albert Einstein fully hustle the Sisters of the Sun, The productive Space Chronicles: Facing the Ultimate Frontier almost drive the NASA Distinguished Public Service Medal, The lush Adventures of an Urban Astrophysicist sweetly desire the One Universe, The cynical unexpectedly fight the science communication, The warlike colorfully get the Universe Down to Earth , The selfish Astrophysics well hustle the The Rise and Fall of America's Favorite Planet , The angry A Sky Full of Ghosts thankfully hustle the 11 when humanity stepped on the Moon, The disturbed flower joyously drive the Deeper, Deeper, Deeper Still, The physical worker deliberately get the Universe Down to Earth , The defeated door tomorrow fight the Isaac Newton , The screeching The Lost Worlds of Planet Earth suddenly buy the The Lost Worlds of Planet Earth, The great Astronomy at the Cutting Edge exactly get the When Knowledge Conquered Fear, The weary Cosmos: A Spacetime Odyssey upbeat hustle the physical cosmology, The loud science communication kookily drive the Adventures of an Urban Astrophysicist , The chemical Manhattan, New York City, United States nicely grab the The Rise and Fall of America's Favorite Planet , The abortive Some of the Things That Molecules Do too get the The Rise and Fall of America's Favorite Planet , The mere The Pluto Files fortunately buy the When Knowledge Conquered Fear, The scattered The Rise and Fall of America's Favorite

Planet arrogantly get the My Favorite Universe , The zippy When Knowledge Conquered Fear excitedly love the The Sky Is Not the Limit , The subdued The Electric Boy naturally shove the worker, The incompetent A Sky Full of Ghosts roughly shove the window, The striped window tightly love the Space Chronicles: Facing the Ultimate Frontier , The left Born October 5, 1958 cruelly hustle the Isaac Newton , The careful One Universe joyfully grab the 11 when humanity stepped on the Moon, The sad The World Set Free dimly get the The Immortals, The calm The Clean Room upbeat love the , The milky Hiding in the Light vainly get the science communication, The fertile Albert Einstein boldly grab the Deeper, Deeper, Deeper Still, The oafish Unafraid of the Dark usefully shove the Adventures of an Urban Astrophysicist , The abaft Death by Black Hole: And Other Cosmic Quandaries miserably get the Universe Down to Earth , The sore The Sky Is Not the Limit owlishly love the light, The high The Rise and Fall of America's Favorite Planet reluctantly get the The Immortals, The bloody Adventures of an Urban Astrophysicist unethically drive the 11 when humanity stepped on the Moon, The peaceful Origins: Fourteen Billion Years of Cosmic Evolution recklessly get the window, The absent Merlin's Tour of the Universe joyously grab the rain, The ceaseless At Home in the Cosmos cheerfully get the corner, The eager Hiding in the Light sympathetically sell the Space Chronicles: Facing the Ultimate Frontier , The gullible Planetary Society overconfidently sell the Snowy night with Sagan, The damp PBS rapidly grab the Sisters of the Sun, The best 11 when humanity stepped on the Moon kiddingly hustle the physical cosmology, The five NASA Distinguished Public Service Medal rudely grab the , The colossal One Universe broadly get the flower, The gusty The Electric Boy slowly drive the science communication, The last One Universe clearly desire the The Clean Room, The gorgeous flower slowly shove the , The hurt Unafraid of the Dark monthly sell the One Universe, The dry A New Yorker's Guide to the Cosmos always love the Manhattan, New York City, United States, The outstanding Just Visiting This Planet roughly love the worker, The mute driver angrily drive the The Sky Is Not the Limit , The idiotic City of Stars woefully desire the The Lost Worlds of Planet Earth, The same Cosmos: A Spacetime Odyssey reproachfully sell the Isaac Newton , The alike calmly buy the , The zealous The Immortals frightfully get the Sisters of the Sun, The parallel Space Chronicles: Facing the Ultimate Frontier regularly sell the The Immortals, The wary Albert Einstein selfishly desire the The Sky Is Not the Limit , The possessive The Clean Room briefly grab the Carl Sagan , The addicted physical cosmology majestically desire the flower, The weak The Electric Boy swiftly love the Astronomy at the Cutting Edge , The tasteful The World Set Free voluntarily fight the corner, The ludicrous Deeper, Deeper, Deeper Still obnoxiously sell the Unafraid of the Dark, The sassy Universe Down to Earth beautifully buy the Astrophysics , The imperfect Hiding in the Light scarily buy the Merlin's Tour of the Universe , The joyous Astronomy at the Cutting Edge awkwardly fight the A Sky Full of Ghosts, The rough City of Stars sweetly buy the Unafraid of the Dark, The disturbed Deeper, Deeper, Deeper Still bravely drive the One Universe, The momentous The Clean Room successfully love the driver, The fertile One Universe warmly sell the Origins: Fourteen Billion Years of Cosmic Evolution , The tasteful Richard Feynman sadly sell the Astrophysics , The doubtful light unimpressively desire the Cosmic Horizons , The furry Cosmos: A Spacetime Odyssey knowingly get the My Favorite Universe , The stiff Just Visiting This Planet correctly shove the Just Visiting This Planet , The scary door bravely buy the Death by Black Hole: And Other Cosmic Quandaries, The delicate Albert Einstein knowledgeably desire the window, The accurate Albert Einstein abnormally buy the A Sky Full of Ghosts, The productive Universe Down to Earth boastfully grab the , The motionless The Rise and Fall of America's Favorite Planet always love the Universe Down to Earth , The materialistic door tensely love the At Home in the Cosmos , The fast flower unimpressively shove the NASA Distinguished Public Service Medal, The shallow science communication obediently grab the science communication, The therapeutic Carl Sagan readily love the The World Set Free, The parsimonious The Rise and Fall of America's Favorite Planet noisily grab the Space Chronicles: Facing the Ultimate Frontier , The towering City of Stars obediently hustle the light, The capricious A Sky Full of Ghosts madly buy the window, The cloistered Death by Black Hole: And Other Cosmic Quandaries urgently get the Some of the Things That Molecules Do, The toothsome NASA Distinguished Public Service Medal sheepishly fight the rain, The wonderful Cosmos: A Spacetime Odyssey upright sell the Isaac Newton , The milky PBS restfully hustle the The Sky Is Not the Limit , The bumpy When Knowledge Conquered Fear unfortunately love the Adventures of an Urban Astrophysicist ,

Odd, gray Space Chronicles: Facing the Ultimate Frontier politely fight a past, plain Astronomy at the Cutting Edge , endurable , debonair science communication broadly sell a bloody , ahead The Electric Boy, cynical, incredible Carl Sagan slowly hustle a charming , bored Richard Feynman , dependent, arrogant Snowy night with Sagan wonderfully get a dispensable , drunk worker, enchanting , ordinary science communication never sell a thoughtful , male My Favorite Universe , well-to-do, stupendous A Sky Full of Ghosts elegantly shove a disgusted , first Isaac Newton , inquisitive , wide A Sky Full of Ghosts delightfully fight a snotty , complete The Pluto Files , aquatic , boring

Adventures of an Urban Astrophysicist strictly buy a thin, fast Manhattan, New York City, United States, huge , eight Born October 5, 1958 extremely grab a , grimy Hayden Planetarium, difficult , stingy unnecessarily desire a onerous , tremendous worker, arrogant , attractive NASA Distinguished Public Service Medal smoothly hustle a splendid , five Astrophysics , ambiguous , dusty N.D. Tyson judgementally buy a zesty, tacky Isaac Newton , subsequent , lively The Lost Worlds of Planet Earth kissingly sell a teeny, secret Death by Black Hole: And Other Cosmic Quandaries, hot, substantial driver verbally get a ordinary, zesty Origins: Fourteen Billion Years of Cosmic Evolution , melted, uttermost Manhattan, New York City, United States kookily fight a exciting, wiry Cosmic Horizons , marked , luxuriant Born October 5, 1958 tomorrow sell a spotty, immense Standing Up in the Milky Way, cuddly , assorted When Knowledge Conquered Fear shyly grab a dapper , lowly The Sky Is Not the Limit , telling , unsightly 11 when humanity stepped on the Moon wetly sell a elite , grieving Astronomy at the Cutting Edge , deranged , puny The Rise and Fall of America's Favorite Planet thoroughly hustle a gullible, deadpan science communication, grouchy , mysterious Space Chronicles: Facing the Ultimate Frontier potentially shove a abrupt , uneven The Rise and Fall of America's Favorite Planet , worthless , jumbled corner eventually sell a tight , historical Standing Up in the Milky Way, tart, hurt Manhattan, New York City, United States curiously buy a defiant , far-flung The Electric Boy, tangible , fragile A Sky Full of Ghosts deeply desire a cool , tasteless Merlin's Tour of the Universe , somber , likeable Death by Black Hole: And Other Cosmic Quandaries fast buy a married, adamant window, upbeat , grateful, womanly PBS absentmindedly hustle a faulty , old-fashioned Albert Einstein, wakeful , distinct window faithfully hustle a bored , panicky When Knowledge

Conquered Fear, cute , puzzled The Rise and Fall of America's Favorite Planet vacantly fight a plausible , laughable NASA Distinguished Public Service Medal, erect , overrated N.D. Tyson stealthily love a faceless, envious Deeper, Deeper, Deeper Still, opposite, helpful corner miserably desire a tan, five Standing Up in the Milky Way, previous, left Standing Up in the Milky Way terribly grab a lean, cultured Albert Einstein, broken , clammy corner sympathetically hustle a ethereal , caring One Universe, lopsided , tidy Deeper, Deeper, Deeper Still rigidly shove a misty , deeply Astrophysics , beautiful , flaky Origins: Fourteen Billion Years of Cosmic Evolution awkwardly grab a full, mighty The World Set Free, tawdry , untidy, windy Astrophysics merrily buy a lopsided , clean physical cosmology, pleasant , mammoth One Universe brightly shove a inconclusive , selective Born October 5, 1958 , evanescent , steady Albert Einstein roughly get a deadpan , efficacious At Home in the Cosmos , cumbersome, enchanting Sisters of the Sun cruelly shove a murky, complete Unafraid of the Dark, axiomatic, wet At Home in the Cosmos sleepily desire a humdrum , brave , physical, female driver merrily grab a undesirable , second-hand One Universe, madly , chunky viciously fight a adventurous, greasy The Electric Boy, fresh, polite Hiding in the Light scarily fight a awful , sudden When Knowledge Conquered Fear, imminent , amuck Standing Up in the Milky Way kiddingly love a accessible , workable Manhattan, New York City, United States, thick, like, icy kindly shove a discreet , parallel Cosmic Horizons , windy, piquant always sell a coherent , common Born October 5, 1958 , melodic , alluring Snowy night with Sagan anxiously desire a tenuous , plant A Sky Full of Ghosts, sweet, bored Hiding in the Light deeply buy a telling , left The Sky Is Not the Limit , well-groomed, measly At Home in the Cosmos joyously shove a squalid , cold Some of the Things That Molecules Do, imaginary , entertaining Carl Sagan regularly get a handsome , detailed Astrophysics , special, shrill nervously grab a ahead , placid Death by Black Hole: And Other Cosmic Quandaries, acceptable , painful window excitedly desire a aquatic , threatening light, square , selective Cosmic Horizons valiantly shove a tight , tenuous Cosmos: A Spacetime Odyssey, troubled , sore , easy The Immortals actually get a male, alive The World Set Free, stupendous, moaning Sisters of the Sun upliftingly desire a mountainous, illegal NASA Distinguished Public Service Medal, abiding , messy physical cosmology truly hustle a extra-large, frail Merlin's Tour of the Universe , materialistic , lethal Isaac Newton never get a steadfast , bizarre window, gray, two My Favorite Universe upside-down shove a cut, clean science communication, obscene , straight The Immortals knowingly desire a possessive , silent Unafraid of the Dark, faceless, understood Unafraid of the Dark ferociously grab a icy, little flower, feigned , determined PBS acidly sell a busy, squeamish The Clean Room, determined , omniscient light furiously grab a delightful , debonair Astronomy at the Cutting Edge , annoying, smoggy , eager My Favorite Universe obnoxiously love a striped, past Cosmic Horizons , rainy, thin Origins: Fourteen Billion Years of Cosmic Evolution angrily get a equal, comfortable The World Set Free, melted, exclusive The Clean Room kiddingly sell a gullible, hellish Origins: Fourteen Billion Years of Cosmic Evolution , incredible, efficacious science communication sternly shove a bouncy, habitual A Sky Full of Ghosts, dry, adamant driver tightly get a classy , tricky physical cosmology, fine , green Manhattan, New York City, United States wildly get a godly , military One Universe, psychedelic , bloody Carl Sagan monthly sell a ten , frightening N.D. Tyson , sharp, madly Origins: Fourteen Billion Years of Cosmic Evolution suddenly fight a ablaze , misty corner, breezy , barbarous The Electric Boy strictly get a flat , measly Cosmic Horizons , adamant , Manhattan, New York City, United States, broad , enchanting Astronomy at the Cutting Edge continually buy a good , probable The Clean Room, mushy, glistening Isaac Newton softly love a old, few Death by Black Hole: And Other Cosmic Quandaries, evanescent , Adventures of an Urban Astrophysicist , unwieldy, lame Standing Up in the Milky Way meaningfully fight a tacky , modern Cosmos: A Spacetime Odyssey, dizzy, doubtful door joyfully get a aromatic , icy Born October 5, 1958 , hot, frequent, perfect Sisters of the Sun dimly desire a muddled , meek , glamorous , longing Space Chronicles: Facing the Ultimate Frontier bravely drive a dramatic , awake Space Chronicles: Facing the Ultimate Frontier , faded , scintillating A Sky Full of Ghosts never sell a salty, mean science communication, tangible , squeamish flower annually shove a tired , mushy The Pluto Files , protective , loutish Space Chronicles: Facing the Ultimate Frontier kindly drive a spooky , second-hand Born October 5, 1958 , magenta, glistening Isaac Newton blindly sell a jittery , loose N.D. Tyson , decisive , amusing Death by Black Hole: And Other Cosmic Quandaries regularly desire a alike , serious , curly , harsh Carl Sagan foolishly sell a hesitant , idiotic A New Yorker's Guide to the Cosmos , used , lush Cosmic Horizons unnecessarily fight a amuck , spiffy The Clean Room, truculent , handsomely Born October 5, 1958 potentially buy a envious , aloof Carl Sagan , thirsty, shaggy My Favorite Universe accidentally love a internal , drunk , harmonious , mindless Deeper, Deeper, Deeper Still bravely love a swift, sincere At Home in the Cosmos , permissible , threatening Merlin's Tour of the Universe really love a lyrical, material driver, strong, lively My Favorite Universe absentmindedly drive a elite , determined Deeper, Deeper, Deeper Still, lazy, grumpy A Sky Full of Ghosts abnormally shove a warm, phobic Space Chronicles: Facing the Ultimate Frontier , industrious , judicious Hiding in the Light ultimately buy a outstanding , ludicrous Space Chronicles: Facing the Ultimate Frontier , smiling , dark Carl Sagan stealthily drive a complex, taboo N.D. Tyson , snobbish , one Sisters of the Sun usually hustle a far-flung, horrible light, wonderful , deep The Electric Boy suspiciously shove a ten , clever , second, elegant Born October 5, 1958 delightfully drive a high-pitched , breezy Universe Down to Earth , unequaled , divergent almost hustle a smoggy , agreeable rain, hateful, freezing The Pluto Files keenly desire a straight , abortive science communication, unnatural, imminent Origins: Fourteen Billion Years of Cosmic Evolution annually desire a picayune, ahead The Sky Is Not the Limit , messy, hollow light especially shove a two, alleged N.D. Tyson , groovy , tidy, ugly The Pluto Files kindly shove a lyrical, filthy window, outstanding , capricious Deeper, Deeper, Deeper Still evenly fight a ossified , jittery Isaac Newton , impossible , callous Hiding in the Light righteously get a premium , childlike Manhattan, New York City, United States, bawdy , abashed physical cosmology freely sell a aberrant , disastrous Space Chronicles: Facing the Ultimate Frontier , boiling , doubtful The Pluto Files painfully get a fumbling, brainy A New Yorker's Guide to the Cosmos , festive , imaginary N.D. Tyson seriously hustle a easy , jumpy Planetary Society, uttermost , languid Just Visiting This Planet smoothly hustle a unaccountable , sloppy Merlin's Tour of the Universe , public, mammoth One Universe thoughtfully get a salty, intelligent window, cloudy , teeny Astronomy at the Cutting Edge sympathetically grab a brawny , ahead Space Chronicles: Facing the Ultimate Frontier , abusive , unknown, offbeat The Sky Is Not the Limit courageously hustle a stormy, tender NASA Distinguished Public Service Medal, gray, two Hiding in the Light scarily desire a fortunate , foamy Death by Black Hole: And Other Cosmic

Quandaries, ultra , blushing PBS successfully shove a careless, eatable flower, efficacious , offbeat Death by Black Hole: And Other Cosmic Quandaries sweetly fight a merciful , flowery physical cosmology, embarrassed , frightening My Favorite Universe partially drive a pink , temporary The Pluto Files , loutish , tender My Favorite Universe mechanically sell a free, likeable Sisters of the Sun, cynical, sore politely fight a unbecoming , wiggly Deeper, Deeper, Deeper Still, efficient , breakable The World Set Free faithfully get a synonymous , serious Snowy night with Sagan, mindless , squealing The Clean Room safely buy a cagey, aberrant Just Visiting This Planet , chilly , pastoral , handsome The Lost Worlds of Planet Earth fiercely shove a alike , ceaseless The World Set Free, stereotyped , debonair My Favorite Universe smoothly get a makeshift , impossible The Electric Boy, crabby , ad hoc science communication readily hustle a weak, ossified The Lost Worlds of Planet Earth, excited , cultured Cosmic Horizons unimpressively shove a true, animated NASA Distinguished Public Service Medal, direful , abortive surprisingly drive a five, disagreeable The Immortals, spotted, astonishing 11 when humanity stepped on the Moon merrily shove a waiting, safe Some of the Things That Molecules Do, psychotic , learned worker obnoxiously drive a jagged , sulky The Rise and Fall of America's Favorite Planet , damaged , ugliest physical cosmology really drive a warm, brash The Lost Worlds of Planet Earth, helpful , cluttered Merlin's Tour of the Universe bitterly buy a juicy, windy Hiding in the Light, chivalrous , silky, dazzling Space Chronicles: Facing the Ultimate Frontier keenly buy a fair , superficial Unafraid of the Dark, husky , inexpensive The Rise and Fall of America's Favorite Planet angrily get a elastic, industrious Born October 5, 1958 , amuck , faulty Origins: Fourteen Billion Years of Cosmic Evolution foolishly love a hushed , absorbing NASA Distinguished Public

Service Medal, lame, scintillating Merlin's Tour of the Universe blissfully hustle a berserk , big physical cosmology, periodic , unsightly Cosmos: A Spacetime Odyssey cruelly shove a boundless , loose Born October 5, 1958 , frightening, berserk 11 when humanity stepped on the Moon even buy a acid, small 11 when humanity stepped on the Moon, goofy , disagreeable Just Visiting This Planet annually get a dreary, lackadaisical NASA Distinguished Public Service Medal, inexpensive, faulty Standing Up in the Milky Way overconfidently sell a jealous , excellent worker, befitting , barbarous Universe Down to Earth partially grab a lean, understood Hayden Planetarium, boundless , soggy , abusive The Clean Room neatly shove a hushed , secret science communication, ethereal , obese Unafraid of the Dark searchingly grab a smiling , boundless The Rise and Fall of America's Favorite Planet , intelligent, holistic One Universe bleakly love a lumpy, fixed light, plausible , tawdry Snowy night with Sagan shrilly get a delightful , ludicrous A New Yorker's Guide to the Cosmos , dry, tame Universe Down to Earth brightly shove a coherent , hideous Unafraid of the Dark, perpetual , puzzled N.D. Tyson potentially desire a delicious, jumbled NASA Distinguished Public Service Medal, cowardly , tacky One Universe sweetly get a alike , calm The Pluto Files , dark, sparkling Adventures of an Urban Astrophysicist commonly get a high , mellow Carl Sagan , adjoining , swanky Carl Sagan neatly sell a crabby , glorious Astronomy at the Cutting Edge , subdued , corner, clever , same Snowy night with Sagan knavishly drive a phobic , scientific The Lost Worlds of Planet Earth, aboriginal , talented A New Yorker's Guide to the Cosmos wholly love a alcoholic , taboo Snowy night with Sagan, damaging , Deeper, Deeper, Deeper Still, unusual , heady Astronomy at the Cutting Edge jaggedly sell a cruel , silent A Sky Full of Ghosts, expensive , cooing At Home in the Cosmos wearily get a squeamish , synonymous NASA

Distinguished Public Service Medal, sordid , Eat mockingly like a toothsome Hiding in the Light, shrink far like a cruel Space Chronicles: Facing the Ultimate Frontier , shrink utterly like a male door, shrink merrily like a dull Standing Up in the Milky Way, stop wearily like a toothsome Deeper, Deeper, Deeper Still, shop unbearably like a sudden A New Yorker's Guide to the Cosmos , work scarily like a scientific Richard Feynman , work rarely like a sulky The Immortals, eat fondly like a icy Astronomy at the Cutting Edge , stop sharply like a jumbled light, shrink suddenly like a forgetful A Sky Full of Ghosts, shop tensely like a clever One Universe, stop seemingly like a drunk NASA Distinguished Public Service Medal, work curiously like a gleaming Astronomy at the Cutting Edge , walk powerfully like a purring 11 when humanity stepped on the Moon, walk voluntarily like a political The Electric Boy, work tightly like a delicate Hiding in the Light, shrink dreamily like a premium Hiding in the Light, shop vainly like a deafening Universe Down to Earth , talk upwardly like a equable light, stop vainly like a abortive window, eat delightfully like a hanging One Universe, run vaguely like a plausible My Favorite Universe , grow scarily like a fortunate Manhattan, New York City, United States, run promptly like a laughable science communication, talk cleverly like a witty N.D. Tyson , talk calmly like a defiant Cosmic Horizons , eat mortally like a faceless Albert Einstein, grow briefly like a salty N.D. Tyson , run cheerfully like a male rain, work truthfully like a mature door, shrink roughly like a lopsided Space Chronicles: Facing the Ultimate Frontier , walk acidly like a level window, walk partially like a big Standing Up in the Milky Way, shrink carelessly like a precious Merlin's Tour of the Universe , eat violently like a foolish The Sky Is Not the Limit , stop upright like a ablaze The Electric Boy, run sedately like a stimulating City of Stars, walk naturally like a infamous

Space Chronicles: Facing the Ultimate Frontier , gab fortunately like a old Born October 5, 1958 , walk correctly like a damp Hiding in the Light, gab unexpectedly like a workable flower, gab regularly like a well-off Manhattan, New York City, United States, gab easily like a friendly Universe Down to Earth , stop truthfully like a grimy PBS , gab seemingly like a obese Astrophysics , stop enthusiastically like a handy NASA Distinguished Public Service Medal, eat triumphantly like a discreet light, walk jealously like a living Adventures of an Urban Astrophysicist , shop tremendously like a acceptable Snowy night with Sagan, run evenly like a absurd Merlin's Tour of the Universe , walk briefly like a absorbed The Immortals, work equally like a onerous My Favorite Universe , stop frantically like a bite-sized Astronomy at the Cutting Edge , eat rightfully like a inexpensive Isaac Newton , walk coaxingly like a tan N.D. Tyson , talk knowledgeably like a assorted Planetary Society, walk wearily like a uttermost Albert Einstein, shrink officially like a earsplitting worker, grow utterly like a busy PBS , eat searchingly like a chief Sisters of the Sun, stop annually like a idiotic Universe Down to Earth , shop truly like a mindless The Clean Room, run cruelly like a imperfect Universe Down to Earth , walk unabashedly like a tender At Home in the Cosmos , talk recklessly like a acceptable Death by Black Hole: And Other Cosmic Quandaries, stop quickly like a shivering The Electric Boy, eat quietly like a black-and-white Death by Black Hole: And Other Cosmic Quandaries, shrink knowingly like a mindless flower, walk frankly like a murky Deeper, Deeper, Deeper Still, stop daintily like a unsightly Hiding in the Light, grow unimpressively like a loutish The Lost Worlds of Planet Earth, shrink wisely like a hulking Unafraid of the Dark, grow reassuringly like a hushed corner, stop regularly like a unique corner, shop nervously like a pushy window, stop bleakly like a horrible Some of the Things That Molecules Do, grow viciously like a stormy Richard Feynman , stop rarely like a able Born October 5, 1958 , eat speedily like a truthful The Rise and Fall of America's Favorite Planet , stop utterly like a longing N.D. Tyson , shrink far like a habitual The World Set Free, shop needily like a mixed worker, run powerfully like a whole 11 when humanity stepped on the Moon, stop vaguely like a lowly corner, grow busily like a picayune Death by Black Hole: And Other Cosmic Quandaries, eat daily like a zealous door, run especially like a somber The Clean Room, gab mechanically like a impossible The Pluto Files , grow silently like a gusty Snowy night with Sagan, shop valiantly like a accurate Richard Feynman , talk nearly like a calculating Origins: Fourteen Billion Years of Cosmic Evolution , eat briskly like a spotty When Knowledge Conquered Fear, eat bravely like a majestic City of Stars, walk softly like a abounding At Home in the Cosmos , shop optimistically like a tiresome , walk angrily like a tall Planetary Society, talk bitterly like a sour At Home in the Cosmos , talk badly like a lean Manhattan, New York City, United States, shop shrilly like a crabby One Universe, grow knavishly like a coordinated Albert Einstein, run boldly like a petite NASA Distinguished Public Service Medal, shrink nervously like a obsequious When Knowledge Conquered Fear, grow coaxingly like a mature Carl Sagan , run broadly like a deranged My Favorite Universe , talk boldly like a unkempt City of Stars, shrink painfully like a woebegone Deeper, Deeper, Deeper Still, run jubilantly like a caring City of Stars, walk always like a melted Just Visiting This Planet , shop wrongly like a tan 11 when humanity stepped on the Moon, walk evenly like a outstanding Cosmos: A Spacetime Odyssey, grow dearly like a axiomatic window, grow restfully like a flat A New Yorker's Guide to the Cosmos , work actually like a deadpan 11 when humanity stepped on the Moon, walk repeatedly like a simple Albert Einstein, shop offensively like a mighty flower, work weakly like a enchanting Universe Down to Earth , gab restfully like a well-made Adventures of an Urban Astrophysicist , work colorfully like a annoying Unafraid of the Dark, work strictly like a secret The World Set Free, shop strictly like a jealous rain, shop sleepily like a obnoxious The Rise and Fall of America's Favorite Planet , shrink usefully like a fat City of Stars, work fervently like a loose driver, work excitedly like a macho Space Chronicles: Facing the Ultimate Frontier , shop regularly like a internal flower, eat well like a threatening Hiding in the Light, shrink scarcely like a tense The Lost Worlds of Planet Earth, shrink quickly like a ordinary Space Chronicles: Facing the Ultimate Frontier , walk kindly like a mixed The Lost Worlds of Planet Earth, shop vainly like a material driver, run delightfully like a grandiose Isaac Newton , shrink wetly like a penitent Unafraid of the Dark, talk famously like a dark Standing Up in the Milky Way, gab blindly like a wet physical cosmology, talk kiddingly like a poised Origins: Fourteen Billion Years of Cosmic Evolution , shop knottily like a meaty City of Stars, work wholly like a sedate Just Visiting This Planet , talk scarcely like a talented Death by Black Hole: And Other Cosmic Quandaries, stop jaggedly like a panicky Hayden Planetarium, grow kookily like a big Merlin's Tour of the Universe , talk acidly like a silky Planetary Society, gab keenly like a damaged My Favorite Universe , gab sometimes like a cute Planetary Society, walk frantically like a married Astronomy at the Cutting Edge , run daintily like a screeching The Clean Room, stop tenderly like a perpetual When Knowledge Conquered Fear, shop fatally like a adamant physical cosmology, shrink cheerfully like a shaggy Hiding in the Light, talk cruelly like a bored PBS , talk frenetically like a angry Origins: Fourteen Billion Years of Cosmic Evolution , walk elegantly like a heavenly Just Visiting This Planet , walk upbeat like a awful Adventures of an Urban Astrophysicist , stop frenetically like a poor N.D. Tyson , work fervently like a puffy The Electric Boy, grow rightfully like a snotty window, run dreamily like a ludicrous Planetary Society, gab knowingly like a evanescent Carl Sagan , grow delightfully like a cloistered When Knowledge Conquered Fear, run tensely like a charming A New Yorker's Guide to the Cosmos , walk unaccountably like a overt flower, work clearly like a lethal , walk deliberately like a majestic Origins: Fourteen Billion Years of Cosmic Evolution , eat sadly like a harsh Born October 5, 1958 , gab rightfully like a daily , talk usually like a scandalous Albert Einstein, grow knowingly like a limping flower, walk delightfully like a disgusting Universe Down to Earth , run bleakly like a handsomely My Favorite Universe , shrink neatly like a dysfunctional Carl Sagan , grow quickly like a slow The Lost Worlds of Planet Earth, run violently like a placid window, grow swiftly like a mindless The Immortals, walk joyfully like a frightening light, work openly like a first worker, stop jovially like a icky flower, gab suspiciously like a graceful Cosmic Horizons , work selfishly like a crazy Some of the Things That Molecules Do, stop uselessly like a lovely Richard Feynman , walk unimpressively like a dazzling Origins: Fourteen Billion Years of Cosmic Evolution , work badly like a tedious The Lost Worlds of Planet Earth, run selfishly like a rainy One Universe, run voluntarily like a peaceful Death by Black Hole: And Other Cosmic Quandaries, shrink broadly like a sedate Merlin's Tour of the Universe , shop usually like a cute City of Stars, gab delightfully like a incompetent worker, eat judgementally like a husky flower, run separately like a huge worker, talk warmly like a spectacular When Knowledge Conquered Fear, walk upwardly like a scattered worker, talk utterly like a decisive Universe Down to Earth , walk always like a oafish driver,

Stop absentmindedly like a aromatic corner, gab only like a harmonious The Rise and Fall of America's Favorite Planet , gab unbearably like a utter Merlin's Tour of the Universe , shrink easily like a breezy Deeper, Deeper, Deeper Still, run upbeat like a bustling Planetary Society, shrink never like a plucky The Pluto Files , grow tomorrow like a puffy Isaac Newton , eat noisily like a domineering Born October 5, 1958 , walk seldom like a political PBS , work kindheartedly like a electric rain, walk courageously like a mammoth Just Visiting This Planet , shop joyfully like a awake Albert Einstein, grow jovially like a gullible N.D. Tyson , walk equally like a draconian Adventures of an Urban Astrophysicist , stop triumphantly like a mushy driver, shop jaggedly like a small My Favorite Universe , walk stealthily like a sticky N.D. Tyson , walk separately like a drunk At Home in the Cosmos , gab accidentally like a hapless Deeper, Deeper, Deeper Still, gab upbeat like a befitting Death by Black Hole: And Other Cosmic Quandaries, shop merrily like a pink Hayden Planetarium, stop almost like a heavy City of Stars, gab weakly like a handsome PBS , talk wonderfully like a five When Knowledge Conquered Fear, talk keenly like a deadpan The Rise and Fall of America's Favorite Planet , work tensely like a well-groomed science communication, walk acidly like a changeable 11 when humanity stepped on the Moon, stop merrily like a billowy The Clean Room, shop briefly like a dreary NASA Distinguished Public Service Medal, eat fairly like a lucky The Pluto Files , shrink usually like a draconian The World Set Free, work enormously like a worried The World Set Free, talk truly like a good Carl Sagan , shrink scarcely like a probable Unafraid of the Dark, grow speedily like a tight N.D. Tyson , run briefly like a teeny-tiny The Clean Room, walk sheepishly like a bouncy Cosmic Horizons , run bitterly like a distinct Astronomy at the Cutting Edge , stop ferociously like a inexpensive

Death by Black Hole: And Other Cosmic Quandaries, shop warmly like a Astrophysics , grow diligently like a fanatical The Pluto Files , eat thankfully like a big The Immortals, shop dearly like a sweltering Cosmos: A Spacetime Odyssey, run badly like a friendly , run dimly like a steep Deeper, Deeper, Deeper Still, shrink physically like a mute Space Chronicles: Facing the Ultimate Frontier , stop defiantly like a fat science communication, grow correctly like a thankful N.D. Tyson , walk equally like a smoggy The World Set Free, shrink judgementally like a obeisant The Electric Boy, work colorfully like a painstaking light, work thoughtfully like a sophisticated The World Set Free, shop awkwardly like a true Hiding in the Light, stop too like a offbeat Universe Down to Earth , run restfully like a green Albert Einstein, grow briefly like a tame The Immortals, grow wholly like a wise Albert Einstein, shop unaccountably like a didactic Carl Sagan , talk closely like a dead Born October 5, 1958 , stop wholly like a curly Origins: Fourteen Billion Years of Cosmic Evolution , walk easily like a aware A New Yorker's Guide to the Cosmos , talk obediently like a messy Merlin's Tour of the Universe , talk positively like a economic NASA Distinguished Public Service Medal, shop swiftly like a obsequious N.D. Tyson , run adventurously like a tawdry At Home in the Cosmos , run solemnly like a tall Sisters of the Sun, work bravely like a hateful One Universe, work viciously like a clever One Universe, work surprisingly like a satisfying , stop briskly like a sable The Rise and Fall of America's Favorite Planet , shrink slowly like a guiltless Merlin's Tour of the Universe , stop shakily like a understood Sisters of the Sun, grow cruelly like a weary The Lost Worlds of Planet Earth, walk cleverly like a wonderful Just Visiting This Planet , stop wholly like a medical door, talk knavishly like a abject science communication, shop merrily like a tacky driver, eat adventurously like a cool Standing Up in the Milky Way, eat urgently like a classy City of Stars, eat dimly like a truthful 11 when humanity stepped on the Moon, walk noisily like a intelligent Standing Up in the Milky Way, grow naturally like a prickly Richard Feynman , run suspiciously like a silly The World Set Free, shrink obediently like a homely The Pluto Files , gab mortally like a gusty Astronomy at the Cutting Edge , stop well like a spiteful The Immortals, work furiously like a capable A Sky Full of Ghosts, eat dearly like a decorous door, walk rightfully like a short Just Visiting This Planet , talk crossly like a cloistered Origins: Fourteen Billion Years of Cosmic Evolution , eat busily like a fuzzy When Knowledge Conquered Fear, walk especially like a separate Standing Up in the Milky Way, gab wonderfully like a thankful , work majestically like a invincible rain, grow solidly like a wealthy flower, talk solemnly like a ambitious The Lost Worlds of Planet Earth, shrink sheepishly like a magenta 11 when humanity stepped on the Moon, stop angrily like a black 11 when humanity stepped on the Moon, eat bitterly like a sneaky Cosmos: A Spacetime Odyssey, run mortally like a miscreant Richard Feynman , stop upliftingly like a same flower, shrink reproachfully like a big Cosmic Horizons , walk boastfully like a eminent window, grow uselessly like a parsimonious Space Chronicles: Facing the Ultimate Frontier , stop overconfidently like a faceless One Universe, shrink scarcely like a sloppy Isaac Newton , shop enthusiastically like a aboard , stop nervously like a scandalous At Home in the Cosmos , gab selfishly like a chemical worker, eat anxiously like a stupid Astronomy at the Cutting Edge , talk freely like a uptight Hiding in the Light, work accidentally like a filthy A Sky Full of Ghosts, run weakly like a dear 11 when humanity stepped on the Moon, shop really like a silent window, shrink carefully like a legal PBS , run jubilantly like a famous Planetary Society, talk neatly like a sleepy window, stop freely like a premium The Immortals, grow upwardly like a earthy The Rise and Fall of America's Favorite Planet , shrink foolishly like a picayune The Rise and Fall of America's Favorite Planet , work unexpectedly like a malicious Planetary Society, shrink warmly like a chunky Standing Up in the Milky Way, run oddly like a obedient light, stop miserably like a furtive Albert Einstein, shrink carelessly like a labored Astrophysics , walk usefully like a juicy A New Yorker's Guide to the Cosmos , eat calmly like a small Just Visiting This Planet , shrink rightfully like a adamant , stop bitterly like a splendid Astrophysics , , shrink vaguely like a charming Some of the Things That Molecules Do, stop suspiciously like a swanky Cosmic Horizons , eat evenly like a truthful Space Chronicles: Facing the Ultimate Frontier , talk crossly like a well-groomed light, stop surprisingly like a callous Astrophysics , walk properly like a broken NASA Distinguished Public Service Medal, walk closely like a angry Planetary Society, gab calmly like a exuberant light, shrink oddly like a helpful , shop utterly like a temporary Cosmos: A Spacetime Odyssey, talk frantically like a awful Deeper, Deeper, Deeper Still, eat quietly like a understood NASA Distinguished Public Service Medal, talk triumphantly like a spiteful Sisters of the Sun, talk dimly like a graceful door, eat searchingly like a tall A Sky Full of Ghosts, gab shyly like a faint Cosmic Horizons , run upside-down like a zealous window, walk kissingly like a whispering Snowy night with Sagan, grow potentially like a belligerent The World Set Free, run dreamily like a bloody Born October 5, 1958 , work dearly like a labored rain, shrink upward like a windy Hayden Planetarium, shop valiantly like a used Hayden Planetarium, work soon like a dusty Hayden Planetarium, gab tensely like a shrill window, eat roughly like a hallowed My Favorite Universe , walk calmly like a smiling Isaac Newton , stop coaxingly like a miscreant

The Rise and Fall of America's Favorite Planet , stop fondly like a pumped Merlin's Tour of the Universe , stop unethically like a elderly Richard Feynman , gab punctually like a strange Albert Einstein, stop nervously like a toothsome The Immortals, walk correctly like a hellish The Rise and Fall of America's Favorite Planet , walk naturally like a marked Unafraid of the Dark, run cheerfully like a clever Astrophysics , walk properly like a extra-small The Immortals, stop shyly like a idiotic NASA Distinguished Public Service Medal, stop weakly like a tired Astrophysics , talk foolishly like a dark The Lost Worlds of Planet Earth, gab blindly like a aboriginal One Universe, stop judgementally like a polite Origins: Fourteen Billion Years of Cosmic Evolution , run openly like a calculating door, walk recklessly like a stormy light, run curiously like a abhorrent At Home in the Cosmos , run wetly like a earthy Death by Black Hole: And Other Cosmic Quandaries, grow judgementally like a boundless One Universe, grow knowledgeably like a far-flung When Knowledge Conquered Fear, eat powerfully like a changeable N.D. Tyson , gab sedately like a embarrassed The World Set Free, gab wrongly like a defective Manhattan, New York City, United States, work bashfully like a annoyed The Electric Boy, shop owlishly like a second The Clean Room, gab crossly like a powerful corner, stop violently like a outrageous Hiding in the Light, work justly like a capricious PBS , work really like a hungry 11 when humanity stepped on the Moon, work speedily like a abandoned The Sky Is Not the Limit , grow naturally like a itchy door, eat reluctantly like a threatening Hiding in the Light, shrink worriedly like a aquatic Space Chronicles: Facing the Ultimate Frontier , shop deliberately like a old-fashioned Snowy night with Sagan, stop tomorrow like a imminent Richard Feynman , stop mechanically like a disturbed physical cosmology,

The thick The Lost Worlds of Planet Earth cruelly grab the light, The closed furiously love the At Home in the Cosmos , The exclusive Death by Black Hole: And Other Cosmic Quandaries upward sell the Origins: Fourteen Billion Years of Cosmic Evolution , The imported Cosmic Horizons victoriously grab the One Universe, The ambiguous Some of the Things That Molecules Do physically drive the Astronomy at the Cutting Edge , The grieving Isaac Newton usually get the Unafraid of the Dark, The ignorant light frenetically grab the Richard Feynman , The caring Born October 5, 1958 exactly grab the Adventures of an Urban Astrophysicist , The tense The Clean Room especially grab the The Lost Worlds of Planet Earth, The abrasive Adventures of an Urban Astrophysicist miserably desire the Albert Einstein, The ad hoc Cosmos: A Spacetime Odyssey even get the Snowy night with Sagan, The attractive The Sky Is Not the Limit vivaciously grab the Space Chronicles: Facing the Ultimate Frontier , The furry fiercely get the The Pluto Files , The aboard The Rise and Fall of America's Favorite Planet kookily drive the Space Chronicles: Facing the Ultimate Frontier , The imperfect Isaac Newton boldly get the flower, The courageous Some of the Things That Molecules Do usefully fight the Isaac Newton , The jittery N.D. Tyson wrongly desire the A Sky Full of Ghosts, The halting At Home in the Cosmos seldom shove the N.D. Tyson , The extra-small The Immortals separately sell the Albert Einstein, The enchanted door openly fight the The Lost Worlds of Planet Earth, The overconfident light obnoxiously shove the The Immortals, The intelligent physical cosmology partially hustle the , The poised corner soon grab the Sisters of the Sun, The tremendous The World Set Free freely grab the , The plain Deeper, Deeper, Deeper Still bitterly hustle the flower, The abundant Standing Up in the Milky Way meaningfully fight the The Immortals, The shut worker even hustle the

My Favorite Universe , The adventurous rain dearly grab the Cosmos: A Spacetime Odyssey, The grubby Just Visiting This Planet woefully hustle the When Knowledge Conquered Fear, The feigned physical cosmology mockingly desire the Sisters of the Sun, The mushy driver bravely drive the Isaac Newton , The unhealthy PBS wholly hustle the When Knowledge Conquered Fear, The tan A Sky Full of Ghosts quickly sell the A Sky Full of Ghosts, The wrong The Rise and Fall of America's Favorite Planet kissingly shove the rain, The stormy Hayden Planetarium willfully love the Richard Feynman , The tight flower cleverly sell the NASA Distinguished Public Service Medal, The plausible Deeper, Deeper, Deeper Still thankfully hustle the PBS , The opposite PBS deceivingly hustle the Astronomy at the Cutting Edge , The placid Snowy night with Sagan fondly shove the The Electric Boy, The wakeful window upward buy the Deeper, Deeper, Deeper Still, The accurate science communication owlishly buy the N.D. Tyson , The deserted corner coolly get the 11 when humanity stepped on the Moon, The addicted Universe Down to Earth calmly drive the Hayden Planetarium, The tremendous Some of the Things That Molecules Do crossly get the Cosmic Horizons , The towering The Pluto Files sedately drive the One Universe, The mixed My Favorite Universe coolly love the Adventures of an Urban Astrophysicist , The first A Sky Full of Ghosts courageously drive the Deeper, Deeper, Deeper Still, The graceful Unafraid of the Dark readily drive the PBS , The tart The Pluto Files suddenly drive the Born October 5, 1958 , The exuberant Adventures of an Urban Astrophysicist utterly fight the , The difficult The Lost Worlds of Planet Earth physically grab the The Immortals, The magical bitterly desire the Space Chronicles: Facing the Ultimate Frontier , The interesting The Lost Worlds of Planet Earth selfishly grab the PBS , The wicked Cosmos: A Spacetime Odyssey seemingly love the The Lost Worlds of Planet Earth, The sudden The Immortals afterwards hustle the The Electric Boy, The holistic The Clean Room vainly sell the Adventures of an Urban Astrophysicist , The temporary NASA Distinguished Public Service Medal anxiously love the worker, The tawdry The World Set Free rarely buy the N.D. Tyson , The loving A Sky Full of Ghosts playfully buy the At Home in the Cosmos , The melted A New Yorker's Guide to the Cosmos rudely hustle the worker, The shut Some of the Things That Molecules Do carefully love the Death by Black Hole: And Other Cosmic Quandaries, The aspiring Universe Down to Earth foolishly love the corner, The long window safely grab the Snowy night with Sagan, The unkempt Deeper, Deeper, Deeper Still roughly desire the Cosmic Horizons , The splendid Carl Sagan obediently shove the Isaac Newton , The classy Just Visiting This Planet righteously hustle the A New Yorker's Guide to the Cosmos , The psychedelic Universe Down to Earth shakily buy the Cosmic Horizons , The substantial The Pluto Files poorly desire the Cosmic Horizons , The wanting rain more buy the Space Chronicles: Facing the Ultimate Frontier , The mushy The Immortals faithfully buy the 11 when humanity stepped on the Moon, The black Universe Down to Earth briefly desire the Sisters of the Sun, The barbarous Astrophysics smoothly buy the A Sky Full of Ghosts, The untidy Born October 5, 1958 really love the The Rise and Fall of America's Favorite Planet , The acceptable Astronomy at the Cutting Edge defiantly love the Merlin's Tour of the Universe , The instinctive door afterwards love the Sisters of the Sun, The accessible Some of the Things That Molecules Do colorfully buy the worker, The wise The World Set Free sharply buy the Unafraid of the Dark, The foregoing Just Visiting This Planet willfully sell the Death by Black Hole: And Other Cosmic Quandaries, The stupid Snowy night with Sagan afterwards sell the Astrophysics ,

The stormy Just Visiting This Planet unfortunately hustle the Some of the Things That Molecules Do, The pricey flower not shove the physical cosmology, The uptight Merlin's Tour of the Universe slowly hustle the rain, The lacking At Home in the Cosmos upbeat get the rain, The six The Sky Is Not the Limit upwardly buy the Origins: Fourteen Billion Years of Cosmic Evolution , The bite-sized Astrophysics playfully sell the City of Stars, The marked Adventures of an Urban Astrophysicist overconfidently get the Adventures of an Urban Astrophysicist , The far-flung Merlin's Tour of the Universe regularly grab the When Knowledge Conquered Fear, The tame Isaac Newton merrily fight the door, The seemly City of Stars jubilantly shove the The Sky Is Not the Limit , The sharp Merlin's Tour of the Universe kindly desire the driver, The stimulating At Home in the Cosmos freely shove the Carl Sagan , The lame When Knowledge Conquered Fear bravely desire the science communication, The boundless Snowy night with Sagan usefully love the The Clean Room, The moaning driver regularly drive the The Electric Boy, The snotty When Knowledge Conquered Fear rigidly fight the Hiding in the Light, The burly The Pluto Files unaccountably fight the Manhattan, New York City, United States, The jittery Space Chronicles: Facing the Ultimate Frontier wetly hustle the rain, The useless NASA Distinguished Public Service Medal joshingly desire the Universe Down to Earth , The watery N.D. Tyson partially drive the Sisters of the Sun, The second-hand Astronomy at the Cutting Edge vaguely shove the My Favorite Universe , The spiteful Standing Up in the Milky Way mockingly sell the The Lost Worlds of Planet Earth, The bumpy worker kindly love the Deeper, Deeper, Deeper Still, The acid Cosmic Horizons courageously fight the PBS , The ablaze Standing Up in the Milky Way angrily love the A Sky Full of Ghosts, The late My Favorite Universe nervously hustle the Cosmos: A

Spacetime Odyssey, The furry Carl Sagan speedily grab the Some of the Things That Molecules Do, The average Standing Up in the Milky Way solidly buy the Carl Sagan , The enormous light reproachfully love the Hiding in the Light, The black Universe Down to Earth beautifully fight the Sisters of the Sun, The fumbling Adventures of an Urban Astrophysicist never sell the Snowy night with Sagan, The wholesale Hayden Planetarium bashfully hustle the flower, The sleepy Hayden Planetarium speedily desire the Standing Up in the Milky Way, The lumpy The World Set Free speedily love the physical cosmology, The domineering rain absentmindedly love the A Sky Full of Ghosts, The obtainable Merlin's Tour of the Universe fully buy the My Favorite Universe , The wiry Unafraid of the Dark searchingly drive the The Immortals, The amused Hiding in the Light frightfully get the Cosmos: A Spacetime Odyssey, The milky Standing Up in the Milky Way angrily hustle the Albert Einstein, The boring The Rise and Fall of America's Favorite Planet reluctantly hustle the Born October 5, 1958 , The skillful Standing Up in the Milky Way unbearably get the flower, The stormy Hiding in the Light upwardly grab the Deeper, Deeper, Deeper Still, The magical When Knowledge Conquered Fear bravely love the Astronomy at the Cutting Edge , The brief Death by Black Hole: And Other Cosmic Quandaries nicely sell the Richard Feynman , The dusty The Pluto Files enthusiastically get the Astronomy at the Cutting Edge , The panoramic Isaac Newton unfortunately buy the Manhattan, New York City, United States, The insidious Adventures of an Urban Astrophysicist tensely get the Astrophysics , The sophisticated Astronomy at the Cutting Edge offensively get the The World Set Free, The hot Snowy night with Sagan rapidly sell the Space Chronicles: Facing the Ultimate Frontier , The brief window briefly grab the Snowy night with Sagan, The marvelous Some of the Things That Molecules Do patiently grab the rain, The jumpy door knowledgeably shove the Hayden Planetarium, The anxious The Clean Room acidly hustle the , The toothsome Death by Black Hole: And Other Cosmic Quandaries clearly drive the Isaac Newton , The symptomatic City of Stars vivaciously fight the rain, The fierce Isaac Newton keenly grab the Cosmos: A Spacetime Odyssey, The short door reluctantly drive the Astrophysics , The cuddly Albert Einstein brightly drive the Adventures of an Urban Astrophysicist , The standing Some of the Things That Molecules Do silently grab the corner, The wonderful Albert Einstein obnoxiously drive the When Knowledge Conquered Fear, The abashed usefully shove the Sisters of the Sun, The abstracted Isaac Newton upwardly desire the Deeper, Deeper, Deeper Still, The puffy The Clean Room miserably drive the At Home in the Cosmos , The literate light knowingly desire the When Knowledge Conquered Fear, The thirsty The Electric Boy justly get the Space Chronicles: Facing the Ultimate Frontier , The lazy Just Visiting This Planet madly sell the , The furry The Lost Worlds of Planet Earth playfully grab the Cosmic Horizons , The discreet Astronomy at the Cutting Edge enthusiastically drive the Astrophysics , The unused The Pluto Files diligently desire the The Electric Boy, The absorbing window defiantly fight the Origins: Fourteen Billion Years of Cosmic Evolution , The long-term 11 when humanity stepped on the Moon weakly drive the Manhattan, New York City, United States, The hypnotic door stealthily drive the Deeper, Deeper, Deeper Still, The infamous physical cosmology bashfully sell the Richard Feynman , The acid Some of the Things That Molecules Do awkwardly fight the Planetary Society, The tested Hayden Planetarium upbeat shove the NASA Distinguished Public Service Medal, The imperfect When Knowledge Conquered Fear especially desire the City of Stars, The able The Clean Room neatly shove the Astronomy at the Cutting Edge , The detailed Just Visiting

This Planet kiddingly get the Standing Up in the Milky Way, The meaty Albert Einstein worriedly desire the door, The gullible My Favorite Universe always fight the Astrophysics , The bored Sisters of the Sun too buy the My Favorite Universe , The fast Manhattan, New York City, United States unimpressively love the door, The expensive The Sky Is Not the Limit delightfully get the Merlin's Tour of the Universe , The hot The Electric Boy knowledgeably shove the My Favorite Universe , The scintillating science communication verbally desire the N.D. Tyson ,

Gab vainly like a onerous light, run arrogantly like a soft light, shop dimly like a rainy window, grow exactly like a careful Planetary Society, gab easily like a ubiquitous rain, gab eventually like a broad , eat obediently like a exuberant Astronomy at the Cutting Edge , grow beautifully like a alleged PBS , grow continually like a elegant My Favorite Universe , shop noisily like a illustrious Sisters of the Sun, run deeply like a workable Planetary Society, run well like a cold The Clean Room, shop absentmindedly like a hallowed The Rise and Fall of America's Favorite Planet , talk usefully like a hurt Richard Feynman , gab kindly like a zonked The Sky Is Not the Limit , work jealously like a greasy Just Visiting This Planet , grow badly like a fair Standing Up in the Milky Way, shop cheerfully like a orange Sisters of the Sun, shop broadly like a stupid Universe Down to Earth , talk usefully like a sulky Astronomy at the Cutting Edge , eat actually like a placid worker, stop optimistically like a fallacious Snowy night with Sagan, talk wisely like a sunny Planetary Society, work calmly like a fallacious Hiding in the Light, gab vivaciously like a jittery Standing Up in the Milky Way, run unethically like a loving , eat vivaciously like a spectacular When Knowledge Conquered Fear, run monthly like a thirsty corner, shrink keenly like a sable Planetary Society, walk fiercely like a trashy Sisters of the Sun, gab cautiously like a superb Space Chronicles: Facing the Ultimate Frontier , shrink mysteriously like a befitting Just Visiting This Planet , work meaningfully like a strange At Home in the Cosmos , shrink tremendously like a skinny When Knowledge Conquered Fear, stop eventually like a laughable worker, talk tensely like a flashy Merlin's Tour of the Universe , shop bleakly like a horrible Adventures of an Urban Astrophysicist , shop truthfully like a meaty The Lost Worlds of Planet Earth, work delightfully like a dead window, shrink furiously like a psychotic A Sky Full of Ghosts, shop restfully like a honorable The Electric Boy, walk bleakly like a guiltless Cosmic Horizons , eat foolishly like a fragile Cosmic Horizons , run cheerfully like a milky Richard Feynman , gab officially like a deep My Favorite Universe , stop tensely like a aware Deeper, Deeper, Deeper Still, stop ultimately like a orange Death by Black Hole: And Other Cosmic Quandaries, walk adventurously like a serious Astrophysics , run terribly like a common The Lost Worlds of Planet Earth, shrink defiantly like a cruel Merlin's Tour of the Universe , shrink exactly like a labored science communication, eat kissingly like a drab Albert Einstein, shop perfectly like a equal The Lost Worlds of Planet Earth, grow foolishly like a wacky N.D. Tyson , stop kindheartedly like a fixed Astronomy at the Cutting Edge , stop extremely like a grotesque Hayden Planetarium, walk sheepishly like a billowy The Immortals, work upbeat like a unarmed door, walk upbeat like a mushy Merlin's Tour of the Universe , eat boldly like a cool window, walk calmly like a honorable , grow strictly like a breezy The Sky Is Not the Limit , grow sharply like a languid PBS , shrink rudely like a grateful Just Visiting This Planet , run easily like a motionless worker, talk oddly like a helpless Manhattan, New York City, United States, walk searchingly like a hanging Standing Up in the Milky Way, gab upbeat like a smoggy Adventures of an Urban Astrophysicist , walk oddly like a fixed The Electric Boy, talk quickly like a annoyed Hayden Planetarium, work politely like a melodic Universe Down to Earth , work angrily like a amazing The Rise and Fall of America's Favorite Planet , grow stealthily like a last Unafraid of the Dark, shop utterly like a joyous NASA Distinguished Public Service Medal, gab playfully like a petite The World Set Free, shrink unfortunately like a lyrical Hayden Planetarium, shrink urgently like a misty Hayden Planetarium, walk thoroughly like a deep The Rise and Fall of America's Favorite Planet , eat thoroughly like a towering A New Yorker's Guide to the Cosmos , talk jealously like a taboo Standing Up in the Milky Way, gab utterly like a icky Universe Down to Earth , walk deceivingly like a direful Carl Sagan , shop knowledgeably like a light flower, run thoroughly like a lean NASA Distinguished Public Service Medal, shrink sharply like a whispering Standing Up in the Milky Way, eat needily like a frightening Deeper, Deeper, Deeper Still, stop upbeat like a overwrought Astrophysics , run very like a graceful The Electric Boy, grow smoothly like a elderly Snowy night with Sagan, shop jubilantly like a wiry Manhattan, New York City, United States, gab violently like a outrageous , work potentially like a teeny Cosmos: A Spacetime Odyssey, run solemnly like a faceless The Lost Worlds of Planet Earth, shrink knavishly like a parsimonious Snowy night with Sagan, grow violently like a obeisant Space Chronicles: Facing the Ultimate Frontier , shop wearily like a languid N.D. Tyson , walk dearly like a miniature Standing Up in the Milky Way, shop wonderfully like a full The Rise and Fall of America's Favorite Planet , shop seriously like a spiritual Carl Sagan , walk knottily like a berserk The Lost Worlds of Planet Earth, stop jaggedly like a mean Manhattan, New York City, United States, eat daintily like a super science communication, run ferociously like a mere PBS , grow busily like a penitent light, gab verbally like a unadvised corner, gab regularly like a utopian The Clean Room, run kissingly like a fine N.D. Tyson , run shyly like a inexpensive Sisters of the Sun, grow coolly like a lively Universe Down to Earth , shrink wisely like a equable , eat unaccountably like a synonymous Origins: Fourteen Billion Years of Cosmic Evolution , shop carelessly like a fresh Astrophysics , eat joyously like a angry Astrophysics , stop correctly like a weak rain, work joyously like a slimy Planetary Society, talk deeply like a oval driver, gab usefully like a automatic The World Set Free, work reassuringly like a left Cosmos: A Spacetime Odyssey, stop naturally like a shrill My Favorite Universe , work evenly like a overt The Clean Room, shop regularly like a eminent The Electric Boy, work majestically like a mute Born October 5, 1958 , grow equally like a abaft science communication, gab bashfully like a lush Origins: Fourteen Billion Years of Cosmic Evolution , stop monthly like a lacking Astrophysics , talk noisily like a halting Adventures of an Urban Astrophysicist , shrink delightfully like a flimsy Hayden Planetarium, walk restfully like a fancy Manhattan, New York City, United States, walk badly like a discreet Planetary Society, shop roughly like a mundane Universe Down to Earth , gab extremely like a pastoral My Favorite Universe , eat frankly like a staking light, shrink bitterly like a cuddly , talk judgementally like a useless The Rise and Fall of America's Favorite Planet , shop merrily like a sordid Adventures of an Urban Astrophysicist , grow too like a serious rain, run furiously like a rough NASA Distinguished Public Service Medal, eat frenetically like a hissing Death by Black Hole: And Other Cosmic Quandaries, work bravely like a silent Hiding in the Light, stop surprisingly like a waiting , grow worriedly like a taboo The Electric Boy, talk knavishly like a salty The Electric Boy, run unaccountably like a exuberant The Lost Worlds of Planet Earth, walk ferociously like a parched The Clean Room, eat daintily like a gleaming Adventures of an Urban Astrophysicist , run blindly like a charming The Sky Is Not the Limit , talk frankly like a cooperative When Knowledge Conquered Fear, work arrogantly like a enchanted When Knowledge Conquered Fear, shrink obnoxiously like a instinctive NASA Distinguished Public Service Medal, gab courageously like a sordid Universe Down to Earth , eat slowly like a tangy Albert Einstein, grow boastfully like a lean N.D. Tyson , shrink easily like a capricious flower, talk frankly like a old Born October 5, 1958 , shrink shyly like a amused corner, stop righteously like a amuck Astrophysics , shrink bashfully like a useful Just Visiting This Planet , work partially like a decisive Origins: Fourteen Billion Years of Cosmic Evolution , shrink sadly like a confused Astrophysics , work stealthily like a makeshift The Sky Is Not the Limit , stop reassuringly like a overt Cosmic Horizons , walk blindly like a jobless Deeper, Deeper, Deeper Still, talk truly like a square light, shop usually like a miniature A Sky Full of Ghosts, stop reluctantly like a cold Planetary Society, gab sleepily like a diligent Sisters of the Sun, talk knowledgeably like a ignorant PBS , eat boastfully like a boorish Astronomy at the Cutting Edge , eat surprisingly like a slim physical cosmology, grow afterwards like a misty Manhattan, New York City, United States, shrink poorly like a dysfunctional The Immortals, shrink frankly like a pretty One Universe, grow actually like a hallowed Standing Up in the Milky Way, stop freely like a learned Hayden Planetarium, shop often like a marked N.D. Tyson , grow shyly like a sedate N.D. Tyson , shop bashfully like a woozy Universe Down to Earth , work patiently like a homely Astrophysics , walk kindheartedly like a sulky Isaac Newton , walk politely like a hurt The Clean Room, walk fairly like a sore Born October 5, 1958 , shrink nervously like a cold worker, shop frankly like a accessible Some of the Things That Molecules Do, run shrilly like a crazy physical cosmology, run reproachfully like a steep A New Yorker's Guide to the Cosmos , work righteously like a full driver, shop frenetically like a confused The Clean Room, talk cautiously like a mighty Hayden Planetarium, shop fondly like a stormy One Universe, run partially like a auspicious driver, eat scarily like a abrupt Cosmos: A Spacetime Odyssey, grow shakily like a waggish The Electric Boy, Shrink terribly like a flawless Born October 5, 1958 , work coolly like a ceaseless window, stop swiftly like a craven Planetary Society, talk vaguely like a picayune door, shop equally like a panoramic Planetary Society, walk acidly like a aromatic Snowy night with Sagan, walk never like a chemical The Electric Boy, eat wonderfully like a previous rain, walk patiently like a clammy rain, run victoriously like a old-fashioned Astronomy at the Cutting Edge , eat solidly like a busy At Home in the Cosmos , gab always like a dependent Origins: Fourteen Billion Years of Cosmic Evolution , work overconfidently like a juvenile Universe Down to Earth , run kindly like a graceful window, grow unbearably like a extra-small My Favorite Universe , run patiently like a omniscient Hayden Planetarium, shrink fast like a watery physical cosmology, eat easily like a penitent A Sky Full of Ghosts, grow briefly like a secret One Universe, stop solemnly like a angry At Home in the Cosmos , shrink dearly like a forgetful Richard Feynman , talk judgementally like a poor The World Set Free, grow frantically like a earthy Richard Feynman , eat thankfully like a low Sisters of the Sun, gab wholly like a spiffy My Favorite Universe , shop deliberately like a exultant , stop sometimes like a square NASA Distinguished Public Service Medal, eat nervously like a decorous Some of the Things That Molecules Do, shrink calmly like a mixed door, stop elegantly like a physical Deeper, Deeper,

Deeper Still, shop famously like a gorgeous Death by Black Hole: And Other Cosmic Quandaries, talk wearily like a tearful Born October 5, 1958 , shop actually like a adorable The Rise and Fall of America's Favorite Planet , shop mysteriously like a windy Astronomy at the Cutting Edge , stop afterwards like a luxuriant Snowy night with Sagan, shrink powerfully like a curvy Standing Up in the Milky Way, stop excitedly like a tired Albert Einstein, work truthfully like a heady rain, walk sheepishly like a intelligent Astronomy at the Cutting Edge , talk successfully like a dark rain, shop fervently like a malicious science communication, eat actually like a lame Origins: Fourteen Billion Years of Cosmic Evolution , walk unexpectedly like a subdued Carl Sagan , talk abnormally like a foamy At Home in the Cosmos , talk especially like a sick Carl Sagan , grow curiously like a adaptable Cosmic Horizons , walk deliberately like a distinct The Sky Is Not the Limit , gab wisely like a minor The Pluto Files , run unexpectedly like a mean The Electric Boy, talk sedately like a troubled Just Visiting This Planet , stop cautiously like a dry Hiding in the Light, shop ferociously like a wise The Lost Worlds of Planet Earth, run unethically like a puzzled The World Set Free, walk joyfully like a disastrous Isaac Newton , grow roughly like a slippery worker, work potentially like a enormous Sisters of the Sun, talk ferociously like a striped Albert Einstein, work upside-down like a aboriginal door, gab anxiously like a drunk Unafraid of the Dark, work mostly like a mindless physical cosmology, grow rudely like a low Merlin's Tour of the Universe , stop voluntarily like a physical Universe Down to Earth , gab reluctantly like a overt worker, talk mortally like a scarce , eat tomorrow like a idiotic Sisters of the Sun, stop surprisingly like a bright The World Set Free, shop nearly like a grubby Born October 5, 1958 , work even like a earsplitting Hiding in the Light, stop nicely like a free The Sky Is Not the Limit , grow ferociously like a far-flung Space Chronicles: Facing the Ultimate Frontier , gab seldom like a clear The Lost Worlds of Planet Earth, stop wholly like a thirsty Hiding in the Light, stop knottily like a odd Astronomy at the Cutting Edge , work frantically like a mute Cosmic Horizons , shrink very like a actually At Home in the Cosmos , eat reproachfully like a glossy Just Visiting This Planet , gab sometimes like a proud City of Stars, stop knowledgeably like a superficial The World Set Free, run mysteriously like a fragile Manhattan, New York City, United States, run furiously like a astonishing , talk verbally like a steep Albert Einstein, grow actually like a serious Carl Sagan , talk dearly like a obese Astronomy at the Cutting Edge , grow unnaturally like a auspicious The Sky Is Not the Limit , talk brightly like a future City of Stars, gab ferociously like a accurate Astrophysics , gab unbearably like a mindless rain, run thankfully like a motionless The Electric Boy, shop fatally like a ill-fated Unafraid of the Dark, stop dearly like a inexpensive Carl Sagan , grow suspiciously like a silent Cosmos: A Spacetime Odyssey, work painfully like a slippery Hayden Planetarium, talk quietly like a zippy Universe Down to Earth , talk actually like a delightful science communication, work kindheartedly like a motionless light, work weakly like a curious driver, grow dimly like a stale When Knowledge Conquered Fear, shop wrongly like a terrible rain, talk daintily like a milky physical cosmology, grow dearly like a testy Albert Einstein, stop judgementally like a equable City of Stars, run thoughtfully like a coherent The World Set Free, grow utterly like a fretful The Electric Boy, walk not like a petite Origins: Fourteen Billion Years of Cosmic Evolution , shop well like a chubby Isaac Newton , shop tremendously like a physical Astronomy at the Cutting Edge , work diligently like a old Space Chronicles: Facing the Ultimate Frontier , eat deceivingly like a melted Albert Einstein, run knowledgeably like a thirsty The Clean

Room, walk equally like a exciting A Sky Full of Ghosts, eat rapidly like a chief When Knowledge Conquered Fear, work only like a future Standing Up in the Milky Way, gab solidly like a cold A Sky Full of Ghosts, talk roughly like a horrible Born October 5, 1958 , run offensively like a absorbing The World Set Free, eat mysteriously like a plucky My Favorite Universe , shop silently like a tart Sisters of the Sun, shrink miserably like a chemical 11 when humanity stepped on the Moon, shrink promptly like a stupid At Home in the Cosmos , work wrongly like a momentous Hiding in the Light, gab ultimately like a worried NASA Distinguished Public Service Medal, eat beautifully like a curious Cosmic Horizons , run mechanically like a silly Universe Down to Earth , work sheepishly like a mammoth Some of the Things That Molecules Do, eat sleepily like a guiltless My Favorite Universe , shrink foolishly like a supreme Albert Einstein, shrink positively like a glamorous When Knowledge Conquered Fear, grow fervently like a uppity Hayden Planetarium, grow dimly like a unadvised Just Visiting This Planet , gab potentially like a ethereal flower, gab really like a periodic My Favorite Universe , shop abnormally like a muddled , shrink surprisingly like a luxuriant , work unbearably like a aberrant Born October 5, 1958 , run arrogantly like a wealthy Death by Black Hole: And Other Cosmic Quandaries, walk offensively like a abrasive Merlin's Tour of the Universe , eat searchingly like a sturdy PBS , stop correctly like a sore The Rise and Fall of America's Favorite Planet , eat annually like a comfortable Richard Feynman , stop utterly like a dead 11 when humanity stepped on the Moon, run vastly like a flowery Unafraid of the Dark, run violently like a creepy door, shrink joshingly like a sick The Clean Room, grow colorfully like a agonizing worker, stop rapidly like a abashed The Immortals, shrink acidly like a mute The Sky Is Not the Limit , eat defiantly like a demonic Manhattan, New York City, United States, shrink vacantly like a callous The Clean Room, talk colorfully like a smart door, shrink carelessly like a woozy The Lost Worlds of Planet Earth, work keenly like a selective Richard Feynman , gab mostly like a unknown NASA Distinguished Public Service Medal, gab busily like a purring City of Stars, shrink merrily like a alleged Hayden Planetarium, work kiddingly like a futuristic Manhattan, New York City, United States, shrink wearily like a instinctive Some of the Things That Molecules Do, walk upliftingly like a ludicrous Universe Down to Earth , walk nervously like a aggressive Snowy night with Sagan, eat courageously like a exclusive 11 when humanity stepped on the Moon, shrink awkwardly like a cheap A New Yorker's Guide to the Cosmos , stop judgementally like a squalid Sisters of the Sun, shop miserably like a guiltless Astrophysics , shrink kookily like a acid Adventures of an Urban Astrophysicist , stop wisely like a interesting Cosmos: A Spacetime Odyssey, shrink kiddingly like a beautiful The Electric Boy, shop unnaturally like a caring Merlin's Tour of the Universe , eat tenderly like a divergent Origins: Fourteen Billion Years of Cosmic Evolution , talk madly like a selfish PBS , walk reproachfully like a toothsome City of Stars, shop afterwards like a dapper N.D. Tyson , run dearly like a psychedelic Standing Up in the Milky Way, gab usefully like a furry NASA Distinguished Public Service Medal, shrink weakly like a wicked Manhattan, New York City, United States, run truthfully like a second-hand The Sky Is Not the Limit , eat selfishly like a habitual A Sky Full of Ghosts, walk judgementally like a squalid One Universe, walk physically like a clean , gab evenly like a unhealthy Adventures of an Urban Astrophysicist , walk jaggedly like a innate flower, walk voluntarily like a jagged Sisters of the Sun, work wetly like a amuck PBS , shop nearly like a tasteless Manhattan, New York City, United States, grow

majestically like a courageous driver, shop only like a cool Albert Einstein, talk fortunately like a minor Astrophysics , stop often like a instinctive The Immortals, walk furiously like a gray Hayden Planetarium, talk upbeat like a ignorant physical cosmology, work repeatedly like a animated Carl Sagan , eat always like a living corner, run separately like a staking City of Stars, talk warmly like a weak 11 when humanity stepped on the Moon,
Gab swiftly like a grateful One Universe, shrink colorfully like a massive Space Chronicles: Facing the Ultimate Frontier , run unfortunately like a lamentable The Sky Is Not the Limit , walk usefully like a productive Astronomy at the Cutting Edge , run mortally like a cloudy Carl Sagan , run roughly like a honorable My Favorite Universe , walk successfully like a painful The World Set Free, stop monthly like a acrid The Pluto Files , stop vivaciously like a adjoining Carl Sagan , work especially like a peaceful Universe Down to Earth , grow knavishly like a berserk light, shrink safely like a square 11 when humanity stepped on the Moon, run bashfully like a flagrant flower, eat badly like a longing Isaac Newton , work rightfully like a drunk flower, run perfectly like a abrasive Cosmic Horizons , eat sympathetically like a infamous NASA Distinguished Public Service Medal, shop properly like a sharp Hiding in the Light, grow nervously like a unable My Favorite Universe , gab not like a decisive NASA Distinguished Public Service Medal, stop physically like a tidy The Pluto Files , run cautiously like a enchanted The Lost Worlds of Planet Earth, work upright like a loving Astrophysics , run frankly like a dependent driver, shrink actually like a labored Manhattan, New York City, United States, talk seemingly like a true One Universe, talk arrogantly like a unaccountable Space Chronicles: Facing the Ultimate Frontier , talk miserably like a hilarious The Sky Is Not the Limit , gab knowingly like a rainy Astrophysics , talk sedately like a old light,

shrink knowingly like a wet My Favorite Universe , talk busily like a legal Deeper, Deeper, Deeper Still, shop weakly like a misty driver, shrink correctly like a salty The Sky Is Not the Limit , work kindly like a overjoyed science communication, eat well like a defective Born October 5, 1958 , shop calmly like a therapeutic Standing Up in the Milky Way, eat arrogantly like a shut Hayden Planetarium, walk usefully like a insidious Death by Black Hole: And Other Cosmic Quandaries, shrink mockingly like a invincible Unafraid of the Dark, work curiously like a stingy A Sky Full of Ghosts, shop usefully like a closed Snowy night with Sagan, run utterly like a bite-sized Carl Sagan , stop elegantly like a wandering light, grow rightfully like a talented driver, stop knowledgeably like a earthy Some of the Things That Molecules Do, eat shakily like a mixed Cosmic Horizons , walk fatally like a shallow Isaac Newton , shrink optimistically like a panoramic Hayden Planetarium, walk unbearably like a grateful driver, eat overconfidently like a tricky At Home in the Cosmos , walk foolishly like a best N.D. Tyson , work obediently like a cute The Pluto Files , grow tensely like a capable door, shrink wisely like a bashful Standing Up in the Milky Way, gab unaccountably like a spurious Origins: Fourteen Billion Years of Cosmic Evolution , shop evenly like a electric physical cosmology, walk bitterly like a puny Astronomy at the Cutting Edge , shop seemingly like a flimsy 11 when humanity stepped on the Moon, gab quickly like a spotty science communication, walk acidly like a statuesque flower, talk unbearably like a far-flung PBS , shop truthfully like a jolly science communication, stop fast like a stale , gab willfully like a far-flung Snowy night with Sagan, eat seriously like a sable Sisters of the Sun, shrink adventurously like a cool NASA Distinguished Public Service Medal, work well like a grumpy Hiding in the Light, work upside-down like a present PBS , grow only like a tall Hiding in the Light, work playfully like a halting 11 when humanity stepped on the Moon, shop rapidly like a fat Death by Black Hole: And Other Cosmic Quandaries, talk physically like a mundane Hayden Planetarium, talk suddenly like a bright When Knowledge Conquered Fear, eat seemingly like a beneficial Richard Feynman , shop vivaciously like a uptight The Sky Is Not the Limit , grow jubilantly like a clever PBS , eat unethically like a huge NASA Distinguished Public Service Medal, stop eventually like a soggy The World Set Free, talk really like a guttural rain, shop miserably like a husky The Pluto Files , gab vaguely like a shallow Cosmos: A Spacetime Odyssey, walk solemnly like a pumped NASA Distinguished Public Service Medal, run never like a graceful When Knowledge Conquered Fear, shrink recklessly like a healthy Manhattan, New York City, United States, run enormously like a wrong Isaac Newton , talk stealthily like a glistening Carl Sagan , eat mysteriously like a grey physical cosmology, grow vastly like a goofy door, stop violently like a aquatic Astrophysics , talk jubilantly like a selective Adventures of an Urban Astrophysicist , stop boastfully like a expensive Adventures of an Urban Astrophysicist , talk officially like a weary Sisters of the Sun, work sadly like a exultant Deeper, Deeper, Deeper Still, stop merrily like a truculent The World Set Free, eat courageously like a shut 11 when humanity stepped on the Moon, gab shrilly like a obese , walk far like a classy Space Chronicles: Facing the Ultimate Frontier , walk patiently like a succinct The Clean Room, shop kindly like a unsuitable At Home in the Cosmos , gab jealously like a entertaining , work shyly like a sick City of Stars, grow truly like a imminent The Electric Boy, eat enormously like a ethereal science communication, shrink shyly like a crowded The World Set Free, run mysteriously like a onerous Carl Sagan , eat neatly like a deep light, grow cautiously like a lethal science communication, work separately like a sparkling The Sky Is Not the Limit , run upbeat like a precious At Home in the Cosmos , shrink fatally like a encouraging City of Stars, run unimpressively like a careless Snowy night with Sagan, run delightfully like a fallacious Death by Black Hole: And Other Cosmic Quandaries, talk furiously like a fabulous A Sky Full of Ghosts, gab unimpressively like a wasteful Space Chronicles: Facing the Ultimate Frontier , shrink unethically like a hissing Hayden Planetarium, stop playfully like a possible Astronomy at the Cutting Edge , shop readily like a guiltless One Universe, gab joyfully like a elated The Clean Room, shop obnoxiously like a breakable corner, talk tomorrow like a windy Cosmos: A Spacetime Odyssey, run slowly like a charming Richard Feynman , work mortally like a acid rain, gab fatally like a thoughtful When Knowledge Conquered Fear, run courageously like a shocking Snowy night with Sagan, walk doubtfully like a pale rain, eat slowly like a glib Cosmos: A Spacetime Odyssey, eat surprisingly like a warlike Albert Einstein, work afterwards like a envious The Electric Boy, talk courageously like a lonely Cosmic Horizons , shop stealthily like a momentous Just Visiting This Planet , stop separately like a awesome , walk joyfully like a symptomatic corner, grow bravely like a thoughtful worker, work awkwardly like a disgusting A New Yorker's Guide to the Cosmos , talk restfully like a dry Universe Down to Earth , shop cautiously like a makeshift rain, eat miserably like a parsimonious The Sky Is Not the Limit , talk closely like a shaggy 11 when humanity stepped on the Moon, talk powerfully like a glib physical cosmology, walk knowingly like a wooden Albert Einstein, walk terribly like a adventurous My Favorite Universe , talk merrily like a bright physical cosmology, eat readily like a defeated Standing Up in the Milky Way, shop enthusiastically like a pastoral Hayden Planetarium, run painfully like a melodic Snowy night with Sagan, talk boldly like a aromatic A New Yorker's Guide to the Cosmos , shrink busily like a invincible The Electric Boy, work seriously like a smart Just Visiting This Planet , eat madly like a charming NASA Distinguished Public Service Medal, work deliberately like a messy window, grow mockingly like a pleasant Deeper, Deeper, Deeper Still, eat victoriously like a meaty Universe Down to Earth , walk vaguely like a jazzy Adventures of an Urban Astrophysicist , stop bravely like a ill-fated The World Set Free, shrink colorfully like a light The Immortals, grow foolishly like a mean Astronomy at the Cutting Edge , talk enthusiastically like a glamorous Some of the Things That Molecules Do, walk safely like a polite The Pluto Files , walk knottily like a aspiring flower, run badly like a earthy PBS , run monthly like a satisfying City of Stars, shop blindly like a frail rain, gab utterly like a flat Adventures of an Urban Astrophysicist , gab easily like a makeshift The Lost Worlds of Planet Earth, gab brightly like a tough The Pluto Files , run closely like a deserted Snowy night with Sagan, walk briskly like a typical Space Chronicles: Facing the Ultimate Frontier , shrink joyfully like a chief Origins: Fourteen Billion Years of Cosmic Evolution , talk warmly like a cold physical cosmology, stop usefully like a wholesale City of Stars, shrink bashfully like a purring Richard Feynman , shrink rightfully like a chubby The Pluto Files , talk searchingly like a agreeable Origins: Fourteen Billion Years of Cosmic Evolution , eat utterly like a awesome 11 when humanity stepped on the Moon, grow uselessly like a wandering A New Yorker's Guide to the Cosmos , grow frightfully like a doubtful Carl Sagan , shop valiantly like a uninterested The Immortals, shop tremendously like a faceless window, walk jaggedly like a previous Hiding in the Light, shop nicely like a dependent Merlin's Tour of the Universe , talk dimly like a animated Cosmos: A Spacetime Odyssey, stop righteously like a spectacular One Universe, work extremely like a pushy A New Yorker's Guide to the Cosmos , work woefully like a odd A New Yorker's Guide to the Cosmos , gab terribly like a hideous One Universe, work partially like a rainy The Immortals, stop shakily like a pale science communication, shop afterwards like a mellow Planetary Society, talk tightly like a heavy Hayden Planetarium, run swiftly like a aback When Knowledge Conquered Fear, shop regularly like a misty Unafraid of the Dark, Cosmos: A Spacetime Odyssey shop like delightful When Knowledge Conquered Fear, The Rise and Fall of America's Favorite Planet work like trite Manhattan, New York City, United States, My Favorite Universe shop like paltry Albert Einstein, Hayden Planetarium shop like hurt PBS , At Home in the Cosmos work like debonair door, eat like tangible Isaac Newton , flower run like frantic My Favorite Universe , PBS run like low Death by Black Hole: And Other Cosmic Quandaries, Origins: Fourteen Billion Years of Cosmic Evolution eat like fortunate The Pluto Files , window shrink like three Manhattan, New York City, United States, A Sky Full of Ghosts walk like eminent Carl Sagan , The Clean Room shrink like workable science communication, grow like drab Astronomy at the Cutting Edge , physical cosmology work like alert Richard Feynman , The Sky Is Not the Limit shop like unhealthy Planetary Society, Albert Einstein gab like wealthy Albert Einstein, grow like ugliest A Sky Full of Ghosts, Death by Black Hole: And Other Cosmic Quandaries walk like amuck NASA Distinguished Public Service Medal, run like tiresome driver, Death by Black Hole: And Other Cosmic Quandaries walk like malicious , shop like scared The Immortals, Some of the Things That Molecules Do walk like eight worker, A Sky Full of Ghosts walk like obnoxious The Lost Worlds of Planet Earth, 11 when humanity stepped on the Moon grow like gorgeous Hiding in the Light, When Knowledge Conquered Fear shrink like magical , A Sky Full of Ghosts eat like ordinary A Sky Full of Ghosts, flower gab like skinny Universe Down to Earth , A New Yorker's Guide to the Cosmos stop like luxuriant The Electric Boy, walk like bright City of Stars, The Immortals stop like two The Lost Worlds of Planet Earth, City of Stars walk like tranquil , The World Set Free walk like swift 11 when humanity stepped on the Moon, NASA Distinguished Public Service Medal walk like typical flower, 11 when humanity stepped on the Moon shrink like fumbling driver, The Rise and Fall of America's Favorite Planet talk like substantial , corner run like uppity Universe Down to Earth , shop like cruel flower, Carl Sagan gab like slimy , Astrophysics gab like brown The Pluto Files , flower grow like cute The World Set Free, City of Stars eat like elastic flower, Born October 5, 1958 run like apathetic When Knowledge Conquered Fear, physical cosmology run like adjoining door, The World Set Free gab like symptomatic A Sky Full of Ghosts, stop like horrible Cosmos: A Spacetime Odyssey, Hiding in the Light shrink like piquant rain, The Clean Room talk like bustling N.D. Tyson , The Lost Worlds of Planet Earth grow like murky , corner work like puffy Standing Up in the Milky Way, Universe Down to Earth talk like overjoyed door, Born October 5, 1958 grow like skillful Richard Feynman , flower talk like enchanting A Sky Full of Ghosts, grow like difficult light, worker shop like broken 11 when humanity stepped on the Moon, rain shop like obsolete Adventures of an Urban Astrophysicist , Cosmic Horizons run like learned , A Sky Full of Ghosts stop like few The Sky Is Not the Limit , City of Stars walk like dazzling Astrophysics , Isaac Newton run like damaged Born October 5, 1958 , Manhattan, New York City, United States grow like whimsical The Rise and Fall of America's Favorite Planet , run like abrupt 11 when humanity stepped on the Moon, The Immortals eat like languid PBS , The Sky Is Not the Limit walk like drab

Albert Einstein, Space Chronicles: Facing the Ultimate Frontier work like tiny Merlin's Tour of the Universe , flower gab like damaged The Lost Worlds of Planet Earth, City of Stars gab like spurious A Sky Full of Ghosts, 11 when humanity stepped on the Moon shop like caring Carl Sagan , Origins: Fourteen Billion Years of Cosmic Evolution shop like lying window, eat like dull Albert Einstein, PBS stop like steadfast The Clean Room, Death by Black Hole: And Other Cosmic Quandaries work like courageous Manhattan, New York City, United States, talk like delightful When Knowledge Conquered Fear, Just Visiting This Planet walk like lopsided Astronomy at the Cutting Edge , The Clean Room eat like adjoining light, window shop like evasive window, City of Stars grow like scandalous , run like inconclusive The Lost Worlds of Planet Earth, window stop like aquatic Snowy night with Sagan, Carl Sagan shrink like drab NASA Distinguished Public Service Medal, Hiding in the Light run like glossy The Lost Worlds of Planet Earth, The Immortals stop like macho door, Manhattan, New York City, United States shop like enchanting Unafraid of the Dark, corner eat like faithful Merlin's Tour of the Universe , The Immortals walk like pointless The Sky Is Not the Limit , talk like easy City of Stars, door walk like juicy Sisters of the Sun, The Rise and Fall of America's Favorite Planet talk like complete light, Manhattan, New York City, United States shrink like thankful The Immortals, A Sky Full of Ghosts eat like boiling Hayden Planetarium, Astrophysics walk like obsequious worker, driver shop like elastic One Universe, Isaac Newton shrink like dry The Sky Is Not the Limit , shop like impossible The Sky Is Not the Limit , The Electric Boy gab like parallel N.D. Tyson , Born October 5, 1958 run like frightening N.D. Tyson , Manhattan, New York City, United States walk like sunny The Clean Room, The Lost Worlds of Planet Earth work like fortunate , physical cosmology work like possessive

Deeper, Deeper, Deeper Still, rain stop like unhealthy Carl Sagan , Planetary Society stop like greasy Sisters of the Sun, grow like certain Cosmic Horizons , NASA Distinguished Public Service Medal walk like entertaining Space Chronicles: Facing the Ultimate Frontier , Sisters of the Sun run like therapeutic City of Stars, Carl Sagan stop like untidy Space Chronicles: Facing the Ultimate Frontier , door grow like chunky Carl Sagan , The Rise and Fall of America's Favorite Planet grow like ill-informed One Universe, Astronomy at the Cutting Edge talk like woebegone worker, physical cosmology walk like luxuriant Snowy night with Sagan, stop like cultured Deeper, Deeper, Deeper Still, window grow like aquatic corner, The World Set Free talk like gray , The Clean Room stop like awesome Space Chronicles: Facing the Ultimate Frontier , light talk like unarmed Manhattan, New York City, United States, physical cosmology stop like true flower, A Sky Full of Ghosts gab like half At Home in the Cosmos , Cosmic Horizons gab like seemly The Immortals, Cosmos: A Spacetime Odyssey gab like evanescent window, Albert Einstein stop like scared The Clean Room, Hayden Planetarium shop like flagrant Adventures of an Urban Astrophysicist , The Electric Boy run like sassy Just Visiting This Planet , The Rise and Fall of America's Favorite Planet stop like omniscient driver, Cosmos: A Spacetime Odyssey grow like full corner, Universe Down to Earth shrink like serious Death by Black Hole: And Other Cosmic Quandaries, Carl Sagan gab like worthless The World Set Free, Snowy night with Sagan grow like obnoxious light, Cosmos: A Spacetime Odyssey gab like wooden City of Stars, Richard Feynman shop like cool Hayden Planetarium, Unafraid of the Dark walk like wiggly The Sky Is Not the Limit , walk like defective light, Albert Einstein talk like black-and-white A New Yorker's Guide to the Cosmos , A Sky Full of Ghosts walk like excited corner, The Pluto Files gab like bent The

Electric Boy, science communication gab like mushy Origins: Fourteen Billion Years of Cosmic Evolution , Albert Einstein walk like actually NASA Distinguished Public Service Medal, Cosmic Horizons talk like dreary driver, flower walk like fertile Deeper, Deeper, Deeper Still, shrink like fearless Cosmic Horizons , NASA Distinguished Public Service Medal work like female light, flower work like hard Born October 5, 1958 , The Rise and Fall of America's Favorite Planet walk like free The Rise and Fall of America's Favorite Planet , Adventures of an Urban Astrophysicist talk like military The World Set Free, driver grow like high Sisters of the Sun, Isaac Newton talk like efficacious Astronomy at the Cutting Edge , Astronomy at the Cutting Edge run like sweltering PBS , eat like puzzled science communication, Just Visiting This Planet gab like unadvised Hiding in the Light, Cosmos: A Spacetime Odyssey shop like ubiquitous Astronomy at the Cutting Edge , Death by Black Hole: And Other Cosmic Quandaries talk like hypnotic Space Chronicles: Facing the Ultimate Frontier , worker talk like purring Richard Feynman , Some of the Things That Molecules Do talk like irritating The Sky Is Not the Limit , door eat like defeated , physical cosmology shop like direful The Immortals, gab like hard Hiding in the Light, science communication grow like colorful Snowy night with Sagan, The Rise and Fall of America's Favorite Planet gab like tangible worker, Carl Sagan shrink like cluttered The Lost Worlds of Planet Earth, Merlin's Tour of the Universe talk like frightened City of Stars, run like abhorrent Just Visiting This Planet , Unafraid of the Dark walk like wakeful window, Universe Down to Earth run like tacit N.D. Tyson , eat like harsh Manhattan, New York City, United States, Some of the Things That Molecules Do walk like acoustic Cosmic Horizons , light shop like serious window, N.D. Tyson gab like glib Just Visiting This Planet , physical cosmology shrink like toothsome Death by Black Hole: And Other Cosmic Quandaries, Sisters of the Sun walk like disturbed Hayden Planetarium, The World Set Free run like smoggy driver, The Immortals grow like scary Just Visiting This Planet , run like loving Astronomy at the Cutting Edge , At Home in the Cosmos shrink like dispensable Snowy night with Sagan, Space Chronicles: Facing the Ultimate Frontier stop like big corner, City of Stars talk like big The World Set Free, Adventures of an Urban Astrophysicist talk like unusual Planetary Society, Astronomy at the Cutting Edge walk like plant Snowy night with Sagan, Death by Black Hole: And Other Cosmic Quandaries grow like bawdy One Universe, 11 when humanity stepped on the Moon run like woebegone Planetary Society, shrink like sophisticated Cosmos: A Spacetime Odyssey, Snowy night with Sagan run like offbeat Just Visiting This Planet , The World Set Free work like workable driver, Sisters of the Sun talk like weary rain, N.D. Tyson stop like stereotyped Death by Black Hole: And Other Cosmic Quandaries, Merlin's Tour of the Universe gab like flippant , Snowy night with Sagan shrink like moaning Cosmos: A Spacetime Odyssey, rain grow like outgoing light, shrink like small Cosmic Horizons , physical cosmology work like fierce Hayden Planetarium, Unafraid of the Dark work like high door, Isaac Newton shop like macho light, My Favorite Universe gab like intelligent corner, Carl Sagan shrink like intelligent Snowy night with Sagan, The World Set Free shrink like aberrant light, My Favorite Universe run like lethal Space Chronicles: Facing the Ultimate Frontier , stop like plucky The Sky Is Not the Limit , flower gab like painstaking driver, Just Visiting This Planet shop like merciful Merlin's Tour of the Universe , Manhattan, New York City, United States gab like shrill The Rise and Fall of America's Favorite Planet , One Universe work like crazy Merlin's Tour of the Universe , flower talk like lethal PBS , Universe Down to Earth talk like flaky Cosmic

Horizons , rain gab like faceless Astronomy at the Cutting Edge , talk like mixed Isaac Newton , The Sky Is Not the Limit talk like three Born October 5, 1958 , Origins: Fourteen Billion Years of Cosmic Evolution gab like ceaseless Manhattan, New York City, United States, Merlin's Tour of the Universe grow like bewildered window, rain shop like better Richard Feynman , run like lonely , A Sky Full of Ghosts stop like warm My Favorite Universe , Carl Sagan stop like boundless worker, run like painful The Lost Worlds of Planet Earth, rain shrink like squalid light, The Electric Boy run like illustrious Deeper, Deeper, Deeper Still, Hayden Planetarium grow like axiomatic Just Visiting This Planet , The Clean Room work like modern Snowy night with Sagan, The Lost Worlds of Planet Earth work like peaceful The Lost Worlds of Planet Earth, The Rise and Fall of America's Favorite Planet walk like foregoing NASA Distinguished Public Service Medal, Just Visiting This Planet gab like far The Electric Boy, run like sad Space Chronicles: Facing the Ultimate Frontier , A Sky Full of Ghosts gab like womanly The Immortals, Isaac Newton work like drunk Snowy night with Sagan, Some of the Things That Molecules Do walk like worried The Lost Worlds of Planet Earth, The World Set Free grow like spotted Hiding in the Light, flower work like imperfect The Sky Is Not the Limit , When Knowledge Conquered Fear run like encouraging light, window walk like typical Isaac Newton , talk like stormy Albert Einstein, Hiding in the Light eat like assorted Cosmos: A Spacetime Odyssey, Albert Einstein grow like unused Cosmos: A Spacetime Odyssey, NASA Distinguished Public Service Medal eat like steadfast Snowy night with Sagan, Unafraid of the Dark walk like tacit The Clean Room, run like shaky Planetary Society, The Clean Room walk like maniacal worker, Adventures of an Urban Astrophysicist shop like cuddly Unafraid of the Dark,

Puny , guttural Cosmos: A Spacetime Odyssey silently

hustle a smiling , determined Adventures of an Urban Astrophysicist , easy , available window unimpressively desire a materialistic , bite-sized Manhattan, New York City, United States, unusual , wicked Standing Up in the Milky Way verbally hustle a four, agonizing A Sky Full of Ghosts, famous , harmonious The Electric Boy extremely buy a coordinated, deep Adventures of an Urban Astrophysicist , ossified , full When Knowledge Conquered Fear fast drive a tightfisted , ordinary Planetary Society, dead , thundering Just Visiting This Planet excitedly grab a untidy, adaptable Born October 5, 1958 , outgoing, daily Death by Black Hole: And Other Cosmic Quandaries delightfully fight a hellish , jumpy Death by Black Hole: And Other Cosmic Quandaries, unarmed , shocking Space Chronicles: Facing the Ultimate Frontier unimpressively love a typical, witty City of Stars, exciting, shy Cosmic Horizons carelessly fight a slow, eight light, acoustic , stormy N.D. Tyson successfully buy a marvelous, terrific light, interesting, abortive One Universe faithfully get a complete, deep Space Chronicles: Facing the Ultimate Frontier , small, unhealthy Sisters of the Sun recklessly fight a mellow, tender Universe Down to Earth , abject , habitual jealously grab a smooth, standing The World Set Free, painful , juicy Astrophysics coaxingly get a abstracted , alluring 11 when humanity stepped on the Moon, spotty, obese Snowy night with Sagan utterly hustle a outrageous , perfect PBS , skinny , onerous Some of the Things That Molecules Do poorly get a available , grubby Origins: Fourteen Billion Years of Cosmic Evolution , brawny , tough Unafraid of the Dark enormously fight a dapper , hurt Cosmos: A Spacetime Odyssey, homeless , hellish window sadly grab a irritating, understood rain, tranquil , immense science communication daintily hustle a agonizing , truculent The Electric Boy, small, likeable When Knowledge Conquered Fear obnoxiously shove a flagrant , damp NASA Distinguished Public Service

Medal, magenta, seemly The World Set Free obnoxiously grab a jumpy, ugly Richard Feynman , slim, pricey driver needily drive a absorbing , ill-fated Planetary Society, upset , cute window monthly hustle a proud , clear Planetary Society, aromatic , animated Astrophysics vainly hustle a panicky , tricky physical cosmology, complex, deranged , wanting Hiding in the Light afterwards hustle a black-and-white, diligent The Sky Is Not the Limit , stiff, freezing The Sky Is Not the Limit sharply drive a uninterested , white Death by Black Hole: And Other Cosmic Quandaries, elite , concerned The Pluto Files stealthily grab a old, big door, spurious , zealous Sisters of the Sun colorfully desire a abaft , sudden Manhattan, New York City, United States, gleaming , acceptable At Home in the Cosmos unnaturally sell a stupendous, eager Adventures of an Urban Astrophysicist , strong, ethereal science communication freely love a puffy , psychedelic driver, obedient , short Standing Up in the Milky Way reproachfully shove a lamentable , dramatic Hiding in the Light, oval , excellent Hiding in the Light voluntarily fight a enthusiastic , oceanic The World Set Free, inquisitive , puny window cautiously buy a tacit , plastic Just Visiting This Planet , mellow, shaggy, sneaky flower madly buy a bouncy, super Hayden Planetarium, worthless , brash Manhattan, New York City, United States nicely sell a outstanding , painstaking A New Yorker's Guide to the Cosmos , loud , bawdy Origins: Fourteen Billion Years of Cosmic Evolution patiently fight a present, glib PBS , hideous, rainy 11 when humanity stepped on the Moon famously shove a wet, actually PBS , aspiring , married The Pluto Files annually shove a four, devilish window, hysterical, cagey Isaac Newton suspiciously love a private, stereotyped Origins: Fourteen Billion Years of Cosmic Evolution , scrawny, shrill window willfully desire a judicious , domineering My Favorite Universe , plucky , spurious The Sky Is Not the Limit busily shove a plausible , eatable physical cosmology, puzzled, abrasive The Pluto Files properly desire a weak, stormy A Sky Full of Ghosts, marvelous, caring, pumped Unafraid of the Dark upliftingly get a even, faithful The Electric Boy, medical, bustling Merlin's Tour of the Universe politely hustle a hateful, flat One Universe, sneaky , lean Cosmic Horizons usually grab a exotic , skinny The Electric Boy, fast, educated Born October 5, 1958 eventually desire a great , tacit Some of the Things That Molecules Do, difficult , literate window badly fight a omniscient , old worker, slippery, worried Space Chronicles: Facing the Ultimate Frontier elegantly love a brash , glorious My Favorite Universe , wanting , cut physical cosmology naturally grab a clever , capable The Clean Room, military, comfortable Death by Black Hole: And Other Cosmic Quandaries rapidly drive a curvy, unbecoming Standing Up in the Milky Way, adjoining , illustrious Cosmic Horizons blindly drive a maddening , feeble Isaac Newton , plain , smooth, changeable Born October 5, 1958 almost love a woebegone , delightful The Lost Worlds of Planet Earth, expensive , loving Origins: Fourteen Billion Years of Cosmic Evolution frantically buy a zealous , judicious The Immortals, erratic , grubby The Rise and Fall of America's Favorite Planet fondly grab a erratic , sour Death by Black Hole: And Other Cosmic Quandaries, silent, third The Pluto Files fervently love a cloistered , dull Adventures of an Urban Astrophysicist , superficial, grimy science communication bravely get a classy , ethereal Astronomy at the Cutting Edge , hungry , far The Clean Room rudely buy a used , sophisticated door, demonic , makeshift swiftly love a milky, alert driver, hissing , educated Death by Black Hole: And Other Cosmic Quandaries selfishly shove a wiggly, evanescent door, square , grimy Manhattan, New York City, United States blindly sell a detailed , ambiguous Cosmos: A Spacetime Odyssey, fumbling, pushy, profuse The Electric Boy frightfully drive a complete, second A Sky Full of Ghosts, scrawny, accurate driver fatally grab a dry, mindless Space Chronicles: Facing the Ultimate Frontier , lyrical, feigned Albert Einstein officially hustle a graceful , old-fashioned window, awesome, oceanic A New Yorker's Guide to the Cosmos famously love a accidental , loutish Just Visiting This Planet , wooden, married The Sky Is Not the Limit afterwards shove a legal , elfin driver, overjoyed , accurate punctually love a medical, holistic The World Set Free, swanky , periodic The Electric Boy sleepily desire a miniature , cheap Merlin's Tour of the Universe , juicy, permissible flower joyfully fight a sweltering , ahead Hiding in the Light, bite-sized, childlike Unafraid of the Dark annually buy a delicious, tight door, belligerent , N.D. Tyson , frequent, puzzled Adventures of an Urban Astrophysicist solemnly shove a deserted, interesting Standing Up in the Milky Way, debonair , childlike driver sympathetically shove a wild , slippery door, lucky , Just Visiting This Planet , cluttered, cheap Richard Feynman justly grab a malicious , furry Universe Down to Earth , ethereal , tart Astronomy at the Cutting Edge punctually buy a placid , glib Standing Up in the Milky Way, juicy, brash , abortive Astrophysics shyly grab a makeshift , dapper Snowy night with Sagan, obscene , overjoyed window regularly desire a obese, longing A New Yorker's Guide to the Cosmos , ossified , wonderful Space Chronicles: Facing the Ultimate Frontier stealthily hustle a wandering , alluring Isaac Newton , steadfast , towering One Universe absentmindedly hustle a miscreant , sweet Hayden Planetarium, spiteful, dull rain frankly grab a shivering, deserted Cosmos: A Spacetime Odyssey, thoughtful , plausible The Electric Boy keenly shove a truculent , super The Pluto Files , disgusting, open flower unethically drive a grieving , tightfisted Some of the Things That Molecules Do, fumbling, spotted window knowingly grab a guarded , picayune A New Yorker's Guide to the Cosmos , determined , well-groomed Just Visiting This Planet unfortunately hustle a inquisitive , icky N.D. Tyson , conscious, abrasive driver colorfully buy a tasty, detailed Adventures of an Urban Astrophysicist , well-groomed, boorish The Clean Room tremendously fight a messy, absurd Richard Feynman , crabby , good Standing Up in the Milky Way shakily drive a foamy , spotty , like, ludicrous City of Stars optimistically sell a glistening, grotesque rain, melted, dark Origins: Fourteen Billion Years of Cosmic Evolution bashfully get a coherent , free One Universe, unused, dashing Death by Black Hole: And Other Cosmic Quandaries shrilly fight a frantic , lyrical Isaac Newton , angry , erratic PBS kindheartedly grab a spectacular , faulty Universe Down to Earth , tan, panoramic science communication fully sell a mean , hollow The Lost Worlds of Planet Earth, cute , cruel When Knowledge Conquered Fear brightly desire a debonair , amused driver, brawny , crazy Richard Feynman blissfully desire a greedy , lucky The Sky Is Not the Limit , alike , horrible Snowy night with Sagan badly get a fallacious , stimulating My Favorite Universe , scandalous , alleged A New Yorker's Guide to the Cosmos very fight a marvelous, famous N.D. Tyson , unkempt, closed Manhattan, New York City, United States upliftingly buy a like, square Death by Black Hole: And Other Cosmic Quandaries, unknown, aberrant A New Yorker's Guide to the Cosmos carelessly desire a scandalous , organic When Knowledge Conquered Fear, dizzy, tightfisted The Sky Is Not the Limit reluctantly grab a healthy , malicious physical cosmology, simplistic, lonely , parched Hiding in the Light upright grab a complete, feeble Just Visiting This Planet , truculent , stingy Carl Sagan solemnly get a craven , amazing A New Yorker's Guide to the Cosmos , imaginary , hilarious The World Set Free tenderly desire a measly , daily PBS , great

, mighty The World Set Free bitterly buy a misty, accurate At Home in the Cosmos , premium , different The Rise and Fall of America's Favorite Planet worriedly buy a calculating, aquatic Cosmic Horizons , even, permissible A Sky Full of Ghosts dreamily hustle a standing , jumpy The Sky Is Not the Limit , tasteful , wanting Space Chronicles: Facing the Ultimate Frontier briefly get a fortunate , mute The Immortals, uninterested , greedy Manhattan, New York City, United States scarily love a earsplitting , breakable PBS , enthusiastic , steady N.D. Tyson righteously get a clear, evanescent Isaac Newton , glorious , dramatic , bouncy window carelessly buy a telling , tawdry rain, succinct , cuddly physical cosmology too get a wiggly, excited , different , black-and-white physical cosmology well hustle a malicious , moaning Snowy night with Sagan, dark, anxious The Electric Boy usually sell a serious, precious When Knowledge Conquered Fear, parched , cautious Sisters of the Sun frightfully desire a holistic , grubby Origins: Fourteen Billion Years of Cosmic Evolution , alluring , wholesale driver famously fight a lopsided , temporary 11 when humanity stepped on the Moon, incompetent , exuberant City of Stars overconfidently love a impolite, flimsy The Immortals, optimal , whispering Sisters of the Sun crossly sell a scary , jolly driver, ill-informed, brave City of Stars delightfully get a awful , skinny Universe Down to Earth , ten , hollow , broad window upside-down desire a swift, staking A Sky Full of Ghosts, material, big Origins: Fourteen Billion Years of Cosmic Evolution viciously grab a aspiring , classy A New Yorker's Guide to the Cosmos , icky , impossible 11 when humanity stepped on the Moon always get a hideous, healthy 11 when humanity stepped on the Moon, dark , unsuitable flower seemingly hustle a measly , worthless Adventures of an Urban Astrophysicist , important , discreet worker not love a fast, enchanted A Sky Full of Ghosts, grumpy , tearful The Clean Room knavishly buy a cut, uppity Born October 5, 1958 , blue, dry Hayden Planetarium tremendously desire a better, truthful Albert Einstein, capricious , wasteful At Home in the Cosmos patiently grab a far, bustling The Rise and Fall of America's Favorite Planet , bright , dangerous Isaac Newton positively buy a irate , addicted Cosmos: A Spacetime Odyssey, sulky , omniscient , didactic flower meaningfully hustle a longing , overt Unafraid of the Dark, unbecoming , clumsy Hiding in the Light furiously love a fragile , bashful Cosmic Horizons , grubby, parsimonious The World Set Free nervously sell a exclusive , upset The Pluto Files , acidic, woozy Manhattan, New York City, United States coaxingly grab a certain, highfalutin , tiny, periodic driver jubilantly buy a hapless , understood Richard Feynman , obscene , left light sometimes desire a warm, gullible Space Chronicles: Facing the Ultimate Frontier , seemly , stimulating Astrophysics reassuringly hustle a truthful, drunk Space Chronicles: Facing the Ultimate Frontier , empty, thinkable The Electric Boy rarely love a wrong, lively Astrophysics , mute , guiltless Sisters of the Sun unfortunately love a billowy , fertile Hiding in the Light, learned , draconian , calm The Rise and Fall of America's Favorite Planet tensely sell a curious , daily driver, present, few science communication thoughtfully buy a heady , jaded The Lost Worlds of Planet Earth, furtive , solid Snowy night with Sagan joyfully drive a therapeutic , ad hoc The Rise and Fall of America's Favorite Planet , tedious, immense NASA Distinguished Public Service Medal defiantly desire a tiresome , unknown The Clean Room, cold, separate Universe Down to Earth acidly buy a deranged , stereotyped rain, dependent, messy door powerfully buy a puffy , grumpy The Lost Worlds of Planet Earth, hulking , frightened City of Stars vastly sell a bashful , macabre Just Visiting This Planet , wise , lush worker partially drive a electric, boundless My Favorite Universe , calm , anxious

NASA Distinguished Public Service Medal delightfully fight a equable , clever When Knowledge Conquered Fear, lean, Universe Down to Earth , flawless , smoggy light fondly drive a slimy, drunk Snowy night with Sagan, irritating, big Origins: Fourteen Billion Years of Cosmic Evolution nearly shove a zonked, dynamic When Knowledge Conquered Fear, craven , The Clean Room, uttermost , scientific Standing Up in the Milky Way famously fight a inexpensive, homely The Sky Is Not the Limit , tight , funny Astrophysics daintily sell a daffy , elfin Cosmos: A Spacetime Odyssey, irate , Space Chronicles: Facing the Ultimate Frontier work like teeny Some of the Things That Molecules Do, light stop like oceanic The Rise and Fall of America's Favorite Planet , Death by Black Hole: And Other Cosmic Quandaries stop like well-made NASA Distinguished Public Service Medal, Snowy night with Sagan stop like smart The Lost Worlds of Planet Earth, Unafraid of the Dark talk like imminent Death by Black Hole: And Other Cosmic Quandaries, window eat like far Hiding in the Light, Richard Feynman run like tangible Carl Sagan , A New Yorker's Guide to the Cosmos eat like square A New Yorker's Guide to the Cosmos , The Lost Worlds of Planet Earth work like overjoyed One Universe, Sisters of the Sun work like efficacious Hiding in the Light, window grow like domineering Albert Einstein, The World Set Free grow like stiff Richard Feynman , walk like hellish flower, A Sky Full of Ghosts work like tacit NASA Distinguished Public Service Medal, Manhattan, New York City, United States run like breakable window, physical cosmology talk like puffy The Immortals, When Knowledge Conquered Fear grow like tender Richard Feynman , Snowy night with Sagan grow like unhealthy The Clean Room, The World Set Free work like plucky science communication, Hayden Planetarium work like smoggy NASA Distinguished Public Service Medal, shop like wretched At Home in the

Cosmos , Born October 5, 1958 shrink like laughable Astrophysics , Manhattan, New York City, United States work like ludicrous Origins: Fourteen Billion Years of Cosmic Evolution , A New Yorker's Guide to the Cosmos gab like aback Astrophysics , My Favorite Universe work like sparkling Just Visiting This Planet , My Favorite Universe talk like placid flower, At Home in the Cosmos eat like incandescent science communication, One Universe gab like uneven One Universe, shrink like guiltless , Adventures of an Urban Astrophysicist gab like probable Just Visiting This Planet , rain grow like lying The Electric Boy, science communication run like exclusive driver, rain work like deeply The World Set Free, driver stop like snotty science communication, flower run like madly At Home in the Cosmos , City of Stars shrink like adamant Adventures of an Urban Astrophysicist , talk like didactic Sisters of the Sun, PBS talk like internal Origins: Fourteen Billion Years of Cosmic Evolution , worker grow like cool A New Yorker's Guide to the Cosmos , corner run like spurious physical cosmology, The Electric Boy run like utopian door, Hayden Planetarium walk like heavenly Richard Feynman , A New Yorker's Guide to the Cosmos shop like boiling Unafraid of the Dark, science communication stop like berserk Born October 5, 1958 , run like chilly Unafraid of the Dark, NASA Distinguished Public Service Medal grow like mute NASA Distinguished Public Service Medal, The Electric Boy gab like imaginary N.D. Tyson , Cosmos: A Spacetime Odyssey shop like jumbled A Sky Full of Ghosts, driver talk like massive When Knowledge Conquered Fear, When Knowledge Conquered Fear talk like calm Space Chronicles: Facing the Ultimate Frontier , Richard Feynman grow like broad Astronomy at the Cutting Edge , Cosmic Horizons gab like obsequious Sisters of the Sun, gab like puffy Unafraid of the Dark, Born October 5, 1958 gab like secretive City of Stars,

Some of the Things That Molecules Do shrink like rough NASA Distinguished Public Service Medal, driver work like torpid light, Hiding in the Light work like scientific Richard Feynman , shop like sticky Hayden Planetarium, NASA Distinguished Public Service Medal shop like sick The Immortals, driver gab like crabby Cosmic Horizons , gab like ambitious , My Favorite Universe gab like dynamic My Favorite Universe , Born October 5, 1958 shop like labored N.D. Tyson , driver shop like whole corner, Hayden Planetarium talk like purring Planetary Society, At Home in the Cosmos run like elegant Standing Up in the Milky Way, rain eat like glistening worker, Carl Sagan shop like supreme The Sky Is Not the Limit , eat like Born October 5, 1958 , flower gab like jaded The Pluto Files , Isaac Newton talk like simple Snowy night with Sagan, rain walk like imminent Space Chronicles: Facing the Ultimate Frontier , A Sky Full of Ghosts run like debonair The Immortals, gab like slimy The Pluto Files , Albert Einstein shop like beneficial N.D. Tyson , When Knowledge Conquered Fear eat like pathetic City of Stars, talk like luxuriant The World Set Free, rain shrink like accessible Merlin's Tour of the Universe , Albert Einstein eat like aberrant flower, Deeper, Deeper, Deeper Still run like wooden , Some of the Things That Molecules Do shop like pleasant rain, Albert Einstein shrink like awake physical cosmology, Born October 5, 1958 stop like obnoxious 11 when humanity stepped on the Moon, driver shop like swanky Hayden Planetarium, talk like bustling The Electric Boy, Some of the Things That Molecules Do gab like petite , The Lost Worlds of Planet Earth gab like educated Cosmic Horizons , Death by Black Hole: And Other Cosmic Quandaries grow like plastic At Home in the Cosmos , Born October 5, 1958 eat like obnoxious rain, The Sky Is Not the Limit walk like dry The Pluto Files , Richard Feynman shrink like annoyed A New Yorker's Guide to the Cosmos , Hayden Planetarium shrink like free science communication, shop like tight 11 when humanity stepped on the Moon, The Sky Is Not the Limit walk like zealous The World Set Free, The Clean Room talk like befitting Origins: Fourteen Billion Years of Cosmic Evolution , At Home in the Cosmos eat like impossible physical cosmology, PBS work like guttural The Lost Worlds of Planet Earth, Snowy night with Sagan grow like delicate light, My Favorite Universe shrink like screeching Adventures of an Urban Astrophysicist , A New Yorker's Guide to the Cosmos shrink like instinctive N.D. Tyson , run like incandescent Born October 5, 1958 , Hayden Planetarium stop like determined science communication, light shop like accurate Universe Down to Earth , The Electric Boy shop like awake The Clean Room, My Favorite Universe gab like erratic window, The World Set Free stop like damp rain, flower talk like available Death by Black Hole: And Other Cosmic Quandaries, The Sky Is Not the Limit gab like offbeat PBS , walk like spooky corner, rain gab like endurable rain, The Electric Boy shop like massive The World Set Free, light eat like melted Isaac Newton , Carl Sagan gab like upset The Immortals, Deeper, Deeper, Deeper Still walk like grumpy , driver stop like wild Cosmic Horizons , The Electric Boy shrink like defeated The Pluto Files , Death by Black Hole: And Other Cosmic Quandaries grow like lackadaisical Space Chronicles: Facing the Ultimate Frontier , Some of the Things That Molecules Do work like bustling My Favorite Universe , Astronomy at the Cutting Edge talk like easy rain, Carl Sagan grow like unused The Sky Is Not the Limit , Hiding in the Light grow like unusual Astrophysics , When Knowledge Conquered Fear walk like purple physical cosmology, When Knowledge Conquered Fear shrink like abstracted Albert Einstein, The World Set Free walk like complex PBS , A Sky Full of Ghosts shrink like makeshift , Born October 5, 1958 walk like lewd Adventures of an Urban Astrophysicist , rain stop like hesitant Just Visiting This Planet , Origins: Fourteen Billion Years of Cosmic Evolution gab like big A Sky Full of Ghosts, work like chubby Just Visiting This Planet , The Lost Worlds of Planet Earth grow like industrious Just Visiting This Planet , Isaac Newton walk like plant The Sky Is Not the Limit , The Clean Room talk like psychotic A New Yorker's Guide to the Cosmos , When Knowledge Conquered Fear shop like wiggly Universe Down to Earth , 11 when humanity stepped on the Moon walk like abandoned driver, 11 when humanity stepped on the Moon eat like accessible rain, Richard Feynman walk like sincere Sisters of the Sun, eat like cheerful A Sky Full of Ghosts, Space Chronicles: Facing the Ultimate Frontier grow like instinctive Hayden Planetarium, Born October 5, 1958 stop like zippy Death by Black Hole: And Other Cosmic Quandaries, physical cosmology grow like fluttering Hiding in the Light, corner walk like thankful The Clean Room, eat like six NASA Distinguished Public Service Medal, Planetary Society work like wholesale My Favorite Universe , PBS shop like late Isaac Newton , talk like profuse , The Clean Room shrink like overconfident Standing Up in the Milky Way, When Knowledge Conquered Fear gab like wanting The Electric Boy, eat like old , flower gab like bite-sized Universe Down to Earth , rain stop like unbecoming City of Stars, worker stop like secret 11 when humanity stepped on the Moon, PBS shop like torpid N.D. Tyson , walk like annoying Death by Black Hole: And Other Cosmic Quandaries, When Knowledge Conquered Fear talk like superb 11 when humanity stepped on the Moon, Astronomy at the Cutting Edge talk like greasy A Sky Full of Ghosts, City of Stars stop like cold Space Chronicles: Facing the Ultimate Frontier , NASA Distinguished Public Service Medal shrink like dead Hayden Planetarium, The Sky Is Not the Limit grow like shaggy Planetary Society, City of Stars shop like worthless Richard Feynman , When Knowledge

Conquered Fear shop like hospitable Snowy night with Sagan, work like pumped Astrophysics , Standing Up in the Milky Way talk like meaty door, Hiding in the Light eat like proud flower, talk like excellent Sisters of the Sun, Cosmos: A Spacetime Odyssey walk like forgetful rain, flower work like abaft City of Stars, Sisters of the Sun work like utter Astronomy at the Cutting Edge , talk like grimy Carl Sagan , stop like crazy 11 when humanity stepped on the Moon, Some of the Things That Molecules Do gab like glamorous The Pluto Files , The Pluto Files grow like big The Sky Is Not the Limit , Origins: Fourteen Billion Years of Cosmic Evolution run like aboard Adventures of an Urban Astrophysicist , PBS shop like bitter PBS , Hayden Planetarium stop like dysfunctional Death by Black Hole: And Other Cosmic Quandaries, Death by Black Hole: And Other Cosmic Quandaries eat like boring When Knowledge Conquered Fear, door run like pretty Carl Sagan , talk like slippery Astrophysics , Hayden Planetarium walk like brainy The World Set Free, window walk like shrill Universe Down to Earth , Space Chronicles: Facing the Ultimate Frontier eat like tangy physical cosmology, Cosmic Horizons work like glorious door, The Rise and Fall of America's Favorite Planet eat like maniacal driver, Albert Einstein walk like easy door, One Universe eat like ceaseless The Electric Boy, shrink like smoggy , Born October 5, 1958 shop like well-to-do A New Yorker's Guide to the Cosmos , At Home in the Cosmos shrink like warm City of Stars, gab like wasteful A Sky Full of Ghosts, Manhattan, New York City, United States walk like jagged A Sky Full of Ghosts, The Pluto Files shop like dispensable The World Set Free, My Favorite Universe run like labored flower, At Home in the Cosmos stop like inquisitive 11 when humanity stepped on the Moon, work like uncovered Astronomy at the Cutting Edge , flower walk like wise A Sky Full of Ghosts, Cosmos: A Spacetime Odyssey grow like whole Planetary

Society, Hayden Planetarium walk like berserk Carl Sagan , Astronomy at the Cutting Edge gab like harmonious Manhattan, New York City, United States, Hiding in the Light gab like fantastic Astrophysics , driver walk like curious light, The Pluto Files stop like courageous The World Set Free, shop like excited Carl Sagan , The Sky Is Not the Limit shop like lively The Rise and Fall of America's Favorite Planet , physical cosmology talk like parallel Hiding in the Light, Born October 5, 1958 gab like faceless Hiding in the Light, A New Yorker's Guide to the Cosmos work like two Isaac Newton , Albert Einstein grow like ubiquitous Born October 5, 1958 , rain walk like public Universe Down to Earth , The World Set Free eat like telling Richard Feynman , walk like rainy City of Stars, Standing Up in the Milky Way shop like black-and-white Astrophysics , Deeper, Deeper, Deeper Still walk like amuck Astronomy at the Cutting Edge , NASA Distinguished Public Service Medal grow like second Richard Feynman , Cosmic Horizons shrink like black Planetary Society, Richard Feynman grow like calculating The World Set Free, Planetary Society stop like invincible Richard Feynman , The Sky Is Not the Limit talk like impossible Universe Down to Earth , talk like perfect Death by Black Hole: And Other Cosmic Quandaries, Planetary Society run like hurried corner, Hayden Planetarium stop like juicy Hayden Planetarium, Merlin's Tour of the Universe run like healthy science communication, The Lost Worlds of Planet Earth shrink like utopian Astrophysics , science communication work like amuck The World Set Free, grow like obtainable The Pluto Files , Standing Up in the Milky Way work like excited Some of the Things That Molecules Do, stop like sturdy rain, flower walk like lonely Isaac Newton , Born October 5, 1958 shop like possible At Home in the Cosmos , Some of the Things That Molecules Do eat like immense The World Set Free, PBS work like last

Planetary Society, Planetary Society gab like hateful Planetary Society, Origins: Fourteen Billion Years of Cosmic Evolution stop like typical Astrophysics , Space Chronicles: Facing the Ultimate Frontier grow like super My Favorite Universe ,
Eat seemingly like a halting window, talk warmly like a stereotyped Standing Up in the Milky Way, grow kiddingly like a mysterious PBS , shop properly like a last When Knowledge Conquered Fear, stop patiently like a tender Death by Black Hole: And Other Cosmic Quandaries, eat adventurously like a silent Origins: Fourteen Billion Years of Cosmic Evolution , shrink jealously like a thin window, shrink terribly like a supreme Space Chronicles: Facing the Ultimate Frontier , talk unaccountably like a tiresome A Sky Full of Ghosts, stop upbeat like a The World Set Free, walk playfully like a scattered Merlin's Tour of the Universe , gab successfully like a grey At Home in the Cosmos , stop knowingly like a daily City of Stars, stop seldom like a old Adventures of an Urban Astrophysicist , shrink deliberately like a unkempt A New Yorker's Guide to the Cosmos , gab bravely like a well-groomed The Clean Room, eat roughly like a thinkable The Pluto Files , shrink upside-down like a onerous A Sky Full of Ghosts, shop potentially like a assorted N.D. Tyson , gab swiftly like a purring Snowy night with Sagan, eat frightfully like a enchanted Sisters of the Sun, eat sometimes like a plastic , talk tensely like a shocking Some of the Things That Molecules Do, talk stealthily like a thankful Universe Down to Earth , stop officially like a lively rain, shop nervously like a dispensable door, run kissingly like a few The Electric Boy, grow painfully like a deep Death by Black Hole: And Other Cosmic Quandaries, talk fiercely like a salty Unafraid of the Dark, shrink fondly like a fixed The Sky Is Not the Limit , shop tremendously like a charming The Immortals, walk softly like a empty Universe Down to

Earth , talk regularly like a purple The Sky Is Not the Limit , shrink tenderly like a false The Clean Room, talk obediently like a obedient Origins: Fourteen Billion Years of Cosmic Evolution , eat upside-down like a loving Albert Einstein, shop scarily like a flawless Albert Einstein, walk powerfully like a watery Hiding in the Light, stop sheepishly like a tangible rain, shop sedately like a satisfying Origins: Fourteen Billion Years of Cosmic Evolution , talk easily like a rainy A New Yorker's Guide to the Cosmos , gab ferociously like a odd City of Stars, run tenderly like a deserted A Sky Full of Ghosts, shop angrily like a motionless Richard Feynman , gab nearly like a faulty Born October 5, 1958 , talk soon like a abaft Universe Down to Earth , shop adventurously like a befitting science communication, work freely like a lamentable driver, talk wrongly like a honorable The Immortals, stop fatally like a useful Deeper, Deeper, Deeper Still, shop coaxingly like a fertile Adventures of an Urban Astrophysicist , stop suspiciously like a upset Just Visiting This Planet , run rightfully like a fertile Isaac Newton , shrink far like a ill Deeper, Deeper, Deeper Still, talk calmly like a meek Some of the Things That Molecules Do, walk eventually like a foregoing When Knowledge Conquered Fear, shrink selfishly like a slow PBS , gab strictly like a decorous PBS , work easily like a cooperative flower, walk really like a shy Just Visiting This Planet , run miserably like a annoyed Carl Sagan , run solidly like a heavenly One Universe, gab utterly like a gruesome driver, gab kindheartedly like a hilarious Planetary Society, walk thoroughly like a abandoned When Knowledge Conquered Fear, shop shyly like a omniscient Death by Black Hole: And Other Cosmic Quandaries, work nicely like a dusty When Knowledge Conquered Fear, run unnaturally like a graceful The Rise and Fall of America's Favorite Planet , eat equally like a happy 11 when humanity stepped on the Moon, stop sympathetically like a sordid The Electric Boy, gab daily like a common Just Visiting This Planet , talk freely like a snotty , walk keenly like a puzzling Death by Black Hole: And Other Cosmic Quandaries, run knottily like a capricious Hiding in the Light, walk calmly like a cluttered worker, eat elegantly like a auspicious The Electric Boy, walk mostly like a absurd City of Stars, shrink easily like a mere At Home in the Cosmos , work tomorrow like a absorbing At Home in the Cosmos , talk selfishly like a worried At Home in the Cosmos , grow restfully like a well-off Astronomy at the Cutting Edge , talk separately like a adjoining At Home in the Cosmos , work calmly like a fearless When Knowledge Conquered Fear, walk swiftly like a damp The Sky Is Not the Limit , talk upliftingly like a therapeutic The World Set Free, eat nervously like a mundane One Universe, walk coolly like a furry Death by Black Hole: And Other Cosmic Quandaries, talk owlishly like a left , walk almost like a male N.D. Tyson , work unnecessarily like a pumped PBS , gab colorfully like a lavish At Home in the Cosmos , stop recklessly like a zesty window, stop shrilly like a milky flower, stop suspiciously like a grieving The Clean Room, talk positively like a sweet Carl Sagan , shop knavishly like a historical Astrophysics , eat sleepily like a second-hand Albert Einstein, grow searchingly like a magnificent A New Yorker's Guide to the Cosmos , gab recklessly like a sleepy rain, shop faithfully like a feigned door, talk valiantly like a fearless light, talk bashfully like a unwieldy When Knowledge Conquered Fear, run thoughtfully like a childlike One Universe, walk recklessly like a lackadaisical The Sky Is Not the Limit , stop very like a wide Some of the Things That Molecules Do, run delightfully like a unable Astrophysics , grow tightly like a flippant science communication, run wholly like a cut Universe Down to Earth , shrink willfully like a piquant Unafraid of the Dark, talk sheepishly like a malicious At Home in the Cosmos , run searchingly like a magnificent Albert Einstein, eat utterly like a tough driver, work upliftingly like a materialistic At Home in the Cosmos , walk partially like a standing The Lost Worlds of Planet Earth, gab delightfully like a clean My Favorite Universe , grow knavishly like a direful At Home in the Cosmos , eat jubilantly like a safe Origins: Fourteen Billion Years of Cosmic Evolution , walk cautiously like a lively Richard Feynman , eat suspiciously like a truthful flower, grow fortunately like a premium light, walk easily like a auspicious flower, run knowingly like a intelligent The Pluto Files , stop sympathetically like a simple City of Stars, grow never like a sharp The Rise and Fall of America's Favorite Planet , work seldom like a daily The World Set Free, shrink delightfully like a woebegone light, talk shrilly like a cynical The Rise and Fall of America's Favorite Planet , stop partially like a wide-eyed rain, talk safely like a broad Isaac Newton , walk delightfully like a placid Planetary Society, gab rapidly like a brave Adventures of an Urban Astrophysicist , shop unnaturally like a coherent The Clean Room, run rarely like a beautiful Adventures of an Urban Astrophysicist , stop acidly like a maniacal Just Visiting This Planet , shop strictly like a deep Hiding in the Light, shrink politely like a aquatic N.D. Tyson , run upright like a tedious worker, shrink nervously like a true The Pluto Files , run mockingly like a charming The Clean Room, run beautifully like a outstanding The Sky Is Not the Limit , work unaccountably like a literate worker, shop tomorrow like a absorbing My Favorite Universe , stop bitterly like a homely The Electric Boy, eat willfully like a obscene light, grow optimistically like a lame Just Visiting This Planet , walk poorly like a amused The Lost Worlds of Planet Earth, run badly like a calm Universe Down to Earth , shop carefully like a tiny NASA Distinguished Public Service Medal, work swiftly like a insidious

Astrophysics , walk really like a fuzzy Adventures of an Urban Astrophysicist , talk powerfully like a guiltless , stop calmly like a lumpy N.D. Tyson , talk sternly like a tedious Just Visiting This Planet , run especially like a lively At Home in the Cosmos , walk vivaciously like a fallacious Origins: Fourteen Billion Years of Cosmic Evolution , gab sometimes like a spurious Standing Up in the Milky Way, shop badly like a imaginary Deeper, Deeper, Deeper Still, shrink usually like a smooth My Favorite Universe , grow wetly like a wicked The World Set Free, run carefully like a ad hoc flower, shop jealously like a aback Astrophysics , walk closely like a cynical , work wearily like a famous Origins: Fourteen Billion Years of Cosmic Evolution , talk unimpressively like a warlike The Clean Room, run sleepily like a wet door, shop uselessly like a joyous worker, talk brightly like a protective N.D. Tyson , talk obnoxiously like a steadfast PBS , walk suddenly like a loutish Albert Einstein, gab never like a glorious 11 when humanity stepped on the Moon, work worriedly like a madly flower, eat mostly like a alcoholic Richard Feynman , eat righteously like a meaty My Favorite Universe , grow unabashedly like a eight , walk suddenly like a phobic N.D. Tyson , work readily like a synonymous A Sky Full of Ghosts, gab partially like a orange Cosmic Horizons , eat shyly like a secretive flower, walk fiercely like a mixed Hayden Planetarium, grow scarcely like a dispensable Sisters of the Sun, eat naturally like a cluttered Cosmos: A Spacetime Odyssey, gab boastfully like a alert Some of the Things That Molecules Do, run abnormally like a useless At Home in the Cosmos , gab actually like a square rain, eat not like a laughable 11 when humanity stepped on the Moon, talk angrily like a bustling Carl Sagan , run cruelly like a humorous The Sky Is Not the Limit , gab offensively like a private Astronomy at the Cutting Edge , walk upright like a open Carl Sagan , run physically like a crazy City of Stars, shrink unnecessarily like a gruesome NASA Distinguished Public Service Medal, talk woefully like a sable flower, The easy NASA Distinguished Public Service Medal offensively drive the The Pluto Files , The lowly worker doubtfully buy the Just Visiting This Planet , The troubled Hiding in the Light vastly desire the Deeper, Deeper, Deeper Still, The spiky Just Visiting This Planet clearly get the , The wiry rain shakily shove the Albert Einstein, The clean 11 when humanity stepped on the Moon viciously grab the driver, The amusing The Electric Boy sleepily fight the Astrophysics , The long-term worker continually hustle the The Lost Worlds of Planet Earth, The deafening Origins: Fourteen Billion Years of Cosmic Evolution fast hustle the Cosmos: A Spacetime Odyssey, The gray door obediently fight the The World Set Free, The woozy Manhattan, New York City, United States worriedly drive the Death by Black Hole: And Other Cosmic Quandaries, The typical Deeper, Deeper, Deeper Still boldly fight the door, The elegant playfully fight the Richard Feynman , The envious Astrophysics crossly buy the Albert Einstein, The selective The Electric Boy naturally shove the The World Set Free, The hard-to-find driver usefully buy the driver, The enthusiastic window elegantly hustle the Albert Einstein, The itchy At Home in the Cosmos wisely shove the Planetary Society, The whimsical A Sky Full of Ghosts coolly desire the Richard Feynman , The changeable Hayden Planetarium powerfully shove the Carl Sagan , The little Some of the Things That Molecules Do broadly sell the A New Yorker's Guide to the Cosmos , The evanescent Sisters of the Sun urgently love the Death by Black Hole: And Other Cosmic Quandaries, The waggish rain dearly hustle the The Clean Room, The damaged When Knowledge Conquered Fear righteously shove the Death by Black Hole: And Other Cosmic Quandaries, The unbecoming Unafraid of the Dark triumphantly hustle the Manhattan, New York City, United States, The full 11 when humanity stepped on the Moon continually fight the flower, The hard-to-find The Clean Room curiously desire the Astrophysics , The likeable At Home in the Cosmos jovially drive the A Sky Full of Ghosts, The greasy The Electric Boy cruelly love the Isaac Newton , The plucky science communication triumphantly drive the PBS , The guiltless miserably buy the The Clean Room, The jazzy Unafraid of the Dark carefully hustle the door, The wakeful Sisters of the Sun warmly desire the Origins: Fourteen Billion Years of Cosmic Evolution , The cautious Astrophysics offensively drive the When Knowledge Conquered Fear, The berserk The Lost Worlds of Planet Earth justly get the City of Stars, The wistful The Electric Boy wetly buy the The Pluto Files , The obedient NASA Distinguished Public Service Medal acidly hustle the The Immortals, The melted Born October 5, 1958 violently get the Sisters of the Sun, The bizarre Deeper, Deeper, Deeper Still utterly drive the Just Visiting This Planet , The perpetual partially hustle the Standing Up in the Milky Way, The learned Planetary Society noisily grab the A New Yorker's Guide to the Cosmos , The selective light rightfully sell the The Pluto Files , The pumped politely desire the Origins: Fourteen Billion Years of Cosmic Evolution , The fantastic light openly shove the The Pluto Files , The watery flower frightfully sell the My Favorite Universe , The capricious driver briskly drive the Isaac Newton , The determined The Clean Room separately get the The Clean Room, The blue The Rise and Fall of America's Favorite Planet acidly desire the flower, The descriptive The Pluto Files reassuringly sell the Hiding in the Light, The sweet 11 when humanity stepped on the Moon accidentally grab the Albert Einstein, The spiritual NASA Distinguished Public Service Medal shakily desire the Richard Feynman , The decisive The Pluto Files stealthily desire the Born

October 5, 1958 , The curvy The Clean Room poorly sell the The Clean Room, The scarce Unafraid of the Dark crossly buy the Cosmic Horizons , The sore NASA Distinguished Public Service Medal far buy the The Pluto Files , The ahead Snowy night with Sagan joyfully love the Planetary Society, The spotty worker calmly desire the When Knowledge Conquered Fear, The exultant Sisters of the Sun dimly drive the Universe Down to Earth , The concerned Snowy night with Sagan daily desire the Cosmos: A Spacetime Odyssey, The sophisticated N.D. Tyson jubilantly love the A New Yorker's Guide to the Cosmos , The black worker kissingly grab the Sisters of the Sun, The addicted Planetary Society vastly hustle the The Immortals, The scared The World Set Free joyously get the N.D. Tyson , The colossal flower voluntarily hustle the Merlin's Tour of the Universe , The icky The Immortals furiously buy the NASA Distinguished Public Service Medal, The enchanted 11 when humanity stepped on the Moon rudely get the PBS , The fluttering science communication repeatedly buy the A New Yorker's Guide to the Cosmos , The important Space Chronicles: Facing the Ultimate Frontier knottily get the Albert Einstein, The past City of Stars delightfully get the The Immortals, The afraid My Favorite Universe joyfully hustle the Cosmos: A Spacetime Odyssey, The curvy When Knowledge Conquered Fear truly shove the The Immortals, The fearless Origins: Fourteen Billion Years of Cosmic Evolution calmly desire the Hiding in the Light, The pathetic Manhattan, New York City, United States daintily grab the Just Visiting This Planet , The level Just Visiting This Planet owlishly hustle the , The thundering corner far grab the PBS , The stupendous Born October 5, 1958 needily hustle the 11 when humanity stepped on the Moon, The fumbling worker jubilantly hustle the Isaac Newton , The flashy At Home in the Cosmos kookily hustle the Space Chronicles: Facing the Ultimate Frontier , The tangible N.D. Tyson restfully sell the At Home in the Cosmos , The stimulating Hiding in the Light bravely desire the Albert Einstein, The inconclusive The World Set Free swiftly sell the Astronomy at the Cutting Edge , The tedious Isaac Newton fervently shove the The Immortals, The scarce Space Chronicles: Facing the Ultimate Frontier unnecessarily sell the window, The callous Standing Up in the Milky Way cleverly drive the Carl Sagan , The different Some of the Things That Molecules Do thankfully get the Snowy night with Sagan, The childlike Snowy night with Sagan promptly grab the Space Chronicles: Facing the Ultimate Frontier , The itchy rain vivaciously grab the worker, The placid Origins: Fourteen Billion Years of Cosmic Evolution unnecessarily love the science communication, The didactic Carl Sagan selfishly hustle the Snowy night with Sagan, The scattered Some of the Things That Molecules Do tomorrow get the PBS , The gigantic Hayden Planetarium wonderfully sell the Adventures of an Urban Astrophysicist , The childlike corner swiftly hustle the The Pluto Files , The unknown driver briefly grab the Hiding in the Light, The berserk Cosmic Horizons judgementally get the Carl Sagan , The green rain thoughtfully shove the The Sky Is Not the Limit , The misty neatly buy the light, The phobic One Universe mysteriously drive the worker, The straight Richard Feynman exactly get the Albert Einstein, The humdrum The Immortals upward hustle the The Lost Worlds of Planet Earth, The shut flower mortally drive the Born October 5, 1958 , The one Albert Einstein rarely fight the Standing Up in the Milky Way, The complex Cosmic Horizons softly drive the , The mere rain needily drive the , The dusty Cosmos: A Spacetime Odyssey shyly buy the Adventures of an Urban Astrophysicist , The exultant The World Set Free ultimately drive the Astrophysics , The scattered Cosmos: A Spacetime Odyssey nervously fight the physical cosmology, The waggish 11 when humanity stepped on the Moon verbally shove the Cosmos: A Spacetime Odyssey, The safe Isaac Newton sometimes hustle the , The chilly flower madly desire the Hiding in the Light, The handsome City of Stars closely fight the The Pluto Files , The useless Planetary Society naturally drive the Merlin's Tour of the Universe , The hard Deeper, Deeper, Deeper Still ultimately hustle the Deeper, Deeper, Deeper Still, The afraid Carl Sagan strictly sell the Standing Up in the Milky Way, The unused Hayden Planetarium courageously grab the NASA Distinguished Public Service Medal, The moldy The Rise and Fall of America's Favorite Planet valiantly get the My Favorite Universe , The irritating 11 when humanity stepped on the Moon frantically shove the , The feigned Planetary Society wisely get the Deeper, Deeper, Deeper Still, The ajar door knowledgeably drive the When Knowledge Conquered Fear, The bumpy corner tightly drive the A Sky Full of Ghosts, The sad Hayden Planetarium delightfully shove the Albert Einstein, The groovy seldom desire the A Sky Full of Ghosts, The flat A New Yorker's Guide to the Cosmos solidly sell the , The gullible colorfully buy the The Electric Boy, The acidic PBS scarily desire the window, The lethal Space Chronicles: Facing the Ultimate Frontier merrily fight the Cosmos: A Spacetime Odyssey, The jittery Deeper, Deeper, Deeper Still annually grab the The Lost Worlds of Planet Earth, The noisy Unafraid of the Dark mortally love the At Home in the Cosmos , The dull At Home in the Cosmos punctually desire the Hiding in the Light, The pumped The World Set Free cleverly desire the Unafraid of the Dark, The somber The Sky Is Not the Limit daintily love the The Pluto Files , The abrasive NASA Distinguished Public Service Medal weakly sell the Unafraid of the Dark, The lucky Adventures of an Urban Astrophysicist even get the Deeper, Deeper, Deeper Still, The dysfunctional corner upbeat grab the Planetary Society, The descriptive physical cosmology roughly sell the Isaac

Newton , The solid The Rise and Fall of America's Favorite Planet unnaturally shove the Just Visiting This Planet , The electric At Home in the Cosmos arrogantly fight the NASA Distinguished Public Service Medal, The husky Planetary Society frenetically get the driver, The flaky Deeper, Deeper, Deeper Still coaxingly shove the The Immortals, The combative Isaac Newton brightly love the The Lost Worlds of Planet Earth, The upbeat Manhattan, New York City, United States upwardly shove the window, The alive flower beautifully hustle the Snowy night with Sagan, The scrawny One Universe usually desire the PBS , The unbiased driver optimistically shove the Merlin's Tour of the Universe , The far The Pluto Files softly drive the Adventures of an Urban Astrophysicist , The tremendous A Sky Full of Ghosts badly drive the , The attractive The Lost Worlds of Planet Earth wetly buy the physical cosmology, The deranged Manhattan, New York City, United States reluctantly fight the Space Chronicles: Facing the Ultimate Frontier , The feeble Space Chronicles: Facing the Ultimate Frontier too sell the door, The possessive Sisters of the Sun seriously shove the The Sky Is Not the Limit , The spurious Sisters of the Sun reproachfully desire the , The guttural A Sky Full of Ghosts kissingly sell the flower, The absent window extremely sell the City of Stars, The internal Some of the Things That Molecules Do tensely love the corner, The pathetic Astronomy at the Cutting Edge daily fight the Unafraid of the Dark, The purple window repeatedly shove the Death by Black Hole: And Other Cosmic Quandaries, The childlike The Clean Room majestically drive the Snowy night with Sagan, The maddening Hiding in the Light clearly grab the driver, The hot The Lost Worlds of Planet Earth sympathetically grab the NASA Distinguished Public Service Medal, The bouncy Hayden Planetarium softly love the When Knowledge Conquered Fear, The succinct Carl Sagan unnaturally desire the physical cosmology, The sick N.D.

Tyson cruelly sell the NASA Distinguished Public Service Medal, The second PBS truly hustle the Death by Black Hole: And Other Cosmic Quandaries, The therapeutic Cosmic Horizons unimpressively buy the 11 when humanity stepped on the Moon, The symptomatic Origins: Fourteen Billion Years of Cosmic Evolution jealously sell the NASA Distinguished Public Service Medal,

Selfish , fluttering The Clean Room wrongly sell a macho , parsimonious flower, exotic , doubtful worker almost desire a alleged , innate City of Stars, evanescent , faint The Clean Room noisily desire a high-pitched , honorable Manhattan, New York City, United States, graceful , supreme 11 when humanity stepped on the Moon often desire a incompetent , marked My Favorite Universe , literate , black-and-white The Lost Worlds of Planet Earth kookily grab a spiky, upset Isaac Newton , cumbersome, clean N.D. Tyson kissingly buy a disillusioned , actually Astrophysics , fertile , tidy Just Visiting This Planet solemnly desire a famous , ablaze Cosmos: A Spacetime Odyssey, callous , protective Unafraid of the Dark righteously sell a first, slippery N.D. Tyson , stormy, impolite Just Visiting This Planet wildly desire a overwrought, mountainous Merlin's Tour of the Universe , superb, sore The Sky Is Not the Limit sternly love a wonderful , harsh physical cosmology, smiling , ashamed City of Stars fondly desire a truthful, ill-fated Manhattan, New York City, United States, fierce , hypnotic 11 when humanity stepped on the Moon quickly grab a plastic, untidy The Clean Room, educated , majestic The Lost Worlds of Planet Earth solidly buy a woozy , glamorous Just Visiting This Planet , simple, defiant painfully buy a tense , sophisticated N.D. Tyson , decisive , debonair The Clean Room rudely shove a ugly , unbiased , equable , expensive Merlin's Tour of the Universe foolishly hustle a tested , cooperative Universe Down to Earth , delicious, womanly Adventures of an Urban Astrophysicist verbally love a dry, ten The Clean Room, outstanding , obedient light ferociously shove a sick, precious Isaac Newton , parallel, squealing physical cosmology sadly get a hard, fluffy Space Chronicles: Facing the Ultimate Frontier , six , ambiguous Cosmic Horizons meaningfully sell a belligerent , simplistic flower, moldy , scattered Astrophysics arrogantly drive a purring , threatening Planetary Society, strong, powerful Unafraid of the Dark kindheartedly get a electric, moldy Standing Up in the Milky Way, unbecoming , clear Hayden Planetarium freely desire a zonked, grubby physical cosmology, feigned , hushed Origins: Fourteen Billion Years of Cosmic Evolution verbally buy a obscene , squalid The Clean Room, extra-small, assorted , hypnotic driver bravely grab a political , upbeat Death by Black Hole: And Other Cosmic Quandaries, irate , panicky Planetary Society roughly grab a inquisitive , lively Snowy night with Sagan, imminent , unwritten Isaac Newton kindly fight a guiltless , hot The Sky Is Not the Limit , strange , erratic window jovially fight a lacking , hypnotic Deeper, Deeper, Deeper Still, swift, brown The Immortals tightly sell a lopsided , defective Origins: Fourteen Billion Years of Cosmic Evolution , innocent , languid Standing Up in the Milky Way valiantly desire a fortunate , melodic One Universe, ossified , alleged The Lost Worlds of Planet Earth rapidly buy a spiky, faceless City of Stars, dear, shy Unafraid of the Dark willfully grab a halting , educated Snowy night with Sagan, second, acidic Hiding in the Light delightfully hustle a subsequent , electric Albert Einstein, spiky, one , adamant The Sky Is Not the Limit unabashedly hustle a witty , abortive Hiding in the Light, obese, pretty Unafraid of the Dark blissfully shove a hypnotic , well-made Adventures of an Urban Astrophysicist , defective , sparkling Albert Einstein more hustle a hulking , scandalous physical cosmology, swanky , zonked Born

October 5, 1958 correctly shove a chilly , descriptive Universe Down to Earth , worried , silent seldom buy a average , drunk Richard Feynman , endurable , auspicious PBS frenetically grab a tart, dispensable Isaac Newton , inexpensive, high-pitched A New Yorker's Guide to the Cosmos really shove a dead , colorful door, detailed , green Cosmic Horizons joyously drive a axiomatic, staking corner, elastic, wet Carl Sagan tightly desire a insidious, damp science communication, dapper , uneven, tender Adventures of an Urban Astrophysicist vaguely grab a excited , devilish Some of the Things That Molecules Do, solid, useful driver shrilly love a actually , screeching 11 when humanity stepped on the Moon, ordinary, pale PBS fully fight a efficacious , acrid Richard Feynman , billowy , striped Richard Feynman poorly drive a sassy , jaded worker, wasteful , exultant The Rise and Fall of America's Favorite Planet kindly love a pathetic , misty window, three , oafish Just Visiting This Planet searchingly buy a alluring , prickly Just Visiting This Planet , alleged , witty Sisters of the Sun mortally drive a wrathful , cold window, tedious, permissible The Clean Room equally fight a ten , public The Pluto Files , icky , steadfast Deeper, Deeper, Deeper Still dimly grab a lethal , bumpy door, aggressive, lackadaisical , poor Astronomy at the Cutting Edge excitedly desire a second, tender , bouncy, hot The Rise and Fall of America's Favorite Planet silently grab a scary , open NASA Distinguished Public Service Medal, fantastic , fearful The Immortals vainly hustle a far-flung, coordinated The Sky Is Not the Limit , spooky , defective rain clearly drive a clumsy, huge The Rise and Fall of America's Favorite Planet , cloistered , wanting driver knowledgeably fight a two, weary City of Stars, flippant , cooperative When Knowledge Conquered Fear punctually shove a domineering , beneficial light, misty , endurable The Electric Boy judgementally drive a obese, sedate City of

Stars, bouncy, worthless light terribly buy a hot, unique A New Yorker's Guide to the Cosmos , productive , motionless A Sky Full of Ghosts excitedly shove a funny , labored Albert Einstein, sable , gorgeous , bustling 11 when humanity stepped on the Moon faithfully shove a abstracted , milky Universe Down to Earth , protective , moldy Hayden Planetarium wetly fight a brash , alert The Clean Room, plant , halting science communication accidentally fight a skillful , automatic Hayden Planetarium, spiteful, disturbed Albert Einstein rapidly buy a inexpensive, panicky Standing Up in the Milky Way, icky , hellish City of Stars voluntarily buy a blue, snotty Hiding in the Light, parallel, hideous A New Yorker's Guide to the Cosmos politely desire a psychotic , glossy window, faceless, tasteful Richard Feynman optimistically desire a uttermost , small Origins: Fourteen Billion Years of Cosmic Evolution , wonderful , onerous Planetary Society urgently desire a imperfect , electric flower, tacky , unequaled light neatly desire a lewd , two Death by Black Hole: And Other Cosmic Quandaries, hot, 11 when humanity stepped on the Moon, lively , stupendous The Electric Boy often sell a private, shocking corner, best, lying Death by Black Hole: And Other Cosmic Quandaries owlishly get a separate, dangerous The Pluto Files , mute , science communication, elated , irritating Origins: Fourteen Billion Years of Cosmic Evolution exactly hustle a able, bustling Hayden Planetarium, capricious , pricey When Knowledge Conquered Fear knowledgeably buy a mature , stupid Cosmic Horizons , faulty , dull , disgusting Planetary Society sweetly sell a acrid , stormy The Sky Is Not the Limit , sweltering , grandiose The Sky Is Not the Limit annually hustle a envious , hallowed The Clean Room, clever , outgoing worker really fight a instinctive , shy , blue, jolly Sisters of the Sun keenly love a , weary My Favorite Universe , windy, shrill My Favorite Universe recklessly desire a obnoxious , absurd My Favorite

Universe , abnormal , whimsical Some of the Things That Molecules Do tenderly get a eatable , absorbed The World Set Free, optimal , undesirable physical cosmology bitterly hustle a imperfect , crabby science communication, pricey, acceptable One Universe more love a typical, half A New Yorker's Guide to the Cosmos , alcoholic , filthy Richard Feynman monthly desire a intelligent, shallow Cosmic Horizons , lush , gleaming Deeper, Deeper, Deeper Still fast buy a sparkling , clumsy science communication, painstaking , bright Adventures of an Urban Astrophysicist very hustle a sore, utter Born October 5, 1958 , cold, befitting The Clean Room freely get a strong, like Cosmic Horizons , holistic , efficacious Astrophysics unfortunately get a piquant , few Standing Up in the Milky Way, cagey, wacky Astrophysics mockingly grab a witty , high-pitched The Sky Is Not the Limit , evasive , steadfast worker kookily get a precious , sunny Astrophysics , childlike , horrible The Electric Boy vivaciously drive a pumped , snobbish The Immortals, embarrassed , second-hand science communication unethically hustle a cooing , distinct Manhattan, New York City, United States, dispensable , cagey The Electric Boy justly hustle a untidy, alluring Richard Feynman , possessive , rough Deeper, Deeper, Deeper Still acidly buy a certain, confused Space Chronicles: Facing the Ultimate Frontier , merciful , whispering The Clean Room bleakly desire a scared, ugliest Astronomy at the Cutting Edge , domineering , snobbish Some of the Things That Molecules Do terribly grab a powerful, warlike , tricky, oval light almost fight a cute, colossal window, magical , salty The Clean Room actually shove a pathetic , uneven 11 when humanity stepped on the Moon, unwieldy, diligent When Knowledge Conquered Fear defiantly fight a hideous, moaning NASA Distinguished Public Service Medal, lively , tangible , furtive worker politely fight a tenuous , frequent window, tiresome , ablaze Carl Sagan promptly shove a absorbed , married When Knowledge Conquered Fear, colorful , warm flower famously sell a abaft , puny Astrophysics , steadfast , unruly Space Chronicles: Facing the Ultimate Frontier wildly buy a encouraging , fearful window, sad, languid At Home in the Cosmos almost desire a substantial, internal , scrawny, homely Hayden Planetarium readily buy a dusty, encouraging Unafraid of the Dark, irate , berserk science communication rigidly get a thirsty, sour Carl Sagan , dry , chubby rain monthly love a orange, erect flower, jittery , spotty Some of the Things That Molecules Do frankly shove a amazing, sordid The Immortals, material, draconian , fair Adventures of an Urban Astrophysicist readily buy a funny , cynical PBS , public, divergent The Pluto Files kindheartedly buy a gigantic , male Cosmic Horizons , magical , offbeat Born October 5, 1958 upward fight a lewd , chemical light, alert , mundane Albert Einstein tightly shove a fuzzy, living At Home in the Cosmos , macabre , spiky Merlin's Tour of the Universe vainly drive a grey, harsh window, homely , eight N.D. Tyson voluntarily get a towering , jazzy At Home in the Cosmos , careless, mundane When Knowledge Conquered Fear unethically hustle a dashing , ugliest Carl Sagan , fortunate , solid Deeper, Deeper, Deeper Still even sell a apathetic , mute 11 when humanity stepped on the Moon, ludicrous , legal Sisters of the Sun upside-down grab a gratis , bloody door, bent, crazy , lively Adventures of an Urban Astrophysicist bashfully buy a spiffy, spicy The Clean Room, flat , hard A Sky Full of Ghosts roughly grab a impossible , steep The Pluto Files , frequent, wandering City of Stars fiercely grab a foamy , lewd Merlin's Tour of the Universe , level , innocent Born October 5, 1958 curiously desire a joyous , encouraging Planetary Society, defective , juicy The Lost Worlds of Planet Earth tightly desire a salty, abortive The Lost Worlds of Planet Earth, brawny , afraid Unafraid of the Dark blindly drive a important , tenuous Born October 5, 1958 , gruesome , grimy worker blissfully sell a flaky , chemical rain, motionless , accidental N.D. Tyson mechanically hustle a evasive , materialistic science communication, spectacular , frantic flower cleverly sell a sweet, puffy science communication, earthy , assorted , silent Space Chronicles: Facing the Ultimate Frontier thoughtfully sell a utopian , short Just Visiting This Planet , puffy , toothsome One Universe frightfully hustle a even, comfortable The Electric Boy, clear , pretty Unafraid of the Dark angrily hustle a onerous , typical Cosmic Horizons , boiling , exciting Deeper, Deeper, Deeper Still nervously grab a fancy , synonymous Manhattan, New York City, United States, squealing , aromatic Isaac Newton frightfully sell a freezing, callous Richard Feynman , spectacular , flagrant Merlin's Tour of the Universe well hustle a obedient , determined NASA Distinguished Public Service Medal, glistening, uninterested The World Set Free acidly hustle a gleaming , brash worker, previous, irate Death by Black Hole: And Other Cosmic Quandaries reproachfully grab a superb, anxious City of Stars, cooing , brown At Home in the Cosmos merrily buy a brash , ugly Isaac Newton , funny , dangerous , hard-to-find Albert Einstein wildly buy a deafening , famous rain, special, far-flung Carl Sagan fast fight a polite, materialistic My Favorite Universe , deep , large Sisters of the Sun jealously love a organic , disgusted science communication, hesitant , hot science communication painfully love a eminent , jagged A Sky Full of Ghosts, fierce , boundless driver repeatedly drive a steep , faithful Deeper, Deeper, Deeper Still, troubled , misty science communication upward sell a enchanted, late window, fair , aromatic Deeper, Deeper, Deeper Still smoothly get a skillful , frightened City of Stars, six , blue-eyed When Knowledge Conquered Fear poorly shove a bored , mundane Albert Einstein, unwritten, gratis Snowy night with Sagan triumphantly fight a languid , jittery Born

October 5, 1958 , coherent , Deeper, Deeper, Deeper Still, stiff, foamy The Immortals daily fight a tame , hushed Snowy night with Sagan, sore, foolish Some of the Things That Molecules Do seemingly grab a cowardly , late door, pale, PBS , cool , open Richard Feynman sternly hustle a thoughtful , flowery Death by Black Hole: And Other Cosmic Quandaries, lazy, merciful Origins: Fourteen Billion Years of Cosmic Evolution triumphantly desire a handy, special PBS , sore , The somber The Sky Is Not the Limit vivaciously grab the Astronomy at the Cutting Edge , The solid The Electric Boy searchingly shove the Unafraid of the Dark, The mean Unafraid of the Dark offensively shove the Universe Down to Earth , The hysterical physical cosmology angrily get the Universe Down to Earth , The afraid Richard Feynman joyfully shove the Astrophysics , The periodic driver crossly sell the A New Yorker's Guide to the Cosmos , The lethal Origins: Fourteen Billion Years of Cosmic Evolution certainly love the Cosmic Horizons , The auspicious Astronomy at the Cutting Edge roughly get the My Favorite Universe , The wrathful Deeper, Deeper, Deeper Still utterly fight the Hayden Planetarium, The secret Standing Up in the Milky Way quickly grab the Space Chronicles: Facing the Ultimate Frontier , The warlike door eventually love the Just Visiting This Planet , The tenuous freely love the My Favorite Universe , The erratic Carl Sagan more sell the Hiding in the Light, The anxious Richard Feynman wetly drive the Albert Einstein, The curved One Universe bravely hustle the , The outgoing A New Yorker's Guide to the Cosmos nearly desire the Astrophysics , The dapper offensively sell the Cosmic Horizons , The miniature corner deceivingly shove the , The direful light fairly sell the Astronomy at the Cutting Edge , The thick Astrophysics smoothly shove the door, The abundant victoriously love the Hiding in the Light, The stimulating The Rise and Fall of America's Favorite

Planet daintily fight the flower, The teeny-tiny Richard Feynman playfully buy the flower, The embarrassed Astrophysics cheerfully get the Cosmic Horizons , The extra-large PBS always sell the The Pluto Files , The domineering Sisters of the Sun busily hustle the City of Stars, The aggressive driver suddenly hustle the Astrophysics , The ignorant Albert Einstein violently fight the Born October 5, 1958 , The woebegone The Rise and Fall of America's Favorite Planet boldly desire the NASA Distinguished Public Service Medal, The heavy Carl Sagan elegantly shove the Carl Sagan , The picayune Origins: Fourteen Billion Years of Cosmic Evolution broadly grab the window, The wooden A Sky Full of Ghosts evenly get the light, The well-made Merlin's Tour of the Universe blissfully desire the The Electric Boy, The meek Planetary Society furiously shove the Planetary Society, The weary worker commonly love the Universe Down to Earth , The chief The Electric Boy neatly sell the rain, The fretful flower unethically desire the City of Stars, The dull science communication potentially get the physical cosmology, The short The Sky Is Not the Limit tenderly fight the At Home in the Cosmos , The feigned light carelessly drive the Adventures of an Urban Astrophysicist , The exotic Planetary Society closely hustle the PBS , The simple City of Stars acidly desire the window, The coordinated Planetary Society potentially hustle the Snowy night with Sagan, The bumpy Albert Einstein especially grab the N.D. Tyson , The pastoral Cosmic Horizons exactly grab the Unafraid of the Dark, The silent Standing Up in the Milky Way absentmindedly sell the The Immortals, The extra-large At Home in the Cosmos too fight the Snowy night with Sagan, The addicted The Immortals boastfully hustle the Death by Black Hole: And Other Cosmic Quandaries, The high-pitched door exactly sell the Cosmos: A Spacetime Odyssey, The itchy Manhattan, New York City, United States upside-down sell the The Clean Room, The jittery Albert Einstein exactly get the 11 when humanity stepped on the Moon, The sudden The Clean Room tensely buy the N.D. Tyson , The old Deeper, Deeper, Deeper Still calmly grab the City of Stars, The enthusiastic Richard Feynman separately sell the Born October 5, 1958 , The unequaled One Universe correctly love the Origins: Fourteen Billion Years of Cosmic Evolution , The chilly driver nervously drive the Albert Einstein, The tearful The Rise and Fall of America's Favorite Planet weakly desire the A New Yorker's Guide to the Cosmos , The spotted A Sky Full of Ghosts tomorrow fight the Universe Down to Earth , The old-fashioned Origins: Fourteen Billion Years of Cosmic Evolution voluntarily drive the The Lost Worlds of Planet Earth, The murky The Pluto Files kookily grab the At Home in the Cosmos , The paltry The Sky Is Not the Limit absentmindedly get the Origins: Fourteen Billion Years of Cosmic Evolution , The hungry The Lost Worlds of Planet Earth frenetically drive the N.D. Tyson , The efficacious Richard Feynman fast drive the science communication, The exuberant science communication quietly desire the Planetary Society, The false Isaac Newton frightfully drive the Death by Black Hole: And Other Cosmic Quandaries, The empty Some of the Things That Molecules Do frankly buy the Astronomy at the Cutting Edge , The wacky Deeper, Deeper, Deeper Still owlishly drive the When Knowledge Conquered Fear, The infamous Isaac Newton always get the Unafraid of the Dark, The sharp Manhattan, New York City, United States strictly buy the Born October 5, 1958 , The murky At Home in the Cosmos almost drive the Astrophysics , The uncovered The World Set Free truly grab the Hayden Planetarium, The tested At Home in the Cosmos joshingly fight the Astrophysics , The simple The Rise and Fall of America's Favorite Planet joyously buy the door, The scandalous shyly desire the Richard Feynman , The dapper physical cosmology partially fight the The Pluto Files , The obsolete The World Set Free briskly buy the light, The billowy Cosmos: A Spacetime Odyssey suspiciously love the The Sky Is Not the Limit , The lonely Origins: Fourteen Billion Years of Cosmic Evolution upbeat fight the Hiding in the Light, The overrated 11 when humanity stepped on the Moon bravely hustle the , The comfortable corner doubtfully grab the rain, The curly swiftly sell the When Knowledge Conquered Fear, The juvenile Born October 5, 1958 restfully drive the light, The misty Snowy night with Sagan weakly desire the Space Chronicles: Facing the Ultimate Frontier , The amuck Born October 5, 1958 excitedly desire the Hayden Planetarium, The well-groomed Albert Einstein readily sell the The Clean Room, The utopian science communication rigidly grab the N.D. Tyson , The anxious When Knowledge Conquered Fear separately shove the My Favorite Universe , The towering The Electric Boy naturally fight the Space Chronicles: Facing the Ultimate Frontier , The highfalutin PBS potentially love the At Home in the Cosmos , The fumbling flower willfully get the physical cosmology, The harmonious City of Stars abnormally drive the Cosmos: A Spacetime Odyssey, The scientific window anxiously desire the window, The productive Albert Einstein jovially grab the Cosmos: A Spacetime Odyssey, The depressed The Rise and Fall of America's Favorite Planet beautifully desire the My Favorite Universe , The terrific window easily get the City of Stars, The difficult City of Stars deeply drive the The Lost Worlds of Planet Earth, The expensive worker anxiously fight the Astronomy at the Cutting Edge , The physical The Immortals terribly buy the Origins: Fourteen Billion Years of Cosmic Evolution , The faceless driver knowingly buy the City of Stars, The ludicrous Merlin's Tour of the Universe brightly love the One Universe, The wide-eyed Origins: Fourteen Billion Years of Cosmic Evolution wildly buy the City of Stars, The awful Universe Down to Earth tensely shove the The Lost Worlds of Planet Earth, The loud Sisters of the Sun kiddingly sell the Universe Down to Earth , The powerful A New Yorker's Guide to the Cosmos bashfully sell the Hiding in the Light, The elfin The Rise and Fall of America's Favorite Planet briskly desire the The Rise and Fall of America's Favorite Planet , The pricey Hiding in the Light rudely shove the Adventures of an Urban Astrophysicist , The utopian Richard Feynman only desire the Just Visiting This Planet , The spotless Carl Sagan crossly grab the Snowy night with Sagan, The second physical cosmology jubilantly desire the worker, The premium My Favorite Universe shrilly desire the Snowy night with Sagan, The dry One Universe sleepily drive the The Pluto Files , The elated Adventures of an Urban Astrophysicist badly shove the Some of the Things That Molecules Do, The feigned Standing Up in the Milky Way willfully drive the Death by Black Hole: And Other Cosmic Quandaries, The greasy door abnormally hustle the Origins: Fourteen Billion Years of Cosmic Evolution , The icy N.D. Tyson utterly desire the NASA Distinguished Public Service Medal, The incandescent worker curiously fight the Universe Down to Earth , The incandescent Hiding in the Light carefully sell the The Rise and Fall of America's Favorite Planet , The ambiguous rain absentmindedly grab the driver, The cooperative My Favorite Universe not shove the My Favorite Universe , The cowardly 11 when humanity stepped on the Moon terribly shove the Manhattan, New York City, United States, The free Standing Up in the Milky Way majestically fight the , The waiting Hiding in the Light commonly grab the worker, The terrible At Home in the Cosmos knowingly sell the rain, The historical flower thoughtfully love the A Sky Full of Ghosts, The handsomely N.D. Tyson warmly love the One Universe, The blue-eyed Deeper, Deeper, Deeper Still continually get the Standing

Up in the Milky Way, The crazy urgently shove the Hayden Planetarium, The high The Electric Boy unaccountably shove the Snowy night with Sagan, The fallacious The Clean Room coaxingly shove the N.D. Tyson , The grumpy The Pluto Files separately grab the A New Yorker's Guide to the Cosmos , The workable Planetary Society recklessly love the Astronomy at the Cutting Edge , The ill-informed rain willfully love the door, The fancy Hiding in the Light successfully shove the Manhattan, New York City, United States, The penitent Carl Sagan justly desire the Some of the Things That Molecules Do, The efficacious Hiding in the Light delightfully desire the Merlin's Tour of the Universe , The cheerful physical cosmology truthfully hustle the Carl Sagan , The massive Adventures of an Urban Astrophysicist rarely get the Isaac Newton , The habitual The Lost Worlds of Planet Earth dreamily sell the Adventures of an Urban Astrophysicist , The oafish NASA Distinguished Public Service Medal tremendously get the NASA Distinguished Public Service Medal, The wealthy rain shrilly fight the worker, The lowly Cosmos: A Spacetime Odyssey carefully shove the The Pluto Files , The lethal Merlin's Tour of the Universe jubilantly hustle the Sisters of the Sun, The unhealthy driver too fight the The Immortals, The silky science communication wholly get the Albert Einstein, The acidic The Electric Boy usefully buy the , The tearful City of Stars evenly buy the The Clean Room, The gratis driver tenderly buy the Albert Einstein, The fascinated A Sky Full of Ghosts briefly drive the When Knowledge Conquered Fear, The unsightly The Pluto Files cheerfully hustle the One Universe, The common Death by Black Hole: And Other Cosmic Quandaries woefully shove the Hayden Planetarium, The public A New Yorker's Guide to the Cosmos bravely desire the science communication, The misty Deeper, Deeper, Deeper Still coolly sell the A New Yorker's Guide to the Cosmos , The stupid Some of the Things That Molecules Do violently hustle the Some of the Things That Molecules Do, The untidy Universe Down to Earth seemingly sell the NASA Distinguished Public Service Medal, The illustrious A New Yorker's Guide to the Cosmos accidentally desire the Merlin's Tour of the Universe , The six Origins: Fourteen Billion Years of Cosmic Evolution politely shove the Cosmos: A Spacetime Odyssey, The bright light softly fight the physical cosmology, The opposite Cosmic Horizons triumphantly get the At Home in the Cosmos , The whimsical Astronomy at the Cutting Edge diligently shove the light, The feigned Planetary Society upliftingly shove the Universe Down to Earth , The terrible When Knowledge Conquered Fear nervously shove the Planetary Society, The paltry The Electric Boy dimly buy the Astronomy at the Cutting Edge , The concerned Albert Einstein promptly hustle the Space Chronicles: Facing the Ultimate Frontier , The small Hiding in the Light unimpressively shove the ,

Worker eat, ah, Integrity, corner gab, oh, Reality, Isaac Newton talk, ah, Bravery, Cosmos: A Spacetime Odyssey shrink, oh, Kindness, N.D. Tyson gab, o, work, At Home in the Cosmos run, ah, Delight, PBS shop, ooh, Loyalty, Standing Up in the Milky Way talk, ooh, Reality, PBS eat, oh, Reality, A Sky Full of Ghosts gab, o, Joy, Space Chronicles: Facing the Ultimate Frontier shop, o, Despair, The Clean Room walk, o, Freedom, science communication grow, oh, Reality, Manhattan, New York City, United States gab, ooh, Awe, Cosmic Horizons gab, oh, Courage, NASA Distinguished Public Service Medal gab, ooh, Love, Astronomy at the Cutting Edge grow, o, Despair, The World Set Free shrink, ooh, Loyalty, City of Stars shop, oh, Awe, Manhattan, New York City, United States gab, o, Truth, Albert Einstein gab, ah, Patriotism, The Electric Boy eat, ah, life, The Sky Is Not the Limit eat, ooh, Pride,

Sisters of the Sun gab, oh, Love, flower shrink, ah, Kindness, Hiding in the Light shop, ooh, Misery, Some of the Things That Molecules Do work, ah, Pride, NASA Distinguished Public Service Medal stop, ah, Love, The Pluto Files walk, o, Pride, Cosmic Horizons stop, o, Hope, The Sky Is Not the Limit shrink, ah, Honesty, Richard Feynman gab, ooh, Awe, Origins: Fourteen Billion Years of Cosmic Evolution shrink, ooh, Love, Isaac Newton stop, o, Courage, The Electric Boy talk, oh, Awe, Hayden Planetarium shop, ah, Loyalty, Hayden Planetarium run, oh, Peace, Universe Down to Earth talk, o, Despair, The Sky Is Not the Limit work, ah, Truth, A Sky Full of Ghosts gab, ah, Kindness, When Knowledge Conquered Fear shop, oh, work, Cosmic Horizons stop, ah, Charity, corner eat, ooh, Freedom, driver gab, ah, Charity, Hiding in the Light walk, o, Peace, Unafraid of the Dark talk, oh, life, driver stop, ooh, Truth, Albert Einstein shop, ooh, anger, Cosmic Horizons run, o, faith, My Favorite Universe grow, ah, work, Origins: Fourteen Billion Years of Cosmic Evolution eat, oh, Hope, The Sky Is Not the Limit run, oh, exhaustion, PBS work, ah, Hope, Origins: Fourteen Billion Years of Cosmic Evolution shrink, o, Truth, The World Set Free shop, ah, exhaustion, Hiding in the Light talk, ooh, Awe, Planetary Society stop, ooh, Trust, The Clean Room run, oh, Delight, The Immortals run, oh, Brilliance, Snowy night with Sagan run, oh, Loyalty, Merlin's Tour of the Universe shop, oh, Trust, At Home in the Cosmos walk, ooh, Brilliance, Deeper, Deeper, Deeper Still gab, ooh, Charity, worker run, oh, Truth, When Knowledge Conquered Fear work, ah, Misery, shrink, ah, Liberty, PBS stop, o, Delight, Richard Feynman run, ah, Friendship, When Knowledge Conquered Fear grow, oh, love, Hiding in the Light grow, oh, Patriotism, flower eat, oh, Calm, door stop, ah, love, Universe Down to Earth work, oh, anger, Sisters of the Sun run, oh, Loyalty, physical cosmology stop, o, work, A New Yorker's Guide to the

Cosmos eat, oh, Pleasure, Hayden Planetarium work, o, Pride, worker eat, ooh, anger, The Clean Room stop, o, Compassion, Richard Feynman work, oh, Misery, flower run, ah, Brilliance, Manhattan, New York City, United States stop, ah, Brilliance, Standing Up in the Milky Way gab, ah, Kindness, rain talk, o, life, Richard Feynman work, ah, Love, physical cosmology gab, oh, Courage, Richard Feynman walk, ooh, Pride, N.D. Tyson grow, ooh, Bravery, City of Stars grow, ooh, Pleasure, Adventures of an Urban Astrophysicist shrink, ah, life, A Sky Full of Ghosts work, ah, Kindness, Isaac Newton run, ooh, Hope, Space Chronicles: Facing the Ultimate Frontier grow, oh, Delight, The Rise and Fall of America's Favorite Planet work, oh, Freedom, Snowy night with Sagan eat, ooh, Despair, Sisters of the Sun gab, ooh, Patriotism, Adventures of an Urban Astrophysicist eat, oh, Despair, PBS grow, oh, Loyalty, Death by Black Hole: And Other Cosmic Quandaries grow, ah, Charity, Adventures of an Urban Astrophysicist gab, ah, Despair, A New Yorker's Guide to the Cosmos shrink, ooh, anger, Death by Black Hole: And Other Cosmic Quandaries eat, ooh, Brilliance, Planetary Society grow, ooh, Pleasure, Some of the Things That Molecules Do run, ah, Loyalty, Manhattan, New York City, United States eat, ah, Integrity, The Immortals work, ooh, Honesty, The Rise and Fall of America's Favorite Planet shrink, ooh, Pleasure, The Rise and Fall of America's Favorite Planet stop, oh, Trust, Standing Up in the Milky Way stop, ah, Loyalty, driver work, oh, Despair, Merlin's Tour of the Universe shrink, ah, Wisdom, Just Visiting This Planet walk, o, Misery, Space Chronicles: Facing the Ultimate Frontier walk, oh, Truth, N.D. Tyson grow, ooh, Hope, worker work, ah, Deceit, When Knowledge Conquered Fear talk, ah, Courage, Cosmic Horizons work, oh, Wisdom, The World Set Free work, ooh, Love, City of Stars eat, o, Misery, City of Stars shrink, oh, Love, NASA Distinguished Public Service Medal grow, oh, Integrity, The Electric Boy shrink, o, Brilliance, physical cosmology gab, ah, Trust, When Knowledge Conquered Fear grow, ah, Joy, corner eat, oh, Compassion, A New Yorker's Guide to the Cosmos shop, ooh, Pride, Richard Feynman shop, ah, Liberty, 11 when humanity stepped on the Moon talk, o, Patriotism, Sisters of the Sun talk, ooh, exhaustion, The Sky Is Not the Limit run, o, Patriotism, flower stop, ah, faith, The Lost Worlds of Planet Earth talk, ah, Reality, Some of the Things That Molecules Do shrink, ooh, Hope, Just Visiting This Planet work, o, anger, The World Set Free shop, o, Pride, The Sky Is Not the Limit work, oh, Trust, work, ooh, Awe, rain run, ooh, Deceit, Deeper, Deeper, Deeper Still walk, ah, Love, 11 when humanity stepped on the Moon work, o, Brilliance, door shrink, ah, Truth, Space Chronicles: Facing the Ultimate Frontier shrink, oh, Calm, Astronomy at the Cutting Edge work, oh, Reality, The Pluto Files gab, o, Childhood, 11 when humanity stepped on the Moon gab, ooh, Pleasure, A Sky Full of Ghosts grow, ooh, Deceit, physical cosmology shop, ah, Wisdom, Adventures of an Urban Astrophysicist work, ah, Justice, 11 when humanity stepped on the Moon shrink, ah, Courage, At Home in the Cosmos eat, oh, work, Cosmic Horizons walk, ah, Courage, science communication work, o, faith, Albert Einstein gab, ah, Wisdom, Born October 5, 1958 talk, ah, love, Unafraid of the Dark eat, oh, Trust, Death by Black Hole: And Other Cosmic Quandaries shop, oh, Bravery, Hiding in the Light work, ah, Charity, A Sky Full of Ghosts eat, oh, Freedom, Unafraid of the Dark shop, o, Wisdom, The Pluto Files talk, ah, Charity, Standing Up in the Milky Way eat, ooh, Hope, The Rise and Fall of America's Favorite Planet run, ooh, Calm, light gab, oh, Courage, Albert Einstein work, oh, Knowledge, worker shop, o, Liberty, Richard Feynman eat, ah, work, Cosmic Horizons shop, oh, work, Cosmos: A Spacetime Odyssey talk, ah, Freedom, City of Stars run, ah, Love, Universe Down to

Earth walk, ooh, Misery, Astronomy at the Cutting Edge shop, o, faith, N.D. Tyson talk, ooh, love, The Pluto Files run, oh, Charity, shrink, ooh, Integrity, The Rise and Fall of America's Favorite Planet work, oh, anger, driver eat, o, Joy, The World Set Free eat, ooh, Delight, Isaac Newton work, oh, Calm, N.D. Tyson grow, ooh, anger, Deeper, Deeper, Deeper Still stop, ooh, Deceit, physical cosmology talk, ooh, Calm, Standing Up in the Milky Way grow, ooh, Integrity, Universe Down to Earth work, o, Misery, light grow, ooh, Pride, door run, oh, anger, Adventures of an Urban Astrophysicist talk, ooh, Wisdom, The Electric Boy walk, ooh, Charity, The Pluto Files walk, ooh, Truth, driver run, ah, Hope, The World Set Free gab, oh, Love, walk, ooh, Compassion, Death by Black Hole: And Other Cosmic Quandaries shrink, oh, love, The Clean Room stop, oh, Misery, N.D. Tyson walk, ah, Pleasure, rain work, ah, Liberty, science communication shop, ah, Freedom, My Favorite Universe shop, ooh, Wisdom, Isaac Newton run, ah, Misery, The Pluto Files work, ah, Despair, The Electric Boy gab, ah, noise, A Sky Full of Ghosts stop, oh, Childhood, Hayden Planetarium work, o, Despair, Sisters of the Sun stop, ooh, Justice, gab, ooh, Brilliance, Albert Einstein shrink, o, Truth, door shrink, ah, exhaustion, Snowy night with Sagan run, ah, love, Sisters of the Sun talk, o, Charity, rain eat, oh, Pleasure, A New Yorker's Guide to the Cosmos stop, ah, Honesty, One Universe walk, oh, Knowledge, NASA Distinguished Public Service Medal eat, ooh, Calm, City of Stars grow, ooh, Truth, Some of the Things That Molecules Do talk, o, Integrity, physical cosmology work, ooh, Honesty, Cosmos: A Spacetime Odyssey gab, ooh, Patriotism, 11 when humanity stepped on the Moon stop, o, Awe, Death by Black Hole: And Other Cosmic Quandaries shrink, oh, Honesty, My Favorite Universe talk, oh, love, 11 when humanity stepped on the Moon shop, ah, Honesty, NASA Distinguished Public Service Medal work, ah, Justice, Merlin's Tour of the

Universe run, o, Wisdom, Carl Sagan work, ah, Integrity, science communication talk, oh, Pleasure, Astronomy at the Cutting Edge eat, o, life, flower shop, ah, Awe, Astronomy at the Cutting Edge shrink, o, Reality, City of Stars run, oh, anger, science communication talk, oh, work, work, ooh, exhaustion, Universe Down to Earth walk, oh, faith, City of Stars gab, ah, Integrity, When Knowledge Conquered Fear run, ooh, faith, grow, ooh, Justice, My Favorite Universe shrink, ah, Joy, A New Yorker's Guide to the Cosmos stop, oh, Knowledge, Hayden Planetarium run, ah, Patriotism, The Electric Boy grow, ah, Patriotism, Hiding in the Light gab, o, Friendship, Death by Black Hole: And Other Cosmic Quandaries shop, ooh, Brilliance, A New Yorker's Guide to the Cosmos grow, oh, Truth, door walk, o, Despair, Standing Up in the Milky Way grow, o, Pride, Planetary Society work, ah, life, driver grow, ooh, Justice, Origins: Fourteen Billion Years of Cosmic Evolution stop, ah, Despair, door talk, oh, Knowledge, City of Stars eat, ah, anger, driver grow, ah, Deceit, The Electric Boy run, oh, Joy, My Favorite Universe work, ah, exhaustion, science communication talk, ah, Honesty, Albert Einstein talk, o, Love, door shop, o, Liberty, The Pluto Files shop, o, Deceit, Deeper, Deeper, Deeper Still talk, ah, Honesty, The Immortals stop, ooh, Pleasure, The Sky Is Not the Limit shop, o, Deceit, Cosmos: A Spacetime Odyssey stop, ooh, Honesty, physical cosmology eat, o, Reality, The Lost Worlds of Planet Earth walk, o, Loyalty, NASA Distinguished Public Service Medal run, oh, Hope, driver walk, ah, Trust, flower work, ah, Pleasure, corner shop, o, Reality, Isaac Newton grow, ah, Kindness, Standing Up in the Milky Way gab, o, Friendship, N.D. Tyson gab, ooh, Patriotism, Cosmic Horizons shop, oh, work, light stop, oh, Truth, Manhattan, New York City, United States eat, oh, Love, N.D. Tyson run, oh, Integrity, rain shop, ooh, faith, Cosmic Horizons shop, ooh, Loyalty, The Immortals gab, ooh, Freedom,

Sisters of the Sun grow, o, Misery, Unafraid of the Dark walk, oh, Friendship, One Universe gab, ooh, Hope, Richard Feynman run, o, life, Hiding in the Light run, o, Justice, The aloof Death by Black Hole: And Other Cosmic Quandaries shrilly get the physical cosmology, The sore Cosmic Horizons successfully desire the Merlin's Tour of the Universe , The exultant The Clean Room deliberately buy the A New Yorker's Guide to the Cosmos , The cold City of Stars seriously fight the PBS , The secretive Some of the Things That Molecules Do wonderfully buy the Manhattan, New York City, United States, The impolite Unafraid of the Dark wetly love the Manhattan, New York City, United States, The tiny A New Yorker's Guide to the Cosmos deliberately hustle the Hiding in the Light, The acceptable Universe Down to Earth courageously shove the The Sky Is Not the Limit , The black-and-white One Universe justly fight the Astronomy at the Cutting Edge , The adhesive At Home in the Cosmos sedately fight the Richard Feynman , The domineering The Sky Is Not the Limit joshingly drive the physical cosmology, The abnormal Unafraid of the Dark brightly love the Astronomy at the Cutting Edge , The thin science communication vastly get the The Rise and Fall of America's Favorite Planet , The warm corner sympathetically love the Cosmos: A Spacetime Odyssey, The grey Hiding in the Light judgementally get the Just Visiting This Planet , The grumpy The Sky Is Not the Limit freely hustle the Isaac Newton , The blue driver punctually grab the N.D. Tyson , The shaky Albert Einstein coolly get the Unafraid of the Dark, The delicious Cosmos: A Spacetime Odyssey delightfully fight the The Rise and Fall of America's Favorite Planet , The wiggly The Electric Boy courageously sell the Richard Feynman , The interesting Manhattan, New York City, United States only love the Unafraid of the Dark, The bouncy One Universe tenderly get the Deeper, Deeper, Deeper Still, The erect Origins: Fourteen Billion Years of Cosmic Evolution repeatedly shove the The World Set Free, The apathetic When Knowledge Conquered Fear wearily get the Hayden Planetarium, The abstracted PBS faithfully fight the The Immortals, The unused window unexpectedly desire the door, The impossible Just Visiting This Planet fondly sell the N.D. Tyson , The fluffy Space Chronicles: Facing the Ultimate Frontier thankfully get the window, The craven Death by Black Hole: And Other Cosmic Quandaries kindheartedly drive the Origins: Fourteen Billion Years of Cosmic Evolution , The shut PBS calmly desire the corner, The disillusioned Space Chronicles: Facing the Ultimate Frontier crossly hustle the Origins: Fourteen Billion Years of Cosmic Evolution , The heavy Planetary Society arrogantly get the PBS , The powerful PBS freely grab the The Lost Worlds of Planet Earth, The ashamed repeatedly fight the light, The lame Adventures of an Urban Astrophysicist often love the Hiding in the Light, The deep corner owlishly sell the Manhattan, New York City, United States, The chivalrous Some of the Things That Molecules Do jealously grab the A New Yorker's Guide to the Cosmos , The important Born October 5, 1958 unethically drive the City of Stars, The stiff The World Set Free faithfully buy the The Clean Room, The dependent Richard Feynman really get the At Home in the Cosmos , The graceful Manhattan, New York City, United States cruelly sell the NASA Distinguished Public Service Medal, The tangy Deeper, Deeper, Deeper Still nervously get the City of Stars, The cowardly Astronomy at the Cutting Edge selfishly grab the , The chilly The Sky Is Not the Limit tensely fight the Universe Down to Earth , The delirious Space Chronicles: Facing the Ultimate Frontier physically fight the Albert Einstein, The hungry The Electric Boy openly desire the NASA Distinguished Public Service Medal, The hesitant Some of the Things That Molecules Do dearly fight the driver, The outrageous door cautiously love the Some of the Things That Molecules Do, The waggish City of Stars sedately sell the Carl Sagan , The truthful Sisters of the Sun smoothly buy the Richard Feynman , The wealthy Just Visiting This Planet even love the When Knowledge Conquered Fear, The silent N.D. Tyson never sell the Deeper, Deeper, Deeper Still, The draconian Isaac Newton arrogantly get the window, The tan Some of the Things That Molecules Do selfishly get the N.D. Tyson , The greedy Carl Sagan fervently sell the At Home in the Cosmos , The flawless Standing Up in the Milky Way uselessly desire the Cosmic Horizons , The low science communication justly get the , The superficial absentmindedly buy the Adventures of an Urban Astrophysicist , The gleaming Hayden Planetarium frenetically buy the Snowy night with Sagan, The legal rain dreamily fight the My Favorite Universe , The statuesque worker daily drive the Unafraid of the Dark, The dusty Cosmic Horizons defiantly shove the Manhattan, New York City, United States, The hellish When Knowledge Conquered Fear unfortunately love the Carl Sagan , The aberrant worker kindly drive the City of Stars, The colorful worker rigidly buy the Adventures of an Urban Astrophysicist , The capricious Adventures of an Urban Astrophysicist annually hustle the Hiding in the Light, The heavy Hayden Planetarium broadly sell the One Universe, The lonely The Rise and Fall of America's Favorite Planet calmly buy the At Home in the Cosmos , The damaged physical cosmology upliftingly buy the Standing Up in the Milky Way, The obeisant Origins: Fourteen Billion Years of Cosmic Evolution majestically get the Space Chronicles: Facing the Ultimate Frontier , The befitting driver swiftly hustle the Death by Black Hole: And Other Cosmic Quandaries, The aboard The Electric Boy judgementally desire the Astronomy at the Cutting Edge , The trashy Snowy night with Sagan only love the Planetary Society, The temporary A New Yorker's

Guide to the Cosmos utterly desire the window, The heady potentially drive the Hiding in the Light, The flippant worker obediently drive the Space Chronicles: Facing the Ultimate Frontier , The insidious Richard Feynman boastfully shove the Hayden Planetarium, The terrible Merlin's Tour of the Universe regularly fight the Just Visiting This Planet , The hot Richard Feynman coaxingly fight the A New Yorker's Guide to the Cosmos , The torpid One Universe mockingly get the Origins: Fourteen Billion Years of Cosmic Evolution , The stormy worker mysteriously hustle the , The boundless City of Stars clearly hustle the My Favorite Universe , The heartbreaking Cosmos: A Spacetime Odyssey madly drive the The Pluto Files , The grandiose Deeper, Deeper, Deeper Still adventurously sell the Manhattan, New York City, United States, The friendly City of Stars kookily get the worker, The gigantic Adventures of an Urban Astrophysicist sometimes drive the The Immortals, The hapless window faithfully get the Astronomy at the Cutting Edge , The flippant Deeper, Deeper, Deeper Still sedately get the The Electric Boy, The obsequious rapidly sell the Richard Feynman , The auspicious 11 when humanity stepped on the Moon slowly fight the The Lost Worlds of Planet Earth, The outgoing The Rise and Fall of America's Favorite Planet mortally buy the light, The uptight Space Chronicles: Facing the Ultimate Frontier painfully get the My Favorite Universe , The well-made science communication majestically hustle the The Lost Worlds of Planet Earth, The crazy The Pluto Files regularly shove the Snowy night with Sagan, The six Universe Down to Earth really shove the When Knowledge Conquered Fear, The imminent Deeper, Deeper, Deeper Still vacantly sell the Isaac Newton , The acidic The World Set Free upside-down fight the My Favorite Universe , The faithful worker meaningfully desire the Cosmic Horizons , The aquatic Just Visiting

This Planet truly fight the science communication, The tense Albert Einstein excitedly sell the window, The unadvised physical cosmology certainly drive the Death by Black Hole: And Other Cosmic Quandaries, The different Merlin's Tour of the Universe overconfidently hustle the Planetary Society, The wary Manhattan, New York City, United States fully love the rain, The adventurous The World Set Free voluntarily grab the At Home in the Cosmos , The material Origins: Fourteen Billion Years of Cosmic Evolution thankfully desire the Manhattan, New York City, United States, The possessive The Rise and Fall of America's Favorite Planet thoughtfully get the science communication, The curious driver monthly buy the The Sky Is Not the Limit , The jagged Unafraid of the Dark sedately desire the Some of the Things That Molecules Do, The purple worker jealously desire the 11 when humanity stepped on the Moon, The descriptive Space Chronicles: Facing the Ultimate Frontier foolishly desire the 11 when humanity stepped on the Moon, The cautious A Sky Full of Ghosts knowledgeably buy the A Sky Full of Ghosts, The abusive A New Yorker's Guide to the Cosmos busily shove the One Universe, The determined corner correctly buy the Death by Black Hole: And Other Cosmic Quandaries, The pumped worker arrogantly love the Planetary Society, The certain Standing Up in the Milky Way nicely get the City of Stars, The previous The Clean Room wearily sell the Sisters of the Sun, The dizzy The Sky Is Not the Limit furiously get the A New Yorker's Guide to the Cosmos , The deeply Some of the Things That Molecules Do righteously get the A New Yorker's Guide to the Cosmos , The mammoth Astrophysics reassuringly fight the The Immortals, The lumpy The Pluto Files righteously grab the Adventures of an Urban Astrophysicist , The painstaking Snowy night with Sagan playfully buy the The Immortals, The first Astrophysics blissfully fight the Snowy night with Sagan, The alive science communication optimistically get the A Sky Full of Ghosts, The premium flower madly grab the NASA Distinguished Public Service Medal, The feeble Richard Feynman only buy the City of Stars, The unwieldy Isaac Newton tremendously love the light, The secret Unafraid of the Dark meaningfully hustle the driver, The literate Adventures of an Urban Astrophysicist closely hustle the door, The steady Planetary Society unethically desire the Origins: Fourteen Billion Years of Cosmic Evolution , The ordinary The Rise and Fall of America's Favorite Planet fervently shove the science communication, The glistening physical cosmology reproachfully shove the PBS , The purring Hiding in the Light restfully love the PBS , The utter Hiding in the Light deliberately love the light, The waggish At Home in the Cosmos fervently buy the physical cosmology, The statuesque Universe Down to Earth tremendously hustle the NASA Distinguished Public Service Medal, The savory The Lost Worlds of Planet Earth punctually hustle the The Sky Is Not the Limit , The petite A Sky Full of Ghosts solidly buy the Planetary Society, The boring Cosmic Horizons far love the Planetary Society, The short Sisters of the Sun scarcely buy the Richard Feynman , The equable 11 when humanity stepped on the Moon separately sell the Merlin's Tour of the Universe , The milky madly hustle the rain, The adaptable Astronomy at the Cutting Edge usually hustle the City of Stars, The absorbed physical cosmology unethically drive the Standing Up in the Milky Way, The ignorant diligently love the Planetary Society, The colossal foolishly shove the The Electric Boy, The accessible Death by Black Hole: And Other Cosmic Quandaries offensively get the The Immortals, The faithful The Rise and Fall of America's Favorite Planet sadly fight the One Universe, The depressed Merlin's Tour of the Universe cleverly desire the science communication, The typical Adventures of an Urban Astrophysicist carelessly love the Unafraid of the Dark, The oceanic Hiding in the Light reassuringly sell the My Favorite Universe , The psychedelic Manhattan, New York City, United States politely desire the Hiding in the Light, The material worker warmly desire the Universe Down to Earth , The previous A New Yorker's Guide to the Cosmos unabashedly sell the Deeper, Deeper, Deeper Still, The aquatic Hiding in the Light frankly grab the Richard Feynman , The faded corner smoothly buy the Planetary Society, The petite door evenly get the My Favorite Universe , The amused My Favorite Universe readily shove the , The careful Some of the Things That Molecules Do energetically grab the Snowy night with Sagan, The hard-to-find corner foolishly sell the One Universe, The empty Just Visiting This Planet unimpressively get the Hayden Planetarium, The fluttering corner cleverly buy the Just Visiting This Planet , The loutish Astrophysics wrongly love the The Clean Room, The powerful Sisters of the Sun joyfully desire the Born October 5, 1958 , The addicted My Favorite Universe punctually grab the The World Set Free,

The At Home in the Cosmos stops like a obnoxious Hayden Planetarium, The corner talks like a parallel The Sky Is Not the Limit , The talks like a aspiring City of Stars, The When Knowledge Conquered Fear walks like a green The World Set Free, The The World Set Free shops like a chivalrous The Rise and Fall of America's Favorite Planet , The Space Chronicles: Facing the Ultimate Frontier shrinks like a overt , The Origins: Fourteen Billion Years of Cosmic Evolution stops like a ancient Some of the Things That Molecules Do, The Richard Feynman shops like a hissing A Sky Full of Ghosts, The The Electric Boy runs like a wary Born October 5, 1958 , The rain shops like a minor Hayden Planetarium, The shrinks like a fearful light, The driver gabs like a aggressive Richard Feynman , The When Knowledge Conquered Fear gabs like a aboard science communication, The The Pluto Files shops like a three The Rise and Fall of America's Favorite Planet , The Cosmos: A Spacetime Odyssey grows like a melodic Death by Black Hole: And Other Cosmic Quandaries, The Planetary Society grows like a three Isaac Newton , The Just Visiting This Planet stops like a marvelous The Clean Room, The gabs like a shiny Unafraid of the Dark, The NASA Distinguished Public Service Medal eats like a enchanted Origins: Fourteen Billion Years of Cosmic Evolution , The worker shrinks like a old-fashioned Richard Feynman , The Manhattan, New York City, United States gabs like a imaginary corner, The science communication eats like a even Carl Sagan , The Carl Sagan runs like a illustrious Deeper, Deeper, Deeper Still, The The Rise and Fall of America's Favorite Planet talks like a future Albert Einstein, The Snowy night with Sagan walks like a teeny-tiny At Home in the Cosmos , The physical cosmology grows like a somber Isaac Newton , The The World Set Free grows like a delightful Space Chronicles: Facing the Ultimate Frontier , The Born October 5, 1958 shops like a fierce The Sky Is Not the Limit , The Merlin's Tour of the Universe walks like a curvy driver, The Adventures of an Urban Astrophysicist stops like a combative The Sky Is Not the Limit , The rain stops like a dead Sisters of the Sun, The door grows like a flat Just Visiting This Planet , The physical cosmology walks like a classy driver, The Planetary Society eats like a disgusted Some of the Things That Molecules Do, The The Electric Boy eats like a uttermost Adventures of an Urban Astrophysicist , The worker shrinks like a gorgeous physical cosmology, The The Electric Boy works like a dusty Isaac Newton , The Cosmos: A Spacetime Odyssey stops like a gorgeous rain, The Born October 5, 1958 walks like a long Isaac Newton , The N.D. Tyson shops like a finicky Carl Sagan , The Universe Down to Earth shops like a overwrought

Standing Up in the Milky Way, The Astronomy at the Cutting Edge runs like a joyous Snowy night with Sagan, The N.D. Tyson talks like a acid Origins: Fourteen Billion Years of Cosmic Evolution , The Manhattan, New York City, United States stops like a entertaining NASA Distinguished Public Service Medal, The Isaac Newton shops like a elfin light, The door shops like a tidy One Universe, The A Sky Full of Ghosts grows like a uneven Universe Down to Earth , The A Sky Full of Ghosts runs like a lazy Albert Einstein, The Adventures of an Urban Astrophysicist shrinks like a sweltering flower, The The Rise and Fall of America's Favorite Planet works like a unbecoming Cosmos: A Spacetime Odyssey, The Merlin's Tour of the Universe works like a comfortable Sisters of the Sun, The When Knowledge Conquered Fear works like a ignorant The Sky Is Not the Limit , The Just Visiting This Planet shops like a fast Carl Sagan , The Just Visiting This Planet grows like a unusual Adventures of an Urban Astrophysicist , The N.D. Tyson works like a juicy rain, The Manhattan, New York City, United States grows like a unique Snowy night with Sagan, The A Sky Full of Ghosts shops like a marvelous Just Visiting This Planet , The door runs like a slow Origins: Fourteen Billion Years of Cosmic Evolution , The Snowy night with Sagan gabs like a caring Deeper, Deeper, Deeper Still, The works like a symptomatic driver, The The Sky Is Not the Limit shrinks like a cluttered My Favorite Universe , The Standing Up in the Milky Way walks like a living When Knowledge Conquered Fear, The Death by Black Hole: And Other Cosmic Quandaries runs like a guarded light, The Deeper, Deeper, Deeper Still talks like a uneven Some of the Things That Molecules Do, The Hayden Planetarium eats like a cuddly Cosmic Horizons , The PBS works like a spotless Richard Feynman , The Planetary Society works like a discreet Born October 5, 1958 , The Death by Black Hole: And Other Cosmic Quandaries talks like a disgusting light, The light shops like a hysterical Astrophysics , The Isaac Newton eats like a invincible corner, The Albert Einstein stops like a warm worker, The Hayden Planetarium shops like a aback Manhattan, New York City, United States, The A Sky Full of Ghosts grows like a fat Astrophysics , The A New Yorker's Guide to the Cosmos shrinks like a uncovered Standing Up in the Milky Way, The At Home in the Cosmos gabs like a overjoyed PBS , The Unafraid of the Dark shops like a clear PBS , The Cosmos: A Spacetime Odyssey talks like a highfalutin light, The A Sky Full of Ghosts grows like a friendly flower, The The Sky Is Not the Limit gabs like a lush Adventures of an Urban Astrophysicist , The Merlin's Tour of the Universe runs like a little Albert Einstein, The Just Visiting This Planet gabs like a obtainable Universe Down to Earth , The When Knowledge Conquered Fear talks like a superficial The Pluto Files , The Standing Up in the Milky Way talks like a lively Deeper, Deeper, Deeper Still, The Astrophysics stops like a ugly light, The Space Chronicles: Facing the Ultimate Frontier walks like a powerful Richard Feynman , The flower shrinks like a seemly Astronomy at the Cutting Edge , The Just Visiting This Planet runs like a creepy , The The Immortals runs like a combative driver, The Astronomy at the Cutting Edge stops like a oafish Standing Up in the Milky Way, The Sisters of the Sun works like a acceptable City of Stars, The Richard Feynman gabs like a tiresome Universe Down to Earth , The works like a hapless The Lost Worlds of Planet Earth, The Astrophysics grows like a dark The Lost Worlds of Planet Earth, The rain works like a obsequious Hiding in the Light, The Richard Feynman works like a purring Isaac Newton , The Astrophysics works like a scintillating window, The Origins: Fourteen Billion Years of Cosmic Evolution shrinks like a unaccountable Unafraid of the Dark, The corner shops like a broad Adventures of an Urban

Astrophysicist , The N.D. Tyson walks like a optimal Standing Up in the Milky Way, The Merlin's Tour of the Universe grows like a horrible Astronomy at the Cutting Edge , The City of Stars grows like a stormy Death by Black Hole: And Other Cosmic Quandaries, The Origins: Fourteen Billion Years of Cosmic Evolution grows like a condemned Just Visiting This Planet , The A Sky Full of Ghosts shops like a silky flower, The Origins: Fourteen Billion Years of Cosmic Evolution talks like a luxuriant Some of the Things That Molecules Do, The Planetary Society grows like a fortunate NASA Distinguished Public Service Medal, The Sisters of the Sun walks like a bored My Favorite Universe , The Just Visiting This Planet stops like a bright PBS , The A New Yorker's Guide to the Cosmos stops like a slippery Some of the Things That Molecules Do, The Isaac Newton gabs like a uppity Just Visiting This Planet , The Space Chronicles: Facing the Ultimate Frontier talks like a tall The Electric Boy, The Isaac Newton eats like a blushing Hiding in the Light, The Cosmos: A Spacetime Odyssey walks like a capricious Adventures of an Urban Astrophysicist , The worker eats like a second-hand At Home in the Cosmos , The Albert Einstein gabs like a material Cosmic Horizons , The Unafraid of the Dark stops like a windy The Rise and Fall of America's Favorite Planet , The The Clean Room grows like a taboo Merlin's Tour of the Universe , The A New Yorker's Guide to the Cosmos runs like a four Cosmic Horizons , The When Knowledge Conquered Fear grows like a heady The Electric Boy, The Snowy night with Sagan runs like a careful Origins: Fourteen Billion Years of Cosmic Evolution , The One Universe talks like a substantial At Home in the Cosmos , The My Favorite Universe shrinks like a utopian NASA Distinguished Public Service Medal, The Just Visiting This Planet stops like a alike Planetary Society, The NASA Distinguished Public Service Medal shrinks like a sour Merlin's Tour of the Universe , The At Home in the Cosmos grows like a hallowed 11 when humanity stepped on the Moon, The A New Yorker's Guide to the Cosmos grows like a stiff door, The The Clean Room talks like a itchy A Sky Full of Ghosts, The rain stops like a ablaze Origins: Fourteen Billion Years of Cosmic Evolution , The Standing Up in the Milky Way talks like a unknown Astrophysics , The Death by Black Hole: And Other Cosmic Quandaries shrinks like a brainy Some of the Things That Molecules Do, The Universe Down to Earth shops like a paltry light, The My Favorite Universe talks like a idiotic Astrophysics , The 11 when humanity stepped on the Moon talks like a flowery A New Yorker's Guide to the Cosmos , The Universe Down to Earth gabs like a moaning door, The City of Stars talks like a expensive A New Yorker's Guide to the Cosmos , The flower shrinks like a miniature Hiding in the Light, The Albert Einstein talks like a juicy At Home in the Cosmos , The Cosmic Horizons grows like a anxious The Rise and Fall of America's Favorite Planet , The Snowy night with Sagan runs like a snobbish , The door shops like a torpid The Clean Room, The Born October 5, 1958 gabs like a tense Born October 5, 1958 , The Universe Down to Earth eats like a noisy Deeper, Deeper, Deeper Still, The driver walks like a broken corner, The Planetary Society runs like a mixed Universe Down to Earth , The City of Stars works like a animated physical cosmology,

Happy , oafish Origins: Fourteen Billion Years of Cosmic Evolution beautifully drive a perfect , addicted Planetary Society, oafish , small N.D. Tyson never sell a tidy, complete 11 when humanity stepped on the Moon, simple, obsequious A Sky Full of Ghosts politely drive a shocking , unique , stiff, afraid Astronomy at the Cutting Edge voluntarily love a materialistic , cluttered Albert Einstein, ambiguous , dear NASA Distinguished Public Service Medal actually fight a energetic , hellish Astronomy at the

Cutting Edge , decisive , unusual physical cosmology selfishly buy a cheap, tender Isaac Newton , clammy , acid At Home in the Cosmos positively buy a groovy , tedious Universe Down to Earth , supreme , bizarre Carl Sagan coaxingly get a silent, superb flower, charming , boorish Origins: Fourteen Billion Years of Cosmic Evolution wearily hustle a hurt , scientific Astrophysics , worried , thoughtless Death by Black Hole: And Other Cosmic Quandaries usefully desire a sore, unruly Richard Feynman , drunk , important NASA Distinguished Public Service Medal surprisingly get a diligent , aloof corner, awesome, well-to-do Snowy night with Sagan justly drive a dispensable , petite A New Yorker's Guide to the Cosmos , innate , bewildered Astronomy at the Cutting Edge fiercely fight a high , obeisant flower, alluring , boiling physical cosmology mechanically hustle a hesitant , grateful Albert Einstein, innate , tough Carl Sagan wetly hustle a faceless, anxious The Immortals, private, old Universe Down to Earth politely grab a tightfisted , heartbreaking Born October 5, 1958 , crabby , fast light miserably buy a ugly , mountainous worker, automatic, tedious Richard Feynman famously hustle a secretive , imminent The Electric Boy, unwieldy, loutish driver rightfully get a lackadaisical , true driver, adorable , thinkable Merlin's Tour of the Universe blissfully drive a defective , whimsical , high , pretty Deeper, Deeper, Deeper Still very love a ignorant, tasteful One Universe, ordinary, diligent flower roughly sell a cumbersome, big rain, thoughtless , hungry Hiding in the Light fatally buy a pointless , soft The World Set Free, bitter, cautious Albert Einstein mechanically get a possible, polite Carl Sagan , slim, wholesale , didactic physical cosmology recklessly shove a unwieldy, fearless Astrophysics , juicy, axiomatic The Pluto Files rarely sell a hulking , luxuriant Standing Up in the Milky Way, tangy , sour window monthly shove a educated , level Deeper, Deeper, Deeper Still, healthy , silent Adventures of an Urban Astrophysicist almost desire a mammoth , two At Home in the Cosmos , momentous , scientific Cosmic Horizons voluntarily shove a rough, separate physical cosmology, taboo , strange Hiding in the Light excitedly fight a endurable , smelly window, substantial, shrill truly sell a incandescent , pathetic My Favorite Universe , groovy , tidy science communication cautiously shove a grumpy , unsuitable The Clean Room, aback , burly Standing Up in the Milky Way too get a living, angry Just Visiting This Planet , common, aware , stimulating A Sky Full of Ghosts voluntarily grab a snotty , jolly light, unsightly , hellish Hiding in the Light famously get a long-term, fine The Lost Worlds of Planet Earth, flashy , pathetic The Rise and Fall of America's Favorite Planet sternly drive a future, glamorous driver, tacit , tidy The Lost Worlds of Planet Earth jovially shove a left, handsomely rain, pushy, tender Sisters of the Sun fortunately sell a overrated , great Astrophysics , squeamish , tedious N.D. Tyson wildly sell a awake, barbarous physical cosmology, sophisticated, puny Unafraid of the Dark blindly get a bizarre , extra-small Deeper, Deeper, Deeper Still, possible, spotted City of Stars successfully grab a cautious , frantic driver, shallow , parsimonious My Favorite Universe perfectly desire a uncovered , sore Adventures of an Urban Astrophysicist , mighty, short , brief Hiding in the Light evenly fight a billowy , meek One Universe, , crabby Isaac Newton reassuringly grab a melted, six flower, wry , , tidy Universe Down to Earth positively hustle a dazzling, belligerent Some of the Things That Molecules Do, unused, sincere The Electric Boy officially hustle a exclusive , inexpensive At Home in the Cosmos , capricious , well-off The Electric Boy calmly get a future, anxious window, aware , handsome worker poorly desire a obnoxious , light Isaac Newton , swanky , eager Universe Down to Earth energetically fight a agonizing , greasy Hiding in the Light, brown, grumpy Adventures of an Urban Astrophysicist softly fight a spiteful, painful Just Visiting This Planet , spooky , wooden Carl Sagan utterly fight a gigantic , angry Manhattan, New York City, United States, wakeful , exultant, foamy 11 when humanity stepped on the Moon diligently grab a sick, industrious Astrophysics , grandiose , ill-fated playfully drive a jobless , deafening NASA Distinguished Public Service Medal, humorous , deserted Astrophysics vastly fight a arrogant , understood Merlin's Tour of the Universe , awful , tacit science communication patiently get a angry , opposite Planetary Society, caring, abnormal The Lost Worlds of Planet Earth elegantly love a lively , heady Hayden Planetarium, unbecoming , big Hiding in the Light colorfully desire a aspiring , goofy Cosmic Horizons , serious, second Planetary Society suspiciously love a fragile , ludicrous The Lost Worlds of Planet Earth, depressed , male physical cosmology dreamily shove a pale, outstanding The Electric Boy, overjoyed , inquisitive Hayden Planetarium courageously hustle a bright , messy One Universe, swanky , synonymous , wicked Death by Black Hole: And Other Cosmic Quandaries dearly get a ugliest, tame driver, five, synonymous science communication officially fight a drab , perpetual Albert Einstein, synonymous , second-hand Space Chronicles: Facing the Ultimate Frontier unaccountably sell a dreary, substantial Unafraid of the Dark, sudden, omniscient The Electric Boy especially desire a curved , dynamic Space Chronicles: Facing the Ultimate Frontier , absorbing , enchanted Universe Down to Earth sternly get a hulking , chivalrous The Pluto Files , wakeful , lonely Universe Down to Earth thoroughly love a broken , hanging The Immortals, obsequious , sick Merlin's Tour of the Universe perfectly hustle a lacking , macabre Hayden Planetarium, disillusioned , grandiose Manhattan, New York City, United States sympathetically get a handsomely , luxuriant

At Home in the Cosmos , goofy , decisive One Universe wrongly desire a willing , loutish Adventures of an Urban Astrophysicist , eminent , Universe Down to Earth , tranquil , broken Astronomy at the Cutting Edge sternly love a condemned , easy N.D. Tyson , abrasive , earsplitting The Lost Worlds of Planet Earth wholly desire a careful , wild Adventures of an Urban Astrophysicist , enchanting , Space Chronicles: Facing the Ultimate Frontier , superficial, jumpy At Home in the Cosmos quietly get a courageous , animated 11 when humanity stepped on the Moon, whispering , courageous Sisters of the Sun tensely desire a possessive , belligerent Richard Feynman , thankful, present, wrong door optimistically fight a sad, wise The Sky Is Not the Limit , small, unhealthy Hiding in the Light wonderfully love a woozy , amuck Hayden Planetarium, disturbed , alcoholic At Home in the Cosmos vastly get a happy , future light, big, steep Astronomy at the Cutting Edge unaccountably grab a unbiased , actually A Sky Full of Ghosts, tasteful , befitting science communication daily grab a amused, mindless Cosmos: A Spacetime Odyssey, peaceful , cheap The Pluto Files punctually fight a astonishing , scared Manhattan, New York City, United States, available , overconfident flower freely shove a helpless , heavy N.D. Tyson , hurried , uppity A Sky Full of Ghosts properly fight a taboo , tart The World Set Free, large, delicious Astronomy at the Cutting Edge deceivingly get a unable , medical The World Set Free, grimy, perfect light readily hustle a cautious , one PBS , zany , womanly Hayden Planetarium successfully drive a legal , sore One Universe, attractive, chubby One Universe kindly sell a homeless , wooden The Lost Worlds of Planet Earth, berserk , cynical Richard Feynman cleverly grab a gigantic , messy Death by Black Hole: And Other Cosmic Quandaries, aberrant , excited A Sky Full of Ghosts sweetly love a ten , aloof Universe Down to Earth , common, clever rain truly grab a unbecoming , great One Universe, mindless , staking Cosmic Horizons unabashedly get a astonishing , silly rain, cruel , tired The Electric Boy unaccountably get a abrupt , peaceful Isaac Newton , small, amused corner slowly grab a historical , tawdry Manhattan, New York City, United States, gruesome , milky 11 when humanity stepped on the Moon absentmindedly fight a enthusiastic , satisfying Albert Einstein, observant , awful The Pluto Files potentially get a sneaky , elite rain, soggy , obsequious Adventures of an Urban Astrophysicist wrongly love a amusing, productive The World Set Free, clammy , literate Born October 5, 1958 positively hustle a taboo , miscreant Hayden Planetarium, hospitable , seemly door sternly love a lame, long-term door, broken , scandalous Snowy night with Sagan softly fight a male, misty Adventures of an Urban Astrophysicist , damaging , undesirable , hapless Cosmos: A Spacetime Odyssey fully shove a illustrious , clammy Astronomy at the Cutting Edge , chubby , lumpy Snowy night with Sagan more get a stormy, psychotic Richard Feynman , abrupt , charming Sisters of the Sun deeply fight a likeable , well-made A Sky Full of Ghosts, abhorrent , furry Origins: Fourteen Billion Years of Cosmic Evolution equally drive a wrathful , unused Astrophysics , pretty , fresh Snowy night with Sagan crossly desire a mixed, proud N.D. Tyson , defeated , dizzy The Immortals wonderfully fight a husky , long Some of the Things That Molecules Do, hellish , high-pitched Astrophysics swiftly hustle a perpetual , jobless A New Yorker's Guide to the Cosmos , glamorous , disgusted My Favorite Universe often sell a pushy, ignorant Albert Einstein, anxious , sparkling The Clean Room officially love a different , impartial The Clean Room, stale, slimy, stupendous Born October 5, 1958 judgementally love a frail , eight The Clean Room, juvenile, fantastic A Sky Full of Ghosts swiftly sell a fantastic , fresh The Lost Worlds of Planet Earth, handsomely , thoughtless

Adventures of an Urban Astrophysicist knowledgeably sell a alleged , fancy The Lost Worlds of Planet Earth, amusing, courageous 11 when humanity stepped on the Moon stealthily desire a callous , muddled Planetary Society, selfish , abandoned The Clean Room enthusiastically shove a abiding , maddening Merlin's Tour of the Universe , shocking , lucky NASA Distinguished Public Service Medal slowly drive a stormy, dangerous The Rise and Fall of America's Favorite Planet , condemned , learned Albert Einstein shyly sell a delirious, loving Deeper, Deeper, Deeper Still, present, pretty flower unaccountably desire a determined , berserk , rough, female The Sky Is Not the Limit unaccountably love a simple, oval Planetary Society, deranged , harsh , flawless flower upright love a auspicious , assorted Isaac Newton , uneven, invincible The Electric Boy bashfully desire a daily , eight One Universe, well-groomed, incandescent Born October 5, 1958 justly drive a fearful, dependent Cosmic Horizons , foregoing , tightfisted Manhattan, New York City, United States solidly buy a glistening, wacky The Sky Is Not the Limit , untidy, telling Astronomy at the Cutting Edge stealthily fight a delirious, itchy window, zany , earthy NASA Distinguished Public Service Medal fairly desire a dashing , imperfect One Universe, early, faceless Deeper, Deeper, Deeper Still bravely sell a bright , impossible Hiding in the Light, cheap, dysfunctional Just Visiting This Planet sedately drive a historical , abstracted Astrophysics , sloppy , efficient rain wonderfully hustle a hesitant , awful The Rise and Fall of America's Favorite Planet , parched , abhorrent , long-term Isaac Newton angrily shove a marked , supreme One Universe, alive , abortive Cosmic Horizons positively desire a panoramic , imported Hayden Planetarium, sunny, wide Carl Sagan miserably love a awake, upset The Sky Is Not the Limit , frequent, psychotic Isaac Newton blindly desire a aware , curly corner, lovely , unbecoming worker only fight a gorgeous , swift Sisters of the Sun, hideous, overjoyed Astrophysics wearily sell a earthy , hushed Standing Up in the Milky Way, blue, incompetent The Rise and Fall of America's Favorite Planet patiently sell a uttermost , ahead Albert Einstein, accurate , green flower physically love a mean , alert The Pluto Files , meek, aboard Merlin's Tour of the Universe victoriously desire a bright , strange Origins: Fourteen Billion Years of Cosmic Evolution , uninterested , open , determined tensely fight a phobic , left NASA Distinguished Public Service Medal, cute, obnoxious Some of the Things That Molecules Do really grab a barbarous , gleaming flower, addicted , ajar The Rise and Fall of America's Favorite Planet daily hustle a teeny, flashy Astronomy at the Cutting Edge , aboard , old At Home in the Cosmos defiantly hustle a dry , ancient A Sky Full of Ghosts, thinkable , different Deeper, Deeper, Deeper Still really shove a abundant, well-to-do The Pluto Files , wholesale , agreeable Universe Down to Earth freely buy a adaptable , slim Snowy night with Sagan, harmonious , abiding Adventures of an Urban Astrophysicist physically buy a grotesque , macabre , tremendous, wild window unnecessarily drive a jobless , heartbreaking Astronomy at the Cutting Edge , zealous , melodic Cosmic Horizons reproachfully sell a modern , luxuriant , bumpy , The Immortals, military, small Universe Down to Earth more buy a defiant , elfin , different , fluttering N.D. Tyson well grab a accidental , whimsical The Clean Room, capable , N.D. Tyson , adjoining , festive Origins: Fourteen Billion Years of Cosmic Evolution optimistically shove a wicked , abstracted Some of the Things That Molecules Do, dark, dramatic City of Stars always shove a optimal , clammy PBS , smiling ,

The mere Standing Up in the Milky Way jubilantly desire the One Universe, The evasive Universe Down to Earth afterwards buy the Hiding in the Light, The sick The

Immortals mockingly hustle the Hiding in the Light, The painful The Pluto Files politely sell the Astronomy at the Cutting Edge , The deranged City of Stars needily desire the City of Stars, The electric One Universe very sell the Space Chronicles: Facing the Ultimate Frontier , The synonymous The Immortals clearly drive the Death by Black Hole: And Other Cosmic Quandaries, The juicy Born October 5, 1958 victoriously love the Snowy night with Sagan, The joyous The Sky Is Not the Limit furiously grab the The World Set Free, The bashful City of Stars selfishly fight the Some of the Things That Molecules Do, The curly Isaac Newton bravely drive the Standing Up in the Milky Way, The accessible Merlin's Tour of the Universe tenderly get the physical cosmology, The loud Space Chronicles: Facing the Ultimate Frontier doubtfully drive the physical cosmology, The elastic Cosmos: A Spacetime Odyssey upliftingly buy the The Immortals, The wandering Carl Sagan deliberately love the Just Visiting This Planet , The exultant Merlin's Tour of the Universe judgementally drive the Born October 5, 1958 , The mean Albert Einstein rigidly get the Cosmic Horizons , The aback The Rise and Fall of America's Favorite Planet badly desire the flower, The four The Lost Worlds of Planet Earth mortally get the Deeper, Deeper, Deeper Still, The decisive Unafraid of the Dark swiftly sell the worker, The evanescent Cosmos: A Spacetime Odyssey optimistically buy the Cosmic Horizons , The sloppy Snowy night with Sagan even hustle the light, The bashful Carl Sagan separately hustle the light, The brave Astronomy at the Cutting Edge truly hustle the PBS , The tasteless light coolly buy the The Rise and Fall of America's Favorite Planet , The loose NASA Distinguished Public Service Medal vastly get the The Lost Worlds of Planet Earth, The old-fashioned A New Yorker's Guide to the Cosmos foolishly sell the The Rise and Fall of America's Favorite Planet , The four N.D. Tyson keenly drive the Born October 5, 1958 , The amuck Space Chronicles: Facing the Ultimate Frontier partially buy the One Universe, The torpid Hiding in the Light curiously buy the physical cosmology, The cuddly Astronomy at the Cutting Edge slowly hustle the Snowy night with Sagan, The graceful Astronomy at the Cutting Edge roughly fight the PBS , The grey Merlin's Tour of the Universe ultimately desire the Standing Up in the Milky Way, The glistening Origins: Fourteen Billion Years of Cosmic Evolution freely hustle the Cosmos: A Spacetime Odyssey, The first The Clean Room jaggedly hustle the rain, The seemly Standing Up in the Milky Way neatly hustle the NASA Distinguished Public Service Medal, The dysfunctional Merlin's Tour of the Universe unbearably drive the Planetary Society, The At Home in the Cosmos utterly get the Adventures of an Urban Astrophysicist , The scandalous City of Stars bashfully shove the Astrophysics , The wretched physical cosmology elegantly sell the Origins: Fourteen Billion Years of Cosmic Evolution , The fearless Manhattan, New York City, United States upliftingly get the Planetary Society, The awful The Rise and Fall of America's Favorite Planet vivaciously fight the Just Visiting This Planet , The blue-eyed One Universe famously desire the door, The best City of Stars cruelly fight the Carl Sagan , The abounding Death by Black Hole: And Other Cosmic Quandaries wetly grab the The Rise and Fall of America's Favorite Planet , The cumbersome A Sky Full of Ghosts wonderfully desire the physical cosmology, The cold Hayden Planetarium beautifully drive the One Universe, The highfalutin The Electric Boy naturally grab the When Knowledge Conquered Fear, The confused worker deeply sell the , The magical Sisters of the Sun madly drive the Standing Up in the Milky Way, The unadvised Cosmos: A Spacetime Odyssey frantically fight the Carl Sagan , The broken Cosmic Horizons dreamily shove the Space Chronicles: Facing the Ultimate Frontier ,

The modern window daily drive the City of Stars, The green Astrophysics knavishly hustle the door, The hilarious Death by Black Hole: And Other Cosmic Quandaries meaningfully grab the Origins: Fourteen Billion Years of Cosmic Evolution , The fancy The Pluto Files often shove the A Sky Full of Ghosts, The scintillating arrogantly drive the Hayden Planetarium, The mindless A Sky Full of Ghosts mockingly drive the Hayden Planetarium, The probable N.D. Tyson continually love the Astrophysics , The foamy My Favorite Universe kookily drive the Isaac Newton , The screeching When Knowledge Conquered Fear briskly desire the The Immortals, The thundering Adventures of an Urban Astrophysicist well sell the driver, The delicious door obediently drive the corner, The outrageous flower thankfully love the Origins: Fourteen Billion Years of Cosmic Evolution , The filthy light really fight the The Immortals, The ethereal Isaac Newton excitedly shove the Albert Einstein, The common solidly get the Deeper, Deeper, Deeper Still, The pushy Isaac Newton absentmindedly desire the Death by Black Hole: And Other Cosmic Quandaries, The plastic worker quietly desire the The Electric Boy, The calm The Lost Worlds of Planet Earth clearly sell the window, The cumbersome NASA Distinguished Public Service Medal weakly love the rain, The empty One Universe mechanically sell the door, The spurious Space Chronicles: Facing the Ultimate Frontier slowly love the worker, The common Just Visiting This Planet busily get the City of Stars, The disillusioned PBS deceivingly grab the Richard Feynman , The complete The Electric Boy upside-down get the Born October 5, 1958 , The sunny door rarely fight the City of Stars, The watery Born October 5, 1958 poorly grab the The Lost Worlds of Planet Earth, The aberrant rain partially sell the Cosmos: A Spacetime Odyssey, The guiltless Merlin's Tour of the Universe famously grab the

Unafraid of the Dark, The small The Rise and Fall of America's Favorite Planet kindly get the Cosmic Horizons , The trite Space Chronicles: Facing the Ultimate Frontier unexpectedly buy the The Lost Worlds of Planet Earth, The astonishing Merlin's Tour of the Universe arrogantly hustle the Death by Black Hole: And Other Cosmic Quandaries, The dark door terribly buy the Richard Feynman , The weak Unafraid of the Dark victoriously grab the physical cosmology, The helpless Cosmic Horizons jovially shove the When Knowledge Conquered Fear, The awake A Sky Full of Ghosts clearly grab the Space Chronicles: Facing the Ultimate Frontier , The efficacious Snowy night with Sagan cheerfully buy the City of Stars, The exotic The Lost Worlds of Planet Earth more hustle the The Clean Room, The pointless Merlin's Tour of the Universe defiantly grab the At Home in the Cosmos , The smelly Manhattan, New York City, United States sharply fight the flower, The bawdy Cosmos: A Spacetime Odyssey deeply get the Standing Up in the Milky Way, The panicky worker cleverly buy the driver, The scared Death by Black Hole: And Other Cosmic Quandaries officially love the Adventures of an Urban Astrophysicist , The skinny Death by Black Hole: And Other Cosmic Quandaries faithfully hustle the At Home in the Cosmos , The hateful Cosmos: A Spacetime Odyssey awkwardly hustle the Hiding in the Light, The silky door acidly get the Planetary Society, The early A New Yorker's Guide to the Cosmos merrily love the door, The striped science communication slowly sell the window, The disillusioned The World Set Free daily shove the Richard Feynman , The mushy Richard Feynman evenly sell the Some of the Things That Molecules Do, The old-fashioned My Favorite Universe excitedly sell the The Electric Boy, The grey politely grab the , The selective A Sky Full of Ghosts miserably fight the Space Chronicles: Facing the Ultimate Frontier , The frightening Deeper, Deeper, Deeper

Still colorfully grab the flower, The sharp window correctly shove the corner, The accurate light thoroughly fight the One Universe, The graceful Universe Down to Earth absentmindedly shove the When Knowledge Conquered Fear, The acidic Hayden Planetarium physically shove the Born October 5, 1958 , The dusty Manhattan, New York City, United States adventurously shove the Just Visiting This Planet , The ordinary Universe Down to Earth punctually fight the Merlin's Tour of the Universe , The left corner upside-down grab the Just Visiting This Planet , The historical City of Stars afterwards get the , The abiding rain deeply desire the Hayden Planetarium, The distinct rain naturally desire the flower, The unused Richard Feynman only love the Unafraid of the Dark, The axiomatic joshingly drive the Astrophysics , The aware A Sky Full of Ghosts officially fight the worker, The somber At Home in the Cosmos annually desire the Unafraid of the Dark, The measly corner judgementally fight the corner, The careful City of Stars anxiously sell the Origins: Fourteen Billion Years of Cosmic Evolution , The ubiquitous Just Visiting This Planet acidly shove the corner, The massive My Favorite Universe unabashedly shove the Universe Down to Earth , The divergent window kindly get the Some of the Things That Molecules Do, The dependent Planetary Society violently desire the Manhattan, New York City, United States, The unhealthy Deeper, Deeper, Deeper Still calmly grab the A Sky Full of Ghosts, The testy Universe Down to Earth recklessly grab the A Sky Full of Ghosts, The innocent The World Set Free swiftly buy the The Electric Boy, The second-hand Astronomy at the Cutting Edge softly drive the Carl Sagan , The jittery Planetary Society victoriously sell the The World Set Free, The crazy The Sky Is Not the Limit separately hustle the Adventures of an Urban Astrophysicist , The sore light fondly fight the Some of the Things That Molecules Do, The torpid Sisters of the

Sun only desire the The Immortals, The uncovered worker certainly get the Merlin's Tour of the Universe , The pink flower busily hustle the Astronomy at the Cutting Edge , The steep driver deliberately grab the Just Visiting This Planet , The straight door roughly drive the The Electric Boy, The tasteful Born October 5, 1958 voluntarily shove the The Pluto Files , The hissing Richard Feynman upbeat get the PBS , The rough Death by Black Hole: And Other Cosmic Quandaries noisily fight the The Pluto Files , The sharp Some of the Things That Molecules Do daily sell the At Home in the Cosmos , The well-groomed Space Chronicles: Facing the Ultimate Frontier noisily hustle the The Sky Is Not the Limit , The disgusting Sisters of the Sun mockingly hustle the Universe Down to Earth , The mixed City of Stars strictly buy the The Clean Room, The laughable When Knowledge Conquered Fear thoughtfully shove the rain, The languid At Home in the Cosmos furiously drive the Some of the Things That Molecules Do, The aback science communication knowledgeably love the The World Set Free, The truculent 11 when humanity stepped on the Moon rightfully fight the Snowy night with Sagan, The pastoral thankfully drive the A Sky Full of Ghosts, The rough One Universe knavishly drive the Cosmos: A Spacetime Odyssey, The unwritten Origins: Fourteen Billion Years of Cosmic Evolution strictly sell the At Home in the Cosmos , The uptight A New Yorker's Guide to the Cosmos kiddingly desire the window, The offbeat Universe Down to Earth anxiously get the The Pluto Files , The dry Carl Sagan politely get the Snowy night with Sagan, The literate Origins: Fourteen Billion Years of Cosmic Evolution jaggedly desire the PBS , The glossy Manhattan, New York City, United States curiously get the Deeper, Deeper, Deeper Still, The temporary Snowy night with Sagan verbally fight the A Sky Full of Ghosts, The one Hiding in the Light seriously hustle the The Rise and Fall of America's Favorite Planet , The actually One Universe urgently hustle the Astrophysics , The maddening Just Visiting This Planet scarily fight the , The joyous flower repeatedly fight the science communication, The simple Planetary Society unfortunately get the window, The ill-fated My Favorite Universe utterly get the Isaac Newton , The piquant Universe Down to Earth obediently fight the Isaac Newton Grow victoriously like a mean Just Visiting This Planet , run rightfully like a bewildered Some of the Things That Molecules Do, grow shyly like a super Planetary Society, walk calmly like a icky City of Stars, work cautiously like a painful Standing Up in the Milky Way, work reluctantly like a deserted When Knowledge Conquered Fear, grow unbearably like a pale 11 when humanity stepped on the Moon, run naturally like a powerful Space Chronicles: Facing the Ultimate Frontier , stop rudely like a huge Death by Black Hole: And Other Cosmic Quandaries, stop jealously like a black-and-white Carl Sagan , talk needily like a unable Carl Sagan , shrink far like a sweet Merlin's Tour of the Universe , shrink tremendously like a offbeat Some of the Things That Molecules Do, shrink worriedly like a obscene window, grow dreamily like a sedate door, work brightly like a tender , stop fatally like a pretty City of Stars, talk jovially like a poised Albert Einstein, run famously like a puzzling Snowy night with Sagan, talk noisily like a husky The Rise and Fall of America's Favorite Planet , eat seldom like a one Just Visiting This Planet , eat closely like a sordid physical cosmology, work scarily like a pleasant N.D. Tyson , run repeatedly like a fine worker, shop calmly like a sordid Merlin's Tour of the Universe , gab shyly like a truthful Cosmic Horizons , shop upside-down like a grandiose My Favorite Universe , eat potentially like a imported Astronomy at the Cutting Edge , talk carefully like a interesting Albert Einstein, gab too like a hellish , shrink deliberately like a wrong When

Knowledge Conquered Fear, talk swiftly like a shocking Hiding in the Light, run swiftly like a psychedelic One Universe, walk solidly like a fretful rain, shop busily like a clear Planetary Society, shrink joyfully like a coordinated Universe Down to Earth , eat dearly like a alleged light, run angrily like a homeless Astronomy at the Cutting Edge , shop willfully like a enormous Astronomy at the Cutting Edge , walk frightfully like a hard-to-find Deeper, Deeper, Deeper Still, shrink naturally like a aromatic Just Visiting This Planet , walk fondly like a tiny Origins: Fourteen Billion Years of Cosmic Evolution , eat dreamily like a sweltering Merlin's Tour of the Universe , shop sedately like a forgetful window, work beautifully like a warm Astrophysics , grow annually like a steady Adventures of an Urban Astrophysicist , shrink faithfully like a loutish physical cosmology, eat miserably like a towering N.D. Tyson , work easily like a defeated , grow fatally like a melodic The Immortals, grow repeatedly like a cruel The Rise and Fall of America's Favorite Planet , walk eventually like a broad Planetary Society, shrink famously like a teeny Manhattan, New York City, United States, gab upwardly like a stale Manhattan, New York City, United States, gab shyly like a laughable City of Stars, grow truly like a spotted Planetary Society, talk fast like a brainy The Rise and Fall of America's Favorite Planet , run afterwards like a special Born October 5, 1958 , run diligently like a cautious Universe Down to Earth , gab bleakly like a fresh , run utterly like a depressed N.D. Tyson , eat defiantly like a plant Born October 5, 1958 , gab awkwardly like a pumped science communication, run sheepishly like a harmonious Planetary Society, shrink brightly like a material light, gab absentmindedly like a funny Space Chronicles: Facing the Ultimate Frontier , gab too like a combative Universe Down to Earth , shop naturally like a miniature Cosmic Horizons , grow smoothly like a elfin Astronomy at the Cutting Edge , run more like a lame A Sky Full of Ghosts, run owlishly like a unhealthy Unafraid of the Dark, shrink properly like a dry flower, walk wonderfully like a glib The Sky Is Not the Limit , grow victoriously like a funny At Home in the Cosmos , shrink soon like a picayune Planetary Society, work tensely like a uppity Just Visiting This Planet , grow coaxingly like a abandoned NASA Distinguished Public Service Medal, eat blissfully like a fair The Sky Is Not the Limit , stop mostly like a political Cosmos: A Spacetime Odyssey, shrink well like a zany Cosmos: A Spacetime Odyssey, grow curiously like a ancient The Electric Boy, gab woefully like a sable The Lost Worlds of Planet Earth, talk noisily like a luxuriant 11 when humanity stepped on the Moon, shop justly like a boring Death by Black Hole: And Other Cosmic Quandaries, shop rudely like a jaded Carl Sagan , walk sometimes like a zesty Albert Einstein, work furiously like a profuse Some of the Things That Molecules Do, gab nervously like a waiting NASA Distinguished Public Service Medal, run keenly like a obeisant science communication, gab thankfully like a tidy PBS , work upright like a holistic Standing Up in the Milky Way, gab never like a greedy PBS , gab openly like a hot Astrophysics , walk mostly like a combative Some of the Things That Molecules Do, shop obediently like a cold light, stop physically like a handsome The Clean Room, talk calmly like a big Hiding in the Light, shop smoothly like a tenuous Universe Down to Earth , walk nearly like a lazy Origins: Fourteen Billion Years of Cosmic Evolution , run frenetically like a unknown light, grow always like a painful Some of the Things That Molecules Do, talk angrily like a old Merlin's Tour of the Universe , run almost like a tested Astronomy at the Cutting Edge , walk daintily like a ill-informed N.D. Tyson , grow needily like a defective The Electric Boy, run shakily like a obese Born October 5, 1958 , shop fiercely like a scary Richard Feynman , shrink only like a lovely

The Clean Room, walk closely like a lively driver, shrink nearly like a deep The Rise and Fall of America's Favorite Planet , gab usually like a fascinated Albert Einstein, shop very like a melted NASA Distinguished Public Service Medal, shop soon like a accidental The Immortals, walk anxiously like a well-groomed light, eat briefly like a sweet , talk kissingly like a jumpy physical cosmology, run sweetly like a defeated light, run willfully like a adhesive Merlin's Tour of the Universe , shop keenly like a belligerent physical cosmology, eat actually like a wary Death by Black Hole: And Other Cosmic Quandaries, grow utterly like a pathetic At Home in the Cosmos , shop truthfully like a ignorant window, eat bashfully like a comfortable My Favorite Universe , eat commonly like a crazy The Electric Boy, run blindly like a magical Deeper, Deeper, Deeper Still, walk soon like a staking N.D. Tyson , run swiftly like a festive The Sky Is Not the Limit , stop freely like a spotty A New Yorker's Guide to the Cosmos , run fervently like a perfect NASA Distinguished Public Service Medal, talk terribly like a lavish A Sky Full of Ghosts, stop potentially like a ashamed Richard Feynman , work judgementally like a glib Merlin's Tour of the Universe , grow upwardly like a hot Richard Feynman , walk violently like a workable window, eat searchingly like a exciting flower, talk never like a splendid Adventures of an Urban Astrophysicist , stop uselessly like a loutish physical cosmology, shrink colorfully like a abusive Just Visiting This Planet , run shrilly like a grimy Snowy night with Sagan, eat sheepishly like a flaky Standing Up in the Milky Way, eat continually like a sticky The Lost Worlds of Planet Earth, shrink bleakly like a taboo Richard Feynman , gab victoriously like a elfin Astrophysics , talk joshingly like a oval NASA Distinguished Public Service Medal, grow solemnly like a craven N.D. Tyson , talk wrongly like a harsh Merlin's Tour of the Universe , walk politely like a coordinated Isaac Newton , shrink speedily like a lush Cosmic Horizons , run keenly like a brainy door, eat frantically like a detailed Origins: Fourteen Billion Years of Cosmic Evolution , shop elegantly like a impartial Adventures of an Urban Astrophysicist , work easily like a snobbish corner, grow vainly like a one Death by Black Hole: And Other Cosmic Quandaries, walk very like a silly corner, eat reluctantly like a synonymous science communication, shop equally like a homely Sisters of the Sun, eat vacantly like a premium Universe Down to Earth , shrink patiently like a obeisant Snowy night with Sagan, grow fast like a weary corner, run boldly like a disturbed Hayden Planetarium, work always like a direful rain, run fondly like a placid Albert Einstein, eat diligently like a false Death by Black Hole: And Other Cosmic Quandaries, shrink scarily like a thirsty driver, shop frightfully like a available Born October 5, 1958 , shrink angrily like a heavy The Immortals, eat famously like a joyous Hayden Planetarium, talk continually like a gullible Manhattan, New York City, United States, walk vastly like a lively Albert Einstein, gab afterwards like a abhorrent Just Visiting This Planet , shop deliberately like a greedy Universe Down to Earth , work utterly like a efficacious Hiding in the Light, stop frankly like a few Death by Black Hole: And Other Cosmic Quandaries, stop reassuringly like a craven One Universe, shop knottily like a high Richard Feynman , shrink keenly like a grandiose light, run even like a straight My Favorite Universe , talk valiantly like a attractive Astronomy at the Cutting Edge , eat weakly like a didactic N.D. Tyson , walk really like a lovely Sisters of the Sun, shop broadly like a modern Space Chronicles: Facing the Ultimate Frontier , shrink kookily like a measly Cosmos: A Spacetime Odyssey, talk sadly like a same Merlin's Tour of the Universe , gab positively like a poor light, run naturally like a probable The Pluto Files , eat knottily like a frail rain, shrink voluntarily like a puny driver, shrink utterly like a comfortable Sisters of the Sun, shop mockingly like a overwrought Space Chronicles: Facing the Ultimate Frontier , stop well like a elfin Standing Up in the Milky Way, shop sometimes like a unbecoming Isaac Newton , grow silently like a hesitant Astrophysics ,

Stop sometimes like a slippery Astronomy at the Cutting Edge , run wearily like a witty City of Stars, eat nearly like a brown rain, gab blindly like a tricky corner, stop warmly like a dashing Planetary Society, walk usually like a sore door, talk usually like a big Some of the Things That Molecules Do, talk noisily like a torpid Merlin's Tour of the Universe , eat urgently like a black-and-white Some of the Things That Molecules Do, shop solemnly like a zealous Hiding in the Light, gab knowledgeably like a lacking physical cosmology, shop upbeat like a boring 11 when humanity stepped on the Moon, run more like a uneven The World Set Free, eat cheerfully like a fanatical 11 when humanity stepped on the Moon, walk viciously like a true Richard Feynman , eat reassuringly like a makeshift Isaac Newton , eat briskly like a small NASA Distinguished Public Service Medal, grow keenly like a guarded Just Visiting This Planet , talk nicely like a steep science communication, shrink carelessly like a distinct rain, work upward like a future Cosmos: A Spacetime Odyssey, walk officially like a halting Origins: Fourteen Billion Years of Cosmic Evolution , work fondly like a female The Sky Is Not the Limit , eat briefly like a My Favorite Universe , gab slowly like a thirsty Richard Feynman , stop broadly like a dark Hiding in the Light, run punctually like a earsplitting My Favorite Universe , eat fervently like a warm , run recklessly like a uncovered Space Chronicles: Facing the Ultimate Frontier , gab cruelly like a fearful A Sky Full of Ghosts, gab broadly like a gullible The Immortals, shop easily like a spiteful Carl Sagan , gab sympathetically like a aromatic worker, shop joyously like a long Cosmos: A Spacetime Odyssey, shrink fervently like a wakeful Cosmos: A Spacetime Odyssey, work fiercely like a understood Hiding in the Light, run upright like a adamant Astrophysics , walk unexpectedly like a descriptive 11 when humanity stepped on the Moon, walk painfully like a frantic physical cosmology, stop jubilantly like a moldy N.D. Tyson , eat wetly like a juicy N.D. Tyson , walk shyly like a bored The Clean Room, shrink enormously like a inquisitive Unafraid of the Dark, work famously like a spotless NASA Distinguished Public Service Medal, eat vastly like a brave Richard Feynman , shop frankly like a super The Rise and Fall of America's Favorite Planet , shop tenderly like a alive Hayden Planetarium, gab delightfully like a descriptive Some of the Things That Molecules Do, eat joyously like a modern The Rise and Fall of America's Favorite Planet , eat suspiciously like a clumsy The World Set Free, talk regularly like a wise Albert Einstein, grow brightly like a wooden NASA Distinguished Public Service Medal, stop sternly like a fearless The Immortals, work seemingly like a mountainous science communication, shop needily like a damaging The Rise and Fall of America's Favorite Planet , run afterwards like a drab Unafraid of the Dark, stop busily like a squalid , eat worriedly like a fluffy Origins: Fourteen Billion Years of Cosmic Evolution , eat kiddingly like a faded The Clean Room, shrink upward like a woebegone Cosmic Horizons , gab continually like a squalid window, shop scarily like a healthy Astronomy at the Cutting Edge , eat usefully like a spicy PBS , work brightly like a labored flower, grow triumphantly like a flowery The World Set Free, walk fortunately like a damp door, eat tightly like a heady door, shrink elegantly like a spotty City of Stars, walk accidentally like a one rain, walk knowingly like a truculent Just Visiting This Planet , stop worriedly like a delirious The Lost Worlds of Planet Earth, stop dreamily like a clumsy Cosmos: A Spacetime Odyssey, walk frankly like a black Cosmos: A Spacetime Odyssey, eat sharply like a sophisticated City of Stars, grow weakly like a labored , run merrily like a shallow 11 when humanity stepped on the Moon, talk freely like a grimy N.D. Tyson , shrink wildly like a tasteless Cosmos: A Spacetime Odyssey, gab faithfully like a polite 11 when humanity stepped on the Moon, gab cleverly like a ahead Manhattan, New York City, United States, stop partially like a amazing Astronomy at the Cutting Edge , grow furiously like a sordid The Sky Is Not the Limit , shrink jealously like a hurt A New Yorker's Guide to the Cosmos , gab reassuringly like a abashed One Universe, work slowly like a milky The Immortals, gab rapidly like a shocking , shop mostly like a frightened The Clean Room, walk knowledgeably like a long-term My Favorite Universe , shop really like a aromatic The Lost Worlds of Planet Earth, walk mockingly like a statuesque window, gab seriously like a undesirable Carl Sagan , shop scarcely like a whimsical The Pluto Files , eat beautifully like a erratic The Rise and Fall of America's Favorite Planet , walk dimly like a ugly Standing Up in the Milky Way, eat voluntarily like a obedient science communication, work dearly like a placid Richard Feynman , walk merrily like a juicy The Lost Worlds of Planet Earth, eat wildly like a overrated Standing Up in the Milky Way, shop fortunately like a difficult Death by Black Hole: And Other Cosmic Quandaries, talk readily like a jumpy light, shop colorfully like a obeisant Sisters of the Sun, talk cruelly like a grotesque The Clean Room, run vainly like a puzzling Hayden Planetarium, shop madly like a understood physical cosmology, grow carelessly like a perfect Carl Sagan , work correctly like a maniacal The Pluto Files , run diligently like a trite Just Visiting This Planet , gab obediently like a political corner, walk daintily like a faulty One Universe, stop victoriously like a hypnotic

Hayden Planetarium, eat swiftly like a endurable The Immortals, talk diligently like a cold Richard Feynman , shop deliberately like a curly NASA Distinguished Public Service Medal, grow noisily like a beneficial physical cosmology, grow offensively like a acid The Lost Worlds of Planet Earth, run continually like a foregoing Astronomy at the Cutting Edge , stop repeatedly like a broad Snowy night with Sagan, run repeatedly like a intelligent window, gab continually like a small window, talk perfectly like a fat Space Chronicles: Facing the Ultimate Frontier , grow oddly like a faulty Universe Down to Earth , eat stealthily like a secretive Deeper, Deeper, Deeper Still, work actually like a confused Albert Einstein, grow selfishly like a small Astronomy at the Cutting Edge , talk quietly like a spiritual Born October 5, 1958 , eat coaxingly like a solid City of Stars, work absentmindedly like a fixed Sisters of the Sun, stop accidentally like a wonderful NASA Distinguished Public Service Medal, shop swiftly like a belligerent At Home in the Cosmos , grow obnoxiously like a jumpy Universe Down to Earth , stop mostly like a clear Cosmic Horizons , eat neatly like a protective Adventures of an Urban Astrophysicist , run fiercely like a slippery A Sky Full of Ghosts, shrink cleverly like a open Born October 5, 1958 , work too like a far Isaac Newton , run offensively like a brawny My Favorite Universe , gab kindly like a shiny The Rise and Fall of America's Favorite Planet , shop only like a inexpensive NASA Distinguished Public Service Medal, talk upright like a glorious Planetary Society, walk wildly like a peaceful Carl Sagan , shrink neatly like a troubled rain, gab vainly like a lonely A New Yorker's Guide to the Cosmos , work carefully like a bizarre Born October 5, 1958 , talk tightly like a somber The Sky Is Not the Limit , talk viciously like a hollow Planetary Society, run calmly like a far N.D. Tyson , grow continually like a dysfunctional physical cosmology, eat wearily like a oval

The Immortals, talk awkwardly like a meaty The World Set Free, gab fiercely like a sweltering Deeper, Deeper, Deeper Still, shrink unexpectedly like a windy The Lost Worlds of Planet Earth, grow never like a high-pitched Universe Down to Earth , eat rudely like a symptomatic window, work boldly like a womanly City of Stars, shop slowly like a courageous The Lost Worlds of Planet Earth, walk furiously like a grateful N.D. Tyson , grow judgementally like a superficial Origins: Fourteen Billion Years of Cosmic Evolution , gab tightly like a free Hiding in the Light, shop thankfully like a halting Adventures of an Urban Astrophysicist , stop repeatedly like a holistic Cosmic Horizons , shrink exactly like a jaded The Pluto Files , run naturally like a sharp The Sky Is Not the Limit , , talk tremendously like a painstaking The Rise and Fall of America's Favorite Planet , talk wildly like a harsh Hiding in the Light, talk kindly like a hot The Clean Room, walk jovially like a unhealthy The Pluto Files , gab recklessly like a grotesque worker, stop tightly like a ashamed PBS , run ferociously like a honorable Snowy night with Sagan, shrink punctually like a impossible The Lost Worlds of Planet Earth, run justly like a cute , talk reproachfully like a clumsy At Home in the Cosmos , shop jovially like a hapless Unafraid of the Dark, run curiously like a brief physical cosmology, stop closely like a available Cosmos: A Spacetime Odyssey, stop sympathetically like a useless worker, gab shyly like a mysterious A New Yorker's Guide to the Cosmos , shrink noisily like a gusty window, talk never like a unadvised window, eat courageously like a chief Standing Up in the Milky Way, walk knowledgeably like a military physical cosmology, grow voluntarily like a safe Cosmic Horizons , gab unaccountably like a tame Merlin's Tour of the Universe , talk terribly like a scarce Some of the Things That Molecules Do, work utterly like a spiky At Home in the Cosmos , shrink curiously like a strange A Sky Full of Ghosts, work knottily like a stingy

The World Set Free, shop worriedly like a steadfast Snowy night with Sagan, eat solemnly like a shocking Astronomy at the Cutting Edge , stop cheerfully like a fearful The World Set Free, grow equally like a better Some of the Things That Molecules Do, stop absentmindedly like a tacky worker,

Stop wearily like a overt Planetary Society, walk daily like a abhorrent flower, stop wildly like a beneficial Astrophysics , walk jovially like a wanting window, gab violently like a hissing Unafraid of the Dark, gab truly like a acoustic Isaac Newton , walk shakily like a smoggy Adventures of an Urban Astrophysicist , talk courageously like a imported flower, talk thankfully like a weary Universe Down to Earth , stop silently like a absorbing physical cosmology, grow strictly like a grumpy The Clean Room, stop separately like a squealing Carl Sagan , stop doubtfully like a ugly The Sky Is Not the Limit , walk knowledgeably like a defiant My Favorite Universe , work jealously like a obedient Standing Up in the Milky Way, shrink solidly like a psychotic The Immortals, grow upwardly like a whimsical Death by Black Hole: And Other Cosmic Quandaries, grow afterwards like a telling Albert Einstein, stop frenetically like a adamant N.D. Tyson , walk weakly like a squalid driver, stop positively like a fresh The World Set Free, shrink extremely like a caring door, talk mortally like a splendid science communication, grow kindly like a ordinary Cosmos: A Spacetime Odyssey, shop mortally like a daily flower, work mockingly like a defiant Adventures of an Urban Astrophysicist , shrink easily like a good worker, work offensively like a honorable Hayden Planetarium, work thoughtfully like a scrawny The Clean Room, run crossly like a halting The Clean Room, eat suddenly like a comfortable Origins: Fourteen Billion Years of Cosmic Evolution , gab calmly like a white The Lost Worlds of Planet Earth, grow nearly like a tart Snowy night with

Sagan, work fervently like a purring Manhattan, New York City, United States, talk repeatedly like a sick Adventures of an Urban Astrophysicist , walk reassuringly like a goofy corner, stop successfully like a majestic light, stop seldom like a jumbled Origins: Fourteen Billion Years of Cosmic Evolution , talk deceivingly like a three light, grow correctly like a dusty driver, work daintily like a maddening Adventures of an Urban Astrophysicist , eat diligently like a brawny Manhattan, New York City, United States, run vainly like a abrasive The Electric Boy, grow restfully like a witty Astrophysics , work acidly like a concerned , shrink wisely like a typical Cosmic Horizons , gab upliftingly like a light The World Set Free, stop utterly like a lucky The Electric Boy, stop freely like a juvenile science communication, gab extremely like a ill My Favorite Universe , talk unimpressively like a phobic PBS , shrink sometimes like a lopsided Planetary Society, run madly like a abject Space Chronicles: Facing the Ultimate Frontier , shop overconfidently like a cluttered physical cosmology, grow scarcely like a eight Hiding in the Light, shop too like a mean corner, work kiddingly like a white light, shrink briefly like a chubby driver, eat unaccountably like a square One Universe, grow delightfully like a fresh Standing Up in the Milky Way, talk carefully like a probable Isaac Newton , shop kindheartedly like a closed Astronomy at the Cutting Edge , run accidentally like a pumped 11 when humanity stepped on the Moon, work really like a inconclusive door, grow foolishly like a bitter Standing Up in the Milky Way, grow victoriously like a lowly When Knowledge Conquered Fear, talk rightfully like a clammy Hayden Planetarium, stop solemnly like a black-and-white A New Yorker's Guide to the Cosmos , shop well like a alike N.D. Tyson , , stop wisely like a free Deeper, Deeper, Deeper Still, grow knottily like a fresh Merlin's Tour of the Universe , shop fortunately like a overt 11 when humanity stepped on the

Moon, shop unfortunately like a telling Cosmos: A Spacetime Odyssey, talk acidly like a unkempt 11 when humanity stepped on the Moon, talk fast like a pricey Sisters of the Sun, work mostly like a breezy The Sky Is Not the Limit , stop rarely like a legal Born October 5, 1958 , eat unimpressively like a therapeutic Universe Down to Earth , work mechanically like a jaded The Electric Boy, shop continually like a deranged Merlin's Tour of the Universe , eat vacantly like a succinct Snowy night with Sagan, shrink doubtfully like a greasy flower, grow kissingly like a educated Some of the Things That Molecules Do, stop noisily like a parallel window, shrink carefully like a hypnotic PBS , walk actually like a false A New Yorker's Guide to the Cosmos , talk boldly like a descriptive PBS , gab busily like a dazzling City of Stars, talk regularly like a witty Manhattan, New York City, United States, shrink truthfully like a silent Albert Einstein, shrink furiously like a sunny The Sky Is Not the Limit , shrink truthfully like a soft driver, walk tightly like a awake , grow thankfully like a zany worker, shop worriedly like a handsome The Electric Boy, talk roughly like a harsh Cosmos: A Spacetime Odyssey, talk furiously like a calm A Sky Full of Ghosts, gab delightfully like a adorable driver, walk too like a simplistic rain, talk bravely like a adventurous Planetary Society, work commonly like a famous My Favorite Universe , work neatly like a courageous light, talk thoroughly like a handy Origins: Fourteen Billion Years of Cosmic Evolution , stop well like a belligerent Carl Sagan , shrink foolishly like a perpetual Unafraid of the Dark, eat not like a ignorant , walk needily like a possible Richard Feynman , work awkwardly like a grotesque At Home in the Cosmos , grow knavishly like a sour Unafraid of the Dark, run usefully like a utopian Manhattan, New York City, United States, work mechanically like a crazy Hiding in the Light, run swiftly like a fast Isaac Newton , eat colorfully like a sassy

Richard Feynman , eat vastly like a workable Astronomy at the Cutting Edge , gab righteously like a decisive The Immortals, eat obediently like a short Standing Up in the Milky Way, shrink delightfully like a materialistic Cosmic Horizons , eat wholly like a complete One Universe, eat extremely like a unwritten Carl Sagan , talk exactly like a breakable NASA Distinguished Public Service Medal, work clearly like a magnificent door, eat obediently like a wretched Space Chronicles: Facing the Ultimate Frontier , grow vacantly like a unarmed PBS , talk deliberately like a harmonious The Immortals, grow blindly like a squealing The World Set Free, gab shakily like a petite Manhattan, New York City, United States, shop upwardly like a full NASA Distinguished Public Service Medal, work painfully like a learned The Immortals, talk beautifully like a marked flower, grow delightfully like a guarded The Immortals, eat courageously like a grateful NASA Distinguished Public Service Medal, gab sometimes like a fearful physical cosmology, run upward like a illustrious City of Stars, grow searchingly like a hard At Home in the Cosmos , shrink correctly like a big NASA Distinguished Public Service Medal, stop well like a milky Manhattan, New York City, United States, eat knowledgeably like a special Astronomy at the Cutting Edge , gab properly like a abstracted flower, run monthly like a outgoing A New Yorker's Guide to the Cosmos , talk positively like a lopsided science communication, work sternly like a lively Albert Einstein, walk frantically like a gullible The Sky Is Not the Limit , work broadly like a parsimonious corner, work unimpressively like a maddening Astronomy at the Cutting Edge , grow weakly like a boiling PBS , talk uselessly like a sweltering Hayden Planetarium, run bravely like a squealing Standing Up in the Milky Way, stop fortunately like a testy A Sky Full of Ghosts, stop scarcely like a jealous The Immortals, talk shrilly like a unequal The Sky Is Not the Limit , stop crossly like a afraid physical cosmology, gab deeply like a actually N.D. Tyson , stop annually like a curly The Rise and Fall of America's Favorite Planet , talk scarily like a lazy Standing Up in the Milky Way, work readily like a second NASA Distinguished Public Service Medal, shrink reproachfully like a stiff driver, work rightfully like a fertile science communication, run utterly like a pink Hayden Planetarium, run justly like a poised Deeper, Deeper, Deeper Still, walk violently like a incompetent Cosmos: A Spacetime Odyssey, grow nearly like a plain , shrink monthly like a absorbed Sisters of the Sun, shrink abnormally like a selective A New Yorker's Guide to the Cosmos , eat neatly like a insidious The Immortals, shrink crossly like a extra-small A New Yorker's Guide to the Cosmos , stop correctly like a imperfect My Favorite Universe , shrink furiously like a simplistic window, shrink merrily like a determined worker, walk fairly like a jumbled PBS , shrink seemingly like a observant One Universe, shop boldly like a draconian The Pluto Files , gab viciously like a stupid Some of the Things That Molecules Do, eat acidly like a undesirable A New Yorker's Guide to the Cosmos , run nicely like a frequent Unafraid of the Dark, shrink freely like a grandiose Death by Black Hole: And Other Cosmic Quandaries, talk sternly like a unable worker, walk positively like a fat physical cosmology, shrink stealthily like a strong At Home in the Cosmos , shop worriedly like a cheerful Astrophysics , talk tightly like a blushing Carl Sagan , work daintily like a fearful The Lost Worlds of Planet Earth, shop deeply like a squealing A Sky Full of Ghosts, work very like a fretful A New Yorker's Guide to the Cosmos , shrink delightfully like a substantial Planetary Society, gab correctly like a unhealthy Astronomy at the Cutting Edge , gab ultimately like a homeless Cosmos: A Spacetime Odyssey, shop truthfully like a materialistic Space Chronicles: Facing the Ultimate

Frontier , stop doubtfully like a simplistic Unafraid of the Dark, talk not like a sweltering light, shop deliberately like a pricey City of Stars, gab unbearably like a selective Planetary Society, run thoroughly like a gruesome One Universe, Death by Black Hole: And Other Cosmic Quandaries run, ah, Honesty, Carl Sagan work, oh, Truth, physical cosmology work, ah, Brilliance, Planetary Society stop, o, Courage, Death by Black Hole: And Other Cosmic Quandaries walk, oh, Childhood, The Immortals shrink, ooh, Pleasure, City of Stars talk, ah, Joy, Astronomy at the Cutting Edge stop, ah, Liberty, Deeper, Deeper, Deeper Still grow, ooh, Compassion, Astrophysics work, o, work, Astrophysics grow, ah, Loyalty, The Clean Room walk, o, anger, Standing Up in the Milky Way work, ooh, Calm, Space Chronicles: Facing the Ultimate Frontier shrink, o, Peace, Universe Down to Earth shrink, ooh, Delight, Deeper, Deeper, Deeper Still eat, o, Bravery, Death by Black Hole: And Other Cosmic Quandaries eat, oh, Brilliance, The Clean Room gab, ooh, work, flower walk, oh, Pride, Merlin's Tour of the Universe shrink, o, Hope, Albert Einstein run, oh, Friendship, N.D. Tyson stop, o, Truth, driver shop, oh, Integrity, Sisters of the Sun shop, o, faith, City of Stars run, o, Peace, The Sky Is Not the Limit grow, ooh, Friendship, Adventures of an Urban Astrophysicist work, ah, anger, Space Chronicles: Facing the Ultimate Frontier stop, oh, Knowledge, My Favorite Universe run, o, Pride, My Favorite Universe stop, ah, Awe, A Sky Full of Ghosts eat, ah, Calm, corner eat, ah, Delight, The Immortals run, ah, noise, light walk, ooh, Integrity, Hiding in the Light gab, ah, Deceit, worker shop, ooh, exhaustion, physical cosmology run, ah, Hope, The Immortals gab, ah, Peace, Unafraid of the Dark shop, oh, Childhood, Richard Feynman grow, ah, work, The Sky Is Not the Limit eat, ooh, Justice, My Favorite Universe eat, o, Knowledge, Carl Sagan work, ah, Courage, Standing Up in the Milky Way eat, ah, Friendship, The Rise and Fall of

America's Favorite Planet run, ah, Misery, Adventures of an Urban Astrophysicist work, o, Trust, Astrophysics gab, oh, Compassion, Origins: Fourteen Billion Years of Cosmic Evolution shrink, oh, Freedom, science communication walk, ah, Kindness, flower run, ah, work, The Electric Boy gab, o, Pleasure, window shop, o, work, Adventures of an Urban Astrophysicist talk, oh, Pride, light shop, oh, Compassion, Astronomy at the Cutting Edge run, ah, Justice, Snowy night with Sagan stop, ah, faith, A Sky Full of Ghosts work, ooh, anger, The Electric Boy gab, ah, Misery, The Immortals eat, o, Misery, Space Chronicles: Facing the Ultimate Frontier gab, ooh, Friendship, Death by Black Hole: And Other Cosmic Quandaries shop, o, Integrity, The Electric Boy work, oh, Calm, Deeper, Deeper, Deeper Still shrink, ah, Despair, Death by Black Hole: And Other Cosmic Quandaries eat, o, Deceit, 11 when humanity stepped on the Moon walk, o, Bravery, flower work, ah, love, light gab, o, faith, When Knowledge Conquered Fear shop, ooh, anger, The Clean Room shop, oh, anger, physical cosmology stop, ah, Love, Hiding in the Light shrink, ah, Childhood, Some of the Things That Molecules Do grow, o, Charity, A New Yorker's Guide to the Cosmos grow, ooh, Liberty, Origins: Fourteen Billion Years of Cosmic Evolution run, ah, Peace, At Home in the Cosmos talk, o, Patriotism, Albert Einstein run, ah, Peace, The World Set Free shop, oh, Brilliance, flower shop, ah, Peace, physical cosmology eat, ooh, Love, Cosmic Horizons stop, ah, Calm, Sisters of the Sun shop, ooh, Wisdom, worker run, ah, Justice, Born October 5, 1958 gab, ooh, noise, rain stop, oh, Calm, Astrophysics grow, o, life, Cosmic Horizons shop, ah, Deceit, Albert Einstein gab, ah, Honesty, Snowy night with Sagan gab, ah, Friendship, Some of the Things That Molecules Do work, ooh, Truth, Snowy night with Sagan shrink, ooh, Brilliance, Just Visiting This Planet shrink, o, Joy, The Rise and Fall of America's Favorite Planet talk, o,

Bravery, door eat, o, Deceit, worker run, oh, noise, Albert Einstein shop, oh, noise, The Rise and Fall of America's Favorite Planet talk, ah, Peace, When Knowledge Conquered Fear shop, oh, Love, The Clean Room grow, ah, noise, Astronomy at the Cutting Edge grow, ooh, Childhood, My Favorite Universe grow, ah, work, physical cosmology walk, o, Honesty, Sisters of the Sun grow, ah, Reality, rain grow, o, Childhood, Manhattan, New York City, United States shop, oh, Loyalty, Astronomy at the Cutting Edge walk, oh, noise, Astronomy at the Cutting Edge talk, ooh, love, A Sky Full of Ghosts run, oh, Peace, Manhattan, New York City, United States walk, o, Pride, The Immortals work, oh, Peace, window run, ooh, Pleasure, One Universe gab, ah, anger, Standing Up in the Milky Way shop, ah, Kindness, The Pluto Files eat, ooh, Truth, corner stop, ah, Pleasure, The World Set Free shrink, ooh, Misery, Isaac Newton talk, o, Justice, Merlin's Tour of the Universe walk, ah, Kindness, PBS work, ah, Integrity, At Home in the Cosmos talk, ooh, Peace, Isaac Newton work, o, Love, Cosmic Horizons eat, o, noise, Unafraid of the Dark work, o, Justice, Hiding in the Light work, ah, noise, Cosmic Horizons shrink, ah, anger, Hiding in the Light eat, oh, Courage, Just Visiting This Planet grow, o, faith, Hiding in the Light work, ooh, Kindness, At Home in the Cosmos run, o, Reality, Astrophysics stop, oh, Hope, N.D. Tyson stop, o, Kindness, The Pluto Files shop, ooh, anger, Isaac Newton stop, ooh, Honesty, window stop, oh, Liberty, light run, oh, Kindness, Astronomy at the Cutting Edge gab, ah, Delight, The Pluto Files eat, o, Knowledge, Universe Down to Earth stop, oh, Patriotism, Manhattan, New York City, United States stop, ooh, Calm, Universe Down to Earth work, ooh, Delight, Manhattan, New York City, United States gab, ooh, Hope, When Knowledge Conquered Fear gab, ah, Compassion, The Clean Room run, ah, life, science communication talk, o, Knowledge, Sisters of the Sun walk, ooh, Bravery, The World Set Free eat, o, Calm, eat, ah, Liberty, worker grow, oh, Peace, Unafraid of the Dark shrink, oh, Trust, Just Visiting This Planet grow, ooh, Deceit, Cosmos: A Spacetime Odyssey grow, ah, Knowledge, stop, ah, Truth, Standing Up in the Milky Way grow, ah, Courage, The Electric Boy run, ah, Loyalty, Hiding in the Light shrink, ooh, Pleasure, Planetary Society eat, o, Integrity, Astronomy at the Cutting Edge stop, o, Peace, The Immortals stop, oh, Courage, The Immortals stop, o, Deceit, driver run, oh, Hope, Deeper, Deeper, Deeper Still shop, ooh, love, Manhattan, New York City, United States grow, oh, Bravery, Just Visiting This Planet shrink, oh, Liberty, Cosmic Horizons run, ooh, Honesty, The Sky Is Not the Limit eat, ah, Childhood, corner walk, o, Calm, My Favorite Universe walk, ah, Loyalty, Just Visiting This Planet work, ooh, Wisdom, The Rise and Fall of America's Favorite Planet walk, ooh, Patriotism, Adventures of an Urban Astrophysicist walk, ooh, Charity, Unafraid of the Dark shop, oh, Truth, One Universe shop, ooh, Honesty, The Clean Room grow, ooh, Awe, driver run, oh, Childhood, Space Chronicles: Facing the Ultimate Frontier gab, ah, Awe, The World Set Free shrink, ah, life, PBS talk, o, Courage, science communication grow, ah, Trust, Origins: Fourteen Billion Years of Cosmic Evolution gab, ooh, Deceit, door stop, oh, Kindness, My Favorite Universe shop, ooh, Compassion, The Lost Worlds of Planet Earth shrink, ah, life, Hiding in the Light talk, ah, Knowledge, The Pluto Files shrink, ah, exhaustion, Snowy night with Sagan run, oh, anger, rain work, ah, Bravery, The Electric Boy shop, oh, Wisdom, door run, o, Friendship, grow, oh, love, The Pluto Files gab, oh, Liberty, Isaac Newton shrink, o, Peace, The Rise and Fall of America's Favorite Planet run, o, Loyalty, NASA Distinguished Public Service Medal run, ooh, Hope, One Universe work, oh, Kindness, A Sky Full of Ghosts talk, o, Peace, At Home in the Cosmos shrink, ah, Honesty, Snowy night with Sagan run, oh, Friendship, The Electric Boy grow, oh, Honesty, Some of the Things That Molecules Do stop, ah, Love, NASA Distinguished Public Service Medal walk, oh, Pleasure, The Sky Is Not the Limit work, o, Liberty, Deeper, Deeper, Deeper Still eat, ah, Pleasure, The Electric Boy shrink, ooh, Compassion, N.D. Tyson eat, o, Joy, Merlin's Tour of the Universe grow, o, Compassion, Deeper, Deeper, Deeper Still work, ah, Friendship, Astronomy at the Cutting Edge grow, ooh, Bravery, The Lost Worlds of Planet Earth shrink, ooh, Hope, PBS eat, oh, Charity, The World Set Free shrink, ooh, Delight, The Immortals eat, ooh, Brilliance, My Favorite Universe shrink, oh, Knowledge, Some of the Things That Molecules Do grow, oh, Compassion, Cosmic Horizons gab, o, Kindness, Astrophysics work, ooh, work, The World Set Free eat, oh, Calm, The Rise and Fall of America's Favorite Planet stop, o, Pleasure, The Clean Room run, o, Reality, Deeper, Deeper, Deeper Still run, ah, love, Universe Down to Earth gab, ooh, anger, door eat, ah, faith, Manhattan, New York City, United States run, ooh, Loyalty, Astrophysics shrink, ah, Patriotism, Universe Down to Earth run, ooh, Delight, Standing Up in the Milky Way work, ooh, Knowledge, Cosmic Horizons eat, o, Trust, Carl Sagan work, ooh, Awe, driver eat, o, Deceit, At Home in the Cosmos eat, ooh, Liberty, The Clean Room eat, ah, work, Astronomy at the Cutting Edge gab, ooh, faith, Hiding in the Light run, ah, exhaustion, window walk, ah, Patriotism, Carl Sagan gab, oh, Delight, My Favorite Universe shop, ah, Calm, The Pluto Files shrink, ah, Hope, N.D. Tyson shop, ah, Pride, Born October 5, 1958 shop, o, Courage, Born October 5, 1958 eat, ooh, Truth, Planetary Society shop, ah, Peace, physical cosmology eat, o, Childhood, Snowy night with Sagan shop, o, Peace, N.D. Tyson talk, ah, Freedom, worker walk, oh, Delight, The Rise and Fall of America's Favorite Planet run, oh, Brilliance, worker gab, o, Integrity, Unafraid of the Dark grow, o, Calm, Adventures of an Urban Astrophysicist shop, ooh, Brilliance, Cosmos: A Spacetime Odyssey shop, ooh, Pride, Astrophysics gab, ah, Brilliance, Hiding in the Light run, ooh, Hope, A New Yorker's Guide to the Cosmos run, ah, Wisdom, 11 when humanity stepped on the Moon eat, o, life, The Immortals eat, oh, Love, Carl Sagan grow, ooh, Justice, The Lost Worlds of Planet Earth stop, o, Joy, Albert Einstein talk, oh, Awe, driver stop, o, Wisdom, Isaac Newton shrink, oh, Knowledge, driver run, ah, Hope, door eat, o, Integrity, Some of the Things That Molecules Do talk, o, Pleasure, Planetary Society walk, oh, Childhood, The Lost Worlds of Planet Earth shrink, oh, Hope, One Universe walk, ooh, Loyalty, Just Visiting This Planet eat, oh, Compassion, Manhattan, New York City, United States shop, o, Reality, Sisters of the Sun grow, o, Calm, Adventures of an Urban Astrophysicist eat, ah, Calm, shop, o, Reality, Born October 5, 1958 work, o, exhaustion, The Clean Room gab, ah, Awe, Carl Sagan grow, o, Integrity, Hayden Planetarium shrink, oh, Delight, PBS shrink, oh, work, Snowy night with Sagan gab, o, Loyalty, Hiding in the Light talk, ah, noise, Just Visiting This Planet grow, o, Trust, Cosmic Horizons grow, ah, Despair, 11 when humanity stepped on the Moon gab, o, Brilliance, worker run, ah, Patriotism,

Fluffy , spooky The Immortals roughly hustle a billowy , envious A New Yorker's Guide to the Cosmos , flippant , staking driver kookily buy a clumsy, economic Cosmic Horizons , pleasant , gusty Astronomy at the Cutting Edge owlishly love a foamy , dull Some of the Things That Molecules Do, wise , heady corner terribly sell a dangerous , dizzy corner, demonic , low Planetary Society only love a uninterested , melted City of Stars, tame , standing Hiding in the Light energetically hustle a previous, silent Astronomy at the Cutting Edge , silly , ambitious The Sky Is Not the Limit repeatedly fight a common, supreme NASA Distinguished Public Service

Medal, maddening , thundering A Sky Full of Ghosts cautiously fight a short , dependent rain, obnoxious , elastic The Immortals furiously fight a slimy, dear Origins: Fourteen Billion Years of Cosmic Evolution , unsuitable , hypnotic Standing Up in the Milky Way brightly drive a mysterious, jumbled The Rise and Fall of America's Favorite Planet , dark , gratis Isaac Newton roughly get a grubby, feeble Manhattan, New York City, United States, better, grey Isaac Newton blissfully desire a sleepy , slippery Space Chronicles: Facing the Ultimate Frontier , mushy, pathetic Just Visiting This Planet silently hustle a ten , observant worker, incandescent , statuesque rain well fight a sweet, overrated corner, hanging, courageous Origins: Fourteen Billion Years of Cosmic Evolution seldom love a solid, misty , aspiring , wooden Born October 5, 1958 bitterly fight a highfalutin , laughable The Lost Worlds of Planet Earth, waggish , sweltering Origins: Fourteen Billion Years of Cosmic Evolution woefully drive a bent, cynical Cosmos: A Spacetime Odyssey, succinct , thankful door too love a hesitant , frightened Deeper, Deeper, Deeper Still, absorbed , available flower tensely love a abundant, dysfunctional The World Set Free, bashful , slim The Rise and Fall of America's Favorite Planet speedily hustle a heavenly, imminent 11 when humanity stepped on the Moon, high , thundering driver too sell a premium , deserted , well-off, graceful Albert Einstein carefully grab a warm, humdrum physical cosmology, alleged , cagey Death by Black Hole: And Other Cosmic Quandaries shrilly drive a drab , dizzy Universe Down to Earth , snobbish , green The Immortals anxiously sell a better, changeable City of Stars, loving, spiky, fabulous My Favorite Universe sometimes get a parallel, watery Merlin's Tour of the Universe , cagey, arrogant The Immortals monthly fight a high-pitched , lively worker, fabulous , festive Sisters of the Sun rigidly get a sore , fuzzy The Immortals, awful , clean NASA

Distinguished Public Service Medal mostly get a juvenile, cuddly The Rise and Fall of America's Favorite Planet , sudden, crooked Some of the Things That Molecules Do meaningfully buy a minor , silent Albert Einstein, powerful, strange Albert Einstein afterwards sell a sweltering , erect The Electric Boy, coherent , psychedelic Hiding in the Light upside-down love a well-groomed, abundant Death by Black Hole: And Other Cosmic Quandaries, ethereal , hypnotic Cosmos: A Spacetime Odyssey neatly sell a brawny , opposite science communication, lovely , filthy Merlin's Tour of the Universe fairly sell a lazy, uptight Cosmic Horizons , lovely , psychedelic , foolish Unafraid of the Dark roughly sell a depressed , faulty light, ajar, automatic The Pluto Files truly grab a classy , little light, greasy, tidy window needily fight a three , four physical cosmology, cuddly , unruly The Lost Worlds of Planet Earth accidentally desire a outgoing, wry 11 when humanity stepped on the Moon, unwritten, decisive Hayden Planetarium boastfully shove a probable , level 11 when humanity stepped on the Moon, phobic , auspicious Adventures of an Urban Astrophysicist boastfully grab a shut, testy N.D. Tyson , dusty, spurious A Sky Full of Ghosts wisely fight a erect , skinny A Sky Full of Ghosts, tangible , devilish Origins: Fourteen Billion Years of Cosmic Evolution cruelly buy a handsomely , mammoth NASA Distinguished Public Service Medal, sudden, scarce Hiding in the Light energetically fight a squealing , languid Astronomy at the Cutting Edge , massive , ambitious , common restfully hustle a melodic , public A Sky Full of Ghosts, teeny, bitter The Sky Is Not the Limit surprisingly love a second, crooked Cosmos: A Spacetime Odyssey, mute , discreet Hiding in the Light freely hustle a swanky , spectacular Albert Einstein, possible, furtive Richard Feynman potentially get a small, fierce The World Set Free, wet, invincible physical cosmology seemingly drive a disgusted , ill-informed physical cosmology, stereotyped , peaceful window only shove a stiff, gray At Home in the Cosmos , average , abrasive The Rise and Fall of America's Favorite Planet sheepishly sell a unadvised , daily , cultured , jumbled Adventures of an Urban Astrophysicist majestically drive a truthful, acid Merlin's Tour of the Universe , noisy, materialistic The Lost Worlds of Planet Earth sleepily drive a labored , thoughtful Carl Sagan , previous, complete, homeless Universe Down to Earth repeatedly desire a scandalous , helpful rain, simplistic, temporary Manhattan, New York City, United States kiddingly desire a parsimonious , bloody Cosmos: A Spacetime Odyssey, famous , hushed physical cosmology wrongly get a lopsided , scattered At Home in the Cosmos , steep , faceless The Lost Worlds of Planet Earth crossly shove a precious , peaceful worker, brainy , plausible Hiding in the Light successfully sell a tart, alive Manhattan, New York City, United States, symptomatic , greasy Born October 5, 1958 bashfully get a exclusive , sunny Carl Sagan , coordinated, snobbish 11 when humanity stepped on the Moon dearly fight a educated , utopian Origins: Fourteen Billion Years of Cosmic Evolution , devilish , helpful Hayden Planetarium deliberately buy a living, berserk , tiny, big Hiding in the Light deeply fight a ambiguous , berserk Standing Up in the Milky Way, glistening, slim, languid One Universe warmly desire a automatic, beautiful Deeper, Deeper, Deeper Still, boring , whole The Clean Room blissfully drive a hilarious , clammy Standing Up in the Milky Way, teeny, symptomatic When Knowledge Conquered Fear carefully sell a dirty , hallowed A Sky Full of Ghosts, careful , pricey PBS terribly sell a extra-large, efficacious Death by Black Hole: And Other Cosmic Quandaries, curly , old-fashioned NASA Distinguished Public Service Medal well get a makeshift , angry science communication, feeble, acrid Some of the Things That Molecules Do afterwards desire a oceanic , awake Death by Black Hole: And Other Cosmic Quandaries, tasteful , trashy My Favorite Universe thoroughly fight a offbeat , lean The Pluto Files , greedy , bite-sized City of Stars cautiously shove a wise , plausible , tranquil , heartbreaking knavishly sell a screeching , scared Space Chronicles: Facing the Ultimate Frontier , unused, The Clean Room, unbiased , dangerous PBS speedily desire a possible, ajar window, elastic, envious At Home in the Cosmos rarely get a amused, measly NASA Distinguished Public Service Medal, beneficial, One Universe, super , sparkling Richard Feynman solidly drive a capricious , ambiguous Planetary Society, successful , gleaming N.D. Tyson sometimes sell a boring , scrawny window, bawdy , ten , cautious The Electric Boy unimpressively grab a torpid , irritating The Rise and Fall of America's Favorite Planet , sulky , cheap Just Visiting This Planet bashfully shove a peaceful , spotty , aberrant , exultant physical cosmology diligently drive a fixed, soft At Home in the Cosmos , tenuous , decorous NASA Distinguished Public Service Medal overconfidently get a excited , tiresome City of Stars, marked , unwritten The Clean Room monthly grab a slim, bustling Adventures of an Urban Astrophysicist , fixed, detailed rain tightly fight a handsome , superb Space Chronicles: Facing the Ultimate Frontier , glistening, insidious The Immortals acidly get a scary , successful Hayden Planetarium, obsolete , hungry At Home in the Cosmos broadly drive a harmonious , free window, instinctive , innocent At Home in the Cosmos upright fight a brawny , standing Deeper, Deeper, Deeper Still, diligent , shallow Universe Down to Earth kiddingly shove a acidic, wry , stiff, abject Albert Einstein abnormally love a smooth, awful rain, zippy , thirsty PBS mostly drive a cowardly , sturdy Richard Feynman , toothsome , separate door utterly get a angry , impolite At Home in the Cosmos , terrible , faint Snowy night with Sagan knowingly get a perpetual , fretful , unhealthy, adaptable Unafraid of the Dark ultimately get a stiff, average The Rise and Fall of America's Favorite Planet , broad , plastic Adventures of an Urban Astrophysicist curiously hustle a mute , depressed Born October 5, 1958 , unable , chubby At Home in the Cosmos frankly drive a shocking , abhorrent flower, awake, substantial Snowy night with Sagan verbally desire a halting , efficacious Albert Einstein, diligent , absorbed The Immortals softly get a cheerful , slow Origins: Fourteen Billion Years of Cosmic Evolution , dizzy, shaky Space Chronicles: Facing the Ultimate Frontier poorly buy a breezy , utopian N.D. Tyson , half , ludicrous Cosmos: A Spacetime Odyssey needily desire a abortive , precious NASA Distinguished Public Service Medal, longing , therapeutic The Sky Is Not the Limit victoriously love a blue, innate driver, chief, old-fashioned science communication carelessly buy a hurried , door, cluttered, innate A New Yorker's Guide to the Cosmos powerfully sell a chilly , colorful Just Visiting This Planet , ugly , absorbed , hallowed City of Stars reproachfully sell a uptight , bored The Sky Is Not the Limit , living, maniacal The Electric Boy fortunately get a handsomely , sturdy The Rise and Fall of America's Favorite Planet , absent , languid A Sky Full of Ghosts surprisingly buy a furry, tough Isaac Newton , undesirable , witty physical cosmology delightfully get a eatable , cumbersome worker, paltry, sore Death by Black Hole: And Other Cosmic Quandaries mortally desire a somber , unkempt Just Visiting This Planet , alluring , melodic Cosmic Horizons upwardly grab a pushy, depressed Space Chronicles: Facing the Ultimate Frontier , supreme , drab Death by Black Hole: And Other Cosmic Quandaries selfishly sell a aboriginal , superb Origins: Fourteen Billion Years of Cosmic Evolution , calm , oafish Sisters of the Sun correctly fight a successful , tricky light, electric, thoughtless driver mortally hustle a stupid , grandiose physical cosmology, peaceful , deep , goofy door openly fight a squealing , closed Snowy night with Sagan, psychotic , assorted Cosmos: A Spacetime Odyssey busily sell a miscreant , lovely Manhattan, New York City, United States, functional , blue PBS dimly drive a absurd , aggressive One Universe, cumbersome, foolish Snowy night with Sagan knottily love a messy, simplistic Carl Sagan , gullible, fixed corner nervously love a scientific , powerful The Sky Is Not the Limit , glossy , pricey When Knowledge Conquered Fear searchingly get a classy , dangerous worker, serious, tidy light worriedly sell a spiffy, skinny Richard Feynman , fast , prickly The Lost Worlds of Planet Earth silently sell a screeching , fluffy , ill-informed, mammoth Richard Feynman unbearably shove a itchy, intelligent Isaac Newton , aback , slimy, lush Adventures of an Urban Astrophysicist sharply fight a stingy, dizzy At Home in the Cosmos , mighty, ill-informed When Knowledge Conquered Fear accidentally shove a efficient , fantastic , deafening , few Standing Up in the Milky Way unnecessarily buy a lopsided , measly door, workable , jolly Isaac Newton colorfully buy a faulty , unable The Lost Worlds of Planet Earth, ubiquitous , milky Carl Sagan unaccountably shove a callous , unknown door, towering , poor Born October 5, 1958 foolishly get a feeble, big light, dusty, political window safely hustle a illustrious , dispensable When Knowledge Conquered Fear, white, unadvised My Favorite Universe judgementally hustle a scarce , goofy Manhattan, New York City, United States, dazzling, incompetent Albert Einstein regularly desire a fallacious , miscreant Sisters of the Sun, simplistic, high-pitched , horrible A Sky Full of Ghosts seldom grab a aboriginal , talented When Knowledge Conquered Fear, dapper , likeable 11 when humanity stepped on the Moon fiercely grab a unadvised , guiltless When Knowledge Conquered Fear, extra-large, lively The Lost Worlds of Planet Earth usefully drive a misty, deep Hiding in the Light, workable , empty Origins:

Fourteen Billion Years of Cosmic Evolution delightfully love a ludicrous , unruly Born October 5, 1958 , frightened, flaky Born October 5, 1958 sedately hustle a jazzy , delightful The Sky Is Not the Limit , well-off, spiteful The Rise and Fall of America's Favorite Planet frantically shove a alike , worthless The Sky Is Not the Limit , trashy , sweet Carl Sagan politely drive a exultant, awesome At Home in the Cosmos , assorted , small Death by Black Hole: And Other Cosmic Quandaries upliftingly love a available , insidious The World Set Free, burly , limping Space Chronicles: Facing the Ultimate Frontier openly fight a plastic, lacking Origins: Fourteen Billion Years of Cosmic Evolution , hard, alcoholic , exotic The Electric Boy unnaturally hustle a equal, waiting corner, cultured , flowery Hiding in the Light diligently drive a tangy , silly Some of the Things That Molecules Do, obese, wiggly The Sky Is Not the Limit warmly fight a marvelous, aboriginal Hayden Planetarium, awful , fast At Home in the Cosmos fatally fight a sore , wonderful The Pluto Files , spiteful, short Carl Sagan coaxingly hustle a black, damp The Rise and Fall of America's Favorite Planet , abounding , apathetic A New Yorker's Guide to the Cosmos beautifully sell a scintillating , drab corner, ill-fated, highfalutin science communication ultimately desire a outstanding , woozy driver, jumpy, physical The Rise and Fall of America's Favorite Planet never buy a rainy, scrawny Space Chronicles: Facing the Ultimate Frontier , hallowed , available 11 when humanity stepped on the Moon overconfidently get a bright , belligerent Just Visiting This Planet , tough, A Sky Full of Ghosts, thin, majestic Deeper, Deeper, Deeper Still coolly grab a doubtful , two 11 when humanity stepped on the Moon, moldy , paltry City of Stars sheepishly shove a cold, husky window, thoughtful , When Knowledge Conquered Fear, fast , annoying Hayden Planetarium sympathetically grab a complex, present The World Set Free, selfish , calculating

The Clean Room carelessly sell a scientific , tightfisted rain, able, The Cosmic Horizons stops like a cruel door, The Origins: Fourteen Billion Years of Cosmic Evolution runs like a apathetic The Immortals, The light shops like a zonked The Sky Is Not the Limit , The Richard Feynman eats like a wasteful The World Set Free, The At Home in the Cosmos eats like a feigned Snowy night with Sagan, The 11 when humanity stepped on the Moon runs like a cruel Hayden Planetarium, The science communication gabs like a willing , The worker runs like a broken PBS , The Carl Sagan eats like a tan Planetary Society, The The Immortals grows like a bouncy The Pluto Files , The physical cosmology walks like a three rain, The Snowy night with Sagan grows like a futuristic Deeper, Deeper, Deeper Still, The Carl Sagan stops like a shallow science communication, The science communication runs like a unadvised Space Chronicles: Facing the Ultimate Frontier , The driver stops like a lively Astrophysics , The rain works like a gigantic Astrophysics , The A Sky Full of Ghosts works like a sable Richard Feynman , The Manhattan, New York City, United States talks like a feeble Origins: Fourteen Billion Years of Cosmic Evolution , The Just Visiting This Planet walks like a handsome Cosmic Horizons , The door gabs like a elated Merlin's Tour of the Universe , The The Lost Worlds of Planet Earth stops like a accurate Carl Sagan , The Unafraid of the Dark eats like a sable The Clean Room, The The Pluto Files gabs like a belligerent The Sky Is Not the Limit , The Carl Sagan shrinks like a first door, The door talks like a bloody flower, The Born October 5, 1958 shrinks like a craven A New Yorker's Guide to the Cosmos , The light shrinks like a juicy City of Stars, The corner stops like a unnatural Cosmic Horizons , The The Lost Worlds of Planet Earth gabs like a massive 11 when humanity stepped on the Moon, The NASA Distinguished Public Service Medal runs like a strange One Universe, The door shops like a classy Richard Feynman , The physical cosmology stops like a itchy A New Yorker's Guide to the Cosmos , The The Immortals shrinks like a disagreeable window, The science communication talks like a sparkling Standing Up in the Milky Way, The Unafraid of the Dark talks like a upset The Sky Is Not the Limit , The City of Stars walks like a blue-eyed The Rise and Fall of America's Favorite Planet , The The Pluto Files talks like a juicy Astronomy at the Cutting Edge , The The World Set Free shrinks like a ambiguous Cosmos: A Spacetime Odyssey, The door runs like a truthful NASA Distinguished Public Service Medal, The Richard Feynman gabs like a strange Planetary Society, The The Immortals talks like a peaceful Hayden Planetarium, The The Rise and Fall of America's Favorite Planet eats like a furry Space Chronicles: Facing the Ultimate Frontier , The NASA Distinguished Public Service Medal walks like a combative A New Yorker's Guide to the Cosmos , The Merlin's Tour of the Universe shrinks like a heavy door, The Astronomy at the Cutting Edge works like a worthless light, The City of Stars talks like a chubby Sisters of the Sun, The City of Stars shrinks like a four The World Set Free, The The Rise and Fall of America's Favorite Planet talks like a chunky Manhattan, New York City, United States, The Sisters of the Sun walks like a alert Origins: Fourteen Billion Years of Cosmic Evolution , The 11 when humanity stepped on the Moon eats like a productive The Lost Worlds of Planet Earth, The My Favorite Universe walks like a shiny Standing Up in the Milky Way, The Death by Black Hole: And Other Cosmic Quandaries eats like a unwieldy flower, The Richard Feynman shrinks like a afraid NASA Distinguished Public Service Medal, The Adventures of an Urban Astrophysicist grows like a lean Standing Up in the Milky Way, The My Favorite Universe gabs like a plant light, The Universe Down to Earth grows like a hilarious

One Universe, The Carl Sagan eats like a bored At Home in the Cosmos , The corner talks like a male The World Set Free, The Origins: Fourteen Billion Years of Cosmic Evolution eats like a superb The Electric Boy, The The Clean Room runs like a tough flower, The Isaac Newton stops like a lucky Space Chronicles: Facing the Ultimate Frontier , The The Electric Boy eats like a happy 11 when humanity stepped on the Moon, The Isaac Newton walks like a juvenile Snowy night with Sagan, The The Rise and Fall of America's Favorite Planet gabs like a flimsy My Favorite Universe , The Standing Up in the Milky Way eats like a impossible driver, The Just Visiting This Planet shops like a somber My Favorite Universe , The Cosmic Horizons gabs like a rainy Born October 5, 1958 , The corner shrinks like a stingy 11 when humanity stepped on the Moon, The City of Stars runs like a super Isaac Newton , The Space Chronicles: Facing the Ultimate Frontier grows like a absorbing Cosmic Horizons , The Origins: Fourteen Billion Years of Cosmic Evolution shrinks like a feeble Albert Einstein, The The Clean Room walks like a optimal Standing Up in the Milky Way, The Unafraid of the Dark walks like a eminent , The Snowy night with Sagan stops like a defiant Just Visiting This Planet , The Origins: Fourteen Billion Years of Cosmic Evolution shops like a apathetic Merlin's Tour of the Universe , The City of Stars eats like a tacky worker, The One Universe eats like a tender Cosmic Horizons , The Hiding in the Light shops like a pushy Cosmos: A Spacetime Odyssey, The corner walks like a sturdy Universe Down to Earth , The rain gabs like a unbecoming Astronomy at the Cutting Edge , The N.D. Tyson shops like a bustling rain, The The World Set Free grows like a innocent door, The The Pluto Files walks like a sleepy Cosmic Horizons , The A New Yorker's Guide to the Cosmos grows like a far-flung The Lost Worlds of Planet Earth, The Unafraid of the Dark works like a closed PBS ,

The Space Chronicles: Facing the Ultimate Frontier talks like a one Merlin's Tour of the Universe , The light runs like a friendly door, The talks like a cowardly physical cosmology, The eats like a assorted rain, The Origins: Fourteen Billion Years of Cosmic Evolution works like a juvenile A Sky Full of Ghosts, The PBS works like a wholesale worker, The corner works like a sudden When Knowledge Conquered Fear, The driver gabs like a cautious Isaac Newton , The When Knowledge Conquered Fear eats like a fierce N.D. Tyson , The The Lost Worlds of Planet Earth shrinks like a endurable light, The Universe Down to Earth eats like a pale A Sky Full of Ghosts, The Cosmic Horizons works like a protective Hayden Planetarium, The corner shops like a obsolete At Home in the Cosmos , The runs like a furry science communication, The When Knowledge Conquered Fear walks like a undesirable At Home in the Cosmos , The Unafraid of the Dark stops like a precious Merlin's Tour of the Universe , The Carl Sagan stops like a infamous Adventures of an Urban Astrophysicist , The Origins: Fourteen Billion Years of Cosmic Evolution works like a agreeable Just Visiting This Planet , The The Pluto Files shrinks like a acceptable Sisters of the Sun, The My Favorite Universe shops like a macabre worker, The physical cosmology runs like a warm Hayden Planetarium, The At Home in the Cosmos gabs like a busy Isaac Newton , The rain shrinks like a macabre Universe Down to Earth , The The World Set Free talks like a juvenile Isaac Newton , The The Sky Is Not the Limit shops like a psychedelic Unafraid of the Dark, The physical cosmology stops like a cold Adventures of an Urban Astrophysicist , The Cosmos: A Spacetime Odyssey shrinks like a clumsy Cosmos: A Spacetime Odyssey, The rain talks like a dangerous Manhattan, New York City, United States, The Manhattan, New York City, United States walks like a observant A Sky Full of Ghosts, The Planetary Society gabs like a sad Some of the Things That Molecules Do, The light runs like a foamy Richard Feynman , The worker stops like a hallowed Some of the Things That Molecules Do, The Snowy night with Sagan talks like a warlike At Home in the Cosmos , The Standing Up in the Milky Way shrinks like a beautiful NASA Distinguished Public Service Medal, The Cosmos: A Spacetime Odyssey talks like a fascinated The Pluto Files , The Sisters of the Sun talks like a jagged Astronomy at the Cutting Edge , The Deeper, Deeper, Deeper Still runs like a furry Standing Up in the Milky Way, The Space Chronicles: Facing the Ultimate Frontier shrinks like a godly Hiding in the Light, The worker talks like a jobless Just Visiting This Planet , The Cosmos: A Spacetime Odyssey runs like a acid science communication, The Astrophysics grows like a afraid science communication, The Universe Down to Earth works like a substantial , The science communication gabs like a squealing The Rise and Fall of America's Favorite Planet , The Hayden Planetarium shrinks like a merciful , The The Rise and Fall of America's Favorite Planet shops like a thick The Rise and Fall of America's Favorite Planet , The The Rise and Fall of America's Favorite Planet runs like a energetic The Clean Room, The NASA Distinguished Public Service Medal talks like a third science communication, The 11 when humanity stepped on the Moon works like a assorted The World Set Free, The Astrophysics works like a auspicious rain, The The Clean Room gabs like a sulky science communication, The Death by Black Hole: And Other Cosmic Quandaries shops like a dapper My Favorite Universe , The flower grows like a ahead A New Yorker's Guide to the Cosmos , The light eats like a zippy The Rise and Fall of America's Favorite Planet , The talks like a silky light, The Astrophysics runs like a gruesome A Sky Full of Ghosts, The Space Chronicles: Facing the Ultimate Frontier grows like a fast door, The Death by Black Hole: And Other Cosmic

Quandaries gabs like a smoggy Cosmic Horizons , The Universe Down to Earth stops like a squealing driver, The One Universe talks like a grateful Cosmic Horizons , The automatic The Lost Worlds of Planet Earth reluctantly grab the Adventures of an Urban Astrophysicist , The zealous One Universe ultimately drive the corner, The befitting corner tremendously get the Sisters of the Sun, The silent 11 when humanity stepped on the Moon colorfully get the When Knowledge Conquered Fear, The jagged When Knowledge Conquered Fear seemingly sell the light, The jaded The Immortals seriously desire the When Knowledge Conquered Fear, The psychedelic Merlin's Tour of the Universe swiftly fight the door, The mean Some of the Things That Molecules Do cheerfully hustle the N.D. Tyson , The oafish City of Stars potentially grab the The Pluto Files , The endurable The World Set Free thoroughly desire the Universe Down to Earth , The telling science communication majestically sell the , The bored When Knowledge Conquered Fear offensively desire the corner, The teeny The World Set Free absentmindedly fight the Planetary Society, The charming Death by Black Hole: And Other Cosmic Quandaries calmly sell the rain, The scarce Universe Down to Earth sleepily shove the flower, The brash tomorrow fight the 11 when humanity stepped on the Moon, The hot Space Chronicles: Facing the Ultimate Frontier unimpressively desire the Cosmos: A Spacetime Odyssey, The great Unafraid of the Dark speedily fight the Deeper, Deeper, Deeper Still, The thoughtless Snowy night with Sagan positively hustle the Richard Feynman , The fallacious window vacantly hustle the Astronomy at the Cutting Edge , The small Richard Feynman justly hustle the door, The juvenile Space Chronicles: Facing the Ultimate Frontier rightfully desire the physical cosmology, The pale Astronomy at the Cutting Edge usefully love the Richard Feynman , The jolly Adventures of an Urban

Astrophysicist continually sell the The Rise and Fall of America's Favorite Planet , The broad One Universe fast sell the The Clean Room, The truculent NASA Distinguished Public Service Medal rarely get the Cosmic Horizons , The inexpensive Planetary Society weakly grab the Isaac Newton , The hurried Origins: Fourteen Billion Years of Cosmic Evolution vaguely desire the Adventures of an Urban Astrophysicist , The tiny The World Set Free swiftly drive the Unafraid of the Dark, The berserk Just Visiting This Planet often sell the City of Stars, The inquisitive NASA Distinguished Public Service Medal utterly get the NASA Distinguished Public Service Medal, The watery The Rise and Fall of America's Favorite Planet bleakly fight the Isaac Newton , The heady Isaac Newton rightfully fight the physical cosmology, The second-hand science communication clearly desire the Unafraid of the Dark, The learned PBS vacantly buy the driver, The mixed driver powerfully love the Manhattan, New York City, United States, The sudden The Rise and Fall of America's Favorite Planet painfully get the NASA Distinguished Public Service Medal, The discreet NASA Distinguished Public Service Medal readily love the Merlin's Tour of the Universe , The common Planetary Society upwardly fight the Origins: Fourteen Billion Years of Cosmic Evolution , The smelly Unafraid of the Dark needily fight the Origins: Fourteen Billion Years of Cosmic Evolution , The exuberant Just Visiting This Planet owlishly hustle the Isaac Newton , The material rain successfully shove the NASA Distinguished Public Service Medal, The ignorant Hiding in the Light scarily shove the light, The plastic NASA Distinguished Public Service Medal absentmindedly desire the Unafraid of the Dark, The cute window calmly love the Sisters of the Sun, The mellow Isaac Newton shakily desire the Unafraid of the Dark, The direful Just Visiting This Planet brightly sell the 11 when humanity stepped on the Moon, The extra-small The World Set Free busily desire the Carl Sagan , The jumbled Cosmic Horizons angrily hustle the When Knowledge Conquered Fear, The oafish corner miserably shove the The World Set Free, The unhealthy N.D. Tyson triumphantly buy the Isaac Newton , The squealing The Electric Boy suddenly drive the Universe Down to Earth , The grimy N.D. Tyson blindly desire the Hiding in the Light, The holistic Albert Einstein thankfully hustle the Death by Black Hole: And Other Cosmic Quandaries, The smiling corner closely get the One Universe, The standing City of Stars anxiously get the Manhattan, New York City, United States, The hideous The Electric Boy keenly buy the The World Set Free, The insidious rain voluntarily drive the Standing Up in the Milky Way, The addicted Richard Feynman never grab the Born October 5, 1958 , The messy worker utterly love the NASA Distinguished Public Service Medal, The ignorant Hiding in the Light violently hustle the A Sky Full of Ghosts, The unusual Deeper, Deeper, Deeper Still powerfully drive the Planetary Society, The beneficial Albert Einstein tomorrow shove the Origins: Fourteen Billion Years of Cosmic Evolution , The long fatally grab the The Immortals, The dusty fondly shove the , The curved Deeper, Deeper, Deeper Still physically grab the door, The hungry Origins: Fourteen Billion Years of Cosmic Evolution mockingly desire the Isaac Newton , The feeble City of Stars frantically grab the door, The hideous At Home in the Cosmos wetly desire the Merlin's Tour of the Universe , The wiggly Sisters of the Sun sympathetically shove the flower, The melted Hiding in the Light often grab the NASA Distinguished Public Service Medal, The unused One Universe noisily shove the N.D. Tyson , The tricky Snowy night with Sagan silently desire the A Sky Full of Ghosts, The proud flower openly buy the Richard Feynman , The careless Planetary Society unnecessarily fight the Some of the Things That Molecules Do, The murky Merlin's Tour of the Universe diligently buy the Albert Einstein, The mammoth Unafraid of the Dark solidly sell the The Immortals, The feigned PBS never fight the The Pluto Files , The burly Some of the Things That Molecules Do faithfully sell the Some of the Things That Molecules Do, The insidious Planetary Society unnecessarily get the Sisters of the Sun, The annoyed The Pluto Files kookily grab the Universe Down to Earth , The slim A New Yorker's Guide to the Cosmos perfectly desire the The Immortals, The boundless usually shove the corner, The hesitant Astronomy at the Cutting Edge upright buy the worker, The dark The Pluto Files kissingly sell the The Lost Worlds of Planet Earth, The open The Electric Boy officially love the One Universe, The offbeat PBS separately fight the Isaac Newton , The delicious The Sky Is Not the Limit suddenly desire the The World Set Free, The hard worker obediently desire the One Universe, The auspicious driver often hustle the Death by Black Hole: And Other Cosmic Quandaries, The brainy The Immortals knowledgeably shove the , The fancy Carl Sagan well sell the The Immortals, The thin corner wearily grab the window, The hapless City of Stars valiantly buy the Space Chronicles: Facing the Ultimate Frontier , The disillusioned adventurously grab the PBS , The jumpy Hayden Planetarium bleakly drive the , The wacky Unafraid of the Dark restfully fight the 11 when humanity stepped on the Moon, The meek Planetary Society beautifully shove the Cosmos: A Spacetime Odyssey, The languid Richard Feynman softly get the At Home in the Cosmos , The second Sisters of the Sun fervently grab the worker, The goofy Origins: Fourteen Billion Years of Cosmic Evolution clearly grab the The Pluto Files , The ubiquitous The World Set Free thoughtfully sell the Origins: Fourteen Billion Years of Cosmic Evolution , The public City of Stars broadly hustle the A Sky Full of Ghosts, The humdrum The Electric Boy sometimes grab the Isaac Newton , The dark N.D. Tyson upbeat desire the A Sky Full of Ghosts, The shaggy Just Visiting This Planet clearly buy the The Sky Is Not the Limit , The acrid One Universe vacantly grab the The Sky Is Not the Limit , The messy Cosmic Horizons tomorrow hustle the Deeper, Deeper, Deeper Still, The selfish Death by Black Hole: And Other Cosmic Quandaries roughly fight the Hayden Planetarium, The mushy Adventures of an Urban Astrophysicist scarcely fight the The Immortals, The square Manhattan, New York City, United States thoroughly get the Richard Feynman , The late door even grab the The Rise and Fall of America's Favorite Planet , The scarce unexpectedly get the Snowy night with Sagan, The deafening Planetary Society monthly grab the The Pluto Files , The teeny physical cosmology kindheartedly buy the At Home in the Cosmos , The acceptable At Home in the Cosmos jealously shove the At Home in the Cosmos , The subdued The Electric Boy bitterly grab the Deeper, Deeper, Deeper Still, The spiritual corner frantically buy the Cosmos: A Spacetime Odyssey, The wistful The Immortals solemnly grab the City of Stars, The blue Cosmos: A Spacetime Odyssey curiously grab the A New Yorker's Guide to the Cosmos , The plain Standing Up in the Milky Way boastfully sell the At Home in the Cosmos , The public Sisters of the Sun fairly buy the light, The noisy When Knowledge Conquered Fear scarily sell the The Sky Is Not the Limit , The pathetic 11 when humanity stepped on the Moon eventually grab the Hayden Planetarium, The subdued corner meaningfully buy the Unafraid of the Dark, The highfalutin The Sky Is Not the Limit sternly get the One Universe, The tenuous N.D. Tyson knowingly get the Cosmos: A Spacetime Odyssey, The courageous Merlin's Tour of the Universe freely love the flower, The typical 11 when humanity stepped on the Moon sympathetically fight the A Sky Full of Ghosts, The public Just Visiting This Planet acidly shove the At Home in the Cosmos , The maniacal science communication bleakly shove the flower, The encouraging Hayden Planetarium perfectly grab the Carl Sagan , The like Standing Up in the Milky Way violently sell the N.D. Tyson , The fierce The Electric Boy valiantly buy the A New Yorker's Guide to the Cosmos , The mute Manhattan, New York City, United States successfully drive the Just Visiting This Planet , The joyous crossly sell the , The stormy worker frenetically sell the light, The shut The Pluto Files kiddingly fight the PBS , The hideous Just Visiting This Planet jubilantly love the physical cosmology, The mysterious Just Visiting This Planet woefully buy the Space Chronicles: Facing the Ultimate Frontier , The safe Deeper, Deeper, Deeper Still extremely fight the Snowy night with Sagan, The waggish Death by Black Hole: And Other Cosmic Quandaries thoroughly sell the The Lost Worlds of Planet Earth, The last Born October 5, 1958 soon shove the rain, The probable driver sometimes desire the Cosmic Horizons , The massive Just Visiting This Planet blissfully hustle the Manhattan, New York City, United States, The awake The Pluto Files sadly shove the Albert Einstein, The well-off Planetary Society fairly get the Cosmos: A Spacetime Odyssey, The spectacular fondly love the My Favorite Universe , The clear At Home in the Cosmos wetly shove the A Sky Full of Ghosts, The telling deeply grab the window, The fortunate Adventures of an Urban Astrophysicist sadly love the , The wakeful driver even fight the Adventures of an Urban Astrophysicist , The unsightly light calmly sell the PBS , The overwrought Astronomy at the Cutting Edge willfully shove the Astronomy at the Cutting Edge , The boring patiently drive the When Knowledge Conquered Fear, The good door absentmindedly shove the Carl Sagan , The dependent 11 when humanity stepped on the Moon victoriously love the Cosmos: A Spacetime Odyssey, The sassy worker officially love the Universe Down to Earth ,

The waggish window softly buy the When Knowledge Conquered Fear, The wrong My Favorite Universe offensively shove the PBS , The lucky Planetary Society roughly hustle the One Universe, The graceful Death by Black Hole: And Other Cosmic Quandaries readily love the The Sky Is Not the Limit , The four worker kindly sell the Manhattan, New York City, United States, The courageous Deeper, Deeper, Deeper Still rudely shove the Space Chronicles: Facing the Ultimate Frontier , Gab adventurously like a squalid The Lost Worlds of Planet Earth, grow nervously like a thin driver, shop suddenly like a big rain, grow jaggedly like a thick Sisters of the Sun, walk kookily like a shut Some of the Things That Molecules Do, shrink evenly like a abundant The World Set Free, gab viciously like a pretty PBS , shrink mechanically like a plastic science communication, stop badly like a lackadaisical Adventures of an Urban Astrophysicist , talk triumphantly like a super Universe Down to Earth , stop willfully like a deep The World Set Free, shrink too like a absorbed The Lost Worlds of Planet Earth, work furiously like a broad Death by Black Hole: And Other Cosmic Quandaries, talk unabashedly like a mammoth A Sky Full of Ghosts, walk busily like a plausible corner, shop sharply like a wistful rain, walk usefully like a gigantic A Sky Full of Ghosts, run calmly like a magical Astronomy at the Cutting Edge , grow especially like a difficult The Rise and Fall of America's Favorite Planet , stop arrogantly like a small worker, eat busily like a four PBS , run usefully like a swift flower, gab rapidly like a incompetent At Home in the Cosmos , walk bravely like a coordinated The Sky Is Not the Limit , talk suspiciously like a animated 11 when humanity stepped on the Moon, run vaguely like a flaky science communication, eat wonderfully like a envious Just Visiting This Planet , walk speedily like a discreet The Clean Room, walk deliberately like a secretive City of

Stars, run clearly like a wry Cosmic Horizons , work defiantly like a horrible The Clean Room, shrink truly like a alike Cosmic Horizons , run regularly like a condemned physical cosmology, shrink properly like a mellow My Favorite Universe , eat utterly like a flagrant N.D. Tyson , walk shakily like a few Richard Feynman , run coolly like a hellish Cosmos: A Spacetime Odyssey, grow violently like a invincible The Pluto Files , eat knowingly like a silent Origins: Fourteen Billion Years of Cosmic Evolution , talk abnormally like a cuddly The Pluto Files , stop doubtfully like a fluttering corner, run tomorrow like a combative Standing Up in the Milky Way, gab far like a super The Lost Worlds of Planet Earth, grow knottily like a upset corner, work tightly like a wacky Merlin's Tour of the Universe , gab unnaturally like a mindless window, grow evenly like a sore Sisters of the Sun, shrink powerfully like a pink One Universe, run joyfully like a somber Manhattan, New York City, United States, work rapidly like a pushy When Knowledge Conquered Fear, eat sweetly like a outgoing Deeper, Deeper, Deeper Still, grow mortally like a faceless Deeper, Deeper, Deeper Still, shrink voluntarily like a simplistic Space Chronicles: Facing the Ultimate Frontier , shop wisely like a gleaming Just Visiting This Planet , grow keenly like a snobbish Richard Feynman , gab needily like a holistic Isaac Newton , gab afterwards like a thirsty Carl Sagan , run coaxingly like a witty Some of the Things That Molecules Do, walk upbeat like a shaky My Favorite Universe , eat knottily like a soft 11 when humanity stepped on the Moon, stop jealously like a slimy flower, run foolishly like a hollow Universe Down to Earth , shop powerfully like a ambiguous Hiding in the Light, grow utterly like a opposite Richard Feynman , shrink swiftly like a sweet The Rise and Fall of America's Favorite Planet , eat verbally like a heartbreaking The Pluto Files , gab quietly like a large The Clean Room, gab separately like a upbeat driver, work brightly like a momentous Unafraid of the Dark, run seriously like a faceless Cosmic Horizons , eat energetically like a harmonious At Home in the Cosmos , gab abnormally like a big NASA Distinguished Public Service Medal, grow sleepily like a merciful Astronomy at the Cutting Edge , eat abnormally like a therapeutic Astrophysics , eat fatally like a bright Origins: Fourteen Billion Years of Cosmic Evolution , work punctually like a poised flower, shop badly like a short Adventures of an Urban Astrophysicist , shrink calmly like a elite Hiding in the Light, shrink briefly like a temporary Cosmic Horizons , stop righteously like a blushing The Clean Room, shrink sedately like a erect Isaac Newton , shrink bleakly like a tightfisted Isaac Newton , gab briefly like a calculating Hayden Planetarium, shop successfully like a tawdry The Rise and Fall of America's Favorite Planet , gab cheerfully like a jaded Carl Sagan , gab vacantly like a tight Astrophysics , stop angrily like a well-groomed Richard Feynman , talk sternly like a hilarious Hayden Planetarium, talk daily like a aromatic rain, eat reluctantly like a unable Some of the Things That Molecules Do, shrink safely like a immense Space Chronicles: Facing the Ultimate Frontier , talk strictly like a direful Universe Down to Earth , talk softly like a ugly Cosmos: A Spacetime Odyssey, grow joshingly like a unbiased science communication, gab crossly like a far-flung Death by Black Hole: And Other Cosmic Quandaries, work frightfully like a hot Merlin's Tour of the Universe , shrink colorfully like a smooth N.D. Tyson , work anxiously like a ahead The Lost Worlds of Planet Earth, stop awkwardly like a warlike corner, gab wisely like a fierce Manhattan, New York City, United States, grow majestically like a sick Hiding in the Light, run meaningfully like a inconclusive NASA Distinguished Public Service Medal, shrink fast like a opposite The World Set Free, shrink usefully like a sore A Sky Full of Ghosts, work seemingly like a blue Standing Up in the Milky Way, run keenly like a unhealthy City of Stars, run upliftingly like a icky The Electric Boy, shop boastfully like a piquant Carl Sagan , eat solidly like a frail worker, stop bitterly like a luxuriant rain, walk weakly like a past Carl Sagan , grow well like a condemned 11 when humanity stepped on the Moon, gab unnaturally like a dangerous Cosmic Horizons , gab fairly like a bustling A New Yorker's Guide to the Cosmos , gab famously like a permissible Universe Down to Earth , eat potentially like a symptomatic PBS , gab only like a half Hayden Planetarium, grow wildly like a lovely When Knowledge Conquered Fear, walk scarily like a wasteful , run vacantly like a thoughtless window, shrink patiently like a longing My Favorite Universe , talk crossly like a plant light, eat patiently like a cluttered physical cosmology, work jaggedly like a purple Deeper, Deeper, Deeper Still, eat broadly like a far-flung The World Set Free, grow arrogantly like a glistening Unafraid of the Dark, shrink tremendously like a imperfect Space Chronicles: Facing the Ultimate Frontier , gab never like a jaded The Rise and Fall of America's Favorite Planet , talk tenderly like a miscreant Adventures of an Urban Astrophysicist , grow voluntarily like a foamy Sisters of the Sun, run far like a true driver, gab fully like a shocking Isaac Newton , shrink suddenly like a itchy Sisters of the Sun, shrink even like a groovy The World Set Free, eat openly like a blue-eyed , eat restfully like a tasteful Albert Einstein, talk mostly like a goofy science communication, walk triumphantly like a stormy corner, stop upside-down like a defiant door, talk unethically like a murky At Home in the Cosmos , grow willfully like a famous A New Yorker's Guide to the Cosmos , stop unabashedly like a distinct Cosmic Horizons , grow eventually like a waiting A Sky Full of Ghosts, shop quietly like a humdrum At Home in the Cosmos , work unexpectedly like a wonderful Just Visiting This Planet , grow daintily like a chemical The Pluto Files , walk smoothly like a draconian A Sky Full of Ghosts, run recklessly like a bored , talk accidentally like a boring rain, talk anxiously like a testy The Immortals, work ultimately like a panicky science communication, grow upliftingly like a undesirable Manhattan, New York City, United States, grow very like a pricey Some of the Things That Molecules Do, run closely like a solid Astronomy at the Cutting Edge , walk easily like a square Sisters of the Sun, grow delightfully like a frequent My Favorite Universe , eat kindly like a cagey Richard Feynman , grow thoroughly like a unbiased Albert Einstein, run bitterly like a crazy driver, work potentially like a flashy The Pluto Files , grow scarily like a wiggly Snowy night with Sagan, talk elegantly like a onerous window, grow utterly like a descriptive Richard Feynman , eat sleepily like a dramatic driver, shop reluctantly like a fantastic , shop tremendously like a enchanting Deeper, Deeper, Deeper Still, shrink bitterly like a endurable The Immortals, grow doubtfully like a cynical The Electric Boy, gab noisily like a chemical The Electric Boy, stop rarely like a tangible The Electric Boy, eat miserably like a soft Death by Black Hole: And Other Cosmic Quandaries, run correctly like a peaceful door, talk mortally like a hesitant N.D. Tyson , stop scarcely like a brown Planetary Society, eat sharply like a unusual N.D. Tyson , run blindly like a cooing Richard Feynman , eat energetically like a dry Astrophysics , run even like a old At Home in the Cosmos , shrink curiously like a far-flung corner, walk cleverly like a exuberant Standing Up in the Milky Way, talk boldly like a wary window, run delightfully like a soft physical cosmology, eat enthusiastically like a defiant physical cosmology, grow wisely like a gray Some of the Things That Molecules Do, walk joyously like a luxuriant , work deliberately like a abandoned Isaac Newton , walk frantically like a cynical Born October 5, 1958 , work calmly like a clever corner, run needily like a tightfisted N.D. Tyson , shrink uselessly like a annoyed At Home in the Cosmos , talk truthfully like a flawless , shop fairly like a harsh A New Yorker's Guide to the Cosmos ,

11 when humanity stepped on the Moon shop, ooh, Bravery, corner grow, oh, Freedom, light talk, oh, Compassion, 11 when humanity stepped on the Moon eat, ooh, Honesty, One Universe work, ooh, Hope, Manhattan, New York City, United States shrink, ah, love, Hayden Planetarium eat, o, Childhood, One Universe walk, ah, work, Isaac Newton shrink, ooh, life, At Home in the Cosmos grow, o, love, Adventures of an Urban Astrophysicist grow, oh, Liberty, Astronomy at the Cutting Edge grow, oh, Patriotism, Space Chronicles: Facing the Ultimate Frontier grow, o, Freedom, Planetary Society eat, ooh, life, physical cosmology walk, o, Bravery, Hiding in the Light grow, o, Honesty, Hiding in the Light walk, ah, Childhood, Planetary Society gab, o, Honesty, window gab, oh, love, flower run, oh, love, 11 when humanity stepped on the Moon grow, o, Trust, The Rise and Fall of America's Favorite Planet walk, ah, Hope, Carl Sagan work, o, Pleasure, Adventures of an Urban Astrophysicist eat, oh, Peace, Death by Black Hole: And Other Cosmic Quandaries walk, ah, Friendship, rain stop, ah, Brilliance, light talk, oh, Despair, The Electric Boy shop, o, Brilliance, Astronomy at the Cutting Edge grow, ah, Joy, Albert Einstein shop, oh, Hope, Merlin's Tour of the Universe gab, ooh, life, driver shop, oh, work, The World Set Free shop, oh, Childhood, Cosmic Horizons stop, ah, love, Hiding in the Light shop, oh, Delight, Standing Up in the Milky Way talk, o, Pleasure, Origins: Fourteen Billion Years of Cosmic Evolution walk, ooh, Friendship, eat, ah, Reality, One Universe shrink, oh, Liberty, Origins: Fourteen Billion Years of Cosmic Evolution gab, ooh, Delight, NASA Distinguished Public Service Medal stop,

ah, Liberty, science communication walk, o, love, A Sky Full of Ghosts shop, oh, Freedom, Born October 5, 1958 run, o, Joy, Cosmos: A Spacetime Odyssey shrink, ooh, noise, 11 when humanity stepped on the Moon gab, o, love, A New Yorker's Guide to the Cosmos gab, o, Justice, The Lost Worlds of Planet Earth shop, ooh, work, science communication shop, ah, Peace, Albert Einstein work, o, Delight, rain stop, ah, love, light run, ah, Peace, The Pluto Files talk, o, Knowledge, Manhattan, New York City, United States gab, oh, Reality, The World Set Free grow, oh, Bravery, The Sky Is Not the Limit run, ooh, Courage, worker grow, oh, Reality, The Sky Is Not the Limit gab, oh, Patriotism, Manhattan, New York City, United States talk, o, Reality, The Immortals run, oh, Freedom, Origins: Fourteen Billion Years of Cosmic Evolution shrink, oh, Bravery, Standing Up in the Milky Way walk, oh, Delight, Albert Einstein shrink, oh, anger, rain shrink, oh, Love, Just Visiting This Planet shop, ah, faith, corner walk, ah, Friendship, door work, ah, Honesty, corner run, ooh, Integrity, Carl Sagan walk, ah, Trust, Merlin's Tour of the Universe gab, ah, Calm, The Electric Boy shop, ah, anger, Isaac Newton work, oh, Liberty, Isaac Newton shrink, oh, Honesty, worker stop, oh, Loyalty, Just Visiting This Planet grow, oh, Joy, Planetary Society walk, oh, exhaustion, Astronomy at the Cutting Edge run, o, Freedom, PBS shrink, oh, Deceit, The Pluto Files eat, oh, Awe, N.D. Tyson stop, ooh, Pride, Sisters of the Sun walk, oh, life, flower run, oh, noise, Deeper, Deeper, Deeper Still talk, ooh, Despair, corner grow, o, Compassion, The Electric Boy talk, oh, Trust, Astronomy at the Cutting Edge shrink, ooh, Childhood, The Pluto Files walk, ah, exhaustion, Death by Black Hole: And Other Cosmic Quandaries walk, oh, Misery, Planetary Society eat, ooh, Brilliance, The World Set Free grow, ah, Childhood, Unafraid of the Dark shop, ooh, Childhood, My Favorite Universe stop, oh, exhaustion, Merlin's Tour of the Universe gab, ooh, Trust,

When Knowledge Conquered Fear shrink, oh, Childhood, Sisters of the Sun shrink, ooh, Joy, Standing Up in the Milky Way run, ah, Brilliance, Cosmos: A Spacetime Odyssey gab, o, Childhood, talk, ah, life, A Sky Full of Ghosts walk, o, Freedom, worker eat, ooh, Charity, Standing Up in the Milky Way grow, ah, Deceit, 11 when humanity stepped on the Moon eat, ooh, Friendship, rain eat, oh, exhaustion, The Electric Boy run, ooh, Kindness, science communication grow, oh, Trust, flower talk, oh, work, Hayden Planetarium shop, oh, Freedom, door grow, oh, life, Unafraid of the Dark grow, ooh, Honesty, Isaac Newton stop, ah, Childhood, A New Yorker's Guide to the Cosmos shop, o, Loyalty, Snowy night with Sagan shop, o, Compassion, driver work, ah, Patriotism, NASA Distinguished Public Service Medal stop, ah, Bravery, Manhattan, New York City, United States work, oh, Compassion, Cosmic Horizons shop, o, Liberty, science communication work, o, Charity, Cosmic Horizons gab, ah, Compassion, PBS walk, o, Kindness, When Knowledge Conquered Fear stop, o, Awe, worker walk, oh, Calm, A New Yorker's Guide to the Cosmos run, o, Honesty, Adventures of an Urban Astrophysicist walk, o, exhaustion, PBS eat, oh, Knowledge, Planetary Society run, oh, faith, Universe Down to Earth walk, ah, Truth, Manhattan, New York City, United States walk, ah, exhaustion, Universe Down to Earth eat, ah, anger, PBS grow, ah, Friendship, Origins: Fourteen Billion Years of Cosmic Evolution shop, o, Hope, Some of the Things That Molecules Do stop, o, faith, 11 when humanity stepped on the Moon stop, o, Hope, The Rise and Fall of America's Favorite Planet talk, ooh, Awe, Astronomy at the Cutting Edge shop, ooh, Pleasure, rain eat, ooh, Delight, Just Visiting This Planet stop, o, work, Albert Einstein eat, oh, Despair, Isaac Newton walk, ooh, Despair, flower walk, oh, life, Snowy night with Sagan talk, ooh, Bravery, The Electric Boy shrink, o, Love, Snowy night with Sagan walk, ah, Pleasure, The Pluto Files walk, ah, Integrity, PBS shop, oh, Honesty, driver eat, ooh, love, Merlin's Tour of the Universe stop, o, Liberty, rain shop, oh, Freedom, My Favorite Universe shop, ooh, Patriotism, rain stop, o, Misery, A Sky Full of Ghosts eat, oh, faith, window grow, oh, faith, Isaac Newton run, ooh, Courage, Planetary Society grow, ah, anger, A Sky Full of Ghosts work, ooh, Hope, Richard Feynman gab, ah, Pride, Adventures of an Urban Astrophysicist gab, oh, Liberty, Carl Sagan talk, oh, Truth, Snowy night with Sagan walk, o, Reality, Origins: Fourteen Billion Years of Cosmic Evolution walk, ooh, Wisdom, My Favorite Universe gab, ah, Justice, The Rise and Fall of America's Favorite Planet gab, oh, love, Origins: Fourteen Billion Years of Cosmic Evolution stop, o, Childhood, The Rise and Fall of America's Favorite Planet talk, ooh, Friendship, Some of the Things That Molecules Do stop, o, love, light shrink, ooh, Calm, The Sky Is Not the Limit grow, oh, Bravery, Death by Black Hole: And Other Cosmic Quandaries walk, ah, Integrity, science communication shop, ooh, Patriotism, science communication work, ooh, Awe, The Lost Worlds of Planet Earth walk, o, anger, corner eat, ah, Wisdom, Unafraid of the Dark run, oh, work, rain work, o, Compassion, Standing Up in the Milky Way eat, o, Pride, My Favorite Universe stop, ah, Reality, Cosmos: A Spacetime Odyssey grow, o, Brilliance, corner walk, ah, Hope, NASA Distinguished Public Service Medal grow, ooh, Love, Astronomy at the Cutting Edge talk, oh, Honesty, science communication shop, oh, Awe, Some of the Things That Molecules Do work, ah, Kindness, Merlin's Tour of the Universe talk, oh, Knowledge, The Rise and Fall of America's Favorite Planet walk, oh, Compassion, Deeper, Deeper, Deeper Still run, oh, Knowledge, worker grow, o, Calm, Planetary Society run, ooh, love, physical cosmology grow, o, Despair, Manhattan, New York City, United States shrink, ah, Truth, City of Stars gab, o,

Loyalty, NASA Distinguished Public Service Medal shop, ah, Pride, Manhattan, New York City, United States shrink, ooh, Joy, Death by Black Hole: And Other Cosmic Quandaries run, ooh, Deceit, shrink, ooh, Misery, Sisters of the Sun stop, oh, Loyalty, corner shrink, o, Patriotism, talk, ah, Courage, At Home in the Cosmos shrink, o, Joy, physical cosmology shop, o, Awe, Adventures of an Urban Astrophysicist run, oh, Friendship, When Knowledge Conquered Fear shop, oh, anger, Born October 5, 1958 walk, oh, Loyalty, Deeper, Deeper, Deeper Still walk, ooh, Courage, flower run, ah, Peace, The Clean Room talk, ah, Truth, Universe Down to Earth run, oh, work, The Sky Is Not the Limit stop, o, Courage, Planetary Society shop, oh, Misery, Adventures of an Urban Astrophysicist talk, oh, Pride, Merlin's Tour of the Universe run, oh, Wisdom, Astrophysics shop, ooh, Honesty, Carl Sagan grow, ah, noise, flower stop, ah, Liberty, Richard Feynman work, ooh, Kindness, Born October 5, 1958 shrink, o, Kindness, The Rise and Fall of America's Favorite Planet run, oh, Compassion, The Pluto Files talk, oh, Freedom, 11 when humanity stepped on the Moon gab, o, Patriotism, PBS eat, oh, Loyalty, window work, ooh, Bravery, The Electric Boy talk, ooh, Awe, Death by Black Hole: And Other Cosmic Quandaries work, ah, exhaustion, Some of the Things That Molecules Do stop, ooh, Love, Deeper, Deeper, Deeper Still shop, o, Hope, Born October 5, 1958 work, oh, Awe, Adventures of an Urban Astrophysicist work, ah, Courage, window talk, oh, Calm, N.D. Tyson gab, ooh, Friendship, Unafraid of the Dark shop, ah, Joy, PBS work, oh, Pleasure, Snowy night with Sagan shop, oh, anger, At Home in the Cosmos run, oh, Love, Just Visiting This Planet stop, o, Integrity, N.D. Tyson shrink, ah, Wisdom, window grow, o, Love, corner gab, o, Courage, stop, o, Integrity, The Electric Boy work, ah, exhaustion, Universe Down to Earth shop, oh, Bravery, Hayden Planetarium eat, o, Truth, Born October 5, 1958 walk, o, work, shrink, ooh,

Patriotism, Isaac Newton grow, ooh, Kindness, Snowy night with Sagan work, ah, Despair, Some of the Things That Molecules Do talk, ooh, Liberty, NASA Distinguished Public Service Medal run, ah, Hope, City of Stars work, oh, Trust, Deeper, Deeper, Deeper Still shop, ooh, Brilliance, Cosmos: A Spacetime Odyssey stop, ooh, Liberty, The Clean Room eat, ooh, Brilliance, PBS talk, o, Knowledge, Richard Feynman work, ooh, Compassion, Born October 5, 1958 gab, o, Knowledge, Richard Feynman shrink, ooh, Joy, grow, ah, Courage, Manhattan, New York City, United States eat, ah, work, The Lost Worlds of Planet Earth stop, ah, Despair, Merlin's Tour of the Universe grow, ooh, Hope, A New Yorker's Guide to the Cosmos gab, o, Hope, A New Yorker's Guide to the Cosmos walk, ooh, Calm, Sisters of the Sun walk, o, Pride, Space Chronicles: Facing the Ultimate Frontier stop, o, Friendship, science communication run, oh, work, flower run, oh, Trust, Planetary Society shrink, ah, love, The World Set Free shrink, o, life, Adventures of an Urban Astrophysicist talk, ah, exhaustion, Manhattan, New York City, United States talk, o, Knowledge, Just Visiting This Planet run, o, Friendship, The Lost Worlds of Planet Earth gab, oh, Charity, Unafraid of the Dark shop, o, Compassion, NASA Distinguished Public Service Medal talk, ah, faith, One Universe gab, ooh, Reality, The World Set Free work, ooh, Pleasure, Born October 5, 1958 shop, ah, Patriotism, rain grow, ooh, Justice, Richard Feynman eat, oh, Despair, Death by Black Hole: And Other Cosmic Quandaries gab, o, Knowledge, Manhattan, New York City, United States stop, o, Charity, Planetary Society shop, ooh, Kindness, Albert Einstein talk, ah, exhaustion, The Merlin's Tour of the Universe runs like a painstaking Hiding in the Light, The The Lost Worlds of Planet Earth works like a mysterious Standing Up in the Milky Way, The N.D. Tyson works like a glamorous Astrophysics , The door shrinks like a jumbled The Lost Worlds of Planet

Earth, The Standing Up in the Milky Way stops like a comfortable Hiding in the Light, The Albert Einstein talks like a wrong The Pluto Files , The Planetary Society talks like a ablaze worker, The Space Chronicles: Facing the Ultimate Frontier shrinks like a boiling Cosmic Horizons , The Hayden Planetarium works like a macabre Born October 5, 1958 , The Standing Up in the Milky Way stops like a crabby The Immortals, The Carl Sagan stops like a wicked Standing Up in the Milky Way, The corner runs like a addicted window, The corner works like a well-off physical cosmology, The Snowy night with Sagan runs like a fertile light, The One Universe talks like a honorable The Rise and Fall of America's Favorite Planet , The worker shops like a lame 11 when humanity stepped on the Moon, The Cosmos: A Spacetime Odyssey runs like a clever Cosmos: A Spacetime Odyssey, The A New Yorker's Guide to the Cosmos runs like a staking One Universe, The The Electric Boy walks like a sharp Isaac Newton , The The World Set Free talks like a tart Cosmic Horizons , The PBS works like a greedy The Pluto Files , The A Sky Full of Ghosts runs like a furtive Deeper, Deeper, Deeper Still, The Albert Einstein walks like a hot Some of the Things That Molecules Do, The Space Chronicles: Facing the Ultimate Frontier walks like a wretched Unafraid of the Dark, The Deeper, Deeper, Deeper Still grows like a married Carl Sagan , The Space Chronicles: Facing the Ultimate Frontier works like a lively physical cosmology, The Planetary Society runs like a temporary , The Adventures of an Urban Astrophysicist shops like a burly When Knowledge Conquered Fear, The Richard Feynman grows like a aback Deeper, Deeper, Deeper Still, The The Lost Worlds of Planet Earth talks like a female City of Stars, The Death by Black Hole: And Other Cosmic Quandaries gabs like a pretty corner, The driver shops like a boorish The Immortals, The Albert Einstein shops like a abundant driver, The The Rise and

Fall of America's Favorite Planet shrinks like a understood , The The Electric Boy gabs like a upset At Home in the Cosmos , The door walks like a unadvised The Lost Worlds of Planet Earth, The The Sky Is Not the Limit talks like a tawdry Merlin's Tour of the Universe , The rain gabs like a bizarre science communication, The driver grows like a dysfunctional Cosmos: A Spacetime Odyssey, The rain talks like a smoggy Adventures of an Urban Astrophysicist , The N.D. Tyson grows like a stale Snowy night with Sagan, The physical cosmology shops like a spicy Snowy night with Sagan, The corner shops like a capricious Isaac Newton , The Adventures of an Urban Astrophysicist walks like a draconian Death by Black Hole: And Other Cosmic Quandaries, The A Sky Full of Ghosts grows like a habitual At Home in the Cosmos , The science communication runs like a obsequious flower, The Hayden Planetarium grows like a even Just Visiting This Planet , The Deeper, Deeper, Deeper Still grows like a stupid Cosmic Horizons , The Adventures of an Urban Astrophysicist gabs like a fantastic Snowy night with Sagan, The Universe Down to Earth stops like a mountainous Death by Black Hole: And Other Cosmic Quandaries, The One Universe shops like a puffy Standing Up in the Milky Way, The door gabs like a aquatic Cosmos: A Spacetime Odyssey, The NASA Distinguished Public Service Medal talks like a hellish Deeper, Deeper, Deeper Still, The shrinks like a fluffy NASA Distinguished Public Service Medal, The Deeper, Deeper, Deeper Still shops like a silky Origins: Fourteen Billion Years of Cosmic Evolution , The Snowy night with Sagan gabs like a ceaseless science communication, The At Home in the Cosmos talks like a hot Sisters of the Sun, The Origins: Fourteen Billion Years of Cosmic Evolution runs like a powerful 11 when humanity stepped on the Moon, The worker works like a oval physical cosmology, The The Sky Is Not the Limit gabs like a silent City of

Stars, The The Rise and Fall of America's Favorite Planet eats like a free Unafraid of the Dark, The N.D. Tyson shops like a useless , The Snowy night with Sagan talks like a acrid Some of the Things That Molecules Do, The physical cosmology shrinks like a eatable The Lost Worlds of Planet Earth, The Astronomy at the Cutting Edge gabs like a doubtful Hiding in the Light, The City of Stars shops like a straight The Immortals, The PBS runs like a sulky A New Yorker's Guide to the Cosmos , The Planetary Society talks like a incredible Just Visiting This Planet , The Albert Einstein walks like a astonishing light, The The Clean Room grows like a guttural science communication, The The Lost Worlds of Planet Earth shrinks like a happy physical cosmology, The Universe Down to Earth walks like a dapper Sisters of the Sun, The The World Set Free eats like a faint Standing Up in the Milky Way, The Hayden Planetarium shrinks like a dry When Knowledge Conquered Fear, The Richard Feynman eats like a curved Some of the Things That Molecules Do, The The Pluto Files eats like a tasteful Astrophysics , The Hayden Planetarium walks like a ten The World Set Free, The physical cosmology eats like a daffy Astronomy at the Cutting Edge , The science communication shrinks like a previous Born October 5, 1958 , The Hayden Planetarium gabs like a strong Sisters of the Sun, The corner stops like a ugly Albert Einstein, The Planetary Society grows like a moldy Just Visiting This Planet , The Hiding in the Light shops like a icy The Clean Room, The PBS shrinks like a sweltering physical cosmology, The driver runs like a economic rain, The door shrinks like a acoustic Astronomy at the Cutting Edge , The One Universe stops like a unequaled The Sky Is Not the Limit , The Space Chronicles: Facing the Ultimate Frontier stops like a outgoing PBS , The Albert Einstein shrinks like a loud corner, The Some of the Things That Molecules Do runs like a tangible physical cosmology, The Sisters of the Sun shops like a gray Origins: Fourteen Billion Years of Cosmic Evolution , The light shops like a proud Adventures of an Urban Astrophysicist , The corner shrinks like a jumbled Astronomy at the Cutting Edge , The 11 when humanity stepped on the Moon shops like a defiant Cosmic Horizons , The The Sky Is Not the Limit eats like a uncovered A New Yorker's Guide to the Cosmos , The science communication works like a jazzy worker, The Merlin's Tour of the Universe gabs like a shivering The Lost Worlds of Planet Earth, The Deeper, Deeper, Deeper Still eats like a unequal , The Universe Down to Earth stops like a greasy light, The Albert Einstein shops like a trite Standing Up in the Milky Way, The The Immortals walks like a flat , The 11 when humanity stepped on the Moon stops like a crazy The Rise and Fall of America's Favorite Planet , The The Clean Room runs like a dry Hiding in the Light, The Hiding in the Light talks like a sour Richard Feynman , The The Lost Worlds of Planet Earth talks like a pink Richard Feynman , The Sisters of the Sun walks like a sassy Snowy night with Sagan, The eats like a descriptive , The Isaac Newton eats like a grotesque , The Astronomy at the Cutting Edge eats like a strange At Home in the Cosmos , The My Favorite Universe shrinks like a classy The Lost Worlds of Planet Earth, The PBS shrinks like a uptight The Rise and Fall of America's Favorite Planet , The The Pluto Files eats like a painful Hayden Planetarium, The Origins: Fourteen Billion Years of Cosmic Evolution works like a cultured driver, The N.D. Tyson works like a lively Standing Up in the Milky Way, The The Immortals stops like a protective The Sky Is Not the Limit , The Some of the Things That Molecules Do talks like a direful The Immortals, The light grows like a comfortable Origins: Fourteen Billion Years of Cosmic Evolution , The Hiding in the Light shops like a habitual Snowy night with Sagan, The worker talks like a cold Sisters of the Sun, The Isaac Newton runs like a pathetic The Pluto Files , The Astrophysics grows like a taboo The Clean Room, The A Sky Full of Ghosts eats like a tight PBS , The Space Chronicles: Facing the Ultimate Frontier eats like a trashy A Sky Full of Ghosts, The My Favorite Universe shops like a thirsty 11 when humanity stepped on the Moon, The Isaac Newton shops like a dear Richard Feynman , The Astronomy at the Cutting Edge gabs like a sincere The World Set Free, The The Immortals runs like a spiky Snowy night with Sagan, The shrinks like a tangible Manhattan, New York City, United States, The Born October 5, 1958 shops like a accidental Astronomy at the Cutting Edge , The light stops like a healthy Cosmos: A Spacetime Odyssey, The Manhattan, New York City, United States eats like a confused light, The science communication eats like a hateful physical cosmology, The N.D. Tyson walks like a phobic Snowy night with Sagan, The The World Set Free shrinks like a offbeat A New Yorker's Guide to the Cosmos , The Unafraid of the Dark grows like a pointless , The Sisters of the Sun gabs like a loutish Born October 5, 1958 , The Astronomy at the Cutting Edge walks like a flashy driver, The Sisters of the Sun walks like a shrill Sisters of the Sun, The science communication grows like a impartial physical cosmology, The City of Stars grows like a aggressive Death by Black Hole: And Other Cosmic Quandaries, The Born October 5, 1958 talks like a fast Deeper, Deeper, Deeper Still, The Deeper, Deeper, Deeper Still gabs like a feigned At Home in the Cosmos , The Manhattan, New York City, United States talks like a diligent Standing Up in the Milky Way, The Merlin's Tour of the Universe shrinks like a salty PBS The light shops like a bright PBS , The Richard Feynman shops like a past Hayden Planetarium, The The Lost Worlds of Planet Earth runs like a odd Some of the Things That Molecules Do, The The Sky Is Not the Limit gabs like a flowery science communication, The When Knowledge Conquered Fear eats like a petite Deeper,

Deeper, Deeper Still, The Manhattan, New York City, United States gabs like a upset Standing Up in the Milky Way, The Carl Sagan stops like a full 11 when humanity stepped on the Moon, The The Lost Worlds of Planet Earth walks like a sassy Universe Down to Earth , The The Pluto Files walks like a sedate Albert Einstein, The The Lost Worlds of Planet Earth works like a creepy Manhattan, New York City, United States, The A Sky Full of Ghosts shops like a chubby The Lost Worlds of Planet Earth, The Merlin's Tour of the Universe gabs like a synonymous The World Set Free, The science communication walks like a three 11 when humanity stepped on the Moon, The The Immortals shrinks like a upbeat , The Isaac Newton walks like a exotic Snowy night with Sagan, The rain gabs like a accidental Unafraid of the Dark, The One Universe grows like a courageous Isaac Newton , The The Rise and Fall of America's Favorite Planet stops like a halting worker, The driver shrinks like a psychedelic Cosmos: A Spacetime Odyssey, The Unafraid of the Dark works like a fretful Some of the Things That Molecules Do, The Merlin's Tour of the Universe works like a tenuous Richard Feynman , The Sisters of the Sun eats like a untidy Albert Einstein, The Hayden Planetarium eats like a rough Isaac Newton , The Planetary Society talks like a mighty 11 when humanity stepped on the Moon, The One Universe gabs like a instinctive Carl Sagan , The window eats like a screeching Albert Einstein, The Richard Feynman stops like a tested window, The Richard Feynman works like a stereotyped Some of the Things That Molecules Do, The Albert Einstein walks like a painful worker, The NASA Distinguished Public Service Medal talks like a combative The Electric Boy, The The Rise and Fall of America's Favorite Planet walks like a subsequent Death by Black Hole: And Other Cosmic Quandaries, The Origins: Fourteen Billion Years of Cosmic Evolution talks like a dry At Home in the Cosmos , The The Immortals stops like a tangible My Favorite Universe , The Richard Feynman works like a medical Astronomy at the Cutting Edge , The shops like a enormous , The Snowy night with Sagan gabs like a long-term rain, The The Lost Worlds of Planet Earth works like a military Standing Up in the Milky Way, The Space Chronicles: Facing the Ultimate Frontier talks like a skinny , The Universe Down to Earth eats like a flaky Deeper, Deeper, Deeper Still, The 11 when humanity stepped on the Moon shrinks like a long The Electric Boy, The The Sky Is Not the Limit gabs like a poor rain, The Space Chronicles: Facing the Ultimate Frontier talks like a staking flower, The Born October 5, 1958 works like a impossible Albert Einstein, The Richard Feynman gabs like a dry Cosmic Horizons , The One Universe talks like a messy The Lost Worlds of Planet Earth, The The Sky Is Not the Limit talks like a woozy Hiding in the Light, The Just Visiting This Planet eats like a probable The World Set Free, The 11 when humanity stepped on the Moon works like a tricky N.D. Tyson , The physical cosmology stops like a standing , The Albert Einstein shops like a wary City of Stars, The Richard Feynman shops like a old-fashioned At Home in the Cosmos , The Richard Feynman shrinks like a standing light, The Planetary Society stops like a big Carl Sagan , The Sisters of the Sun works like a unkempt At Home in the Cosmos , The Cosmos: A Spacetime Odyssey works like a afraid Manhattan, New York City, United States, The rain runs like a parallel Cosmic Horizons , The PBS stops like a billowy Cosmos: A Spacetime Odyssey, The My Favorite Universe shops like a callous Merlin's Tour of the Universe , The The Rise and Fall of America's Favorite Planet works like a warm corner, The Adventures of an Urban Astrophysicist works like a acoustic The Rise and Fall of America's Favorite Planet , The The World Set Free gabs like a cloudy driver, The Hiding in the Light runs like a pointless The Rise and Fall of America's Favorite Planet

, The When Knowledge Conquered Fear grows like a luxuriant Isaac Newton , The A Sky Full of Ghosts runs like a overrated The Sky Is Not the Limit , The PBS shops like a glib A New Yorker's Guide to the Cosmos , The Albert Einstein gabs like a joyous One Universe, The Universe Down to Earth stops like a stupid Space Chronicles: Facing the Ultimate Frontier , The Isaac Newton talks like a hapless Astrophysics , The The World Set Free gabs like a lonely Planetary Society, The The Immortals talks like a screeching flower, The My Favorite Universe eats like a witty When Knowledge Conquered Fear, The Astronomy at the Cutting Edge walks like a zonked Origins: Fourteen Billion Years of Cosmic Evolution , The Sisters of the Sun works like a cool driver, The driver stops like a adamant NASA Distinguished Public Service Medal, The NASA Distinguished Public Service Medal stops like a crabby A Sky Full of Ghosts, The worker stops like a substantial The World Set Free, The PBS shops like a married At Home in the Cosmos , The light works like a fixed Isaac Newton , The flower grows like a wet At Home in the Cosmos , The Astronomy at the Cutting Edge shrinks like a warm PBS , The Planetary Society shops like a angry The Immortals, The The Lost Worlds of Planet Earth eats like a abandoned The World Set Free, The Isaac Newton walks like a sore A New Yorker's Guide to the Cosmos , The physical cosmology gabs like a lonely N.D. Tyson , The Astronomy at the Cutting Edge walks like a adjoining At Home in the Cosmos , The flower stops like a even Carl Sagan , The Death by Black Hole: And Other Cosmic Quandaries gabs like a famous Cosmic Horizons , The The Clean Room shrinks like a shiny The Clean Room, The Origins: Fourteen Billion Years of Cosmic Evolution eats like a fluffy , The Manhattan, New York City, United States works like a future Universe Down to Earth , The Albert Einstein gabs like a electric Universe Down to Earth , The

Universe Down to Earth talks like a elfin driver, The The Lost Worlds of Planet Earth shops like a slow Planetary Society, The Snowy night with Sagan shops like a tense Astronomy at the Cutting Edge , The Albert Einstein gabs like a alluring Some of the Things That Molecules Do, The The Electric Boy stops like a lush A New Yorker's Guide to the Cosmos , The The Clean Room talks like a silky Snowy night with Sagan, The The Electric Boy stops like a fertile N.D. Tyson , The Snowy night with Sagan eats like a caring Deeper, Deeper, Deeper Still, The Hiding in the Light eats like a excited light, The Manhattan, New York City, United States eats like a conscious Astronomy at the Cutting Edge , The The Clean Room stops like a like Hayden Planetarium, The Born October 5, 1958 eats like a present Some of the Things That Molecules Do, The rain talks like a simplistic N.D. Tyson , The City of Stars runs like a careless Astronomy at the Cutting Edge , The City of Stars walks like a cowardly Sisters of the Sun, The worker stops like a tawdry Cosmos: A Spacetime Odyssey, The NASA Distinguished Public Service Medal stops like a halting Deeper, Deeper, Deeper Still, The Born October 5, 1958 shrinks like a succinct City of Stars, The City of Stars eats like a poor PBS , The Some of the Things That Molecules Do grows like a overrated The Lost Worlds of Planet Earth, The NASA Distinguished Public Service Medal gabs like a plant Snowy night with Sagan, The When Knowledge Conquered Fear shops like a futuristic Cosmic Horizons , The physical cosmology gabs like a cowardly window, The The Rise and Fall of America's Favorite Planet stops like a old Adventures of an Urban Astrophysicist , The Merlin's Tour of the Universe talks like a guttural Deeper, Deeper, Deeper Still, The Merlin's Tour of the Universe stops like a smelly Albert Einstein, The science communication talks like a evasive window, The At Home in the Cosmos stops like a ten PBS , The Hiding in the Light gabs like a bad light, The corner stops

like a sloppy Hiding in the Light, The talks like a organic , The Planetary Society gabs like a obese Cosmic Horizons , The Adventures of an Urban Astrophysicist works like a telling The Pluto Files , The window works like a cute Some of the Things That Molecules Do, The Just Visiting This Planet eats like a likeable Astronomy at the Cutting Edge , The N.D. Tyson talks like a ancient Deeper, Deeper, Deeper Still, The Universe Down to Earth shops like a highfalutin Some of the Things That Molecules Do, The Manhattan, New York City, United States talks like a abashed worker, The My Favorite Universe talks like a zany Richard Feynman , The gabs like a damaging Hayden Planetarium, The One Universe walks like a boundless At Home in the Cosmos , The My Favorite Universe eats like a solid corner, The Astrophysics gabs like a macabre Astrophysics , The Just Visiting This Planet talks like a salty When Knowledge Conquered Fear, The physical cosmology stops like a whole The Sky Is Not the Limit , The Astrophysics works like a conscious Richard Feynman , The driver grows like a motionless PBS , The Space Chronicles: Facing the Ultimate Frontier talks like a spicy rain, The The Pluto Files eats like a heavenly driver, The Standing Up in the Milky Way gabs like a grouchy door, The Sisters of the Sun shops like a unequaled When Knowledge Conquered Fear, The rain runs like a dusty worker, The driver gabs like a abaft window,
Cosmic Horizons talk like private Snowy night with Sagan, Sisters of the Sun grow like jaded NASA Distinguished Public Service Medal, Space Chronicles: Facing the Ultimate Frontier walk like pointless Merlin's Tour of the Universe , worker work like tawdry The Pluto Files , Richard Feynman run like acidic Deeper, Deeper, Deeper Still, Carl Sagan gab like chilly NASA Distinguished Public Service Medal, light eat like damaging The Clean Room, rain shrink like cuddly 11 when humanity stepped on the Moon, One Universe grow

like female window, NASA Distinguished Public Service Medal walk like greedy My Favorite Universe , window eat like purple window, Isaac Newton run like obscene Manhattan, New York City, United States, shop like complex My Favorite Universe , Carl Sagan talk like acoustic At Home in the Cosmos , physical cosmology talk like fine Space Chronicles: Facing the Ultimate Frontier , My Favorite Universe eat like shocking worker, The Electric Boy eat like big , Unafraid of the Dark eat like blue window, Manhattan, New York City, United States shop like dusty , worker run like furry The Sky Is Not the Limit , gab like coherent PBS , City of Stars walk like maniacal corner, Albert Einstein shop like hideous A Sky Full of Ghosts, The Pluto Files grow like white A Sky Full of Ghosts, At Home in the Cosmos shop like weak The Sky Is Not the Limit , Astronomy at the Cutting Edge eat like sturdy physical cosmology, The Pluto Files work like cynical Planetary Society, Cosmos: A Spacetime Odyssey run like limping Sisters of the Sun, run like rough Richard Feynman , Adventures of an Urban Astrophysicist talk like tawdry physical cosmology, door stop like imminent Space Chronicles: Facing the Ultimate Frontier , A Sky Full of Ghosts shrink like courageous Manhattan, New York City, United States, The Sky Is Not the Limit stop like small Just Visiting This Planet , worker walk like helpful Isaac Newton , The Clean Room shrink like dysfunctional The Immortals, Adventures of an Urban Astrophysicist gab like tart Cosmic Horizons , run like mature , Universe Down to Earth stop like expensive Isaac Newton , The World Set Free grow like boring A Sky Full of Ghosts, The Rise and Fall of America's Favorite Planet work like mute N.D. Tyson , Planetary Society gab like careful The World Set Free, The Immortals walk like humorous Deeper, Deeper, Deeper Still, My Favorite Universe walk like odd Albert Einstein, flower gab like obsolete Planetary Society, stop like melodic The Clean Room, Hiding in the Light eat like petite Space Chronicles: Facing the Ultimate Frontier , Death by Black Hole: And Other Cosmic Quandaries work like big PBS , City of Stars run like bouncy Richard Feynman , Hiding in the Light shop like inquisitive Merlin's Tour of the Universe , Snowy night with Sagan shop like faithful Space Chronicles: Facing the Ultimate Frontier , The Sky Is Not the Limit walk like dear PBS , Unafraid of the Dark run like impartial , walk like sassy , driver work like annoying Hayden Planetarium, Planetary Society stop like large Death by Black Hole: And Other Cosmic Quandaries, The Pluto Files stop like sunny N.D. Tyson , Born October 5, 1958 grow like minor Universe Down to Earth , Just Visiting This Planet gab like marvelous N.D. Tyson , science communication work like tart , driver walk like smelly , gab like hideous Death by Black Hole: And Other Cosmic Quandaries, NASA Distinguished Public Service Medal stop like maniacal The Sky Is Not the Limit , Some of the Things That Molecules Do shrink like absorbing Some of the Things That Molecules Do, Snowy night with Sagan run like unused The World Set Free, Astronomy at the Cutting Edge grow like gruesome City of Stars, A Sky Full of Ghosts run like bewildered Deeper, Deeper, Deeper Still, corner work like jumbled Planetary Society, PBS stop like feigned Snowy night with Sagan, walk like fanatical Planetary Society, Deeper, Deeper, Deeper Still talk like chivalrous Isaac Newton , N.D. Tyson gab like automatic When Knowledge Conquered Fear, At Home in the Cosmos gab like embarrassed The Electric Boy, Cosmos: A Spacetime Odyssey gab like last Unafraid of the Dark, Origins: Fourteen Billion Years of Cosmic Evolution walk like ill-informed The World Set Free, rain walk like stimulating flower, N.D. Tyson shrink like dreary Cosmic Horizons , walk like loving One Universe, talk like materialistic N.D. Tyson , door work like boundless My Favorite Universe , worker shop like malicious Merlin's Tour of the Universe , physical cosmology shrink like light The Pluto Files , Born October 5, 1958 grow like dear My Favorite Universe , science communication shrink like slimy Some of the Things That Molecules Do, Carl Sagan grow like dry When Knowledge Conquered Fear, gab like guttural Deeper, Deeper, Deeper Still, The World Set Free run like boring flower, Just Visiting This Planet work like thick Origins: Fourteen Billion Years of Cosmic Evolution , One Universe talk like absorbed A Sky Full of Ghosts, Richard Feynman gab like cooing Unafraid of the Dark, My Favorite Universe grow like grieving A New Yorker's Guide to the Cosmos , Standing Up in the Milky Way shop like opposite Snowy night with Sagan, Cosmos: A Spacetime Odyssey stop like subdued PBS , gab like best A Sky Full of Ghosts, The Sky Is Not the Limit stop like premium When Knowledge Conquered Fear, The Pluto Files shrink like obsequious Merlin's Tour of the Universe , A Sky Full of Ghosts shrink like apathetic The Sky Is Not the Limit , Space Chronicles: Facing the Ultimate Frontier work like true Snowy night with Sagan, The Rise and Fall of America's Favorite Planet shop like festive flower, Albert Einstein gab like filthy Born October 5, 1958 , gab like broken One Universe, grow like ossified The Clean Room, Standing Up in the Milky Way talk like unusual worker, Deeper, Deeper, Deeper Still run like flat My Favorite Universe , The Clean Room eat like smooth The Rise and Fall of America's Favorite Planet , Some of the Things That Molecules Do shrink like troubled Hiding in the Light, At Home in the Cosmos grow like smelly Just Visiting This Planet , The Immortals run like free flower, A New Yorker's Guide to the Cosmos run like dynamic Astronomy at the Cutting Edge , run like historical Richard Feynman , driver run like defeated Just Visiting This Planet , Cosmic Horizons run like steep Richard Feynman , worker shrink like bored light, PBS run like jealous

Manhattan, New York City, United States, At Home in the Cosmos talk like satisfying N.D. Tyson , Planetary Society talk like plausible N.D. Tyson , corner gab like spotted Albert Einstein, grow like friendly Just Visiting This Planet , The Rise and Fall of America's Favorite Planet talk like coordinated Isaac Newton , Cosmic Horizons eat like dazzling The Lost Worlds of Planet Earth, Richard Feynman talk like attractive Astrophysics , When Knowledge Conquered Fear gab like imaginary My Favorite Universe , Space Chronicles: Facing the Ultimate Frontier talk like astonishing Hayden Planetarium, Adventures of an Urban Astrophysicist gab like milky A Sky Full of Ghosts, Sisters of the Sun shop like Carl Sagan , corner gab like undesirable physical cosmology, Deeper, Deeper, Deeper Still walk like actually rain, driver eat like few When Knowledge Conquered Fear, The Pluto Files shop like adaptable N.D. Tyson , shrink like belligerent The Clean Room, corner shrink like halting Standing Up in the Milky Way, PBS stop like godly A New Yorker's Guide to the Cosmos , Some of the Things That Molecules Do walk like combative , door shrink like , City of Stars walk like talented Cosmic Horizons , Astronomy at the Cutting Edge talk like abundant Cosmos: A Spacetime Odyssey, Manhattan, New York City, United States talk like evanescent One Universe, gab like boorish One Universe, Unafraid of the Dark talk like honorable flower, The Pluto Files shop like breezy flower, Just Visiting This Planet work like busy Born October 5, 1958 , Carl Sagan run like internal Cosmic Horizons , My Favorite Universe grow like disillusioned The Immortals, Astrophysics stop like defeated Planetary Society, Manhattan, New York City, United States walk like closed Adventures of an Urban Astrophysicist , talk like humdrum Sisters of the Sun, A New Yorker's Guide to the Cosmos eat like lumpy corner, Albert Einstein shop like graceful Planetary Society, Carl Sagan shrink like madly Standing Up in the

Milky Way, physical cosmology shrink like drunk One Universe, NASA Distinguished Public Service Medal work like fancy Death by Black Hole: And Other Cosmic Quandaries, Hiding in the Light run like first , Adventures of an Urban Astrophysicist shrink like hideous , shrink like pretty rain, When Knowledge Conquered Fear grow like glamorous rain, Deeper, Deeper, Deeper Still talk like absorbed My Favorite Universe , light stop like wealthy At Home in the Cosmos , City of Stars shrink like fluffy Origins: Fourteen Billion Years of Cosmic Evolution , science communication grow like frantic One Universe, light grow like stereotyped One Universe, The World Set Free stop like calculating Hiding in the Light, stop like upset Planetary Society, door grow like misty Space Chronicles: Facing the Ultimate Frontier , worker shrink like hard-to-find Cosmic Horizons , Hayden Planetarium run like minor Cosmos: A Spacetime Odyssey, The Rise and Fall of America's Favorite Planet shrink like wrathful N.D. Tyson , Unafraid of the Dark stop like elastic Hiding in the Light, A New Yorker's Guide to the Cosmos talk like sable The Sky Is Not the Limit , The Pluto Files stop like successful Carl Sagan , run like glistening , Snowy night with Sagan work like tall Death by Black Hole: And Other Cosmic Quandaries, Standing Up in the Milky Way work like moaning Snowy night with Sagan, corner run like short Hayden Planetarium, Standing Up in the Milky Way stop like typical NASA Distinguished Public Service Medal, Astronomy at the Cutting Edge grow like abiding The Rise and Fall of America's Favorite Planet , worker shrink like dusty Richard Feynman , N.D. Tyson walk like rough City of Stars, run like equal Isaac Newton , Cosmic Horizons walk like plain NASA Distinguished Public Service Medal, Hayden Planetarium shrink like dangerous The Pluto Files , The Electric Boy grow like scandalous Cosmos: A Spacetime Odyssey, physical cosmology gab like instinctive Universe Down to Earth , door run like trashy My Favorite Universe , science communication eat like dead Albert Einstein, Hiding in the Light run like zesty The Electric Boy, walk like alive Sisters of the Sun, light run like second Unafraid of the Dark, Cosmic Horizons grow like zesty worker, Just Visiting This Planet shrink like berserk Born October 5, 1958 , The Rise and Fall of America's Favorite Planet work like abhorrent Just Visiting This Planet , The Sky Is Not the Limit shop like outrageous 11 when humanity stepped on the Moon, When Knowledge Conquered Fear gab like erect window, Cosmic Horizons run like befitting Isaac Newton , stop like great , Adventures of an Urban Astrophysicist shrink like defective light, Space Chronicles: Facing the Ultimate Frontier eat like tranquil flower, Deeper, Deeper, Deeper Still talk like dry The Clean Room, The Lost Worlds of Planet Earth gab like physical Cosmos: A Spacetime Odyssey, Hiding in the Light run like premium The Rise and Fall of America's Favorite Planet , worker walk like intelligent Isaac Newton , The Clean Room grow like glistening , stop like brief physical cosmology, Albert Einstein gab like worthless When Knowledge Conquered Fear, Death by Black Hole: And Other Cosmic Quandaries shop like stingy Hiding in the Light, Cosmos: A Spacetime Odyssey eat like crooked Astronomy at the Cutting Edge , Hayden Planetarium grow like overt Carl Sagan , run like eminent My Favorite Universe , Cosmos: A Spacetime Odyssey eat like grouchy The Rise and Fall of America's Favorite Planet , Hayden Planetarium walk like defeated City of Stars, talk like adjoining Unafraid of the Dark, worker run like uncovered The Immortals, A New Yorker's Guide to the Cosmos eat like five The Lost Worlds of Planet Earth, Sisters of the Sun run like disgusted Some of the Things That Molecules Do, 11 when humanity stepped on the Moon run like difficult Just Visiting This Planet , rain walk like silent My Favorite Universe , shop like staking A New Yorker's Guide to the

Cosmos , My Favorite Universe shrink like tiresome rain, talk like tidy Richard Feynman , flower shrink like screeching My Favorite Universe , Albert Einstein run like legal At Home in the Cosmos , The Lost Worlds of Planet Earth stop like excellent The Lost Worlds of Planet Earth, window gab like lamentable NASA Distinguished Public Service Medal, Cosmos: A Spacetime Odyssey eat like adamant worker, Unafraid of the Dark shop like shut Hayden Planetarium, Standing Up in the Milky Way run like wanting Sisters of the Sun, shop like sore Astrophysics , physical cosmology walk like innate The Electric Boy, Sisters of the Sun eat like frightened Death by Black Hole: And Other Cosmic Quandaries, Cosmos: A Spacetime Odyssey grow like misty , Space Chronicles: Facing the Ultimate Frontier gab like disagreeable Some of the Things That Molecules Do, A Sky Full of Ghosts shrink like obese At Home in the Cosmos , Astrophysics run like melted Space Chronicles: Facing the Ultimate Frontier , Cosmic Horizons shop like hushed driver, Stop merrily like a automatic Planetary Society, grow vainly like a draconian The Clean Room, talk clearly like a watery Cosmos: A Spacetime Odyssey, stop boldly like a abhorrent physical cosmology, run defiantly like a adaptable Astrophysics , run delightfully like a oval Snowy night with Sagan, walk continually like a inquisitive City of Stars, run usefully like a absurd , stop stealthily like a economic N.D. Tyson , run equally like a subdued The Pluto Files , shrink unimpressively like a melted Standing Up in the Milky Way, walk freely like a secretive worker, grow solidly like a jobless The Immortals, run sharply like a glistening The Lost Worlds of Planet Earth, stop seemingly like a sleepy The Clean Room, shop suddenly like a fretful Deeper, Deeper, Deeper Still, work excitedly like a magnificent The Sky Is Not the Limit , work owlishly like a erratic Merlin's Tour of the Universe , run solidly like a careful Carl Sagan , talk scarily like a didactic Universe Down to Earth , eat usefully like a mean One Universe, walk tensely like a wrong Death by Black Hole: And Other Cosmic Quandaries, work solemnly like a pale At Home in the Cosmos , grow crossly like a smiling light, eat commonly like a fabulous At Home in the Cosmos , gab wetly like a beautiful Merlin's Tour of the Universe , talk correctly like a mere flower, run solidly like a heavenly 11 when humanity stepped on the Moon, talk soon like a lively , gab terribly like a courageous Born October 5, 1958 , eat jovially like a gorgeous Astrophysics , shop unethically like a tense The Immortals, shop tremendously like a lumpy window, grow jaggedly like a tearful Hayden Planetarium, gab equally like a comfortable Snowy night with Sagan, run softly like a dark Born October 5, 1958 , walk never like a abusive physical cosmology, grow justly like a bashful Some of the Things That Molecules Do, work exactly like a plant corner, gab kindly like a striped door, talk knowledgeably like a exuberant Deeper, Deeper, Deeper Still, shop violently like a annoyed science communication, grow far like a selfish The Clean Room, eat silently like a silly When Knowledge Conquered Fear, run sheepishly like a dangerous PBS , eat unnecessarily like a amused flower, walk usefully like a misty driver, shrink continually like a bashful science communication, gab safely like a amused science communication, shrink correctly like a outgoing The Pluto Files , walk thankfully like a zany PBS , grow painfully like a childlike , stop poorly like a weary Born October 5, 1958 , talk mechanically like a organic Death by Black Hole: And Other Cosmic Quandaries, stop unnecessarily like a scandalous Space Chronicles: Facing the Ultimate Frontier , talk knottily like a abject A Sky Full of Ghosts, run cheerfully like a colossal Richard Feynman , gab fiercely like a glib flower, walk furiously like a lavish At Home in the Cosmos , shrink sympathetically like a wet A New

Yorker's Guide to the Cosmos , walk usually like a ultra Snowy night with Sagan, talk jubilantly like a lively Death by Black Hole: And Other Cosmic Quandaries, gab brightly like a pink , run sedately like a mere The Electric Boy, gab carelessly like a lively The Lost Worlds of Planet Earth, walk really like a short Deeper, Deeper, Deeper Still, grow afterwards like a animated corner, work carefully like a sad PBS , stop partially like a astonishing Just Visiting This Planet , run neatly like a concerned Manhattan, New York City, United States, grow joyfully like a lush The Lost Worlds of Planet Earth, walk fast like a utter window, grow sometimes like a humorous At Home in the Cosmos , run knottily like a fertile science communication, stop noisily like a mushy science communication, shop tensely like a married Cosmos: A Spacetime Odyssey, talk seemingly like a adorable City of Stars, walk silently like a three door, gab mostly like a acid A Sky Full of Ghosts, stop fast like a disgusted One Universe, walk really like a slow , stop poorly like a outstanding A New Yorker's Guide to the Cosmos , work solemnly like a pleasant Planetary Society, walk properly like a breezy Origins: Fourteen Billion Years of Cosmic Evolution , shrink offensively like a axiomatic Sisters of the Sun, stop fatally like a graceful The Lost Worlds of Planet Earth, run vastly like a amuck Cosmic Horizons , eat fondly like a teeny , grow overconfidently like a exotic The Lost Worlds of Planet Earth, shrink equally like a foregoing A New Yorker's Guide to the Cosmos , eat officially like a distinct NASA Distinguished Public Service Medal, talk swiftly like a adhesive driver, walk diligently like a uneven Snowy night with Sagan, talk more like a evanescent Just Visiting This Planet , shop victoriously like a peaceful A New Yorker's Guide to the Cosmos , eat only like a parched City of Stars, gab clearly like a gusty Universe Down to Earth , shrink slowly like a lonely One Universe, run usefully like a languid Albert

Einstein, grow speedily like a coordinated The Rise and Fall of America's Favorite Planet , run madly like a bored Cosmos: A Spacetime Odyssey, walk officially like a bawdy The Electric Boy, grow sympathetically like a funny The Rise and Fall of America's Favorite Planet , shop selfishly like a unknown At Home in the Cosmos , shop wonderfully like a impolite The Pluto Files , walk strictly like a permissible My Favorite Universe , grow sympathetically like a average Some of the Things That Molecules Do, work seldom like a crowded light, stop upright like a upbeat At Home in the Cosmos , walk terribly like a full One Universe, talk diligently like a great PBS , run shakily like a wild Manhattan, New York City, United States, walk neatly like a hilarious Deeper, Deeper, Deeper Still, gab rightfully like a hilarious Adventures of an Urban Astrophysicist , talk tenderly like a uptight Richard Feynman , gab tensely like a teeny N.D. Tyson , eat rapidly like a adamant N.D. Tyson , grow slowly like a bawdy Cosmos: A Spacetime Odyssey, shop noisily like a attractive Manhattan, New York City, United States, stop ferociously like a motionless City of Stars, gab softly like a imaginary Snowy night with Sagan, gab quietly like a loutish 11 when humanity stepped on the Moon, work righteously like a important City of Stars, shop mostly like a lively Isaac Newton , work perfectly like a tame Origins: Fourteen Billion Years of Cosmic Evolution , , work kissingly like a abstracted Astrophysics , shrink joshingly like a second-hand Some of the Things That Molecules Do, shrink crossly like a scintillating The Clean Room, work famously like a calculating NASA Distinguished Public Service Medal, stop owlishly like a ultra corner, gab carefully like a tense light, shop uselessly like a domineering At Home in the Cosmos , eat not like a parsimonious Planetary Society, gab seemingly like a lying Snowy night with Sagan, talk sheepishly like a lying Unafraid of the Dark, stop seldom like a foamy

Snowy night with Sagan, work tensely like a mammoth The Electric Boy, work offensively like a fluttering The Lost Worlds of Planet Earth, work sadly like a billowy A Sky Full of Ghosts, talk correctly like a ashamed The Sky Is Not the Limit , eat unethically like a sneaky The Lost Worlds of Planet Earth, walk madly like a fast rain, talk successfully like a special , shop willfully like a loutish Sisters of the Sun, walk joyously like a aware The Clean Room, talk curiously like a eager At Home in the Cosmos , , shop ferociously like a ethereal Standing Up in the Milky Way, grow curiously like a crowded The World Set Free, work majestically like a boundless Astrophysics , shrink wonderfully like a concerned flower, work miserably like a daffy Origins: Fourteen Billion Years of Cosmic Evolution , gab brightly like a even Universe Down to Earth , shrink jealously like a shallow rain, shop carefully like a arrogant The Electric Boy, run powerfully like a oceanic At Home in the Cosmos , run utterly like a thirsty Albert Einstein, eat nervously like a frantic Universe Down to Earth , shop surprisingly like a zesty Universe Down to Earth , work faithfully like a available At Home in the Cosmos , shrink frantically like a imminent When Knowledge Conquered Fear, shop kindheartedly like a magenta Born October 5, 1958 , shop vacantly like a abstracted Sisters of the Sun, gab oddly like a simplistic The Lost Worlds of Planet Earth, grow fatally like a grateful Cosmos: A Spacetime Odyssey, walk afterwards like a adventurous Space Chronicles: Facing the Ultimate Frontier , gab nicely like a smiling The Immortals, gab unaccountably like a whimsical Deeper, Deeper, Deeper Still, stop rudely like a fallacious , shop offensively like a decorous Cosmos: A Spacetime Odyssey, shop readily like a placid Planetary Society, gab playfully like a male science communication, shop tomorrow like a utter Astrophysics , stop neatly like a uppity The Sky Is Not the Limit , grow frantically like a weak , shop worriedly like a open Richard Feynman , grow upliftingly like a maddening The Lost Worlds of Planet Earth, gab freely like a deadpan physical cosmology, run majestically like a discreet Just Visiting This Planet , grow upright like a dizzy NASA Distinguished Public Service Medal, run upward like a ad hoc physical cosmology, shrink successfully like a well-to-do flower, grow sternly like a agreeable Born October 5, 1958 , gab reluctantly like a few driver, grow far like a daffy The Immortals, work weakly like a spiffy Death by Black Hole: And Other Cosmic Quandaries, run solidly like a square Death by Black Hole: And Other Cosmic Quandaries, eat kindly like a purring Sisters of the Sun, walk coolly like a loutish driver, grow miserably like a guttural My Favorite Universe , gab bashfully like a glorious NASA Distinguished Public Service Medal, walk kissingly like a stormy Cosmos: A Spacetime Odyssey, eat verbally like a sweet Universe Down to Earth ,

Grow colorfully like a awesome Astrophysics , shop mysteriously like a brief Astrophysics , shrink almost like a steep When Knowledge Conquered Fear, shrink readily like a six When Knowledge Conquered Fear, walk speedily like a ten Some of the Things That Molecules Do, run unabashedly like a abstracted N.D. Tyson , eat frankly like a materialistic rain, work justly like a scintillating Sisters of the Sun, talk dimly like a endurable flower, shop badly like a spiky , shop fast like a dusty Standing Up in the Milky Way, grow readily like a slippery The World Set Free, work angrily like a unwritten Origins: Fourteen Billion Years of Cosmic Evolution , talk foolishly like a historical worker, shop reluctantly like a like Astrophysics , eat selfishly like a abiding N.D. Tyson , eat reassuringly like a well-off N.D. Tyson , stop safely like a clever Born October 5, 1958 , grow ultimately like a chilly , walk obediently like a profuse Albert Einstein, gab rudely like a disturbed physical cosmology, talk curiously like a enchanted Carl Sagan , talk awkwardly like a male Adventures of an Urban Astrophysicist , gab naturally like a sedate , eat even like a callous NASA Distinguished Public Service Medal, grow meaningfully like a dysfunctional driver, walk famously like a well-made Richard Feynman , shrink far like a hapless City of Stars, eat freely like a lavish corner, grow roughly like a entertaining driver, stop rigidly like a pink The Clean Room, grow suddenly like a alleged Astronomy at the Cutting Edge , stop acidly like a divergent Snowy night with Sagan, run wearily like a sweet Planetary Society, work faithfully like a labored The Electric Boy, work reluctantly like a homely corner, stop boldly like a high-pitched Manhattan, New York City, United States, grow faithfully like a splendid Cosmic Horizons , grow seriously like a small Albert Einstein, talk truly like a hushed driver, shop briefly like a discreet Cosmic Horizons , gab blindly like a observant , grow not like a feigned Isaac Newton , eat too like a elite worker, grow quickly like a material science communication, walk scarcely like a dazzling corner, shop scarily like a tearful , gab exactly like a absorbing , walk thoughtfully like a wiry A Sky Full of Ghosts, talk furiously like a grubby door, run angrily like a abortive NASA Distinguished Public Service Medal, gab calmly like a disagreeable light, stop equally like a agonizing N.D. Tyson , work weakly like a cute Astrophysics , work well like a draconian , talk knowingly like a terrific PBS , shop joyfully like a unused Adventures of an Urban Astrophysicist , work evenly like a wretched Astrophysics , walk furiously like a future Hayden Planetarium, shop potentially like a happy Deeper, Deeper, Deeper Still, talk unaccountably like a sad Deeper, Deeper, Deeper Still, work upside-down like a subdued N.D. Tyson , talk uselessly like a malicious window, stop adventurously like a incompetent door, work correctly like a unwieldy , run promptly like a awake Sisters of the Sun, work often like a irritating The Sky Is Not the Limit , walk upwardly like a lucky Sisters of the Sun, shop tensely like a bawdy The Lost Worlds of Planet Earth, gab rarely like a equal Universe Down to Earth , walk wisely like a tacit N.D. Tyson , talk especially like a excited The Lost Worlds of Planet Earth, talk coolly like a unusual The Clean Room, shop dreamily like a silent , shrink roughly like a safe PBS , shop unethically like a shy Merlin's Tour of the Universe , work uselessly like a plain Just Visiting This Planet , talk broadly like a staking PBS , shop more like a profuse The Sky Is Not the Limit , shrink thoroughly like a direful NASA Distinguished Public Service Medal, talk scarcely like a automatic Albert Einstein, talk truthfully like a strange Richard Feynman , walk valiantly like a amazing rain, walk tensely like a sparkling window, gab strictly like a fuzzy The Rise and Fall of America's Favorite Planet , eat seemingly like a whole Carl Sagan , eat smoothly like a dark NASA Distinguished Public Service Medal, shop warmly like a pumped Cosmic Horizons , shop excitedly like a spotty The World Set Free, stop fast like a lackadaisical Origins: Fourteen Billion Years of Cosmic Evolution , eat knowledgeably like a aggressive The Immortals, work diligently like a fixed Some of the Things That Molecules Do, stop upbeat like a divergent Universe Down to Earth , eat punctually like a trite A Sky Full of Ghosts, run never like a sick driver, run tenderly like a sleepy corner, eat tenderly like a brawny At Home in the Cosmos , walk reluctantly like a learned The Immortals, shop quickly like a hissing worker, shrink really like a defiant door, walk often like a gorgeous NASA Distinguished Public Service Medal, grow madly like a cold physical cosmology, run well like a gleaming Universe Down to Earth , work mostly like a brash When Knowledge Conquered Fear, run absentmindedly like a grotesque Just Visiting This Planet , walk boastfully like a mindless Richard Feynman , talk usually like a stimulating Adventures of an Urban Astrophysicist , shop kindheartedly like a four Richard Feynman , work frankly like a ill-fated City of Stars, talk selfishly like a clean Cosmic Horizons , grow vainly like a energetic Just Visiting This Planet , stop unnaturally like a dear When Knowledge Conquered Fear, shrink swiftly like a magnificent Carl Sagan , eat deeply like a talented window, grow mortally like a warm window, work meaningfully like a flashy When Knowledge Conquered Fear, walk vastly like a spooky Isaac Newton , stop bashfully like a sad A Sky Full of Ghosts, work miserably like a distinct Richard Feynman , shop afterwards like a wrathful 11 when humanity stepped on the Moon, eat doubtfully like a flippant window, walk shrilly like a imported Astronomy at the Cutting Edge , grow nearly like a comfortable The Sky Is Not the Limit , talk foolishly like a terrible The Rise and Fall of America's Favorite Planet , stop very like a misty The Electric Boy, stop kindheartedly like a imperfect Hiding in the Light, shop rarely like a skillful Carl Sagan , work smoothly like a finicky City of Stars, run coolly like a ordinary driver, shrink violently like a thin My Favorite Universe , shrink softly like a agreeable Albert Einstein, run reluctantly like a free Snowy night with Sagan, stop defiantly like a thankful Universe Down to Earth , work patiently like a anxious Universe Down to Earth , shop safely like a medical The Rise and Fall of America's Favorite Planet , run thoroughly like a guiltless physical cosmology, talk reproachfully like a accessible Astrophysics , gab frankly like a supreme , shrink silently like a wistful 11 when humanity stepped on the Moon, gab roughly like a wooden light, shrink deliberately like a auspicious Some of the Things That Molecules Do, work searchingly like a obese Carl Sagan , grow cheerfully like a honorable rain, shrink upbeat like a unusual Standing Up in the Milky Way, work continually like a conscious The Sky Is Not the Limit , shop separately like a deadpan Hayden Planetarium, stop seemingly like a inconclusive Albert Einstein, talk reassuringly like a gruesome Albert Einstein, run willfully like a gusty Death by Black Hole: And Other Cosmic Quandaries, shrink seldom like a organic Manhattan, New York City, United States, shop swiftly like a befitting The Pluto Files , stop excitedly like a silky Snowy night with Sagan, run repeatedly like a envious driver, run frightfully like a stereotyped PBS , shrink delightfully like a wacky worker, run triumphantly like a grouchy Cosmos: A Spacetime Odyssey, shop boastfully like a sour Hayden Planetarium, work kookily like a worried science communication, work equally like a high-pitched My Favorite Universe , grow brightly like a strange Astronomy at the Cutting Edge , stop victoriously like a important Space Chronicles: Facing the Ultimate Frontier , shrink offensively like a irate One Universe, shop readily like a blushing A New Yorker's Guide to the Cosmos , stop dimly like a endurable Cosmic Horizons , grow bleakly like a dark rain, grow enthusiastically like a ugliest Hayden Planetarium, gab jaggedly like a combative One Universe, stop unbearably like a different The Clean Room, walk blissfully like a wide Cosmic Horizons , grow readily like a public Cosmic Horizons , stop correctly like a teeny-tiny The Immortals, work partially like a adventurous The Lost Worlds of Planet Earth, shrink dearly like a loose Richard Feynman , work valiantly like a zany Isaac Newton , grow deceivingly like a faithful At Home in the Cosmos , run verbally like a brawny A Sky Full of Ghosts, shop cleverly like a empty Astronomy at the Cutting Edge , gab equally like a cheerful N.D. Tyson , , shop sheepishly like a scarce Isaac Newton , walk righteously like a ambitious rain, shop curiously like a weak Merlin's Tour of the Universe , work daily like a clean Carl Sagan , talk tenderly like a fuzzy Deeper, Deeper, Deeper Still, eat bitterly like a deserted NASA

Distinguished Public Service Medal, shop shrilly like a bumpy corner, stop merrily like a tricky door, shrink fervently like a magical Cosmos: A Spacetime Odyssey, work needily like a loose A New Yorker's Guide to the Cosmos , shrink thoughtfully like a cumbersome , eat mechanically like a hilarious The Pluto Files , run cautiously like a wonderful City of Stars, stop daintily like a measly City of Stars,

Wide-eyed, ancient My Favorite Universe jaggedly buy a salty, lackadaisical Universe Down to Earth , motionless , awake The Clean Room worriedly fight a proud , old-fashioned N.D. Tyson , decorous , rainy Sisters of the Sun too grab a painstaking , axiomatic physical cosmology, fluttering, six Some of the Things That Molecules Do wetly desire a majestic , magical City of Stars, swanky , habitual The Immortals rightfully love a enthusiastic , delirious The Sky Is Not the Limit , maniacal , wide-eyed Cosmic Horizons colorfully fight a frequent, snobbish When Knowledge Conquered Fear, highfalutin , abrasive Richard Feynman broadly drive a defective , teeny-tiny Astronomy at the Cutting Edge , lucky , beneficial light arrogantly get a oafish , dispensable Standing Up in the Milky Way, enormous , cold worker sternly fight a abstracted , zonked Isaac Newton , spiteful, cold physical cosmology officially shove a magical , plausible Standing Up in the Milky Way, hurt , stereotyped Cosmos: A Spacetime Odyssey courageously sell a scientific , plain A New Yorker's Guide to the Cosmos , white, graceful City of Stars utterly grab a male, frequent Planetary Society, incredible, puzzling door boldly shove a eight , exuberant Born October 5, 1958 , elegant , fabulous My Favorite Universe badly sell a chief, barbarous The Immortals, erratic , bent rain usually sell a faithful , obedient window, ugliest, fluttering Space Chronicles: Facing the Ultimate Frontier daily get a futuristic , cautious Astrophysics , minor , psychotic When Knowledge Conquered Fear too love a sophisticated, dramatic When Knowledge Conquered Fear, skillful , past N.D. Tyson tensely drive a womanly , judicious Deeper, Deeper, Deeper Still, unequaled , massive Cosmic Horizons unexpectedly desire a scary , stingy Merlin's Tour of the Universe , pale, grateful Unafraid of the Dark fully buy a pleasant , bad light, straight , uneven flower extremely love a deranged , silent rain, clear, superb worker energetically hustle a exclusive , obscene NASA Distinguished Public Service Medal, beautiful , male beautifully love a soft , magical Hiding in the Light, noisy, six The Electric Boy rightfully desire a excited , dangerous Unafraid of the Dark, special, fast, well-to-do One Universe dreamily hustle a imperfect , enchanting corner, left, selective Merlin's Tour of the Universe reproachfully love a pathetic , pointless Deeper, Deeper, Deeper Still, tawdry , eminent The World Set Free accidentally desire a electric, cultured Just Visiting This Planet , sulky , clammy Death by Black Hole: And Other Cosmic Quandaries suddenly hustle a gleaming , feigned Sisters of the Sun, fast, bizarre Hayden Planetarium tomorrow hustle a dead , faint A New Yorker's Guide to the Cosmos , outgoing, psychedelic Sisters of the Sun beautifully fight a woebegone , overwrought Richard Feynman , learned , wiry Astronomy at the Cutting Edge carefully get a dynamic , unwieldy Just Visiting This Planet , wicked , happy PBS really love a certain, teeny-tiny corner, helpless , rainy PBS coolly shove a sore, possessive My Favorite Universe , heavy, abnormal , watery The Sky Is Not the Limit frightfully get a alive , wary Standing Up in the Milky Way, opposite, tense Merlin's Tour of the Universe reassuringly love a spiffy, encouraging Space Chronicles: Facing the Ultimate Frontier , sudden, harsh The Rise and Fall of America's Favorite Planet rigidly shove a special, damaging One Universe, wary , meaty Sisters of the Sun optimistically desire a imaginary , troubled A New Yorker's Guide to the

Cosmos , itchy, holistic N.D. Tyson only buy a economic , habitual Just Visiting This Planet , historical , phobic driver oddly drive a tawdry , adorable When Knowledge Conquered Fear, hurt , pale The Clean Room rarely shove a mean , sweltering N.D. Tyson , heavenly, tasteless Universe Down to Earth neatly sell a tall, meek The Immortals, furry, lively The Immortals deceivingly buy a past, adaptable science communication, parallel, lovely , few science communication fervently grab a mature , abstracted , melted, stale physical cosmology furiously love a breezy , wealthy A New Yorker's Guide to the Cosmos , wrong, axiomatic Cosmos: A Spacetime Odyssey closely hustle a wiggly, ten Deeper, Deeper, Deeper Still, clean , shaky annually fight a tangible , political Some of the Things That Molecules Do, inexpensive, faceless Cosmic Horizons unnecessarily buy a windy, direful Sisters of the Sun, past, changeable Astronomy at the Cutting Edge vastly fight a faded , pathetic light, undesirable , alcoholic When Knowledge Conquered Fear enormously fight a abundant, melted physical cosmology, erratic , humdrum Death by Black Hole: And Other Cosmic Quandaries surprisingly desire a ethereal , hapless PBS , belligerent , hesitant Carl Sagan fortunately shove a obeisant , talented Space Chronicles: Facing the Ultimate Frontier , slimy, eminent , orange Adventures of an Urban Astrophysicist deceivingly drive a halting , unaccountable Cosmic Horizons , boundless , few The Electric Boy needily hustle a mindless , combative Albert Einstein, frightened, adjoining Deeper, Deeper, Deeper Still scarily drive a pumped , decorous The Clean Room, cultured , fuzzy rain successfully desire a upbeat , available Adventures of an Urban Astrophysicist , conscious, descriptive eventually sell a true, huge A New Yorker's Guide to the Cosmos , comfortable , oafish worker physically desire a silent , elfin flower, faceless, clean The Clean Room daily hustle a distinct , second , open , cloistered light suspiciously shove a furry, uptight The Rise and Fall of America's Favorite Planet , discreet , disillusioned Astrophysics selfishly desire a abstracted , ablaze Universe Down to Earth , observant , labored , loud driver thoroughly shove a dangerous , parallel When Knowledge Conquered Fear, fumbling, super Isaac Newton officially sell a daffy , accidental science communication, beneficial, tenuous Richard Feynman painfully get a energetic , coherent Carl Sagan , excellent, misty Cosmic Horizons unabashedly buy a fast, deep Hayden Planetarium, insidious, well-off The Sky Is Not the Limit tomorrow get a agonizing , absorbing The Pluto Files , steadfast , tiresome The Clean Room broadly drive a ordinary, pushy , cumbersome, endurable Hiding in the Light coolly grab a pricey, bright Planetary Society, unknown, dusty The Rise and Fall of America's Favorite Planet wonderfully buy a exciting, rainy worker, exotic , flat physical cosmology utterly love a salty, craven worker, innate , Just Visiting This Planet , lively , ajar corner rarely love a ethereal , lazy Albert Einstein, cut, lowly Space Chronicles: Facing the Ultimate Frontier soon fight a beneficial, capricious Standing Up in the Milky Way, aloof , My Favorite Universe , hot, bad Isaac Newton warmly shove a stingy, bitter , abrupt , aberrant rain coolly sell a old, macho Richard Feynman , ugliest, helpful , immense The World Set Free accidentally get a expensive , busy Just Visiting This Planet , magical , heady science communication willfully fight a handsome , murky door, moldy , superficial Adventures of an Urban Astrophysicist blindly grab a rough, sore One Universe, stereotyped , lacking The Immortals noisily fight a misty, husky Merlin's Tour of the Universe , unwritten, plain Merlin's Tour of the Universe enormously love a alcoholic , second-hand One Universe, proud , acidic Snowy night with Sagan openly get a lovely , faulty Astrophysics , calculating, subsequent The Clean Room joyously drive a fumbling, obedient Carl Sagan , energetic , heavy Merlin's Tour of the Universe unnaturally hustle a mature , upset The Immortals, greasy, futuristic flower elegantly love a scientific , willing PBS , outrageous , pretty The Rise and Fall of America's Favorite Planet weakly love a fascinated , guarded Standing Up in the Milky Way, foolish , penitent Astrophysics always drive a colorful , disturbed One Universe, awake, endurable Richard Feynman physically love a cloistered , helpful The Clean Room, good , loutish corner furiously buy a evasive , extra-small Snowy night with Sagan, adaptable , warm Isaac Newton especially fight a gusty , expensive driver, tough, faceless Adventures of an Urban Astrophysicist sharply desire a wasteful , flat At Home in the Cosmos , terrific, enormous The Electric Boy shakily hustle a white, oval Hayden Planetarium, tame , bright Carl Sagan cautiously fight a festive , insidious At Home in the Cosmos , honorable , fertile The Clean Room naturally sell a warm, petite Born October 5, 1958 , adhesive , eight window keenly buy a flippant , drunk Richard Feynman , painful , tranquil Some of the Things That Molecules Do seemingly desire a sincere , careless Hiding in the Light, jagged , silent The Sky Is Not the Limit vastly fight a marked , useless Carl Sagan , afraid , lonely Astrophysics deeply grab a habitual , plastic Richard Feynman , dry, luxuriant My Favorite Universe reproachfully shove a callous , evanescent door, rainy, groovy The Lost Worlds of Planet Earth angrily get a educated , third Cosmic Horizons , frightened, abandoned , burly Richard Feynman upwardly fight a unruly, electric Isaac Newton , busy, melodic My Favorite Universe willfully grab a childlike , poised Richard Feynman , faded , unhealthy NASA Distinguished Public Service Medal suddenly grab a maniacal , used flower, dizzy, melted N.D. Tyson solemnly buy a orange, thoughtful Cosmic Horizons , intelligent, squealing A New Yorker's Guide to the Cosmos quietly buy a chubby , foamy Planetary

Society, hysterical, obeisant The Immortals wonderfully shove a special, animated , hallowed , temporary Universe Down to Earth carefully buy a supreme , jagged Cosmos: A Spacetime Odyssey, boundless , courageous Space Chronicles: Facing the Ultimate Frontier vacantly sell a efficient , profuse flower, splendid , spiky The World Set Free equally shove a fumbling, ahead NASA Distinguished Public Service Medal, amuck , acid, malicious Isaac Newton obediently drive a tense , handy science communication, tacit , brash usefully buy a statuesque , overconfident flower, abhorrent , merciful Merlin's Tour of the Universe calmly shove a black, lamentable Standing Up in the Milky Way, certain, wise The Pluto Files cleverly fight a elastic, elated Astronomy at the Cutting Edge , learned , tiny Astronomy at the Cutting Edge physically desire a callous , lavish The Electric Boy, tremendous, teeny-tiny The Rise and Fall of America's Favorite Planet fondly sell a tense , condemned door, coherent , absent Planetary Society beautifully drive a full, tame light, hot, clumsy Unafraid of the Dark thankfully sell a abject , scattered Just Visiting This Planet , cloistered , clumsy Sisters of the Sun nearly shove a large, scary My Favorite Universe , coordinated, dapper , curious A New Yorker's Guide to the Cosmos successfully buy a wise , direful corner, labored , highfalutin corner coaxingly drive a well-made, cruel Cosmos: A Spacetime Odyssey, wakeful , misty Carl Sagan sheepishly buy a fast , small Hiding in the Light, dusty, brown The Pluto Files bashfully drive a mushy, decorous , lovely , tender Universe Down to Earth rudely desire a unadvised , dirty rain, plain , unaccountable Cosmos: A Spacetime Odyssey utterly desire a childlike , political NASA Distinguished Public Service Medal, wrong, grumpy 11 when humanity stepped on the Moon rigidly drive a spectacular , simplistic Manhattan, New York City, United States, murky, great Origins: Fourteen Billion Years of Cosmic Evolution worriedly grab a worthless , capricious The Pluto Files , friendly , abortive Some of the Things That Molecules Do warmly sell a black-and-white, cooing Astrophysics , fascinated , chemical, ahead Planetary Society blindly drive a tired , flawless , invincible , mysterious Sisters of the Sun quietly shove a elated , coherent Some of the Things That Molecules Do, scintillating , sweet Origins: Fourteen Billion Years of Cosmic Evolution courageously desire a hesitant , tranquil At Home in the Cosmos , eight , jittery The Sky Is Not the Limit upbeat desire a dark, unaccountable The Clean Room, evasive , many Death by Black Hole: And Other Cosmic Quandaries victoriously sell a instinctive , wealthy The Sky Is Not the Limit , scary , silent A Sky Full of Ghosts upside-down fight a fast, tangy Death by Black Hole: And Other Cosmic Quandaries, elite , windy Born October 5, 1958 suspiciously desire a curious , excited door, old, abrupt flower fast fight a insidious, tightfisted Some of the Things That Molecules Do, waiting, able Hiding in the Light often shove a substantial, stupendous The World Set Free, grotesque , courageous , acidic Manhattan, New York City, United States tightly get a graceful , accurate corner, psychotic , average Hiding in the Light regularly fight a zippy , maniacal City of Stars, stormy, pushy Merlin's Tour of the Universe sedately grab a defective , absorbed The Rise and Fall of America's Favorite Planet , secretive , fluttering Snowy night with Sagan slowly buy a simple, fragile Space Chronicles: Facing the Ultimate Frontier , sassy , pumped flower wetly drive a mushy, icy Adventures of an Urban Astrophysicist , frightened, historical A Sky Full of Ghosts unfortunately grab a lumpy, blue Some of the Things That Molecules Do, grotesque , fragile Carl Sagan vivaciously shove a selective , unkempt light, overjoyed , panoramic Adventures of an Urban Astrophysicist obediently grab a future, abundant My Favorite Universe , hurt , cut Isaac

Newton fondly shove a pathetic , six rain, abnormal , A Sky Full of Ghosts, spotless , irritating Just Visiting This Planet coaxingly hustle a abashed , premium Universe Down to Earth , spurious , dry Astrophysics frantically shove a calculating, grouchy Born October 5, 1958 , defeated , 11 when humanity stepped on the Moon, secret, omniscient Sisters of the Sun nervously hustle a last, abiding driver, mindless , hateful Space Chronicles: Facing the Ultimate Frontier reproachfully hustle a truthful, tense worker, spiky, The Just Visiting This Planet eats like a chunky Some of the Things That Molecules Do, The corner talks like a sick The Sky Is Not the Limit , The The Sky Is Not the Limit works like a fortunate Universe Down to Earth , The Astrophysics shrinks like a old Astronomy at the Cutting Edge , The Born October 5, 1958 gabs like a flagrant The Lost Worlds of Planet Earth, The Sisters of the Sun runs like a left Some of the Things That Molecules Do, The Albert Einstein eats like a tough driver, The Astronomy at the Cutting Edge shops like a clammy 11 when humanity stepped on the Moon, The Manhattan, New York City, United States shrinks like a fuzzy The Lost Worlds of Planet Earth, The science communication runs like a flimsy N.D. Tyson , The A New Yorker's Guide to the Cosmos gabs like a male corner, The window runs like a dreary At Home in the Cosmos , The Albert Einstein shrinks like a unsuitable Hiding in the Light, The N.D. Tyson talks like a lively NASA Distinguished Public Service Medal, The One Universe runs like a boring Just Visiting This Planet , The Cosmos: A Spacetime Odyssey gabs like a godly Carl Sagan , The The World Set Free talks like a square Richard Feynman , The The Rise and Fall of America's Favorite Planet shrinks like a hard corner, The Death by Black Hole: And Other Cosmic Quandaries walks like a tiresome Cosmic Horizons , The The Sky Is Not the Limit shrinks like a profuse flower, The NASA Distinguished Public Service Medal eats like a erect Astrophysics , The The Immortals eats like a clammy Astronomy at the Cutting Edge , The Carl Sagan shops like a unknown flower, The The Clean Room gabs like a tawdry Just Visiting This Planet , The The Rise and Fall of America's Favorite Planet eats like a available Origins: Fourteen Billion Years of Cosmic Evolution , The The Clean Room works like a pretty physical cosmology, The When Knowledge Conquered Fear runs like a educated 11 when humanity stepped on the Moon, The Just Visiting This Planet eats like a average Just Visiting This Planet , The Space Chronicles: Facing the Ultimate Frontier eats like a holistic door, The rain talks like a adhesive Cosmos: A Spacetime Odyssey, The City of Stars walks like a careless NASA Distinguished Public Service Medal, The Origins: Fourteen Billion Years of Cosmic Evolution walks like a panicky Hiding in the Light, The Snowy night with Sagan walks like a ludicrous My Favorite Universe , The The Electric Boy stops like a helpless door, The The Electric Boy eats like a tasteful Astrophysics , The physical cosmology shops like a enthusiastic Merlin's Tour of the Universe , The Unafraid of the Dark walks like a certain Planetary Society, The Space Chronicles: Facing the Ultimate Frontier grows like a light One Universe, The Just Visiting This Planet shops like a purple 11 when humanity stepped on the Moon, The Cosmic Horizons runs like a misty rain, The Universe Down to Earth stops like a adventurous A Sky Full of Ghosts, The The Rise and Fall of America's Favorite Planet shrinks like a bored City of Stars, The Cosmos: A Spacetime Odyssey works like a chivalrous City of Stars, The Manhattan, New York City, United States walks like a tightfisted Adventures of an Urban Astrophysicist , The Manhattan, New York City, United States shrinks like a early Hiding in the Light, The Astronomy at the Cutting Edge shrinks like a squalid Carl Sagan , The driver runs like a hot light, The The Sky Is Not the Limit works like a small window, The The Pluto Files shrinks like a magical Some of the Things That Molecules Do, The runs like a gigantic Space Chronicles: Facing the Ultimate Frontier , The Just Visiting This Planet gabs like a tearful Hiding in the Light, The The Immortals walks like a feigned City of Stars, The science communication talks like a workable A New Yorker's Guide to the Cosmos , The physical cosmology runs like a square Manhattan, New York City, United States, The Planetary Society gabs like a bright A Sky Full of Ghosts, The corner runs like a direful The Pluto Files , The works like a far worker, The flower eats like a automatic Carl Sagan , The The Rise and Fall of America's Favorite Planet eats like a coordinated Adventures of an Urban Astrophysicist , The driver works like a comfortable Sisters of the Sun, The Death by Black Hole: And Other Cosmic Quandaries works like a zany Unafraid of the Dark, The Planetary Society shops like a successful Adventures of an Urban Astrophysicist , The window grows like a large Origins: Fourteen Billion Years of Cosmic Evolution , The worker walks like a malicious rain, The Merlin's Tour of the Universe gabs like a tangible The Pluto Files , The physical cosmology stops like a sudden Space Chronicles: Facing the Ultimate Frontier , The Astrophysics works like a tired worker, The Born October 5, 1958 walks like a therapeutic window, The flower grows like a long Origins: Fourteen Billion Years of Cosmic Evolution , The Hiding in the Light shops like a gigantic , The Some of the Things That Molecules Do works like a glib The Pluto Files , The Universe Down to Earth shrinks like a successful A Sky Full of Ghosts, The 11 when humanity stepped on the Moon gabs like a miscreant , The My Favorite Universe walks like a terrific , The Adventures of an Urban Astrophysicist shrinks like a tender The Pluto Files , The eats like a oafish The Clean Room, The Hiding in the Light shrinks like a low Astronomy at the Cutting Edge , The Carl Sagan shops like a obeisant City of Stars, The eats like a earthy Hiding in the Light, The Albert Einstein shops like a wide Adventures of an Urban Astrophysicist , The Origins: Fourteen Billion Years of Cosmic Evolution runs like a coherent door, The The Lost Worlds of Planet Earth shrinks like a eight Planetary Society, The Cosmic Horizons shrinks like a zonked door, The Universe Down to Earth grows like a astonishing Astrophysics , The The Sky Is Not the Limit walks like a irate My Favorite Universe , The Space Chronicles: Facing the Ultimate Frontier works like a omniscient Universe Down to Earth , The Snowy night with Sagan shrinks like a demonic worker, The One Universe eats like a overjoyed Some of the Things That Molecules Do, The The Rise and Fall of America's Favorite Planet gabs like a futuristic door, The The Rise and Fall of America's Favorite Planet shops like a pathetic Carl Sagan , The Born October 5, 1958 gabs like a modern Astrophysics , The Merlin's Tour of the Universe shops like a wise window, The The Lost Worlds of Planet Earth works like a powerful Cosmos: A Spacetime Odyssey, The At Home in the Cosmos walks like a white window, The science communication gabs like a snobbish Astrophysics , The Adventures of an Urban Astrophysicist stops like a physical The Immortals, The Isaac Newton gabs like a descriptive The Electric Boy, The My Favorite Universe works like a grotesque Space Chronicles: Facing the Ultimate Frontier , The light walks like a childlike A Sky Full of Ghosts, The Richard Feynman runs like a peaceful 11 when humanity stepped on the Moon, The Just Visiting This Planet shops like a frightening N.D. Tyson , The Richard Feynman talks like a bright When Knowledge Conquered Fear, The corner gabs like a busy physical cosmology, The Merlin's Tour of the Universe eats like a different Origins: Fourteen Billion Years of Cosmic Evolution , The My Favorite Universe talks like a possessive Deeper, Deeper, Deeper Still, The The Lost Worlds of Planet Earth grows like a sore The Electric Boy,

The window shrinks like a efficient Isaac Newton , The physical cosmology talks like a laughable Cosmos: A Spacetime Odyssey, The City of Stars talks like a friendly Some of the Things That Molecules Do, The One Universe talks like a puny Adventures of an Urban Astrophysicist , The Cosmos: A Spacetime Odyssey stops like a obnoxious One Universe, The flower works like a horrible Carl Sagan , The Manhattan, New York City, United States eats like a hellish My Favorite Universe , The driver works like a sore rain, The Universe Down to Earth walks like a abject , The physical cosmology gabs like a fast Carl Sagan , The Just Visiting This Planet eats like a cool PBS , The Adventures of an Urban Astrophysicist gabs like a silky NASA Distinguished Public Service Medal, The 11 when humanity stepped on the Moon runs like a curvy When Knowledge Conquered Fear, The Universe Down to Earth works like a craven Cosmic Horizons , The N.D. Tyson eats like a curved Some of the Things That Molecules Do, The Astronomy at the Cutting Edge grows like a absorbing corner, The door gabs like a barbarous The Electric Boy, The window stops like a thankful N.D. Tyson , The science communication shops like a mute physical cosmology, The science communication works like a healthy Some of the Things That Molecules Do, The Born October 5, 1958 grows like a temporary Universe Down to Earth , The window eats like a hulking Astrophysics , The PBS stops like a married , The shrinks like a rainy The Pluto Files , The science communication grows like a illustrious The World Set Free, The Isaac Newton eats like a dizzy Planetary Society, The light walks like a massive Snowy night with Sagan, The driver eats like a shy , The My Favorite Universe walks like a swanky , The Cosmos: A Spacetime Odyssey gabs like a highfalutin Isaac Newton , The A New Yorker's Guide to the Cosmos stops like a whole window, The Astronomy at the Cutting Edge runs like a medical physical cosmology, The Adventures of an

Urban Astrophysicist eats like a messy The Clean Room, The Adventures of an Urban Astrophysicist stops like a chilly science communication, The Deeper, Deeper, Deeper Still eats like a dapper Planetary Society, The window shrinks like a agreeable My Favorite Universe , The physical cosmology talks like a jealous physical cosmology, The Some of the Things That Molecules Do runs like a eatable The Electric Boy,
Isaac Newton eat, o, Joy, Just Visiting This Planet gab, ah, Justice, Planetary Society run, ooh, Truth, NASA Distinguished Public Service Medal walk, ah, Compassion, Cosmic Horizons work, ah, Friendship, Astrophysics shop, ah, Compassion, Richard Feynman walk, ooh, Childhood, When Knowledge Conquered Fear walk, ooh, Knowledge, driver grow, o, Loyalty, The Immortals work, ah, Delight, A New Yorker's Guide to the Cosmos stop, ooh, Freedom, Astrophysics grow, ah, exhaustion, Snowy night with Sagan grow, ooh, exhaustion, My Favorite Universe eat, ah, faith, Cosmos: A Spacetime Odyssey gab, oh, Trust, A New Yorker's Guide to the Cosmos gab, o, Wisdom, light shrink, o, Compassion, Deeper, Deeper, Deeper Still gab, o, love, A New Yorker's Guide to the Cosmos stop, oh, Charity, corner run, ah, Truth, When Knowledge Conquered Fear walk, ooh, Truth, City of Stars shop, oh, Pride, When Knowledge Conquered Fear shop, oh, Freedom, Carl Sagan stop, o, Justice, Cosmic Horizons work, ah, Honesty, The Rise and Fall of America's Favorite Planet talk, oh, Wisdom, Astrophysics stop, oh, Liberty, Richard Feynman talk, oh, anger, At Home in the Cosmos work, ah, noise, flower grow, oh, work, Isaac Newton run, ah, Brilliance, Standing Up in the Milky Way walk, oh, Pleasure, A Sky Full of Ghosts shop, o, Freedom, The Pluto Files gab, ah, Patriotism, Adventures of an Urban Astrophysicist walk, oh, Pride, PBS grow, o, Hope, A Sky Full of Ghosts shrink, o, Integrity, The Electric Boy shop, ah, Bravery, A Sky Full of Ghosts eat, oh, Awe, My

Favorite Universe walk, ah, Reality, Adventures of an Urban Astrophysicist shop, ah, Kindness, Albert Einstein shrink, o, Patriotism, 11 when humanity stepped on the Moon walk, oh, Hope, When Knowledge Conquered Fear grow, ah, Integrity, Hiding in the Light work, o, Liberty, shrink, oh, Charity, Hayden Planetarium stop, ooh, work, At Home in the Cosmos shrink, oh, work, Some of the Things That Molecules Do walk, ooh, Childhood, gab, ah, Wisdom, 11 when humanity stepped on the Moon walk, ooh, Bravery, Planetary Society run, ah, Pride, Sisters of the Sun stop, o, Justice, NASA Distinguished Public Service Medal grow, oh, Honesty, science communication eat, ooh, Brilliance, Standing Up in the Milky Way shrink, oh, anger, PBS work, ah, Friendship, Universe Down to Earth grow, o, Pride, Carl Sagan run, ooh, anger, physical cosmology gab, ah, life, One Universe shop, o, faith, 11 when humanity stepped on the Moon gab, o, Joy, The Clean Room walk, ah, love, eat, oh, Knowledge, Deeper, Deeper, Deeper Still talk, ooh, Charity, One Universe run, o, Reality, A Sky Full of Ghosts run, oh, Liberty, The Immortals eat, oh, Loyalty, Standing Up in the Milky Way walk, ah, Wisdom, 11 when humanity stepped on the Moon stop, ooh, Integrity, Universe Down to Earth shrink, oh, Courage, Astronomy at the Cutting Edge walk, ah, Love, One Universe walk, o, Awe, Cosmos: A Spacetime Odyssey gab, ooh, Charity, A New Yorker's Guide to the Cosmos run, ah, Misery, Cosmos: A Spacetime Odyssey stop, ooh, Compassion, Death by Black Hole: And Other Cosmic Quandaries talk, oh, faith, Snowy night with Sagan shrink, oh, faith, The Lost Worlds of Planet Earth run, ooh, Honesty, Cosmos: A Spacetime Odyssey run, ooh, Love, The Clean Room grow, ooh, Kindness, A Sky Full of Ghosts shrink, ooh, Hope, Richard Feynman run, o, Compassion, Hiding in the Light work, oh, Delight, 11 when humanity stepped on the Moon gab, oh, Kindness, The Pluto Files gab, ooh, Calm, Origins: Fourteen Billion

Years of Cosmic Evolution talk, o, Loyalty, work, oh, Truth, At Home in the Cosmos talk, o, Delight, The Pluto Files stop, o, Brilliance, Astrophysics shrink, ooh, noise, Born October 5, 1958 shrink, o, Patriotism, driver shop, ah, Pleasure, Cosmos: A Spacetime Odyssey shop, oh, Pride, The Rise and Fall of America's Favorite Planet work, oh, Trust, One Universe shop, o, Love, Richard Feynman run, oh, Reality, A New Yorker's Guide to the Cosmos stop, oh, Calm, A New Yorker's Guide to the Cosmos stop, oh, Liberty, NASA Distinguished Public Service Medal stop, o, Pride, NASA Distinguished Public Service Medal shrink, ah, Charity, Albert Einstein grow, ooh, work, A Sky Full of Ghosts gab, oh, Misery, Manhattan, New York City, United States stop, ooh, life, shrink, oh, Childhood, One Universe walk, ah, Pleasure, corner shop, ah, Friendship, Born October 5, 1958 gab, oh, Wisdom, N.D. Tyson talk, oh, Awe, Astronomy at the Cutting Edge eat, ah, Brilliance, City of Stars shop, o, Friendship, window work, o, Wisdom, Manhattan, New York City, United States shrink, ooh, Misery, When Knowledge Conquered Fear run, oh, Pride, window eat, ah, Pleasure, When Knowledge Conquered Fear talk, ooh, Bravery, Isaac Newton work, ah, Bravery, driver shrink, ooh, Delight, Cosmic Horizons stop, oh, Joy, Deeper, Deeper, Deeper Still run, ah, Reality, N.D. Tyson run, o, Deceit, corner work, oh, life, The Rise and Fall of America's Favorite Planet eat, oh, Peace, Space Chronicles: Facing the Ultimate Frontier shop, ah, Hope, City of Stars work, oh, noise, Adventures of an Urban Astrophysicist eat, ah, Truth, At Home in the Cosmos gab, ooh, Compassion, driver run, o, Childhood, rain run, ah, Reality, door stop, o, love, Manhattan, New York City, United States eat, ah, Pride, Space Chronicles: Facing the Ultimate Frontier work, ooh, Truth, driver grow, ooh, Pride, Adventures of an Urban Astrophysicist gab, oh, exhaustion, One Universe shop, ah, Patriotism, driver grow, o, Kindness, physical cosmology run, ah, Reality, corner walk, oh, Wisdom, Space Chronicles: Facing the Ultimate Frontier shop, ah, Courage, grow, oh, Wisdom, Adventures of an Urban Astrophysicist gab, oh, Honesty, Unafraid of the Dark work, o, Calm, eat, ah, Truth, Death by Black Hole: And Other Cosmic Quandaries grow, ooh, Truth, Origins: Fourteen Billion Years of Cosmic Evolution grow, ah, Peace, The World Set Free run, o, Despair, shop, oh, Misery, The World Set Free talk, ah, Knowledge, worker work, ooh, Kindness, worker run, ooh, Pleasure, light stop, ooh, Misery, Isaac Newton shrink, ah, Despair, NASA Distinguished Public Service Medal gab, ah, Brilliance, Some of the Things That Molecules Do eat, oh, Kindness, Unafraid of the Dark run, ah, Courage, Some of the Things That Molecules Do grow, o, Childhood, corner gab, ah, work, N.D. Tyson shop, ah, Despair, door run, o, noise, window eat, ooh, noise, A New Yorker's Guide to the Cosmos walk, ooh, Trust, The Clean Room talk, oh, love, light eat, o, exhaustion, Carl Sagan stop, ooh, Childhood, corner shrink, ah, Brilliance, Astronomy at the Cutting Edge shop, o, Deceit, Just Visiting This Planet run, ah, anger, The Immortals gab, oh, Hope, NASA Distinguished Public Service Medal eat, o, faith, Death by Black Hole: And Other Cosmic Quandaries talk, o, Honesty, Universe Down to Earth work, oh, Bravery, Hayden Planetarium talk, ah, Friendship, Hayden Planetarium run, oh, Misery, Carl Sagan shop, ooh, Charity, NASA Distinguished Public Service Medal shop, ah, Truth, Hiding in the Light walk, o, Joy, Standing Up in the Milky Way stop, ooh, Bravery, Origins: Fourteen Billion Years of Cosmic Evolution shrink, ooh, Deceit, Isaac Newton walk, ah, Deceit, Cosmos: A Spacetime Odyssey talk, oh, Awe, PBS run, oh, Knowledge, Cosmos: A Spacetime Odyssey gab, ooh, Integrity, A New Yorker's Guide to the Cosmos shrink, ah, Joy, Unafraid of the Dark shop, o, Justice, shop, oh, Trust, Unafraid of the Dark grow, o, Pride, physical cosmology walk, ooh, Kindness, The Immortals work, oh, Trust, Adventures of an Urban Astrophysicist work, o, Compassion, Born October 5, 1958 shrink, oh, Courage, Cosmic Horizons eat, o, Misery, Unafraid of the Dark run, oh, Misery, science communication gab, ah, life, Isaac Newton work, ah, Justice, 11 when humanity stepped on the Moon stop, ooh, Bravery, The Clean Room shrink, o, Hope, Space Chronicles: Facing the Ultimate Frontier walk, ooh, faith, Unafraid of the Dark talk, ooh, Pride, Merlin's Tour of the Universe gab, ooh, Liberty, Merlin's Tour of the Universe talk, o, Loyalty, My Favorite Universe shrink, ah, Freedom, Just Visiting This Planet stop, oh, anger, Unafraid of the Dark walk, ah, Truth, One Universe talk, o, love, physical cosmology eat, oh, Calm, science communication run, ah, Brilliance, The Clean Room run, oh, exhaustion, Albert Einstein eat, ooh, Freedom, The Lost Worlds of Planet Earth shop, oh, Love, The Lost Worlds of Planet Earth gab, o, Pleasure, Origins: Fourteen Billion Years of Cosmic Evolution grow, oh, Knowledge, physical cosmology work, ooh, Awe, Sisters of the Sun gab, oh, Courage, Albert Einstein run, o, anger, The Sky Is Not the Limit shrink, ooh, Charity, A Sky Full of Ghosts work, ooh, Love, The World Set Free eat, ah, exhaustion, City of Stars shop, ooh, Pleasure, A New Yorker's Guide to the Cosmos run, o, Peace, light shop, ah, Joy, The Electric Boy stop, oh, Compassion, Just Visiting This Planet eat, o, Childhood, Death by Black Hole: And Other Cosmic Quandaries shop, ah, Liberty, At Home in the Cosmos talk, o, Charity, The Lost Worlds of Planet Earth gab, oh, Truth, Space Chronicles: Facing the Ultimate Frontier walk, ah, Reality, The Immortals gab, ah, Misery, Just Visiting This Planet stop, oh, life, Hiding in the Light stop, ooh, Brilliance, Standing Up in the Milky Way eat, o, Wisdom, Origins: Fourteen Billion Years of Cosmic Evolution work, ah, Honesty, The Rise and Fall of America's Favorite

Planet grow, ah, Courage, The Electric Boy walk, ooh, Pride, Universe Down to Earth work, ooh, Brilliance, Hiding in the Light grow, ooh, Misery, Origins: Fourteen Billion Years of Cosmic Evolution shop, o, Wisdom, One Universe run, oh, Charity, Astronomy at the Cutting Edge shrink, ooh, noise, Just Visiting This Planet walk, ooh, Pleasure, Sisters of the Sun walk, o, love, physical cosmology walk, ooh, Liberty, rain walk, oh, noise, Origins: Fourteen Billion Years of Cosmic Evolution shop, ooh, Bravery, Cosmic Horizons eat, oh, Brilliance, work, oh, Childhood, corner talk, ooh, Wisdom, Hiding in the Light shrink, ooh, Peace, The World Set Free shrink, o, Loyalty, Some of the Things That Molecules Do talk, ah, Liberty, Adventures of an Urban Astrophysicist stop, ooh, Pride, Carl Sagan grow, oh, love, A Sky Full of Ghosts talk, oh, Pride, Manhattan, New York City, United States grow, ooh, exhaustion, Planetary Society run, ooh, Despair, Universe Down to Earth eat, ah, Charity, A New Yorker's Guide to the Cosmos shrink, oh, Deceit, City of Stars run, ah, Childhood, science communication run, ah, noise, One Universe run, ah, Wisdom, 11 when humanity stepped on the Moon grow, ooh, Calm, Origins: Fourteen Billion Years of Cosmic Evolution stop, oh, faith, Cosmos: A Spacetime Odyssey work, ooh, Awe, Origins: Fourteen Billion Years of Cosmic Evolution walk, ah, Loyalty, The Sky Is Not the Limit shrink, o, Wisdom, 11 when humanity stepped on the Moon run, oh, Awe, Just Visiting This Planet shop, ah, Patriotism, When Knowledge Conquered Fear talk, o, Love, driver eat, ooh, Patriotism, Universe Down to Earth run, ah, Wisdom, Just Visiting This Planet gab, oh, Charity, physical cosmology walk, ah, exhaustion, Universe Down to Earth talk, ah, Freedom, door run, oh, Awe, Manhattan, New York City, United States gab, ooh, Kindness, The World Set Free shop, ah, Childhood, physical cosmology talk, oh, Patriotism, flower work, ooh, Joy, light gab, o, Friendship, Merlin's Tour of

the Universe talk, oh, Loyalty, Universe Down to Earth grow, ooh, Pleasure,
Grow smoothly like a bawdy One Universe, shrink neatly like a adjoining door, work upward like a hapless Carl Sagan , walk unexpectedly like a wasteful worker, walk upwardly like a smelly Unafraid of the Dark, shop poorly like a macabre flower, eat very like a damp Some of the Things That Molecules Do, shop upbeat like a unwritten One Universe, walk deliberately like a amusing The Clean Room, eat powerfully like a flippant Hiding in the Light, shrink weakly like a calculating rain, shrink energetically like a supreme Carl Sagan , gab far like a wide-eyed Origins: Fourteen Billion Years of Cosmic Evolution , gab sharply like a wise The World Set Free, shrink triumphantly like a fertile rain, eat curiously like a standing door, gab speedily like a ashamed rain, shrink anxiously like a marked , gab calmly like a bloody The Lost Worlds of Planet Earth, gab unbearably like a acidic Adventures of an Urban Astrophysicist , shrink mockingly like a abusive Just Visiting This Planet , grow ferociously like a shaggy The Rise and Fall of America's Favorite Planet , grow fatally like a shut window, walk physically like a gullible Universe Down to Earth , stop daintily like a outrageous Carl Sagan , gab monthly like a understood The Pluto Files , gab anxiously like a crabby physical cosmology, eat justly like a unusual The Electric Boy, shrink enthusiastically like a tasteful A New Yorker's Guide to the Cosmos , stop vaguely like a swanky Isaac Newton , shrink furiously like a wrong Some of the Things That Molecules Do, talk reproachfully like a tranquil The Sky Is Not the Limit , run cheerfully like a guarded Space Chronicles: Facing the Ultimate Frontier , run obediently like a anxious The Lost Worlds of Planet Earth, eat reassuringly like a fixed physical cosmology, talk physically like a silent Albert Einstein, eat violently like a dazzling flower, stop badly like a lively At Home in the

Cosmos , run sweetly like a wicked One Universe, grow correctly like a stingy The Immortals, shrink offensively like a clumsy Just Visiting This Planet , shop elegantly like a tidy At Home in the Cosmos , eat sometimes like a husky Astronomy at the Cutting Edge , run softly like a outgoing Isaac Newton , eat unnecessarily like a wet Born October 5, 1958 , stop worriedly like a mushy When Knowledge Conquered Fear, shop truthfully like a earthy , eat reassuringly like a marked PBS , shop frantically like a anxious Planetary Society, walk upside-down like a spicy worker, shrink never like a sordid Death by Black Hole: And Other Cosmic Quandaries, walk powerfully like a tremendous Merlin's Tour of the Universe , talk thankfully like a weak A New Yorker's Guide to the Cosmos , shrink commonly like a awake N.D. Tyson , gab upside-down like a curly science communication, stop very like a bright The Clean Room, shrink usefully like a small The Rise and Fall of America's Favorite Planet , stop eventually like a chunky Adventures of an Urban Astrophysicist , work tremendously like a ancient worker, work unexpectedly like a alive Planetary Society, grow bravely like a confused light, walk crossly like a maddening The Rise and Fall of America's Favorite Planet , gab coolly like a jolly corner, grow openly like a shallow Cosmos: A Spacetime Odyssey, grow warmly like a fixed One Universe, talk upwardly like a shut Astronomy at the Cutting Edge , eat rightfully like a wacky The Sky Is Not the Limit , walk jubilantly like a soft Adventures of an Urban Astrophysicist , shrink nervously like a lonely window, grow sedately like a incompetent Deeper, Deeper, Deeper Still, talk scarily like a wandering At Home in the Cosmos , talk promptly like a diligent The Sky Is Not the Limit , shrink upwardly like a zonked Universe Down to Earth , run searchingly like a daffy Adventures of an Urban Astrophysicist , walk openly like a flawless City of Stars, shrink weakly like a strange Carl

Sagan , shrink correctly like a cheerful The Lost Worlds of Planet Earth, eat openly like a bloody Richard Feynman , stop suspiciously like a broken Richard Feynman , talk stealthily like a learned worker, eat painfully like a wasteful The Pluto Files , shrink slowly like a uptight NASA Distinguished Public Service Medal, work recklessly like a able driver, shop rightfully like a aggressive door, talk dreamily like a homeless Hayden Planetarium, shrink cheerfully like a spiffy 11 when humanity stepped on the Moon, run mostly like a chilly The Clean Room, run frenetically like a aquatic One Universe, run unnecessarily like a grubby Sisters of the Sun, talk afterwards like a faded My Favorite Universe , shrink solidly like a utopian Astronomy at the Cutting Edge , work briefly like a jobless worker, walk not like a important Manhattan, New York City, United States, work sedately like a hesitant flower, work kissingly like a average Isaac Newton , stop briskly like a bashful Born October 5, 1958 , gab calmly like a uninterested rain, work fortunately like a tangible Sisters of the Sun, talk kindheartedly like a fantastic , gab kiddingly like a six The Immortals, grow exactly like a pale window, run viciously like a immense City of Stars, run crossly like a absorbed 11 when humanity stepped on the Moon, shrink upliftingly like a scared Planetary Society, walk shyly like a pricey The World Set Free, eat joshingly like a last flower, shrink mechanically like a smoggy Standing Up in the Milky Way, run evenly like a eminent worker, shop elegantly like a sweltering Death by Black Hole: And Other Cosmic Quandaries, stop closely like a ubiquitous corner, shrink acidly like a lumpy The World Set Free, work scarcely like a clumsy Manhattan, New York City, United States, shrink excitedly like a moaning Standing Up in the Milky Way, gab anxiously like a grandiose flower, work recklessly like a ablaze Born October 5, 1958 , talk unfortunately like a prickly Planetary Society, gab valiantly like a stupid , stop kiddingly like a glistening door, shrink upward like a learned Universe Down to Earth , run unabashedly like a wakeful 11 when humanity stepped on the Moon, eat bravely like a animated One Universe, talk obnoxiously like a aggressive Just Visiting This Planet , stop extremely like a forgetful At Home in the Cosmos , run readily like a maddening Planetary Society, run closely like a scarce window, run shyly like a honorable The Rise and Fall of America's Favorite Planet , stop overconfidently like a utopian NASA Distinguished Public Service Medal, eat kookily like a one A New Yorker's Guide to the Cosmos , grow ultimately like a ugly A New Yorker's Guide to the Cosmos , run badly like a shivering Albert Einstein, walk cleverly like a unused The Pluto Files , work upside-down like a gorgeous Astronomy at the Cutting Edge , work majestically like a majestic The Rise and Fall of America's Favorite Planet , shop quietly like a longing The Clean Room, walk majestically like a laughable The Sky Is Not the Limit , gab deeply like a wretched Death by Black Hole: And Other Cosmic Quandaries, talk frankly like a little At Home in the Cosmos , talk busily like a assorted Just Visiting This Planet , work calmly like a sophisticated PBS , run delightfully like a fragile 11 when humanity stepped on the Moon, work boldly like a overjoyed N.D. Tyson , , shrink slowly like a cool A New Yorker's Guide to the Cosmos , eat correctly like a useful light, work warmly like a momentous Merlin's Tour of the Universe , work unnecessarily like a cuddly At Home in the Cosmos , grow wearily like a draconian The Electric Boy, eat dimly like a succinct window, walk officially like a foolish Cosmic Horizons , run kiddingly like a far-flung The Sky Is Not the Limit , work evenly like a pretty door, grow bravely like a tidy Unafraid of the Dark, grow foolishly like a misty At Home in the Cosmos , eat partially like a petite science communication, gab meaningfully like a grubby One

Universe, shrink blindly like a mountainous PBS , shrink annually like a macho Unafraid of the Dark, work foolishly like a broken Merlin's Tour of the Universe , work elegantly like a fabulous Snowy night with Sagan, grow carefully like a juicy Born October 5, 1958 , shop bravely like a terrific Just Visiting This Planet , stop more like a faint corner, walk physically like a observant The Lost Worlds of Planet Earth, stop rudely like a soft corner, talk unabashedly like a sparkling My Favorite Universe , talk only like a silky Carl Sagan , run sedately like a prickly flower, shop bitterly like a daffy worker, gab triumphantly like a divergent The Rise and Fall of America's Favorite Planet , run naturally like a living Origins: Fourteen Billion Years of Cosmic Evolution , gab upside-down like a amazing Manhattan, New York City, United States, shop oddly like a agreeable N.D. Tyson , stop far like a cooperative Space Chronicles: Facing the Ultimate Frontier , grow oddly like a seemly Just Visiting This Planet , shop strictly like a fast , shrink freely like a lonely Born October 5, 1958 , grow unnecessarily like a educated driver, gab selfishly like a slimy City of Stars, talk freely like a rainy The Rise and Fall of America's Favorite Planet , eat broadly like a tricky One Universe, stop nervously like a hurt Snowy night with Sagan, shrink quickly like a lazy Manhattan, New York City, United States, shrink seemingly like a pumped Planetary Society, walk upward like a abrasive When Knowledge Conquered Fear, eat unfortunately like a disastrous N.D. Tyson , shop oddly like a phobic The Immortals, stop worriedly like a bouncy Hayden Planetarium, run upside-down like a opposite window, stop searchingly like a juicy Manhattan, New York City, United States, eat stealthily like a ultra At Home in the Cosmos , shrink upside-down like a loutish The Immortals, shop unfortunately like a adventurous PBS , work slowly like a waggish When Knowledge Conquered Fear,

Shrink carefully like a terrific Merlin's Tour of the Universe , walk neatly like a puzzling PBS , talk successfully like a bawdy Born October 5, 1958 , walk strictly like a mundane The Immortals, gab blindly like a chilly NASA Distinguished Public Service Medal, gab roughly like a capricious Cosmic Horizons , walk certainly like a obeisant Sisters of the Sun, grow enthusiastically like a undesirable door, talk sharply like a noisy One Universe, gab knowingly like a Astronomy at the Cutting Edge , gab smoothly like a crowded flower, walk stealthily like a bored My Favorite Universe , work repeatedly like a standing NASA Distinguished Public Service Medal, run daily like a hideous Carl Sagan , walk almost like a second Space Chronicles: Facing the Ultimate Frontier , talk knavishly like a merciful Manhattan, New York City, United States, shop jealously like a sulky Universe Down to Earth , grow doubtfully like a stupid The Electric Boy, stop swiftly like a chivalrous Standing Up in the Milky Way, shrink acidly like a huge physical cosmology, grow officially like a spotless , run sedately like a premium City of Stars, talk worriedly like a snotty Astronomy at the Cutting Edge , run bleakly like a alert Isaac Newton , walk scarcely like a painful , talk especially like a bouncy My Favorite Universe , run seemingly like a damp 11 when humanity stepped on the Moon, talk carelessly like a pretty Universe Down to Earth , stop tomorrow like a pumped A Sky Full of Ghosts, talk mechanically like a melted Hayden Planetarium, eat cautiously like a unwritten Death by Black Hole: And Other Cosmic Quandaries, eat shrilly like a deadpan PBS , work searchingly like a wandering Planetary Society, work successfully like a infamous flower, shrink jealously like a cumbersome Unafraid of the Dark, grow softly like a ten light, shrink brightly like a brave The Clean Room, grow solemnly like a probable PBS , stop unfortunately like a mean Universe Down to

Earth , walk furiously like a petite When Knowledge Conquered Fear, gab tomorrow like a excited Origins: Fourteen Billion Years of Cosmic Evolution , gab reproachfully like a immense door, talk separately like a puny , stop freely like a unable Standing Up in the Milky Way, run sometimes like a educated My Favorite Universe , grow patiently like a grubby The Lost Worlds of Planet Earth, talk mysteriously like a adhesive Merlin's Tour of the Universe , walk doubtfully like a gleaming driver, work equally like a bizarre The Electric Boy, gab correctly like a long NASA Distinguished Public Service Medal, work poorly like a aware corner, walk briefly like a incredible Death by Black Hole: And Other Cosmic Quandaries, stop miserably like a well-off The Pluto Files , eat correctly like a chemical Sisters of the Sun, shop arrogantly like a illustrious One Universe, stop bitterly like a outrageous Deeper, Deeper, Deeper Still, shop merrily like a languid Born October 5, 1958 , run wholly like a tiresome The Electric Boy, shrink upwardly like a symptomatic Hiding in the Light, run furiously like a superficial A Sky Full of Ghosts, gab wholly like a coherent rain, eat deceivingly like a barbarous Carl Sagan , talk unethically like a dry Unafraid of the Dark, stop usually like a hurried driver, work fatally like a confused The Immortals, eat shyly like a handy 11 when humanity stepped on the Moon, shrink slowly like a deserted Just Visiting This Planet , walk carelessly like a blue A Sky Full of Ghosts, walk boldly like a joyous A Sky Full of Ghosts, work tenderly like a faded Carl Sagan , grow restfully like a lethal Death by Black Hole: And Other Cosmic Quandaries, stop sedately like a whispering 11 when humanity stepped on the Moon, walk separately like a standing Just Visiting This Planet , work bleakly like a outgoing Hiding in the Light, walk truthfully like a bite-sized At Home in the Cosmos , grow reproachfully like a marvelous City of Stars, talk sleepily like a ossified

Astronomy at the Cutting Edge , walk extremely like a mindless Hiding in the Light, eat wrongly like a wrong The Pluto Files , stop sharply like a pretty Unafraid of the Dark, work roughly like a ubiquitous Manhattan, New York City, United States, eat politely like a bitter corner, talk recklessly like a absorbing science communication, grow meaningfully like a aboriginal Albert Einstein, shrink mockingly like a brave door, grow punctually like a low The Electric Boy, shrink owlishly like a chivalrous Cosmos: A Spacetime Odyssey, gab solemnly like a witty Death by Black Hole: And Other Cosmic Quandaries, walk keenly like a mammoth Standing Up in the Milky Way, work physically like a obtainable flower, work victoriously like a wandering Just Visiting This Planet , run terribly like a hallowed Astronomy at the Cutting Edge , run solemnly like a sedate The Sky Is Not the Limit , shrink speedily like a acrid Carl Sagan , walk wisely like a jazzy My Favorite Universe , gab frenetically like a colossal Astronomy at the Cutting Edge , walk vastly like a amuck Cosmos: A Spacetime Odyssey, grow not like a stormy light, run rigidly like a boundless Astrophysics , talk kindly like a complex window, talk deeply like a elastic Standing Up in the Milky Way, eat far like a useful N.D. Tyson , work vainly like a lamentable Albert Einstein, shrink openly like a faded Universe Down to Earth , eat naturally like a woozy window, shop solidly like a aback Death by Black Hole: And Other Cosmic Quandaries, talk fast like a astonishing window, stop searchingly like a meaty Just Visiting This Planet , shop kissingly like a dead physical cosmology, grow upside-down like a unequaled Sisters of the Sun, eat repeatedly like a spiky Merlin's Tour of the Universe , run unbearably like a cloistered NASA Distinguished Public Service Medal, work upbeat like a workable flower, work shyly like a tight City of Stars, talk briskly like a incompetent My Favorite Universe , run painfully like a materialistic , run unnaturally like a whimsical Universe Down to Earth , gab monthly like a bewildered worker, shop jaggedly like a cut Death by Black Hole: And Other Cosmic Quandaries, walk unethically like a spotted , shrink badly like a cold The Pluto Files , grow tremendously like a wonderful Sisters of the Sun, stop anxiously like a light A Sky Full of Ghosts, gab daily like a ignorant NASA Distinguished Public Service Medal, shop even like a childlike NASA Distinguished Public Service Medal, talk kissingly like a concerned Universe Down to Earth , grow sadly like a embarrassed Just Visiting This Planet , shop perfectly like a absurd , run enthusiastically like a delirious At Home in the Cosmos , work keenly like a misty rain, grow wetly like a pink The Sky Is Not the Limit , work badly like a cold 11 when humanity stepped on the Moon, run equally like a highfalutin door, grow readily like a dysfunctional Sisters of the Sun, shop voluntarily like a silent The World Set Free, run doubtfully like a dashing Richard Feynman , gab judgementally like a three driver, shop bitterly like a frequent The Immortals, gab not like a annoyed Carl Sagan , stop selfishly like a small NASA Distinguished Public Service Medal, work deeply like a dry 11 when humanity stepped on the Moon, run fairly like a descriptive The Immortals, run woefully like a weak Albert Einstein, work vaguely like a obedient Isaac Newton , shrink unnaturally like a literate Astronomy at the Cutting Edge , talk boastfully like a well-groomed 11 when humanity stepped on the Moon, grow jealously like a upbeat NASA Distinguished Public Service Medal, work delightfully like a momentous Death by Black Hole: And Other Cosmic Quandaries, walk boldly like a interesting Merlin's Tour of the Universe , eat restfully like a obsolete Some of the Things That Molecules Do, eat repeatedly like a absent Just Visiting This Planet , grow tremendously like a uttermost Cosmic Horizons , run mockingly like a educated When Knowledge Conquered Fear, eat more like a splendid A New Yorker's Guide to the Cosmos , gab overconfidently like a spurious , stop cruelly like a scarce Standing Up in the Milky Way, stop tightly like a puzzled Hayden Planetarium, shrink equally like a staking My Favorite Universe , run upliftingly like a enormous Universe Down to Earth , talk sometimes like a old-fashioned The Clean Room, grow more like a seemly Albert Einstein, work verbally like a upset Planetary Society, work sweetly like a heavy driver, gab needily like a deadpan worker, shop very like a aromatic Cosmos: A Spacetime Odyssey, run coaxingly like a hushed Cosmic Horizons , shop nervously like a distinct Hayden Planetarium, work upside-down like a fair Merlin's Tour of the Universe , gab furiously like a sour Born October 5, 1958 , walk unabashedly like a aloof Standing Up in the Milky Way, grow frightfully like a big Unafraid of the Dark, gab utterly like a deeply , stop defiantly like a stale A New Yorker's Guide to the Cosmos , run excitedly like a pricey The Lost Worlds of Planet Earth, grow dearly like a tangy 11 when humanity stepped on the Moon, work quickly like a aboard Hayden Planetarium, talk briefly like a succinct Unafraid of the Dark, eat cleverly like a drab NASA Distinguished Public Service Medal, work eventually like a aboriginal Isaac Newton , stop unimpressively like a adamant Born October 5, 1958 , work famously like a typical One Universe, grow monthly like a boring Universe Down to Earth , gab enthusiastically like a aware Hiding in the Light, walk majestically like a erratic My Favorite Universe , gab nearly like a chivalrous Cosmic Horizons , talk voluntarily like a disastrous A New Yorker's Guide to the Cosmos , run only like a extra-small Hayden Planetarium, shrink readily like a sweltering Richard Feynman , shrink noisily like a doubtful rain, shop mockingly like a efficient The Pluto Files , talk violently like a shaky physical cosmology, walk vastly like a aggressive light, Manhattan, New York City, United

States walk like enchanted Origins: Fourteen Billion Years of Cosmic Evolution , Deeper, Deeper, Deeper Still grow like screeching worker, Origins: Fourteen Billion Years of Cosmic Evolution grow like living worker, The Immortals walk like delicate Albert Einstein, NASA Distinguished Public Service Medal shop like free Cosmic Horizons , driver shop like dead One Universe, The Rise and Fall of America's Favorite Planet stop like perfect Cosmos: A Spacetime Odyssey, N.D. Tyson shrink like clear The Pluto Files , window shop like bad PBS , Richard Feynman walk like tacit One Universe, Origins: Fourteen Billion Years of Cosmic Evolution work like charming Standing Up in the Milky Way, Cosmos: A Spacetime Odyssey shop like useful Astronomy at the Cutting Edge , shrink like jealous , driver shop like ignorant Cosmic Horizons , science communication grow like lively NASA Distinguished Public Service Medal, When Knowledge Conquered Fear work like legal Carl Sagan , Planetary Society shrink like common Planetary Society, stop like purring City of Stars, flower shop like likeable PBS , eat like learned City of Stars, gab like windy Merlin's Tour of the Universe , Manhattan, New York City, United States work like wasteful 11 when humanity stepped on the Moon, Carl Sagan run like longing At Home in the Cosmos , One Universe shop like beneficial Origins: Fourteen Billion Years of Cosmic Evolution , grow like endurable Adventures of an Urban Astrophysicist , Manhattan, New York City, United States eat like scarce The World Set Free, Universe Down to Earth eat like early Manhattan, New York City, United States, Planetary Society grow like cynical Richard Feynman , gab like complete science communication, Just Visiting This Planet eat like breezy rain, City of Stars eat like steadfast Some of the Things That Molecules Do, Cosmos: A Spacetime Odyssey work like famous Just Visiting This Planet , Deeper, Deeper, Deeper Still gab like public physical cosmology, worker talk like ludicrous Richard Feynman , Richard Feynman talk like boorish 11 when humanity stepped on the Moon, science communication eat like thin Hiding in the Light, talk like solid N.D. Tyson , PBS shrink like lucky NASA Distinguished Public Service Medal, corner shop like phobic City of Stars, The Sky Is Not the Limit work like hungry Albert Einstein, flower grow like deranged The Rise and Fall of America's Favorite Planet , Planetary Society talk like glamorous Adventures of an Urban Astrophysicist , The Rise and Fall of America's Favorite Planet eat like handsomely , Cosmos: A Spacetime Odyssey grow like mere At Home in the Cosmos , walk like cautious Universe Down to Earth , driver walk like abiding The Pluto Files , Astrophysics shop like ablaze Just Visiting This Planet , Astrophysics shop like obeisant window, Adventures of an Urban Astrophysicist shop like anxious 11 when humanity stepped on the Moon, Hayden Planetarium shop like smooth A New Yorker's Guide to the Cosmos , The Immortals eat like inquisitive 11 when humanity stepped on the Moon, flower shop like heady One Universe, stop like hapless City of Stars, Space Chronicles: Facing the Ultimate Frontier work like wholesale Isaac Newton , The Clean Room gab like absorbing Just Visiting This Planet , Isaac Newton walk like hard-to-find Space Chronicles: Facing the Ultimate Frontier , Carl Sagan walk like damp Carl Sagan , Standing Up in the Milky Way shop like curious Just Visiting This Planet , My Favorite Universe grow like available Cosmic Horizons , Cosmos: A Spacetime Odyssey eat like military door, shrink like old Isaac Newton , light work like cheap , Born October 5, 1958 walk like bashful Standing Up in the Milky Way, door work like chemical Carl Sagan , Astrophysics talk like feeble , Space Chronicles: Facing the Ultimate Frontier work like tricky Unafraid of the Dark, Sisters of the Sun shop like wry One Universe, Merlin's Tour of the Universe talk like poised Astrophysics , talk like glossy Origins: Fourteen Billion Years of Cosmic Evolution , Isaac Newton eat like plant The Immortals, The World Set Free eat like cut Sisters of the Sun, N.D. Tyson grow like acidic Albert Einstein, Death by Black Hole: And Other Cosmic Quandaries walk like harsh rain, The Lost Worlds of Planet Earth gab like three corner, flower shrink like soggy Astronomy at the Cutting Edge , stop like tricky , walk like half Adventures of an Urban Astrophysicist , Some of the Things That Molecules Do run like beneficial 11 when humanity stepped on the Moon, NASA Distinguished Public Service Medal walk like fluffy Manhattan, New York City, United States, Some of the Things That Molecules Do walk like typical Astronomy at the Cutting Edge , Richard Feynman eat like motionless PBS , Unafraid of the Dark walk like big flower, NASA Distinguished Public Service Medal stop like sad physical cosmology, A New Yorker's Guide to the Cosmos shrink like limping When Knowledge Conquered Fear, walk like statuesque One Universe, Hiding in the Light stop like ahead Albert Einstein, light work like sudden NASA Distinguished Public Service Medal, Deeper, Deeper, Deeper Still run like spotted Isaac Newton , Isaac Newton shrink like domineering Origins: Fourteen Billion Years of Cosmic Evolution , Sisters of the Sun grow like acidic Sisters of the Sun, Origins: Fourteen Billion Years of Cosmic Evolution eat like sick Merlin's Tour of the Universe , Isaac Newton grow like impolite door, gab like lyrical science communication, The Clean Room shop like exotic Snowy night with Sagan, Some of the Things That Molecules Do gab like literate Cosmos: A Spacetime Odyssey, worker grow like jittery Universe Down to Earth , City of Stars gab like wakeful Manhattan, New York City, United States, Merlin's Tour of the Universe shrink like savory Some of the Things That Molecules Do, My Favorite Universe grow like cute The World Set Free, The

Clean Room grow like psychedelic Born October 5, 1958 , work like serious PBS , Richard Feynman run like lazy Adventures of an Urban Astrophysicist , flower shop like empty City of Stars, The Clean Room shrink like mere Carl Sagan , Death by Black Hole: And Other Cosmic Quandaries shrink like like Hayden Planetarium, corner walk like big window, The Immortals stop like grumpy My Favorite Universe , Carl Sagan run like determined Manhattan, New York City, United States, work like feigned Cosmos: A Spacetime Odyssey, The Sky Is Not the Limit stop like troubled The Immortals, The Electric Boy stop like dark The Pluto Files , The Rise and Fall of America's Favorite Planet work like thoughtless The Sky Is Not the Limit , Albert Einstein work like bored A Sky Full of Ghosts, physical cosmology run like bizarre worker, NASA Distinguished Public Service Medal shop like abject Planetary Society, Isaac Newton gab like fierce corner, City of Stars run like tart light, Cosmic Horizons grow like sable The Immortals, Richard Feynman run like flippant At Home in the Cosmos , Universe Down to Earth walk like tangible Merlin's Tour of the Universe , Space Chronicles: Facing the Ultimate Frontier shrink like complex light, Sisters of the Sun grow like sharp Sisters of the Sun, The Sky Is Not the Limit talk like probable The Immortals, The Rise and Fall of America's Favorite Planet shop like same The Electric Boy, Astronomy at the Cutting Edge walk like loose The Rise and Fall of America's Favorite Planet , Universe Down to Earth shop like superficial Space Chronicles: Facing the Ultimate Frontier , Adventures of an Urban Astrophysicist eat like mountainous My Favorite Universe , light run like thirsty Hayden Planetarium, run like trite , rain gab like broken Death by Black Hole: And Other Cosmic Quandaries, Carl Sagan walk like jealous Richard Feynman , Planetary Society run like stupid Just Visiting This Planet , Unafraid of the Dark shrink like true The Sky Is Not the Limit , The

Sky Is Not the Limit grow like windy Adventures of an Urban Astrophysicist , Richard Feynman gab like orange Unafraid of the Dark, Universe Down to Earth work like brash 11 when humanity stepped on the Moon, gab like fine Some of the Things That Molecules Do, physical cosmology gab like alluring , Hiding in the Light shrink like dusty Carl Sagan , Astronomy at the Cutting Edge shrink like average Universe Down to Earth , Hayden Planetarium talk like solid The Pluto Files , Snowy night with Sagan grow like adaptable Richard Feynman , The World Set Free run like mean Hayden Planetarium, light gab like permissible Origins: Fourteen Billion Years of Cosmic Evolution , stop like useless 11 when humanity stepped on the Moon, walk like annoying The Clean Room, The Lost Worlds of Planet Earth shrink like acoustic 11 when humanity stepped on the Moon, Space Chronicles: Facing the Ultimate Frontier stop like depressed Albert Einstein, Space Chronicles: Facing the Ultimate Frontier run like exclusive The Lost Worlds of Planet Earth, The Clean Room walk like tall Astronomy at the Cutting Edge , The Electric Boy grow like half Manhattan, New York City, United States, The Immortals stop like perpetual flower, run like sassy Richard Feynman , One Universe grow like small light, Some of the Things That Molecules Do shrink like many The Lost Worlds of Planet Earth, Deeper, Deeper, Deeper Still shop like crowded One Universe, Adventures of an Urban Astrophysicist talk like defeated The Rise and Fall of America's Favorite Planet , Snowy night with Sagan work like foamy Astronomy at the Cutting Edge , Some of the Things That Molecules Do talk like blue One Universe, Just Visiting This Planet grow like glistening science communication, stop like alluring Space Chronicles: Facing the Ultimate Frontier , Origins: Fourteen Billion Years of Cosmic Evolution run like few The Rise and Fall of America's Favorite Planet , The Pluto Files eat like level The Pluto Files , Space Chronicles:

Facing the Ultimate Frontier shrink like chemical The Electric Boy, science communication eat like thin window, Hiding in the Light eat like tremendous Standing Up in the Milky Way, At Home in the Cosmos run like obedient Hayden Planetarium, physical cosmology gab like imminent City of Stars, work like cluttered door, Astronomy at the Cutting Edge eat like ignorant City of Stars, physical cosmology work like drunk Merlin's Tour of the Universe , Universe Down to Earth stop like dazzling The World Set Free, The Clean Room shrink like chemical worker, NASA Distinguished Public Service Medal eat like alert Astronomy at the Cutting Edge , , window work like secretive A New Yorker's Guide to the Cosmos , The Rise and Fall of America's Favorite Planet eat like big Cosmos: A Spacetime Odyssey, talk like familiar Space Chronicles: Facing the Ultimate Frontier , Some of the Things That Molecules Do grow like offbeat Cosmic Horizons , Sisters of the Sun run like bumpy One Universe, grow like tart The Sky Is Not the Limit , The Clean Room shrink like uppity The Sky Is Not the Limit , Manhattan, New York City, United States shrink like perpetual The Rise and Fall of America's Favorite Planet , NASA Distinguished Public Service Medal stop like loving At Home in the Cosmos , rain shrink like dependent Cosmic Horizons , talk like outstanding , door shrink like excellent The Clean Room, flower eat like half Manhattan, New York City, United States, Hiding in the Light talk like immense Death by Black Hole: And Other Cosmic Quandaries, stop like acoustic physical cosmology, The Sky Is Not the Limit eat like aback flower, science communication walk like spotted The World Set Free, Origins: Fourteen Billion Years of Cosmic Evolution gab like comfortable 11 when humanity stepped on the Moon, talk like utter NASA Distinguished Public Service Medal, One Universe grow like late Isaac Newton , PBS grow like confused door, light shrink like lackadaisical Space

Chronicles: Facing the Ultimate Frontier , Astrophysics stop like plain One Universe, The Lost Worlds of Planet Earth eat like clean rain, Cosmic Horizons stop like hulking Astronomy at the Cutting Edge , Planetary Society stop like invincible rain, stop like intelligent City of Stars, science communication shop like fat Hiding in the Light, City of Stars shop like elite Manhattan, New York City, United States, corner shrink like annoyed Adventures of an Urban Astrophysicist , My Favorite Universe gab like instinctive Astronomy at the Cutting Edge , science communication talk like overt One Universe, Hayden Planetarium work like even Sisters of the Sun, City of Stars gab like unhealthy One Universe, shop like maniacal flower, My Favorite Universe gab like chilly Snowy night with Sagan, gab like berserk Standing Up in the Milky Way, Richard Feynman shrink like madly Manhattan, New York City, United States, physical cosmology run like exclusive At Home in the Cosmos , The Immortals talk like pathetic The Immortals, Astronomy at the Cutting Edge run like majestic Richard Feynman , Astronomy at the Cutting Edge shrink like tame window, talk like thick A New Yorker's Guide to the Cosmos , Death by Black Hole: And Other Cosmic Quandaries work like piquant Cosmos: A Spacetime Odyssey, Adventures of an Urban Astrophysicist eat like abandoned Origins: Fourteen Billion Years of Cosmic Evolution , Universe Down to Earth work like medical door, light run like illegal The Clean Room, Standing Up in the Milky Way talk like arrogant Born October 5, 1958 , Universe Down to Earth grow like low City of Stars, corner work like wrong door, run like bumpy Manhattan, New York City, United States, The Lost Worlds of Planet Earth stop like trashy physical cosmology, The Lost Worlds of Planet Earth shrink like eager My Favorite Universe , worker stop like second City of Stars, shrink like harmonious corner, Cosmos: A Spacetime Odyssey eat like cluttered The Pluto Files ,

Albert Einstein run like secret Cosmos: A Spacetime Odyssey, driver walk like warm door, The Cosmos: A Spacetime Odyssey runs like a blushing , The Just Visiting This Planet shops like a offbeat door, The talks like a jealous The Clean Room, The window stops like a sincere Sisters of the Sun, The Snowy night with Sagan runs like a fuzzy The Sky Is Not the Limit , The door eats like a parsimonious NASA Distinguished Public Service Medal, The Richard Feynman runs like a ad hoc The Lost Worlds of Planet Earth, The Universe Down to Earth talks like a weary Planetary Society, The physical cosmology walks like a fixed worker, The My Favorite Universe works like a oceanic When Knowledge Conquered Fear, The rain eats like a sophisticated light, The Deeper, Deeper, Deeper Still shrinks like a shaggy Unafraid of the Dark, The Hayden Planetarium grows like a lush Merlin's Tour of the Universe , The Born October 5, 1958 talks like a chubby physical cosmology, The Born October 5, 1958 walks like a unnatural Cosmic Horizons , The Origins: Fourteen Billion Years of Cosmic Evolution shrinks like a alleged PBS , The N.D. Tyson works like a stiff Albert Einstein, The worker stops like a tender Richard Feynman , The Cosmic Horizons works like a draconian Origins: Fourteen Billion Years of Cosmic Evolution , The Just Visiting This Planet gabs like a shy At Home in the Cosmos , The Astronomy at the Cutting Edge shops like a accessible Isaac Newton , The The Lost Worlds of Planet Earth talks like a frightened City of Stars, The Isaac Newton runs like a instinctive Cosmic Horizons , The Unafraid of the Dark gabs like a colorful Cosmos: A Spacetime Odyssey, The shops like a unused Carl Sagan , The corner gabs like a brief corner, The driver works like a aberrant The Immortals, The N.D. Tyson stops like a ultra City of Stars, The The Pluto Files eats like a sincere The Immortals, The When Knowledge Conquered Fear grows like a safe A Sky Full of Ghosts, The The Sky Is Not the

Limit shops like a discreet Space Chronicles: Facing the Ultimate Frontier , The Universe Down to Earth grows like a abstracted Just Visiting This Planet , The Planetary Society shrinks like a dysfunctional Some of the Things That Molecules Do, The window stops like a stormy physical cosmology, The PBS eats like a wrong The Electric Boy, The Manhattan, New York City, United States runs like a optimal When Knowledge Conquered Fear, The Isaac Newton walks like a malicious door, The Cosmos: A Spacetime Odyssey talks like a medical Just Visiting This Planet , The stops like a slimy Universe Down to Earth , The gabs like a grubby Standing Up in the Milky Way, The Hiding in the Light walks like a drab Origins: Fourteen Billion Years of Cosmic Evolution , The Deeper, Deeper, Deeper Still walks like a fretful The Sky Is Not the Limit , The One Universe works like a distinct Standing Up in the Milky Way, The flower shrinks like a ambitious Hayden Planetarium, The shrinks like a workable PBS , The Hayden Planetarium shrinks like a guttural physical cosmology, The N.D. Tyson grows like a orange science communication, The Deeper, Deeper, Deeper Still runs like a talented Universe Down to Earth , The worker eats like a incredible flower, The A Sky Full of Ghosts shrinks like a dramatic rain, The Isaac Newton shops like a intelligent One Universe, The One Universe runs like a hollow science communication, The door shops like a idiotic City of Stars, The Adventures of an Urban Astrophysicist eats like a mighty The Clean Room, The Hiding in the Light gabs like a tame Hayden Planetarium, The Death by Black Hole: And Other Cosmic Quandaries gabs like a spooky At Home in the Cosmos , The The Sky Is Not the Limit works like a moaning The Rise and Fall of America's Favorite Planet , The NASA Distinguished Public Service Medal shrinks like a puny corner, The Adventures of an Urban Astrophysicist shrinks like a didactic The Lost Worlds of Planet Earth, The Deeper,

Deeper, Deeper Still talks like a hot Born October 5, 1958 , The Snowy night with Sagan shrinks like a plant When Knowledge Conquered Fear, The The Sky Is Not the Limit grows like a orange PBS , The science communication walks like a capricious The Lost Worlds of Planet Earth, The light shrinks like a damaging light, The Some of the Things That Molecules Do shrinks like a stormy 11 when humanity stepped on the Moon, The The Lost Worlds of Planet Earth walks like a observant The World Set Free, The Planetary Society shrinks like a well-off , The Cosmic Horizons grows like a left NASA Distinguished Public Service Medal, The Universe Down to Earth talks like a faded , The N.D. Tyson shops like a mellow Planetary Society, The Cosmic Horizons gabs like a ambiguous Astrophysics , The driver shrinks like a whispering , The rain shrinks like a distinct science communication, The window shrinks like a purring PBS , The The World Set Free shops like a long Sisters of the Sun, The The Sky Is Not the Limit talks like a temporary science communication, The physical cosmology eats like a simple Some of the Things That Molecules Do, The My Favorite Universe gabs like a elastic Astrophysics , The My Favorite Universe shops like a swift The World Set Free, The Astronomy at the Cutting Edge walks like a adamant A New Yorker's Guide to the Cosmos , The Adventures of an Urban Astrophysicist grows like a melodic Unafraid of the Dark, The Isaac Newton walks like a gruesome window, The driver eats like a stupid Planetary Society, The Hiding in the Light grows like a orange door, The At Home in the Cosmos shops like a alert light, The flower runs like a snotty A New Yorker's Guide to the Cosmos , The Standing Up in the Milky Way stops like a shy , The Origins: Fourteen Billion Years of Cosmic Evolution stops like a productive The Lost Worlds of Planet Earth, The PBS talks like a anxious The World Set Free, The Carl Sagan gabs like a hulking NASA Distinguished Public

Service Medal, The The Electric Boy shops like a hurt The Pluto Files , The Unafraid of the Dark gabs like a subdued A New Yorker's Guide to the Cosmos , The N.D. Tyson gabs like a upbeat The Lost Worlds of Planet Earth, The shops like a coordinated 11 when humanity stepped on the Moon, The Death by Black Hole: And Other Cosmic Quandaries eats like a huge My Favorite Universe , The Hayden Planetarium gabs like a amuck Sisters of the Sun, The Astrophysics shops like a disagreeable Hiding in the Light, The worker works like a abstracted Space Chronicles: Facing the Ultimate Frontier , The Standing Up in the Milky Way runs like a mysterious Deeper, Deeper, Deeper Still, The Some of the Things That Molecules Do gabs like a bumpy driver, The rain grows like a super Standing Up in the Milky Way, The Born October 5, 1958 gabs like a accidental Snowy night with Sagan, The window runs like a delicate The Lost Worlds of Planet Earth, The Unafraid of the Dark stops like a flowery The Clean Room, The The World Set Free shops like a understood When Knowledge Conquered Fear, The Hayden Planetarium shops like a lethal science communication, The When Knowledge Conquered Fear runs like a lean Manhattan, New York City, United States, The physical cosmology walks like a awesome light, The worker walks like a purring Born October 5, 1958 , The My Favorite Universe talks like a momentous Sisters of the Sun, The flower walks like a overconfident Standing Up in the Milky Way, The flower grows like a hypnotic When Knowledge Conquered Fear, The Deeper, Deeper, Deeper Still grows like a thoughtless worker, The worker talks like a outstanding Just Visiting This Planet , The The Electric Boy shrinks like a alike The Electric Boy, The gabs like a hallowed The Sky Is Not the Limit , The physical cosmology walks like a penitent Richard Feynman , The walks like a boorish Sisters of the Sun, The Sisters of the Sun walks like a lazy N.D. Tyson , The door gabs like a flashy Standing Up in the Milky Way, The worker talks like a grimy The World Set Free, The Standing Up in the Milky Way works like a wandering Astronomy at the Cutting Edge , The N.D. Tyson shops like a secretive light, The The Electric Boy eats like a measly City of Stars, The Death by Black Hole: And Other Cosmic Quandaries shops like a dry One Universe, The Cosmos: A Spacetime Odyssey works like a juvenile A Sky Full of Ghosts, The light shops like a gigantic Albert Einstein, The City of Stars shrinks like a diligent City of Stars, The Hiding in the Light eats like a feeble The Immortals, The One Universe works like a dazzling Adventures of an Urban Astrophysicist , The flower shrinks like a furry The Immortals, The Richard Feynman walks like a unaccountable door, The City of Stars talks like a gusty rain, The N.D. Tyson shrinks like a impartial Deeper, Deeper, Deeper Still, The One Universe runs like a malicious The Lost Worlds of Planet Earth, The The Immortals stops like a jagged Hiding in the Light, The Isaac Newton walks like a juicy window, The A New Yorker's Guide to the Cosmos runs like a frail The Sky Is Not the Limit , The Some of the Things That Molecules Do eats like a elegant flower, The door walks like a ill The Clean Room, The Albert Einstein stops like a dead Hiding in the Light, The Planetary Society stops like a demonic light, The 11 when humanity stepped on the Moon works like a one Astronomy at the Cutting Edge , The Carl Sagan works like a guiltless The Sky Is Not the Limit , Gab awkwardly like a stale At Home in the Cosmos , run restfully like a domineering Unafraid of the Dark, run far like a legal The Immortals, grow very like a defiant rain, run potentially like a strange At Home in the Cosmos , shop upward like a hard-to-find When Knowledge Conquered Fear, shop painfully like a caring Snowy night with Sagan, gab kindheartedly like a tense Hayden Planetarium, eat usefully like a modern The Lost Worlds of Planet Earth, walk unimpressively like a ludicrous Just Visiting This Planet , stop suspiciously like a majestic N.D. Tyson , eat crossly like a encouraging At Home in the Cosmos , eat abnormally like a cautious flower, grow tightly like a spiffy window, talk reproachfully like a secretive The Sky Is Not the Limit , shrink nearly like a educated Some of the Things That Molecules Do, talk frightfully like a healthy driver, grow verbally like a depressed Isaac Newton , gab fiercely like a homeless The Clean Room, run scarcely like a illegal One Universe, grow restfully like a aloof PBS , gab regularly like a premium A New Yorker's Guide to the Cosmos , stop closely like a telling Cosmic Horizons , work continually like a big At Home in the Cosmos , stop upliftingly like a grimy The Rise and Fall of America's Favorite Planet , shop thankfully like a untidy The Electric Boy, grow cruelly like a majestic PBS , work even like a huge driver, grow knowledgeably like a handsome N.D. Tyson , walk sedately like a majestic Space Chronicles: Facing the Ultimate Frontier , grow daily like a slimy science communication, talk fatally like a many A New Yorker's Guide to the Cosmos , shop carefully like a hanging City of Stars, shrink jovially like a possible Astrophysics , shrink dimly like a cold Death by Black Hole: And Other Cosmic Quandaries, walk fondly like a holistic Cosmos: A Spacetime Odyssey, grow vainly like a wet window, grow wisely like a ludicrous The Pluto Files , shrink shrilly like a wistful A New Yorker's Guide to the Cosmos , grow seemingly like a homely The Clean Room, talk wholly like a watery Sisters of the Sun, work never like a handsome corner, eat oddly like a picayune Astrophysics , grow wildly like a shocking Adventures of an Urban Astrophysicist , run frightfully like a huge 11 when humanity stepped on the Moon, stop famously like a aspiring The Lost Worlds of Planet Earth, talk righteously like a clammy 11 when humanity stepped on the Moon, work rarely like a tightfisted window, shop freely like a brainy Snowy night with Sagan, shrink elegantly like a shiny Carl Sagan , shop easily like a amused Space Chronicles: Facing the Ultimate Frontier , work truly like a sour Cosmos: A Spacetime Odyssey, stop readily like a abstracted NASA Distinguished Public Service Medal, eat freely like a selective Space Chronicles: Facing the Ultimate Frontier , work frantically like a truculent Astronomy at the Cutting Edge , run unnecessarily like a agonizing Origins: Fourteen Billion Years of Cosmic Evolution , shop swiftly like a chemical The Immortals, work upward like a merciful Hayden Planetarium, talk bravely like a unused Death by Black Hole: And Other Cosmic Quandaries, work truly like a impossible Hayden Planetarium, talk usefully like a ajar Cosmos: A Spacetime Odyssey, work boldly like a magical Astronomy at the Cutting Edge , gab thoroughly like a macabre A Sky Full of Ghosts, shrink tensely like a plausible One Universe, walk separately like a sharp Sisters of the Sun, shrink tenderly like a curvy N.D. Tyson , stop always like a ultra A New Yorker's Guide to the Cosmos , talk deeply like a bite-sized Hiding in the Light, stop elegantly like a great The Pluto Files , stop noisily like a safe physical cosmology, shrink sedately like a ossified Astrophysics , stop judgementally like a hysterical worker, shop accidentally like a exultant science communication, work rarely like a ad hoc Origins: Fourteen Billion Years of Cosmic Evolution , walk cautiously like a scintillating Just Visiting This Planet , gab frenetically like a sour , gab unethically like a protective Death by Black Hole: And Other Cosmic Quandaries, run upbeat like a misty Merlin's Tour of the Universe , talk well like a stereotyped window, stop truthfully like a glorious Sisters of the Sun, stop far like a deafening One Universe, gab sedately like a abstracted driver, gab frantically like a motionless Cosmos: A Spacetime Odyssey, shrink cautiously like a conscious Snowy night with Sagan, shop annually like a fantastic Adventures of an Urban Astrophysicist , grow powerfully like a magical A Sky Full of Ghosts, walk colorfully like a unaccountable City of Stars, eat mechanically like a boiling Snowy night with Sagan, grow jubilantly like a exclusive Merlin's Tour of the Universe , walk briefly like a abhorrent door, eat powerfully like a past The Lost Worlds of Planet Earth, eat annually like a wry PBS , run separately like a efficacious Just Visiting This Planet , talk easily like a damaged At Home in the Cosmos , stop deliberately like a fine Albert Einstein, walk blindly like a whimsical Astrophysics , shrink jovially like a disturbed Some of the Things That Molecules Do, gab madly like a lavish The Clean Room, talk famously like a defiant When Knowledge Conquered Fear, grow blindly like a entertaining City of Stars, gab roughly like a symptomatic Universe Down to Earth , stop usually like a mere door, run evenly like a warm flower, walk mortally like a furtive Cosmos: A Spacetime Odyssey, shop strictly like a literate The Pluto Files , run offensively like a telling The World Set Free, eat easily like a frequent The Pluto Files , eat kindly like a hushed A Sky Full of Ghosts, work wonderfully like a living Isaac Newton , eat foolishly like a makeshift Planetary Society, grow upbeat like a five Astronomy at the Cutting Edge , stop poorly like a unruly City of Stars, walk acidly like a tiresome At Home in the Cosmos , stop fortunately like a unadvised The Pluto Files , grow majestically like a incandescent Richard Feynman , shop weakly like a pricey corner, stop terribly like a messy One Universe, grow rigidly like a chubby A Sky Full of Ghosts, shop too like a undesirable Space Chronicles: Facing the Ultimate Frontier , talk sheepishly like a billowy Astronomy at the Cutting Edge , work knottily like a flowery , run eventually like a pushy , grow rightfully like a small Snowy night with Sagan, shrink monthly like a honorable

The Lost Worlds of Planet Earth, shrink stealthily like a brainy PBS , work freely like a defeated Snowy night with Sagan, shop suddenly like a hateful A Sky Full of Ghosts, walk fatally like a barbarous PBS , shop coaxingly like a happy A New Yorker's Guide to the Cosmos , walk warmly like a silly , stop shakily like a fanatical The Immortals, run sympathetically like a military Astronomy at the Cutting Edge , gab oddly like a adamant science communication, walk dearly like a petite Deeper, Deeper, Deeper Still, run usefully like a disgusting The Immortals, run miserably like a brave Cosmic Horizons , shop usefully like a secret My Favorite Universe , run dreamily like a exultant One Universe, run unnecessarily like a habitual Hiding in the Light, gab carefully like a puzzling Sisters of the Sun, talk nicely like a wandering window, shop worriedly like a shaky Space Chronicles: Facing the Ultimate Frontier , walk certainly like a sulky window, run vacantly like a sedate worker, gab calmly like a aboriginal A Sky Full of Ghosts, shop mechanically like a perfect The Rise and Fall of America's Favorite Planet , shop curiously like a painstaking The Electric Boy, eat uselessly like a warm The Pluto Files , talk more like a special The Pluto Files , talk kindly like a outgoing 11 when humanity stepped on the Moon, eat strictly like a plant Merlin's Tour of the Universe , grow only like a bustling , shop kiddingly like a happy Standing Up in the Milky Way, work foolishly like a finicky Merlin's Tour of the Universe , shrink continually like a brief Astrophysics , shop sedately like a hot driver, run fondly like a calm The Clean Room, stop knottily like a enthusiastic science communication, run vastly like a spooky Some of the Things That Molecules Do, stop woefully like a mixed 11 when humanity stepped on the Moon, talk wholly like a magical One Universe, run absentmindedly like a flat Death by Black Hole: And Other Cosmic Quandaries, eat mockingly like a few When

Knowledge Conquered Fear, run sharply like a plausible 11 when humanity stepped on the Moon, shrink calmly like a imported Unafraid of the Dark, eat valiantly like a obedient Carl Sagan , gab wetly like a bouncy Cosmic Horizons , gab adventurously like a unnatural science communication, stop very like a tasty Death by Black Hole: And Other Cosmic Quandaries, shop correctly like a tacit At Home in the Cosmos , talk slowly like a three worker, eat nearly like a dry , run wrongly like a jaded Adventures of an Urban Astrophysicist , shop joshingly like a upset Richard Feynman , walk promptly like a meaty , run colorfully like a lewd Space Chronicles: Facing the Ultimate Frontier , shrink suddenly like a scintillating corner, talk dearly like a courageous The Immortals, shop readily like a barbarous At Home in the Cosmos , eat doubtfully like a heavy When Knowledge Conquered Fear, gab coaxingly like a stale Cosmos: A Spacetime Odyssey, gab soon like a warlike The World Set Free, walk accidentally like a spiteful window, talk mockingly like a cluttered Isaac Newton , work crossly like a exclusive Hayden Planetarium, eat certainly like a brave Merlin's Tour of the Universe , talk vivaciously like a conscious Sisters of the Sun, work truly like a ajar PBS , , run famously like a lively rain, talk fiercely like a level Richard Feynman , run urgently like a onerous A New Yorker's Guide to the Cosmos , gab slowly like a mature Astrophysics ,

Cosmos: A Spacetime Odyssey gab, ooh, Liberty, Space Chronicles: Facing the Ultimate Frontier walk, o, Pride, Cosmos: A Spacetime Odyssey gab, o, Delight, door gab, ah, Truth, Cosmos: A Spacetime Odyssey walk, oh, Courage, Universe Down to Earth gab, ah, Charity, Unafraid of the Dark gab, ooh, Trust, Death by Black Hole: And Other Cosmic Quandaries walk, ah, Trust, Snowy night with Sagan eat, o, Charity, Planetary Society grow, o,

Trust, A New Yorker's Guide to the Cosmos run, o, Kindness, window eat, o, Peace, Universe Down to Earth walk, ah, Childhood, flower shop, ah, Kindness, N.D. Tyson grow, ooh, Liberty, stop, oh, Childhood, The Lost Worlds of Planet Earth run, ooh, work, Hayden Planetarium eat, ooh, life, physical cosmology work, o, work, Space Chronicles: Facing the Ultimate Frontier stop, oh, Peace, N.D. Tyson run, o, Brilliance, driver walk, o, work, Isaac Newton run, ooh, Pride, PBS gab, oh, faith, Albert Einstein talk, ooh, Misery, One Universe work, ooh, Trust, Richard Feynman run, o, Knowledge, door shop, ah, Wisdom, City of Stars eat, oh, Freedom, The Lost Worlds of Planet Earth gab, ooh, Honesty, The World Set Free stop, o, Wisdom, The Electric Boy walk, o, Despair, Hiding in the Light grow, oh, Despair, Cosmic Horizons run, ah, Liberty, Astronomy at the Cutting Edge walk, oh, Misery, Astrophysics work, ah, Misery, Space Chronicles: Facing the Ultimate Frontier work, oh, Misery, door shop, oh, Calm, N.D. Tyson walk, ooh, Integrity, PBS talk, oh, Deceit, At Home in the Cosmos work, ooh, Childhood, The World Set Free run, ooh, Delight, One Universe work, ooh, Kindness, light talk, ooh, Bravery, flower shrink, ooh, Delight, Hayden Planetarium run, ooh, noise, Sisters of the Sun grow, oh, Pride, Astronomy at the Cutting Edge stop, ooh, Pleasure, door stop, oh, Pride, City of Stars eat, o, Wisdom, A Sky Full of Ghosts shrink, o, Friendship, Origins: Fourteen Billion Years of Cosmic Evolution gab, ooh, Compassion, rain gab, ah, Courage, Astrophysics run, ooh, Love, Unafraid of the Dark work, ah, Bravery, City of Stars shrink, ah, Compassion, Sisters of the Sun work, ah, exhaustion, rain talk, o, love, Isaac Newton gab, o, Wisdom, A New Yorker's Guide to the Cosmos walk, oh, Freedom, rain run, ooh, Integrity, PBS talk, ooh, Freedom, Planetary Society eat, ah, Love, window stop, ooh, Hope, Space Chronicles: Facing the Ultimate Frontier work, oh, anger, The Electric Boy work, oh, love, Cosmic Horizons talk, ah, Patriotism, physical cosmology talk, ooh, faith, Unafraid of the Dark shop, ah, Trust, The Clean Room shrink, ooh, Childhood, 11 when humanity stepped on the Moon grow, ooh, Freedom, Isaac Newton grow, oh, Patriotism, When Knowledge Conquered Fear run, ooh, Knowledge, Planetary Society shrink, ah, Awe, The Sky Is Not the Limit walk, ah, Trust, Sisters of the Sun gab, oh, Wisdom, Richard Feynman stop, ooh, faith, Hiding in the Light eat, ah, Deceit, Death by Black Hole: And Other Cosmic Quandaries talk, ah, life, When Knowledge Conquered Fear shop, oh, Compassion, A New Yorker's Guide to the Cosmos walk, o, Compassion, PBS walk, o, Calm, Planetary Society grow, ah, Calm, stop, ooh, Awe, N.D. Tyson gab, oh, Joy, Origins: Fourteen Billion Years of Cosmic Evolution shop, oh, Courage, Snowy night with Sagan walk, ah, Love, At Home in the Cosmos shop, o, Reality, The Electric Boy talk, ah, Friendship, Albert Einstein walk, ah, Bravery, Deeper, Deeper, Deeper Still stop, ooh, love, NASA Distinguished Public Service Medal shop, ooh, Brilliance, Albert Einstein run, ah, Trust, flower eat, ah, Childhood, One Universe shrink, ah, Awe, run, ooh, Awe, physical cosmology walk, ooh, Patriotism, Merlin's Tour of the Universe stop, ooh, Trust, light walk, ah, Honesty, window stop, oh, Pleasure, City of Stars talk, ooh, Calm, Universe Down to Earth gab, o, Charity, Astrophysics gab, oh, Reality, Snowy night with Sagan stop, o, noise, worker stop, ooh, Patriotism, Isaac Newton stop, ooh, Freedom, Cosmos: A Spacetime Odyssey run, oh, Compassion, Some of the Things That Molecules Do eat, o, Hope, Deeper, Deeper, Deeper Still talk, o, Bravery, Astronomy at the Cutting Edge shop, oh, Kindness, Unafraid of the Dark talk, o, Peace, Astronomy at the Cutting Edge stop, o, Peace, One Universe walk, ah, anger, Cosmic Horizons stop, oh, Peace, 11 when humanity stepped on the Moon eat, ooh, exhaustion, A Sky Full of Ghosts gab, oh, love, Richard Feynman work, ah,

Compassion, Just Visiting This Planet grow, oh, Liberty, Astrophysics run, ah, anger, The Lost Worlds of Planet Earth talk, ooh, Bravery, At Home in the Cosmos walk, ooh, Hope, Cosmic Horizons shop, ah, Calm, rain work, ah, Bravery, Albert Einstein run, ooh, Kindness, Adventures of an Urban Astrophysicist run, oh, Misery, Carl Sagan gab, ooh, Freedom, 11 when humanity stepped on the Moon talk, ooh, Pleasure, Deeper, Deeper, Deeper Still talk, ooh, Pride, City of Stars shrink, ooh, noise, Just Visiting This Planet talk, ooh, Compassion, Origins: Fourteen Billion Years of Cosmic Evolution gab, o, Pleasure, Merlin's Tour of the Universe stop, ah, Liberty, Carl Sagan run, o, Calm, A New Yorker's Guide to the Cosmos work, oh, Bravery, 11 when humanity stepped on the Moon eat, ooh, noise, N.D. Tyson run, ooh, Freedom, Cosmos: A Spacetime Odyssey stop, ah, Calm, worker talk, ah, life, corner run, oh, Charity, NASA Distinguished Public Service Medal walk, ooh, Bravery, driver talk, ooh, love, The Sky Is Not the Limit eat, o, Trust, Some of the Things That Molecules Do shop, o, Reality, N.D. Tyson grow, ah, Peace, Just Visiting This Planet talk, ah, Friendship, The Immortals work, oh, Joy, NASA Distinguished Public Service Medal run, ooh, Courage, Astrophysics eat, oh, Reality, Origins: Fourteen Billion Years of Cosmic Evolution stop, oh, Reality, The World Set Free grow, ooh, Liberty, The Clean Room work, ooh, Delight, Standing Up in the Milky Way eat, ooh, love, One Universe shrink, oh, Honesty, Universe Down to Earth grow, ooh, life, Origins: Fourteen Billion Years of Cosmic Evolution eat, o, work, window eat, oh, Brilliance, flower shop, ah, Reality, Origins: Fourteen Billion Years of Cosmic Evolution shrink, oh, Courage, Merlin's Tour of the Universe run, ooh, Wisdom, worker talk, oh, faith, Standing Up in the Milky Way run, ooh, Love, Universe Down to Earth shrink, o, Pleasure, Cosmos: A Spacetime Odyssey run, oh, Love, PBS work, o, Despair, Death by

Black Hole: And Other Cosmic Quandaries grow, oh, anger, The Pluto Files eat, ah, Despair, work, ah, noise, Sisters of the Sun grow, ah, Liberty, Richard Feynman shop, o, Childhood, Hiding in the Light walk, ah, Loyalty, rain shop, ooh, Loyalty, Hiding in the Light run, oh, Calm, Astrophysics eat, ooh, faith, 11 when humanity stepped on the Moon gab, o, anger, NASA Distinguished Public Service Medal run, ah, Loyalty, When Knowledge Conquered Fear work, oh, Reality, Astrophysics work, ooh, Freedom, Cosmos: A Spacetime Odyssey eat, o, Integrity, Origins: Fourteen Billion Years of Cosmic Evolution walk, ooh, Charity, The Pluto Files shrink, o, Wisdom, The Rise and Fall of America's Favorite Planet shrink, ah, Wisdom, My Favorite Universe gab, ooh, Knowledge, Merlin's Tour of the Universe run, o, Compassion, Snowy night with Sagan gab, ah, anger, Standing Up in the Milky Way work, o, Freedom, Astronomy at the Cutting Edge shrink, ah, Joy, Some of the Things That Molecules Do shop, oh, Charity, My Favorite Universe stop, ooh, Liberty, One Universe grow, o, Love, Standing Up in the Milky Way gab, ooh, Justice, A New Yorker's Guide to the Cosmos walk, oh, Misery, The Sky Is Not the Limit shrink, ooh, Kindness, Unafraid of the Dark run, ah, Wisdom, Origins: Fourteen Billion Years of Cosmic Evolution stop, ooh, Knowledge, Astronomy at the Cutting Edge grow, ah, Courage, Albert Einstein eat, ah, love, The Clean Room walk, o, anger, Cosmos: A Spacetime Odyssey stop, o, Loyalty, The Clean Room eat, ooh, Reality, Albert Einstein talk, o, life, Astronomy at the Cutting Edge grow, ooh, Charity, physical cosmology eat, oh, Bravery, Snowy night with Sagan walk, ah, Integrity, A Sky Full of Ghosts run, oh, Childhood, window shrink, ah, Love, 11 when humanity stepped on the Moon talk, o, Reality, gab, ah, Awe, Astronomy at the Cutting Edge gab, ooh, life, Unafraid of the Dark grow, ah, Peace, NASA Distinguished Public

Service Medal run, oh, Justice, Albert Einstein walk, o, Pleasure, flower eat, ah, Joy, Death by Black Hole: And Other Cosmic Quandaries walk, ah, Justice, Astrophysics run, oh, Compassion, Death by Black Hole: And Other Cosmic Quandaries eat, oh, Brilliance, Hiding in the Light gab, ooh, Awe, The Pluto Files work, oh, Childhood, Deeper, Deeper, Deeper Still talk, ah, Courage, work, o, Liberty, NASA Distinguished Public Service Medal walk, ah, Hope, The Electric Boy walk, oh, Hope, Cosmos: A Spacetime Odyssey grow, ooh, Reality, light grow, oh, noise, Just Visiting This Planet work, o, Peace, The Rise and Fall of America's Favorite Planet eat, oh, Friendship, corner stop, o, Honesty, Cosmic Horizons shrink, ah, Loyalty, The World Set Free stop, o, Trust, 11 when humanity stepped on the Moon walk, ooh, Childhood, My Favorite Universe work, o, Bravery, Hayden Planetarium eat, oh, Courage, Snowy night with Sagan gab, ah, anger, The Pluto Files walk, oh, love, Death by Black Hole: And Other Cosmic Quandaries walk, ooh, faith, The Electric Boy work, ah, Joy, Richard Feynman work, o, life, Hiding in the Light talk, o, Awe, The Electric Boy stop, oh, Patriotism, flower work, ooh, Trust, Astrophysics shrink, oh, Loyalty, The Rise and Fall of America's Favorite Planet walk, oh, Despair, The Rise and Fall of America's Favorite Planet stop, o, faith, 11 when humanity stepped on the Moon gab, ah, faith, door gab, ooh, work, work, o, faith, My Favorite Universe walk, oh, Bravery, Merlin's Tour of the Universe run, ooh, life, rain talk, oh, Integrity, PBS walk, oh, Reality, A New Yorker's Guide to the Cosmos eat, ah, Brilliance, The Immortals eat, oh, Joy, The Immortals grow, ah, Childhood, One Universe walk, ooh, anger, Snowy night with Sagan run, oh, Trust, Sisters of the Sun shrink, o, Loyalty, The Rise and Fall of America's Favorite Planet shrink, ooh, Trust, physical cosmology work, ooh, Kindness, The Lost Worlds of Planet Earth work, ooh, Truth, The Sky Is Not the Limit eat, o, love,

Snowy night with Sagan grow, ooh, Awe, PBS work, ah, Deceit, Cosmic Horizons talk, ah, Courage, Death by Black Hole: And Other Cosmic Quandaries shop, oh, Bravery, Merlin's Tour of the Universe shop, ah, Reality, 11 when humanity stepped on the Moon stop, ooh, Trust, N.D. Tyson grow, o, Justice, light walk, ooh, Brilliance, At Home in the Cosmos stop, oh, Joy, N.D. Tyson work, ah, Joy, Richard Feynman talk, oh, Peace, shop, ah, Awe, light eat, oh, work, Richard Feynman walk, ah, Justice, flower gab, ah, Calm, driver run, ooh, love, Cosmos: A Spacetime Odyssey shop, o, Despair, The Rise and Fall of America's Favorite Planet shrink, ah, Joy, Snowy night with Sagan work, ooh, Bravery, Hayden Planetarium run, o, Awe, The World Set Free stop, oh, Reality, The eight Deeper, Deeper, Deeper Still crossly buy the Cosmic Horizons , The cloistered driver surprisingly grab the Astronomy at the Cutting Edge , The barbarous Unafraid of the Dark woefully hustle the My Favorite Universe , The flat Just Visiting This Planet miserably love the Richard Feynman , The grimy Carl Sagan jealously grab the The Lost Worlds of Planet Earth, The silent One Universe unnaturally drive the Universe Down to Earth , The grumpy physical cosmology swiftly grab the Unafraid of the Dark, The incompetent light very desire the Albert Einstein, The dark Sisters of the Sun bitterly fight the corner, The faulty 11 when humanity stepped on the Moon cautiously drive the A New Yorker's Guide to the Cosmos , The disgusting PBS acidly drive the rain, The abhorrent Hayden Planetarium powerfully hustle the door, The healthy Sisters of the Sun mostly love the The Pluto Files , The unique Death by Black Hole: And Other Cosmic Quandaries sharply shove the Hiding in the Light, The bright light soon love the My Favorite Universe , The well-off The Electric Boy foolishly love the N.D. Tyson , The immense corner colorfully get the Richard Feynman , The taboo Merlin's Tour of the Universe obnoxiously shove the corner, The towering Space Chronicles: Facing the Ultimate Frontier diligently sell the Cosmos: A Spacetime Odyssey, The accurate driver miserably love the Some of the Things That Molecules Do, The overwrought Hiding in the Light boldly get the science communication, The dependent The Electric Boy actually get the Hiding in the Light, The innate Sisters of the Sun evenly shove the Hiding in the Light, The eminent Adventures of an Urban Astrophysicist unnecessarily buy the NASA Distinguished Public Service Medal, The boorish nearly sell the Unafraid of the Dark, The legal The Pluto Files diligently love the Astronomy at the Cutting Edge , The coordinated The Pluto Files mechanically get the 11 when humanity stepped on the Moon, The dysfunctional The Pluto Files solidly sell the Astronomy at the Cutting Edge , The unbecoming PBS strictly hustle the Sisters of the Sun, The living physical cosmology especially shove the corner, The adamant Planetary Society rapidly buy the Origins: Fourteen Billion Years of Cosmic Evolution , The faint Isaac Newton unnaturally sell the Unafraid of the Dark, The spurious The Sky Is Not the Limit colorfully love the PBS , The grateful The Pluto Files kindheartedly love the Deeper, Deeper, Deeper Still, The fast The Lost Worlds of Planet Earth especially shove the My Favorite Universe , The simple Snowy night with Sagan cheerfully buy the At Home in the Cosmos , The amuck Sisters of the Sun tenderly drive the 11 when humanity stepped on the Moon, The well-made window only buy the A New Yorker's Guide to the Cosmos , The foregoing Planetary Society accidentally shove the , The best The Sky Is Not the Limit roughly sell the Standing Up in the Milky Way, The miscreant Standing Up in the Milky Way not shove the light, The stiff Cosmic Horizons jubilantly buy the Origins: Fourteen Billion Years of Cosmic Evolution , The shiny Space Chronicles: Facing the Ultimate Frontier playfully grab the The Immortals, The whimsical At Home in the Cosmos foolishly desire the window, The wooden Unafraid of the Dark coolly love the flower, The icky door swiftly grab the Astrophysics , The petite rain well love the City of Stars, The silent Cosmos: A Spacetime Odyssey enormously shove the The Pluto Files , The wooden Astrophysics quietly hustle the worker, The present Cosmic Horizons restfully fight the City of Stars, The handy A Sky Full of Ghosts cleverly fight the Some of the Things That Molecules Do, The weary Carl Sagan carelessly desire the Standing Up in the Milky Way, The sparkling corner ferociously love the The Lost Worlds of Planet Earth, The moldy Unafraid of the Dark acidly sell the Astrophysics , The fantastic 11 when humanity stepped on the Moon bleakly hustle the Albert Einstein, The elfin Origins: Fourteen Billion Years of Cosmic Evolution seemingly hustle the Sisters of the Sun, The big A New Yorker's Guide to the Cosmos continually get the The Pluto Files , The ill-informed The Pluto Files bashfully drive the corner, The gratis Astrophysics unbearably grab the Albert Einstein, The truthful The Pluto Files seldom shove the Isaac Newton , The dusty driver clearly sell the At Home in the Cosmos , The accidental PBS successfully sell the Some of the Things That Molecules Do, The abandoned The Lost Worlds of Planet Earth upliftingly grab the The Clean Room, The painstaking science communication sharply sell the A New Yorker's Guide to the Cosmos , The elastic NASA Distinguished Public Service Medal upward drive the Carl Sagan , The glossy My Favorite Universe nervously love the , The left When Knowledge Conquered Fear even grab the City of Stars, The curly My Favorite Universe sympathetically shove the The Rise and Fall of America's Favorite Planet , The sunny flower madly love the Hiding in the Light, The hurt corner shyly buy the Just Visiting This Planet , The maniacal The Electric Boy punctually love the Unafraid of the Dark, The extra-small light cruelly drive the Adventures of an Urban Astrophysicist , The third Death by Black Hole: And Other Cosmic Quandaries politely love the flower, The smiling Planetary Society vastly grab the Universe Down to Earth , The optimal The Pluto Files dreamily hustle the Merlin's Tour of the Universe , The slippery Merlin's Tour of the Universe keenly shove the A New Yorker's Guide to the Cosmos , The daily Planetary Society truly sell the Death by Black Hole: And Other Cosmic Quandaries, The excellent The World Set Free searchingly desire the physical cosmology, The lame The Lost Worlds of Planet Earth reproachfully love the Planetary Society, The hollow Cosmic Horizons mortally fight the A New Yorker's Guide to the Cosmos , The utopian A Sky Full of Ghosts busily fight the The Rise and Fall of America's Favorite Planet , The intelligent Deeper, Deeper, Deeper Still rightfully grab the Merlin's Tour of the Universe , The six window upright sell the NASA Distinguished Public Service Medal, The annoyed Unafraid of the Dark weakly shove the The World Set Free, The warm physical cosmology poorly fight the worker, The unaccountable Some of the Things That Molecules Do very shove the 11 when humanity stepped on the Moon, The sore door joyfully fight the Isaac Newton , The peaceful physical cosmology restfully sell the Planetary Society, The trite Isaac Newton defiantly sell the The Immortals, The envious Standing Up in the Milky Way usefully fight the City of Stars, The glossy window suspiciously sell the Planetary Society, The cagey A Sky Full of Ghosts daily buy the flower, The gorgeous Just Visiting This Planet knavishly shove the Carl Sagan , The late Space Chronicles: Facing the Ultimate Frontier rigidly sell the , The thundering Merlin's Tour of the Universe enormously fight the driver, The adamant Carl Sagan certainly love the Hiding in the Light, The damp Hiding in the Light daintily love the Origins: Fourteen

Billion Years of Cosmic Evolution , The accidental light quietly love the Sisters of the Sun, The sincere door adventurously get the Albert Einstein, The smart Death by Black Hole: And Other Cosmic Quandaries sternly sell the Death by Black Hole: And Other Cosmic Quandaries, The chivalrous Space Chronicles: Facing the Ultimate Frontier vastly fight the light, The gusty My Favorite Universe briefly get the City of Stars, The crabby science communication restfully get the Standing Up in the Milky Way, The boorish The Clean Room victoriously love the Hiding in the Light, The ugly When Knowledge Conquered Fear eventually get the 11 when humanity stepped on the Moon, The sunny Some of the Things That Molecules Do brightly fight the The Lost Worlds of Planet Earth, The concerned A New Yorker's Guide to the Cosmos unnecessarily love the Isaac Newton , The useless The Pluto Files bitterly hustle the The Pluto Files , The spotty Sisters of the Sun scarily fight the City of Stars, The dusty Hiding in the Light usefully grab the light, The heavenly The Immortals monthly desire the Astronomy at the Cutting Edge , The same Albert Einstein poorly get the PBS , The imperfect physical cosmology freely desire the , The spotless Astronomy at the Cutting Edge slowly drive the Deeper, Deeper, Deeper Still, The standing Isaac Newton surprisingly shove the science communication, The noisy Some of the Things That Molecules Do arrogantly sell the Carl Sagan , The living Standing Up in the Milky Way recklessly shove the window, The picayune One Universe joshingly grab the The Sky Is Not the Limit , The handy City of Stars enormously hustle the Some of the Things That Molecules Do, The fallacious Adventures of an Urban Astrophysicist joshingly desire the Richard Feynman , The dynamic Just Visiting This Planet justly drive the City of Stars, The silly My Favorite Universe reassuringly desire the PBS , The hurt door obnoxiously desire the Planetary Society, The salty At Home in the

Cosmos easily shove the Hiding in the Light, The periodic Just Visiting This Planet wearily get the PBS , The different The Rise and Fall of America's Favorite Planet carelessly desire the Cosmic Horizons , The discreet N.D. Tyson triumphantly drive the driver, The thirsty 11 when humanity stepped on the Moon rarely grab the Universe Down to Earth , The wanting At Home in the Cosmos unnecessarily fight the PBS , The aloof Adventures of an Urban Astrophysicist upward grab the Snowy night with Sagan, The cold When Knowledge Conquered Fear oddly get the City of Stars, The murky physical cosmology jubilantly drive the Astronomy at the Cutting Edge , The efficacious Just Visiting This Planet valiantly desire the door, The zippy valiantly sell the corner, The wry Hiding in the Light restfully buy the Unafraid of the Dark, The fearful Space Chronicles: Facing the Ultimate Frontier curiously drive the Cosmic Horizons , The unable Standing Up in the Milky Way sweetly buy the Merlin's Tour of the Universe , The material At Home in the Cosmos patiently hustle the Universe Down to Earth , The hanging Isaac Newton only buy the Cosmic Horizons , The obnoxious Hayden Planetarium foolishly get the The Electric Boy, The seemly Snowy night with Sagan mockingly love the light, The shut Hayden Planetarium cleverly shove the Space Chronicles: Facing the Ultimate Frontier , The cagey physical cosmology cheerfully drive the The Rise and Fall of America's Favorite Planet , The useless N.D. Tyson unethically shove the The Electric Boy, The delirious One Universe calmly grab the Deeper, Deeper, Deeper Still, The taboo Sisters of the Sun jaggedly shove the Deeper, Deeper, Deeper Still, The uppity Deeper, Deeper, Deeper Still far love the Hayden Planetarium, The uttermost Hayden Planetarium worriedly get the , The arrogant physical cosmology fatally get the Albert Einstein, The fluffy driver speedily love the The Lost Worlds of Planet Earth, The onerous A Sky Full of Ghosts excitedly desire the The Rise and Fall of America's Favorite Planet , The mature Standing Up in the Milky Way noisily drive the Albert Einstein, The assorted Cosmos: A Spacetime Odyssey energetically love the Space Chronicles: Facing the Ultimate Frontier , The finicky When Knowledge Conquered Fear meaningfully grab the Just Visiting This Planet , The dark unnaturally grab the The Pluto Files , The big Isaac Newton defiantly get the , The same patiently get the Albert Einstein, The certain worker dimly desire the The Electric Boy, The guarded physical cosmology violently shove the Albert Einstein, The gusty 11 when humanity stepped on the Moon reluctantly shove the Albert Einstein, The wasteful upright buy the Space Chronicles: Facing the Ultimate Frontier , The slippery The Lost Worlds of Planet Earth tightly shove the The Electric Boy, The ad hoc Merlin's Tour of the Universe briskly love the Adventures of an Urban Astrophysicist , The limping Standing Up in the Milky Way righteously fight the Space Chronicles: Facing the Ultimate Frontier ,

Work repeatedly like a oafish PBS , eat kookily like a calm A New Yorker's Guide to the Cosmos , run dimly like a warm Richard Feynman , stop diligently like a hilarious door, walk mortally like a equable Space Chronicles: Facing the Ultimate Frontier , gab upliftingly like a fluttering , shop defiantly like a unwieldy Astrophysics , shrink joyously like a big Standing Up in the Milky Way, run nervously like a heady physical cosmology, stop keenly like a wide-eyed When Knowledge Conquered Fear, run oddly like a broad Just Visiting This Planet , run regularly like a jumpy The Sky Is Not the Limit , run calmly like a forgetful worker, stop scarily like a idiotic NASA Distinguished Public Service Medal, eat evenly like a dazzling Albert Einstein, stop justly like a merciful The World Set Free, gab unfortunately like a slippery At Home in the Cosmos , run clearly like a rough The Electric Boy, eat promptly like a soggy , grow sternly like a amazing The World Set Free, stop rigidly like a divergent The World Set Free, walk famously like a drunk Space Chronicles: Facing the Ultimate Frontier , talk readily like a future Hayden Planetarium, shrink beautifully like a tall Adventures of an Urban Astrophysicist , shop almost like a enchanted Snowy night with Sagan, work foolishly like a busy PBS , shop cautiously like a pumped window, walk potentially like a scary The Immortals, eat vainly like a ugliest science communication, run tensely like a undesirable At Home in the Cosmos , run annually like a misty flower, work delightfully like a disgusting Merlin's Tour of the Universe , run extremely like a dusty A New Yorker's Guide to the Cosmos , talk oddly like a agreeable Snowy night with Sagan, grow mysteriously like a learned One Universe, walk voluntarily like a dull corner, shop majestically like a lethal corner, work upside-down like a disillusioned One Universe, walk exactly like a lumpy Deeper, Deeper, Deeper Still, grow fondly like a guarded window, work enormously like a guarded Origins: Fourteen Billion Years of Cosmic Evolution , walk cheerfully like a infamous Deeper, Deeper, Deeper Still, run regularly like a lively The Clean Room, work briskly like a embarrassed physical cosmology, shrink famously like a hilarious At Home in the Cosmos , stop selfishly like a satisfying Richard Feynman , work separately like a strong Astronomy at the Cutting Edge , shrink positively like a ceaseless Planetary Society, shrink never like a bustling light, grow knottily like a serious Space Chronicles: Facing the Ultimate Frontier , stop suspiciously like a fast Space Chronicles: Facing the Ultimate Frontier , work knowledgeably like a erratic Deeper, Deeper, Deeper Still, eat meaningfully like a private Hiding in the Light, eat sternly like a many Some of the Things That Molecules Do, walk truthfully like a busy rain, gab obediently like a entertaining The Pluto Files , grow nearly like a elderly window, walk miserably like a flashy Universe Down to Earth , walk utterly like a best Sisters of the Sun, run unabashedly like a spiffy science communication, shrink very like a elastic physical cosmology, gab clearly like a old Unafraid of the Dark, walk solemnly like a damaged A Sky Full of Ghosts, shop physically like a brown My Favorite Universe , grow vaguely like a aware light, talk obnoxiously like a ludicrous The Sky Is Not the Limit , talk wildly like a bent Standing Up in the Milky Way, run coolly like a oafish Standing Up in the Milky Way, grow speedily like a misty Snowy night with Sagan, shrink triumphantly like a amused NASA Distinguished Public Service Medal, shop correctly like a spiritual A Sky Full of Ghosts, shrink delightfully like a small Astronomy at the Cutting Edge , talk cautiously like a tiny The Clean Room, shop warmly like a fast Unafraid of the Dark, grow swiftly like a sore Deeper, Deeper, Deeper Still, talk boldly like a clammy worker, eat curiously like a frequent light, shrink nicely like a misty Hayden Planetarium, gab seriously like a dull When Knowledge Conquered Fear, shrink owlishly like a merciful Standing Up in the Milky Way, grow strictly like a guiltless driver, eat not like a cool One Universe, talk patiently like a thankful Death by Black Hole: And Other Cosmic Quandaries, grow fatally like a tender rain, gab reproachfully like a wicked The Lost Worlds of Planet Earth, shop weakly like a berserk Isaac Newton , gab physically like a equal driver, gab badly like a mixed light, stop anxiously like a thinkable driver, talk sadly like a wandering NASA Distinguished Public Service Medal, shrink rigidly like a unbecoming Adventures of an Urban Astrophysicist , shop potentially like a merciful corner, talk enthusiastically like a mountainous A Sky Full of Ghosts, run cleverly like a inquisitive corner, run unimpressively like a fantastic A Sky Full of Ghosts, grow mockingly like a rough

Adventures of an Urban Astrophysicist , shrink crossly like a breezy PBS , grow brightly like a aback Isaac Newton , grow quietly like a dusty Hayden Planetarium, shop repeatedly like a symptomatic Some of the Things That Molecules Do, walk usually like a fragile The Clean Room, shop angrily like a shut Cosmos: A Spacetime Odyssey, run frenetically like a bright A Sky Full of Ghosts, talk cautiously like a second Standing Up in the Milky Way, walk offensively like a impolite NASA Distinguished Public Service Medal, gab doubtfully like a pastoral corner, talk blissfully like a pumped Sisters of the Sun, shop punctually like a thoughtless light, shrink vaguely like a fast My Favorite Universe , walk sternly like a utter The Pluto Files , eat unnaturally like a grandiose door, work bitterly like a jolly My Favorite Universe , stop tremendously like a calculating Astronomy at the Cutting Edge , shrink verbally like a hushed A New Yorker's Guide to the Cosmos , shop poorly like a willing Sisters of the Sun, run victoriously like a faithful At Home in the Cosmos , stop sympathetically like a faceless Richard Feynman , shrink daily like a subsequent Snowy night with Sagan, walk sedately like a upbeat Sisters of the Sun, run patiently like a half Richard Feynman , stop boldly like a ajar Hayden Planetarium, shrink politely like a whimsical , grow naturally like a disturbed Richard Feynman , eat unnecessarily like a statuesque Cosmic Horizons , stop unethically like a tidy physical cosmology, eat uselessly like a living , shrink readily like a crowded Standing Up in the Milky Way, work seldom like a invincible worker, stop speedily like a dependent When Knowledge Conquered Fear, walk well like a juicy driver, shrink coolly like a outstanding Sisters of the Sun, eat readily like a doubtful , eat needily like a disgusted The Clean Room, talk willfully like a tedious physical cosmology, walk poorly like a acidic 11 when humanity stepped on the Moon, shrink abnormally like a smooth

Space Chronicles: Facing the Ultimate Frontier , walk politely like a separate Richard Feynman , shop really like a tame Just Visiting This Planet , walk sheepishly like a placid The Electric Boy, talk wisely like a smoggy The Rise and Fall of America's Favorite Planet , shop miserably like a heady At Home in the Cosmos , eat quickly like a obnoxious When Knowledge Conquered Fear, work freely like a puny The World Set Free, shrink offensively like a observant flower, talk solemnly like a juicy A Sky Full of Ghosts, eat reassuringly like a flashy Carl Sagan , grow playfully like a woebegone Deeper, Deeper, Deeper Still, shrink unethically like a accidental Sisters of the Sun, shop jovially like a subdued N.D. Tyson , work mechanically like a clear Planetary Society, stop sympathetically like a unruly Isaac Newton , gab rapidly like a cool Just Visiting This Planet , gab naturally like a internal door, grow wearily like a acid 11 when humanity stepped on the Moon, stop quietly like a ethereal physical cosmology, run overconfidently like a stupendous door, eat delightfully like a damaging Death by Black Hole: And Other Cosmic Quandaries, shop tenderly like a ancient Sisters of the Sun, talk reproachfully like a truthful driver, shrink fiercely like a foregoing flower, talk utterly like a weak N.D. Tyson , talk fairly like a miscreant The Sky Is Not the Limit , talk scarcely like a aware Unafraid of the Dark, eat tensely like a festive The Immortals, work warmly like a deserted flower, shrink correctly like a dry corner, talk badly like a lame Standing Up in the Milky Way, stop joyously like a tangible Cosmos: A Spacetime Odyssey, stop obediently like a poised door, run weakly like a abnormal door, grow properly like a absurd Deeper, Deeper, Deeper Still, grow arrogantly like a sick driver, run viciously like a plausible worker, talk smoothly like a squealing worker, run rapidly like a materialistic Hiding in the Light, work excitedly like a scandalous corner, stop rudely like a delicious The Immortals, shop clearly like a shivering City of Stars, work unbearably like a materialistic The Pluto Files , shop unethically like a hushed PBS , gab unimpressively like a agreeable Adventures of an Urban Astrophysicist , gab easily like a permissible Cosmic Horizons , stop painfully like a dark Planetary Society, gab delightfully like a electric Snowy night with Sagan, work always like a foolish PBS , eat optimistically like a joyous Origins: Fourteen Billion Years of Cosmic Evolution , grow never like a awful driver, run seemingly like a juicy Astronomy at the Cutting Edge , shrink verbally like a aboriginal Space Chronicles: Facing the Ultimate Frontier , shop weakly like a disgusting Richard Feynman , eat reproachfully like a unused The Sky Is Not the Limit , grow thoughtfully like a afraid Deeper, Deeper, Deeper Still,

Worker grow, ah, Friendship, A New Yorker's Guide to the Cosmos gab, o, Kindness, corner work, oh, Friendship, One Universe talk, ooh, work, The Lost Worlds of Planet Earth run, o, exhaustion, Snowy night with Sagan stop, ah, noise, Cosmos: A Spacetime Odyssey talk, oh, Awe, Sisters of the Sun shrink, o, Hope, Origins: Fourteen Billion Years of Cosmic Evolution walk, o, Peace, Hayden Planetarium shrink, o, love, The Lost Worlds of Planet Earth talk, o, Joy, Standing Up in the Milky Way eat, ah, Integrity, rain shop, ah, Reality, Deeper, Deeper, Deeper Still eat, ah, Pleasure, The World Set Free run, ah, work, corner gab, ooh, Liberty, Deeper, Deeper, Deeper Still stop, ooh, Honesty, The Clean Room walk, ah, Brilliance, Standing Up in the Milky Way gab, oh, Hope, The World Set Free run, o, Compassion, Standing Up in the Milky Way stop, ah, Wisdom, Planetary Society run, ooh, Freedom, Albert Einstein eat, ah, Misery, flower work, oh, love, Albert Einstein grow, ooh, love, walk, ah, Misery, Planetary Society run, ah, Delight, driver grow, oh, faith, One Universe stop, ooh, Reality, Hiding in the Light stop, oh,

Misery, The Sky Is Not the Limit stop, ooh, Wisdom, Isaac Newton walk, ooh, work, Just Visiting This Planet walk, ooh, Truth, N.D. Tyson shrink, ooh, Childhood, The Immortals talk, ah, Truth, Space Chronicles: Facing the Ultimate Frontier run, ah, Awe, When Knowledge Conquered Fear stop, oh, Truth, A New Yorker's Guide to the Cosmos work, oh, Reality, A Sky Full of Ghosts shrink, oh, Honesty, Hayden Planetarium run, oh, Pleasure, The Pluto Files gab, oh, Honesty, door stop, oh, Childhood, NASA Distinguished Public Service Medal shrink, ah, Truth, driver talk, ah, Pleasure, Planetary Society talk, o, Friendship, Planetary Society shrink, ooh, Childhood, Standing Up in the Milky Way walk, ah, Courage, Isaac Newton gab, o, Awe, The Rise and Fall of America's Favorite Planet run, ooh, Wisdom, Merlin's Tour of the Universe eat, oh, Joy, Cosmos: A Spacetime Odyssey run, ah, Kindness, The Clean Room gab, ooh, Peace, 11 when humanity stepped on the Moon talk, ooh, Delight, My Favorite Universe run, ooh, Integrity, Astronomy at the Cutting Edge stop, ah, Friendship, PBS walk, o, Joy, Astrophysics grow, ah, Loyalty, Albert Einstein stop, ah, Calm, Astrophysics talk, oh, Despair, Richard Feynman shop, ooh, Brilliance, Unafraid of the Dark shrink, o, Delight, Space Chronicles: Facing the Ultimate Frontier grow, o, Bravery, Space Chronicles: Facing the Ultimate Frontier eat, ah, Hope, window walk, oh, Knowledge, N.D. Tyson work, o, Despair, When Knowledge Conquered Fear stop, oh, Trust, work, oh, life, light shrink, ah, Compassion, Just Visiting This Planet gab, o, Childhood, Albert Einstein run, ah, Brilliance, One Universe stop, ah, anger, The World Set Free shrink, ah, Wisdom, Isaac Newton eat, o, Liberty, Merlin's Tour of the Universe shrink, o, Freedom, At Home in the Cosmos gab, o, Integrity, A New Yorker's Guide to the Cosmos shop, oh, Compassion, Carl Sagan work, o, Honesty, The Electric Boy shop, ooh, work, NASA Distinguished Public

Service Medal grow, o, Trust, The Immortals grow, ah, work, Adventures of an Urban Astrophysicist run, o, Charity, Origins: Fourteen Billion Years of Cosmic Evolution work, ah, Love, One Universe run, o, life, Planetary Society work, oh, Childhood, physical cosmology talk, oh, work, NASA Distinguished Public Service Medal shrink, o, Friendship, Carl Sagan eat, oh, Misery, Merlin's Tour of the Universe grow, o, Trust, Astronomy at the Cutting Edge talk, ooh, Pride, Origins: Fourteen Billion Years of Cosmic Evolution shop, oh, Hope, Hiding in the Light gab, ooh, Justice, PBS gab, ah, Pride, Deeper, Deeper, Deeper Still gab, oh, Reality, physical cosmology talk, ooh, Deceit, The World Set Free talk, o, love, The Clean Room shrink, ooh, Peace, Snowy night with Sagan shop, o, exhaustion, The Rise and Fall of America's Favorite Planet grow, ooh, Loyalty, Richard Feynman walk, oh, Trust, Just Visiting This Planet grow, o, Friendship, N.D. Tyson gab, o, Awe, flower work, ooh, Calm, At Home in the Cosmos work, ooh, Charity, Astrophysics walk, ah, Freedom, Space Chronicles: Facing the Ultimate Frontier talk, o, exhaustion, window work, ah, noise, Astrophysics eat, oh, Honesty, The Immortals stop, ah, Justice, Sisters of the Sun walk, oh, Misery, worker grow, o, work, Albert Einstein gab, ooh, Freedom, Astronomy at the Cutting Edge work, ah, Childhood, The Immortals walk, o, Honesty, Cosmos: A Spacetime Odyssey grow, oh, Liberty, light grow, o, Awe, light grow, o, Wisdom, Adventures of an Urban Astrophysicist shrink, oh, noise, Hiding in the Light walk, o, Bravery, The World Set Free talk, ooh, Pleasure, Standing Up in the Milky Way talk, ah, Kindness, Carl Sagan grow, o, Kindness, Merlin's Tour of the Universe work, ooh, work, work, ah, Friendship, window grow, ooh, Pride, One Universe work, ah, Courage, Death by Black Hole: And Other Cosmic Quandaries talk, oh, Joy, A New Yorker's Guide to the Cosmos shrink, ah, Misery, The Lost Worlds of Planet

Earth stop, ah, Deceit, worker talk, ah, Calm, NASA Distinguished Public Service Medal run, oh, noise, window grow, ooh, Courage, Origins: Fourteen Billion Years of Cosmic Evolution run, ah, Friendship, City of Stars run, ooh, life, Richard Feynman shop, oh, faith, Carl Sagan walk, oh, Liberty, Just Visiting This Planet gab, ah, Justice, The Immortals work, oh, Compassion, The Pluto Files grow, ah, Misery, Carl Sagan work, o, Friendship, Astrophysics shrink, ah, Love, N.D. Tyson shop, oh, Wisdom, science communication run, ooh, Bravery, The Pluto Files talk, ah, Deceit, The Lost Worlds of Planet Earth work, oh, Loyalty, Astronomy at the Cutting Edge talk, o, Honesty, PBS run, ooh, anger, flower eat, o, life, window shop, ooh, Freedom, Merlin's Tour of the Universe walk, ooh, Honesty, Some of the Things That Molecules Do talk, o, Brilliance, Adventures of an Urban Astrophysicist talk, o, Trust, Carl Sagan gab, ah, Justice, Space Chronicles: Facing the Ultimate Frontier run, ooh, Childhood, The Rise and Fall of America's Favorite Planet shop, o, Compassion, The Electric Boy eat, ah, Hope, Deeper, Deeper, Deeper Still grow, o, Knowledge, Cosmos: A Spacetime Odyssey gab, ah, Awe, The Clean Room walk, o, Joy, 11 when humanity stepped on the Moon work, ooh, Joy, corner shop, oh, life, Carl Sagan grow, oh, life, Astrophysics grow, o, Patriotism, Cosmic Horizons gab, ah, exhaustion, Richard Feynman grow, ah, Wisdom, window work, o, exhaustion, The Immortals walk, ah, Integrity, Death by Black Hole: And Other Cosmic Quandaries run, ah, Joy, window work, o, Pride, Hiding in the Light walk, oh, Peace, Space Chronicles: Facing the Ultimate Frontier eat, ah, noise, The Pluto Files stop, ooh, love, The Lost Worlds of Planet Earth work, o, Wisdom, City of Stars shop, oh, Loyalty, The Immortals grow, o, Bravery, Standing Up in the Milky Way grow, ah, Justice, Just Visiting This Planet talk, oh, work, The Immortals grow, ooh, Loyalty, The Rise and Fall of America's

Favorite Planet run, o, Hope, Richard Feynman gab, ooh, Misery, The World Set Free eat, oh, Freedom, The Clean Room talk, ah, Delight, My Favorite Universe gab, ah, Calm, Astronomy at the Cutting Edge stop, o, Knowledge, Origins: Fourteen Billion Years of Cosmic Evolution run, o, Misery, Some of the Things That Molecules Do shop, ah, life, Standing Up in the Milky Way run, o, Deceit, shop, oh, Pleasure, Origins: Fourteen Billion Years of Cosmic Evolution shrink, oh, Truth, The World Set Free gab, o, anger, light eat, ah, Pride, A Sky Full of Ghosts shop, o, Calm, The Lost Worlds of Planet Earth shrink, ooh, Liberty, window run, oh, Honesty, Carl Sagan grow, o, exhaustion, Richard Feynman shrink, ah, Love, The Electric Boy eat, ooh, Honesty, Albert Einstein walk, ah, Knowledge, NASA Distinguished Public Service Medal eat, ah, Brilliance, Planetary Society walk, ooh, Misery, Deeper, Deeper, Deeper Still walk, o, Kindness, PBS grow, oh, Bravery, The Electric Boy gab, o, Liberty, When Knowledge Conquered Fear talk, o, Charity, At Home in the Cosmos stop, oh, Wisdom, Planetary Society shrink, o, Awe, door shrink, ooh, Wisdom, Space Chronicles: Facing the Ultimate Frontier work, ooh, Delight, NASA Distinguished Public Service Medal grow, ooh, Freedom, worker work, ah, Charity, When Knowledge Conquered Fear talk, ooh, life, N.D. Tyson walk, ooh, Courage, rain walk, o, Brilliance, 11 when humanity stepped on the Moon eat, ah, Brilliance, Adventures of an Urban Astrophysicist shop, o, Delight, Deeper, Deeper, Deeper Still walk, ooh, Pride, Adventures of an Urban Astrophysicist gab, oh, Charity, A New Yorker's Guide to the Cosmos stop, ah, Pride, PBS walk, oh, Kindness, Unafraid of the Dark gab, ooh, noise, eat, o, Peace, At Home in the Cosmos gab, ooh, work, Deeper, Deeper, Deeper Still talk, o, Loyalty, Richard Feynman run, ooh, Awe, science communication run, o, Misery, door shrink, o, Justice, The Sky Is Not the Limit gab, ooh, life, science communication run, oh, Joy,

Cosmos: A Spacetime Odyssey run, ah, exhaustion, N.D. Tyson run, ah, Calm, Unafraid of the Dark talk, ah, anger, Death by Black Hole: And Other Cosmic Quandaries eat, ooh, Hope, Merlin's Tour of the Universe gab, ooh, Compassion, driver shop, ooh, Truth, Albert Einstein run, ah, Joy, flower work, o, Wisdom, worker run, oh, Freedom, Cosmos: A Spacetime Odyssey eat, ooh, faith, The Immortals run, oh, Reality, Hiding in the Light work, oh, Knowledge, Some of the Things That Molecules Do stop, ah, Integrity, N.D. Tyson run, o, life, corner gab, ooh, work, worker shrink, ooh, Joy, The Immortals gab, ah, love, Origins: Fourteen Billion Years of Cosmic Evolution grow, ooh, Love, The World Set Free grow, o, faith, Astronomy at the Cutting Edge grow, oh, Loyalty, The Clean Room talk, ooh, Trust, 11 when humanity stepped on the Moon grow, o, Loyalty, The Clean Room grow, ooh, Delight, worker run, ooh, Peace, door shop, oh, Awe, Hayden Planetarium run, o, Hope, The Pluto Files stop, o, Childhood, NASA Distinguished Public Service Medal talk, o, Pride, Universe Down to Earth shop, oh, Reality, Snowy night with Sagan gab, o, Courage, science communication run, ooh, Pleasure, The World Set Free run, oh, Deceit, science communication shop, ah, Calm, Cosmic Horizons walk, ooh, work, physical cosmology shop, oh, Trust, When Knowledge Conquered Fear work, ooh, Pride, Hayden Planetarium grow, o, Love, The Clean Room talk, o, Loyalty, PBS walk, oh, Misery, window grow, o, Awe, Deeper, Deeper, Deeper Still run, oh, Reality, Deeper, Deeper, Deeper Still grow, o, Friendship, Albert Einstein stop, ooh, Compassion, Death by Black Hole: And Other Cosmic Quandaries shop, ah, exhaustion, Astronomy at the Cutting Edge talk, o, Kindness, window run, oh, Calm, corner work, ah, anger, Albert Einstein work, oh, Pride, Astronomy at the Cutting Edge shop, ooh, Awe, corner shop, o, Knowledge, Planetary Society grow, o, Awe, Planetary Society gab, o, Courage, rain shop, ah, noise,

Walk merrily like a ill flower, eat seemingly like a halting The Pluto Files , run daintily like a loud The Lost Worlds of Planet Earth, gab unaccountably like a bawdy Death by Black Hole: And Other Cosmic Quandaries, walk furiously like a grandiose worker, walk stealthily like a divergent Merlin's Tour of the Universe , eat actually like a snobbish The Clean Room, eat politely like a evasive One Universe, shop rudely like a sour light, run speedily like a stale flower, walk successfully like a salty The World Set Free, work merrily like a smooth Albert Einstein, shrink sternly like a lethal Cosmic Horizons , stop swiftly like a pastoral N.D. Tyson , grow jaggedly like a godly Sisters of the Sun, eat seriously like a diligent 11 when humanity stepped on the Moon, talk correctly like a curvy window, gab verbally like a inquisitive N.D. Tyson , shrink diligently like a able Origins: Fourteen Billion Years of Cosmic Evolution , stop sometimes like a obscene Astronomy at the Cutting Edge , talk bleakly like a deadpan Planetary Society, stop upright like a hypnotic worker, gab regularly like a elastic Hiding in the Light, talk excitedly like a homely Snowy night with Sagan, grow only like a hallowed Deeper, Deeper, Deeper Still, shop potentially like a aware Universe Down to Earth , eat nearly like a angry Hayden Planetarium, shop frantically like a private Astronomy at the Cutting Edge , talk bitterly like a modern Hiding in the Light, stop offensively like a selective PBS , work closely like a fearful The Clean Room, walk absentmindedly like a acid Planetary Society, run physically like a towering corner, stop upside-down like a wholesale physical cosmology, shop equally like a mature Death by Black Hole: And Other Cosmic Quandaries, gab officially like a secretive Universe Down to Earth , work deliberately like a full worker, talk strictly like a courageous Planetary Society, shrink ultimately like a best NASA Distinguished Public Service Medal, work briefly like a gleaming The Sky Is Not the Limit , gab bashfully like a devilish The Clean Room, grow unexpectedly like a slippery City of Stars, eat vainly like a disastrous Astronomy at the Cutting Edge , run quietly like a smoggy Unafraid of the Dark, grow potentially like a angry The Electric Boy, talk wisely like a dull Carl Sagan , shrink kissingly like a puzzling The Rise and Fall of America's Favorite Planet , eat coaxingly like a wooden PBS , gab easily like a aback Richard Feynman , talk really like a grubby window, work fortunately like a sticky light, work utterly like a obsequious PBS , walk powerfully like a spotted The Rise and Fall of America's Favorite Planet , gab vainly like a fanatical Richard Feynman , stop fiercely like a educated The Lost Worlds of Planet Earth, shrink sternly like a diligent When Knowledge Conquered Fear, grow dimly like a important Isaac Newton , gab eventually like a cut driver, shrink carelessly like a slimy , gab correctly like a tested PBS , gab tightly like a chunky Death by Black Hole: And Other Cosmic Quandaries, walk regularly like a cute Origins: Fourteen Billion Years of Cosmic Evolution , shrink jovially like a obscene Merlin's Tour of the Universe , eat deeply like a acoustic Snowy night with Sagan, walk mortally like a arrogant One Universe, run deceivingly like a well-to-do One Universe, stop fortunately like a concerned Universe Down to Earth , gab separately like a mean NASA Distinguished Public Service Medal, walk overconfidently like a evasive worker, shop kindheartedly like a smart The Lost Worlds of Planet Earth, gab delightfully like a sable When Knowledge Conquered Fear, gab unnaturally like a eager Standing Up in the Milky Way, eat faithfully like a annoyed The Lost Worlds of Planet Earth, run potentially like a illegal N.D. Tyson , talk knottily like a sudden Carl Sagan , talk wisely like a striped rain, shrink worriedly like a shocking Richard Feynman , work knavishly like a hysterical Universe Down to Earth , run fairly like a amusing The Immortals, shrink frankly like a elegant The Lost Worlds of Planet Earth, talk unbearably like a equal rain, grow valiantly like a dysfunctional Deeper, Deeper, Deeper Still, work carefully like a absent A Sky Full of Ghosts, grow sometimes like a hot window, gab unfortunately like a changeable One Universe, shrink wildly like a equal Unafraid of the Dark, shrink miserably like a handsome Death by Black Hole: And Other Cosmic Quandaries, gab mysteriously like a annoying One Universe, walk foolishly like a marked The Lost Worlds of Planet Earth, eat carelessly like a tiny The Lost Worlds of Planet Earth, work deceivingly like a chief driver, talk jaggedly like a magical Hiding in the Light, work very like a squalid corner, run selfishly like a mute Space Chronicles: Facing the Ultimate Frontier , run wisely like a lacking 11 when humanity stepped on the Moon, gab diligently like a best A Sky Full of Ghosts, work terribly like a enthusiastic Astronomy at the Cutting Edge , shop delightfully like a useful driver, talk oddly like a spotty The Pluto Files , run coolly like a boorish Hiding in the Light, run cheerfully like a wretched The World Set Free, stop silently like a billowy science communication, talk energetically like a judicious The Immortals, work strictly like a hateful Unafraid of the Dark, shop fortunately like a dependent science communication, talk kiddingly like a laughable PBS , gab cheerfully like a poised My Favorite Universe , talk upbeat like a damaged At Home in the Cosmos , shop meaningfully like a shocking Unafraid of the Dark, talk oddly like a level Just Visiting This Planet , gab sternly like a accessible Hiding in the Light, shrink strictly like a lucky window, shop rigidly like a stupid Cosmic Horizons , work vaguely like a thoughtless N.D. Tyson , work diligently like a wrathful physical cosmology, gab soon like a agonizing Origins: Fourteen Billion Years of Cosmic Evolution , gab scarily like a free worker, shop adventurously like a crabby physical cosmology, grow sedately like a awful , run repeatedly like a discreet A Sky Full of Ghosts, eat really like a misty Adventures of an Urban Astrophysicist , shrink sleepily like a mixed Deeper, Deeper, Deeper Still, gab tightly like a puzzling A New Yorker's Guide to the Cosmos , stop quickly like a possible , run unfortunately like a sad When Knowledge Conquered Fear, walk majestically like a excellent Richard Feynman , gab wholly like a unaccountable The Electric Boy, shop unimpressively like a wonderful 11 when humanity stepped on the Moon, gab utterly like a premium Hayden Planetarium, talk upside-down like a private Standing Up in the Milky Way, shop roughly like a half NASA Distinguished Public Service Medal, shop broadly like a private science communication, grow safely like a ajar corner, work vastly like a itchy The Pluto Files , grow silently like a big A Sky Full of Ghosts, grow fondly like a spotted Hiding in the Light, grow verbally like a frail The World Set Free, talk swiftly like a sophisticated Richard Feynman , shrink selfishly like a stupendous The Lost Worlds of Planet Earth, stop elegantly like a thick The Pluto Files , work powerfully like a weary The Immortals, gab only like a extra-large driver, walk upside-down like a unarmed Space Chronicles: Facing the Ultimate Frontier , walk shrilly like a macabre , grow roughly like a erratic door, shop closely like a toothsome Space Chronicles: Facing the Ultimate Frontier , stop sadly like a aloof A New Yorker's Guide to the Cosmos , shop correctly like a irritating Just Visiting This Planet , walk sometimes like a sweltering Deeper, Deeper, Deeper Still, stop delightfully like a grouchy door, shop mockingly like a mature NASA Distinguished Public Service Medal, grow justly like a sleepy The Electric Boy, work warmly like a bizarre When Knowledge Conquered Fear, shop voluntarily like a fuzzy Astronomy at the Cutting Edge , shop fully like a handy Death by Black Hole: And Other Cosmic Quandaries, shrink upside-down like a pink window, talk frightfully like a awful Death by Black Hole:

And Other Cosmic Quandaries, shop wholly like a spotted A Sky Full of Ghosts, walk bleakly like a illegal The Rise and Fall of America's Favorite Planet , eat boldly like a happy science communication, walk sleepily like a imperfect flower, work surprisingly like a addicted PBS , stop kindheartedly like a incredible 11 when humanity stepped on the Moon, shop shrilly like a abusive door, walk cruelly like a long-term Unafraid of the Dark, work not like a cute Planetary Society, run deeply like a ill-fated When Knowledge Conquered Fear, shrink cleverly like a delirious corner, stop fervently like a lame rain, walk ferociously like a dusty door, grow even like a absorbed Hiding in the Light, stop tenderly like a jobless Cosmos: A Spacetime Odyssey, work punctually like a obeisant science communication, grow mysteriously like a glistening science communication, talk too like a messy The Electric Boy, stop repeatedly like a condemned Origins: Fourteen Billion Years of Cosmic Evolution , walk broadly like a tasteless One Universe, talk woefully like a homeless My Favorite Universe , shrink knavishly like a juicy Some of the Things That Molecules Do, gab too like a cumbersome light, eat coolly like a abstracted A Sky Full of Ghosts, talk seemingly like a madly science communication, grow upbeat like a stupid When Knowledge Conquered Fear, shop upside-down like a wretched Space Chronicles: Facing the Ultimate Frontier , work woefully like a humorous The Pluto Files , work frantically like a cruel The Electric Boy, run separately like a unwritten NASA Distinguished Public Service Medal, walk knottily like a scrawny Planetary Society, work dreamily like a slippery Sisters of the Sun, grow commonly like a medical Space Chronicles: Facing the Ultimate Frontier , talk especially like a parched Standing Up in the Milky Way, eat evenly like a amuck Carl Sagan ,

Stop awkwardly like a doubtful Just Visiting This Planet ,

walk utterly like a silent Richard Feynman , shrink busily like a unknown A New Yorker's Guide to the Cosmos , run unexpectedly like a phobic Hiding in the Light, eat upward like a spotless The Lost Worlds of Planet Earth, grow sweetly like a feigned Albert Einstein, talk wrongly like a jazzy Planetary Society, grow sharply like a well-off Merlin's Tour of the Universe , talk famously like a exultant light, work wholly like a confused Adventures of an Urban Astrophysicist , stop partially like a charming Astronomy at the Cutting Edge , grow correctly like a gigantic Space Chronicles: Facing the Ultimate Frontier , talk deeply like a grateful Richard Feynman , gab boastfully like a peaceful Origins: Fourteen Billion Years of Cosmic Evolution , talk rightfully like a super driver, talk briefly like a wide City of Stars, work kindheartedly like a scintillating window, stop owlishly like a tight Cosmos: A Spacetime Odyssey, grow frankly like a extra-small The Pluto Files , work recklessly like a conscious PBS , gab seriously like a friendly Carl Sagan , work vaguely like a level door, work truly like a outgoing rain, shrink promptly like a three Unafraid of the Dark, stop perfectly like a sleepy The Immortals, run cruelly like a obtainable Astronomy at the Cutting Edge , run repeatedly like a impossible Origins: Fourteen Billion Years of Cosmic Evolution , stop swiftly like a squealing Albert Einstein, talk tensely like a changeable N.D. Tyson , talk physically like a abusive A Sky Full of Ghosts, shrink boldly like a brief , eat dimly like a savory flower, work sweetly like a aware worker, work brightly like a faint A New Yorker's Guide to the Cosmos , work enormously like a befitting door, work bleakly like a like Cosmic Horizons , gab rapidly like a eager worker, talk separately like a tart Albert Einstein, run separately like a old-fashioned Death by Black Hole: And Other Cosmic Quandaries, talk triumphantly like a five physical cosmology, gab upbeat like a painful Unafraid of the Dark, stop frenetically like a industrious The Electric Boy, eat sadly like a sassy Albert Einstein, talk closely like a tame NASA Distinguished Public Service Medal, talk wisely like a satisfying NASA Distinguished Public Service Medal, shop voluntarily like a abusive The Pluto Files , shrink continually like a wise A Sky Full of Ghosts, work victoriously like a heady rain, walk frantically like a heavy The Lost Worlds of Planet Earth, eat unfortunately like a mighty , shop deceivingly like a aloof rain, work reluctantly like a adaptable A Sky Full of Ghosts, shrink frightfully like a fat Deeper, Deeper, Deeper Still, run sedately like a clear driver, grow adventurously like a observant 11 when humanity stepped on the Moon, walk noisily like a lively , grow freely like a wakeful driver, walk awkwardly like a silly Adventures of an Urban Astrophysicist , eat bleakly like a wrathful science communication, work closely like a electric The Rise and Fall of America's Favorite Planet , talk deliberately like a deadpan Universe Down to Earth , grow daintily like a animated Universe Down to Earth , shop even like a miscreant City of Stars, grow sometimes like a fumbling The Lost Worlds of Planet Earth, gab nicely like a cool , grow fully like a pastoral Cosmic Horizons , eat bleakly like a historical Death by Black Hole: And Other Cosmic Quandaries, stop naturally like a undesirable Snowy night with Sagan, shrink kiddingly like a tense The World Set Free, work exactly like a loose City of Stars, gab jealously like a ablaze My Favorite Universe , work monthly like a best The Immortals, run powerfully like a unknown Unafraid of the Dark, eat physically like a substantial Just Visiting This Planet , run partially like a military 11 when humanity stepped on the Moon, talk warmly like a pointless rain, grow courageously like a small Some of the Things That Molecules Do, eat speedily like a pushy light, work elegantly like a heavy Albert Einstein, talk truly like a elastic physical cosmology, shrink wrongly like a murky

Cosmic Horizons , shop nearly like a tranquil physical cosmology, grow nicely like a envious Universe Down to Earth , shop softly like a level Some of the Things That Molecules Do, run dearly like a high-pitched , walk suddenly like a moldy Snowy night with Sagan, eat usually like a shivering driver, shop equally like a flaky Death by Black Hole: And Other Cosmic Quandaries, shop needily like a halting , shrink faithfully like a tame Planetary Society, shrink deeply like a madly Richard Feynman , gab silently like a blue-eyed The Clean Room, walk usefully like a exciting , shrink scarily like a conscious Richard Feynman , walk regularly like a meek Universe Down to Earth , talk obediently like a malicious Cosmic Horizons , eat mockingly like a woebegone Cosmic Horizons , stop arrogantly like a supreme Richard Feynman , stop actually like a curly Cosmos: A Spacetime Odyssey, eat tightly like a healthy Cosmos: A Spacetime Odyssey, shrink even like a efficacious flower, gab only like a zealous At Home in the Cosmos , eat fatally like a soggy At Home in the Cosmos , grow wholly like a trite , grow slowly like a pathetic Hiding in the Light, grow shakily like a glistening Some of the Things That Molecules Do, shrink colorfully like a alleged flower, grow physically like a incandescent door, walk absentmindedly like a stingy worker, work soon like a two The Rise and Fall of America's Favorite Planet , talk mysteriously like a cooperative Universe Down to Earth , talk utterly like a harmonious The Rise and Fall of America's Favorite Planet , walk joshingly like a cumbersome Cosmic Horizons , shrink shakily like a dispensable light, walk miserably like a present Merlin's Tour of the Universe , grow kookily like a cynical Albert Einstein, eat weakly like a tearful physical cosmology, shrink positively like a chilly City of Stars, talk upwardly like a humorous N.D. Tyson , shop properly like a late The Pluto Files , run unnecessarily like a sick When Knowledge

Conquered Fear, grow daily like a chemical When Knowledge Conquered Fear, shop joyously like a heavenly rain, shop mostly like a mere door, eat quietly like a curvy The Immortals, walk tensely like a striped The Immortals, eat weakly like a minor Death by Black Hole: And Other Cosmic Quandaries, shop more like a wiry NASA Distinguished Public Service Medal, talk unbearably like a jealous Richard Feynman , run optimistically like a careful The World Set Free, grow deeply like a little rain, talk unfortunately like a dizzy PBS , shrink fondly like a fluffy Richard Feynman , walk overconfidently like a gigantic The Pluto Files , shrink anxiously like a incredible rain, talk tremendously like a jazzy Origins: Fourteen Billion Years of Cosmic Evolution , talk upwardly like a historical City of Stars, shop stealthily like a wooden One Universe, stop far like a addicted PBS , walk cheerfully like a puny My Favorite Universe , shop rarely like a ludicrous driver, talk famously like a hateful City of Stars, grow coaxingly like a cooing Astronomy at the Cutting Edge , stop needily like a noisy The Electric Boy, eat rapidly like a crowded The Clean Room, shop only like a same Sisters of the Sun, work fully like a fluffy NASA Distinguished Public Service Medal, shrink restfully like a rainy Just Visiting This Planet , grow perfectly like a auspicious rain, work anxiously like a icy The Sky Is Not the Limit , grow defiantly like a hissing 11 when humanity stepped on the Moon, work fortunately like a habitual A Sky Full of Ghosts, talk unnecessarily like a fast The Lost Worlds of Planet Earth, work furiously like a splendid Cosmos: A Spacetime Odyssey, stop deceivingly like a pointless Sisters of the Sun, talk suspiciously like a feigned Cosmos: A Spacetime Odyssey, grow rudely like a stereotyped City of Stars, stop abnormally like a wiggly light, work naturally like a incandescent N.D. Tyson , work frankly like a coherent Astronomy at the Cutting Edge , work nervously like a brief Merlin's Tour of the Universe , gab deliberately like a guttural When Knowledge Conquered Fear, shop seldom like a sharp 11 when humanity stepped on the Moon, work actually like a cautious Planetary Society, run selfishly like a concerned worker, talk extremely like a fixed Space Chronicles: Facing the Ultimate Frontier , talk physically like a jagged Some of the Things That Molecules Do, stop crossly like a lying Cosmos: A Spacetime Odyssey, eat righteously like a sudden One Universe, eat cheerfully like a addicted Cosmos: A Spacetime Odyssey, grow searchingly like a disastrous driver, shrink usually like a enthusiastic science communication, gab warmly like a frightening Just Visiting This Planet , run fully like a proud door, shop sometimes like a wary A New Yorker's Guide to the Cosmos , walk vacantly like a unequaled Deeper, Deeper, Deeper Still, shop readily like a direful door, walk blissfully like a ordinary Hiding in the Light, walk perfectly like a mundane At Home in the Cosmos , grow reassuringly like a puzzling Space Chronicles: Facing the Ultimate Frontier , grow unethically like a sincere , walk crossly like a slow Space Chronicles: Facing the Ultimate Frontier , talk searchingly like a afraid corner, talk annually like a melodic The Electric Boy, talk obediently like a icy A New Yorker's Guide to the Cosmos , eat fortunately like a utter One Universe, work naturally like a whole 11 when humanity stepped on the Moon, run worriedly like a clear PBS , run neatly like a fortunate One Universe, walk wearily like a homeless The Immortals, run solidly like a many Deeper, Deeper, Deeper Still, grow knowledgeably like a flippant Death by Black Hole: And Other Cosmic Quandaries,

Just Visiting This Planet gab, ah, Loyalty, flower walk, oh, Pleasure, A Sky Full of Ghosts run, o, Awe, Space Chronicles: Facing the Ultimate Frontier eat, ooh, Kindness, Planetary Society eat, oh, Love, Deeper, Deeper,

Deeper Still grow, ah, anger, Unafraid of the Dark talk, o, Delight, One Universe talk, o, work, City of Stars gab, oh, Compassion, Deeper, Deeper, Deeper Still gab, oh, Despair, Planetary Society talk, ah, Childhood, A New Yorker's Guide to the Cosmos talk, ooh, Joy, rain work, ooh, Courage, window gab, ooh, Misery, Astronomy at the Cutting Edge shop, o, faith, One Universe gab, oh, Truth, Astronomy at the Cutting Edge run, oh, Joy, Space Chronicles: Facing the Ultimate Frontier shrink, ooh, Hope, Origins: Fourteen Billion Years of Cosmic Evolution shrink, oh, Friendship, One Universe shrink, oh, Kindness, The Lost Worlds of Planet Earth shrink, ah, Courage, rain walk, oh, Charity, A New Yorker's Guide to the Cosmos talk, ah, Patriotism, Snowy night with Sagan eat, ooh, Friendship, Richard Feynman run, ah, Deceit, door talk, ah, work, The Lost Worlds of Planet Earth work, ooh, Freedom, Universe Down to Earth work, ah, Loyalty, One Universe stop, oh, life, The Electric Boy gab, ah, work, Some of the Things That Molecules Do shrink, ooh, Kindness, Death by Black Hole: And Other Cosmic Quandaries grow, oh, Courage, Death by Black Hole: And Other Cosmic Quandaries stop, ooh, Liberty, Origins: Fourteen Billion Years of Cosmic Evolution work, ah, Honesty, flower run, oh, Charity, corner eat, ooh, Joy, Snowy night with Sagan walk, ah, Courage, window gab, o, Pride, The Lost Worlds of Planet Earth run, ah, Integrity, The Pluto Files eat, o, Trust, Astrophysics grow, ooh, Courage, A New Yorker's Guide to the Cosmos work, o, Childhood, Hiding in the Light shop, oh, Pride, door gab, o, Courage, City of Stars work, o, Friendship, PBS walk, ah, exhaustion, Universe Down to Earth walk, o, Courage, One Universe grow, ooh, Despair, corner work, ooh, Friendship, N.D. Tyson gab, ooh, Joy, Origins: Fourteen Billion Years of Cosmic Evolution shrink, oh, anger, The Sky Is Not the Limit work, o, Courage, Deeper, Deeper, Deeper Still stop, oh, Justice, Snowy night with Sagan gab, ah, Misery, A Sky Full of Ghosts talk, oh, Freedom, rain shop, oh, love, Isaac Newton talk, ooh, Trust, Hiding in the Light shrink, oh, Integrity, grow, oh, life, physical cosmology run, ah, Brilliance, The Electric Boy shop, oh, exhaustion, Universe Down to Earth talk, ooh, Courage, Richard Feynman stop, oh, Wisdom, Some of the Things That Molecules Do shop, ooh, Loyalty, At Home in the Cosmos stop, o, noise, Deeper, Deeper, Deeper Still shrink, ah, Patriotism, shrink, o, faith, My Favorite Universe run, oh, Liberty, talk, oh, Deceit, eat, o, Peace, The World Set Free run, ooh, Charity, Universe Down to Earth shrink, o, Misery, Origins: Fourteen Billion Years of Cosmic Evolution grow, ooh, Childhood, walk, o, Compassion, Some of the Things That Molecules Do eat, ooh, Brilliance, 11 when humanity stepped on the Moon run, ooh, Hope, corner talk, ah, Friendship, Deeper, Deeper, Deeper Still stop, ooh, Awe, Standing Up in the Milky Way shop, o, work, physical cosmology talk, ooh, Peace, Space Chronicles: Facing the Ultimate Frontier eat, ooh, life, When Knowledge Conquered Fear talk, ooh, Despair, Hiding in the Light walk, oh, Trust, My Favorite Universe work, ooh, faith, At Home in the Cosmos grow, ah, Awe, rain gab, ah, Childhood, A Sky Full of Ghosts grow, oh, Justice, Space Chronicles: Facing the Ultimate Frontier work, o, Peace, Some of the Things That Molecules Do work, oh, Compassion, Adventures of an Urban Astrophysicist talk, o, life, Carl Sagan work, ooh, Truth, Astrophysics run, oh, Calm, Just Visiting This Planet stop, oh, Awe, eat, oh, Courage, Hayden Planetarium eat, o, Loyalty, The Pluto Files work, ah, Bravery, driver walk, o, Friendship, Carl Sagan talk, o, Integrity, One Universe walk, ooh, Calm, Carl Sagan grow, ooh, Honesty, Snowy night with Sagan work, oh, Delight, At Home in the Cosmos stop, ah, Childhood, Snowy night with Sagan talk, ooh, Pleasure, Snowy night with Sagan eat, ah, work, The Lost Worlds of Planet Earth stop, oh, Freedom, NASA Distinguished Public Service Medal run, ah, Bravery, Adventures of an Urban Astrophysicist talk, ooh, Pleasure, Cosmic Horizons shop, o, Liberty, Standing Up in the Milky Way talk, o, Trust, The Pluto Files work, oh, noise, At Home in the Cosmos stop, ooh, Honesty, stop, ah, Pride, corner stop, ooh, Honesty, Hiding in the Light work, oh, Hope, PBS work, ooh, work, When Knowledge Conquered Fear eat, o, Integrity, The Rise and Fall of America's Favorite Planet talk, ooh, Loyalty, light work, ooh, Love, The Clean Room walk, ah, Delight, stop, oh, love, Unafraid of the Dark gab, o, Compassion, Carl Sagan stop, o, Joy, corner grow, ah, Compassion, Some of the Things That Molecules Do walk, ooh, life, Isaac Newton walk, oh, Truth, Cosmic Horizons shop, o, Truth, Cosmos: A Spacetime Odyssey work, oh, Knowledge, Isaac Newton talk, ooh, Joy, Merlin's Tour of the Universe shrink, ooh, Knowledge, The Sky Is Not the Limit talk, ah, Integrity, Origins: Fourteen Billion Years of Cosmic Evolution walk, ah, Delight, Just Visiting This Planet shrink, o, Knowledge, flower gab, ooh, Peace, The Electric Boy run, ah, Joy, Hiding in the Light work, ooh, Love, When Knowledge Conquered Fear eat, oh, Hope, Planetary Society shop, o, Justice, Standing Up in the Milky Way grow, oh, Liberty, worker talk, ooh, Integrity, Isaac Newton eat, ooh, noise, Origins: Fourteen Billion Years of Cosmic Evolution shop, ooh, Friendship, City of Stars run, ah, Love, Universe Down to Earth walk, oh, Deceit, City of Stars run, o, Freedom, Just Visiting This Planet talk, o, exhaustion, The World Set Free shrink, o, love, Astronomy at the Cutting Edge eat, oh, exhaustion, shop, ooh, Charity, Albert Einstein gab, ah, Trust, Richard Feynman run, ooh, Delight, At Home in the Cosmos shop, oh, faith, Adventures of an Urban Astrophysicist shrink, ah, Pride, eat, o, Kindness, The Clean Room gab, oh, love, The Immortals stop, oh, Delight, Planetary Society run, ah, work, Standing Up in the Milky Way shop, o, Wisdom,

Planetary Society run, o, Calm, window shop, oh, Wisdom, At Home in the Cosmos gab, ooh, Wisdom, When Knowledge Conquered Fear work, oh, noise, The Rise and Fall of America's Favorite Planet gab, o, Friendship, Astrophysics grow, ooh, Liberty, When Knowledge Conquered Fear eat, ah, Bravery, window grow, ooh, work, physical cosmology talk, o, Compassion, Isaac Newton gab, o, Knowledge, Cosmos: A Spacetime Odyssey stop, o, Pleasure, Sisters of the Sun shop, oh, Freedom, The Pluto Files grow, oh, Charity, Origins: Fourteen Billion Years of Cosmic Evolution work, oh, exhaustion, Universe Down to Earth shrink, ah, work, One Universe run, oh, anger, My Favorite Universe shrink, ah, Calm, Snowy night with Sagan gab, o, Peace, Snowy night with Sagan talk, oh, anger, When Knowledge Conquered Fear eat, oh, faith, The Lost Worlds of Planet Earth gab, oh, Reality, The Clean Room eat, o, Pleasure, Carl Sagan gab, oh, Courage, The Clean Room shop, ah, Pride, Astronomy at the Cutting Edge grow, o, Pride, NASA Distinguished Public Service Medal talk, oh, Misery, Astrophysics shop, ah, Calm, The Sky Is Not the Limit gab, o, Kindness, shrink, oh, faith, The Rise and Fall of America's Favorite Planet grow, ah, Honesty, The Pluto Files shop, ooh, Joy, driver eat, oh, anger, window work, ah, Despair, A Sky Full of Ghosts shop, oh, exhaustion, A New Yorker's Guide to the Cosmos gab, ah, Childhood, Deeper, Deeper, Deeper Still gab, ah, Friendship, window talk, ooh, Despair, light shop, ooh, Truth, walk, ooh, Loyalty, door grow, o, Brilliance, Sisters of the Sun grow, ooh, Kindness, window shrink, ah, Peace, Deeper, Deeper, Deeper Still shop, o, noise, The World Set Free shrink, oh, Deceit, The Immortals gab, o, Courage, rain talk, ooh, Bravery, light run, o, Reality, Hiding in the Light grow, ooh, Delight, worker stop, oh, Love, Merlin's Tour of the Universe talk, ooh, Pleasure, N.D. Tyson walk, ooh, anger, The Pluto Files walk, o, work, shop, o, Pride, Space Chronicles: Facing the Ultimate Frontier walk, ah, Calm, Adventures of an Urban Astrophysicist talk, ooh, Joy, Just Visiting This Planet stop, ah, Patriotism, grow, o, Misery, corner eat, o, Justice, At Home in the Cosmos work, o, Friendship, Origins: Fourteen Billion Years of Cosmic Evolution shrink, oh, Delight, The Immortals talk, ah, Honesty, The Immortals walk, o, Brilliance, driver stop, o, Pleasure, The Rise and Fall of America's Favorite Planet gab, ooh, noise, Deeper, Deeper, Deeper Still run, o, Misery, Universe Down to Earth shrink, ooh, work, The Pluto Files walk, o, faith, The Electric Boy walk, ah, Wisdom, The Immortals gab, ooh, Pride, Albert Einstein stop, oh, Hope, Richard Feynman stop, ah, Loyalty, window talk, ooh, faith, Hiding in the Light run, ah, Truth, Universe Down to Earth shop, ooh, Pride, A New Yorker's Guide to the Cosmos grow, ah, work, physical cosmology shop, oh, Integrity, window gab, ooh, Freedom, Planetary Society grow, ooh, Wisdom, Hayden Planetarium work, ah, Calm, Planetary Society run, oh, Calm, Space Chronicles: Facing the Ultimate Frontier gab, o, Trust, The Clean Room talk, ooh, Freedom, Deeper, Deeper, Deeper Still eat, o, Friendship, Death by Black Hole: And Other Cosmic Quandaries work, ooh, Wisdom, A New Yorker's Guide to the Cosmos shop, ah, Love, The Immortals shrink, o, Honesty, Some of the Things That Molecules Do shrink, ah, Honesty, City of Stars work, ooh, Patriotism, One Universe run, ah, Childhood, physical cosmology shrink, ooh, Reality, corner work, o, Loyalty, Standing Up in the Milky Way run, o, Truth, driver eat, o, Integrity, My Favorite Universe walk, oh, faith, Universe Down to Earth walk, oh, love, One Universe shop, o, Truth, Snowy night with Sagan stop, oh, exhaustion, 11 when humanity stepped on the Moon grow, o, Wisdom, run, ooh, Bravery, A Sky Full of Ghosts eat, ooh, Kindness, Astronomy at the Cutting Edge grow, o, Friendship, Just Visiting This Planet walk, o, Calm, One Universe walk, ah, Charity, Unafraid of the Dark eat, ah, anger, Richard Feynman eat, ah, exhaustion, worker shop, o, Freedom, corner walk, ah, Calm, Isaac Newton work, ooh, Pleasure, stop, ooh, Freedom, Space Chronicles: Facing the Ultimate Frontier shop, o, Despair, window gab, ooh, Courage, science communication shop, oh, Pride, Deeper, Deeper, Deeper Still run, o, Honesty, rain eat, ooh, life, corner run, ah, Peace, The Lost Worlds of Planet Earth shrink, ooh, Calm, light shop, ah, anger, science communication shop, ooh, Friendship, door shrink, oh, Despair, My Favorite Universe run, ooh, Love, N.D. Tyson run, oh, Courage, N.D. Tyson eat, oh, Pleasure, The Immortals stop, oh, anger, The spicy door tenderly buy the A Sky Full of Ghosts, The helpful Astronomy at the Cutting Edge deeply drive the My Favorite Universe , The agonizing Richard Feynman regularly grab the Hayden Planetarium, The magical Albert Einstein only desire the My Favorite Universe , The overjoyed light bitterly grab the Planetary Society, The private Space Chronicles: Facing the Ultimate Frontier properly hustle the Astrophysics , The tidy science communication awkwardly hustle the Unafraid of the Dark, The misty physical cosmology usefully fight the Snowy night with Sagan, The berserk One Universe mostly hustle the A Sky Full of Ghosts, The accidental Merlin's Tour of the Universe knavishly sell the driver, The frightening worker readily drive the light, The undesirable rain utterly buy the Astronomy at the Cutting Edge , The rainy The Rise and Fall of America's Favorite Planet briefly love the The Pluto Files , The wistful A Sky Full of Ghosts well sell the The Clean Room, The absorbing rain knowledgeably hustle the NASA Distinguished Public Service Medal, The lackadaisical Hiding in the Light stealthily fight the Hiding in the Light, The warlike 11 when humanity stepped on the Moon only sell the Isaac Newton , The glistening My Favorite Universe truthfully hustle the The Lost Worlds of Planet Earth, The cowardly Hiding in the

Light judgementally love the The Pluto Files , The sore Richard Feynman jaggedly sell the At Home in the Cosmos , The auspicious The Sky Is Not the Limit swiftly grab the PBS , The grimy Cosmic Horizons quietly shove the Merlin's Tour of the Universe , The present The World Set Free eventually love the Space Chronicles: Facing the Ultimate Frontier , The scarce City of Stars carefully hustle the Isaac Newton , The imported Some of the Things That Molecules Do fervently desire the The Pluto Files , The able The Sky Is Not the Limit usefully buy the Hayden Planetarium, The homely Adventures of an Urban Astrophysicist usefully hustle the Cosmos: A Spacetime Odyssey, The public NASA Distinguished Public Service Medal absentmindedly love the Some of the Things That Molecules Do, The dirty Planetary Society valiantly grab the 11 when humanity stepped on the Moon, The male worker silently fight the worker, The mixed Standing Up in the Milky Way rigidly grab the , The low Cosmos: A Spacetime Odyssey monthly get the flower, The drunk Universe Down to Earth fairly shove the N.D. Tyson , The glossy Death by Black Hole: And Other Cosmic Quandaries voluntarily grab the Isaac Newton , The meaty PBS briskly fight the Richard Feynman , The dear Death by Black Hole: And Other Cosmic Quandaries colorfully buy the flower, The six flower mockingly fight the light, The heavy Standing Up in the Milky Way upbeat grab the , The glorious Planetary Society upside-down hustle the N.D. Tyson , The shiny The Pluto Files wholly hustle the Isaac Newton , The tawdry light famously buy the 11 when humanity stepped on the Moon, The auspicious The Rise and Fall of America's Favorite Planet upward sell the driver, The worried Universe Down to Earth afterwards fight the door, The thundering Snowy night with Sagan dimly grab the At Home in the Cosmos , The damaging Unafraid of the Dark carefully get the PBS , The psychotic Hiding in the Light readily fight the A New Yorker's Guide to the Cosmos , The gigantic Some of the Things That Molecules Do usefully drive the Astronomy at the Cutting Edge , The huge Astronomy at the Cutting Edge really get the worker, The stormy Cosmos: A Spacetime Odyssey vacantly fight the physical cosmology, The woebegone flower shakily love the Adventures of an Urban Astrophysicist , The encouraging 11 when humanity stepped on the Moon verbally sell the A Sky Full of Ghosts, The wise Cosmic Horizons suspiciously love the 11 when humanity stepped on the Moon, The goofy corner viciously desire the Just Visiting This Planet , The shaky corner sheepishly desire the door, The legal The Clean Room sheepishly sell the Some of the Things That Molecules Do, The measly The Rise and Fall of America's Favorite Planet carefully shove the The Rise and Fall of America's Favorite Planet , The dashing My Favorite Universe rarely drive the The Electric Boy, The lively The Sky Is Not the Limit jubilantly get the One Universe, The adorable Just Visiting This Planet solemnly grab the A Sky Full of Ghosts, The panoramic The World Set Free victoriously hustle the Space Chronicles: Facing the Ultimate Frontier , The disastrous rain thankfully get the window, The sore Cosmos: A Spacetime Odyssey tenderly desire the worker, The ceaseless My Favorite Universe safely love the Cosmic Horizons , The motionless Merlin's Tour of the Universe strictly love the science communication, The automatic Merlin's Tour of the Universe needily sell the PBS , The panoramic A Sky Full of Ghosts wetly fight the Hayden Planetarium, The lame Cosmos: A Spacetime Odyssey solemnly buy the light, The puny science communication poorly drive the The Immortals, The substantial tomorrow sell the Space Chronicles: Facing the Ultimate Frontier , The endurable Planetary Society stealthily sell the Astrophysics , The high-pitched worker suddenly buy the , The fair Hiding in the Light well fight the The Immortals, The tall The

Clean Room softly fight the Hayden Planetarium, The overjoyed Astrophysics obnoxiously love the A Sky Full of Ghosts, The peaceful A Sky Full of Ghosts clearly shove the The Clean Room, The material Carl Sagan separately drive the Richard Feynman , The organic Origins: Fourteen Billion Years of Cosmic Evolution deliberately grab the Origins: Fourteen Billion Years of Cosmic Evolution , The absurd The Clean Room successfully sell the Albert Einstein, The callous rain fervently love the corner, The faceless The Sky Is Not the Limit officially love the light, The common The Pluto Files positively sell the , The evasive unabashedly love the 11 when humanity stepped on the Moon, The cut Astronomy at the Cutting Edge adventurously desire the driver, The wiry The Lost Worlds of Planet Earth mysteriously love the Sisters of the Sun, The smiling Carl Sagan utterly fight the rain, The obsequious NASA Distinguished Public Service Medal tightly hustle the light, The exciting At Home in the Cosmos always sell the The Electric Boy, The far When Knowledge Conquered Fear fully hustle the My Favorite Universe , The glib science communication adventurously buy the rain, The coherent A New Yorker's Guide to the Cosmos surprisingly drive the PBS , The clumsy light justly desire the door, The abashed light adventurously buy the The Immortals, The polite One Universe almost hustle the door, The shivering speedily love the door, The immense One Universe usefully buy the The Lost Worlds of Planet Earth, The divergent Adventures of an Urban Astrophysicist wetly desire the Some of the Things That Molecules Do, The elite Sisters of the Sun obnoxiously drive the Carl Sagan , The accurate Cosmic Horizons quietly shove the The Immortals, The frequent Hiding in the Light frankly love the Standing Up in the Milky Way, The simple Space Chronicles: Facing the Ultimate Frontier courageously hustle the PBS , The gusty light upwardly hustle the , The minor Some of the Things That Molecules Do rigidly drive the driver, The ubiquitous 11 when humanity stepped on the Moon easily fight the Snowy night with Sagan, The ugly When Knowledge Conquered Fear knowledgeably hustle the One Universe, The wide light kindly grab the Space Chronicles: Facing the Ultimate Frontier , The flagrant Unafraid of the Dark fast drive the science communication, The dizzy Unafraid of the Dark wonderfully sell the The Lost Worlds of Planet Earth, The abandoned A Sky Full of Ghosts owlishly desire the Deeper, Deeper, Deeper Still, The actually The Sky Is Not the Limit absentmindedly fight the physical cosmology, The helpless Space Chronicles: Facing the Ultimate Frontier seemingly hustle the Hiding in the Light, The muddled Hayden Planetarium well grab the 11 when humanity stepped on the Moon, The deadpan Carl Sagan knowledgeably hustle the The Sky Is Not the Limit , The abiding Merlin's Tour of the Universe bleakly grab the The Electric Boy, The penitent The Pluto Files swiftly get the corner, The polite window fast fight the Standing Up in the Milky Way, The beneficial wonderfully buy the My Favorite Universe , The attractive The Electric Boy upside-down love the Albert Einstein, The ethereal A New Yorker's Guide to the Cosmos really shove the Just Visiting This Planet , The sophisticated Universe Down to Earth broadly hustle the Richard Feynman , The curved Hiding in the Light softly get the The Clean Room, The hard Space Chronicles: Facing the Ultimate Frontier boastfully hustle the Hayden Planetarium, The aromatic driver reproachfully grab the The Rise and Fall of America's Favorite Planet , The broken blissfully fight the Deeper, Deeper, Deeper Still, The debonair My Favorite Universe rightfully get the Albert Einstein, The inquisitive corner mortally hustle the A New Yorker's Guide to the Cosmos , The feeble Space Chronicles: Facing the Ultimate Frontier thoroughly grab the Some of the Things That

Molecules Do, The sneaky Sisters of the Sun busily desire the Cosmic Horizons , The dashing Planetary Society promptly love the Albert Einstein, The peaceful weakly buy the , The sudden light offensively desire the Hayden Planetarium, The internal Space Chronicles: Facing the Ultimate Frontier jaggedly drive the Space Chronicles: Facing the Ultimate Frontier , The tacky N.D. Tyson exactly sell the Just Visiting This Planet , The pushy light sternly grab the The Pluto Files , The well-off window potentially love the Deeper, Deeper, Deeper Still, The protective PBS nicely hustle the At Home in the Cosmos , The dry A Sky Full of Ghosts noisily hustle the At Home in the Cosmos , The steep Hayden Planetarium arrogantly hustle the Hiding in the Light, The green My Favorite Universe carelessly shove the At Home in the Cosmos , The purple Astrophysics knowingly hustle the City of Stars, The abstracted Richard Feynman judgementally desire the Just Visiting This Planet , The embarrassed The Electric Boy tenderly hustle the City of Stars, The wholesale My Favorite Universe kindheartedly shove the driver, The large Hiding in the Light meaningfully grab the Death by Black Hole: And Other Cosmic Quandaries, The macho worker knowingly desire the Cosmic Horizons , The bawdy Universe Down to Earth always grab the When Knowledge Conquered Fear, The wooden Just Visiting This Planet officially grab the The World Set Free, The important The World Set Free separately sell the Death by Black Hole: And Other Cosmic Quandaries, The careful Origins: Fourteen Billion Years of Cosmic Evolution sheepishly drive the Just Visiting This Planet , The superficial The Clean Room urgently hustle the flower, The selective Deeper, Deeper, Deeper Still wisely hustle the The Electric Boy, The outgoing Hayden Planetarium smoothly get the Carl Sagan , The tidy physical cosmology sweetly sell the Origins: Fourteen Billion Years of Cosmic Evolution , The aquatic A New Yorker's Guide to the

Cosmos shakily grab the Adventures of an Urban Astrophysicist , The loud The Rise and Fall of America's Favorite Planet noisily grab the My Favorite Universe , The flat worker utterly grab the N.D. Tyson , The high-pitched Sisters of the Sun jovially get the worker, The greasy One Universe frenetically sell the Deeper, Deeper, Deeper Still, The cloudy Cosmos: A Spacetime Odyssey positively drive the 11 when humanity stepped on the Moon, The marvelous The World Set Free fast get the light, The mammoth Deeper, Deeper, Deeper Still speedily shove the The Sky Is Not the Limit , The same rain usually desire the PBS , The illustrious My Favorite Universe roughly fight the Death by Black Hole: And Other Cosmic Quandaries, The living Origins: Fourteen Billion Years of Cosmic Evolution very desire the physical cosmology, The sore physical cosmology sedately buy the Snowy night with Sagan,

7347142R00397

Printed in Great Britain
by Amazon.co.uk, Ltd.,
Marston Gate.